the conclusion," writes the author, "that the usual interpretation of American history which aligns farmers and debtors on one side and mercantile and financial groups on another is wrong."

Mr. Govan describes the Bank of the United States as a public, not a private, institution. Biddle's policies, he insists, were determined by his concern for the welfare of the nation. Biddle fought for a national bank, believing that only such an institution could promote sound economic progress. The defeat of his views (which Henry Clay called the "American System") climaxed a crucial phase in American history and transcended by far the historical significance of Biddle's personal tragedy.

About the author . . .

THOMAS PAYNE GOVAN is a native of Georgia and was educated at southern universities. He has taught history at Tulane, the University of the South, and the University of Virginia. Mr. Govan is at present associated with the Division of College Work of the Protestant Episcopal Church.

NICHOLAS BIDDLE

NICHOLAS BIDDLE

Nationalist and Public Banker

1786–1844

By THOMAS PAYNE GOVAN

THE UNIVERSITY OF CHICAGO PRESS

Library of Congress Catalog Number: 59-12286

THE UNIVERSITY OF CHICAGO PRESS, CHICAGO 37
Cambridge University Press, London, N.W. 1, England
The University of Toronto Press, Toronto 5, Canada

© *1959 by The University of Chicago. Published 1959. Com-*
posed and printed by THE UNIVERSITY OF CHICAGO PRESS,
Chicago, Illinois, U.S.A.

Preface

*M*y interest in Nicholas Biddle was first aroused when, as a graduate student in history at Vanderbilt University, I began research on the panic of 1837 as part of a thesis on banking, credit, and cotton in ante bellum Georgia. The year was 1936, and in the contemporary world the Democratic administration of Franklin D. Roosevelt, deriving, I was told and believed, from the tradition of Jefferson and Jackson, was seeking to restore the profits of the growers of cotton and other agricultural produce. What puzzled me, at this time a Jeffersonian individualist with leanings toward socialism, was that the contemporary policies being used to overcome a depression were essentially identical with those that had been advocated and followed almost a century before by Biddle, a banker and Hamiltonian nationalist, in a similar economic situation. The contrast between what I learned from my observation and research and what I had read and been taught stimulated my curiosity about Biddle, but it was not until 1946 that I had an opportunity to do anything more than make a cursory examination of his papers. In that year, through a grant from the Library of Congress, I began the research upon which this book is based, with the intention of writing an objective, impartial biography that would do justice to Biddle and his opponents alike. This ambition has not been fulfilled. I have written an apologia, a defense (one reader has called it "a lawyer's brief"), but I could do nothing else and remain loyal to the evidence.

Many historians have previously studied Biddle and the conflict between him, as president of the Bank of the United States, and Andrew Jackson, but only a few have followed Hermann E. von Holst in rendering a verdict in Biddle's favor. The others have taken the Jacksonian side, largely, I believe, for reasons extraneously injected into their study of the American past. Some—William Graham Sumner is the chief example—have accepted the deterministic doctrines of the classical economists as being of universal validity and have considered regulation and control of currency and credit by a nationally chartered institution to be a harmful and impossible attempt to circumvent natural law. Others, deceived by Karl Marx's equally deterministic doctrine of class conflict, have thought that a wealthy aristocrat at the head of a powerful financial institution could have no other motive

[vii]

than the increase of his own wealth and power and those of the fellow members of his class. The great majority, however, have shared the instinctive American prejudice against wealth and position, uncritically accepting the Jeffersonian dogma that freedom and virtue can be achieved only in a simple rural society of landowning farmers unrestrained by a national government and have looked on Biddle as the spokesman for the eastern cities, which sought to destroy freedom by ignoring the constitutionally established rights of individuals and states.

These historians have acted on the usually valid assumption that where there is so much smoke, there must be some fire and have taken the false charges brought against Biddle and the Bank as proved and valid. They have judged Biddle by harsher moral standards than those used to measure his opponents, and the failure of the United States Bank of Pennsylvania in 1841 has been taken as proof of the weakness and corruption of that bank, of Biddle himself, and of its national predecessor. Historians have almost universally ignored Albert Gallatin's statement: "We know from the experience of nearly forty years, that so long as the Bank of the United States has been in operation we have had a sound currency; and that it was thrown into utter confusion when left to the control of the several states." Nor have they been willing to connect the disordered and unsatisfactory currency of the United States from 1836 to 1913 with Jackson's financial policies or to point out that it was only through a return to a federally chartered central banking system that this fundamental economic defect was removed. The silence in regard to the number and severity of financial panics when the national banks were in effective operation and after their demise has been even more prevalent, and few have remembered John Sergeant's words at the last meeting of the stockholders of the Bank of the United States: "When danger threatened, when credit was trembling, when confidence was shaken, whenever, in a word, a revulsion was threatened with its disastrous train of circumstances, this Bank, strong in its power, stronger in its inclination to do good, anticipated and averted the crisis."

These positive accomplishments, which cannot be denied, have not been sufficient evidence to overcome the fact that in the end the Bank failed, and even those historians (in particular, Ralph C. H. Catterall, Fritz Redlich, Walter B. Smith, and Bray Hammond) who have been generally favorable in their interpretation of Biddle and his policies as head of the national bank have found in him some weakness, some mistake in judgment or act, some fault in character that was serious enough to be the effective cause of his political defeat and financial failure. My own study of Biddle, I know, would seem more believable if I had been able to follow their example. Biddle had faults and weaknesses, he did make mistakes, but none of these has seemed sufficient to me to account for the final result. There probably can be no explanation. This may be one of those circumstances of which many centuries ago an anonymous Persian chronicler wrote: "When a mortal's star enters the constellation of misfortune, fate decrees that all his undertakings shall have an effect opposite to that which he desires, and nothing can save him—not the most penetrating intelligence, nor the most extensive experience. His merits are annihilated by the rigour of destiny."

This fatalistic statement of destined defeat is only partially true in this particular circumstance, and its truth is true only after the event. It obscures the closeness to victory that is now hidden in Biddle's defeat, and what is best learned from this story is that the successful are not necessarily those who have the right of a matter or the losers those who are in the wrong. It is also my hope that this study will lead historians to challenge the deeply held American belief that institutions are hostile to freedom and the restraints they impose necessarily harmful. Liberty and authority are not opposed concepts, rather one cannot exist without the other. There can be no freedom unless there is an authority to establish and maintain it, but authority can exist only where it avoids perversion into authoritarianism through honoring and protecting the freedom of those who subject themselves to it. This calls for some method of checks and balances such as that so beautifully exemplified in the Constitution of the United States, which establishes powerful officers and institutions but provides for their restraint, for freedom disappears under either of the alternative systems: unrestrained individualism or an unrestrained state.

One more word about the book. It is in biographical form, but it is not a full story of Biddle's life. I have written of him as nationalist and public banker, for it is here, in my opinion, that his significance lies. I could not write of him as son, husband, parent, private citizen, or even as man without having these remarks appear as irrelevant intrusions into the already too complex narrative. I have also avoided characterizing the other persons in the book, except as they reveal themselves through their acts and words. Each of these men is a whole human being and is not to be judged on the basis of what he did or said in regard to Biddle and the Bank. For similar reasons I have eschewed the use of those words of censure and praise—the adjectives, adverbs, nouns, and verbs—that do impart color and life to a narrative but also permit an *unscrupulous partisan* to *insinuate slyly* what he believes, yet hesitates to say.

In preparing this study I have incurred many obligations to hundreds of people, far more than I can name, but my chief debt is to Nicholas Biddle himself, who in his retirement examined and arranged his papers, taking from them only the personal letters exchanged between him and his wife. Neither he nor his sons and grandsons, who also examined the collection, took from it the relatively small number of letters containing material that could be construed as discreditable, and if there are omissions of this sort, they are to be explained by my inadequacies as a researcher rather than by any deliberate withholding of the record. I have also been generously helped by Biddle's descendants in this generation, in particular Nicholas Biddle Wainwright, research librarian of the Historical Society of Pennsylvania and editor of the *Pennsylvania Magazine of History and Biography*. His continuing interest and unfailing support have been of immense aid. He gave me free access to his private collection of Biddle letters and papers, as did Colonel Nicholas Biddle of Philadelphia, Mr. Charles Biddle of "Andalusia," and other members of the family, and not once was I questioned by any of them as to the use and interpretation I would make of the materials so provided.

The staff at the Library of Congress, the Historical Society of Pennsylvania, and numerous other libraries in which I have studied, read, or written, have been kind, sympathetic, and patient, as have been my students, colleagues, and friends, in the long years during which I bothered them with my inordinate desire to find out and talk about Nicholas Biddle. My graduate teachers, William C. Binkley and Fletcher M. Green, set me on this road, and have continued as advisers and friends. The late Nicholas Wreden corrected and improved the initial draft of the manuscript, and Livia Appel guided me in the preparation of the final draft. Financial assistance for my research and writing has been given by the Julius Rosenwald Foundation, the Social Science Research Council, the Library of Congress, the Carnegie Research Fund of the University of the South, and the Fund for the Advancement of Education. In particular I want to express my appreciation to the American History Research Center and to Forrest McDonald, formerly its executive secretary, for providing the means through which the final revision of the manuscript was made possible. None of these is to be held responsible for what is written herein, but without them there would have been nothing at all.

Contents

CONTENTS

~ 1 ~

The End
and the
Beginning

$\mathcal{N}$icholas Biddle, sitting at his desk on January 8, 1839, wrote the first words in a new journal. "This is my birthday," he recorded. "Born in 1786. I am now fifty-three years of age. I know this and yet as I write down the number of years it seems strange to me." He looked back with pride upon a long and successful public career as president of the Bank of the United States and of its successor, the United States Bank of Pennsylvania, without presentiment of the disasters that were soon to overwhelm the national economy. The preceding ten years, during which he had defended these banks from attacks by a "popular party led on by a popular chief," had been the happiest in his life. He had resolved "not merely not to be conquered" by Andrew Jackson and the Democratic party "but to beat them." And so he thought it had ended. He resigned on March 29, 1839, but within six months a financial catastrophe struck the nation, destroying the Bank, Biddle's personal reputation, and his private fortune. Reality in this instance followed a tragic pattern, and John Quincy Adams, among the wisest of Americans, recognized the fact. Biddle, he wrote, was brooding "with smiling face and stifled groans over the wreck of splendid blasted expectations and ruined hopes. A fair mind, a brilliant genius, a generous temper, waylaid and led astray by prosperity, suffering the penalty of scarcely voluntary error."[1]

This tragedy involved much more than the frustration of one man's am-

[1] N. Biddle, Journal, in the Biddle Manuscripts in the Historical Society of Pennsylvania; N. Biddle to the Board of Directors of the United States Bank of Pennsylvania, March 29, 1839, in the Biddle Manuscripts at "Andalusia"; Charles Francis Adams (ed.), *The Memoirs of John Quincy Adams, Comprising Portions of His Diary from 1795 to 1848* (12 vols.; Philadelphia, 1874–77), X, 361.

bition. When Andrew Jackson became President of the United States on March 4, 1829, the national currency was elastic, uniform, trustworthy, and altogether adequate for the needs of an expanding economy. The Bank of the United States was the balance wheel of a complex but effective financial and mercantile system, but eight years later, when Jackson retired from office, this system was destroyed. All the banks in the United States were forced shortly afterward to suspend specie payments, and the uniform national currency was replaced by local currencies fluctuating in value from place to place and from month to month. The state banks were left without restraint, guidance, or support, and Biddle's attempt to restore order in the financial realm, though temporarily successful, ultimately failed.

The subsequent history of the United States offers no evidence that the influence of wealth was lessened by Jackson's reforms. The sole result of his effort was the elimination of the one bank that had public responsibility for the general welfare and sufficient capital and strength to protect and sustain the national economy. The effects of his policy are to be found not only in the financial crises of 1837 and 1839 but also in the disordered economy that plagued the United States throughout the rest of the century. Only the speculators and those so rich that they could not be hurt profited as the nation moved through unrestrained cycles of "boom and bust" to the financial injury of those who engaged in productive enterprises: farmers, merchants, manufacturers, shippers, bankers, and investors.

Jackson's administration brought one phase of American history to an end. Beginning with the Washington administration and continuing through that of John Quincy Adams, the Federalist and Republican proponents of what was called the "American System" had been dominant most of the time. Their goal was the economic and political strength of the nation as a whole, and the instrument that they used was the national government. They did not seek to advance the particular interests of any one section, class, or group, and their policies effectively prevented domination of the nation by an oligarchy of wealth. But their political opponents, motivated variously by ideology or party interest, successfully misrepresented their purposes and, in the Jackson administration, reversed and defeated their entire program.

Biddle's life and his political and economic views thus have a significance that transcends his personal fate. He was the leading spokesman for a major point of view at one of the decisive turning points in American history, and his defeat and failure had momentous consequences for generations of his fellow citizens.

Biddle was born in the Northern Liberties of Philadelphia, the fourth son of Charles and Hannah Shepard Biddle. His forebears on this continent were respected men and women of some social position and more than average means, but the boy inherited no privilege or status, unless freedom from hardship and an adequate education can be so interpreted. The first Biddle to come to America was Nicholas' great-great-grandfather William, a member of the Society of Friends and one of the proprietors of West Jersey. He arrived from England about 1681, accompanied by his wife and two children, and established his homestead at Mount Hope on the Delaware River. He was a member of the Governor's Council, the General Assembly, and the Council of Proprietors of West Jersey. His son, also named William, took little part in public life but was a successful farmer and left each of his seven children a substantial sum at his death.[2]

The oldest son of this family—the third William Biddle and grandfather of Nicholas—moved to Philadelphia. He left the Society of Friends on his marriage in 1730 to Mary Scull, a communicant of the Church of England and a daughter of Nicholas Scull, surveyor-general of Pennsylvania, of whom Benjamin Franklin wrote that he loved books and sometimes made verses. William Biddle was unfortunate in business and lost his inheritance by going bail for one untrustworthy man and forming a partnership with another. He died in 1756, leaving his widow with nine children, the oldest twenty-five and the youngest four. Six of her sons grew to manhood. Of these, Thomas, the youngest, died in 1775 just after he had begun the practice of medicine, and John, always referred to by Charles Biddle as "my unfortunate brother John," broke with his family during the Revolution. He alone among the Biddles was a loyalist, and he moved to Nova Scotia. The others supported the Colonial cause, and Edward, who had been a captain in the army during the French and Indian War, was a delegate to both the Continental Congresses. Illness in 1775 deprived him of an opportunity to assume an important military command in the American army, but he continued to serve in the Congress until his death in 1779.

Another of Mary Biddle's sons, named Nicholas for his grandfather, was one of the youngest commanders in the Continental navy, and his death at the age of twenty-eight, when his thirty-six-gun frigate "Randolph" exploded while engaged in unequal combat with the British ship "Yarmouth," was a grievous blow to the country as well as to the family.[3] Nicholas learned of these ancestors from his father, who talked more freely of their exploits than of his own. But occasionally Charles Biddle told of his own experiences as a seaman, and these tales of shipwreck and rescue, of fighting on land and sea, and of trade in peace and war fascinated the attentive boy. Charles Biddle had long retired from his life on the sea, and when Nicholas was a youngster his father was a successful merchant and vice-president of the Supreme Executive Council of Pennsylvania. He was

[2] This account of the Biddle family in America is based upon genealogical records in the Historical Society of Pennsylvania and in James S. Biddle (ed.), *Autobiography of Charles Biddle, Vice-President of the Supreme Executive Council of Pennsylvania, 1745–1821* (Philadelphia, 1883), pp. 361–402.

[3] The career of this first Nicholas Biddle is described in William Bell Clark, *Captain Dauntless: The Story of Nicholas Biddle of the Continental Navy* (Baton Rouge, 1949).

one of the leading citizens of Philadelphia, active in political and mercantile life, but his wife, the daughter of an upcountry North Carolina merchant, was different. She had met and married Charles Biddle in New Bern during the revolution and never quite accustomed herself to life in the city. She was timid and shy with strangers and would have preferred to remain in the modest neighborhood of the Northern Liberties, had not her husband's public duties and his increasing private business made it necessary for them to move closer to the center of the city.

Soon after Nicholas' birth they purchased one of a pleasant row of brick houses on Market Street between Sixth and Seventh, and here their nine children were reared. The house was in the fashionable section of the city, well away from the shops and warehouses on the river but within easy walking distance of the State House and other public buildings. Governor Thomas Mifflin lived directly across the street, the house of Dr. Caspar Wistar, one of the city's noted physicians, was only a few doors away, and that occupied by President Washington was in the next block. Philadelphia, with forty-five thousand inhabitants, was the largest city in the country in this last decade of the eighteenth century. It was built on a broad plain between the Delaware and Schuylkill rivers, and its streets were laid out with geometrical precision, intersecting at right angles. The houses were almost as uniform as the streets, being constructed of brick and few having more than two floors.

Nicholas gradually became familiar with every street and building in the city as he accompanied members of the household to the public market which gave their street its name, went to and from school with the other children, and on Sunday walked with the family to Christ Church. In the spring and fall, when the ships from foreign ports arrived, he and the other boys went down to the wharfs to watch the unloading of the cargoes. The pavement from Arch to Walnut Street was filled with boxes and bales. Sailors, colorfully dressed and speaking strange tongues, crowded the grogshops, and the city boys dreamed of the time when they too would be men sailing to the far corners of the world.[4]

In his later years Nicholas did not remember many such carefree episodes and, in reviewing his life, said: "My boyhood was not I think happy." The fault, if any there were, lay in his temperament, which made him mature and serious beyond his years. Like his grandfather and namesake, he loved books, and his earliest recollection was of an aunt who placed him on a table to recite verses for the entertainment of visitors.[5] He always preferred reading to play and frequently sat quietly in his father's room

[4] Philadelphia as seen by a boy of approximately Biddle's age is described in Horace Binney's Autobiography, in the Binney Manuscripts in the Historical Society of Pennsylvania.

[5] N. Biddle, Journal, in the Biddle Manuscripts in the Historical Society of Pennsylvania; N. Biddle to Mrs. John Craig, March 17, 1811, in the Biddle-Craig Manuscripts in the Historical Society of Pennsylvania.

listening to adult conversations about war, politics, or business. This precocious seriousness set him apart from Edward, James, and Charles, the three brothers closest to him in age, and made William, the eldest son, his chosen companion. The older boy was gentle and kind. He also loved study and reading more than games and mischief, and the two were almost inseparable, despite the five years' difference in their ages.

When William entered the college department of the University of Pennsylvania in 1794 at the age of thirteen, Nicholas intensified his study and was ready for entrance two years later, though he was only ten. Three years later he wanted to join William in the study of law, but this time the family refused.[6] In April, 1799, they withdrew him from the university, where he was a Senior, and enrolled him in the Sophomore class at the College of New Jersey. The other boys in his class were much older, and they had the advantage of a year's acquaintance with one another, so it was a frightened and shy Nicholas Biddle who, five months after his thirteenth birthday, descended from the Philadelphia coach at Princeton. He felt very much alone as he looked across the large bare yard studded with trees in front of Nassau Hall and saw the other students greet one another with easy familiarity after their five-week vacation. His roommate was a Senior, Arthur Rose Fitzhugh, of Stafford County, Virginia, and under his guidance Nicholas became acquainted with the customs and practices of the college.

His talents as a writer were an invaluable asset, and he soon achieved local fame as the author of a doggerel poem protesting against the five o'clock rising hour and the hurried and full schedule. Two literary and debating societies—the Cliosophic and the Whig—were the leading extracurricular activities, and Biddle was elected to Clio during his first term. In accordance with the practice of the group, he was given a classical name, "Grammaticus" (one who knows his letters), possibly as a semi-ironic commentary upon his precocious learning and his grave and pedagogic manner. The welfare of Clio became his chief interest at Princeton, and he took a prominent part in the society's activities.[7] His college life also included occasional dinners at the local tavern, sleigh rides to Kingston, and calls upon the young ladies of Princeton. His closest friends—Richard B. Bayly and Edward Watts of Virginia and Edward C. Thomas of Maryland—usually accompanied him on these expeditions. Little is known of the girls except their names: Susan, Anne "the affected," Miss Vorhees, and

6 *University of Pennsylvania: Biographical Catalogue of the Matriculates of the College, 1749–1893* (Philadelphia, 1894), p. 40; James B. Longacre and James Herring (eds.), "Nicholas Biddle," in *The National Portrait Gallery of Distinguished Americans* (Philadelphia, 1856), Vol. IV, no pagination.

7 Nicolani Biddle, "Specimum Noblissimum Communum," in the Biddle Manuscripts in the Historical Society of Pennsylvania; Arthur R. Fitzhugh to N. Biddle, November 8, 1800, in the Biddle Family Manuscripts in the Library of Congress; the Minutes of the Cliosophic Society in the Cliosophic Society Manuscripts in the Princeton University Library.

the president's daughter, Betsy Smith, whom the boys considered "rather wild." Nicholas seems to have been well regarded by the young ladies and once was introduced as a "smart beau" with a "highly improved mind." On another occasion his brother James warned him that Miss Johanna Turner was coming to Princeton and advised him "to read some piece against Early Marriages in order to strengthen yourself against the *All Powerful* charms of the *All Accomplished* Miss Johanna—Amen."[8]

To his contemporaries and to himself Nicholas seemed a mature, serious adult, but to his parents he remained a child in need of constant advice. His father was concerned about his reluctance to take exercise and urged him to walk or run whenever possible, to preserve his health. And his mother was concerned about his diet. "Cant you get your washerwoman to buy and boil you a ham and keep in your room?" she wrote. "Have you had any molasses? These two things would be good and very proper together."[9]

They also insisted that he keep regular accounts of his money, but, though he carefully recorded all that he had received and spent, the totals somehow were never in balance. His most frequent expenditures were for food, but he also was charitable; several times a month he recorded gifts of twenty-five cents to poor men and women. But, to judge from the appearance of the account, one contribution was unwillingly made. In large handwriting betraying annoyance, he made the entry, "To subscription for propagating Christianity among the Indians, there being a subscription in the college and all signing, I among the rest—$3.00."[10]

His main interest at Princeton, however, was not social life, suppers in student rooms, or even the support of missionaries. He was primarily a student, and the college under the influence of John Witherspoon, president from 1768 to 1794, had been transformed into an institution for the training of leaders of the new nation in all fields of endeavor. Witherspoon, who himself took an active part in the American Revolution, believed that scholarship was most valuable when it provided effective guides for action and that scholars had a special obligation to their fellow citizens and the state. He broadened the curriculum by an increased emphasis on history, mathematics, natural science, composition and grammar, and public speaking. His son-in-law and successor, Samuel Smith, continued these educational policies and taught an identical philosophy. As president and professor of moral philosophy, he taught all branches of belles-lettres,

[8] Edward Watts to N. Biddle, December 8; Maria Gibbon to Maria Mayo, September 26, in the Biddle Manuscripts in the private collection of Nicholas B. Wainwright; J. Biddle to N. Biddle, n.d., in the Biddle Manuscripts at "Andalusia."

[9] Hannah Biddle to N. Biddle, January 21, 1800, Sunday evening, Thursday; Charles Biddle to N. Biddle, November 13, 1800, in the Biddle Manuscripts in the private collection of Nicholas B. Wainwright.

[10] N. Biddle, Expense Account at the College of New Jersey, in the Biddle Family Papers in the Library of Congress.

including composition and criticism, and also directed the study of metaphysics, natural theology, the philosophy of civil government, the law of nature and nations, logic, geography, history, and the evidences and principles of revealed religion.

The other professorship, that of mathematics and natural philosophy, was equally broad. Under the supervision of Dr. John Maclean, a Scotch physician and scientist, the Princeton undergraduates studied the elements of speculative and practical geometry, trigonometry, surveying, conic sections, algebra, natural and experimental philosophy, astronomy, and chemistry. These senior members of the faculty were assisted by two recent graduates, who were in charge of student discipline and were tutors in Latin and Greek.[11]

Nicholas Biddle was almost an ideal student for a college organized on this plan. To him the study of the liberal arts (or, as one of his former classmates at the University of Pennsylvania wrote, "Logick, Theoretick, Natural and Moral Philosophy, and the devil knows what all at the College of Princeton")[12] was a practical preparation for the study and practice of law. A knowledge of the dead languages, he conceded in a paper on this subject, was of little value to those who planned to engage in trade; their time could be more profitably spent on other subjects. But doctors and lawyers and "those who intend to move in a higher sphere" needed Latin and Greek, and the study of these languages should be confined to such persons.

Like most of his classmates, Biddle was a Federalist, and his papers on history and politics were strongly partisan. One of his friends gave extravagant expression to his hatred of Thomas Jefferson and Thomas Paine, saying that these two were paving the way for scenes similar to those that had occurred in France, and Biddle himself accused the Republican party of seeking to impose an absolute and tyrannical government upon the country.[13] Another of his compositions stated that republics were in con-

11 This description of Princeton at the close of the eighteenth century is taken from John Maclean, *History of the College of New Jersey* (Philadelphia, 1877); Varnum L. Collins, *Princeton* (New York, 1914); Thomas J. Wertenbaker, *Princeton, 1746–1896* (Princeton, 1946); Charles R. Williams, *The Cliosophic Society, Princeton University* (Princeton, 1916). Much of the material here used is also to be found in Thomas P. Govan, "Nicholas Biddle at Princeton," *Princeton University Library Chronicle*, IX (1947), 49–61.

12 Condy Raguet to N. Biddle, December 9, 1800, in the Biddle Family Papers in the Library of Congress.

13 Richard D. Bayly to N. Biddle, December 12, 1800, in the Biddle Manuscripts at "Andalusia"; Richard D. Bayly to N. Biddle, January 1, 1802; John Stoops to N. Biddle, August 9, 1802; N. Biddle to Richard B. Jones, November 26, 1802, in the Biddle Family Papers in the Library of Congress. Biddle's classroom compositions and his essays and addresses prepared for the Cliosophic Society are to be found in the Biddle Manuscripts in the private collection of Nicholas B. Wainwright and in the Biddle Family Papers in the Library of Congress.

stant danger from demagogues; even in America the alarm of insurrection had already sounded in Pennsylvania. "The fires of discord," he concluded, "rage with dreadful fury and unless extinguished by the wisdom of citizens may involve our country in one general conflagration."

Other papers that Biddle wrote for the classroom and the Cliosophic Society were concerned with the general problem of freedom and social order. In one "On the Discovery of America," he argued that Columbus had sought a new continent to provide a refuge for men seeking to escape the despotism of selfish princes, the religious inquisition, and the general depravity of Europe. The free and independent-minded men came to the New World, and those who desired to be slaves remained behind. Another paper was in the form of a letter from a Russian general to the Czar warning against the evil consequences of oppression and tyranny; and a third attacked the institution of ostracism in the Athenian Republic because it enabled an intriguer to banish those who opposed his infamous designs or obstructed his road to power. Such a man, raised into power by the affections of the mob, could excite against the best of men the envy of the populace, who resented the appearance of goodness and were weary of virtue itself.

He also wrote on subjects, such as "The Evils of Intemperance and the Joys of Drinking Wine," "Commerce," "The Civilized and Savage State," and the relative advantages of "Public and Private Punishment." The papers, youthful and naïve though they were, demonstrate the thoroughness of the training he received at Princeton. His opinions were not important— these would be altered with the growth of judgment and information—but in trying to establish the relation of the present to the past, in coming to a realization of the universality of the problems of humanity, and in grappling with the complex phenomena of politics and history, Biddle laid a basic foundation for subsequent studies.

He completed his assigned course in September, 1801, at the age of fifteen, the youngest person to graduate from Princeton up to his time and possibly since. Despite his youth, he shared the first honors with Edward Watts and was named to deliver the valedictory address. This, according to custom, was written for him by the Rev. Henry Kollock, a Presbyterian minister in New Jersey, who later became professor of theology at Princeton. Kollock, after many delays, sent a four-page oration on the lamentable literary taste of the times, of which he said, "I like neither the subject nor the execution. Such as it is, it is all yours."[14] Biddle's opinion is not recorded, but he delivered the address, eliciting the customary praise from what is always the most friendly of audiences, and returned to Philadelphia to begin the study of law.

[14] Henry Kollock to N. Biddle, September 17, 1801, Wednesday (September 23, 1801), in the Manuscript Collection, Princeton University Library.

~ 2 ~

Preparation

*T*he fifteen-year-old Nicholas Biddle could do little but study and read in this first fall and winter after his graduation from Princeton. The family was in mourning for his brother Edward, who had died while on his initial voyage as a midshipman in the United States Navy. The Biddles were an affectionate family, and this first break was a grievous one. Nicholas' mother was distraught, and his father, usually undemonstrative, disposed of the house on Market Street because it "brought to the recollection of the family our dear, lost Edward," and the family moved to another at 159 Chestnut.[1]

Nicholas shared his parents' grief and employed the enforced abstinence from all social life to concentrate his attention on his studies. He drove himself with fiery impatience as if he must learn everything there was to learn within a limited time. His teacher was William Lewis, one of the leaders of the Philadelphia bar, and his brother William, who had already begun to practice, was a constant adviser and tutor. The two young men discussed abstruse points of jurisprudence and the proper form of writs in the same spirit of affectionate rivalry that had characterized their study together at the University of Pennsylvania.

Under this stimulus Nicholas continued his study of French and Italian and kept on with his general reading in history, political economy, and natural science, for William was determined that his younger brother should become more than a mere practitioner of the law.[2] William also introduced him to Joseph Dennie, a strange and erratic person but a wonderful teacher, who, as founder of the *Port Folio*, a literary magazine, and guiding spirit of the Tuesday Club, was the arbiter of taste for Biddle's generation in Philadelphia. Every Tuesday a group of young men gathered

[1] Charles Biddle, *Autobiography*, pp. 290–93, 296.

[2] N. Biddle, "List of My Books, September 9, 1803," in the Biddle Manuscripts at Andalusia. Many of these books were a bequest from a family friend, Dr. Enoch Edwards of Frankford, and this legacy—more specifically the delay in its receipt—led Biddle to write a humorous and self-revealing poem which is to be found in the Biddle Family Papers in the Library of Congress.

with Dennie to discuss books and writers. Sometimes they dined together at the home of Joseph Hopkinson or of William Meredith, but more often they met just to talk and smoke in Asbury Dickins' bookstore at 25 North Second Street opposite Christ Church.[3]

Here Nicholas came to know the young men who were to be his associates in Philadelphia for more than forty years: Thomas Cadwalader, Nathaniel Chapman, Horace Binney, Richard Rush, Charles J. Ingersoll, and many other lawyers, physicians, teachers, and merchants, all of whom had been encouraged by Dennie to write for the *Port Folio*. Biddle himself contributed two humorous essays: one, signed "A Young Bachelor," was a description of a tea party with its awkward pauses, dull conversation, and boring entertainment; and the other a mock review of the nursery rhyme "Jack and Jill," which used technical terms and methods of serious criticism with a keen sense of the burlesque. He also wrote a series of public letters defending Commodore Truxton in one of the periodic conflicts between that quarrelsome officer and the Navy Department. These attracted the attention of Aaron Burr, a close friend of Charles Biddle, who wrote in a letter of introduction that his young friend Nicholas Biddle had attained a reputation for uncommon talents and acquirements and that if he were the author of some pieces ascribed to him, he was "certainly a very extraordinary youth."[4]

During these same years Nicholas began to think of himself as a young man about town. He commented critically on the merits of the plays and actors appearing in the local theaters and argued with his friends about the relative speed and blood lines of Maryland, Virginia, and Pennsylvania horses. He continued to find the young ladies of the city attractive, particularly Miss Turner, but pretended to take no pleasure in their company and grumbled at the necessity of attending teas, receptions, and the Assembly balls.

This life of study and pleasure contented him for three years, but the more he read of the law and the more he saw of a lawyer's life, the more certain he became that he wanted something different. He began to believe that his only prospects were "those of completing my profession, pleading the defenseless cases of vice and misfortune, and then dying like a mush-

---

[3] Studies of the *Port Folio*, the Tuesday Club, and Joseph Dennie are to be found in Albert H. Smyth, *The Philadelphia Magazines and Their Contributors* (Philadelphia, 1872); Ellis P. Oberholtzer, *The Literary History of Philadelphia* (Philadelphia, 1906); Frank L. Mott, *A History of American Magazines* (Cambridge, 1938); Robert E. Spiller *et al.* (eds.), *Literary History of the United States* (New York, 1948); Harold M. Ellis, *Joseph Dennie and His Circle: A Study of American Literature from 1792 to 1812* (Austin, Tex., 1915); Randolph C. Randall, "Authors of the Port Folio Revealed by the Hall Files," *American Literature*, XI (1940), 379–416; and Thomas P. Govan (ed.), "The Death of Joseph Dennie: A Memoir by Nicholas Biddle," *Pennsylvania Magazine of History and Biography*, LXXV (1951), 36–46.

[4] *Port Folio*, IV (1804), 49, 217; A. Burr to W. T. Broome, July 30, 1804, in the Biddle Manuscripts at Andalusia.

room on the soil which had seen me grow."[5] But this youthful pessimism was partially overcome in July, 1804, when General John Armstrong of New York, the newly appointed United States minister to France, invited him to serve as an unpaid secretary in Paris. Nicholas, of course, was eager to go, but his father was reluctant to permit him to do so. He and Mrs. Biddle had not recovered from the death of Edward, and they had just learned that their third son, James, who was also in the navy, had been captured and imprisoned when the "Philadelphia" went aground off Tripoli.

Nicholas was insistent, and his father finally consented. The statement in Charles Biddle's *Autobiography* concerning this momentous event in his son's life was characteristically brief and matter of fact. "In July 1804," he wrote, "my friend General Armstrong was appointed Ambassador to France. Wishing to get my son Nicholas with him as his secretary, I spoke to him and he agreed to take him. Nicholas left us the last of July."[6]

William Lewis was less restrained. He reminded his law student that he had played a part in bringing about the appointment and felt responsible for Biddle's good conduct. "Remember also," he added, "what is due to yourself and to your country, and should you ever think of me I beg of you to remember that I shall by no means be satisfied with hearing that you are in good health and conduct yourself with propriety—I shall expect much more, I shall whenever I hear your name mentioned expect to hear that you are in the pursuit of *noble ends by noble means* and that your success and your merit bid fair to render your character eminently prominent among the sons of America."

Lewis' letter with its well-meant advice provided Biddle with one of those opportunities that no serious young man with pretensions to a prose style could resist. "Be assured, my dear sir," he replied, "that your interference in my behalf shall not be forgotten; it has added another to the thousand notions which stimulate me to honorable exertions and I feel myself bound to prove that it has not been applied unworthily. I shall enter on the duties of my new situation with the timid diffidence of conscious inexperience and the trembling solicitude which a wish to give general satisfaction can alone inspire."[7]

Not all Biddle's friends were as enthusiastic as Lewis about his decision to go with Armstrong. Some of them believed that by accepting an appointment as secretary to a Republican minister he was betraying his party

[5] E. C. Thomas to N. Biddle, January 3, 29, June 9, July 2, 1802, February 1, 1803, in the Manuscript Collection, Princeton University Library; N. Biddle to Rebecca Biddle, a poem, June 25, 1804; N. Biddle, Journal of His Journey to Greece, in the Biddle Manuscripts in the Historical Society of Pennsylvania.

[6] Charles Biddle, *Autobiography*, p. 306; J. Armstrong to W. Lewis, July 15, 1804, in the Biddle Manuscripts in the Historical Society of Pennsylvania.

[7] W. Lewis to N. Biddle, July 19, 1804; N. Biddle to W. Lewis, July 20, 1804, in the Biddle Manuscripts in the Library of Congress.

and the cause of respectable government, but Biddle was impatient at such extreme partisan zeal. His father had taught him that men could differ about politics and principles without descending to personal hatred, and too many friends of the Biddle family were Republicans to permit Nicholas to believe that association with members of that party was dangerous.

The evil effects of excessive political feeling were made real to him in the weeks before he left Philadelphia, when Aaron Burr, a fugitive from New York because of his duel with Hamilton, was given refuge in the Biddle house on Chestnut Street. The offer of the Biddle house was made by Charles Biddle because Burr was his friend, not because of political sympathy, but his action was immediately denounced by many of his party friends. He was unmoved by these criticisms, and later, when a report was spread that several persons from New York were coming to kidnap Burr, he armed himself and came into town from his summer home. He stayed with Burr until the danger was past, and in his *Autobiography* wrote, "He would not have been easily taken."[8]

Nicholas left Philadelphia on July 30, soon after Burr had arrived, but on the day after his departure his father received a letter from General Armstrong announcing that the ship's sailing had been postponed. This news was an added sorrow to his mother. "I lament very much," she wrote, "that you did not wait untill General Armstrong's letter to your papa arrived. . . . It is impossible my beloved son to express what I felt at being separated from you and my constant anxiety for your welfare. To advise you is not in my power. I must therefore rely on the strength of your own mind and the goodness of your heart under that power alone that is able to protect you from all the temptations to which you will be exposed."

The month of August passed slowly, with the ship's sailing being delayed from day to day, but Nicholas' stay in New York was enlivened by a visit from Miss Turner. During this time he received letters of guidance and counsel from his father and William; but Thomas, a younger brother, wrote "merely to convince you of the increasing love of your affectionate brother."[9]

The ship finally sailed on September 2. Thirty-eight uneventful days later it arrived in Nantes, and General Armstrong and his party departed for the American ministry in Paris to take up their duties. Biddle was less than nineteen years old when he arrived in Paris. He was full grown, standing five feet seven inches in height, and was described in his passport as having chestnut eyes, a middling mouth, a middling nose, high forehead, round chin, fair complexion, chestnut hair and eyebrows, and oval face. This official description gives little idea of the romantic appearance dis-

[8] Charles Biddle, *Autobiography*, pp. 303–4, 402.

[9] Hannah Biddle to N. Biddle, August 5, 1804; Thomas Biddle to N. Biddle, August 5, 1804; Charles Biddle to N. Biddle, August 25, 1804, in the Biddle Manuscripts in the private collection of Nicholas B. Wainwright; William S. Biddle to N. Biddle, August 28, 1804, in the Biddle Family Papers in the Library of Congress.

played in his early portraits. Nicholas was a handsome young man, with eyes that reflected an eager and excited intelligence. He was sensitive about his too youthful appearance and tried to make himself seem older by assuming a grave and serious manner. And whenever he was questioned about his age, he would add four or five years in order to get the respect to which he felt entitled.[10]

He remained in Europe from October, 1804, to July, 1807, three years during which the political world was turned upside down. Two months after he arrived in Paris he witnessed the self-coronation of the Emperor, and the next year the war of the Third Coalition began. Napoleon moved swiftly. In three campaigns between October, 1805, and June, 1807, he defeated the Austrian, Prussian, and Russian armies, and then at Tilsit on the Niemen River he divided all Europe between himself and Alexander I of Russia. Great Britain was isolated but took comfort in Nelson's victory at Trafalgar in October, 1805, which made her as dominant on the sea as her enemy was on land. The war continued in a different form. The British blockaded the ports under French jurisdiction, and Napoleon, in attempted retaliation, established the Continental System.

These measures were intended to bring economic pressure upon the respective belligerents, but they had the incidental effect of crippling American and other neutral trade. Biddle followed the developments closely and with disappointment; he had thought, like many other Americans, that the renewed outbreak of war would enable the United States to win concessions from each of the powers engaged. President Jefferson and Secretary of State James Madison, however, had committed the nation to a policy of peace, and Napoleon and his enemies alike interpreted this renunciation of force as an admission of weakness.

The failure of American diplomacy at this critical period had a lasting influence on Biddle's thought and life. It made him an ardent nationalist determined to gain respect for his country and its free institutions, and a lifelong advocate of a strong army and navy to be used for the protection and advancement of the national interest. During this period in Paris Biddle obtained a valuable introduction to the problems and techniques of international finance. His particular assignment was the certification and payment of the claims of American merchants against the French government. These had been assumed by the United States as part of the payment for Louisiana, and Biddle was thus able to acquire a detailed knowledge of international commercial and financial practices and the laws and customs that governed them.[11]

10 United States, French, and British passports issued to N. Biddle, 1804–7, in the private collection of Nicholas B. Wainwright and in the Biddle Family Papers in the Library of Congress.

11 N. Biddle, Journal of His Journey to Greece, in the Biddle Manuscripts in the Historical Society of Pennsylvania; Henry S. Waddell to N. Biddle, July 18, August 1, 1805, in the Biddle Manuscripts in the Library of Congress.

Not all his attention was given to such grave matters of state policy. While in Europe he devoted much time to pleasure, study, and travel and left the fullest record of these activities. His teachers, family, and friends had warned him of the temptations that would confront him, apparently thinking, as did Thomas Jefferson, that a young American visiting abroad inevitably acquired a fondness for European luxury and dissipation and a contempt for the simplicity of his own country. Their fears were unwarranted so far as Biddle was concerned. His tastes and desires were moderate. His vices, if he had any, went unnoticed, and his observation of European manners only strengthened his affection for the United States.

He read constantly during his first year in Paris and supplemented his reading by eagerly questioning whomever he met on every subject from politics and history to agriculture and mineralogy. His mind was on fire with a fervid, eager wish to study and learn, but he soon came to the conclusion that "all which concerns real solid useful knowledge may be learnt from books, since the social period which confined to a single soil the knowledge of the people is past." The purpose of this statement was to justify his determination to leave Paris and to occupy whatever remained of his time in "seeing as far as possible the different varieties of people" who inhabited Europe. He had already learned something about them. When he left America, he had applied for and had been granted a degree of Master of Arts from Princeton in the belief that a scholar would be honored by Europeans, but when he planned his trip he was more realistic. He wrote his father and Governor Joseph Bloomfield of New Jersey for military commissions, and they responded immediately. The governor sent an appointment as colonel in the militia with authority to design his own uniform, and his father persuaded General James Wilkinson, a kinsman by marriage, to procure Nicholas a brevet captaincy in the United States Artillery.[12]

Dressed as a soldier, he left Paris in July, 1805, and traveled through northern and eastern France and Switzerland. His companion was George Gibbs of Newport, a wealthy young mineralogist, and such was their initial pleasure in each other's company that they decided to tour Italy together the next winter. Biddle had to obtain his father's permission and additional money. They returned to Paris, and he occupied the interval between his return and the receipt of a favorable reply from Charles Biddle in making arrangements for a number of plaster casts of statuary in the Louvre to be prepared for exhibition in the newly formed Pennsylvania Academy of the Fine Arts. Biddle was delighted with this task. He spent many hours in consultation with Houdon, the sculptor of Washington and Jefferson, deciding which were the choice pieces for reproduction, and signed a con-

[12] J. Bloomfield to N. Biddle, May 13, 1805, in the Manuscript Collection, Princeton University Library; C. Biddle to N. Biddle, June 10, 1805, in the Biddle Manuscripts in the private collection of Nicholas B. Wainwright.

tract with an Italian artist to supervise the making of the casts. Just then the letter arrived from Charles Biddle granting him permission to take the additional journey. The same letter brought the welcome news that his brother James had been released from captivity in Tripoli and was once more safe at home.[13]

Biddle left Paris at once for the south of France, but he soon tired of Gibbs as a companion. Society in travel, he confided to his journal, must be "very delicately composed." All women should be excluded because "with females you can never see the whole of everything. The courtesies of society distract attention, and although many objects are seen more agreeably when seen with friends, yet all are seen less profoundly." The reason for this outburst against the sex usually so attractive to a young man of twenty was not recorded. He immediately turned to a discussion of Gibbs and wrote that "the most useless and unprofitable of all society in travelling is that with persons of your own age and your own standing in point of improvement."[14]

They parted when they left France. Gibbs went to Genoa, Leghorn, Rome, and Naples, and Biddle followed at a more leisurely pace. In Florence and Rome he spent most of his time in the museums, and under the tutelage of John Vanderlyn, a fellow American who had been a pupil of Gilbert Stuart, he continued the education begun under Houdon. The first time Biddle walked through the Louvre, he reported, he did so "with indifference, or rather with surprise at finding that all the great things . . . were nothing but marble cut into the form of men, or pieces covered with figures." But after visiting Italy he began to understand what the artists were attempting to do and could say that "now, without pretending to any skill, I think I could tell a good from a bad picture or statue."[15]

He found the whole of Italy exciting, but he soon grew restive as he reflected that everything he saw had been seen by many thousands before him. He inquired about the possibility of a trip to Greece, influenced by the thought that "knowledge is doubly valuable when it is exclusive. All that we do know is indeed so small that we must be contented sometimes to build our reputation on the ignorance of our neighbor." He had diffi-

[13] C. Biddle to N. Biddle, September 5, 1805, in the private collection of Nicholas B. Wainwright; W. S. Biddle to N. Biddle, May 13, 1807, in the Biddle Family Papers in the Library of Congress; Helen W. Henderson, *The Pennsylvania Academy of the Fine Arts* (Boston, 1911), pp. 10–12.

[14] N. Biddle, Journal of His Journey to Greece (written in the form of letters to his brother Thomas), in the Biddle Manuscripts in the Historical Society of Pennsylvania. Portions of this journal were published in William N. Bates (ed.), "Nicholas Biddle's Journey to Greece," *Proceedings of the Numismatic and Antiquarian Society of Pennsylvania*, XXVIII (1919), 167–83.

[15] Bates, *op. cit.*; G. Gibbs to N. Biddle, November 20, December 17, 1805, February 22, 1806, in the Biddle Family Papers in the Library of Congress; John Vanderlyn to N. Biddle, August 2, 1806, in the Vanderlyn Manuscripts in the New York Historical Society.

culty in procuring passage but finally located the Greek brig "Themis-
tocles," which departed from Naples for Zante on March 28, 1806. The
United States consul in Sicily was on board, but Biddle's closest companion was a Greek priest, who for some obscure political reason had been
smuggled onto the ship in Naples. The priest was an intelligent man and
willingly instructed the young American in the pronunciation of modern
Greek. Biddle was surprised to find how little it differed from the language
he had learned in school. "The ancient Greek," he informed William, "has
only suffered what everything traditionally will suffer in its passage from
a civilized nation to a barbarous posterity; the embellishments, the beauties
are gradually forgotten as the refinement which creates them ceases."[16]

The two scholars were pleased with each other's company on the
tedious voyage until one day they chanced to discuss religion. Biddle was
unwise enough to express his doubt when the priest said he had a piece of
the true Cross which would resist flame and that a certain patriarch in
Constantinople had lighted the lamps in a large room with fire from his
beard after they had been extinguished by Satan. The modern-minded
American was astounded by what he considered the barbarous superstition
of the Greek, and the Greek was frightened to learn that he was traveling
on the same ship with an infidel. His fears were communicated to the captain and the crew, and when Biddle went ashore at Messina on the northeastern tip of Sicily, his luggage was secretly unloaded and the ship sailed
without him.

He found Messina distressing. The poverty of the people, the corruption
of the government, and the dirt and filth offended him, and he noted in his
diary that "though I have never seen so much misery, I have rarely given
so little in charity. What indeed can I do? I cannot extinguish and therefore will not wet the flame." His impatience to get on prevented him from
visiting any of the rest of Sicily, but it was not until Thursday, April 17,
that he obtained a passage to Malta in one of the small boats that traded
between the two islands.[17]

Upon his arrival he was greatly pleased to find the United States frigate
"Constitution" in port; he dined almost daily with Captain John Rodgers
and his officers, many of whom were friends and former shipmates of
James Biddle. Captain Rodgers was an enthusiastic horseman and wanted
company, which led Biddle to write plaintively to his younger brother:
"You, my dear Tom, who remember my want of horsemanship will
imagine my ideas at sight of a fine horse which I was to mount. Much as I
dislike equitation, there was no declining."[18]

Time passed slowly on Malta, and he was relieved to sail for the island

[16] N. Biddle to W. S. Biddle, July 25, 1806, in the Biddle Family Papers in the Library
of Congress.

[17] N. Biddle, Journal of His Journey to Greece, in the Biddle Manuscripts in the
Historical Society of Pennsylvania.

[18] Ibid.

of Zante. Here he remained three days, observing the customs and habits of the people and familiarizing himself with the constitution and laws of the Seven Islands Republic. This small state had been created in 1800 to govern the islands formerly belonging to Venice, and its constitution, Biddle wrote, "was one of those productions which has many of the liberal principles of the modern schools but which like too many of their works is badly fortified against attack and innovation." Its elaborate definitions of human rights and its equally elaborate provision for their protection would prove unavailing, he predicted, since constitutions were made of paper and paper had not yet been able to secure or defend the freedom of a nation.

Russian troops had been landed on the islands, ostensibly to protect their independence, and Biddle was alarmed at this extension of Russian power into the Mediterranean. He believed that it was only a prelude to their further advance into western Europe and that this advance, under the guise of protecting freedom, would actually end in the establishment of autocratic power. He soon exhausted the sights and tourist attractions of Zante and took the first obtainable boat across the narrow channel to the ancient port of Cyllene. Upon landing, he was surprised to find that a customs house and two huts were all that remained of what had once been a flourishing city. He spent the night with the Turkish customs officer, dined on freshly killed mutton, and departed the next morning for Patras. He rode horseback through the broad and well-cultivated plains of Elis, accompanied only by a servant, and, since he had no contemporary map of Greece, he was forced to rely upon his own knowledge of classical geography. He was frequently surprised by the appearance of villages where he expected none or by complete emptiness where he looked for towns, but he was never lost, and only infrequently was he obliged to ask for directions from inhabitants of the countryside.

From Patras he went to Aegium and then crossed the Gulf of Corinth to Delphos. Turning eastward, he traveled through the Turkish province of Lavadia to Chaeronea, and then north to Thermopylae. After viewing the battlefield, he turned southeast to Thebes and then to Athens. Here he remained several weeks, taking side excursions to the island of Aegina and to Marathon by way of Mount Pentelicus. His guide in Athens was M. Fauvel, the French consul, who was an amateur archeologist and antiquarian, and through him he met M. Lusieri, a painter who had supervised the removal of the statuary from the Parthenon by Lord Elgin. Biddle, who had already been shocked by the unrepaired damage that time and neglect had done to the monuments of antiquity, was highly indignant at what he considered the vandalism of the English nobleman. The destruction of the Temple of Ephesus, he wrote, was a high and honorable deed as compared with Elgin's thefts, and he hoped that "some historian may one day do justice by declaring that 'Herostratus burnt for glory, Elgin robbed for gold.'"

He left Athens in mid-June for Sparta, traveling by way of Eleusis,

Megara, Corinth, Sicyon, Nemea, Mycenae, Argos, Nauplia, and Tripoliza, the Turkish capital. He then followed the Eurota River north to Belmina and Megalopolis, crossed Arcadia to Elis, and returned to Patras. Here he boarded a ship sailing to Trieste, where he arrived late in July, and from there he went overland to Paris.[19]

These months in Italy and Greece were of immense value to Biddle. The measurements and drawings he made of classical buildings aroused an enthusiasm for architecture which found expression in his subsequent contribution to the Greek revival movement in the United States. But the chief value of the journey was the solitude he enjoyed, which gave him an opportunity for prolonged self-examination. The same romantic impulse that had prompted him to break away from the usual path of tourist travel and become the first American to visit Greece also led him to contemplate solemnly his past and his future.

Before he left Italy he wrote: "Every good citizen owes himself to his country and his family, and I feel that every step of my path I become a better citizen." Freedom came to have a greater meaning for him as he traveled through the areas which had given it birth and from which it had long since departed. He hated the tyranny of the Turks, but he despised the servility of the Greeks. Are these Athenians, he asked, "these men, the wretches, little superior to the beasts whom they drive heedlessly over the ruins? . . . Unable to act, they scarcely dare to think freely and everything, even down to their music (the miserable nasal noise of a slave afraid to speak out loud) tells us they have a master."[20]

He came to understand the importance of leadership in a republic as he realized how tenuous a hold freedom and its political institutions have on the affections of men, and he determined to take a share in the molding of events, to participate in that form of activity which seemed to him more important than any other. To William he wrote: "If, at this moment, I feel any ambition, any wish to gain the applause of others, it is by becoming not an Attorney, not a Lawyer, not a Pleader, but an Orator. To you I need not explain the majesty of the name." And to Edward Watts, using less antique language, he announced his determination to devote himself "wholly to the world and politics and building a sort of a name as a statesman."[21]

[19] *Ibid.*

[20] *Ibid.*

[21] N. Biddle to E. Watts, June 3, 1806, in the Manuscript Collection in the Princeton University Library; N. Biddle to W. S. Biddle, August, 1806, in the Biddle Family Papers in the Library of Congress.

～ 3 ～

The Young Lawyer

*L*ate in the summer of 1806, when Biddle returned to Paris, his plans for an immediate departure to America were postponed because Armstrong needed his services. His duties were less burdensome and his desire for knowledge less acute than during his earlier residence, and he had more time for purely social activities. He visited Lafayette at LaGrange and had dinner with Mme de Staël, but he spent most of his spare time at the home of a Mrs. Stewart, a fellow American. Mademoiselle Caroline du Sait lived in the same house, and she and Nicholas pretended that they were brother and sister as they played together in a mild flirtation under the approving eye of their hostess.[1] But even the delights of this association did not keep Biddle's thoughts from straying toward home. He finished his special assignment for the minister at the close of the year and resigned in January, 1807, planning to visit Belgium, Germany, Holland, England, and Ireland before returning home.

Mrs. Stewart gave him a farewell dinner, and he promised never to forget his little sister. The two vowed that each night at ten they would drink a toast of remembrance, but there the romance ended. The northern European countries were dull and gray with winter drabness, and Biddle found them boring. He was tired of traveling, and in London, when he was asked by James Monroe, the American minister, to act as a temporary secretary, he readily accepted. He was very happy in London and developed a warm and personal friendship with the whole Monroe family. Robert Walsh of Baltimore was also at the legation, and the two secretaries had much in common. Walsh had read law after his graduation from Georgetown, but his real ambition was to follow the example of Joseph Dennie and earn a livelihood by writing and editing. He had already contributed several articles and reviews to the *Port Folio,* and he and Biddle spent much of their time talking of writing, painting, and the other arts.[2]

---

[1] Mrs. D. Stewart to N. Biddle, February 18, April 6, 1807, in the Biddle Manuscripts in the Library of Congress.

[2] Robert Walsh to N. Biddle, September 18, 1809, in the Biddle Family Papers in the Library of Congress; Sister M. Frederick Lochemes, *Robert Walsh, His Story* (New York, 1941), pp. 57, 60.

London society, even that of scholars and literary men, was largely closed to them, and they resented the disdain with which they and other Americans were treated. Both conceived a distaste for English intellectual and social snobbery that colored much of their later thinking and writing, and both were triumphant over a minor scholastic victory which Biddle gained over a group of Cambridge dons when he accompanied Monroe to the university. During a discussion at dinner a debate arose as to the difference between the Greek of Homer and the modern idiom. When none of the classicists present could settle the point, Biddle modestly joined the conversation and "exhibited a knowledge of the subject so profound and critical, that the learned gentlemen present listened in silent amazement, while Monroe, overjoyed at what he considered a kind of American triumph, with difficulty repressed his exultation and delight."[3]

Soon thereafter Biddle departed from London, taking with him letters and reports from Monroe to Jefferson and Madison. In late September he disembarked from his Baltimore-bound ship off Cape Henry, at the entrance to Chesapeake Bay, and hurried overland to Washington. The Secretary of State and the President were absent in Virginia, and Biddle had to wait for their arrival. The whole city was excited over the recent attack by the British man-of-war "Leopard" upon the United States frigate "Chesapeake" and the impressment from its crew of four alleged deserters. War between the two countries seemed probable, and Biddle, now definitely anti-British, rejoiced at the prospect.

The sense of national humiliation born of this affair increased the bitterness of the opponents of Jefferson and Madison within the Republican party and outside it, thus adding strength to a movement initiated by John Randolph of Roanoke to substitute Monroe for Madison as the party's candidate to succeed Jefferson in 1809. Biddle, as a person coming directly from Monroe, was eagerly questioned by many of the members of this antiadministration group, and in reporting these conversations, he wrote: "Very little has been said in the public prints, but the candidates are very clearly designated by public opinion. I hope that you persist in your intention of returning home shortly. It is everywhere said that your interests suffer by your absence."[4]

Public questions ceased to occupy Biddle's attention after his arrival in Philadelphia. He found his father and brother involved in the complex affairs of Aaron Burr, and Biddle, while insisting that he was not partial to Burr and found certain parts of his conduct abhorrent, associated himself with these attempts to aid his father's friend. "I am afraid that I have

[3] Longacre and Herring (eds.), *National Portrait Gallery*, Vol. IV.

[4] C. Biddle to N. Biddle, July 18, 1807; T. Biddle to N. Biddle, September 27, 1807, in the Biddle Manuscripts in the private collection of Nicholas B. Wainwright; R. O. Forrest to N. Biddle, October 9, 1807, in the Biddle Manuscripts in the Library of Congress; N. Biddle to J. Monroe, October 31, 1807, in the Monroe Manuscripts in the Library of Congress.

begun my legal career somewhat inauspiciously," he said to Monroe. "After his acquittal at Richmond, Burr came here broken in fortune and character and has been pursued by his creditors. . . . I thought it my duty not to refuse any aid within the limits of my profession, particularly as he is ruined and any assistance I gave would be gratuitous."[5]

Other business was soon turned over to him. William Biddle went to the legislature in 1807 and 1808, and left Nicholas in charge of a large practice. Soon many of his associates in Europe sent Nicholas legal matters to handle for them. He was the authorized representative of Fulmer Skipworth, former American consul in Paris; of his successor, David Warden; and of General David Lyman, the consul in London. The bulk of his practice was thus connected with civil law and the collection of debts, but the case which brought him the most notice was a particularly sordid murder trial in which he and Richard Rush were appointed as defense counsel. The evidence against the accused men was overwhelming, so the lawyers decided that their only course was to admit that the men were guilty in an effort to reduce the charge to murder in the second degree. Biddle as junior counsel opened the case and, Rush later reported, "worked out a capital speech; his language, even at that early day, disciplined and classic, and his delivery animated and impressive."[6]

The plea was unsuccessful. The prisoners were convicted of murder in the first degree. Fortunately, not all Biddle's cases ended so disastrously, and he soon found himself with a profitable practice. The embargo enacted by Congress on December 22, 1807, was injurious to the commercial interests of Philadelphia and the rest of the country, but, as Horace Binney noted, it "gave an unparalleled harvest to the bar." Many problems arose that involved novel interpretations of the law, particularly in regard to insurance policies, and the lawyers received their compensation regardless of the outcome of the battle between insurance company and policyholder.[7]

Biddle shared in this general prosperity and derived more pleasure from the practice of law than he had expected. He enjoyed renewing his acquaintance with the lawyers and other professional men who had continued their literary meetings with Dennie while Biddle was in Europe. But the *Port Folio* was dangerously close to suspension of publication. Dennie's poor health, aggravated by his increasing intemperance, was

[5] N. Biddle to J. Monroe, January 2, 1808, in the Monroe Manuscripts in the Library of Congress.

[6] R. Rush to P. A. Browne, December 4, 1856, in the Gratz Manuscript Collection in the Historical Society of Pennsylvania. Other letters and documents dealing with Biddle's legal practice are to be found in the Biddle Family Papers in the Library of Congress and in the Biddle Manuscripts in the Historical Society of Pennsylvania.

[7] Horace Binney, Autobiography, in the Binney Manuscripts in the Historical Society of Pennsylvania; Louis M. Sears, *Jefferson and the Embargo* (Durham, 1927), pp. 212–13.

making it impossible for him to attend to the business end of the enterprise, and he had offended many readers by his extreme antidemocratic views in politics. Only a drastic reorganization could save it, and in this emergency Dennie's friends made a new arrangement with the publishing firm of Bradford and Inskeep that enabled the magazine to continue.

Dennie informed his mother that he was now very powerfully supported. "We have Bishops and Lawyers in our Confederacy," he wrote. "The Chief Justice of the United States, Judge Washington, Judge Peters and the Honourable Mr. Penn are with us." The prime movers, however, were less distinguished men. It was Biddle, Alexander Wilson the ornithologist, and Condy Raguet, merchant and economist, who assumed most of the burden of editing and publishing the magazine. They expressly excluded from its pages all references to party politics and religion, transforming the *Port Folio* into a national periodical appealing to varied groups and interests. Literature continued to predominate, but sporting notes, travelers' accounts, and technical and mechanical articles were also published.[8]

Biddle was one of the most frequent contributors to the new magazine. He wrote reviews of new books, translated Greek and French poetry, and supplied filler material. He wrote a long biographical article on his uncle, the first Nicholas Biddle, and a second on Machiavelli, in which he asserted that the Florentine's purpose in writing *The Prince* was not to teach but to warn. Dennie was enthusiastic in his praise, and Biddle found the work with the *Port Folio* so satisfying that he began to think once more of abandoning the practice of law. This sentiment was strengthened in July, 1809, when Robert Walsh returned from London. Their friendship was renewed, and their conversations and correspondence on literary subjects contributed to the dissatisfaction with which each viewed the legal profession.[9]

Biddle was thus caught between his desire to devote most of his time to writing and the pressure from his family and many of his friends to continue the practice of law when, in February, 1810, he was asked by Colonel William Clark to edit the journals of the Lewis and Clark expedition. He was greatly tempted, but on March 3, after much internal debate, he definitely rejected the offer. He began to regret the decision as soon as he had made it, and two weeks later he wrote Clark that he would accept if no other arrangements had been made. He left Philadelphia almost immediately, long before he could have received an answer, and traveled by stage to Clark's home in the Valley of Virginia.[10]

[8] Ellis, *Dennie*, p. 205; *Port Folio* (1809), 3d ser., Vol. I, title page.

[9] *Port Folio*, II (1809), 120–33, 285–93, 578; R. Walsh to N. Biddle, July 11, August 1, 15, September 18, October 2, November 7, 1809, January 8, 27, February 4, 7, 1810, in the Biddle Family Papers in the Library of Congress; N. Biddle to R. Walsh, October 29, 1809, in the Biddle Manuscripts in the private collection of Nicholas B. Wainwright.

[10] W. Clark to N. Biddle, February 20, 1810; N. Biddle to W. Clark, March 3, 17, 1810, in the Biddle Manuscripts in the Library of Congress.

The original journals and memoranda, totaling more than a million words, were turned over to Biddle, and he began to appreciate the magnitude of the task he had undertaken. The explorers had recorded every event in their long journey. They had made careful notes concerning the Indians, the geography of the area, and the flora and fauna encountered, but much explanatory material had to be supplied. David Shannon, a member of the expedition, was sent to Philadelphia to assist Biddle with his personal knowledge, and additional information was obtained from the published works on the history, ethnology, and geography of the Missouri and Columbia River valleys. Some of these were available in Philadelphia, but others had to be obtained from Paris and London. There were times when Biddle began to doubt whether the task would ever be finished.[11]

He arose each morning at five and devoted seven hours or longer to the work. Gradually the book began to take shape, and at the end of the summer was so nearly completed that Biddle accepted the nomination of the American Republicans as a candidate for a seat in the lower house of the state legislature. His father was a candidate for the state senate on the same ticket, and in early October they were both elected.[12] Biddle's pleasure in this first political success was tempered, however, by the knowledge that he must pass the winter in Lancaster. He had been very busy since his return from Europe three years before, and his social engagements and interests had been few, particularly as Johannah Turner had not waited for him and no other young lady had taken her place in his affections. But now, just when he was to be absent from the city during the height of the social season, he had found an acquaintance that made him reluctant to leave.[13]

Her name was Jane Craig, and she was only seventeen years old, but Biddle loved her almost from their first meeting and soon was spending with her every hour he could spare from the Lewis and Clark manuscripts. She had only one rival, and that was her mother, Margaret Craig, a cultivated, cosmopolitan, and beautiful woman unlike anyone Biddle had previously known, and he hardly knew which he loved more.[14] Mrs. Craig

11 W. Clark to N. Biddle, May 22, 1810; N. Biddle to W. Clarke, July 7, 1810; N. Biddle to D. Warden, July 7, 1810, in the Biddle Manuscripts in the Library of Congress.

12 N. Biddle to E. Watts, October 5, 1810, in the Biddle Family Papers in the Library of Congress.

13 N. Biddle to Rebecca Biddle, August 30, 1808, in the Biddle Manuscripts in the Historical Society of Pennsylvania; W. Miller to Mrs. John Craig, October 10, 1810, in the Biddle-Craig Manuscripts in the Historical Society of Pennsylvania.

14 Gouverneur Morris, no inexperienced observer, wrote the following verse as a tribute to Mrs. Craig's charms:

> "With lively grace to beauty joined
> A feeling heart, a noble mind.
> To chastened wit and social ease
> You form't at once to love and please,
> In nature's lavish bounty deckt
> From princes might command respect."

later denied that she had been a matchmaker between Jane and Nicholas, and perhaps she was right, but it is also evident that her own heart was engaged from the very beginning of the affair.

Her husband, John Craig, had died only a short time before, and her oldest son, James, was in Europe, so she adopted Nicholas as one of the family, and his interests and work became her main concern. He was encouraged to talk at will of the problems of editing the Lewis and Clark journals, of his travels in Europe, and of his political ambitions, and, when he was tired, they read poetry and novels. This intimacy between the Craigs and Biddle had hardly been established before it was interrupted by his departure for Lancaster. The night before leaving, he went to Jane's house to bid her goodbye. Her mother was resting in preparation for a late party, and Biddle, not wishing to disturb her, departed without acquainting her of his presence. He had hardly arrived home before he received a reproachful note affectionately chiding him for his neglect.[15]

She ordered him to return to pay his respects and threatened that if he did not do so, she would burn the plans he had drawn for a Greek summer house at her country home, "Andalusia," and build a mud cottage according to her own fancy. Biddle was unable to comply with her command, but the letter gave him pleasure. The conventions of the time and place forbade his writing to Jane, but Mrs. Craig had opened the way for continued communication between them. All the next day, as he rode toward Lancaster, he thought of his answer, and immediately after dining at the inn in Downingstown he asked for pen and paper. Across the top of the sheet he copied the harsh phrases of her condemnation and then began a long doggerel poem of affectionate protest, the limping meter of which testified to its composition on horseback. As he finished, he looked up to see a bemused traveler who seemed to think it strange that a person should write so long; so he closed with the statement that "though the deaf and the blind might see it was not poetry, I can assure you my dear madame it is not fiction."[16]

He waited with anxiety for her answer and was relieved a few days later when she replied that he must consider all formality at an end between them. "I have long hoped that it would be so," she wrote, "but the restraints of the world and the caution so necessary to our sex at every period often retard the progress of friendship in minds most congenial to each other." Biddle was overjoyed and told Mrs. Craig that he had read and reread her letter "with feelings, which, if you were of my own age, I would have less difficulty in understanding." The exchange of letters continued at regular intervals, and their occasional references to Jane were

[15] Mrs. J. Craig to N. Biddle, November 30, 1810, in the Biddle-Craig Manuscripts in the Historical Society of Pennsylvania.

[16] N. Biddle to Mrs. J. Craig, December 1, 1810, in the Biddle-Craig Manuscripts in the Historical Society of Pennsylvania.

tinged with amused and loving condescension as if they were writing of a favorite child. Jane had her mother send Nicholas a copy of her favorite novel, and, in acknowledging the gift, he wrote: "My grave occupations have not given me time to do more than cast my eyes over the first pages of Mathilde but accompany my thanks to the unknown donor with the assurance that my chief inducement to read it will be her recommendation and that my principal reason for considering the hero as a model would be that she approves of him."[17]

His reference to his grave occupations was not entirely ironic, for he was unusually active for a new assemblyman. He had gone to Lancaster thinking that he would accomplish little. All but fifteen members of the legislature were Republicans, and the Philadelphia delegation, who considered themselves Federalists, seemed a powerless minority. But Biddle's father wanted certain local measures to be passed, and he persuaded his associates to take a conciliatory attitude toward what his son called "the Germans and other strange animals in the state councils." The policy worked, and the city delegation, Nicholas later reported, was able "to preserve even in matters of mere party, a respectful attention, and on all other occasions, a degree of influence far beyond our numerical strength."[18]

His own part, he said, had been "that of a plain, frank, and independent member careless of party distinctions, always speaking my sentiments with freedom but at the same time avoiding every offensive expression that could tend to irritate," and he favorably impressed many of his older colleagues. His first assignment was the chairmanship of the Committee on the Education of the Poor. The Pennsylvania constitution had directed the legislature to provide for the establishment of schools "in such a manner that the poor may be taught gratis," but in twenty years not a single free school had been established in the state. No one besides the chairman seemed interested in the least, but Biddle had studied the free schools of Europe and New England, and had read the works of Noah Webster, Benjamin Rush, Samuel Harrison Smith, and other proponents of a national system of free education in the United States.

He determined to make a serious proposal, for he was convinced that American society could not be truly equal so long as it continued "the most odious of all distinctions, the practical inequality between the educated and the ignorant." His plan provided for the division of all the

17 Mrs. J. Craig to N. Biddle, December 3, 10, 1810; N. Biddle to Mrs. J. Craig, December 15, 1810, in the Biddle-Craig Manuscripts in the Historical Society of Pennsylvania.

18 N. Biddle to E. Watts, October 5, 1810, in the Biddle Family Papers in the Library of Congress; N. Biddle to J. Monroe, June 6, 1811, in the Monroe Manuscripts in the Library of Congress; N. Biddle, Pennsylvania Political Factions and Parties, 1806–1810, manuscript notebook in the Biddle Manuscripts in the Historical Society of Pennsylvania. For a recent study of Pennsylvania politics in this period see Sanford W. Higginbotham, *The Keystone in the Democratic Arch: Pennsylvania Politics, 1800–1816* (Harrisburg, 1952).

counties of the state into small neighborhoods so that each family would be convenient to a school, the schoolmaster was to be paid a sufficient sum to enable him to teach the poor free of charge, and the rest of the pupils would pay a small tuition. Such schools, Biddle believed, combining children of all economic classes, would make for mutual sympathy and understanding between them. This proposal was too expensive to be considered by a legislature dominated by small property-holders, more interested in avoiding taxes than in the welfare of the state and its people. No action was taken on the bill, but twenty-five years later, when Thomas H. Burrows established a free system of public schools in Pennsylvania, he acknowledged his indebtedness to Biddle's pioneer work in the field.[19]

Biddle was also a member of the Committee on the Reorganization of the Militia, in which capacity he carried on an extensive correspondence with officials of other states in a vain attempt to provide an effective defense force for the war with Great Britain or France, or perhaps both, that he thought was approaching. He was similarly unsuccessful in his attempt to arouse the interest of the legislature in internal improvements. He was particularly concerned with the proposal to build a canal to connect the Delaware and Susquehanna rivers, but the same unwillingness to spend money that had defeated his efforts for the schools and the militia defeated this proposal too.[20]

The Republican party in Pennsylvania, at this stage in its history, was insistently loyal to the dogmas which its leaders had promulgated in the 1790's. Governmental economy was the principal aim of political activity, and all proposals for the expenditure of funds, however necessary or useful they might be, were relentlessly opposed. Biddle had no patience with this shortsighted policy. Pennsylvanians, he insisted, were too indifferent to the improvement of their state. They were idle and inactive while their rivals were making progress. New York had already built a connection between Lake Erie and the Mohawk River and could supply Pittsburgh more cheaply than Philadelphia could. Maryland was constructing turnpikes to attract the produce of the Susquehanna Valley to Baltimore, but the Pennsylvania legislature did nothing.[21]

The same provincial attitude was being exhibited by Pennsylvanians in

[19] *Journal of the Twenty-first House of Representatives of the Commonwealth of Pennsylvania* (Lancaster, 1811), pp. 108–14; N. Biddle to J. Dennie, February 13, 1811, in the Biddle Manuscripts in the Historical Society of Pennsylvania; N. Biddle to T. H. Burrows, March 6, 1836, April 8, 1837, in the Stauffer Manuscript Collection in the Historical Society of Pennsylvania.

[20] *Journal of the House*, pp. 3, 5, 13, 92, 153, 159, 333–38, 526; draft of a letter from N. Biddle to an unnamed correspondent, December 12, 1810, in the Biddle Manuscripts in the private collection of Nicholas B. Wainwright; Colonel Williams to N. Biddle, December 12, 1810, in the Biddle Family Papers in the Library of Congress.

[21] N. Biddle to Mrs. J. Craig, February 15, 1811, in the Biddle-Craig Manuscripts in the Historical Society of Pennsylvania.

regard to the Bank of the United States, which was under attack in the national Congress. The Bank's headquarters were in Philadelphia, but to most of the legislators it was a foreign corporation imposed on their state by the national authorities. Biddle alone rose to its defense, and his speech on the Bank of the United States in this legislative session became the most important in his entire public career. It established his reputation as an authority on banking, currency, and governmental finance and later led President Monroe to appoint him to the board of the second national bank.

Defender
of the
National Bank

*B*iddle owned no stock of the Bank of the United States, nor was he closely connected by ties of blood or friendship with its officers or directors. His concern was a disinterested one, based on the conviction that the Bank was a necessary public institution performing essential public functions, and that the national economy would be injured if the charter was not renewed. It had been established by the Congress in 1791 upon the recommendation of the Secretary of the Treasury, Alexander Hamilton, and had been placed under private control because this seemed to be the only effective means of protection from political pressure for partisan ends.

One of the Bank's duties was to act as the fiscal agent of the national Treasury; another to protect and transfer the national revenues without cost to the government; and a third to provide a national currency. In addition, it held a considerable proportion of the specie reserves of the whole banking system and acted as the general guardian of commercial credit, the other banks, and the mercantile and financial community. The term "central bank" had not yet been invented, and the concept embodied in it was only partially understood, but this was the position that the Bank of the United States occupied in the American banking and credit system.[1]

Thomas Jefferson, Secretary of State in Washington's Cabinet, and

[1] Bray Hammond, *Banks and Politics in America from the Revolution to the Civil War* (Princeton, 1957), pp. 114–43; Fritz Redlich, *The Molding of American Banking: Men and Ideas* (New York, 1947), I, 98; Burton A. Konkle, *Thomas Willing and the First American Financial System* (Philadelphia, 1937); James O. Weteraau, "New Light on the First Bank of the United States," *Pennsylvania Magazine of History and Biography,* LXI (1937), 263–85; "Branches of the First Bank of the United States," *Journal of Economic History,* 1942 (suppl. to Vol. II), pp. 66–100.

James Madison, a member of the House of Representatives, had led the opposition to the original charter of the Bank. They believed, as Jefferson once stated, that a paper currency, regardless of how issued, would necessarily be abused and that specie was the only safe medium of exchange. They also objected to the Bank on political grounds and brought three charges against it: that its charter was unconstitutional; that it would be controlled by its foreign stockholders; and that in some vague and mysterious manner it would permit the financial classes to subvert the interests of farmers.[2]

Twenty years of experience had belied their predictions. The directors and officers of the Bank had faithfully performed every duty assigned to them by the public authorities. So effectively did the Bank operate that Albert Gallatin, Secretary of the Treasury under Jefferson and Madison, was certain that its continuance was essential to the successful conduct of his office, and he persuaded a reluctant Madison to recommend its recharter in 1810. The Bank question, which for more than ten years had not been debated in the Congress, now became the central issue in American politics, but not as a dispute between the two political parties. The weakened Federalists remained quiet as Bank and anti-Bank Republicans attacked one another in violent and bitter language.

The real target of these attacks was not the Bank of the United States. The purpose of many of the Republican leaders who opposed the recharter was to seize control of the party, drive Gallatin out of the administration, and prevent the renomination of Madison in 1812. The Bank was used toward these ends because opposition to this Federalist-created institution was one of the fundamental tenets of republicanism, and here Gallatin and Madison could be convicted of departure from the tradition that they and Jefferson had originally fostered.[3]

Pennsylvania Republicans were involved in this intra-party feud, and on December 13, 1810, Jacob Holgate of Philadelphia County introduced a series of resolutions into the lower house of the legislature denouncing the Bank of the United States and instructing the Pennsylvania senators to vote against the recharter. The resolutions were accompanied by a preamble which said that the state banks could safely perform every function of the national bank and that their notes or specie could be used as an effective substitute for the national currency that it provided. Holgate also repeated in demagogic language the charges originally advanced by Jeffer-

---

[2] *Annals of Congress* (1st Cong., 3d sess.), pp. 1939–2011; Paul L. Ford (ed.), *The Works of Thomas Jefferson* (New York, 1904), VI, 197–204; T. Jefferson to J. W. Eppes, November 6, 1813, in H. A. Washington (ed.), *The Writings of Thomas Jefferson* (Washington, 1853), VI, 228–47.

[3] Henry Adams, *The Life of Albert Gallatin* (Philadelphia, 1880), pp. 428–29, and *History of the United States in the Administrations of Thomas Jefferson and James Madison* (New York, 1889–92), V, 328–60; John S. Pancake, "The 'Invisibles': A Chapter in the Opposition to President Madison," *Journal of Southern History*, XXI (1955), 33–34.

son and Madison—that the Bank was unconstitutional, that it was under the influence of its foreign stockholders, and that it permitted a financial oligarchy to dominate the United States.[4]

Biddle knew that the Bank had been caught in this fight between political factions through no fault of the directors or their policies and that the question of its value to the country had been lost sight of while a struggle for party power was being resolved. He determined to oppose the adoption of the resolutions, and every night after the completion of the day's business he retired to compose his arguments. He left no record of the books he used, but in the rough notes from which he spoke there were quotations from Adam Smith, David Hume, Sir James Steuart, and Jean Baptiste Say and many references to the arguments of Alexander Hamilton, Fisher Ames, and other American defenders of the national bank.[5]

He soon completed his preparation, but day followed day without mention of the resolutions until January 8, Biddle's twenty-fifth birthday. On this Thursday the house was preparing to adjourn when Holgate suddenly demanded a vote. Biddle was sitting by the open fire which warmed the room when the resolutions were read, and the Yea's and Nay's had just been called when he demanded the floor. His opponents thought he would speak for only a few minutes, but he continued for three hours, and, as word of the speech spread through the lobby, his audience grew.[6]

In form, the speech was an answer to the preamble of Holgate's resolutions, moving from one allegation to another and disposing of each in turn. But in substance it constituted an analysis of the banking and credit system, the currency, and the nature and functions of the national bank. Biddle began by scornfully rejecting the contention that the Bank's charter was unconstitutional. Every responsible authority—executive, judicial, and legislative—in the national government and in the states, whenever it had been called on to express an opinion, had agreed that the Bank had been legally chartered, and he challenged his opponents to find a single contrary judicial decision or executive or legislative act. The Constitution contained no specific authorization to charter corporations, but no government could function if it were confined to the means and agencies provided by the exact wording of its fundamental document, and Biddle cited numerous examples of the resort to implied and inherent powers by each President and Congress and by all the states.[7]

[4] William Hamilton (reporter), *Debates of the Legislature of Pennsylvania in the Session of 1810–11 at Lancaster* (Lancaster, 1811), pp. 3–4.

[5] N. Biddle, Notes for Speech on the Bank of the United States, in the Biddle Manuscripts in the Library of Congress.

[6] C. Biddle to J. Biddle, January 8, 1811; C. Biddle to Hannah Biddle, January 9, 1811, in the Biddle Manuscripts in the private collection of Nicholas B. Wainwright; N. Biddle to Mrs. J. Craig, January 19, 1811, in the Biddle-Craig Manuscripts in the Historical Society of Pennsylvania.

[7] Biddle's speech, on which this and the following paragraphs are based, is reported in full in Hamilton's *Debates*, cited in n. 4.

He also contemptuously dismissed the charge that foreign ownership of the Bank's stock endangered the freedom and independence of the United States. The charter provided not only that directors must be citizens but also that stockholders must be residents if they were to vote in the annual elections; so non-resident, alien stockholders had no voice in the management of the institution. Instead they had turned over their money to American control and in so doing had enriched and strengthened the nation's economy. Biddle further denied that banks were peculiarly advantageous to the rich and powerful. "As to a monied aristocracy," he said, "is it not obvious that the funds of a bank are of all kinds of property the least calculated to promote the influence which is feared?" An extensive proprietor of land could oppress and control his tenantry; the holder of mortgages could influence a whole neighborhood; but a stockholder in a bank had no direct connection with the borrowers. He could not influence their opinions or control their acts. No principle of political economy was clearer, he insisted, than that which looked on banks as "the most natural way of protecting the poorer classes of society" from oppression by the rich. Credit provided by these institutions, either directly or through merchants, enabled farmers, craftsmen, and manufacturers to reserve their products for an advantageous market instead of sacrificing them to meet immediate needs; and bank loans at a moderate and legally controlled rate of interest relieved every economic group from the pressure of usury.

Bank notes, likewise, were more advantageous to the less wealthy groups, for they, unlike gold and silver, could not be monopolized by the powerful few. The amount in circulation fluctuated with the volume of bank loans, and they were available to all who could borrow. Another objection to an exclusively metallic currency was the universal acceptability of gold and silver as a means of payment in international commerce. An unfavorable balance of trade would drain these metals out of the country, thus depriving the domestic economy of its means of payment. Whenever this happened, creditors could not collect from their debtors; farmers, manufacturers, and merchants could not sell their products; and the government could not pay out or receive funds. An economic depression would ensue. Debtors would for a time sacrifice their property to meet their commitments, but finally what Biddle called the "contest between suffering credit and honest punctuality" would be finished. In this situation, he said: "Without credit or money, while your commerce is stopped and your manufactures languish, do you think its effect will be confined to the city? It will be known beyond the mountains; there is not a fibre in the whole body which will not feel its deleterious influence. In the total want of money, the demand for specie will place the poorer classes at the mercy of the rich, and the great money lenders will issue abroad to prey upon their fellow citizens. In the general submersion of small traders, the only beings who will be seen floating on the wreck are these very 'monied aristocrats' whom the resolutions denounce with such indignation."

Biddle had no experience of such a depression. The nearest approach to it occurred during the financial crisis precipitated by the embargo, and he had learned then how intelligently operated banks could intervene to protect the entire economy when business was temporarily interrupted. Their refusal to press their debtors for payment during this emergency had prevented insolvency, and their bank notes had provided an effective internal currency when most of the country's specie had been drained abroad to pay international debts. Gold and silver, he had then realized, could not be used as a domestic medium of payment, and the only proper sort of money for a commercial nation was one identical with that already being provided by the national bank. It was uniform and stable, maintaining an almost equal value throughout the whole country, and it could not be drained away because it had no intrinsic value outside the national boundaries.

No other form of paper money was so safe. The federal government had the power to issue bills of credit or Treasury notes, but the exercise of this power was a dangerous expedient. If the bills and notes were redeemable in gold and silver, as bank notes were, the government would have to maintain excessive specie reserves, for it could not expand and contract its expenditures and collections so rapidly or so efficiently as a bank in response to changing economic conditions. But if this government-issued money were not made so redeemable, as had happened during the Revolution, there would be no check upon it, and Biddle could rightly assume that none of the Bank's opponents wanted to repeat this disastrous experience.

If there was to be some form of paper money, it must be issued by banks, and, unless the Bank of the United States was rechartered, it would be supplied by the essentially unregulated and uncontrolled state banks. None of those who denounced the evils of paper money in the United States, not even Jefferson, ever faced up to this fact. They had attacked the national bank and its currency but had suggested no practical means for stopping the emission of notes by the state institutions. Not one of the many Republican-dominated legislatures ever passed such a law; in fact, as Biddle predicted, the immediate result of the refusal of Congress to recharter the national bank was an increase in every state of these weaker, less responsible banks with inadequate specie reserves against their notes.

He remarked at the time upon the singularity of this reasoning. There was only one bank in the country that maintained adequate specie reserves, that bank was being eliminated, and at the same moment new banks were being established to increase the emission of paper. The inevitable consequence of this course was to increase the quantity of paper and to diminish the quantity of specie, and it was no wonder that he thought the opponents of the national bank to be either ignorant or demagogic.

He knew also that state bank notes could not be substituted for the national currency provided by the Bank of the United States. Confidence in these notes and their value would necessarily decrease in proportion to the distance from the place of their issue and redemption, and buyers and sellers outside the state would be reluctant to use them. Nor could the state banks be safely or effectively used as federal depositories. Could the United States, Biddle asked, "afford to place its millions in a bank whose capital may not exceed the amount of a single day's deposit, whose affairs they have no right to inspect, over whose operations they have no constitutional control?" The Bank of the United States and its branches were directly subject to the authority of the national government. They were required to make periodic reports to the Secretary of the Treasury, and this official had a right to inspect the books or to remove the deposits if he thought they were unsafe. The Bank was also required to place at the disposition of the Treasury in any part of the nation the whole amount of its deposits, and this with no expense to the government. Since no state bank would or could do this, the inevitable result of the elimination of the national bank would be the establishment of seventeen depositories, one in each of the states, and the government would have to bear the expense of the transfer of funds.

An even more powerful argument against the proposed substitution of state banks for the Bank of the United States was presented in the discussion of the effect that such action would have upon the ability of the federal Treasury to borrow money. Governments needed loans most urgently in moments of crisis, not in times of public peace, prosperity, and security, and individuals, even the most public spirited, could not be relied upon in such emergencies. Their funds were invested in commercial, manufacturing, and agricultural ventures, which in times of public danger could not be liquidated and placed at the service of the nation. Under such circumstances the only sources of immediate credit were banks, where money could always be borrowed, but here again a national institution was necessary. The states might prohibit banks, or, if they chose to continue these institutions, they could forbid loans to the national government. The United States in this event would have the power to borrow but would be unable to exercise this power without the consent of the states, and that consent would not always be forthcoming. Would Massachusetts and the other commercial states, Biddle pointedly asked, in their discontent with the embargo have permitted their banks to lend a dollar to the United States? And if these banks could not lend to the government in a national emergency, then to whom would it turn?

Biddle had completed his task of proving that the Bank of the United States was a necessary and useful institution and that no acceptable substitute for it or its currency could be devised. But he was not quite through. He was a patriot, much concerned for the welfare, strength, and safety of the nation, and this was a dangerous and critical moment in its life. The

United States had just concluded a most insecure agreement with France. It had then adopted measures that threatened to involve it in war with Great Britain. The government needed all its strength to meet this real danger, but the opponents of the Bank seemed unconcerned. "Is this a time to disorder the finances?" Biddle asked. "When the nerves of the whole nation should be braced and strong, are we to prepare for combat by cutting the main artery of all its resources?" And then, almost in despair, he said, "But you are anxious to witness the results of this dissolution . . . just as a child wishes to wind up a watch to hear the noise and set it going again. Take care that in this process you do not break the main spring of your happiness and security."[8]

His speech was enthusiastically applauded. Even his opponents congratulated him upon the excellence of his arguments, and some of them thought for a time that the resolutions might be defeated. Party loyalty, however, proved too strong. The resolutions against the recharter were passed by both houses, but the preamble with its hostile phrases was eliminated altogether. The small group favorable to the national bank looked upon this gain as a triumph, and Biddle emerged from the debate with enhanced prestige.[9] This single term in the legislature (he refused the offer of a renomination in 1811) taught Biddle many useful lessons. Soon after he arrived in Lancaster he wrote that he and those who thought as he did had little to do but "laugh at our adversaries." He was contemptuous of the ignorance and crudeness of many of the rural legislators, but in the course of the session he learned to honor and respect many of these men. He was very much pleased when one of the backcountry members said, "I like your candor and reality always," and when another told him of one of his constituents who had asked the name of *that little fellow* who set them to rights in the business."[10]

Such commendations as these made him feel that his winter in Lancaster had not been wholly wasted, but they did not keep him from being impatient for the end of the session. He was eager to return to the editing of the Lewis and Clark manuscript and to his general and miscellaneous studies which, "tho' they are certainly less useful and have less immediate bearing upon the objects of ordinary concern possess a charm which public occupations can never retain."[11] These were the reasons he gave for his impatience, but the real reason for his desire to return to Philadelphia was Jane Craig. During the session his status had changed. He was no longer just a favored suitor; he had become an engaged man.

[8] *Ibid.*

[9] R. Rush to N. Biddle, January 20, 1811; J. Hollingsworth to N. Biddle, January 21, 1811; John Hanley to C. Biddle, February 14, 1811, in the Biddle Manuscripts in the Library of Congress.

[10] N. Biddle to Mrs. J. Craig, December 9, 19, 1810, February 21, March 19, 1811, in the Biddle-Craig Manuscripts in the Historical Society of Pennsylvania.

[11] N. Biddle to Mrs. J. Craig, March 17, 1811, in the Biddle-Craig Manuscripts in the Historical Society of Pennsylvania.

5

Courtship

and

Marriage

*D*on't be alarmed at the question I am going to put to you," Hannah Biddle wrote to her son on February 7; "I am told you are much attached to a young lady in this city and that a positive engagement was entered into on Saturday or Sunday last. *Is it so or not?* Remember it is an anxious mother that questions you." His secret that he thought had been jealously guarded was not a secret at all. He had gone back to Philadelphia the preceding weekend, apparently thinking that it would not seem strange to his family to ride horseback through severe winter weather to visit a young lady that they hardly knew. But they had found out what he had tried to hide. He had become engaged; and in his first letter to Mrs. Craig after his return to Lancaster he wrote: "I have resumed all my Lancaster operations, but much more reluctantly than I did, for my visit to Philadelphia has a little disqualified me."[1]

The next day he was less restrained. "No, my dearest friend," he protested, "I can no longer write to you 'as I used to do.' . . . Before strangers, indeed, I ought to and will disguise these feelings till you may yourself approve the avowal of them. But here, alone, separated from all I love, there is no cautious style of expression, no subject of minor interest which can restrain this heart from pouring out its feelings before those who have excited and rewarded them." Soon he was granted permission to write directly to Jane. The letters continued to be addressed to Mrs. Craig and

[1] Hannah Biddle to N. Biddle, February 7, 1811, in the Biddle Manuscripts in the private collection of Nicholas B. Wainwright; N. Biddle to Mrs. J. Craig, February 9, 1811, in the Biddle-Craig Manuscripts in the Historical Society of Pennsylvania; C. Biddle, Jr., to N. Biddle, February 13, 1811; J. Biddle to N. Biddle, March, 1811, in the Biddle Manuscripts at "Andalusia."

were read by her, but their subject matter was changed. His former freedom of expression was carefully restrained, and he wrote almost exclusively of his daily activities. These carefully phrased letters did not express his
true feelings. He was young, he was in love, and the facts came pouring
out on Saturday, March 30, when the legislative session was almost done:
"I just write you two lines my darling Jane to say that I shall start from
Lancaster on Wednesday morning. . . . I was delighted at learning from
my sister that she had a pleasant party and I cannot express the satisfaction
it gave me to think that you were in the midst of my family where I felt
that

>'When a' the fairest maids were met
>The fairest maid was bonnie Jean.' "[2]

He almost lived at the Craigs' on his return from Lancaster, and late in
April Mrs. Craig gave her consent to an early marriage. Her brother-in-
law, Robert Oliver of Baltimore, came to Philadelphia to consult with
Charles Biddle, and an antenuptial agreement was signed which assigned
Jane's share of her father's estate to a trust fund for her and her children.
Biddle also came to a final decision at this time to abandon the practice of
law and did so without any regrets. The question of earning a living had
little part in the decision. Biddle was one of those fortunate people to
whom personal finances were never a serious problem. When he had been
in school and in Europe, his father had been able to provide easily for all
his wants. His own income, once he began to practice his profession, was
more than sufficient for his needs, and now that he was marrying Jane
Craig, whose father's estate was one of the largest in Philadelphia, his personal contribution, whatever its size, would only add to each year's
surplus.[3]

He did not intend to be idle. He would manage Mrs. Craig's business
affairs, run the farm at "Andalusia," and engage in civic and philanthropic
activities as befitted a young man in his position; but he also intended to
seek political office and to continue his work on the *Port Folio*. He finished the editing of the Lewis and Clark manuscript shortly after his return
from the legislature, and when it was published (which was not until
several years later), most readers were unaware that they were not reading
the original journals themselves. The editorial work was skilfully done,
and, though the word count was reduced by half, nothing essential was
omitted. A later editor of the manuscripts has said concerning the book
that it "will always be one of the best digested and most interesting ac-

[2] N. Biddle to Mrs. J. Craig, February 10, 21, March 15, 17, 19, 30, 1811, in the Biddle-
Craig Manuscripts in the Historical Society of Pennsylvania.

[3] Mrs. J. Craig to N. Biddle, May 15, 1811; Mrs. J. Craig to James Craig, May 18,
June 18, 1811, in the Biddle-Craig Manuscripts in the Historical Society of Pennsylvania.

counts of American travel," and it has frequently been reprinted in subsequent generations.[4]

As soon as this task was completed, Biddle began the preparation of a Fourth of July oration for the Pennsylvania State Society of the Cincinnati. He was conscious of the importance of this occasion, his first public address in Philadelphia, and he used as his theme the character and contributions of George Washington to the cause of American freedom. Biddle's father, an honorary member of this association of former officers in the Revolutionary army and navy, had proposed that the Cincinnati erect a memorial monument to Washington, and the younger Biddle indorsed this proposal in eloquent language. He contrasted the condition of free Americans with that of the decadent Europeans, enslaved by the tyrant Napoleon, and attributed the success of the American experiment to the loyalty it had shown to the teachings and example of Washington. Imperial France, Biddle insisted was the enemy of free men everywhere, but he also reminded his hearers that it was Great Britain who, by its disregard of American sensibilities and commercial rights, was steadily forcing the United States into a declaration of war. In such an event, he said, there was but one choice for every patriotic American—support for the national administration regardless of party affiliation.[5]

Biddle had several purposes in mind when he concluded his speech on this note. His recent experience in the legislature had confirmed his belief that the bitter disputes in American politics were born of personal rivalries rather than of true divergences based on principle and interest. These differences, he believed, could be overcome by moderation in language and thought and by the recognition of the common interests that bound together all sections and all persons in the United States. But he also hoped that the speech would attract the attention of the national administration and open the way to appointive office through Monroe, who, his differences with Madison resolved, had become Secretary of State on April 1, 1811.

The close relationship between the Monroe family and Biddle, estab-

[4] Reuben G. Thwaites (ed.), *Original Journals of the Lewis and Clark Expedition, 1804-1806* (New York, 1904), I, xxxviii-xlvi. The journals, though completed in 1811, were not published until 1814. Paul Allen, editorial assistant on the *Port Folio*, supervised it through the press, and his name appeared on the title page, since Biddle, as he told Clark, was "content that my trouble in the business should be recompensed only by the pleasure which attended it." His work did not go unrecognized, and Jefferson, the originator of the expedition, wrote to express "the thanks all owe you for the trouble you have taken with this interesting narrative." N. Biddle to W. Clark, July 4, 1812, March 23, 1814, March 12, 1815, May 29, 1816; W. Clark to N. Biddle, September 5, 1812; J. Conrad to N. Biddle, November 12, 1812, in the Biddle Manuscripts in the Library of Congress; T. Jefferson to N. Biddle, August 20, 1813), in the Biddle Manuscripts at "Andalusia."

[5] N. Biddle, *Oration Delivered before the Pennsylvania State Society of the Cincinnati on the Fourth of July MDCCCXI* (Philadelphia, 1811); Charles Biddle, *Autobiography*, pp. 332-34.

lished in London, had continued after their return to America. He was called on to purchase rugs, lamps, and other furnishings for the home of Mrs. George Hay, the eldest daughter, and his letters to her and other members of the family bespoke a warm friendship. He sent copies of his speech on the Bank of the United States and of his Fourth of July oration to Monroe and received enthusiastic praise and commendation.[6] But no offer of a place was forthcoming, and Biddle, laying aside his desire for political advancement, filled in his time by assisting with the *Port Folio*. Dennie's drinking had been steadily increasing. He went to Bristol for a rest during the summer but, disliking the company, retired to his room to indulge what Mrs. Craig described as "his fatal propensity for strong drink." He refused to attend to editorial duties or to answer mail, and Biddle substituted for him. The proprietor of the magazine, Samuel Bradford, was completely exasperated with Dennie and tried to persuade Biddle and Robert Walsh to edit the *Port Folio*, but they declined.[7]

Jane and her mother were at "Andalusia" during these months, and Biddle visited them almost every weekend. They passed many pleasant hours planning the remodeling of the Regency farmhouse on the place; inspecting the cultivated fields that lay between the woodlot on the public road and the farm buildings; and sitting under the great trees on the lawn which ran down to the river. At night Jane would play and sing for their entertainment and for the guests who came out by boat or carriage from Philadelphia.

The long months gradually passed, and at last on Thursday, October 3, the young couple were married. That night Mrs. Craig wrote in her memorandum book, "I committed the care of my beloved Jane's happiness to the best, the most virtuous of men." Jane and Nicholas remained at "Andalusia" until October 19, when they left for Baltimore in a rented carriage, accompanied by Nicholas' sister and Mrs. Chalmers, a family friend. They visited the Olivers and were extensively entertained. Jane's cousin Peggy had recently married Roswell Colt, son of the president of the Society for Useful Manufactures of Paterson, New Jersey, and the two couples were completely congenial. Not all the parties were pleasant for the young wives. "I spent last evening at Mrs. Carier's with the Walshes, Pahlins, and Politica," Jane wrote petulantly. "It was a terrible stupid evening. I was in one corner with the ladies and Nicholas and the elder Pahlin on one side in deep conversation, Walsh and Politica in the same situation. . . .

[6] N. Biddle to Mrs. G. Hay, November 26, 1810, in the Monroe Manuscripts in the Library of Congress; N. Biddle to G. Hay, February 3, 1811; G. Hay to N. Biddle, February 14, 1811, in the Biddle Manuscripts in the Library of Congress; N. Biddle to J. Monroe, February 14, 1811, in the Biddle Manuscripts in the Historical Society of Pennsylvania.

[7] Bradford and Inskeep to N. Biddle and R. Walsh, n.d., in the Biddle Manuscripts in the Historical Society of Pennsylvania; Mrs. J. Craig to James Craig, January 18, 1812, in the Biddle-Craig Manuscripts in the Historical Society of Pennsylvania.

Wherefore as you may perceive I had no opportunity to judge of their lordships."[8]

They left Baltimore for Washington, where the Monroes called and took them to the executive mansion to meet President and Mrs. Madison, and then returned to Philadelphia to take up their residence in the half of Mrs. Craig's double house which was numbered 183 Chestnut. As soon as they were established, Dennie and Bradford brought pressure on Biddle to become assistant editor of the *Port Folio* at a salary of twenty-five hundred dollars a year. Biddle accepted, and the first number under the joint editorship appeared in January, 1812. Dennie, who was enthusiastically pleased with what he called their "literary coparceny," moderated his habits and "came out among his friends with a new lease of wit and talent." His apparent improvement was of brief duration, however. Shortly after the first issue appeared, he was stricken with a mortal illness and died on January 7, 1812.

Mrs. Craig in a letter to her son expressed the family's sorrow. "Dennie was just the creature you would have worshiped," she wrote, "a perfect child of nature without any knowledge of the world as it is, having lived always in one of his own creating, full of gaiety and benevolence, with the most brilliant imagination and a heart formed for friendship and every social enjoyment." Biddle, in a more formal obituary notice, paid tribute to Dennie's literary abilities and learning and in final summary said: "The great purpose of all his exertions, the uniform pursuit of his life was to disseminate among his countrymen a taste for elegant literature [and] to give to education and to letters their proper elevation in the public esteem."[9]

Dennie's death produced little change in the *Port Folio*. Biddle, now the editor, turned over most of the details of management to Paul Allen, a native of Providence, Rhode Island, and subsequently a newspaper editor in Baltimore and reserved to himself only the "general superintendence over its material with some occasional and voluntary contributions." But the imprint of his personal interests and point of view was plainly evident. He introduced a department of the fine arts into his first issue and increased the number of illustrative plates. One article must have given him great pleasure—an essay "On Architecture" written by George Tucker, political economist and first professor of moral philosophy in the Univer-

---

[8] N. Biddle to Mrs. J. Craig, October, 1811; Mrs. J. Craig, Memorandum Book, October 3, 1811; Jane Biddle to Mrs. J. Craig, November 5, 1811, in the Biddle-Craig Manuscripts in the Historical Society of Pennsylvania.

[9] *Port Folio* (1812), 3d ser., VII, 89–96, 185–90; Thomas P. Govan (ed.), "The Death of Joseph Dennie: A Memoir by Nicholas Biddle," *Pennsylvania Magazine of History and Biography*, V (1951), 36–46; J. Dennie to N. Biddle, December 16, 1811, in the Biddle Manuscripts in the Historical Society of Pennsylvania; Mrs. J. Craig to James Craig, January 18, April 2, 1812, in the Biddle-Craig Manuscripts in the Historical Society of Pennsylvania.

sity of Virginia. Tucker maintained, what Biddle already believed, that the Greek style was the most suitable for an American architecture.[10]

The essay was published at a strategic time. The hostility toward all things British that had been engendered by the conflict between the two countries was diverting American taste from Regency designs to something new in architecture, and Tucker's proposals were soon being adopted, first in Philadelphia and then in the rest of the country. This hostility between Great Britain and the United States also prompted Biddle to put increased emphasis on patriotic themes. He wrote Monroe and other national leaders for materials upon which to base biographical articles, and in April, 1812, under the title "Strictures on the Edinburgh Review," he defended the American language as a more flexible, pleasing, and natural speech than that of the mother country. The occasion of this essay was a British review of Joel Barlow's *Columbiad* in which the reviewer accused the American poet of using a language virtually unknown in Great Britain. Nineteen words in the poem were listed as new coinages, but Biddle took the same list and demonstrated by quotations from Johnson's *Dictionary* and standard British authors from Shakespeare to Pope that all the so-called new words had already been in use except "scow," which referred to a small boat known only in the United States.[11]

Biddle's editorial duties occupied only part of his energies. The rest he devoted, as he informed Monroe, "to the much more agreeable studies, the higher branches of jurisprudence and politics." He and Jane also entertained extensively. They made one visit to Lancaster, where, according to Mrs. Craig, "they were so feasted and caressed that they could scarcely get back again." Her joy in the marriage continually increased. She wrote to James in November, 1811, that Biddle was "one of the most deserving of men" and that he and Jane would live with her until James returned. And again, two months later: "I do most fervently pray that I may live to see you and this dear youth united in the bonds of friendship and relationship. For I never met with two more worthy of each other. What a glorious example of mental and intellectual harmony shall we give should we be able to live together." But by April all doubt about what living arrangements she desired had disappeared, and she wrote: "My dearest child how I rejoice to tell you that I am not the least disappointed in this delightful union. They are the happiest of the happy and he is so sweet a young man,

[10] *Port Folio* (1812), 3d ser., VII, 134–35, 194–96; (1814) 4th ser., IV, 559–69; Talbot Hamlin, *Greek Revival Architecture in America* (New York, 1944), p. 70; Agnes A. Gilchrist, *William Strickland, Architect and Engineer, 1788–1854* (Philadelphia, 1950), p. 3.

[11] N. Biddle to J. Monroe, April 5, 1812, in the Biddle Manuscripts in the Historical Society of Pennsylvania; *Port Folio* (1812), 3d ser., VII, 323–36.

so easy to live with, that I am sure you will love him. We must certainly live all in one house till you are married."[12]

When this final letter was written, James Craig, foreseeing the declaration of war on Great Britain by the United States, had already embarked for home. He arrived late in May and came directly to Philadelphia. Mrs. Craig, worn out by illness during the winter, had gone with her younger son John to Squam Beach on the Jersey coast to rest and recuperate, and James joined them there. Jane and Nicholas followed early in July, and the whole family spent a quiet and pleasant summer. The young men were as congenial as Mrs. Craig and Jane had hoped they would be, each loving and respecting the other. In their private happiness they ignored the public crisis, and refused to permit the outbreak of war to interfere with their summer's plans.

[12] N. Biddle to J. Monroe, January 30, 1812, in the Biddle Manuscripts in the Historical Society of Pennsylvania; Mrs. J. Craig to James Craig, November 17, 1811, January 18, April 2, 1812, in the Biddle-Craig Manuscripts in the Historical Society of Pennsylvania.

~~ 6 ~~

War and Peace

*T*he Biddle family was well represented in the armed forces of the United States at the beginning of the war. James, second in command of the frigate "Wasp," was stationed in Delaware Bay. Thomas and John, officers in the United States Army, were training recruits at Bristol near Philadelphia, and Charles, Jr., and Richard were privates in the Pennsylvania militia. If Nicholas planned to join them—and there is no evidence that he did—he was prevented from doing so by an injury to his leg. In the late summer of 1812 he fell as he stepped out of a carriage, and fifteen months later his physicians, having failed with less stringent treatments, ordered complete rest. After being bedridden for two months, he arose in January, 1814, almost completely cured.[1]

The injury had not interfered with his ordinary activities, and during the war he had continued as editor of the *Port Folio*, managed Mrs. Craig's affairs, and supervised the farm at "Andalusia." The predictions of financial difficulties that he had voiced in his speech on the Bank of the United States were being fulfilled. Between 1812 and 1815, one hundred and twenty new banks were chartered by state legislatures, and, though all these institutions were empowered to issue bank notes, there was no national currency. Money collected by the government in one section of the country was unusable in others, and the national Treasury was forced to issue its own unredeemable paper. The full effect of this overissue of currency was not immediately apparent because its natural corrective, the demand for specie to pay balances abroad, had been eliminated by the war. But eventually the New England merchants by legal and illegal means revived foreign commerce. They became the channel through which European merchandise came into the country and through which specie went out. Purchasers of these goods in the middle and southern states paid for

[1] N. Biddle to W. Miller, November 12, 1812, in the Biddle Family Papers in the Library of Congress; N. Biddle to J. Biddle, November 5, 1813, in the Biddle Manuscripts at "Andalusia"; N. Biddle to Edward Coles, November 6, 1813, January 18, 1814, microfilm in the Historical Society of Pennsylvania of Coles Manuscripts in the private collection of Edward C. Robbins.

them with bank notes of their own locality, but when the New England merchants presented this paper to the issuing banks for redemption, these institutions could not pay. They suspended specie payments, and throughout the remainder of the war their notes and those of the government circulated at discounts varying from 25 to 50 per cent.[2]

The government was virtually bankrupt, being unable to pay interest on what it owed or to borrow more, and Biddle, who had watched these developments with informed interest, urged his political friends in Washington to devise some means to make the New England "Yankees" give their money, if not their sanction, to the war. "Much as I should wish to see peace," he wrote, "I confess she would be an uneasy guest if she is to be hurried upon us by fiscal embarrassments." He sought by his editorials in the *Port Folio* to arouse the country to the need for a more vigorous prosecution of the war, and he denounced those Federalists who out of partisan zeal refused their support to the government as a "miserable gang."[3]

His concern at the apparently disastrous course of the war did not keep him from being personally happy in the years from 1812 to 1814. His and Jane's first child, Nicholas Craig, was born on April 23, 1813, and Mrs. Craig, a proud grandmother, pronounced him to be "one of the most lovely and beautiful boys I ever beheld." Their homes on Chestnut Street and at "Andalusia" were overrun with guests. Edward Coles, President Madison's private secretary, recuperated from a long illness at "Andalusia" and was virtually a member of the family group. The Roswell Colts and other Baltimore friends came frequently to visit, as did Vincent LeRay de Chaumont, grandson of the generous Frenchman who had helped finance the American Revolution. From his father's estate in upper New York he wrote with much pleasure of the gay times he had enjoyed at "Andalusia" and sent a list of descriptions of each member of the family in mixed English and French to be used in charades.[4]

This period of unshadowed family happiness was brief. In late January, 1814, Mrs. Craig had a severe heart attack, and three days later she died. The family's sorrow was eased by the numerous expressions of love and

[2] Ralph C. H. Catterall, *The Second Bank of the United States* (Chicago, 1903), pp. 1–17; Adams, *Gallatin*, pp. 450–92; Hammond, *Banks and Politics*, pp. 227–30.

[3] N. Biddle to J. Biddle, July 12, 1813, in the Biddle Manuscripts at "Andalusia"; N. Biddle to E. Coles, March 8, 1814, microfilm in the Historical Society of Pennsylvania.

[4] Mrs. J. Craig to Mrs. Montgomery, November 16, December 12, 1813, in the Biddle-Craig Manuscripts in the Historical Society of Pennsylvania; Chevalier de Onis to N. Biddle, January 3, 1813; Vincent LeRay de Chaumont to N. Biddle, October 5, 1813, in the Biddle Family Papers in the Library of Congress; N. Biddle to Correa de Serra, October 28, 1813; N. Biddle to Chevalier de Onis, November 18, 21, 1813, in the Biddle Manuscripts in the private collection of Nicholas B. Wainwright; diary of Harriet Manigault, January 26, 1814, in the Historical Society of Pennsylvania and used by the kind permission of its owner, Miss Anna W. Ingersoll.

admiration for Mrs. Craig which her death elicited. Many letters were received from intimate friends and bare acquaintances, and the newspapers reported all Philadelphia to be in mourning. Biddle, in a formal obituary in the *Port Folio*, paid tribute to the person who more than any other except his father and brother had influenced his life. "Our personal attachments," he wrote, "have, we are persuaded, no share in misguiding our deliberate conviction that there has been rarely in any age or country, a being who combined so many distinguishing excellencies . . . whose life was so perfectly pure and beneficent, and who was so exempt from all the frailties which impair the dignity of human virtue."[5]

The initial shock of her death had not been erased when their baby became violently ill and died within a month of his grandmother. The double tragedy was too much for Jane, and Biddle, gravely concerned, took her to "Andalusia" in the hope of reviving her spirits. He resigned from the *Port Folio* so that he would have no distractions, but Jane continued despondent, and her physician advised a complete change of scene. They left Philadelphia at the beginning of June, visited the Olivers in Baltimore for a few weeks, and then went on to the Virginia springs. They remained in this region for the rest of the summer, stopping first at the Warm Spring, then at the White, and ended their trip at the Sweet; but they were not too well satisfied anywhere, and Jane in exasperation wrote, "There is no company, or very little, worth associating with, so that we pass almost the whole day in our room, lolling on the bed and reading the Spectator or some such new publication."[6]

Biddle also reported that the company was not very numerous or by any means a good specimen of Virginia society, but he was heartened by the improvement in Jane's health and spirits. They departed the first week in September, and when they arrived at Staunton in the valley, they learned of the capture of Washington by the British. No word of the invading army had reached them in the mountains, and Biddle had planned a leisurely return through Charlottesville, Washington, and Baltimore. But now Philadelphia was in danger, and he rushed home to the threatened city, though he knew, as he admitted, that he would make an inefficient soldier.

The immediate danger was over when they arrived in Philadelphia. General Samuel Smith's elaborate fortifications in Baltimore had proved too formidable for the British in early September, and the invaders had

[5] N. Biddle to R. Oliver, January 28, 1814, in the Biddle Manuscripts at "Andalusia"; R. Oliver to Jane Biddle, February 4, 1813; J. Abercrombie to Jane Biddle, February 26, 1814, in the Biddle-Craig Manuscripts in the Historical Society of Pennsylvania; R. L. Colt to N. Biddle, February 1, 1814; Miss Bodley to N. Biddle, March 10, 1814, in the Biddle Family Papers in the Library of Congress; *United States Gazette* (Philadelphia), January 29, 1814; *Port Folio* (1814), 4th ser., III, 284–89.

[6] N. Biddle to E. Coles, March 1, September 24, 1814, microfilm in the Historical Society of Pennsylvania; Jane Biddle to Mary Biddle, August 17, 1814, in the Biddle-Craig Manuscripts in the Historical Society of Pennsylvania.

sailed out of Chesapeake Bay to the south. The United States had gained a decisive victory without severe fighting because Smith, a civilian turned soldier, had been adequately prepared. General Joseph Bloomfield, a former governor of New Jersey, was the United States officer in command at Philadelphia, and he attempted to profit by Smith's experience. His principal coadjutor was Biddle's father, who had been elected chairman of the Committee of Defense, and under their vigorous leadership the militia had been strengthened; the city and surrounding districts had appropriated four hundred and twenty-five thousand dollars for arms and fortifications; and a generous fund had been raised by private subscription for the relief of the families of volunteers and militiamen.[7]

On his return from the springs, Biddle became one of his father's most active assistants, and in October he was elected without opposition to the state senate. The legislative session did not begin until early December, and during this interval he was sent to Washington in a vain effort to persuade Monroe, the acting Secretary of War, to advance additional funds for the defense of Philadelphia. None were available, but Biddle was vastly encouraged by his conversations with Monroe and other national leaders. They, like the citizens of Baltimore and Philadelphia, had been taught by the actual invasion the need for adequate preparations and governmental strength and had already decided to ask Congress to charter a new national bank.

The urgent need for such a fundamental reform in the national financial structure was clearly apparent to Biddle. Robert Oliver had already advised him not to invest any more of the Craig estate in Treasury stock, in the belief that the government would be conquered or overthrown in the next few months. "I have remitted the principal part of my funds to England," Oliver wrote, "and I am endeavouring to purchase cotton at Augusta with a view to let it remain there until peace." What Oliver was doing many other wealthy men had done, and it did no good to denounce them as unpatriotic. The proper remedy was to place the finances of the nation in such a condition that its stock would be an attractive investment. What was needed was a national bank, and Biddle was not alone in this conviction. Stephen Girard of Philadelphia, John Jacob Astor and David Parish of New York, and other prominent merchants and bankers gave Madison and Monroe the same advice, and it was through their influence that Alexander J. Dallas of Philadelphia, a firm advocate of a national bank, was appointed Secretary of the Treasury in October, 1814.[8]

[7] N. Biddle to J. Monroe, September 24, November 27, 1814; J. Monroe to N. Biddle, October 1, 1814, in the Biddle Manuscripts in the Historical Society of Pennsylvania; C. Biddle to N. Biddle, October 31, 1814, in the Biddle Manuscripts in the private collection of Nicholas B. Wainwright; N. Biddle to E. Coles, November 16, 18, 1814, microfilm in the Historical Society of Pennsylvania.

[8] R. Oliver to N. Biddle, November 26, 1814, in the Biddle Family Papers in the Library of Congress; Hammond, *Banks and Politics*, pp. 229–31.

The knowledge that the government was prepared to do something about its finances made up for Biddle's disappointment at the failure of his particular mission, and he returned to Philadelphia to prepare for the winter in the new state capital at Harrisburg.

He arrived at the capital on the opening day of the session and immediately proposed a bill to raise six regiments of regular soldiers in anticipation of congressional authority for individual state armies. His fellow senators, appalled by the cost of this elaborate military establishment, voted it down, and Biddle then moved that a committee be named to inquire into the expediency of raising eight thousand men by lot from the militia to serve for twelve months and to be used in adjoining states as well as Pennsylvania. No expense was involved, so this measure passed, and Biddle, as mover of the resolution, was made chairman of the committee.[9]

He prepared a bill that was a virtual copy of an act passed by the Pennsylvania legislature in 1781, and introduced it with what a visitor described as "a handsome speech in its favor." A vigorous debate ensued, in which Biddle spoke some fifty or more times, and at the close of the day he reported to Jane: "They call it conscription and abuse it in many ways, but if I can raise eight thousand men I do not care a straw what it is called. On this occasion all my political friends have left me except one or two, but I am satisfied with my own course and shall pursue it." Biddle still considered himself a Federalist, and Mathew Carey, one of the most influential members of this party, wrote him: "I applaud your conduct highly, and I think I echo the sense of such of your constituents as it is desirable for you to stand fair with." But the party newspapers did not agree with Carey and attacked Biddle and his bill.[10]

The Republican newspapers were not enthusiastic, but the senate, after a prolonged debate, passed the bill by a vote of twenty-one to nine. It went to the lower house, where once again the cry of conscription was raised, and that "horrible name," Biddle said, "which has frightened all the old women in petticoats and pantaloons, is as fatal as a mad dog." The bill, he believed, was certain to be lost, but just at this moment news arrived of the signing of the peace treaty at Ghent and of Andrew Jackson's triumphant destruction of the British invaders at New Orleans. Biddle was overjoyed. "We are in truth a most favored and happy nation," he wrote, "to have [finished] so triumphantly a war so unequal and inauspicious, and now when our forces began to fail and our means were almost exhausted,

[9] N. Biddle to Jane Biddle, December 15, 1814, in the Biddle-Craig Manuscripts in the Historical Society of Pennsylvania; N. Biddle to J. Monroe, December 17, 1814, in the Biddle Manuscripts in the Historical Society of Pennsylvania.

[10] N. Biddle to Jane Biddle, n.d., in the Biddle-Craig Manuscripts in the Historical Society of Pennsylvania; diary of Thomas F. Pleasants, January 11, 1815, in the Historical Society of Pennsylvania; M. Carey to N. Biddle, February 4, 1815, in the Biddle Manuscripts in the Library of Congress.

to be thus blessed with peace on honorable terms is an abundance of good fortune which we had no right to expect."[11]

He thought that his task was done when the peace was signed. He returned to Philadelphia to be with Jane, who was expecting another child, and from there informed Edward Coles that in a day or two he would go back to his desk to think and speak about such inconsequential matters as roads and fish dams. He turned out to be wrong. Within a few days of his return, letters were received from the Connecticut and Massachusetts legislatures asking for an indorsement of the antiwar and disunionist resolutions of the New England Convention at Hartford, and Biddle was appointed chairman of the committee to prepare Pennsylvania's reply. He accepted the assignment eagerly, believing as he did that the New England doctrines of sectionalism and state sovereignty should be decisively refuted, and his lengthy report concluded with the affirmation that "the maintenance of the general government in the full exercise of its constitutional powers is vital to the freedom and greatness of the nation."[12]

This restatement of the pure nationalistic principles of Hamiltonian federalism was adopted by a legislature controlled by Republicans over the opposing votes of most of the Federalist members. The principles had not changed, but the parties had, and Biddle allied himself with those who defended national power, whatever their name. The submission of this report on March 7, 1815, ended his formal association with the Federalist party in Pennsylvania; thenceforth he was aligned with the Republicans in spirit and in name.

The legislature adjourned four days later, and Biddle returned to Philadelphia to Jane. They stayed with his family until Edward Craig was born on May 8 and then went out to "Andalusia." Jane was proud of her new baby, she was in love with her husband, but she could not forget her past sorrows. She made a real effort, but her continued grief was always apparent. "I am glad the poor little woman has determined to come out once more," was the remark of a friend upon seeing her in Bristol, but many years were to pass before her natural gaiety and high spirits even partially returned.[13]

Only rarely did she utter a complaint, but in 1818, after the birth of another son, James Craig, on July 5, 1817, she wrote in her Occasional Book: "Begun in the year 1811 August the 11th in a happy time, times have sadly changed since then." The next year when their family was again

11 *Journal of the Senate of the Commonwealth of Pennsylvania, 1814–1815* (Harrisburg, 1815), III, 104; *Appendix to the Journal of the Senate,* pp. 50–57; N. Biddle to E. Coles, January 17, 1815, microfilm in the Historical Society of Pennsylvania.

12 N. Biddle to E. Coles, February 19, 1815, microfilm in the Historical Society of Pennsylvania; *Appendix to the Journal of the Senate,* pp. 381–96.

13 Diary of Harriet Manigault, July 28, August 15, 1815, in the Historical Society of Pennsylvania.

increased by the birth of Charles on April 30, she added a note: "They are a little more like that golden year at present . . . but the flowers that may strew my path will never again I fear appear as fresh and beautiful as they did then."[14]

Her one active desire was to travel abroad. Almost everyone in their immediate circle had spent many years in Europe, and she felt cheated when they talked of London, Paris, or Rome. Her protests against remaining in the United States were so vehement that Biddle wrote out a formal contract on October 14, 1815, in which he declared it to be his "serious wish, intention, purpose, design, hope, expectation, desire and determination to take Jane to Europe for her improvement in morals and manners"; and the following month from Washington he reported: "The embassy goes on swimmingly. I have not decided whether I shall go to France or Russia." The facetious tone was a mask behind which he was making a serious effort to obtain a diplomatic appointment, but he had one handicap that could not be overcome. "There was but one obstacle," a friend told him after Monroe had become President, "and that singular as it may appear no doubt has and will hereafter have great weight against you. . . . You are a great favorite with the Chief Magistrate. I mean personally. He has a sort of personal affection for you he fears to indulge."[15]

Jane's disappointment was keener than his. She saw no reason to wait for him to be given an official position before going abroad, but she accepted his decision with patience and good temper. He in his turn made a concession to her. She disliked the noise, confusion, and social life of the city and loved living at "Andalusia," so that from 1815 to 1819 the Biddles stayed in the country the greater part of each year, moving out early in the spring and remaining until late in the fall.

[14] Jane Biddle, Occasional Book, in the Biddle-Craig Manuscripts in the Historical Society of Pennsylvania.

[15] N. Biddle and Jane Biddle, Contract, October 14, 1815; N. Biddle to Jane Biddle, November 3, 1815, in the Biddle-Craig Manuscripts in the Historical Society of Pennsylvania; J. Forsyth to N. Biddle, November 18, 1818, in the Biddle Manuscripts in the Library of Congress.

～ 7 ～

Government Director
of the
Bank of the United States

*R*etirement to the country did not mean that the Biddles cut themselves off from society. The journey from "Andalusia" to Philadelphia was a short one, approximately fourteen miles by road or three hours by boat, and they made frequent visits to their friends in the city.[1] Circe de Ronceray, a family friend, made her home with them, as did John Craig when he was not in school, and their relatives and others came out frequently and stayed as long as they pleased. The farm was Biddle's main occupation, and he proved himself an intelligent and practical cultivator of the soil, who made a profit each year. He wanted to demonstrate the advantages of an adequate capital investment in tools, equipment, and fertilizer to Pennsylvania farmers because he believed that too many of them were attempting to cultivate entirely too much land.

Intensive use of relatively few acres, he was certain, was far more profitable than the current practice, and his farm was transformed into an experimental laboratory to prove the validity of his theory. He bought the latest tools and equipment, testing their usefulness and practicality, and checked the results of using limestone, plaster of paris, marl, and animal manure as fertilizers. Many different varieties of vegetables grew in his gardens, including some he imported from Europe, and in the fields he

[1] The Biddles did not have a town house in the winter of 1815–16, but the following year they rented a double house at 208–10 Chestnut Street which they occupied jointly with James Craig until 1823. They lived on a luxurious scale, their account books showing expenditures of $10,386.05 in 1817; $8,162.04 in 1818; $6,703.03 in 1819; and $3,543.34 in 1820. The diminishing amounts represented an increase in the purchasing power of money rather than an alteration in their style of life until 1820, but the severe reduction in this year was brought about by the need for economy during the depression.

planted such staple crops as wheat, rye, barley, oats, buckwheat, and, above all, Indian corn, which he thought was worth almost all the others in the extent of its yield and the variety of its uses.[2]

He followed a careful plan of rotation, raising grain one year in a field and roots the next, thus preventing the loss from land lying fallow. He found that the root crops—the common turnip, the Swedish turnip, the rutabaga, the mangel-wurzel, and the sugar beet—derived most of their nourishment from the atmosphere and what they did take from the ground was not needed by the grain. They also provided an excellent food for cattle, which, in addition to the profit from the sale of milk and meat, furnished abundant manure to return to the grain crops. All his animals were pure-bred. An inferior hog or cow took as much feed as a good one, but the latter turned at once into milk, beef, or pork everything that was put into them and, by coming earlier into the dairy or market, saved a whole year's expense of feeding.

However assiduously he attended to the farm, he was never far from his books. He read omnivorously during these years after the War of 1812 and followed what he called his "usual habits of laborious indolence . . . mineralogy and the theater, chemistry and clubs, the laws of nations and the rules of tea parties." The organization of the second Bank of the United States in 1816 inspired him to turn back to the study of monetary and currency problems, and he filled a notebook with extracts from the writings of Turgot, Humboldt, Huskisson, and Ricardo on such abstruse subjects as exchange, interest, and the balance of trade.[3]

He believed that a paper currency was the only practical medium of exchange for a commercial nation in the contemporary world, and he was also certain that the United States could not safely permit this currency to be governed by a host of irresponsible bankers. Individual banks could be permitted to issued notes only when each was checked and restrained by a national institution with public responsibilities and power. He agreed with Secretary Dallas, who wrote John C. Calhoun on December 24, 1815: "The national bank ought not to be regarded simply as a commercial bank. It will not operate upon the funds of the stockholders alone, but much more upon the funds of the nation. Its conduct, good or bad, will not affect corporate credit alone, but much more the credit and resources of the government. In fine, it is not an institution created for the purposes of commerce and profit alone, but much more for the purposes of national policy, as an auxiliary in the exercise of some of the highest powers of government."[4]

[2] N. Biddle, "An Address Delivered before the Philadelphia Society for the Promotion of Agriculture, January 15, 1822," *Niles' Register*, 1822 (suppl. to Vol. XXII), pp. 1–9.

[3] N. Biddle, Notebook on Currency, in the Biddle Manuscripts in the Historical Society of Pennsylvania; N. Biddle to J. Forsyth, February 6, 1818, in the Biddle Manuscripts in the Library of Congress.

[4] A. J. Dallas to J. C. Calhoun, December 24, 1815, *Niles' Register*, IX (1816), 365–69.

The constitutional authorities of the United States, congressional and executive, established the national bank in 1816 for these reasons, not for the profit of the private stockholders or to further the interests of any particular economic or social group. Its charter, like that of its predecessor, required it, without any charge to the government, to provide a depository for federal funds in every state in which it had a branch; to transfer these funds from place to place at the order of the Treasury; and to pay the public creditors. To enable the Bank to fulfil these purposes, the capital was set at thirty-five million dollars, its notes were declared to be receivable at par in all payments to the United States, and the Bank was given the right to lend money to individuals and corporations and to buy and sell bills of exchange and bullion.

The Secretary of the Treasury, as an independent administrative officer, was charged with overseeing the operations of the Bank. He was authorized to require periodic reports and to inspect the general accounts to make certain that the information furnished was correct. Further, he was empowered to designate other depositories for the funds in his care whenever he thought proper to do so, informing the Congress of the reasons for his action. The Congress itself was authorized to appoint committees to inspect the books of the Bank, and if any irregularities were found, Congress or the President could institute judicial proceedings for the forfeiture of the charter.

Five of the twenty-five directors were appointed by the President with the consent of the Senate, and, in addition to these formal checks and restraints, the Bank was under the constant supervision of an informed and interested public opinion. Merchants, state bankers, brokers, manufacturers, mechanics, and farmers were dependent upon the proper management of the Bank of the United States, since it had the power and the obligation to provide a national currency, to control the rates of domestic and foreign exchange, to check and guide the state banks, and to protect the national economy from sudden pressures. If it failed to fulfil any of these obligations, the interest of one or another of these groups would be harmed, and they would make their complaints known by public protest and political pressure.

The first president of this powerful institution was not qualified for the post. He was William Jones, an unsuccessful businessman and an inefficient department head, who was chosen for political reasons. It was thought that the best way to insure the popularity of the newly chartered bank was to place at its head a Republican political leader from Philadelphia, and Jones was elected by the directors because he was the designated choice of President Madison and Secretary Dallas. Biddle, an interested observer of these proceedings, was displeased with the election of Jones and refused to serve on the board of directors when requested to do so by representatives of the private stockholders. He partially forgot these misgivings, however, when the Bank, which began active business on January 7, 1817, both persuaded and coerced the state banks into a resumption of specie payments on February 20.[5]

The Bank apparently was fulfilling the purposes for which it was created, and Biddle, pleased by the accuracy of his own predictions, turned his attention to other matters. His political career was not prospering. The nationalistic views which had caused him to leave the Federalist party were equally unacceptable to the majority of Pennsylvania Republicans. His principal interest was internal improvements, and in 1815, under the stimulus of the war, he had been able to persuade his fellow legislators to charter the Schuylkill Navigation Company for the canalization of that important river. But in 1816 and 1817 he could gain no support for a canal from the Delaware River to Chesapeake Bay to connect Philadelphia with the Susquehanna Valley or for another from the upper Susquehanna River to western Pennsylvania, New York, and the Great Lakes. Both were defeated, and he resigned from the Senate in the summer of 1817 because the little he was accomplishing seemed hardly worth the inconvenience and discomfort of the winters in Harrisburg.[6]

His advocacy of the use of governmental power for the improvement of the state and nation not only was ineffective in the legislature but also seemed an insuperable barrier to his political advancement. When his name was proposed as a candidate for the national House of Representatives in 1816, the Old School Democrats, led by William Duane, refused to accept him because of their continued loyalty to the Jeffersonian principles of the 1790's. They were at odds with the national administration, and in 1818, when he won the nomination, they deserted the party and joined Biddle's opponent in denouncing him as a proponent of the national bank, a protective tariff, and internal improvements. They reminded the voters that Biddle had tried to draft them for military service during the war and, through this combination of charges, accomplished his defeat.[7]

Biddle was disappointed by his failure to be elected to Congress and by the unwillingness of President Monroe to appoint him to a national office. He was left essentially unemployed, and in America, he thought, all per-

[5] John Jacob Astor to A. Gallatin, July 31, October 31, 1816, in the Gallatin Manuscripts in the New York Historical Society; N. Biddle to B. Henry, November 27, 1816; N. Biddle to J. Forsyth, January 3, February 6, 1818, in the Biddle Manuscripts in the Library of Congress; *Niles' Register*, XI (1817), 335–36.

[6] J. Roberts to N. Biddle, December 27, 1815; E. Snowden to N. Biddle, February 5, 1840, in the Biddle Manuscripts in the Library of Congress; N. Biddle to I. Weaver, August 14, 1817, in the Biddle Manuscripts in the private collection of Nicholas B. Wainwright; *Journal of the Senate of the Commonwealth of Pennsylvania, 1815–1816* (Harrisburg, 1816), p. 99.

[7] C. Biddle to N. Biddle, August 7, September 12, 1815, September 16, 1816; N. Biddle to C. Biddle, September 13, 1815, in the Biddle Manuscripts in the private collection of Nicholas B. Wainwright; J. Forsyth to N. Biddle, October 13, 1818, in the Biddle Manuscripts in the Library of Congress; C. J. Ingersoll to J. Monroe, November 22, 1818, in the Monroe Manuscripts in the Library of Congress.

sons should be engaged in some useful pursuit. Persons of wealth and distinction had a responsibility to the rest of the nation, particularly when, as in his case, the wealth had been obtained by marriage. Jane's brothers did not share his point of view, and Biddle accused them of "mimicking the dull follies of England."[8]

He was a nationalist, an egalitarian, and politically ambitious, and he continued to seek some place in which to serve. At least twice each year he visited the President in Washington, and hardly a month went by without an exchange of letters between them. When Monroe was preparing his first message to Congress, Biddle urgently recommended that he should propose a general system of internal improvements to be paid for by the federal government; but the President had doubts about the constitutional power and asked for a constitutional amendment to authorize such expenditures. Biddle's congratulatory letter on this portion of the message was relatively cool, but he more than made up for it in his enthusiastic indorsement of Monroe's careful statement in regard to Spain and its revolutionary colonies in Central and South America. The acquisition of the Floridas, the collection of the spoliation claims, and the settlement of the boundaries of Louisiana—disputes with which Biddle had become familiar as Armstrong's secretary in Paris—were still the most important problems of American foreign policy. Spain could be persuaded to settle these questions peaceably, he thought, if the United States avoided premature recognition of, or open support to, the rebels. At the same time, popular sentiment within the country was overwhelmingly in favor of the revolting colonies, and pressure was being exerted to force the administration to intervene on their behalf.[9]

The President, in Biddle's opinion, had taken the most advantageous course. He had written kind words about the rebels to satisfy public opinion but had continued the established policy of strict neutrality to avoid antagonizing Spain. Biddle was well informed on these matters. He was friendly with the Chevalier de Onis, the Spanish minister, and obtained from him confidential information concerning not only the negotiations with the United States but also the relations between Spain and the rest of

[8] N. Biddle to R. Rush, October 13, 1815, in the Biddle Manuscripts in the Library of Congress; N. Biddle, undated, untitled manuscript in the private collection of Nicholas B. Wainwright. In this manuscript Biddle wrote: "The most decisive characteristic of American society is its aristocracy; its downright exclusiveness. We Americans may say what we please, evade it, deny it, modify it, soften it, still it is true in all its force. I know of scarcely any country where the circles of society are more distinctly marked than in the United States, certainly not . . . in the continent of Europe." He returned to this subject somewhat later in the preliminary sketch of a novel which can be found in Thomas P. Govan (ed.), "An Unfinished Novel by Nicholas Biddle," *Princeton University Library Chronicle*, X (1949), 133.

[9] N. Biddle to J. Monroe, February 28, April 10, December 11, 1817; J. Monroe to N. Biddle, April 6, 1817, in the Biddle Manuscripts in the Historical Society of Pennsylvania.

the world. Both he and De Onis were frightened by the advance of the Russians down the Pacific Coast, and Biddle indignantly wrote Monroe, "It is not enough to enjoy a great part of Europe and Asia, not enough to possess the northwest coast down as low as Norfolk Sound and the 57th degree, but they must cross the Columbia and encamp at Bodega within thirty miles of the Spanish settlements in California." To him it was almost an axiom that the United States should be the successor to Spain in control of its remaining territories on the North American continent, in the Caribbean Sea, and in the Gulf of Mexico, and he looked upon the Russians as dangerous intruders and trespassers.[10]

He also had connections with an unnamed South American who was described as "the confidential friend of all the revolutionaries and the depository of all their plans" and, through information obtained from him, kept in touch with all that was going on in South and Central America. He went down to Washington in January, 1818, to talk with Monroe about these and other matters and on his return through Baltimore had a long conversation with De Onis. The minister informed him that he was eager to terminate the dispute between the United States and Spain and that he would go to the full extent of his powers to promote so desirable a conclusion. He suggested that it might be possible to settle the spoliation claims without reference to the other problems and thus remove one obstacle to the negotiations. He also indicated that his government would agree to sell the Floridas if the southern boundary of Louisiana was left for future settlement and if the United States would give up its claims to Texas by accepting a line from the Mermento to Natchitoches as its western limit.[11]

Biddle thought this proposal more definite than any the minister had previously offered, and he sent it to the President with the recommendation that it be used as a basis for settlement. He continued the exchange of ideas with De Onis and in June was convinced that all obstacles to the negotiation had been removed. Just at this moment, General Andrew Jackson, the commander of the Southern Forces of the United States, moved across the border and seized St. Marks and Pensacola. Biddle at first thought that this invasion would cause De Onis to break off the negotiations, but the minister informed him that he was still prepared to cede the Floridas to the United States on the same basis as before. The President, in the meantime, had ordered the posts returned, and Biddle was greatly relieved, for he knew that another American expedition was on its way to the mouth of the Columbia River to force the British trading post at

10 N. Biddle to J. Monroe, December 11, 1817, in the Biddle Manuscripts in the Historical Society of Pennsylvania.

11 N. Biddle to J. Monroe, January 28, 1818, in the Biddle Manuscripts in the Historical Society of Pennsylvania; N. Biddle to J. Monroe, February 7, 25, March 5, 15, 22, 1818, in the Monroe Manuscripts in the Library of Congress.

Astoria to acknowledge the authority of the United States and to act as a threat to the Russians. He would have much regretted, he said to Monroe, "a decision to hold the posts. We have already enemies enough abroad. . . . The seizure of Pensacola, followed as it soon will be, by the accounts from the Columbia River, will furnish the pretext of exaggerated reproaches against our projects of aggrandizement."[12]

He had no further connection with the negotiations between Spain and the United States, which ended with the acquisition of the Floridas the following year. But he continued to send confidential information to Monroe concerning the plans of Spain and the rebels as he obtained it from his sources in Philadelphia. During the remainder of the year he made a digest of the laws of foreign nations affecting the commerce of the United States at the request of Secretary of State John Quincy Adams. The material was in English, French, Spanish, Italian, German, and Dutch (fortunately, the Russian and Scandinavian laws, written in languages of which Biddle had no knowledge, had been recently translated by another student), and he completed this difficult task in six months of arduous study and writing in his library at "Andalusia."[13]

The United States during these same six months was undergoing a financial crisis of major proportions that had as its principal cause the weak and ineffective management of the Bank of the United States. Biddle's original doubts about the wisdom of the election of Jones had been revived soon after the resumption of specie payments in February, 1817. The state banks in the South and West had not been prepared for this sudden revaluation of the currency. Long years of freedom from the requirement to redeem their issues in gold and silver had permitted them to lend freely without regard to the amount of specie in their vaults. The resumption of payments, consequently, forced them to bring pressure upon their borrowers and to refuse to make new loans. This contraction of credit and money imposed a severe strain upon the interior economy, and politically influential protests were immediately raised. A strong and informed president and board of directors of the national bank would have expected and been prepared for these protests, but Jones, for reasons only suspected in 1817, was unwilling to continue an unpopular course. With the consent of a majority of the directors, he ordered each of the interior branches to expand its loans to aid the local business communities and permitted the

[12] N. Biddle to J. Monroe, April 22, 1818, in the Biddle Manuscripts in the private collection of Nicholas B. Wainwright; N. Biddle to J. Monroe, June 18, July 30, 1818, in the Biddle Manuscripts in the Historical Society of Pennsylvania; *Memoirs of John Quincy Adams*, IV, 36, 40.

[13] J. Q. Adams to N. Biddle, July 28, 1818; N. Biddle to J. Q. Adams, July 30, December 26, 1818, February 28, March 6, 1819, in the Biddle Manuscripts in the Library of Congress. The title of the compilation was *Commercial Regulations of Foreign Countries with Which the United States Have Commercial Intercourse* (Washington, 1819).

eastern branches to lend almost without limit upon the stock of the Bank itself.[14]

Stephen Girard, the largest stockholder in the Bank, was one of the five government directors, and he, almost alone among those formally connected with the institution, protested against these policies. In 1816 he had warned a business associate in Charleston that intrigue and corruption had formed a ticket of twenty directors to secure the presidency for William Jones. The following year he solicited proxies for himself and other "independent persons" whose only object was the welfare of the Bank, but this effort likewise was unsuccessful. Jones continued as president and was re-elected at the beginning of 1818, even though Girard, as he had vowed, devoted all his "activity, means, and influence to change and replace the majority of the directors with honest and independent men." The stockholders would not heed his warnings. They thought that nothing was wrong with the Bank so long as the price of the stock was high and they received dividends of 8 per cent, and Girard, in disgust, refused another appointment as a government director.[15]

Biddle was a personal acquaintance of Girard but not in his confidence, and his distrust of Jones was arrived at independently. His single correspondent on these subjects was John Forsyth, a former Princetonian and a representative from Georgia, who had been a member of the select committee which drew up the charter of the Bank of the United States but who had become the most persistent critic of Jones in the Congress. He and Biddle shared information and did what they could to warn the country that the course adopted by the national bank would inevitably lead to financial disaster. They believed that the apparent prosperity of the Bank was a delusion, that its profits came from the unwise expansion of its western and southern loans, and that, if this policy was not revised, the bank would ultimately fail.[16]

The port cities of the Northeast were the principal markets within the nation, and the current of exchanges moved toward them from the South and the West. The notes issued by the interior branches, being acceptable everywhere in payment of debts to the United States, consequently found their way slowly but certainly to Philadelphia, New York, Boston, and Baltimore as they passed from hand to hand in the regular settlement of individual transactions. The southern and western offices thus issued bank

---

[14] N. Biddle to J. Forsyth, October 13, 1819; N. Biddle to A. Gallatin, June 28, July 22, 1830, in the Biddle Manuscripts in the Library of Congress; Adams, *History of the United States*, VII, 386–87; VIII, 214–15; Catterall, *Second Bank*, pp. 1–17; Hammond, *Banks and Politics*, pp. 253–58.

[15] Kenneth L. Brown, "Stephen Girard, Promoter of the Second Bank of the United States," *Journal of Economic History*, II (1942), 125–48.

[16] N. Biddle to J. Forsyth, January 3, February 6, 1818, in the Biddle Manuscripts in the Library of Congress; *Annals of Congress* (14th Cong., 2d sess.), p. 419; *ibid*. (15th Cong., 1st sess.), p. 846; *Niles' Register*, XI (1817), 335–36.

notes but were seldom called on to redeem them, whereas the offices in the northeastern cities were forced to redeem these notes as well as their own. The capital and resources of the Bank were being transferred from the East, where the government had debts to pay, to the interior, where receipts from the sale of public lands far exceeded expenditures. Speculators in land, stocks, and other semipermanent investments were taking advantage of this loosening of credit, and the Bank's current assets, which should have been kept liquid and easily collectible, were in actuality almost completely frozen.

The difficulties predicted by Girard, Forsyth, Biddle, and other informed observers came as an apparent surprise to the board of directors in July, 1818, and they immediately ordered a general curtailment of loans and attempted to force the southern and western branches to strengthen those of the East by a transfer of funds. The resulting pressure on the merchants, the speculators, and the state banks brought the postwar expansion to a sudden halt and precipitated a general financial crisis. Almost at once and from every section of the country there was bitter criticism of the national bank, and state legislatures passed acts taxing or otherwise inhibiting the operations of many of its branches.[17]

John C. Spencer, a congressman from New York, introduced a resolution of inquiry into the House of Representatives that passed by an overwhelming majority, and Spencer was named chairman of the committee of investigation. Upon his arrival in Philadelphia, he called on Biddle, who had just completed his digest of commercial laws, and throughout the investigation he used Biddle as an unofficial aide and adviser. They found evidence of mismanagement in the Bank as a whole, and in Baltimore they uncovered a conspiracy to use the Bank's funds for what seemed to be fraudulent purposes. James A. Buchanan, the president of the branch, James W. McCulloch, its cashier, George Williams, a government director, and D. A. Smith, a son of Senator Samuel Smith, had used one of the provisions of the charter to gain an undue influence over the Bank. The creators of the institution had been afraid of the influence of wealthy men and, to insure popular control of the institution, had given one vote to every holder of one share of stock but had limited to thirty the total number of votes that any one person, copartnership, or body politic might cast, regardless of the number of shares owned. This provision, adopted to prevent monopoly control, was used by the conspirators. They had subscribed for single shares in the names of thousands of individuals with the agreement that the nominal owner would have no interest in its stock and would permit the conspirators to cast his vote.[18] The Baltimore group had

17 *Annals of Congress* (15th Cong., 2d sess.), pp. 317–19.

18 Catterall, *Second Bank*, pp. 28–38, 51–53; Walter B. Smith, *Economic Aspects of the Second Bank of the United States* (Cambridge, 1953), pp. 99–116; Hammond, *Banks and Politics*, pp. 261–62.

thus been enabled to elect a board of directors which, through incompetence, indifference, or a share in the profits, could be relied upon not to interfere with their schemes, and they had borrowed extravagant amounts from the Bank to finance stock speculations.

Biddle was not surprised by these revelations, for he and Forsyth had suspected the truth more than a year before. He was apprehensive, however, about what use would be made of the evidence by the investigating committee and Congress. Jonathan Roberts, United States Senator from Pennsylvania, had told him that the purpose of the investigating committee was not to correct what was wrong with the Bank. Its real aim was to promote the interests of Governor DeWitt Clinton of New York as the successor to Monroe in 1820. A similar political rivalry in 1811 had led to the defeat of the bill rechartering the first national bank, and Biddle feared that the second bank might be destroyed in the same way. He did what he could to prevent this and expressed the hope to Monroe that Congress would be "wise enough to remedy existing evils instead of increasing them, to reform the Bank instead of destroying it." And to Spencer, he wrote: "I think that experience has demonstrated the vital importance of such an institution to the fiscal concerns of this country and that the government which is so jealous of the exclusive privilege of stamping eagles on a few dollars, should be much more tenacious of its rights over the more universal currency, and never again abandon its finances to the mercy of four or five hundred banks, independent, irresponsible and precarious."[19]

He conceded all the faults of the existing administration of the Bank but insisted to Spencer that the question to be asked was whether or not it could be returned to its proper course. He was certain that it could. The abuse had been the misconduct of the directors and the remedy was "simply to enable those most interested to have their due share in managing the Bank." The conflict was between the real stockholders, those who, with the government, had invested their funds in the enterprise, and this group of speculators without character or public responsibility, whose power and influence were derived from money borrowed from the institution itself. "All the measures you so justly reprehend," Biddle concluded, "may be traced distinctly and immediately to the directors named by the government and the men of straw thrust into the Bank by the undue preponderance of the nominal stockholders."[20]

Senator Roberts' suspicions concerning Spencer's motives and purpose fortunately proved to be unfounded, and the Congress, at the recommendation of the committee, passed an amendment to the charter that re-

[19] J. Roberts to N. Biddle, January 20, February 2, 15, 1819; N. Biddle to J. Roberts, January 31, 1819; N. Biddle to J. C. Spencer, January 20, 27, 1819; J. C. Spencer to N. Biddle, January 23, 30, 1819, in the Biddle Manuscripts in the Library of Congress.

[20] N. Biddle to J. Monroe, January 24, 1819, in the Monroe Manuscripts in the Library of Congress; N. Biddle to J. C. Spencer, January 27, 1819, in the Biddle Manuscripts in the Library of Congress.

quired each holder of proxies to swear that he had no interest of any kind in the share or shares he was voting. This simple amendment was all that was needed to enable the real stockholders to control all subsequent elections. In the meantime, however, the power of the conspirators had been overthrown by the combined efforts of Girard and the national administration. Sufficient proxies were intrusted to Girard and others associated with him to enable them to name fourteen of the twenty private directors at the annual election in early January, 1819, but they permitted Jones to continue as president temporarily until the committee of investigation made its report. President Monroe and Secretary of the Treasury William H. Crawford, for the same reason, delayed the appointment of the government directors. They were alarmed by the reports of mismanagement and fraud, which reflected on them as the responsible supervisors of the nation's fiscal affairs, and were belatedly supporting Girard's efforts for reform. As soon as the investigating committee reported its findings, Monroe and Crawford decided that Jones must be removed, and among the directors chosen for this purpose was Nicholas Biddle.[21]

He was notified of his appointment on January 29 and accepted two days later, being unwilling, he told the President, to avoid any duty by which he could be of service. "The truth is," he continued, "that with all its faults, the Bank is of vital importance to the finances of the government and an object of great interest to the community. That it has been perverted to selfish purposes cannot be doubted, that it may and must be renovated is equally certain. But they who undertake to reform abuses and particularly of that description, must encounter much hostility and submit to much labor."[22]

This appointment defined Biddle's career for the next twenty years. He who for so long had been seeking the proper employment of his talents in the service of the nation was at last named to a place for which he was fitted by nature, capacity, and training, but neither he nor the personal friend who appointed him had any presentiment of the far-reaching consequences of his nomination to this relatively unimportant post.

[21] Brown, "Stephen Girard," *op. cit.*, pp. 125–48.

[22] J. Monroe to N. Biddle, January 29, 1819, in the Biddle Manuscripts at "Andalusia"; N. Biddle to J. Monroe, January 31, 1819, in the Monroe Manuscripts in the Library of Congress.

Rescuing the Bank
of the
United States

*D*isgraced and humiliated by the report of the Spencer committee, William Jones made no attempt to continue as president with a board of directors composed of opponents. He resigned at the beginning of February, and a search was started for a suitable successor. Girard's candidate was Langdon Cheves of Charleston, a former Speaker of the House of Representatives. Other influential stockholders proposed James Lloyd of Boston. But no one wanted a contest at this troubled moment in the Bank's history. The national administration was consulted, and when Monroe and Crawford indicated their approval of Cheves, he was unanimously chosen as the second president of the Bank of the United States.[1]

He was almost an ideal selection as the executive officer in this moment of crisis. Cold, self-confident, uncompromising, and courageous, he had the essential qualities needed by a man whose duty it was to devise and carry through the severe and unpopular measures that would be required to sustain the credit of the Bank. He arrived in Philadelphia on March 6 and found the institution in a desperate condition. Biddle and the other directors had ordered drastic curtailments all over the country; but, when Cheves took over, there was scarcely enough gold and silver in the vaults of the parent bank to settle its adverse balances with the local banks in Philadelphia. Another two million dollars had to be paid on behalf of the government to the holders of the Louisiana debt, and many observers thought that a suspension of specie payments was inevitable. Cheves was undaunted by these difficult circumstances. The resources of the Bank, if they could be made available, far exceeded the demands that could be

[1] N. Biddle to J. Roberts, January 31, 1819; J. Roberts to N. Biddle, February 2, 15, 1819, in the Biddle Manuscripts in the Library of Congress.

brought against it. The curtailments ordered during the preceding months had reduced the loans by eight million dollars, but much of these funds were in the hands of the interior branches, not in the East, where the Bank needed them.[2]

It was as obvious to Cheves as it had been to Biddle and Forsyth that it was this misplacement of the Bank's resources which created the danger, and the proper remedy was applied. He immediately ordered the interior branches to cease issuing notes, to forward three hundred and fifty thousand dollars in specie and two-thirds of their government deposits to the eastern cities, and to demand complete settlement of all adverse balances by the state banks. The regular and general reduction of loans that had been previously ordered was continued, and Cheves forbade the purchase of bills of exchange on any city south or west of Philadelphia. And, as a final step to insure that the Bank remain solvent, he sent Thomas Cadwalader to London with authority to borrow two and a half million dollars.[3]

These measures succeeded. The capital of the Bank was transferred back to the East, and all danger of a suspension of specie payments was ended by July 1. But this desirable end was achieved at a fearful price—the further reduction of business activity and the foreclosure of loans. When the national bank and its branches resorted to so drastic a reduction of discounts and purchases of bills of exchange, the state banks, already in debt to the Bank of the United States and being pressed for payment, were forced to do the same. Bank notes collected by the issuing institutions were kept in their vaults. Bills of exchange were almost unsalable, and bank credit all but disappeared. Debtors all over the country were called upon by their creditors but could not pay. For a time it seemed as though universal bankruptcy must inevitably be the result, and the cry went up from all sections that the Bank had been saved, but the people had been ruined.

Biddle supported Cheves in these severe deflationary measures with full realization of their cost, for he believed the only alternative was the insolvency of the Bank and the complete prostration of the currency. "Whether any less vigorous course," he wrote Secretary Crawford, "could have accomplished the object is a question difficult of solution. But that these measures did directly and palpably save the institution cannot be doubted. The Bank adopted its course with great deliberation, it adhered to it however painful the effort with great steadiness and it was rewarded with rapid and unequivocal success."[4]

His particular duty during the spring of 1819 was the supervision of the inquiry into the Baltimore branch, where John Oliver, George Hoffman,

---

[2] N. Biddle to J. Monroe, July 5, 1819; N. Biddle to the Secretary of the Treasury, December 8, 1819, in the Biddle Manuscripts in the Library of Congress.

[3] Catterall, *Second Bank*, pp. 68–72.

[4] N. Biddle to the Secretary of the Treasury, December 8, 1819, in the Biddle Manuscripts in the Library of Congress.

and John McKim, Jr., were the local directors charged with the investigation. Biddle as Cheves' deputy directed their activities and was the regular channel of communication between them and the parent board. He was shocked by the extent of the loans that some of the directors and the principal officers had secured and accused them of "betraying their trust for their own private emolument." He had no sympathy for such men, who, through misconduct, delinquency, and fraud, had incurred debts far exceeding their ability to pay; but most of the debtors in the country did not fall into this category. They were legitimate businessmen or purchasers of land and stock for investment who had been caught in the crisis, and Biddle, as a public director, thought it his duty to do whatever he could to protect them from loss.[5]

As soon as the Bank had provided for its own security and that of its branches, he recommended to Cheves that its restrictive measures be removed or relaxed and that the Bank resume its normal pattern of operations. The president seemed to agree. Some modifications were made in September, and so confident was Biddle that the regular course of business would be resumed that he wrote Robert Oliver: "From a most careful and minute examination of the affairs of the Bank I am now perfectly satisfied that its losses have been extremely exaggerated. . . . If I could procure at its present depressed rates a considerable quantity of the stock it would enable me to bring down the high price of our first purchase and escape with much less loss than we otherwise would." He requested Jane's uncle to purchase one or two thousand shares in his own name for the Craig estate, but Oliver did not want to appear as a borrower and could not himself advance the requisite funds. He offered to indorse Biddle's personal note for the required amount, but Biddle had been considering the matter further and had decided not to make the purchase. "The object, though perfectly unexceptionable in every point of view," he wrote, "might be hereafter misrepresented. . . . So that on the whole it may be best to wait the operation of time to repair my losses in the Bank."[6]

A different sort of ethical problem arose from Biddle's connection with another Baltimore kinsman, Roswell Colt. They had been almost as close as brothers through the years following their marriages to Jane Craig and Peggy Oliver, and Biddle had participated in a small way, never with much success, in some of Colt's numerous speculations. He was somewhat embarrassed, therefore, when Colt in October, 1821, wrote to ask what the dividend rate might be expected to be at the end of the year. In answer, Biddle first rebuked Colt for making the request, then struck out these harsh-sounding phrases and ended by telling him that he need feel no re-

[5] N. Biddle to J. Monroe, July 5, 1819, in the Biddle Manuscripts in the Library of Congress.

[6] N. Biddle to R. Oliver, December 11, 1819, January 5, 1820; R. Oliver to N. Biddle, December 14, 1819, in the Biddle Manuscripts in the Library of Congress.

luctance in asking information about the Bank, since Biddle would feel none in limiting his communications to what he could properly give. "The fact is," he concluded, "that since my residence in the country I have been very little at the Bank and do not know enough of its actual situation to judge of its prospects."[7]

Biddle was telling Colt the truth when he said that he knew little of what went on at the Bank. He was spending most of his time at "Andalusia" with Jane and the children and came into the city to attend meetings of the board only when it was imperative to do so. The reason did not lie in his loss of interest in the Bank of the United States but in a growing estrangement between him and Cheves. The president had read and approved Biddle's report to Crawford in the fall of 1819, saying that the Bank was ready to remove most of its restrictions, but Cheves had no intention of permitting the resumption of large-scale operations so long as notes issued by the interior branches were universally receivable at par in payments to the government. He feared that if the southern and western branches were permitted to issue notes, the capital and resources would once more be drained from the Northeast, and the Bank would again be plunged into the difficulties from which it had been rescued.[8]

Biddle protested in vain against what he considered a needless restriction of issues. "I believed," he later informed Albert Gallatin, "that there was no danger from the issue of its paper if it were judiciously issued for legitimate purposes and that the Bank could sustain a circulation of great extent and usefulness . . . by possessing a mass of movable funds growing out of the domestic and foreign exchange." The method he recommended was essentially simple and safe. He knew, as Cheves did, that if the interior offices were permitted to issue notes, most of them would find their way to the East. But he also realized, what the president never seemed to do, that the cotton, tobacco, and other products of these regions and the bills of exchange based upon them traveled the same path. All difficulties would be avoided if the interior branches used their notes primarily to purchase bills of exchange payable at Baltimore, Philadelphia, New York, Boston, Liverpool, London, or Paris. The collection or sale of these bills by the parent bank and the eastern offices would build up funds in their vaults for the redemption of the notes issued by the southern and western branches.[9]

The whole nation would profit from such an arrangement. It would provide an elastic and uniform national currency and enable the Bank of the United States to influence the rates of domestic and foreign exchange. In the producing regions of the country the Bank would be the great pur-

[7] R. Colt to N. Biddle, October 27, 1821; N. Biddle to R. Colt, November 2, 1821, in the Biddle Manuscripts in the Library of Congress.

[8] Catterall, *Second Bank*, pp. 74–78.

[9] N. Biddle to A. Gallatin, July 29, 1830, in the Biddle Manuscripts in the Library of Congress.

chaser of bills, and in the East the great seller, preventing too great a fall in the rate at one place and too great a rise in the other. The consequence would be much less fluctuation, a desirable result for the merchant, farmer, and manufacturer and injurious only to the brokers and speculators, to whose interest it was that rates of exchange be low in the interior, where they bought, and high at the seaboard, where they sold.

If Biddle's recommendation had been accepted, the state banks which were then protesting against the national bank's demand for regular settlements, would no longer have had any reason to complain. In each locality notes issued by the Bank of the United States would constitute a reasonable proportion of the money in circulation. Many of these notes would be collected by the local banks, so that at the time of settlement they would have national bank notes to balance against those of their own issue held by the local branch. They would thus be able to expand their issues and provide their customers with the money and credit necessary to carry on a profitable business and trade.

These arguments were not convincing to Cheves. He was certain that the only practical method of insuring the solvency and stability of the national bank was to abandon all thought of providing a national currency. The majority of the board of directors agreed with him, and they petitioned Congress for an amendment to the charter which would authorize the Secretary of the Treasury to accept national bank notes at par only at the place at which they were made payable, thus preventing them from being used as a national currency. Congress was unwilling to act, so Cheves kept the restrictive orders in effect. The branches were ordered to continue the demand for the regular settlement of balances by the state banks and to avoid all loans or purchases of exchange that would require an issue of notes. The result was that the specie in the vaults of each office was kept nearly equal, and often exactly equal, to the amount of its notes in circulation.[10]

These measures would not have aroused so much opposition or have placed so great a strain upon the local communities had it not been for the federal deposits. In the South and the West the government's receipts from the sale of land and the collection of taxes exceeded its expenditures, whereas in the Northeast its expenses were greater than its locally produced revenues. The interior branches, which issued few notes, thus received regular deposits of the notes of the local state banks and had to transfer an equivalent amount to Philadelphia, New York, or Boston for the use of the Treasury. The actual notes collected could not be transferred, so the Bank of the United States was forced to convert them into bills of exchange on the northeastern cities or, as was frequently the case when no bills were available for purchase, to convert them into specie. The resulting pressure upon the specie stocks of the state banks made them

[10] *Ibid.*

restrict issues and deny their customers the necessary credit facilities for carrying on business. The national bank rather than the Treasury policy was looked on as the source of this pressure and was denounced as oppressive by the state bankers, the merchants, the farmers, and all other groups dependent upon a freely available supply of credit.

Their views were expressed by a representative of the state banks in Georgia, who wrote to Secretary Crawford: "They hope that the attempted oppression of the state banking institutions is not a measure resorted to with the view of ultimately destroying them, or advancing to an unreasonable extent the interests of the stockholders of the United States Bank. But the systematic demand for specie, by a daily call for specie settlements while the Branch Bank of the United States issues none of its paper . . . affords very strong evidence to authorize such an apprehension of their motives."[11] Biddle, although he knew that these allegations concerning Cheves' motives were unfounded, welcomed such protests by the state bankers because he believed that the restrictive policies were needlessly injurious to the national economy. He had supported drastic remedies so long as the Bank of the United States was in danger. He had been willing to see mortgages foreclosed and businesses forced into liquidation to preserve the institution which he thought essential to a sound and useful banking system, but, once this end had been accomplished, he could see no sense in the further restriction of credit and the consequent curtailment of useful economic activity.

Unlike Cheves and many of his contemporaries, Biddle was neither afraid of, nor hostile to, debt and credit. As a follower of Alexander Hamilton and in some ways a forerunner of some twentieth-century economic theorists, he looked upon a large and increasing debt as an evidence of a strong and prosperous economy. Credit, properly regulated, would permit the rich and vacant lands of the United States to be transformed into farms, whose products would find markets in the urban and industrial areas of the United States and Europe. Credit would provide the means for the construction of roads, canals, and other internal improvements, not only to facilitate the transportation of goods, but also to strengthen the internal defense of the nation against external enemies. Credit also would enable the manufacturers to increase the size of their factories, and merchants the scale and profitableness of their operations.

This vision of a prosperous and expanding economy could not material-

11 T. Cumming to W. H. Crawford, June 30, 1819; Report of the Board of Directors of the Bank of the United States on the Savannah Situation, May 30, 1820; W. H. Crawford to R. Richardson, August 7, 1821; R. Richardson to W. H. Crawford, July 20, 1821; L. Cheves to W. H. Crawford, August 25, 1821, in *American State Papers, Finance*, IV, 697–98, 957–58, 1040, 1055–56, 1068–70. For a fuller discussion of the problems of the state banks in Georgia during this period see Thomas P. Govan, "Banking and the Credit System in Georgia, 1810–1860," unpublished thesis in the Vanderbilt University Library.

ize until the Bank of the United States repealed its restrictive orders and permitted both the branches and the state banks to resume lending. Biddle remained quiet as long as he could, but in July, 1821, he wrote to Robert Oliver: "I would like very much to have a half-hour's consultation with you about the Bank, which seems every day to be making more enemies than money." And in another letter on the same topic in December he said: "After much reflection I am satisfied it cannot prosper under its present management. The whole of the trading part of the community is totally estranged from it, and it is held in little estimation by all classes of people." Oliver was also dissatisfied with the management of the Bank, but he was unwilling to use his influence against its president. His son-in-law, Roswell Colt, was one of the leaders of a group of speculators and stockbrokers who had been vehement and unrestrained in their denunciations of Cheves. Their declared purpose was to elect a president who would make large profits for the Bank and declare large dividends so that the active trade in shares could be resumed. If Oliver publicly criticized Cheves, he would be aligning himself with a group whose purposes he considered dangerous. Hence he said nothing, and his silence was interpreted as approval of Cheves by the other stockholders in Baltimore.[12]

They assured Cheves that Oliver was decidedly his friend and that Colt's name and Colt's acts were by no means synonymous with those of his father-in-law. Biddle, like Oliver, was unwilling to be associated with Colt and his group. He voted for the re-election of Cheves in January, 1821, but at the same time opposed the adoption of the president's report, which tried to conciliate this hostile group of speculators. No dividends had been distributed since 1818 because Cheves had insisted that all current profits should be used to repair past losses. But in January, 1821, he announced that the capital of the Bank had been re-established and that the losses incurred under his predecessor had been made good. The purpose of his statement was to prepare the way for the resumption of dividends with a distribution of 1½ per cent the following July. Biddle thought Cheves too optimistic. He voted against accepting the report and, after being defeated, asked that his objections be placed in the minutes. This too was denied, and then the board, in spite of Biddle's objections, authorized the resumption of loans on the Bank's stock at par.[13]

This last action was too much for Biddle. As a public director he thought that the president and the board of directors had jeopardized the interests of the country in a misplaced effort to conciliate the persons in-

[12] N. Biddle to R. Oliver, July 24, December 24, 1821, in the Biddle Manuscripts in the Library of Congress.

[13] R. Colt to N. Biddle, December 6, 1820, November 23, 1821; R. Oliver to N. Biddle, December 26, 1821, in the Biddle Manuscripts in the Library of Congress; G. Hoffman to L. Cheves, December 18, 1820, December 29, 1821; R. Gilmor, Jr., to L. Cheves, January 2, 1821; J. Potter to L. Cheves, January 21, 1822, in the Cheves Manuscripts in the South Carolina Historical Society.

terested only in the profits from speculation in stock. He wrote an indignant report for the information of President Monroe in which he said: "By a public and voluntary assurance that its stock is whole, and by a public offer to lend upon it at par, the Bank . . . presents such an invitation to the purchase of its stock and such facilities to purchase without paying for it, as cannot fail to render it the object of active speculation, to raise its price beyond its value and ultimately to revive that unfortunate spirit from which the Bank and the country have already too deeply suffered."[14]

This report alienated Biddle from Cheves. Colt and his associates were likewise opposed to its conclusions, so that both the president of the Bank and his greatest enemies were allied in considering Biddle an opponent. Consequently, Biddle's final year in the Bank was not a happy one, and he looked forward with pleasure to December, 1821, when his commission would expire. He retired from the board with thanksgiving, but within a year he was brought back with authority to implement the policies he thought best for the Bank and the nation.

[14] N. Biddle, Statement on the Resolution of the Directors, January 26, 1821; N. Biddle to W. H. Crawford, January 29, 1821; N. Biddle to J. Roberts, January 29, 1821, in the Biddle Manuscripts in the Library of Congress; N. Biddle to J. Monroe, January 29, 1821, in the Monroe Manuscripts in the Library of Congress; L. Cheves, Report of the Bank of the United States, Janaury 23, 1821, *Niles' Register*, XIX (1821), 374–75.

~ *9* ~

Waiting
and
Seeking

Four years intervened beween Biddle's initial appointment as a government director of the national bank and his election as president of that institution. During these years he continued to seek some place in which he could be of service to the nation. His ambition, though active, did not make him impatient, and during these same years he was happy in his freedom and leisure. He purchased the house on Chestnut Street that they had occupied since 1817, but most of each year was spent at "Andalusia." James and John Craig were now living in a house of their own at Bristol. Circe de Ronceray had married William Biddle. Hence, for the first time in their married life, Jane and Nicholas were living alone with their three children.[1]

The boys were strong and vigorous, and their parents were less worried about their health than by the possibility that one of them would be injured when playing around the barns or the wharf at the river front. Edward, the eldest, was the most daring, and in late June, 1821, when his mother had taken him to visit friends in Frankford, he fell from a gate and broke his leg. He could not be moved, so Jane and the other children, much to their disappointment, were forced to pass the summer away from home. They asked Biddle to promise that they could stay at "Andalusia" the following winter, and he consented. This fall and winter constituted

[1] N. Biddle to J. Forsyth, October 13, 1819; N. Biddle to J. Abercombie, September 10, 1820, in the Biddle Manuscripts in the Library of Congress; W. S. Biddle to N. Biddle, January 30, 1821, in the Biddle Family Papers in the Library of Congress; N. Biddle to Jane Biddle, Monday evening, Tuesday, in the Biddle-Craig Manuscripts in the Historical Society of Pennsylvania; Household Account Books, in the Biddle Manuscripts at "Andalusia,"

one of their happiest periods together,[2] but, at the beginning of February, James, the second son, became ill and was brought into Philadelphia for treatment. Despite an initial improvement, his strength slowly declined, and he died early in April, 1822. Jane had two other children, so the blow, severe as it was, affected her less grievously than had the death of her mother and her first child. Her music and drawing, her churchwork and charities, and her duties as mother and housewife kept her from concentrating upon her grief, and she resumed her normal activities as soon as the conventional period of mourning was over. She still wanted to visit Europe, and Biddle made a serious effort to fulfil the formal contract he had made in 1815. Each spring, except in 1820 when his father was ill, he went to Washington to visit President Monroe. He gave no hint of his desire for a diplomatic post to the President or the Secretary of State, but he talked freely with Richard Forrest, an old friend and one of the permanent officers in the Department of State.[3]

Nothing could be done because, as Forrest reported in March, 1822, the President, though desirous of serving Biddle both on the score of his fitness and on that of private friendship, could not appoint a third Pennsylvanian to a major ministry so long as Albert Gallatin in Paris and Richard Rush in London remained at their posts. Biddle himself was not at this time eager to leave the country because he seemed to have an opportunity for elective office. He had obtained more votes for Congress in 1818 than any other candidate on his ticket, and this evidence of his political strength impelled John Binns, editor of the *Democratic Press,* and other supporters of the national administration to suggest his name as Republican candidate for governor in 1820.[4]

Biddle seriously considered the proposal but eventually decided that he could not command sufficient support to gain the election. He did stand as a candidate for Congress, but once again lost the election, not because of personal hostility to him, as he explained to Monroe, but because he "was well disposed to the administration of the general government." The controlling group in the Republican party in Philadelphia would not abandon their antinationalist and laissez faire views, despite the change in opinion by such national leaders as Madison and Monroe, and Biddle could not win an election without repudiating his political past. He was nominated as a candidate for the United States Senate in both houses of the legislature in 1821, but the Pennsylvania party, as badly divided as that in Philadelphia, could not come to an agreement upon him or any other candidate. Each

[2] N. Biddle to R. Oliver, July 8, December 24, 1821; N. Biddle to P. Butler, September 20, 1821, in the Biddle Manuscripts in the Library of Congress.

[3] R. C. Forrest to N. Biddle, March 29, 1822; J. Forsyth to N. Biddle, August 7, 1822, in the Biddle Manuscripts in the Library of Congress.

[4] N. Biddle, memorandum of a certain proposal, February 19, 1820, in the Biddle Manuscripts in the Historical Society of Pennsylvania.

separate faction was so determined to have its own way that it preferred to let Pennsylvania have only one senator rather than risk the victory of the other.[5]

These successive defeats were disappointing to Biddle. He believed that the economic depression gave the government an opportunity to formulate a consistent and effective national policy, and he wanted to have a share in this task. In the winter of 1820 he observed that unemployment was generating a "factious and desperate" spirit among the workingmen. "Only a few days ago," he informed Jonathan Roberts, "a very respectable gentleman told me that he heard from one of those people a sentiment like this, that as during the Revolution the cargoes of tea were thrown into the river, so the cargoes of manufactured goods ought to be treated." The remedy for this situation seemed obvious to Biddle. It was not to condemn the complaining workers or to arouse fears of revolutionary disorders but to "revive the industry and occupation of the laboring classes" by making credit available and protecting American industry from the dumping of foreign goods.[6]

Biddle's study of political economy led him to reject the deterministic doctrines of the classical liberals, Malthus, Ricardo, and James Mill. He had seen too clearly during the course of the War of 1812 and its aftermath how business activity responded to the expansion and contraction of the money supply to believe that economic activity was governed by natural laws with which men interfered at their peril. He advocated a protective tariff for national reasons, primarily to free the country from economic domination by England. So long as imports were duty-free, the superior technical equipment and greater wealth of the British manufacturers would condemn the United States to an agricultural and mercantile economy. A sound and intelligent protective program, on the other hand, would enable the United States to diversify its economy in time of peace and to insure its supply of tools, equipment, and other essential manufactured goods during war. Wages and profits of workers and factory owners could be maintained at higher levels than in the world outside, and farmers and merchants would receive recompense in the large and constantly increasing home market for foodstuffs and raw materials.[7] Internal improve-

[5] *Poulson's American Daily Advertiser* (Philadelphia), September 30, 1820; N. Biddle to J. Monroe, October 8, 1820, in the Monroe Manuscripts in the Library of Congress; C. B[iddle], Jr., to N. Biddle, November 12, 1820; C. Biddle to N. Biddle, Saturday; H. Waddell to N. Biddle, January 19, 1821, in the Biddle Manuscripts in the Library of Congress; *United States Gazette* (Philadelphia), January 5, 16, 1821. The confused story of state politics in these years is described in Philip S. Klein, *Pennsylvania Politics, 1817–1832* (Philadelphia, 1940).

[6] N. Biddle to J. Roberts, March 16, 1820, in the Biddle Manuscripts in the Library of Congress.

[7] Ralph H. Gabriel, *The Course of American Democratic Thought* (New York, 1940), pp. 80–86; Louis Hart, *Economic Policy and Democratic Thought: Pennsylvania, 1776–1860* (Cambridge, 1948), *passim*.

ments and a national bank were essential elements in such a program. The construction of roads and canals and the improvement of rivers and harbors would facilitate the movement of goods and people, and the Bank of the United States, by providing a uniform currency and regulating the rates of domestic exchange, would similarly facilitate the pecuniary aspects of these same transactions.

No single mind created this concept of a predominantly private economy which was directed, supported, and controlled in the public interest by responsible national authorities. Its origin was in the state papers of Alexander Hamilton of New York. John C. Calhoun and William Lowndes of South Carolina laid its foundations in the Congress after the War of 1812, and Henry Clay of Kentucky designated it the "American System." It was most clearly formulated in the messages of President John Quincy Adams of Massachusetts, and the principal economic writers defending it were Mathew and Henry Carey of Pennsylvania. This diverse group, including Biddle, was united not by loyalty to individuals, party, or class but by American nationalism and a common realization of the complementary aspects of the actual economic relations between farmers, merchants, manufacturers, and bankers in all regions of the country.

At the moment there was little that Biddle or anyone else could do to further this program. President Monroe refused to sanction a general appropriation for internal improvements without a constitutional amendment, and Cheves, as head of the national bank, continued the restrictive policies which kept money short and prices low. The whole country was laboring under a burden of debt which was being liquidated by the painful processes of default, bankruptcy, or partial payment, and almost every individual was forced to alter his manner of living because of reduced earnings.[8]

The farm at "Andalusia" was no longer a mere avocation but had become the source of an important part of the family income, and Biddle's earlier experiments now proved their worth by enabling him to operate at a profit in spite of low market prices. In January, 1822, he was invited to address the Philadelphia Society for Promoting Agriculture, and he drew on his own experience to formulate an ideal program for eastern farmers. Their chief handicap, he believed, was a deficiency of capital. Most farmers exhausted their resources in buying land and reserved too little for stocking and cultivating their acres. This practice had arisen naturally. For a century and a half land had been cheap, capital small, and labor expensive. The market had been uncertain and hard to reach; so farmers had relied upon extensive cultivation for home consumption rather than on intensive production for sale to others. The development of the country had changed these circumstances. As a result of the increase in population

[8] Smith, *Economic Aspects of the Second Bank*, pp. 117–33.

and manufactures and the consequent growth of cities and towns, there was now a permanent home market for farmers. Farmers, he insisted, would make their greatest profits on small farms adequately equipped and cultivated.[9]

Biddle's proposals were based on what he had done at "Andalusia" and called for a larger investment in tools and equipment; artificial fertilization; the rotation of crops; the use of pure-bred animals; the feeding of root crops to the stock in pens, thus permitting the conservation of their manure; and the harnessing of streams for irrigation. The last suggestion was based on bitter experience. Biddle on several occasions had watched his crops wither and die for lack of water during periods of drought, though the streams on his place were still full, but, instead of doing what most farmers did, merely lamenting the loss of his harvest, he had built dams on his creeks and diverted water to his fields.

The speech attracted widespread attention and was reprinted in John S. Skinner's *American Farmer* and Hezekiah Niles's *Weekly Register*. Two years later an anonymous contributor to the *North American Review* wrote a review of the five volumes of Skinner's periodical, the first agricultural journal in America, and singled out for quotation Biddle's eulogy of the American farmer, in which he had said that the country's most steadfast security, its unfailing reliance in time of peril, was "that column of landed proprietors, the men of the soil."[10] Biddle, the Hamiltonian nationalist, the advocate of the American System and the commercial farmer, thus aligned himself with Jefferson in the idealization of the rural and agricultural life and character. But, in spite of love for "Andalusia" and interest in the farm, Biddle's life was centered in Philadelphia, where he occupied a prominent position as a member of two of the foremost families in the city. He and Jane were numbered among that small group which he satirically described as believing that "the world, the whole world, and all the world, live in an extremely small compass. You go to the theater and find it crowded without a soul in the house. The next night it may be thinly filled by all the world."[11]

Neither he nor his wife subscribed to such exaggerated social notions. "Distinctions in society you must have," he once wrote, "because wealth, beauty, notoriety, family connexions create them; different circles in society you must have because no individual can be acquainted with everybody. . . . But it is against the absurd pretension of being the first society,

[9] N. Biddle, "An Address Delivered before the Philadelphia Society for the Promotion of Agriculture, January 15, 1822," *Niles' Register*, 1822 (suppl. to Vol. XII), pp. 1-9.

[10] *North American Review*, XIX (1824), 333-37.

[11] Thomas P. Govan (ed.), "An Unfinished Novel by Nicholas Biddle," *Princeton University Library Chronicle*, X (1949), 134.

against the exclusion from your circle of persons fitted to adorn it because the pursuits of their fathers and brothers is not what is absurdly called genteel, it is against this that I must protest."[12] They had friends among all the various groups in Philadelphia. John Vanderlyn, Charles King, the Peales, Benjamin Trott, Jacob Eichholtz, Thomas Sully, and other painters were not only given commissions but were honored guests in their home. William Strickland the architect, Gerard Troost, a Dutch geologist and mineralogist, Mr. and Mrs. George Bartley, English actors who brought a letter of introduction to Biddle from Washington Irving, and Thomas Cooper, the predecessor of Edmund Kean and Junius Booth as the leading enactor of the tragic Shakespearean roles, were personal friends.

Every Saturday night when Biddle was in town, he went to the meeting of the Wistar Association, which had been formed in 1818 as a memorial to Dr. Caspar Wistar. The home of this noted physician had been a regular gathering place for the older intellectual group in Philadelphia, and after his death John Vaughan, Peter S. DuPonceau, Robert M. Patterson, William Tilghman, Reuben Haines, Robert Walsh, Jr., and Thomas C. James banded themselves together to continue this pleasant custom and agreed to give weekly parties on Saturday evenings throughout the winter. A similar club founded by Thomas Cadwalader in 1817, to which Biddle belonged, disbanded after a brief existence, but gradually its members were absorbed into the Wistar. Robert Hare was invited to join in 1820, and the following year Joseph Hopkinson, William Meredith, Nathaniel Chapman, Mathew Carey, W. P. Dewees, Langdon Cheves, and Nicholas Biddle became members.[13]

The rules of the Wistar were simple and few. In the autumn John Vaughan, the secretary of the American Philosophical Society, sent a card to each member, who marked the week in which it was most convenient for him to entertain, and the schedule for the year was arranged. The meetings began promptly at eight o'clock on Saturday. The host could invite twenty non-member Philadelphia friends, and any member could bring non-resident visitors. No refreshments of any sort were served before supper, and the meal was limited to beef, ham, turkey, chicken, and oysters. No coffee, tea, cakes, or ice cream was permitted, but wines and other liquors were not mentioned on this prohibitory list.

These meetings, which were attended by notable visitors from all parts of the country and abroad, were valued by all the participants. Party politics and specific religious doctrines were not considered, but any literary, scientific, theological, or philosophical topic was freely discussed by capa-

[12] *Ibid.*

[13] Job R. Tyson, *Sketch of the Wistar Party of Philadelphia* (Philadelphia, 1898); the annual printed programs of the Wistar parties are to be found in the Biddle Manuscripts in the Library of Congress.

ble and intelligent students of these special fields, and their thinking and conclusions were checked and corrected by equally informed laymen. This informal bringing-together of the leading Philadelphia citizens gave the city a unity and cohesiveness that seemed to be missing in other American cities and was at least partly responsible for the high quality of its public, philanthropic, and educational institutions. Biddle was also a member of the American Philosophical Society and the Pennsylvania Academy of the Fine Arts, a trustee of the University of Pennsylvania, and one of the group who organized the Historical Society. During the early years of his membership he took only a minor role in these activities, but, like the others of his generation, he was being trained to take over as the older group passed on.

He suffered another personal loss at this time. His father was stricken with paralysis in 1820 and never again rose from his bed. He hung on to life through months of agonizing pain, and his death on April 4, 1821, came almost as a relief to him and the family.[14] His influence upon each of his sons was evident throughout their lives, and, like him, they were as conscious of their public responsibilities as they were of their private careers. Two—John and Richard—were members of Congress. Three—James, Thomas, and again John—were officers in the armed services. William, the eldest, confined his services to the local affairs of Philadelphia and Pennsylvania, but he became the center of the family and, though less widely known than any of the others, was the kindest, the most loyal, and perhaps the strongest of them all. Only one of Charles Biddle's sons was in any sense a disappointment to him. This was the younger Charles, whose extravagant disposition and speculative temperament involved him in financial difficulties. On several occasions his father had been forced to advance money to save him from failure, and, in his will, he stipulated that Charles's share of the estate was to be placed in trust for his wife and children. Charles resented this slur upon his capacity and seemed to hold Nicholas and William responsible. A coolness developed between them which continued for many years, and some of his financial and political adventures were a source of embarrassment to his brothers.[15]

After the death of his father, Biddle turned for guidance and support in his personal and political life to Jane's uncle, Robert Oliver, who was a never failing source of wisdom and strength. He was proud of Biddle's intelligence, capacity, and ambition and was the person most responsible for his election as president of the national bank. Cheves had decided in the

[14] N. Biddle to V. L. de Chaumont, April 13, 1821, in the Biddle Manuscripts in the Library of Congress.

[15] Charles Biddle's will is in the John Cadwalader Manuscripts in the Historical Society of Pennsylvania. The estate was not finally settled until 1835, and a total of $164,267.54 was distributed among the heirs.

fall of 1821 that he would resign at the end of the following year but did not announce his decision until the summer of 1822, two months prior to the triennial meeting of the stockholders. Oliver suggested Biddle's name immediately, but no one seconded the suggestion, and during the rest of the summer and fall he was not thought of as a prominent candidate.[16]

Cheves, almost certainly, did not want Biddle to succeed him. His own choice for the position was Thomas Ellicott of Baltimore, but this Quaker banker was not popular with the large stockholders in that city, who thought Cheves had an exaggerated opinion of his ability. "He is not quick," one of them wrote, "is not considered thoroughly versed in the theory of banking and is too precise and scrupulous to give popularity to the institution."[17] The strongest Baltimore candidate was John White, cashier of the local branch, but he was too young and too little known in New York and Philadelphia. Lynde Catlin, president of the Merchants' Bank in New York and a former cashier of the branch bank there, was also proposed for the place, as was Elihu Chauncey of Philadelphia, who had actively opposed the re-election of Cheves at the beginning of 1822, but neither seemed to command sufficient support. Many of the stockholders, thinking it impossible to find an acceptable person, brought pressure on Cheves to persuade him to stay, but he emphatically refused.[18] Two other persons who could have been elected, Albert Gallatin and James Lloyd, were likewise unwilling to serve,[19] and Thomas Willing, former president of the first Bank of the United States, who was favored by a substantial group in Philadelphia, died in October.

No candidate seemed to be available, and Roswell Colt, at the close of October, asked Biddle: "Who will we have for president of the Bank? Ellicott won't do and I fear we cannot persuade White to run. I wish the Philadelphians would bring forward some person besides Chauncey. Sure you must have characters enough to fill the station with honor to themselves and advantage to the Bank." Biddle's reply to this letter was more carefully written than usually was the case in his correspondence with

[16] L. Cheves to R. Gilmor, Jr., November 16, 1821, July 22, 1822; J. Potter to L. Cheves, June 15, 1822, in the Cheves Manuscripts in the South Carolina Historical Society; *United States Gazette* (Philadelphia), July 1, 1822.

[17] Robert Gilmor to L. Cheves, October 13, 1822; John Donnell to L. Cheves, October 20, 1822; Alexander Brown to L. Cheves, October 21, 1822; R. L. Colt to Alexander Brown, October 19, 1822, in the Cheves Manuscripts in the South Carolina Historical Society.

[18] R. L. Colt to J. White, September 21, 25, 28, 1822, in the White Manuscripts in the Library of Congress; J. Potter to L. Cheves, June 15, 1822; E. Parsons to L. Cheves, September 19, 1822; R. Lenox to L. Cheves, October 26, 1822, in the Cheves Manuscripts in the South Carolina Historical Society.

[19] J. J. Astor to A. Gallatin, July 17, September 9, October 18, 1822, in the Gallatin Manuscripts in the New York Historical Society; R. Gilmor to L. Cheves, July 22, 1822, in the Cheves Manuscripts in the South Carolina Historical Society.

Colt and indicates clearly that he desired the place. The person selected, he wrote, should have "talent for business, standing with the government, and residence in Philadelphia," and the man who most nearly embodied these qualifications was Biddle himself. Colt's reply, nevertheless, was uncertain. "If you would consent to serve," he wrote, "I could secure you a strong support from this quarter and particularly so as I am sure we could have in your favor all the influence of government. . . . I do not ask you to run, but I do ask you not to make up your mind positively against it."[20]

If Colt had any doubts, they were immediately dispelled by Biddle's answer. "Before receiving your letter," he wrote, "I had been spoken of and spoken to by some of the leaders of both the parties which divide the stockholders of the Bank. . . . When pressed to know whether I would allow my name to be brought forward I have said that I should neither seek nor shun, that I would engage in no intrigue and mingle in no parties but if a respectable majority of the stockholders wished me to be placed at the head of the institution I would serve if elected."[21] This letter signaled the opening of Biddle's active campaign, and Cheves, still opposed to Biddle, put his personal influence behind William Meredith, the president of a Philadelphia bank. Robert Oliver, the original proposer of Biddle's name, remained quiet and circumspect, and Robert Gilmor, Cheves' chief confidant in Baltimore, informed the retiring president that Oliver had advised him "by all means to take Meredith, if we thought him more likely to please the Philadelphians, but he told me that Mr. Crawford and Mr. Munroe had written Biddle (I think to him) that they would be perfectly satisfied with his election. Mr. Oliver however does not wish he should stand in the way of the welfare of the Bank, if he will be unpopular."[22]

Biddle's supporters were busy in the next few weeks, and Colt apparently was their leader. "I think it advisable," he wrote to Biddle, "that you should not appear to be supported by Chauncey. Let him and his friends keep his pretensions in public, it may force Cheves to our side under the fear that many of our men will join Chauncey rather than take Meredith. Caballing I don't like but we must manage . . . as well as we can and some management will be necessary to get along with the different tempers and views we have to deal with."[23] The management, whatever it was, was

[20] R. L. Colt to N. Biddle, October 26, November 2, 1822, in the Biddle Family Papers in the Library of Congress; N. Biddle to [R. L. Colt], October 29, 1822, in the Biddle Manuscripts in the Library of Congress.

[21] N. Biddle to R. L. Colt, November 4, 1822, in the Biddle Manuscripts in the Library of Congress. The two parties that divided the stockholders were composed of the supporters of Cheves, on the one side, and the speculators, on the other. Biddle as a government director had offended both and so belonged to neither.

[22] R. Gilmor to L. Cheves, November 19, 1822, in the Cheves Manuscripts in the South Carolina Historical Society.

[23] R. Colt to N. Biddle, November 14, 1822, in the Biddle Manuscripts in the Library of Congress.

successful. Cheves' opposition was overcome, either because he despaired of gaining anything approaching unanimity on any other candidate or because he was convinced that the indorsement of Biddle by Monroe and Crawford was the most important consideration. When Cheves changed his mind, the supporters of other persons changed theirs, and on November 25 the representatives of the stockholders, with the exception of Samuel W. Dana of Connecticut, voted that Nicholas Biddle was a suitable person for the position of president of the Bank of the United States.[24]

24 *United States Gazette* (Philadelphia), November 5, 13, 15, 23, 1822. The president of the Bank was elected annually by the board of directors from among their own number, so what the representatives of the stockholders were actually doing was nominating Biddle as their favored candidate.

～ *10* ～

President
of the
Nation's Bank

*I*n a warm note of congratulation President Monroe expressed his personal and official confidence in Biddle and predicted that he would discharge his duties as president of the Bank with "great ability and perfect integrity." He prophesied that, as Biddle became better known to his fellow citizens, he would be intrusted with other posts in which he could be "still more extensively useful."[1] It was in this spirit that Biddle accepted the nomination of the stockholders, and he thought of the post primarily as a steppingstone to more important office. But there was much that he wanted to do with the Bank of the United States, and the position he was assuming was admirably suited to his talents. He was primarily an intellectual, but his excellent mind was accompanied by marked executive ability. In almost any other public office he would have had to move slowly, to weigh and balance rival political claims and influences, and to outwit or overcome opponents, but as president of the national bank he could formulate policies in the light of what he judged to be the real needs of the economy and put these policies into effect without delay.

Part of this power derived directly from the Bank's charter. The men who had planned and created the institution feared its misuse for partisan ends. They therefore protected it from the direct control of either the executive or the legislative branch by giving to the private stockholders the right to elect twenty of the twenty-five directors. Thus the Bank could operate without regard to politics or political influence, so long as it

[1] J. Monroe to N. Biddle, January 27, 1823, in the Biddle Manuscripts in the Historical Society of Pennsylvania.

[78]

did not violate its charter and performed its proper functions to the satisfaction of the economic community, the Congress, and the President. But the creators of the Bank had paid little attention to the problem of power within the institution itself and had devised a mode of internal government which virtually assured that the person elected as president by the board of directors would dominate and control the Bank. He alone of the directors could serve for an unlimited term—all the others had to retire after three years—and he was the only director who was paid to devote his time and attention exclusively to the Bank. The other directors, naturally more occupied with their private pursuits and interests, were dependent upon the president for information and guidance on all matters of policy and almost never overruled his decisions or acted contrary to his recommendations.

This dependence upon the president was reinforced by the fact that the directors were indebted to him for their selection to this honorable post, which was looked on as the recognition of achieved success in the mercantile community. At every election in the history of the Bank except that in 1819, the president held a majority of the proxies. Cheves, once the representatives of the stockholders had made their nomination, substituted Biddle's name for his own on the proxies, and much of Biddle's correspondence in the six weeks that intervened between his nomination and election dealt with the selection of directors. Twelve of the members of the existing board were eligible for re-election, and Biddle intended to keep these members in an effort to prevent any appearance of a break between him and his predecessor; but the other eight had to retire, and he took great care in his choice of their successors.

His purpose was not to select men with sufficient knowledge and leisure to manage the Bank, since he intended to emulate Cheves and establish the basic policies himself, but rather "to attract to the institution as much respectability and to conciliate as many interests as possible." Numerous names were considered, but he finally selected a list consisting of Richard Willing, Joseph Hemphill, Alexander Henry, and Thomas Cadwalader of Philadelphia; James Lloyd and Jonathan Mason of Boston; and Walter Bowne and Thomas Knox of New York. With respect to most of these men, the specific reasons for Biddle's choice were not clear. They involved a careful weighing of their political and business affiliations against those of directors already on the board, so that there would be an essentially equitable representation of the varied and rival groups in the principal commercial cities. Cadwalader alone was chosen for personal reasons. Throughout the years he was Biddle's most intimate adviser, and their virtues and talents were complementary. Biddle was brilliant, impetuous, and daring; Cadwalader was his equal in intelligence but more cautious and conservative. He was well versed in the affairs of the Bank, and his familiarity with its problems as well as his complete integrity and balanced judgment contributed much to the success of the institution during Biddle's administration.[2]

Only one of the government directors, John Connelly of Philadelphia, was reappointed in 1823. The others, E. Irénée Du Pont of Delaware, John McKim of Baltimore, Henry Eckford of New York, and Biddle himself were apparently selected by Monroe and Crawford for reasons of their own. Neither the President nor the Secretary of the Treasury wrote to Biddle on this subject, and his one letter concerning the government directors stated that from obvious motives he was abstaining from expressing or intimating to the government his own preferences in the matter.[3]

The selection of directors was only one of the many tasks confronting Biddle after his nomination. He was already familiar with the general system of the Bank, but he had much to learn about its routine operations and personnel. Cheves was completely co-operative and helpful in this as in all other matters, and Biddle informed Colt that he had "every reason to be satisfied with Mr. Cheves's conduct which has been not only proper but liberal." Throughout his administration he refrained from criticism of his predecessor, even when reversing his policies, and as late as April, 1826, in furnishing information for an article on the Bank, he cautioned the writer: "I will add only one remark which you will consider a personal request. It is that you would have the goodness to avoid . . . the slightest invidious or disparaging comparison between the past and present administrations of the Bank."[4]

With both men adopting this generous attitude, the transition was carried through smoothly and without friction. On Monday, January 6, 1823, the outgoing board of directors with Cheves presiding convened for the last time. He submitted his final report; the directors declared a dividend of $2\frac{1}{2}$ per cent for the half-year; and then the meeting was adjourned. A few minutes later the annual meeting of the stockholders was convened in the same room. Its proceedings were brief. The chairman recognized Biddle, who presented his nomination of the selected directors. No other nominations were made, and the secretary recorded that each of the nominees received the unanimous vote of the shareholders. The next day these newly elected directors, joined by the five appointed by President Mon-

[2] E. Parsons to N. Biddle, December 21, 1822; N. Biddle to E. Parsons, December 24, 1822; N. Biddle to J. Hemphill, December 27, 1822; N. Biddle to J. Lloyd, January 8, 1823; N. Biddle to W. Bowne, January 6, 1823, in the Biddle Manuscripts in the Library of Congress.

[3] N. Biddle to C. A. Rodney, December 3, 1822, in the Biddle Manuscripts in the Library of Congress.

[4] N. Biddle to R. Colt, December 25, 1822; N. Biddle to P. P. F. DeGrand, April 27, 1826, in the Biddle Manuscripts in the Library of Congress.

roe, formally elected Nicholas Biddle the third president of the Bank of the United States.[5]

Biddle himself took little interest in these proceedings and no pleasure at all. His heart and mind were occupied by fears for his wife, who was expecting another child and whose confinement was two weeks overdue. The attending physician was puzzled and concerned at the delay, and Biddle was alarmed. Their worry proved to be needless. On January 10, two days after Biddle's thirty-seventh birthday and three days after his election as president of the Bank, Jane was safely delivered of another boy, who was named John Craig after her father and her younger brother, and Biddle took over his new duties with a light heart.[6]

The position he assumed was one of the most important in the United States, and many persons were doubtful that he had the requisite qualifications for the place. John Jacob Astor, the New York financier, dismissed him as a statesman who would "not add much to the value of the stock," and Hezekiah Niles, an old-line Republican opponent of the national bank, reported: "This gentleman is highly commended by some and much objected to by others, and it is likely there will be some noise made in the papers about the matter. The 'misery' is, that a few unknown, irresponsible individuals, have the power of an institution that grasps at a regulation of some of the dearest interests of the people of the United States, and can assess, as it were, the price of every man's farm, if . . . brought into the market for sale."[7]

The more general objection was that stated by Astor. Biddle's intimacy with "elegant literature and general politics" and even "the suavity of his manners" were brought forward as evidence of his unfitness, and Robert Walsh, in an effort to dispel these objections, published an editorial which said: "We know directly that the individuals who were most earnest for his nomination as president are sagacious, downright men of business, who judged of him as a man of business from what they had seen of him during his long period of activity in the institution." Biddle's own answer to these charges was contained in a poem, playfully written to a young lady, in which he said:

> I prefer my last letter from Barings or Hope
> To the finest epistles of Pliny or Pope;

[5] *United States Gazette* (Philadelphia), January 8, 1823. For a radically different interpretation of the relations between Cheves and Biddle throughout the period in which Cheves' successor was being chosen see David McCord Wright, "Langdon Cheves and Nicholas Biddle, New Data for a New Interpretation," *Journal of Economic History*, XIII (1953), 305–19.

[6] N. Biddle to R. Colt, December 20, 25, 1822, in the Biddle Manuscripts in the Library of Congress; genealogical records in the Historical Society of Pennsylvania.

[7] J. J. Astor to A. Gallatin, November 27, 1822, in the Gallatin Manuscripts in the New York Historical Society; *Niles' Register*, XXI (1822), 209.

My "much esteemed favors" from Paris, to those
Which brought on poor Helen an Illiad of woes;
One lot of good bills from Prime, Bell or the Biddles,
To whole volumes of epics of satires or idylls;
Nay, two lines of good prose with a good name upon it,
To the tenderest fourteen ever squeezed in a sonnet.[8]

He added the statement that he had renounced all illusions and found peace and content "in that simplest sublimest of truths—six per cent"; but in one phase of his duties—the completion of the construction of the Bank's home on Chestnut Street between Fourth and Fifth streets—he was able to use his informed interest and knowledge of architecture.

Tradition has assigned much of the credit for the style and design of the Bank of the United States in Philadelphia to this "gifted amateur" in the art of building, though he was not a member of the board of directors in 1818, when they decided that it should be "a chaste imitation of Grecian architecture in its simplest and least expensive form." His earlier connection with the beginnings of the Greek Revival movement and his friendship with William Strickland, the architect of the building, may have been responsible for the origin of the tradition that Biddle had a creative hand in the design; but that he was more than casually interested is proved by the fact that, on the morning that Strickland's design was accepted, Biddle's father sent him a note by special messenger to "Andalusia" announcing the result. In any event, whatever Biddle may have had to do with the actual design of the building, he always took a proprietary pride in the pure authentic beauty of the Parthenon Doric exterior, with its porticos supported by eight massive columns over the Chestnut and Library Street entrances to the Bank, and in the efficient, well-lighted, and attractive arrangement of the interior working spaces.[9]

He was chairman of the building committee in each of the three years that he served as a director, and he assumed this position again after his election as president. No single event in the Bank's history gave him as much pleasure as that day in 1824 when it moved out of its temporary quarters on lower Chestnut Street into the new building. He was determined to make the institution itself worthy of its magnificent home by devising "a system of currency and exchanges for the United States better than any that had existed in any other country," and to this purpose he devoted all his time and energies. Cheves had turned over to him a sound, well-organized, and powerful instrument. The Bank's capital was thirty-five million dollars, its total resources exceeded fifty-three million, and its

[8] *United States Gazette* (Philadelphia), January 8, 1823; *Verses by Nicholas Biddle* (Philadelphia, 1889), pp. 11–14.

[9] C. Biddle to N. Biddle, September 10, 1818, in the Biddle Manuscripts in the private collection of Nicholas B. Wainwright; W. Strickland to N. Biddle, April 14, 1837, in the Biddle Manuscripts in the Library of Congress; Hamlin, *Greek Revival Architecture*, pp. 70–71; Gilchrist, *Strickland*, pp. 53–57.

Nicholas Biddle. Early miniature by Henry Inman. (By permission of Colonel Nicholas Biddle and AMERICAN HERITAGE.)

ABOVE, *Second Street north from Market Street, Philadelphia, 1799. (Lithograph by W. Birch & Son. New York Public Library.)* BELOW, *Panorama of Philadelphia, 1838. (Engraving by J. C. Wild. Historical Society of Pennsylvania.)*

Jane Craig Biddle (ABOVE) and Margaret M. Craig (LEFT). 1825 (?) and 1790 (?) miniatures. Painters unknown. (By permission of Mrs. Harold Paumgarten. **Frick Art Reference Library.)**

Mrs. Nicholas Biddle. 1827 portrait by Thomas Sully, at "Andalusia"

Nicholas Biddle. 1826 portrait by Thomas Sully. (By permission of Mrs. Harold Paum-garten. Frick Art Reference Library.) A similar portrait by the same painter is at "Anda-lusia."

ABOVE, *Office of the Bank of the United States at New York. E. M. Thompson, architect. 1825. (Lithograph by A. J. Davis. New York Public Library.)* BELOW, *Office of the Bank of the United States at Savannah. William Jay, architect. 1823. (Engraving from drawing by J. Shaw. New York Public Library.)*

Drawn by J. Shaw.   William Jay Architect   Engraved by I G Mason

Nicholas Biddle. Engraving by John Sartain, from a portrait by Thomas Sully. 1837.

The Greek Revival in Philadelphia: The Merchants' Exchange. William Strickland, architect. 1832. (Lithograph by J. C. Wild. Historical Society of Pennsylvania.)

The Bank of the United States. William Strickland, architect. 1838. (Lithograph by J. C. Wild. Historical Society of Pennsylvania.)

"Andalusia." Thomas U. Walter, architect. (Photograph by Cortlandt V. D. Hubbard for Antiques.*)*

Biddle's "Domestic Den of Iniquity" for billiards and cards. (Photograph by Cortlandt V. D. Hubbard for ANTIQUES.*)*

Chestnut Street, looking toward the Delaware River from the steps of the Bank of the United States, ca. 1842. (Engraving by D. S. Quintin. Historical Society of Pennsylvania.)

Girard College. Thomas U. Walter, architect. (Engraving from the architect's design. New York Public Library.)

Bust of Nicholas Biddle by S. V. Clevenger, completed by the sculptor's widow after Biddle's death. (Historical Society of Pennsylvania.)

St. Peter's Church, Philadelphia. 1829. (Engraving by W. L. Breton. Historical Society of Pennsylvania.)

Bank of the United States. 1839. Popular colored lithograph distributed in England and on the Continent, with English, German, and French titles.

principal depositor was the government, "a partner in the Bank, interested in its prosperity." From his office in Philadelphia, Biddle controlled the operations of eighteen branches, from Portsmouth, New Hampshire, in the Northeast, to New Orleans in the Southwest, and from Louisville on the Ohio to Charleston on the Atlantic. The inherent power of the Bank was increased by the flexibility of its operations, a corollary of the fact that the parent Bank and its branches constituted a single institution completely responsive to the will of its president.[10]

The cashier of each office was elected by the board of directors in Philadelphia, which in practice meant that he was named by Biddle, and his actions were directly controlled by orders from the cashier of the parent Bank. The directors of the branches were also selected by Biddle acting in the name of the board in Philadelphia, and, though these local directors, according to the charter, were empowered to elect one of their number to the presidency of the branch, the choice of this officer was also dictated by Biddle. Only once from 1824 to 1827 was his recommendation disregarded in the Washington office, and he wrote to Thomas Swann, the unwanted president: "With regard to the abstract right of the board of the office to choose any one of their members president, there is no wish to contest it, but like all other strict rights its exercise should be governed by the considerations of the case. The Bank of the United States having two millions of property to manage in the District, names eleven gentlemen to take charge of them, and at the same time informs these gentlemen that inasmuch as one of their number must be the organ of communication with the parent board, must be a correspondent of the board, is to receive a salary from the board, this correspondent, this salaried officer, this confidential agent, should be a gentleman expressly named and selected by them."[11]

He could have prevented the re-election of Swann by omitting his name from the list of Washington directors, but his principle that in regard to any strict right "its exercise should be governed by the considerations of the case" also applied here. He let it be clearly known that Swann was not considered capable of directing the Washington office, but he acquiesced in the contrary decision by the local board until finally, in 1828, they accepted his choice, Samuel Harrison Smith. Few outside the Bank were aware of this internal conflict, and never again was Biddle's right to name the president of the branch contested by the Washington or any other branch board. The president of the parent bank thus exercised direct authority, including the power of removal, over the two principal officers in

10 N. Biddle, "To exhibit the gradual development of the powers . . . of the Bank since the first day of January, 1823," in the Dreer Manuscript Collection in the Historical Society of Pennsylvania.

11 N. Biddle to C. West, May 17, 1823; N. Biddle to T. Swann, February, 1824; N. Biddle to W. Wirt, January 30, 1824; N. Biddle to J. McKim, February 18, 1824, in the Biddle Manuscripts in the Library of Congress.

each of the branches. He also selected one or two directors in each city as private and confidential advisers and correspondents. Whenever he planned a shift in policy, their comments were requested, and adjustments made to meet their objections, or it was explained to them why they had been disregarded. Such an arrangement had many advantages. It enabled him to ascertain local opinion to supplement the formal reports of the president and cashier and also to have informed members of the board ready to explain and defend the Bank's policy when the formal orders were read.

When these channels of authority and communication had been fully established, Biddle began his new system of operations, which not only quieted most of the justifiable criticism of the national bank but also increased its profits. The institution was in excellent condition. Thirteen million dollars of its funds were invested in government loans, and over three and a half million of the Bank's stock were held in its treasury. Since these securities were readily salable in the United States or Europe, the Bank was in a position to increase its liquid resources by more than sixteen million dollars whenever it needed the money. Each of the branches had been given an absolutely fixed capital, thus limiting the amount for local loans, and excellent progress had been made in the collection of the eleven million dollars of suspended debt.

These achievements, all of which had been accomplished by Cheves, had been made at a heavy cost in hatred and denunciation of the Bank of the United States. This was particularly true in the South and West, where conflict over legislation for the relief of debtors and the control of banks had divided the states into warring political factions. The Bank was deemed responsible for all the financial difficulties of the country by many powerful and influential men, and Biddle, who had himself shared these opinions, understood and sympathized with those who expressed bitterness. He believed that the prolongation of depressed business conditions after 1820 had resulted from the needless continuation of the restrictive policies of the national bank. He had protested at the time but had been without power. In 1823, however, he was president and could introduce the system that Cheves had refused to consider.[12]

His first step was to permit the interior branches to issue notes as they had before 1819, but he required them to use most of these notes for the purchase of bills of exchange. The limits upon local loans, which had been established by Cheves, were continued in force, but this made no difference. The complaints had been against the national bank's refusal to issue its currency, not its refusal to lend, and the change ordered by Biddle was all that was needed. The nation once again had a national currency, and the rates of exchange, which previously had been high and irregular, were

[12] N. Biddle, "On the gradual development of the powers of the Bank," in the Dreer Manuscript Collection in the Historical Society of Pennsylvania.

reduced to a nominal and regular sum. Biddle also changed the type of loans made at the eastern offices. Cheves had sought security and certainty of payment, and for this purpose loans upon the security of stock were best. But they had a tendency to become permanent, to tie up the funds of the Bank, and to prevent it from being in a position to influence the course of economic events. Ordinary loans to businessmen, on the other hand, were temporary and usually fully repaid at maturity, so that the Bank, if it wanted to stimulate business activity, could increase the amount of paper it accepted or, if it wanted to impose a check, could refuse applications for loans.[13]

Within six months of Biddle's election, the loans on personal security, business loans, increased by more than two million dollars, and the purchases of domestic exchange increased from less than two million to more than three million. This enlargement of the credit facilities for the real business of the country—the production, manufacture, and distribution of raw materials and finished goods—had an almost magical effect upon the national economy. Prices, which were largely controlled by forces outside the country, remained virtually the same, but the volume of business activity expanded, and profits increased. These policies had a similar effect upon popular feeling toward the Bank. Where before there had been criticism, there was now tacit approval, and the change in public opinion was reflected in the increase in the price of the stock and in the expressions of good will toward the Bank not only in the eastern cities but also west of the mountains.[14]

State banks ceased complaining, now that notes of the Bank of the United States constituted a substantial proportion of the circulating currency, and they no longer protested at the demand for regular settlements. The procedure as Biddle described it was essentially the same as in present-day clearing houses: "Every morning the clerks from this Bank and the

[13] N. Biddle to J. Cumming, May 20, 1825, in the Dreer Manuscript Collection in the Historical Society of Pennsylvania. In this letter Biddle reassured the president of a branch, who had expressed his fears at the dangers resulting from an increased circulation for the purchase of exchange, by writing: "If you were called upon at once to meet your increased circulation, you would be able by your specie, your northern funds, and your claims on the state banks . . . to pay every dollar of it. . . . But you will not, and you cannot be so called upon. . . . The notes thus issued are not immediate debts; they are in circulation, that is, they have a certain career to run before they become chargeable to you. They come gradually in at the northern offices . . . so that your whole object is to provide funds in the northern offices to meet your circulation as it reaches them. As long as you can purchase bills on the north at a profit, as long as you can obtain such bills or specie from the state banks, so long you can fearlessly and profitably issue your notes. This power of circulation is a prodigious lever which if well managed will add so much real capital to the Bank." See also Catterall, *Second Bank*, pp. 93–113; Smith, *Economic Aspects of the Second Bank*, pp. 134–38.

[14] N. Biddle to I. Lawrence, October 13, 1823, in the Biddle Manuscripts in the Library of Congress; Walter B. Smith and Arthur C. Cole, *Fluctuations in American Business, 1790–1860* (Cambridge, 1935); P. P. F. DeGrand, *Boston Weekly Report of Public Sales and Arrivals,* quoted in *United States Gazette* (Philadelphia), July 10, 1823.

State Banks meet and interchange the notes received on the preceding day. The balances are struck accordingly. But no bank ever calculates on its balances remaining for any length of time and whenever it grows a little too large, no bank ever hesitates to send for ten or fifteen or twenty thousand dollars from its debtor. . . . Thus it goes around no one complains and everyone is satisfied. In truth, it is only when these balances accumulate and remain for any time that they become oppressive to both parties and excite mutual ill will."[15]

Each bank, state or national, was thus under constant restraint. The moment its issues exceeded the requirements of the business community, it was confronted with demands for settlement from the other banks and was forced to contract its circulation. The Bank of the United States, the controlling agency in this situation, thus succeeded in keeping in check many institutions which might otherwise have been tempted into extravagant and ruinous excesses. But this necessary and salutary control could not be established so long as the Bank refused to issue its own notes. It took Biddle's innovations, but, once these were introduced, the Bank began to exercise "a mild and gentle but efficient control over the monied institutions of the United States so as to warn rather than force them into a scale of business commensurate with their real means."[16]

The whole relationship of the Bank of the United States to the state banks was thus changed. Under Cheves they had been mutually antagonistic, and neither had been capable of performing its proper function. But Biddle's innovations made them collaborators in the provision of credit facilities for an expanding economy. The local banks supplied local needs, and the national bank concentrated upon supplying the means for the internal exchanges of the products of the labor of citizens in all parts of the country. No mere physical improvement in the means of communication, Biddle proudly reported, "no facilities of traveling and transportation can so completely abridge the wide spaces which separate the parts of this extensive country, as the removal of those great barriers which the want of easy commercial exchanges interpose to their prosperity."[17]

The amazing aspect of Biddle's accomplishment was its speed. Within six months an informed observer noted that the rates of exchange between Charleston and the eastern cities had been brought down to par, and similar reductions were to be found in the rates of exchange between cities in all sections. The Bank of the United States, under Biddle's direction, also

[15] N. Biddle to C. P. White, February 3, 1823, in the Biddle Manuscripts in the Library of Congress. The procedure described was that followed in Philadelphia and was essentially the same elsewhere except that in the smaller towns the settlement was made weekly instead of daily.

[16] N. Biddle to P. P. F. DeGrand, April 27, 1826, in the Biddle Manuscripts in the Library of Congress.

[17] N. Biddle to A. S. Clayton, April 16, 1832, *House Reports* (22d Cong., 1st sess.), No. 460, pp. 315–25.

began to exercise an influence upon the foreign-exchange market and the rates of exchange, and, by so doing, it accomplished more than merely saving its customers' money. Through these operations the Bank was able to protect the national economy from pressures originating abroad and to prevent sudden vibrations in the rate of business activity. When there was an adverse balance of trade, if nothing were done to correct it, the rates of British and European exchange would rise to the point where it was cheaper to ship coin than to buy bills. When such an increase occurred, those owing debts in Europe would draw silver out of the banks, thus forcing these institutions, in their own defense, to diminish their issues and their business, sometimes with great rapidity. This was the natural remedy but, in Biddle's view, an unnecessarily harsh one, in that any great and sudden contraction of the circulating medium reacted on the community with "inconvenient and often oppressive" force. He knew that such a situation, if not managed with "great delicacy," might bring in its train the most disastrous circumstances, so he sought to lessen the force of these results by preparing for them.[18]

The Bank became the largest purchaser and seller of foreign exchange in the country, and it had the additional power to draw on Baring Brothers in London and on Continental bankers. In periods such as that described above, when European exchange was in short supply, the Bank intervened carefully and slowly so as to prevent the rate from remaining long beyond the point where large shipments of coin were required. If unable to prevent the shipments from taking place, and a reduction of issues by the banks was forced, then the Bank used its great powers to come to their aid, so as to make the reduction as gradual as possible and not greater than necessary.

These, Biddle thought, were the proper "functions and benefits of the Bank," and his transformation of the institution from a hated and feared oppressor into the guardian and stabilizer of the national economy was a significant contribution to the entire country. The creative thought was his. The directors, officers, and clerks, who authorized and executed the policies, had previously followed Cheves with equal loyalty, and none of them apparently realized what Biddle was trying to do until it was an accomplished fact.

18 N. Biddle to P. P. F. DeGrand, April 27, 1826, in the Biddle Manuscripts in the Library of Congress.

~ 11 ~

Protecting
the
National Economy

$\mathcal{B}$iddle was an imaginative and creative financial innovator, but in the day-to-day operations of the institution he was a sound and conservative banker. He refused to make long-term real estate loans on the grounds that "it is entirely inconsistent with its design and its safety that a bank should lend its funds on the security of real estate, should lend on permanent accommodation to parties not in business." In his view the object of a commercial bank, such as the Bank of the United States and its branches, was to facilitate the real transactions and exchanges of the community, and its main occupation should always be to discount notes and bills which had short periods to run and which would be payable at maturity. He also resisted demands made by officers and directors in periods of slack business to increase the time limit on commercial loans or to lower the interest rate.[1]

He deliberately abstained from such measures, the sole purpose of which was to increase the profits of the Bank, because he was aware of another responsibility—the necessity for the Bank of the United States "to keep itself in such an attitude that at a moment's warning, it may interpose to preserve the state banks and the country from sudden dangers."[2] He was not unconcerned with profits, and the Bank made money each year, but he

[1] N. Biddle to the president of the Mobile branch, n.d.; N. Biddle to T. Swann, March 1, 1825; N. Biddle to J. S. Johnston, January 9, 1826, in the Biddle Manuscripts in the Library of Congress.

[2] N. Biddle to S. Smith, November 14, 1830, in the Biddle Manuscripts in the Library of Congress.

always preferred "being very strong and able to move with great power in case of emergency to making some additional profit by forcing business." He continued the policy, originated by Cheves, of diverting the larger part of the profits to the surplus funds, and the speculators in the Bank's stock, who had led the attack upon the former president's restriction of dividends, were equally displeased with his successor. They had the impression, as Biddle was informed in an anonymous letter, that his object was "to keep the state banks in check and to regulate the currency *at their cost,*" and they also insisted that "the only test of good banking is good dividends."[3]

They attempted to elect a president more amenable to their influence in January, 1825, but they had little success in persuading stockholders to send them proxies. The ticket of directors that Biddle drew up was easily elected, but the existence of this threat to his control of the Bank led him to begin a campaign to persuade those stockholders who had neglected to send in proxies to do so the following year. He was thus in a position at the beginning of 1826 to thwart the one serious effort made during his administration to subject the national bank to the control of a single private interest. The leader of this conspiracy was Jacob Barker of New York, who, with his associates, began his activities in 1825, and, "as if by the wand of a magician," gained control of some fourteen banks and insurance companies in New York and surrounding areas. The directors of the local branch were seriously alarmed. "They state," one of them wrote, "they will not stop till they get the United States Bank, and I really do not see but they may do it."[4]

Biddle was not alarmed. He knew how the conspirators operated and how they could be defeated. What Barker had done was to take control of one small financial institution, use its resources to buy a controlling block of stock in another, then, having installed new officers and directors in the second, borrow from it to gain control of a third, and so on with an ever mounting structure of financial power. But the scheme had one fatal weakness. In lending money to buy stocks, a bank had to issue its promises to pay specie in the form of bank notes. Slowly but surely throughout 1826 the national bank brought pressure to bear upon the institutions dominated by Barker. Wherever their notes circulated, some of them were deposited in the Bank of the United States and its branches. Regularly these notes were presented to the issuing bank for redemption, and in the fall of

[3] N. Biddle to J. Lloyd, July 5, 1825; "A Stockholder" to N. Biddle, June 17, 1828; R. L. Colt to N. Biddle, January 28, 1823, in the Biddle Manuscripts in the Library of Congress.

[4] I. Lawrence to N. Biddle, June 9, 1825; N. Biddle to I. Lawrence, June 11, 1825; N. Biddle to J. Potter, June 19, 1825; R. Lenox to N. Biddle, July 10, 1825, October 21, 1826; C. P. White to N. Biddle, July 13, 1826; J. Potter to N. Biddle, July 25, 1826, in the Biddle Manuscripts in the Library of Congress.

1826 the conspiracy collapsed in a mass of suits for debt and indictments for fraud.[5]

Biddle had wanted to move against the group earlier, but Barker, who had greater knowledge of national and international finance than most of his contemporaries, had timed his operation shrewdly. He chose the moment when the funds of the Bank of the United States were fully employed in paying off a part of the national debt, and he hoped to gain control of this powerful institution before it was in a position to stop him. He did not come close to success, and his total defeat was but a minor episode in Biddle's triumphant solution of the complex financial problems of 1825 and 1826. These were among the most difficult years in the history of Anglo-American financial relations. Pressures and strains generated within Great Britain threatened to overwhelm the American economy and provided the first test of Biddle's direction of the national bank in a time of crisis.

He had foreseen part of the difficulties. The federal government during 1825 and 1826 was scheduled to pay or refinance two loans incurred during the War of 1812 and also to make a payment of five million dollars to Spain. Biddle had begun to prepare for this operation as early as November, 1823, in order that it might be accomplished without hampering the ordinary business of the Bank or depriving merchants, manufacturers, or farmers of their customary credit facilities.[6] If the Bank, without preparation, were obliged to pay so many million dollars on a particular day, it would have to accumulate the necessary funds by curtailing its loans and stopping its purchases of exchange. This restrictive action would bring pressure upon the state banks and brokers, who would have to curtail in the same way. A temporary scarcity of money would be produced until the day of payment, and then there would be a sudden and drastic change. An immense amount of money would be thrown into the market for investment, and there would be a surplus where before there had been a shortage.

Biddle's aim was to prevent this fluctuation with its attendant disruption of commerce, and in this he was successful. During the months before the first payment was made on January 1, 1825, the Bank of the United States encouraged the fund-holders not to wait for the last moment to find an

---

[5] Jacob Barker, *Letters Developing the Conspiracy Formed in 1826 for His Ruin* (New York, 1827); *Trial of Jacob Barker, Thomas Vermilye and Matthew L. Davis* (New York, 1827); *The Speeches of Mr. Jacob Barker and His Counsel on the Trials for Conspiracy* (New York, 1827); *The Conspiracy Trials of 1826 and 1827* (Philadelphia, 1864); *Incidents in the Life of Jacob Barker* (Washington, 1855).

[6] N. Biddle to W. H. Crawford, November 20, 1823, in the Biddle Manuscripts in the Library of Congress. Twenty-four million dollars of the debt were to be paid during 1825 and 1826. Ten million dollars of this were raised by a new loan, and the total debt at the beginning of 1827 was approximately seventy-one million (Albert S. Bolles, *The Financial History of the United States from 1789 to 1860* [New York, 1894], pp. 303–12).

object of investment but rather to come to the Bank for a loan on the security of their government stock in advance of the payment day and thus avoid the great press for investment which would occur if they all waited until the last moment. Many of the government's creditors took advantage of this offer, with the result that the payments were scattered over a period of four months instead of being concentrated on a particular day.[7]

The solution of this problem was essentially simple in theory and technique, but carrying it out so that there would be no disturbance of ordinary business was a difficult operation. When the national bank increased its loans in the latter part of 1824, the number of its bank notes in circulation also increased, and each of the branches became a debtor of the state banks in its city on every settlement day. If additional funds had not been provided from some other source, the Bank would have had to give up its specie or curtail its regular loans and purchases of exchange. Biddle had anticipated this result and had prepared for it. He had persuaded the Secretary of the Treasury to recommend to the Congress that, in authorizing the two loans necessary to raise the funds for paying off the debt, it should permit the Bank of the United States to bid. The Congress had accepted the recommendation, and both loans, amounting to ten million dollars, were sold in their entirety to the national bank.[8]

Biddle thus had ten million dollars in disposable securities to add to the sixteen million dollars of government loans and forfeited Bank stock which had been turned over to him by Cheves. In addition, the Bank had purchased large amounts of foreign exchange to enable it to pay off the European fund-holders, and its resources in Great Britain and Europe could be increased by drawing on its established credit with Baring Brothers and Company in London. As a result of these preparations, the Bank went through the day of payment without any dangerous increase in its debt to the state banks. In November and December, 1824, Biddle had sold bills of exchange on London and Paris and had sent Bank stock and two million dollars of new government loans to Barings for sale in the English market to meet these bills when they matured. Reuben M. Whitney, a shrewd New England merchant in Philadelphia and a director of the Bank, was sent at the same time to New York with instructions to sell secretly as many shares of the stock as could be disposed of without disturbing the market.[9]

[7] N. Biddle to J. Lloyd, January 19, 1824; N. Biddle to J. Monroe, May 28, 1824; T. Cadwalader to N. Biddle, May 25, 1824; N. Biddle to Baring Brothers and Company, November 29, December 14, 1824, January 1, 7, 1825, in the Biddle Manuscripts in the Library of Congress; N. Biddle to F. Hopkinson, November 2, 1830, in the Gallatin Manuscripts in the New York Historical Society.

[8] *Ibid.*

[9] N. Biddle to I. Lawrence, November 22, 1825; N. Biddle to R. M. Whitney, December 15, 1824, in the Biddle Manuscripts in the Library of Congress.

Through these sales, the permanent investments of the Bank were transformed into current notes of the state banks, and when the respective branches received these notes, they became the creditors of their neighbors, thus avoiding any necessity for curtailment. So easily was the payment accomplished that it attracted almost no public attention, and what under less skilful management could have been a season of severe financial pressure was a period of normal business activity.

The second day of payment was October 1, 1825, and through the troubled months of the spring and summer Biddle had this date constantly in mind. The branches were permitted to expand between January and March, but in April they were ordered to remain substantially stationary, lending each day only what was collected on maturing loans. The spring of the year had always been a difficult time in the money markets of Philadelphia, New York, and Boston, for it was then that the ships for China and the East Indies were being prepared for their voyages. Americans sold very little in these markets. Their profits were made from the sale of goods purchased there, and, before 1825, the owners had purchased specie in the United States to enable their captains to procure a cargo. This annual demand for silver had put a strain upon the banks and the business community. As the banks lost their specie, they were forced to curtail their loans, and business was temporarily slowed. To prevent this from happening, Biddle tried an experiment. He announced his willingness to sell bills of exchange drawn by the Bank of the United States on Barings in London, which could be sold at a profit in the Far East, where London funds were always in demand; and so, by one and the same operation, the Bank of the United States expanded its exchange business, the shipowners increased their profits, and the rest of the community was spared the regular spring curtailment of business.[10]

This successful innovation came at a propitious time, for the banks needed all the strength they could muster during the remaining months of 1825. The difficulties started in Great Britain, where money and credit were cheap and abundant throughout 1824. Even the most conservative businessmen in London and Liverpool became involved in speculative enterprises both at home and in Latin America. The fever and excitement spread, reaching the cotton market in December. Every ship that departed carried extravagant orders to buy cotton at ever increasing prices, and in the exporting cities of the South there was frenzied bidding for the available stocks. During April and May prices almost doubled, and the banks were flooded with requests for loans and offers to sell bills of exchange. But the Bank of the United States refused to expand its operations.

[10] N. Biddle to G. Green, April 11, 1825; N. Biddle to I. Lawrence, September 22, 1825; N. Biddle to T. H. Perkins, December 6, 1825; N. Biddle to P. P. F. DeGrand, April 27, 1828, in the Biddle Manuscripts in the Library of Congress.

"In the midst of the speculations which are abroad . . . ," Biddle wrote on April 22, "prudence requires that we should keep within reasonable limits, and that under the circumstances . . . the Bank should keep itself secure and strong." And, three weeks later, he said: "Our first duty is to take care of the Bank, and at the present moment of wild and exaggerated speculation, if we suffer ourselves to be borne away by the current . . . we shall betray our trust."[11]

He held the Bank in check from April to September, confining new loans almost exclusively to holders of government funds in preparation for the payment on October 1. In Great Britain, meanwhile, powerful forces were operating to bring the excessive speculation to an end. In May the Bank of England, worried by its loss of specie, began restricting its issues and curtailing its rediscounts. At the same time the cotton spinners of Manchester jointly refused to buy cotton at the artificially enhanced prices just when a large supply of the raw material from the United States and Brazil had arrived in Liverpool. The cotton merchants held on briefly, but early in July one of them was forced to sell at a decline in price, and the market was broken. This break in the speculative cycle was felt by everyone engaged in the cotton trade in the United States and Great Britain. Every shipload of cotton arriving in Liverpool was immediately sold regardless of price. The British merchants continued to pay the bills of exchange drawn by their purchasing agents in the United States as long as they could, but, as the restrictive measures of the Bank of England took effect, the supply of credit was exhausted.[12]

Early in August the firm of Crowder, Clough and Company was forced to refuse bills drawn upon it. Their failure brought down other large firms, and the panic was on. The Bank of England continued its pressure until the following March, granting no relief to the sufferers and placing an intolerable strain upon the entire economy. One hundred and four banks failed in London and in the provinces, and their total liabilities were in excess of nineteen million pounds. They carried with them most of the joint-stock companies operating in Latin America, the domestic railroad companies, and thousands of firms and individuals in all occupations and trades.[13]

This financial storm, which struck with full force in Great Britain in November and December, 1825, had threatened the United States a few weeks earlier. As the bills drawn on Crowder, Clough and Company came

11 N. Biddle to I. Lawrence, April 22, May 12, 1825, in the Biddle Manuscripts in the Library of Congress; Vincent Nolte, *The Memoirs of Vincent Nolte* (New York, 1934), pp. 314–18, 323–33; Henry D. McLeod, *Theory and Practice of Banking* (London, 1893), II, 111–25.

12 Sir John Clapham, *The Bank of England* (New York, 1945), II, 93–110; J. H. Clapham, *An Economic History of Modern Britain* (Cambridge, 1939), I, 272–74.

13 *Ibid.*

back protested, their drawers—the Weymans of New York and Charleston and Vincent Nolte of New Orleans—also became insolvent. A wave of fear seized each of the commercial cities in September. Biddle admitted that the times were a "little squally," but he added that he was something of a sailor and he thought the weather would not get much worse. He could do nothing at the moment. The payment of seven million dollars on the government's account on October 1 diminished the Bank's available resources and brought it into debt to the Philadelphia and New York banks. But, as soon as this payment was accomplished, he began to prepare for the relief of the community and to provide against the danger which was obviously approaching. He first strengthened the Bank by selling two million dollars' worth of government loans and Bank stock. This brought it out of debt, but he was immediately confronted with an unexpected and heavy demand for specie. One of these came from the British government, which had large payments to make in Canada, and a second from a newly organized bank in New Orleans, and, by the middle of November, Biddle later testified, everything pointed to an approaching panic. "If the strength and wealth of England," he said, "could not withstand such an alarm, its effects on this country would have been incalculable. That moment seemed to me to be the very crisis of the country, to be met only by some decided and resolute step to rally the confidence of the community."[14]

He himself exhibited no sign of alarm, and his confident air was reflected throughout the Bank. He persuaded Nathaniel Prime, the New York broker who was the agent of the British government, to make his purchases of silver as slowly and gently as possible, and he gave the New Orleans bank a draft on the branch bank in its own city so that it could get its specie there rather than from New York. These negotiations were concluded on November 22, and on that day Biddle wrote to the president of the New York branch: "The pressure is no longer for specie but for bank credits which are much diminished by the want of confidence in the solvency of the borrowers, and in part by the mutual distrust on the part of the banks lest one should invade the specie means of the others. In this state of things it becomes a matter of serious and anxious consideration, whether, as the immediate causes which pressed on the Bank, the payment of the public debt and the demand for specie, have in great degree ceased, it would be necessary for the office to remain any longer in the position forced upon it by circumstances, or whether it might now safely venture to set the example by a more free use of its credits."[15]

He cautioned the New York office against any precipitous action and

14 J. Potter to N. Biddle, September 9, 1825; N. Biddle to J. Potter, September 26, 1825; N. Biddle to J. Hunter, October 10, 1825; R. L. Colt to N. Biddle, November 9, 1825, in the Biddle Manuscripts in the Library of Congress; *House Report* (22d Cong., 1st sess.), No. 460, pp. 433–37.

15 N. Biddle to I. Lawrence, November 22, 1825, in the Biddle Manuscripts in the Library of Congress.

warned them that they would be undertaking a delicate and difficult operation: "The object should be to ease the community, but to let the relief reach them through channels perfectly secure to the Bank. Any extension should therefore be very gentle and gradual and confined to such limits as not to incur any risk, and while it places the state institutions at their ease from any demand on our part, should yet not tempt them into sudden issues or enlarged loans." The next day the New York branch increased its loans by fifty thousand dollars, a relatively small sum, but this expansion of discounts in the face of an approaching panic revived confidence, relieved the pressure upon the state banks, and enabled the community to pass the point of danger. "We are happy to learn," Hezekiah Niles commented the next week from Baltimore, "that the alarm has subsided in New York. The office of the Bank of the United States, with great good sense and liberality extended its discounts. . . . This enabled the other banks to extend theirs. A spirit of accommodation is abroad, and confidence is increased." P. P. F. DeGrand of Boston, shortly afterward, flatly asserted that had the national bank been governed by "unenlightened fear" for its own safety, at least half of the commercial community would have been ruined, but, as it was, the national economy had escaped without serious damage, whereas that of Great Britain had suffered almost irreparable harm.[16]

Another crisis in monetary affairs requiring intervention by the Bank of the United States developed in the winter of 1827–28. The source of the difficulty was a sudden rise in the imports of manufactured goods, which increased the European debt, and a simultaneous decrease in the price and volume of American exports, which reduced the means of paying those debts. Biddle was forced to watch this crisis develop without being capable of preventive action because another large payment on the national debt was due on January 1, 1828. The Bank had to expand its loans, even though Biddle knew it was inappropriate, just when the merchants were building up their stocks of manufactured goods in expectation of an increase in the protective tariff. The manufacturers of Great Britain and Europe, seeking to exploit this market, shipped goods in ever increasing amounts, and as each cargo arrived, it was sold at auction, creating a pressing demand for bills of exchange payable in London or Paris.[17]

16 *Niles' Register*, XXIX (1825), 210–11; *DeGrand's Boston Weekly Report*, VII (1826), 367. Walter B. Smith believes that Biddle, Niles, and DeGrand exaggerated the influence of the Bank of the United States in protecting the nation from this panic. Biddle's "ideas were correct enough," he writes, "but the activities of the Bank, viewed in their entirety, did not live up to Biddle's version of his well conceived policy" (Smith, *Economic Aspects of the Second Bank*, p. 140). I can see no justification for Mr. Smith's views here and believe that the contemporary observers were more nearly correct.

17 R. Lenox to N. Biddle, December 20, 1827; N. Biddle to I. Lawrence, January 4, 1828; W. McIlwaine to N. Biddle, January 26, 1828; N. Biddle to N. Prime, February 15, 1828, in the Biddle Manuscripts in the Library of Congress.

The cotton, tobacco, and rice which normally provided these funds were not being sent forward because the planters, discouraged by the prevailing low prices, were holding their crops. The result was a rapid rise in the rate of exchange, which in November, 1827, reached the point where an export of specie became profitable. The natural corrective for this loss of silver was the reduction of discounts by the banks, but in this situation, with the Bank of the United States having to expand its loans and issues to prepare for the January 1 payment, the state banks merely transferred all the demands for specie to the national bank. They continued to lend in increasing amounts, and Biddle could do nothing but warn of the danger. He knew that the export of silver could not continue indefinitely. Soon it would reach the point where all the banks would be forced to a sudden and drastic curtailment. When this happened, the importation of goods and the export of specie would stop, but it would also force immediate sales by every holder of foreign or domestic goods at a moment when no money or credit was available. Prices would break, and failure would be piled upon failure. Merchants and bankers would go down together, as had happened in Great Britain in 1825.

Biddle was determined to avert the threatened disaster, and he took the initial steps on January 4, three days after the completion of the government payment. He instructed the eastern offices to decline all applications for loans from merchants and brokers engaged in the export of specie, and he sold government stock in the New York market in the expectation that the purchase of these bonds would lessen the demand for imported goods. He used the acquired funds to replenish the Bank's holdings of specie by demands upon the state banks, and he hoped that these moderate measures would act as a warning that the period of easy money and credit was at an end. Much to his disappointment, the warning was not effective. The importation of foreign goods continued, the southern crops remained in the warehouses, and exchange rates stayed at their high level. Ships sailing from the United States carried ever increasing amounts of specie out of the country, and Biddle, on February 12, increased the pressure.[18]

The offices were ordered to hold their loans at the existing level and to let the accumulation of government deposits bring the state banks into their debt, and, when demands were made on their specie, the offices turned the calls over to their debtor banks by presenting notes for redemption. This steady pressure was continued into April, and gradually and gently the state banks reduced their loans. The circle of operations which had threatened disaster was altered, and, though many merchants

---

[18] N. Biddle to J. White, March 3, 1828, in the Biddle Manuscripts in the Library of Congress.

and brokers were inconvenienced, only a few were severely injured.[19] It was not Biddle's purpose in 1828 to control the domestic industry and the foreign trade of the United States, nor was the power of the national bank sufficient to accomplish such a purpose. He was seeking to use the great elasticity of the banking system—the power to expand and contract the credit and money supply safely and soundly with the variations in business activity—for the protection of the national economy. The forces of trade were permitted to generate their own correctives, but the national bank softened the pressures and cushioned the necessary financial readjustments. Time was the essential factor during every period of strain and pressure, since every merchant, banker, and producer operated on credit. If one of them were suddenly called on to pay the whole of his debts, he would have had to default because his assets were never immediately collectible. What Biddle did during moments of danger was to provide time for individuals to make their own adjustments to changed circumstances by protecting them from the full and immediate force of the financial pressure.[20]

This struggle to stop the export of specie between December, 1827, and April, 1828, taught Biddle that there was a clear conflict of interest and purpose between the Bank of the United States and such private dealers in exchange as Alexander Brown and Sons of Baltimore, Philadelphia, New York, and Liverpool. The national bank sought to regulate the rates of exchange so that they would be uniform and low, but the Browns and other brokers profited from fluctuations. Once they had started the export of specie in December, they were determined to continue as long as they could make the "smallest fraction of profit," regardless of its effect upon the rest of the community; and Alexander Brown, the senior partner, thought it impertinent of Biddle to interfere. He was also angry at Biddle's decision to deny his sons and other members of the firm their accustomed places on the Bank's boards of directors, and he sent Biddle a warning that if he thought that, by turning them out of the Bank, he could stop them from exporting specie, he was sadly mistaken. Biddle had made this decision reluctantly. The Browns were among the wealthiest and most respected businessmen in the nation, and Alexander Brown not only had been one of the original subscribers to the stock of the Bank but also had helped to rid the Baltimore branch of the speculators who had dominated

19 N. Biddle to R. Lenox, April 22, 29, May 30, 1828; N. Biddle to C. P. White, May 15, 1828; N. Biddle to J. White, April 24, 1828, in the Biddle Manuscripts in the Library of Congress.

20 N. Biddle to P. P. F. DeGrand, April 27, 1826; N. Biddle to J. White, March 3, 1828, in the Biddle Manuscripts in the Library of Congress; *House Report* (22d Cong., 1st sess.), No. 460, pp. 433–37. Biddle used the term "elasticity" to describe the power of the Bank to expand and contract the currency and credit supply and claimed credit for being the first so to use the term (N. Biddle to W. Bowne, March 25, 1828, in the Biddle Manuscripts in the Library of Congress). For a different view of the Bank's activities in this crisis see Catterall, *Second Bank*, p. 110; Redlich, *Molding of American Banking*, I, 137.

it during the early years. But now the firm was one of the principal competitors of the Bank in the exchange market, and, in view of this fact, Biddle was certain that its members should not be on the boards. The omission of their names from the various lists, he insisted, was based on "as clear and conscientious a principle of duty as ever actuated any man. . . . We consider it as a great instance of presumption in the gentlemen to complain that their families are not permitted to occupy seats at the boards of the three principal cities while they are carrying on the business of exchange brokers."[21]

The Browns could not understand why Biddle opposed their export of silver, since it did not interfere with the profits of the Bank. But Biddle's position was clear. The drain of specie threatened the welfare of the national economy; hence questions of profit for the Bank or for particular firms must not be permitted to interfere with corrective measures. He ordered each of the branches to deny loans to the Browns so long as they were actively engaged in the shipment of coin, and, though he admitted that every person was the sole judge of the employment of his capital, he justified his action by stating that, since some employments were "more inconvenient than others to the community, we consider it our duty as guardians of the interest of that community to afford as little facility as we can to that employment."[22]

The struggle was a long and bitter one, but eventually the greater strength of the national bank prevailed. The Browns and other exporters of specie were forced to cease their operations when the rate of exchange was finally lowered to the point where it was no longer profitable to ship silver. On April 10, when all danger was passed, Biddle published an unsigned article which described the difficulties encountered in the preceding months and made critical remarks concerning certain unnamed individuals and firms that had profited at the expense of the community by the export of silver. The articles led to a newspaper war, during which a writer using the name "Vendex" was personally abusive of Biddle. John A. Brown was credited with the authorship of these articles, and on June 12 Biddle wrote to his Uncle Robert Oliver: "I wish very much to see you here for a few hours and if you can come without inconvenience I think you may do some good and prevent some mischief among your friends here."[23]

He was very tired when he wrote this letter, and he had lost his temper. He had intended to challenge Brown to a duel, but on the same day he had come to this decision he had learned that he had been misinformed. He

21 N. Biddle to J. White, February 26, 1828; N. Biddle to R. Oliver, June 12, 1828, in the Biddle Manuscripts in the Library of Congress.

22 R. Colt to N. Biddle, January 16, 1828, in the Biddle Manuscripts in the Library of Congress.

23 N. Biddle to R. Oliver, June 12, 1828, in the Biddle Manuscripts in the Library of Congress; *United States Gazette* (Philadelphia), April 10, 1828.

wrote immediately to Oliver to inform him that his services would not be required. But he was chagrined that he had lost his habitual self-control, and he professed in half-apologetic fashion that he had not read the newspaper pieces and that he cared nothing about them. "My friends tell me," he said, "they are a series of vulgar falsifications written by some disappointed man which must not be noticed as in this country everybody must expect to be abused in the public prints." The Browns, however, had repeatedly charged Biddle with mismanagement of the Bank, and this accusation rankled. "Mr. Brown," he added, "concluded very naturally that anything which he and all his sons are not allowed to manage in their own way, must be badly managed. It is not for me to say whether the Bank is well managed, but of this I am very sure that it is in a most flourishing condition far beyond what it has ever been before. As to the charter I consider its renewal a thing as certain as anything which has not actually taken place, and the many friends which Mr. Brown thinks that the Bank has lost, are I believe only the very few persons his own personal beliefs can influence."[24]

Biddle's assertions regarding the prosperity of the Bank of the United States were based on the actual figures. Since 1822 its effective resources had been increased by some twenty-one million dollars, and the deposits and circulation of notes by more than sixteen million dollars. The past losses of the Bank had all been made good, and its profits for the year ending July 1, 1828, were more than eight hundred thousand dollars greater than they had been in 1821–22, and almost a million dollars more than the average for the three years preceding July 1, 1822. The dividend rate had been increased to $3\frac{1}{2}$ per cent semiannually, and virtually all criticism of Biddle either from within or from outside the institution had ceased.

The triennial meeting of the stockholders on September 1 and 2, 1828, was almost one paean of praise for the president. The committee appointed to examine the condition of the Bank reported that the stockholders were deriving "important advantages from the successful prosecution of a system of measures, which not only produces profits . . . but furnishes to the community a convenient, sound, and highly useful currency." And the final act of the meeting was the passage of a resolution: "That the thanks of this meeting be presented to the president of the Bank for his able, faithful and devoted service to the administration of the concerns of this institution; and that he be respectfully assured that he has earned the gratitude and the confidence of the stockholders."[25]

[24] N. Biddle to R. Oliver, June 16, 1828, in the Biddle Manuscripts in the Library of Congress.

[25] *Niles' Register*, XXXV (1828), 72–75.

A Moment of Triumph

*B*iddle had been president of the Bank for almost six years when the stockholders gave him their enthusiastic commendation. The reputation and standing of the institution had been restored, and such persistent enemies as Hezekiah Niles, the Baltimore editor, admitted that the national bank "now appears devoted to the purposes for which it was instituted" and that it deserved well of the country. Richard Rush, Secretary of the Treasury under John Quincy Adams, had been converted from a passive opponent into an avowed admirer, who thought that the Bank had become "an indispensable and permanent adjunct of our political and fiscal system." Biddle was justified in assuming that the major part of his work was done and that it was only a question of time until the Bank would be rechartered. All during the summer of 1828 he debated with himself whether or not to resign. He enjoyed the power and prestige of his position, but he was tired of the routine which bound him to his desk in winter and summer and kept him from his library and his books, his fields and his cattle, and, most of all, from his wife and children.[1]

Two daughters, Margaret Craig and Adele, had been born after he had entered the Bank, and his relations with them and the older boys were intimate and loving. He never neglected them, whatever the pressure of business and social affairs, and his one literary exercise was the writing of verse for their amusement. His playful temperament had no other outlet, and one of these poems entitled "An Ode to Bogle," was subsequently printed because its description of this celebrated caterer, head waiter, and undertaker to Philadelphia society gave equal pleasure to the adults who had watched him preside with suavity over christenings, weddings, receptions, and funerals.[2]

Jane Biddle was eager for her husband to retire. Society and its meaning-

[1] *Niles' Register*, XXXV (1828), 37; R. Rush to N. Biddle, December 10, 23, 1828; R. Colt to N. Biddle, September 5, 1828; N. Biddle to G. Hoffman, December 22, 1828, in the Biddle Manuscripts in the Library of Congress.

[2] *Verses of Nicholas Biddle*, pp. 3–10.

less round of entertainments were burdensome to her, though she was a gracious and accomplished hostess, and she was nostalgic for those peaceful years when they had passed most of their time at "Andalusia." The portrait that Thomas Sully painted of her in 1824 caught her true character as well as her lovely features and her charming and elegant costume. The dominant characteristics of her face and posture were quietness and simplicity, and an air of gentle sadness pervaded the whole. Her chief interest outside the family were the missionary and other activities of the Episcopal church, and increasingly each year she turned to religious reading and prayer for solace and comfort.

Biddle thought that he shared his wife's dislike of the artificiality of formal society, but actually he enjoyed his prestige as president of the Bank and was happier than he had ever been before. The old promise of the young man with a brilliant future had been fulfilled. In Washington, New York, and Boston he was regarded as one of the nation's most influential leaders, and in Philadelphia he was thought of as the city's most prominent citizen. Distinguished foreign travelers, diplomats, artists, and actors brought letters of introduction to him, and his town and country houses were described as "the seats of elegant hospitality" in which he displayed the characteristics of a "polished gentleman, amiable, witty, liberal."[3]

He derived too much pleasure from this established position to give up his place as head of the "monied interests of the country" without the prospect of some other public office of at least equal importance. He decided not to resign and justified his decision by the thought that he ought not to leave until his achievements had been recognized through a recharter of the Bank by Congress. But he was still ambitious for political advancement, and he took every opportunity that presented itself to make his name and his views known to the nation. These occasions were rare. The president of the national bank, like the members of the federal judiciary, was barred from partisan activity, and it would have been injurious to the institution for him to take part in the debate on such controversial issues as the protective tariff.

The one issue on which he could speak out was internal improvements. Here the whole nation seemed united in a common effort to connect the East with the West, and no one thought it improper for him to advocate canals, railroads, turnpikes, and the improvement of navigation in rivers and harbors. Biddle wanted such improvements to strengthen the country's economy and its military defenses, but, as president of the Bank, he had another reason for seeking such an outlet for the expenditure of funds. The national government was rapidly retiring the national debt, and if some new opportunities for the investment of these liquid funds were not

[3] Charles J. Ingersoll, *Historical Sketch of the Second War between the United States and Great Britain* (Philadelphia, 1829), II, 285.

created, they would open the way for widespread speculation in land, commodities, and stock. Americans were optimistic by temperament, undeveloped resources were freely at hand, and one of the most difficult tasks confronting the national bank was to keep speculative expansion in check.

Biddle thus had a double reason for his interest in internal improvements, and in November, 1824, he joined Mathew Carey in organizing the Pennsylvania Society for the Promotion of Internal Improvements. He was secretary of the meeting at which the legislature was petitioned to provide funds for the opening of a water route to Pittsburgh by connecting the Susquehanna and Allegheny rivers, but it was not long until he decided that it would be more efficient to build a steam railroad. At the beginning of 1825 he pointed out that, with coal at each end of the state and iron in the middle, the expense of building and operating the "steam waggons" would not be very great and that Philadelphians should take the initiative because, "once established, it would inevitably bring western trade through the heart of Pennsylvania to its commercial capital." The society sent William Strickland to Europe to investigate the costs and efficiency of railroads as compared with canals, and Biddle's willingness as president of the Bank to aid the financing of this newly devised means of transportation was one of the contributing reasons for its rapid introduction into the country.[4]

His most important public statement of his views on internal improvements was his address at the opening of the Chesapeake and Delaware Canal on October 17, 1828. The canal benefited Philadelphia, in that it enabled boats loaded with the produce of the Susquehanna Valley to avoid the long and hazardous voyage of five hundred miles down Chesapeake Bay and up the Atlantic Coast to the Delaware River. But Biddle saw it as another link in a long chain of internal water communications which would prove useful to the whole nation both in peace and in war. A canal connecting the Delaware and the Hudson was being constructed. Another on the Potomac would unite the Ohio River and Chesapeake Bay, and the Baltimore and Ohio Railroad had also been started. When all these projects were completed, the nation would possess several lines of communication to the Great Lakes, the Mississippi, and the Gulf of Mexico; and never again could the blockading fleets of a hostile power prevent the internal movement of troops and supplies.[5]

[4] N. Biddle to S. M. Duncan, January 4, 1825, in the Biddle Manuscripts in the Library of Congress; Richard I. Shelling, "Philadelphia and the Agitation in 1825 for the Pennsylvania Canal," *Pennsylvania Magazine of History and Biography*, LXII (1938), 175–204; James W. Livingood, *The Philadelphia-Baltimore Trade Rivalry, 1780–1860* (Harrisburg, 1947), pp. 21–22; Gilchrist, *Strickland*, p. 6; Hartz, *Economic Policy*, pp. 131–42.

[5] N. Biddle, Speech at the Opening of the Chesapeake and Delaware Canal, *United States Gazette* (Philadelphia), October 19, 1828.

Biddle denied that the Chesapeake and Delaware Canal was injurious to Baltimore, Norfolk, and the other Chesapeake towns. On the contrary, the local interests of one would be best served by promoting the interests of others. "In truth," he declared, "every mile of the railroad westward, every section of a canal in the remotest part of the Union, is serviceable to all the American cities. They add to the movement and the mass of the nation's wealth and industry; they develop its resources; and the share of these advantages which each can obtain is a fit subject of generous competition, not of querulous rivalry." The canal had been built by a company organized by private individuals, but the federal government and the states of Pennsylvania, Delaware, and Maryland were among the subscribers to its stock. Such a mixed company had many advantages. The managers of the canal were constrained to operate it in the public interest, not with the single purpose of profit, but the politicians could not use it as a source of patronage to increase their personal or party power. Each group was well satisfied with the result, and the whole nation profited.

This principle of organization was attractive to Biddle, derived as it was from the principle of the charter of the Bank of the United States; but what he emphasized most in his speech was the part that such improvements played in uniting the separate sections of the nation. "The great problem of the American institutions," he said, "was whether a general government with comparatively feeble means, could accomplish its purpose in so extensive an empire." But that question had been answered permanently, and few things had contributed more than "this great political institution, the steamboat with its auxiliary canals," which measured space by a scale entirely new and brought St. Louis and New Orleans as near to Washington in 1828 as Portland and Savannah had been to Philadelphia in 1776.[6]

The same nationalistic views dominated the most important speech he made in this decade, the eulogy of Thomas Jefferson which he was invited to deliver before the American Philosophical Society. This was an outstanding occasion. The society was the leading intellectual organization in the United States, and Jefferson was its most distinguished past president. Biddle received the invitation almost a year ahead of time, and he thought long and deeply about what he was to say. In it, he finally decided, he would give a complete and clear statement of his most sincere beliefs concerning the nation, its meaning for the rest of the world, and the duties of the individual citizen.[7]

He was forty-one years old when he delivered this oration on April 11, 1827. His last previous appearance before many of his audience had been in 1811, when he had urged the construction of a memorial to George

[6] *Ibid.*

[7] P. S. DuPonceau to N. Biddle, July 11, 1826, in the Biddle Manuscripts in the Library of Congress.

Washington and had warned of the danger of approaching war. Now the country was at peace, enjoying the rich heritage of freedom bequeathed by its founders. Biddle himself had matured in appearance and mind. He was a handsome figure as he stood upon the rostrum, his long chestnut hair lying in close curls about his strong and intelligent face, and his demeanor was calm and serious in accordance with the solemnity of the occasion. As he had grown older, his earlier disdain for Jefferson had been replaced by admiration, and in the great Virginian he had found those qualities of a philosopher-statesman which it was his own ambition to emulate. It was the first glory of Jefferson's life, Biddle said, that he had been one of the founders of a great empire, but it was scarcely less glorious that, "even among his own associates, he was distinguished by being at once a scholar and a statesman." He had devoted his youth to liberal studies and then, being attracted to the public service, had achieved its highest honors. "It is thus that philosophy best fulfills her destiny, when coming from her seclusion into the arena of life she shares and leads in defending the cause of truth and freedom."[8]

Biddle developed this theme, paying particular attention to the literary distinction and the philosophical profundity of Jefferson's writings during the Revolution. "It was among the many distinctions of this great quarrel," he said, "to be announced in a strain corresponding with its dignity. It was essentially an intellectual warfare, a contest of prophecy. . . . Accordingly the Declaration of Independence is among the noblest productions of the human intellect. It embodies the eternal truths which lie at the foundation of all free governments." He deliberately refrained from speaking of the partisan aspects of Jefferson's career, concentrating instead on his great nationalist achievements—the acquisition of Louisiana, the Lewis and Clark Expedition, the establishment of the military academy at West Point—and, most important, his contributions to the struggle against all tyranny over the minds and bodies of men, his efforts to prohibit the further importation of slaves into Virginia and to begin gradual emancipation.

The ending of entails and primogeniture, the statute for religious freedom, and the creation of the University of Virginia were among the accomplishments of Jefferson to which Biddle paid tribute, and he closed with a comparison of the career and character of the Virginian with those of Napoleon, a section that embodied the results of long years of study of the two men. "The life of Jefferson," he said, "was a perpetual devotion, not to his own purposes, but to the pure and noble cause of public freedom. From the first dawning of his youth his undivided heart was given to the

---

[8] *Eulogium on Thomas Jefferson Delivered before the American Philosophical Society on the Eleventh Day of April 1827 by Nicholas Biddle* (Philadelphia, 1827). It has recently been reprinted in Francis C. Rosenberger (ed.), *Jefferson Reader: A Treasury of Writings about Thomas Jefferson* (New York, 1953), who says that Biddle's *Eulogium* "is of all I have seen the finest of the many tributes to Jefferson."

establishment of free principles, free institutions, freedom in all its varieties of untrammelled thought and independent action. His whole life was consecrated to the improvement and happiness of his fellow men; and his intense enthusiasm for knowledge and freedom was sustained to his dying hour." The power of Napoleon, on the other hand, was won by the sword, maintained by the sword, and lost with the sword, and the colossal empire that he exhausted fortune in rearing broke before the first shock of adversity. "Of all his foreign triumphs not one remained, and in his first military conquest, his own country . . . there is now no place for the tomb of this desolate exile."[9]

"The glory of Jefferson," Biddle concluded, "became ever purer as the progress of years mellowed into veneration the love of his countrymen. He died in the midst of a free people whom he had lived to serve; and his only ceremonial . . . was the simple sublimity of his funeral triumph. His power he retained as long as he desired it, and then voluntarily restored the trust with a permanent addition, derived from Napoleon himself, far exceeding the widest limits of the French Empire, that victory of peace which outweighs all the conquests of Napoleon, as one line of the Declaration of Independence is worth all his glory." This address in which the president of the second Bank of the United States paid homage to the man who had created a political party on the basis of opposition to its predecessor, was delivered in the closing days of that period of American politics which has been characterized as the "Era of Good Feeling," and it was only shortly before a new President was to be elected who would renew Jefferson's war against the national bank; but almost no one in the country was aware of the impending change.[10]

The simultaneous deaths of Thomas Jefferson and John Adams on the fiftieth anniversary of the Declaration of Independence had awakened memories, not of the partisan battles between Republican and Federalist, but of the united struggle for freedom, and the great body of the American people were little concerned with the political conflicts which were soon to divide them. The professional politicians, however, were already entered into a new era, and fierce battles for position and power were being fought. The campaigns of 1824 and 1828 engendered much passion and bitterness among the rival candidates and their political associates, but

[9] Biddle had long been fascinated by the career of Napoleon Bonaparte, and he bought many volumes in an effort to find an explanation for the puzzling destiny of the defeated tyrant. A reproduction of Haydon's portrait hung on his study wall with Wordsworth's sonnet on this picture pasted on its back. Whenever he met Joseph Bonaparte, who lived across the Delaware River at Bordentown, New Jersey, Biddle led the conversation to Napoleon and would later record what had been said. Selections of these notes are to be found in Edward Biddle (ed.), "Joseph Bonaparte in America as Recorded in the Private Journal of Nicholas Biddle," *Pennsylvania Magazine of History and Biography*, LV (1931), 208-24.

[10] George W. Pierson, *Tocqueville and Beaumont in America* (New York, 1938), pp. 535-36.

the voters were relatively indifferent and unconcerned. No principles or issues separated the candidates, and there was no common bond of unity, either of class, of economic interest, or of opinion, among their respective supporters.

Politics had become a profession with separate and distinctive interests, and its rewards were won by controlling votes. Jackson was the leading candidate in 1824 and the victor in 1828 because his popularity was a factor with which each leader of a local or personal faction had to reckon, not because of his attitude toward any of the issues being debated during the period.[11] The campaign of 1824 and the election are unique in the annals of American politics. The national Federalist party had distintegrated and disappeared, and each of the presidential candidates either was or had been a prominent officeholder under Monroe: John Quincy Adams, Secretary of State; William H. Crawford, Secretary of the Treasury; John C. Calhoun, Secretary of War; Henry Clay, Speaker of the House of Representatives; and Andrew Jackson, commander of the army in the Southwest and governor of the Territory of Florida.

Biddle took no position in this contest, but Thomas Cadwalader, his closest friend and co-director of the national bank, was one of the earliest supporters of Jackson in Pennsylvania. Cadwalader, like many other Federalists, chose Jackson because he had less formal connections with the Republican party than the other candidates, but, once his name had been brought forward in Pennsylvania, most of the Republican leaders gave their support. Until this moment Calhoun had been considered Pennsylvania's candidate, but all he was able to salvage from the Harrisburg convention in March, 1824, was the nomination for the vice-presidency. Pennsylvania's defection marked the end of Calhoun's first attempt to gain the presidency, and, though no formal bargain was made, from this time on, his supporters worked for Jackson's election. Calhoun became the candidate of all the Jacksonians for vice-president, and he was led to understand that he would be their candidate for President after the one term that Jackson had pledged himself to serve.[12]

None of the candidates received a majority of the votes in the electoral college, except Calhoun for Vice-President, and the choice between the three leaders, Jackson, Adams, and Crawford, was turned over to the House of Representatives as prescribed by the Constitution. The partisans of Clay held the balance of power in the House, and when his support

---

[11] *Ibid.*; see also Pendleton Herring, *The Politics of Democracy* (New York, 1940), pp. 121, 176, 191, where this leading contemporary student of politics writes: "Parties do not contest with each other on basic questions of policy," and that "in the federal sphere, our political parties are temporary alliances of local leaders held together by the hope of winning the presidency."

[12] Charles M. Wiltse, *John C. Calhoun, Nationalist, 1782–1828* (Indianapolis, 1944), pp. 282–84; Jabez D. Hammond, *Political History of New York* (Albany, 1842), II, 254–56; James Parton, *Life of Andrew Jackson* (New York, 1861), III, 11–30.

gave Adams the presidency, there was a new alignment of political factions. The alliance between Jackson and Calhoun held firm and was further strengthened in the first years of the new administration by the addition of Calhoun's most bitter enemies, the supporters of William H. Crawford. The former Secretary of the Treasury had retired from politics because of illness, and his faction, which had great strength in Georgia, Virginia, and New York, was now led by Martin Van Buren, who himself had ambitions for the presidency as a rival to Calhoun after Jackson had finished his term.

Biddle as a voter in Pennsylvania cast his ballot for Andrew Jackson, but as president of the Bank he had no connection with any of the factions or candidates. The complete exemption of the Bank from party politics was his aim, and in 1825 he proudly boasted that "during the late presidential contest . . . the name even of the Bank was never mentioned during the greatest political excitement." Only his closest personal friends knew that he had voted for Jackson, and when the contest with Adams was renewed in 1828, some of Jackson's supporters accused the Bank of using its resources to re-elect the President. Senator Samuel Smith of Maryland, an ally of Van Buren, questioned Biddle concerning these accusations, and received the following reply: "We believe the prosperity of the Bank and its usefulness to the country depend on its being entirely free from the control of the officers of the government. . . . In order to preserve that independence it must never connect itself with any administration and never become a partisan of any set of politicians. In this respect I believe all the officers of the institution have been exemplary. The truth is that, with us, it is considered that we have no concern with politics. Dean Swift said . . . that money is neither Whig nor Tory, and we say with equal truth that the Bank is neither a Jackson nor an Adams man, it is only a bank."[13]

The rule of neutrality applied only to paid employees, not to directors. Thus when Biddle, in January, 1824, gave as his reasons for inviting Benjamin W. Crowninshield to serve on the board, his interest in the Bank, his past connection with it, "and the wish to introduce a distinguished gentleman of the Republican Party in your state," he was in no way violating the rule. In November, 1827, he wrote to Campbell P. White, a Van Buren leader in New York City: "I thank you for the suggestions in regard to the political character of the board. These are considerations which though secondary are not to be overlooked." The following year he renominated White as a member of the New York board and added Churchill C. Cambreleng, Van Buren's principal lieutenant, to the tentative

[13] N. Biddle to P. P. F. DeGrand, April 27, 1826; J. Gales, Jr., to N. Biddle, November 24, 1828; N. Biddle to S. Smith, December 29, 1828; N. Biddle, Memorandum, n.d. (1841 or 1842), in the Biddle Manuscripts in the Library of Congress; Nancy N. Scott (ed.), *A Memoir of Hugh Lawson White* (Philadelphia, 1856), pp. 406-7.

list, with the notation, "not nominated but suggested by N B." The president and cashier of the office protested, "We do not think the one you suggest would answer," and added the plea that Biddle would "avoid placing so decidedly political men in our direction as C P W and C C C."[14]

He acquiesced in their veto of Cambreleng but insisted upon the re-election of White. "It is not the case of introducing for the first time a gentleman engaged in politics," he wrote. "It is the case of a gentleman connected with the Bank for many years, and desirous of continuing the connection at a moment when his political situation may add to his usefulness as a director. To . . . alienate a member of the board at such a time, to offend personally a member of the Congress before whom the Bank may probably come for a renewal of its charter, might prove injurious to the Bank, and we are all of the opinion that he ought not to be omitted particularly at the present moment."[15] Biddle was equally careful and considerate of the sensibilities of the members of the Adams party and made certain in areas where they were a minority that they were not excluded from the board. Neutrality could not be achieved by pretending that political differences did not exist but only by making certain that men of both parties were on the board.

As a result of these policies, the Bank had informed supporters in each of the political factions. It was as popular in Congress as it had become in the commercial community, but it still had a few irreconcilable enemies. One of these was Philip Barbour, a Jackson supporter from Virginia, who introduced a resolution into the House of Representatives instructing the Committee on Ways and Means to inquire into the advisability of selling the government's stock in the Bank. The motion came at an inconvenient moment in December, 1827, when Biddle was engaged in the attempt at one and the same time to make the scheduled payment of the national debt and to stop the export of specie. He wrote to Cambreleng, the chairman of the Committee on Commerce as well as the Van Buren leader in the House, to ask for his aid, and Cambreleng assured him that the motion would not be supported by the Van Buren faction and that it would be "put to rest by a large majority." A Calhoun supporter from South Carolina, James Hamilton, Jr., was even more forceful in his attack upon the motion. He warned that its adoption would cause men to say: "There, you see how it is the moment that these Jackson men have got possession of the House; away goes the Bank of the United States 'sky-high' and we shall next see the 'military chieftain' after his election, making his way,

---

[14] N. Biddle to B. W. Crowninshield, January 5, 1824; N. Biddle to C. P. White, November 27, 1827; N. Biddle to I. Lawrence, November 20, 1828; I. Lawrence and M. Lawrence to N. Biddle, November 21, 1828; M. Lawrence to N. Biddle, November 22, 1828, in the Biddle Manuscripts in the Library of Congress.

[15] N. Biddle to I. Lawrence, November 28, 1828, in the Biddle Manuscripts in the Library of Congress.

sword in hand, into the vaults of the Bank and seizing its coffers as his especial portion of the booty." Hamilton completely repudiated this notion and closed his remarks with the statement: "Be quiet gentlemen. Be assured that we do not mean to run our heads against the Bank of the United States, and this our votes will show."[16]

George McDuffie, another Jacksonian from South Carolina, led the opposition to Barbour's resolution, and it was defeated by the overwhelming vote of one hundred and seventy-four to nine. The Bank was also defended by the leaders of the Jackson party in the Senate. In the spring of 1828, Thomas Hart Benton of Missouri, who, like Barbour, was opposed to the Bank on constitutional grounds, introduced a resolution which would have required the Bank to pay interest on the government deposits. He was answered by Smith of Maryland, chairman of the Finance Committee, who called attention to the numerous services rendered to the government by the Bank of the United States without charge, such as the payment of pensions, the interest on the national debt, the salaries of all federal employees, and the transfer of government funds from one section of the country to another. So convincing were Smith's arguments that no other senator supported Benton, and the resolution was withdrawn without coming to a vote.[17]

Successful as the national bank was in repelling these attacks, it lacked sufficient influence and power to persuade Congress to make desirable alterations in its charter. One of the most burdensome duties imposed upon Biddle was the requirement that he and the cashier of the parent bank sign all the bank notes, including those used by the branches. This requirement had been included in the charter to make counterfeiting more difficult, and for no other reason, but this end could be accomplished without placing so great a physical burden upon the two principal officers of the institution. The problem was a real one. The circulation of national bank notes amounted to more than nine and a half million dollars, and it could have been much larger but for the impossibility of multiplying the signatures for the small notes. To make two million five-dollar notes, it was necessary for Biddle to sign his name four hundred thousand times, which, as he said, "to a person whose time is and must be absorbed during the day by the duties of his station, is wholly impracticable."[18]

A bill was prepared authorizing other persons to sign bank notes. Daniel

[16] E. Everett to N. Biddle, December 13, 1827; N. Biddle to C. C. Cambreleng, December 16, 1827; N. Biddle to E. Everett, December 18, 1827; C. C. Cambreleng to N. Biddle, December 20, 1827; J. Gales, Jr., to N. Biddle, December 20, 1827, in the Biddle Manuscripts in the Library of Congress; *Congressional Debates* (20th Cong., 2d sess.), IV, 815, 854.

[17] N. Biddle to S. Smith, May 2, July 30, 1828, in the Biddle Manuscripts in the Library of Congress; *Senate Documents* (20th Cong., 2d sess.), No. 92.

[18] N. Biddle to D. Webster, February 16, 1826, in the Biddle Manuscripts in the Library of Congress.

Webster, an Adams senator, and Louis McLane, chairman of the Ways and Means Committee of the Jackson-dominated House, agreed to sponsor the measure, but each was requested to move cautiously and avoid controversy. "I have been for three years past," Biddle wrote, "so anxious to keep the Bank out of view in the political world and to bring it down to its true business character as a counting house, that I have been very reluctant to apply to Congress for anything." He thought that the Bank stood better with Congress than it had in the past, but he knew that any excuse might revive the "disputation and odium," so he said to McLane: "If our purpose can be obtained without bringing on two weeks debate upon the constitutionality of the Bank, the usurpations of the Supreme Court, and the omni scibile and quibusdem aliis, it would be a great satisfaction."

The debate did not occur. McLane wrote that his committee had been unwilling to report favorably on the bill and that, rather than make an unfavorable recommendation, he had determined to lay it aside.[19] Biddle acquiesced in McLane's decision, but the inability of the Bank to obtain so simple and necessary a change in its charter made him aware once again how much latent political hostility to the institution still existed. He worked even harder at the task of conciliating the politicians in all sections of the country and in each of the parties, but, despite his desire for their good will, he resisted them firmly when any one of them attempted to encroach improperly upon the freedom or privileges of the Bank.

When, for example, Senator Smith sought information concerning the amount borrowed by the government directors, Biddle's refusal was courteous but firm. "The account which any individual keeps with the Bank," he replied, "is a private concern between him and the Bank of which it would be a violation of confidence to speak. . . . I have for instance been a director of the Bank for nine years. I have been its presiding officer for six years. I have never borrowed a dollar from the Bank and trust I never shall and yet if it were made a question whether I had borrowed one dollar or one million dollars I would not answer the enquiry to be made President of the United States, because it goes to establish an inquisition into the private affairs of individuals which is equally unjust and invidious."[20] He also rejected a protest of Governor John Murphy of Alabama against the establishment of a branch in Mobile in 1826 on the ground that the location of branches was a matter for decision by the board of directors alone. But, having made the Bank's statement of independence, he carefully answered each of the Governor's objections, assuring him that the branch would benefit the whole state by giving "a fresh impulse and increased accommodations to business." The merchants, sustained by the

[19] L. McLane to N. Biddle, January 19, 1827, in the Biddle Manuscripts in the Library of Congress.

[20] N. Biddle to S. Smith, January 5, 1829, in the Biddle Manuscripts in the Library of Congress.

Bank, could "make larger advances to the planter," who through the use of this credit could avoid "the hazards of an immediate sale and sacrifice of his crop," or on its exportation be able "to anticipate at once its proceeds."[21]

In 1826 and 1827 the Bank received from interested cities many applications for branches, two of which entailed relatively difficult political decisions. One of these applications came from Albany and was denied, the other came from Nashville and was accepted, and both actions, Biddle thought, were contrary to what Van Buren and Jackson desired. When the application from Albany was denied, Biddle wrote Van Buren a long letter of explanation, and when that from Nashville was granted, he persuaded Cadwalader to handle the preliminary arrangements for the opening of the office in the hope that he could overcome Jackson's objections. Cadwalader was received graciously at the Hermitage and was thanked for his political services, but when he asked Jackson for his advice on the matter of officers and directors, he received this reply: "Never having been connected with banks, and having very little to do with this one here, I feel unable to give any satisfaction."[22]

Biddle was thus fully aware during the campaign that Jackson, the individual, was hostile to the Bank of the United States, but he voted for him nevertheless in the firm belief that, once in office, he would be forced to change his opinion as Madison, Gallatin, Monroe, Rush, and other opponents of the national bank had done when serving as President of the United States or as Secretary of the Treasury. Moreover, Jackson's closest political friends in Tennessee, as well as most of his supporters among the Crawford and Calhoun factions, were enthusiastic supporters of the institution and advocates of its recharter.[23]

21 J. Murphy to N. Biddle, September 5, 1826; N. Biddle to J. Murphy, October 6, 1826, in the Biddle Manuscripts in the Library of Congress; *Niles' Register*, XXXII (1827), 124–25.

22 N. Biddle to M. Van Buren, October 27, 1826; W. McIlwaine to N. Biddle, January 27, 1827; N. Biddle to T. Cadwalader, February 11, 1827, in the Biddle Manuscripts in the Library of Congress; A. Jackson to T. Cadwalader, November 21, 1828, in John S. Bassett (ed.), *Correspondence of Andrew Jackson* (Washington, 1926–33), III, 438, 445.

23 St. George L. Sioussat, "Tennessee Politics in the Jackson Period," *American Historical Review*, XV (1908), 61–64; Charles G. Sellers, Jr., "Banking and Politics in Jackson's Tennessee, 1817–1827," *Mississippi Valley Historical Review*, XLI (1954), 82–84.

~ 13 ~

The Jacksonians Begin
the Attack

*T*he presidential campaign of 1828, like that of 1824, was based on personalities, and the national bank was not mentioned by either of the candidates or their supporters. But after Jackson's election some of the members of his party thought that their political victory entitled them to control the Bank and its branches, and they raised the false charge that some of the branches had attempted to exercise an improper influence on the election by refusing loans to Jacksonians. Biddle denied the accusation when it was first brought to his attention, but when it continued and he was convinced that these politicians wanted to gain control of the Bank, he became angry and wrote: "I will not give way an inch in what concerns the independence of the Bank to please all the administrations, past, present, or future. The bigots of the last reproached me with not being for them, the bigots of the present will be annoyed that the Bank will not support them. Be it so, I care nothing for either class of partisans and mean to disregard both."[1]

His first reactions to the charge were less violent. He told Senator Smith in December, 1828, that "there is no one principle better understood by every officer in the Bank than that he must abstain from politics, and I have not seen nor heard of any one of them in any part of the union who has been engaged in this controversy." And the following month he courteously replied to Postmaster-General John McLean, who had charged that all the directors in the Louisville and Lexington offices were political supporters of Adams and Clay and that they had rejected most applications for loans from members of the Jackson party. McLean, an officeholder under Adams but a supporter of Jackson, had written at the instigation of

[1] N. Biddle to A. Dickins, September 16, 1829, in the Biddle Manuscripts in the Library of Congress.

Senator Richard M. Johnson and other members of Kentucky's congressional delegation, and he included a list of names that they had recommended as suitable directors for each branch. Biddle had deliberately placed loyal members of the Jackson party on both boards, and he assured McLean that there had not been "the slightest political partiality" in the granting of loans; but he ordered an investigation of the branches and of the character and standing of the persons nominated by Johnson and his colleagues.[2]

The Lexington list was submitted to a committee of five members of the local board, two of whom were "as decided friends of General Jackson as the members of Congress themselves," and they unanimously reported in regard to the suggested directors that "their pursuits in life and their pecuniary situations rendered them unfit for such employment." The men proposed for the Louisville board were characterized as "an unhappy specimen of the kind of person to whose care these politicians would wish to commit the interests of the office," and the charge of political discrimination in making loans at either branch was refuted by the testimony of directors belonging to both political parties.[3]

Biddle knew that President-elect Jackson was not involved in this attempt by the Kentucky congressmen to subject the branches to political control, and he continued to believe that the election of Jackson was not a political threat to the national bank. All the superficial evidence confirmed this view. None of the leaders of the coalition that supported Jackson was opposed to the Bank of the United States, and most of the men chosen by the new President as his personal and political advisers were friends of the institution. William B. Lewis, John Overton, and George Washington Campbell, three of Jackson's Tennessee friends who did much to persuade him to be a candidate and to organize his campaign, had not agreed with him in his opposition to the establishment of the Nashville branch. Each of them, at various times, accepted election as a director of the office, and Lewis, though he was completely loyal to Jackson and accompanied him to Washington, actively aided Biddle in the campaign for the new charter.[4]

John C. Calhoun, the Vice-President and leader of one major faction in the party, had been responsible for the passage of the bill chartering the

[2] N. Biddle to S. Smith, December 28, 1828; J. McLean to N. Biddle, January 5, 1829; N. Biddle to J. McLean, January 10, 11, 1829, in the Biddle Manuscripts in the Library of Congress.

[3] N. Biddle to J. Harper, January 9, 1829; E. Shippen to N. Biddle, January 24, 1829, in the Biddle Manuscripts in the Library of Congress.

[4] Marquis James, *The Life of Andrew Jackson* (Indianapolis, 1938), pp. 553–66; Weymouth T. Jordan, *George Washington Campbell of Tennessee* (Tallahassee, 1955), pp. 183–85; Charles G. Sellers, Jr., "Banking and Politics in Jackson's Tennessee, 1817–1827," *Mississippi Valley Historical Review*, XLI (1954), 82, and "Jackson Men with Feet of Clay," *American Historical Review*, LXII (1957), 537–51.

Bank in 1816 and had supported the institution while a member of Monroe's Cabinet. The nominal leader of the other major faction, William H. Crawford, had fought for the recharter of the first national bank in the Senate and had consistently defended the second while Secretary of the Treasury. Martin Van Buren, who took over leadership of this group from Crawford, had never been forced to take a formal position in regard to the Bank, but he was personally a friend of Biddle's and was not looked on as an enemy of the institution.

The opinions of prospective members of the Jackson Cabinet in regard to the Bank were not ascertained in advance of their appointment and had nothing to do with their selection for these posts. Samuel D. Ingham, a leader of the Calhoun group in Pennsylvania, was appointed Secretary of the Treasury, since Van Buren, the leader of the opposing faction, was given the first office in the Cabinet, that of Secretary of State. John M. Berrien of Georgia, the Attorney-General, was the only other Cabinet member associated with either of the rival factions, but he was in the anomalous position of being a friend of Crawford and having his appointment opposed by Van Buren. He was chosen upon the recommendation of John Eaton of Tennessee, who had been named as Secretary of War, because of his sympathy as a Georgian with Jackson's determination to move all the Indian tribes from east of the Mississippi River. The other cabinet members—John Branch, Secretary of the Navy; John McLean of Ohio, the first Postmaster-General; and his successor, William T. Barry—were supporters of Jackson and had no connection with Calhoun or Van Buren.[5]

Ingham and Berrien were known to be supporters of the Bank of the United States—the Secretary of the Treasury as a Pennsylvanian, where defense for the Philadelphia institution was an article of faith with all but a few political leaders, and the Attorney-General as a former attorney for the Savannah branch in its long and bitter conflicts with the state banks and the legislature in Georgia. The other Cabinet members had no strong feelings for or against the national bank, and not one of them was aware when he accepted the position that he would ever be called on to make a decision in regard to the institution. Biddle was therefore not being politically naïve when he thought that the election of Jackson posed no threat to the Bank. He continued to plan to apply for a renewal of the charter at the first propitious moment, confident that it would be granted without serious opposition. He was certain that the administration would not desire "to set the monied concerns of the country afloat" as they once had been, particularly since the Bank had been forgotten as a political issue and most people were scarcely aware of its existence except when they used its notes for currency.[6]

[5] Thomas P. Govan, "John M. Berrien and the Administration of Andrew Jackson," *Journal of Southern History*, V (1939), 447–67.

[6] N. Biddle to G. Hoffman, December 22, 1828, in the Biddle Manuscripts in the Library of Congress.

Biddle, unfortunately, did not know President Jackson and, even after becoming acquainted, was unable to understand him. He was not alone in this situation, for Jackson and his motives were an enigma to even his closest associates. His silence concerning the Bank of the United States during the campaign masked a determined and relentless opposition to all banks and to the entire mercantile and credit system. He was an uncritical Republican in the Jeffersonian tradition who believed that all debt, governmental and private, and all banks, national and state, were evils from which the nation must be freed. These opinions ("prejudices" would be a more accurate word) had been formed in the 1790's, when opposition to Hamilton's neo-mercantilist policies had led to the formation of the Republican party, and they were strengthened by Jackson's personal experiences in the inflation during the War of 1812 and in the depression that followed. "You know my opinion as to the banks . . ." he wrote to William Lewis in 1820, "that the Constitution of our State, as well as the Constitution of the United States, prohibited the establishment of banks in any State"; and on another occasion he said: "Everyone that knows me, does know that I have been always opposed to the United States Bank, nay all banks."[7]

Jackson wanted to announce his opposition to the Bank in his inaugural address, but his political advisers dissuaded him from doing so, perhaps with the hope that his experience in office would prove to him the usefulness and value of the institution. Whatever their motive, the President remained silent, and none of the party's newspapers attacked the Bank or its currency.[8] Relations between Biddle and Ingham were cordial, and the Secretary of the Treasury made a particular point of expressing his approval of the ease with which the Bank carried off the large payment of the government debt at the beginning of July, 1829. About this time, however, Biddle received a letter from Senator Levi Woodbury of New Hampshire complaining that the conduct of Jeremiah Mason, president of the Portsmouth branch, was injurious to the stockholders, unfavorable to the region, and exceedingly unpopular and that "the political friends of that gentleman have been the first and foremost in opposition to him."[9]

Biddle had been expecting such complaints from New Hampshire and did not at first think that Woodbury's letter was politically motivated. The Portsmouth branch had been badly managed for years, and General Mason, whose reputation as a lawyer in New England was second only to that of Daniel Webster, had been persuaded to take the place to make

[7] A. Jackson to W. B. Lewis, July 16, 1820, in the Ford Manuscript Collection in the New York Public Library; A. Jackson to J. K. Polk, December 23, 1833, in Bassett (ed.), *Correspondence of Jackson*, V, 236.

[8] The report that Jackson planned to attack the Bank in his inaugural address has been doubted by some historians, following Parton's *Jackson*, III, 258–59. The problem is discussed in Catterall, *Second Bank*, p. 184, n. 1, which has been followed here.

[9] L. Woodbury to N. Biddle, June 27, July 3, 1829, in the Woodbury Manuscripts in the Library of Congress.

needed reforms. One of his predecessors had defrauded the pension fund of twenty thousand dollars, which the Bank had had to make good, and the next president had loaned freely on accommodation paper with the understanding that the loans would be continuously renewed if reduced by 10 per cent each four months. This practice had continued so long, despite protests from the parent bank, that a tradition was established, and customers thought they were entitled to such treatment as a matter of right. When Mason became president, the 10 per cent rule was eliminated. The loans were renewed only for sixty days, and a 20 per cent reduction was demanded. He also made no new loans on the semipermanent basis, confining the branch to the discount of real business paper and to the purchase and sale of bills of exchange based upon the actual movement of goods.[10]

These policies were the real source of the criticism and unpopularity of Mason, and Biddle, in his reply to Woodbury, accepted full responsibility for them. But the Senator had also written to Secretary Ingham and had complained of Mason's lack of knowledge of local businessmen, his rudeness, his fluctuating policy in regard to loans and collections, and the partiality and harshness that had characterized all his actions. Then, almost as an aside, he had added that Mason was a particular friend of Webster and that his political character was well known. Ingham sent Biddle a copy of this letter, calling attention to the mention of politics and saying: "Complaints of a similar nature have also been suggested from other places, particularly Kentucky and Louisiana. These, when presented in a more distinct form, will also be communicated to you."[11]

The Jackson administration, Ingham concluded, had no desire "to derive political aid from the Bank." This denial of a charge that had never been made aroused Biddle's suspicions. He and the directors began to believe that the independence of the Bank was being officially threatened, and their remaining doubts were removed when, on July 17, Isaac Hill, second Comptroller of the Currency and former editor of the leading Jackson paper in New Hampshire, sent two petitions to Philadelphia asking for a change in administration of the branch at Portsmouth. One was signed by merchants, the other by Jackson members of the legislature; and Hill, to insure that there would be no mistake as to the reason for the objection to Mason, wrote: "The friends of General Jackson in New Hampshire have had but too much reason to complain of the branch at Portsmouth. All they now ask is, that this institution in that State may not continue to be an engine of political oppression."[12]

[10] G. S. Hillard, *Memoir and Correspondence of Jeremiah Mason* (Cambridge, 1873), pp. 322–27; N. Biddle to S. D. Ingham, July 18, 1829, in *House Report* (22d Cong., 1st sess.), No. 460, pp. 440–43.

[11] L. Woodbury to S. D. Ingham, June 27, 1829; S. D. Ingham to N. Biddle, July 11, 1829, in *House Report* (22d Cong., 1st sess.), No. 460, pp. 438–39.

[12] I. Hill to J. N. Barker and J. Pemberton, July 17, 1829, *ibid.*, p. 472.

Biddle ignored Hill's letter but officially and categorically denied that the Bank had interfered in elections anywhere and informed Ingham that he was determined to resist any attempt to make the Bank an instrument of either party. Ingham replied, sharply questioning the accuracy of this general denial, and Cadwalader, who was acting as president of the Bank while Biddle was on a western trip, wrote: "It requires little prescience to see in these disgusting developments the germ of a course of systematic hostility against the Bank. In the hands of impartial and independent men the institution is not what they would wish to make it, an engine of subserviency to their political objects. They affect to complain of bias on one side; while the real ground of complaint is that there is no bias on the other."[13]

Biddle personally investigated the charges against Mason. He arrived in Portsmouth on August 20 and notified Woodbury and the signers of the memorials that he was ready to hear their complaints. Each person who came forward was encouraged to be completely frank, but not one repeated the charge that loans or renewals had been granted or refused for political reasons. In two days of interviewing, Biddle accumulated eight serious allegations of harshness, unreasonableness, and personal partiality against Mason, and he requested the branch president to make such explanations as he deemed proper. The investigation was as thorough and impartial as Biddle could make it. His one interest was to arrive at the truth, since no public notice had been given to the charges against Mason and none of them involved the general administration of the Bank. If the accusations had been justified, the situation could have been remedied easily and quietly. Mason's term as president and director had already expired, so that the parent board could have elected someone to replace him without giving reasons or explanations. No such action was necessary. The result was a complete vindication of Mason, and Biddle reported to Cadwalader: "I can now say with the utmost confidence that the whole is a paltry intrigue got up by a combination of small bankrupts and smaller demagogues."[14]

Upon his return to Philadelphia, he reviewed the whole episode in a long letter to Ingham and closed with a positive affirmation of the Bank's independence and its determination to resist any attempts at partisan control. "I deem it my duty," he asserted, "to state to you in a manner perfectly respectable to your official and personal character, yet so clear as to leave no possibility of misconception that the board of directors of the Bank of the United States . . . acknowledge not the slightest responsibility of any description whatsoever to the Secretary of the Treasury touching the

13 T. Cadwalader to N. Biddle, August 4, 1829, in the Biddle Manuscripts in the Library of Congress.

14 N. Biddle to J. Mason, August 28, 1829, in the Dreer Manuscript Collection in the Historical Society of Pennsylvania; N. Biddle to T. Cadwalader, August 28, 1829, in the Biddle Manuscripts in the Library of Congress; Hillard, *Mason*, p. 327.

political opinions and conduct of their officers, that being a subject on which they never consult and never desire to know the views of any administration." Ingham sent this letter to Jackson, who apparently had not been informed of the preceding correspondence, and the President's suspicions and hostility were aroused. He instructed Ingham to reply to that part which related to Hill's note and the New Hampshire memorials "to relieve the executive from any interference with the Bank," but to add the remark that the President "reserves his constitutional powers to be exercised through Congress, to redress all grievances complained of by the people of the interference of the branches with the local elections of the states, and all their interference with party politicks in every section of the country, where those complaints have reached the executive."[15]

Ingham's subsequent letters and the private assurances sent by Asbury Dickins, chief clerk of the Treasury Department, convinced Biddle that his and Cadwalader's suspicions concerning the administration were unfounded. He came to believe that Ingham had been made the "unconscious instrument" of a "cabal," just as McLean had been used by Senator Johnson, and he continued the correspondence "to put him on guard against similar machinations in the future." Biddle also realized, for the first time, that Jackson and Ingham believed the reports which accused the branch officers and directors of improper political activities and that they needed evidence to correct these erroneous impressions.[16]

Such evidence was available, and William Lewis, Biddle thought, was the proper intermediary through whom it should reach the President. Lewis was living at the White House, he was Jackson's intimate friend and political adviser, and he was also a convinced believer in the utility and necessity of the national bank. If any person could allay the President's suspicions, he would be the one; so Biddle, in early October, sent him a letter written by Walter Dun, a member of the Lexington, Kentucky, board, in which this known and trusted political supporter of Jackson categorically denied the charge of political partiality so far as it had been raised against the Lexington branch. The President was only partly convinced when he read Dun's letter and instructed Lewis to reply that he was pleased to learn that the reports concerning the partiality with which the Lexington branch had disbursed "its golden favors" were probably "much exaggerated." "He requests me to say," Lewis continued, "that he has too much confidence in you to believe for a moment that you should knowingly tolerate such conduct in the branches of your Bank; but from the complaints which are still made with regard to some of them, particu-

---

[15] N. Biddle to S. D. Ingham, September 15, 1829, in *House Report* (22d Cong., 1st sess.), No. 460, pp. 450–56; A. Jackson to S. D. Ingham, n.d., in Bassett (ed.), *Correspondence of Jackson*, IV, 84–85.

[16] N. Biddle to A. Dickins, September 30, 1829, in the Biddle Manuscripts in the Library of Congress.

larly the one at New Orleans, he thinks it not improbable that party feeling may yet have some influence upon their operations."[17]

Samuel Jaudon, cashier of the New Orleans office and son-in-law of Senator Hugh Lawson White of Tennessee, was in Philadelphia when Lewis' letter was received, and he immediately went to Washington. He was accompanied by John Hagan, a New Orleans director, who was personally acquainted with Jackson and a member of his party. They were cordially greeted by the President, who assured them that "he was entirely convinced that no hostility to his administration was exercised by the board of the parent bank." He also told them, according to Jaudon's report, that he would have been satisfied by Biddle's letter alone "of the want of any foundation for the accusation against the office at New Orleans; and from my unqualified denials as well as my readiness to meet the charges, and from the testimony of Mr. Hagan, not the least doubt remained in his mind."[18]

Biddle himself had a conversation with Jackson on this subject. The President made no reference to the charges which had been brought and refuted against the Lexington and New Orleans branches and dismissed those that had been raised in New Hampshire by saying that Ingham and Biddle had been gotten "into a difficulty through the foolishness, if I may use the term, of Mr. Hill." He repeated his assurances of confidence in the integrity of Biddle and the parent board but mentioned another complaint in Louisville about which he promised to send the particular details. He did not do so, and no explanation or refutation could be made; but that Jackson was unconvinced by the factual testimony he had been given was evidenced by his subsequent references to the Bank as a "hydra of corruption" which was "dangerous to our liberties" because of its political influence everywhere.[19]

The President apparently did not want to learn that what he believed about the Bank and its branches was untrue, and he held on to his belief in the corruption of the Bank in the depths of his mind, though he admitted its partial innocence with his lips. Biddle, on the other hand, thought that the refutation had been effective, that Jackson had changed his mind about the Bank, and he began to believe that Matthew L. Bevan, a Philadelphia merchant, was accurate when, after a conversation with the President in October, he reported that Jackson had "expressed himself in the most clear and decided manner friendly to the Bank, 'that it was a blessing

17 W. Dun to N. Biddle, August 14, 1829; W. B. Lewis to N. Biddle, October 16, 1829, in the Biddle Manuscripts in the Library of Congress.

18 S. Jaudon to N. Biddle, October 26, 1829, in the Biddle Manuscripts in the Library of Congress.

19 N. Biddle, Memorandum of a Conversation with A. Jackson, n.d., in the Biddle Manuscripts in the Library of Congress; A. Jackson to J. A. Hamilton, May 3, 1830, in James A. Hamilton, *Reminiscences* (New York, 1869), p. 164.

to the country administered as it was, diffusing a healthful circulation, sustaining the general credit without partiality or political bias,' that he entertained a high regard for its excellent president (I use his own words) who with the board of the parent bank possessed his entire confidence and indeed his thanks for the readiness and cordiality with which they seemed to meet the views of the government."[20]

Biddle wanted to believe these statements to be true, just as Jackson wanted the Bank to be guilty of improper political activities. The only difference between them was the amount and quality of the evidence upon which each relied, and here it seems certain that Biddle's beliefs more nearly corresponded with what Jackson said and did than the President's beliefs corresponded with the acts of the Bank. Biddle had been waiting and planning for this moment to begin a campaign to persuade Jackson to recommend the recharter of the Bank. He knew that one of the President's greatest ambitions was to do what Jefferson had failed to do, namely, to pay off the national debt; and Biddle, who was more familiar than anyone else with the difficulties of this complex financial operation, had devised an ingenious program that would accomplish the object during the one term that Jackson had pledged himself to serve.

The revenues expected during the four years would be insufficient, but if the government sold its stock in the national bank and if it authorized the Bank to assume the obligation to pay off the remainder of the debt in lieu of a bonus for the recharter, then all that the government owed could be paid. Biddle explained this proposal to Lewis, who indorsed it enthusiastically. "Say to Mr. Biddle," he instructed a Philadelphia friend in early November, "the president is much gratified with the report I have made upon the subject of his Bank, all things with regard to it will be well." And two days later he added: "If you see Mr. Biddle say to him the president would be glad to see his proposition. . . . I think we will find the *old fellow* will do justice to the Bank in his message for the handsome manner in which it assisted the government in paying off the last instalment of the national debt."[21]

Biddle immediately sent his plan to Washington and shortly thereafter went down himself. The President thanked him for his suggestions and said: "I would have no difficulty in recommending it to Congress, but I think it right to be perfectly frank with you. . . . I have read the opinion of John Marshall who I believe was a great and pure mind, and could not agree with him, though if he had said that as it was necessary for the purpose of the national government there ought to be a national bank I should have been disposed to concur; but I do not think that Congress has a right

[20] M. L. Bevan to N. Biddle, October 21, 1829, in the Biddle Manuscripts in the Library of Congress.

[21] W. B. Lewis to H. Toland, November 9, 11, 1829, in the Biddle Manuscripts in the Library of Congress; Catterall, *Second Bank,* pp. 190–91.

to create a corporation out of the ten mile square." This positive refusal to recommend the recharter of the Bank was accompanied by praise of its managers and policies. "I feel very sensibly," Jackson said, "the services rendered by the Bank at the last payment of the national debt, and shall take an opportunity of declaring it publicly in my message to Congress." He added that he had every reason to be satisfied with the board of directors, and Biddle replied: "I am very much gratified at this frank explanation. We shall all be proud of any kind mention in the message, for we should feel like soldiers after an action commended by their general."[22]

Biddle fully understood that Jackson was not going to recommend the recharter of the Bank. He also had been made aware of the emotional nature of the President's views on the subject, for in the course of their conversation Jackson had said: "I do not dislike your bank any more than all banks. But ever since I read the history of the South Sea Bubble I have been afraid of banks." But the natural disappointment with which Biddle came away from the conference was relieved by the knowledge that the message would contain praise of the Bank, and the way was still open for further negotiations when Congress, the majority of whose members were favorable to the recharter, began its session.

[22] N. Biddle, Memorandum of a Conversation with A. Jackson, n.d., in the Biddle Manuscripts in the Library of Congress.

～ *14* ～

Jackson Joins the Fight

*P*resident Jackson was neither accurate nor frank in his conversation with Biddle. He said that he was afraid of all banks and that Congress did not have the power to incorporate an institution to operate outside the District of Columbia, but when he made these statements, he had already decided to recommend the creation of a government-owned substitute bank with branches in the various states. He had spoken favorably of such an institution before he was elected President, but he had not discussed it with Ingham or any other member of his Cabinet. His sole adviser seems to have been Felix Grundy, the Jackson party's candidate for the United States Senate from Tennessee, but (and this is one of the strangest parts of this very confused story) in 1820 when Grundy had proposed a similar state-owned and state-controlled bank, Jackson had denounced it as "wicked, profligate and unconstitutional."[1]

The President's opinion of governmental banks apparently had changed, and Grundy was enthusiastic in May, 1829, when he was first sent Jackson's plan. But as he studied the proposal throughout the summer, his initial enthusiasm was replaced by doubts, for he discovered an unexpected difficulty in devising a safe and effective method of selecting directors for such a bank. A national bank should be free from direct political influence so that it could make financial decisions and act upon them for economic, not political, reasons, but it also should be subject to public restraint so that those in control of the bank could not use it for their private or party advantage. An appropriate and satisfactory balance had been arrived at in the charters of the first and second Banks of the United States, but Jackson's proposed plan provided that all the directors of the principal bank were to be appointed annually by the President of the United States with the advice and consent of the Senate.[2]

[1] A. Jackson to W. B. Lewis, July 15, 1820, in the Ford Manuscript Collection in the New York Public Library; S. Smith to N. Biddle, December 26, 1829, in the Biddle Manuscripts in the Library of Congress; St. George L. Sioussat, "Tennessee Politics in the Jackson Period," *American Historical Review*, XV (1908), 65–66.

[2] F. Grundy to A. Jackson, May 22, October 22, 1829, in Bassett (ed.), *Correspondence of Jackson*, IV, 37, 83–84.

Grundy believed that this provision was dangerous, in that it would make the directors subservient to executive influence. He suggested, instead, that they be elected by Congress, but even he could not devise an acceptable way of selecting the branch directors. Jackson had suggested that they should be elected by the legislature of the state in which the branch was located, but Grundy regarded this as "a very unstatesmanlike idea." It would place the money of the United States under the management of persons over whom it had no control, and "in times of emergency," he said, "the very means necessary to sustain the general government might be withheld or used to its injury, by reason of the disaffection of some of the states." He did not think that the power to elect branch directors should be given to the directors of the principal bank, and if it were turned over to the whole Congress, "it would destroy everything like accountability in making the selections." So he made the proposal, though he did not very much like it, that the branch directors be elected by the congressional delegation of the particular state involved.[3]

Jackson received Grundy's comments about the first of November, but waited more than three weeks to tell Secretary Ingham that this government-owned substitute for the national bank was to be recommended to the Congress. He too objected—particularly to the provision placing the branches under the control of the states. Like Grundy, he feared that a disaffected state in time of war "might frustrate a campaign or sacrifice an army upon some frivolous pretext for refusing the payment of the Treasury drafts." He recommended that all discussion of the project should be postponed until some later time, for the subject was "one of great magnitude" and required "the most mature reflection." This advice to defer any mention of the substitute bank was repeated by Attorney-General Berrien, who also advised caution in reopening the question of the constitutionality of the existing bank. "It must be admitted," he wrote, "that the existence of the power has, at various times and in different forms, been affirmed by every department of the government."[4]

Ingham and Berrien could be disregarded. Their predilections in favor of the Bank were well known, but the same was not true of Amos Kendall, to whom Jackson next turned. This native of New Hampshire, who had moved to Kentucky as a young man to tutor the children of Henry Clay, was a determined enemy of the Bank. He had turned against the institution because of its restrictive policies in the years following the depression of 1819, and the changes which had followed the replacement of Cheves by Biddle had not influenced his views. He was as anxious as Jackson to launch the attack upon the Bank, but even he could not indorse the President's plan. His advice was phrased cautiously but positively and con-

[3] *Ibid.*

[4] S. D. Ingham to A. Jackson, November 26, 27, 1829; J. M. Berrien to A. Jackson, November 27, 1829, in Bassett (ed.), *Correspondence of Jackson*, IV, 92–95.

cluded with the expressed wish that the proposal not "be thrown before the public." Van Buren, Lewis, and other members of the administration joined in the attempt to dissuade Jackson from mentioning his opposition to the Bank of the United States in the message, and, when he would not listen, they called on James A. Hamilton of New York, a son of Alexander Hamilton, for assistance.[5]

Jackson had a high opinion of Hamilton's ability and knowledge and turned over to him the draft of that part of the message which was concerned with the national bank. Jackson's remarks, Hamilton later reported, were written in a "loose, newspaper, slashing style," but no record has been preserved of what this original document contained. Hamilton reduced it to two paragraphs, the first of which said: "The charter of the Bank of the United States expires in 1836, and its stockholders will most probably apply for a renewal of their privileges. In order to avoid the evils resulting from precipitancy in a measure involving such important principles and deep pecuniary interests, I feel that I cannot, in justice to the parties interested, too soon present it to the deliberate consideration of the legislature and the people. Both the constitutionality and the expedience of the law creating this bank are well questioned by a large portion of our fellow-citizens, and it must be admitted that it has failed in the great end of establishing a sound and uniform currency."[6]

The second paragraph was shorter and devoted to Jackson's proposed substitute for the Bank. "Under these circumstances," it said, "if such an institution is deemed essential to the fiscal operations of the government, I submit to the wisdom of the legislature whether a national one, founded upon the credit of the government and its revenues, might not be devised which would avoid all constitutional difficulties and at the same time secure all the advantages to the government and the country that were expected to result from the present bank." Hamilton read what he had written to the President, who asked, "Do you think that is all I ought to say?" And Hamilton replied, "I think you ought to say nothing at present about the Bank." To which Jackson, with complete sincerity, answered, "My friend, I am pledged against the Bank, but if you think that is enough, so let it be."[7]

Thus it was Jackson himself, not his party or any interested group, that made the recharter of the Bank a political issue. The reason for his action was not to be found in any act of commission or omission by the institution itself or in any widespread discontent or dissatisfaction with it and the existing financial and credit system, but rather in his own view of what

[5] A. Kendall to A. Jackson, November 20, 1829, in the Ladies' Hermitage Association Manuscript Collection; Arthur M. Schlesinger, Jr., *The Age of Jackson* (Boston, 1945), p. 32.

[6] Hamilton, *Reminiscences,* pp. 149–51.

[7] *Ibid.*

was moral, constitutional, and proper. All his political advisers had unsuccessfully sought to dissuade him from this course, but he considered himself "pledged" and would not be restrained. When the decision was made to include Hamilton's two paragraphs in the message, Amos Kendall wrote a letter attacking the Bank which was sent to Mordecai Noah, surveyor of the Port of New York and editorial associate of James Watson Webb and James Gordon Bennett on the leading Van Buren newspaper in New York, the *Courier and Enquirer*.[8]

Until this moment, no official position in regard to the Bank had been taken by any of the party press. But Kendall's letter changed this situation. Noah added a lead and conclusion and published it as an editorial. The signal was given for a general attack upon the Bank of the United States, and most of the party papers obeyed as soon as Jackson's message confirmed the fact that this was indeed the new party line. Alexander Hamilton, a brother of James but opposed to him in politics, called Biddle's attention to this editorial when it appeared and warned him that it reflected official party policy in regard to the Bank. Biddle did not believe him. He was certain that Jackson's personal views as to the constitutionality of the Bank were not to be mentioned in the message and that the sole reference to the institution would be praise for its services in the smooth and uncomplicated payment of the national debt.[9]

When he was proved wrong by the appearance of the message, Biddle made no secret of his feeling that the President had been deceitful in their conversation in late November. "It is scarcely three weeks," he wrote, "since he expressed to me in person the greatest confidence in the administration of the Bank and his determination to make public acknowledgement of its services in paying off the debt, nor was there given any intimation of his purpose to speak of it thus." He comforted himself with the conclusion that the statements were those of the President alone, not of his Cabinet or of his party; that the whole argument that the Bank had failed to provide a sound currency was "notoriously wrong"; and that the substitute proposal for a banking machine at Washington was "too bad to find any partisans."[10]

It never occurred to Jackson that his concealment of his intentions might be looked on as deceit. He was engaged in a moral crusade dictated by his conscience and by his concern for "the safety and purity of our free institutions." He told Hamilton that he disliked going against the opinion of so great a majority of his Cabinet, but he had no other choice; and then, as if he were unaware of what he was saying about his own

---

[8] Parton, *Jackson,* III, 268–69.

[9] A. Hamilton to N. Biddle, November 27, 1829; N. Biddle to A. Hamilton, November 28, 1829, in the Biddle Manuscripts in the Library of Congress.

[10] N. Biddle to J. Potter, December 14, 1829, in the Biddle Manuscripts in the Library of Congress.

political friends, he stated that he had been aware that his views in regard to the Bank "would be disapproved by all the sordid and interested who prize self-interest more than the perpetuation of our liberty and the blessings of a free republican government." No member of his party in the Congress ever spoke in favor of his government-controlled bank, and Smith, the chairman of the Finance Committee of the Senate, humorously wrote Biddle, "I have said to myself that if Hamilton or the elder Adams had proposed such a system of power and patronage, what a noise and outcry we democrats would have made."[11]

The Ways and Means Committee of the House, of which George McDuffie was the chairman, almost unanimously condemned the proposal but stated that they were convinced that it "proceeded from the most disinterested patriotism, and was exclusively designed to promote the welfare of the country." This was not, they insisted, "the mere formal and heartless homage, sometimes offered up to official station, either from courtesy or interest, but a tribute which is eminently due, and cheerfully rendered, to the exalted character of the distinguished individual on whom it is bestowed." They were aware of the danger to the party of a split between the President and his legislative leaders so early in the administration, and they dismissed his recommendation as impractical and unwise only because they were compelled to do so by the "highest considerations of public duty."[12]

Biddle was pleased with this repudiation of Jackson's bank by his congressional leaders, but he was more concerned with the President's charge that the currency was unsound. This statement, he thought, must be answered by a committee of Congress, for if the currency was not sound, it was the duty of Congress to make it sound; and if it was sound, the fact should be stated, in order to heal the wound which a contrary assertion from so high a source had inflicted on the character and credit of the country. He corresponded regularly with Senator Smith and on January 25, 1830, sent him a report on the currency. Smith submitted this document to the Finance Committee without naming its author, and it was transmitted to the Senate on March 29 as the committee report.[13]

The currency of the United States, Biddle's analysis began, consisted of

[11] A. Jackson to J. A. Hamilton, December 19, 1829, in Hamilton, *Reminiscences*, pp. 151–52; S. Smith to N. Biddle, December 27, 1829, in the Biddle Manuscripts in the Library of Congress.

[12] *House Report* (21st Cong., 1st sess.), No. 358. Biddle was in close touch with the committee throughout the preparation of its report. He supplied it with information through Representative Joseph Hemphill of Pennsylvania, who, like McDuffie and the majority of the committee, was completely loyal to Jackson at this stage of the administration. N. Biddle to J. Hemphill, December 13, 14, 16, 17, 18, 19, 21, 1829, in the Biddle Manuscripts in the Library of Congress.

[13] S. Smith to N. Biddle, December 26, 1829, January 4, 1830; N. Biddle to S. Smith, January 2, 25, 1830; N. Biddle to N. Silsbee, December 17, 1829, in the Biddle Manuscripts in the Library of Congress; *Senate Document* (21st Cong., 1st sess.), No. 104.

gold and silver and of state and national bank notes redeemable in these metals. This mixed currency was collected by the government through some nine thousand federal employees—customs officers, postmasters, receivers of internal revenue, marshals, clerks of court, and sellers of public lands—and was disbursed through the agency of the Bank of the United States at points thousands of miles from the places in which it had been collected "without the loss of a single dollar and without the expense of a single dollar to the government." It seemed hardly credible, he stated, that "a currency by which the government has been thus enabled to collect and transfer such an amount of revenue to pay its army and navy, and all its expenses, and the national debt, is unsafe and unsound."

The currency was equally useful to the commercial community. It combined the convenience of a portable medium, paper, with the safety of gold and silver, and it was a fact familiar to every citizen that throughout the country the state banks, restrained and supported by the Bank of the United States, supplied a uniform and sound local currency. The notes of the national bank also circulated locally, but they were "more known, more trusted, more valuable than the local currency" and were generally "employed in the exchanges between different parts of the country." All these national bank notes, wherever they were issued, were received at par by every government collector of revenue and were actually, though not legally, redeemable in gold and silver at any branch to which they were presented. They were accepted in most commercial transactions at par, and never did the notes of even the remotest branch vary more than a quarter of 1 per cent from their value in specie. Here, then, the report continued, "is a currency as safe as silver; more convenient and more valuable than silver, which through the whole western and southern and interior parts of the union is eagerly sought in exchange for silver; which in those sections often bears a premium in silver; which is throughout the union equal to silver in the payments to the government and in payments to individuals in business; and which, whenever silver is needed in any part of the country, will command it without the charge of the slightest fraction."

Nor were these all the advantages of this currency. In no other nation in the commercial world could individuals do as they customarily did in the United States: deposit their silver at cities as distant as St. Louis, Nashville, or New Orleans, receive notes which they could take a thousand or fifteen hundred miles to the Atlantic Coast, and there use them at par in payments of purchases or debts. If they did not wish to carry bank notes because of the risk of loss, they could go to the branch of the Bank of the United States and purchase a draft, payable to themselves alone or to an agent, at an expense of no more than half the cost of shipping specie. The owner of funds at St. Louis or Nashville could transfer them to Philadelphia for one-half of 1 per cent; from New Orleans usually without charge; and from Charleston at no more than one-quarter of 1 per cent.

The final proof that the American currency was sound was the state of the foreign exchanges. The current quotation on Great Britain was 1 per cent under par, and this fact was conclusive as to the state of the currency. If the bank notes of a country were not equal to specie, specie would be at a premium. If the currency was unsound, more would have to be paid of that currency in order to produce an equal amount of specie in another country. But in the United States at the moment, the bank notes were convertible into specie, as much could be bought with them as with specie, and in transactions abroad the merchants could pay as much debt by buying bills of exchange with notes as they could pay by shipping metal, so that nothing seemed wanting to prove "the soundness and uniformity of the currency."[14]

The Committee on Ways and Means of the House also denied Jackson's statement concerning the currency. McDuffie, the author of the report, was a bullionist by conviction and believed that gold and silver alone should be used as currency. But he was also a realist and knew that a metallic currency could not be established in the United States. Each of the states had chartered banks of issue, and the nation's economic commitments had been established on the basis of this bank-note currency. To adopt a metallic currency would require the states to reverse their established policies—a political impossibility—and also it would lead to a complete and perhaps disastrous readjustment of all economic agreements and contracts. Hence what the country confronted was not a choice between paper and metal but rather a choice "between a paper currency of uniform value, and subject to the control of the only power competent to its regulation, and a paper currency of varying and fluctuating value . . . subject to no common or adequate control whatever."

McDuffie cited evidence similar to that contained in Biddle's report to prove that the Bank of the United States had properly controlled its own currency and that of the state banks; and even though, as an advocate of state rights, he usually insisted on a strict interpretation of the Constitution, he also defended the constitutionality of the Bank's charter. That could be said of this question, he wrote, which could not be said of most. Both the old political parties, Federalist and Republican, had pronounced the Bank to be constitutional, and there were but a few of the prominent men of the country who were not committed to this position. And to these authorities must be added "the solemn and unanimous opinion of the Supreme Court, in a case which fully and distinctly submitted the constitutional question to their congnizance," so that McDuffie concluded with the question previously asked by Alexander Dallas at the close of the War of 1812, "Can it be deemed a violation of the right of private opinion to con-

14 *Ibid.*

sider the constitutionality of a national bank as a question forever settled and at rest?"[15]

These reports submitted to the Congress by committees controlled by members of the Jackson party effectively answered the President, and Biddle determined to give them as wide a circulation throughout the country as had been given to the President's message. His purpose was to educate, not to influence party politics, since Smith and McDuffie were as much opposed to Adams and Clay and their political followers as was Jackson himself. Biddle was convinced that much of the opposition to the recharter, including the President's, was the result of "downright ignorance," and he hoped to bring about a greater understanding of the Bank's importance "through the free circulation of honest truths by means of the press." With the consent of the directors, he sent copies of the Smith and McDuffie reports to every newspaper, paid some of the editors to insert them in their news columns, and employed other publishers to reprint and distribute the reports as pamphlets.[16]

He made no attempt to conceal these payments, which were not in violation of the customs and practices of the period, and justified them on the ground that the President had undertaken to say of the Bank that which was wholly without foundation. "The whole influence of his government," Biddle wrote, "and of the presses subservient to his government, is employed in endeavoring to break down the Bank. In this situation, the Bank can only find safety in such explanations of its proceedings as will satisfy the country that it has been unjustly assailed and that its operations are highly beneficial. But how is it to make these explanations except through the press, the only channel of communication with the people? And if it employs that channel, why should it ask of printers to insert its explanations gratuitously?"[17]

At the same time that Biddle began the circulation of these reports pointing out the inaccuracies in Jackson's statements about the Bank, he also made a second attempt to persuade the President to recommend the recharter. William Lewis was once again the intermediary, and Biddle wrote that he hoped Jackson, having had the opportunity since delivering the message of "examining more attentively the effects and operations of the institution, of witnessing its utility to the finances of the government, and of knowing the views of sound and practical men from every part of the country," would have become "satisfied that the powers of the Bank

[15] *House Report* (21st Cong., 1st sess.), No. 358.

[16] N. Biddle to J. Gales, March 2, 1831; N. Biddle to J. Hunter, May 4, 1831, in the Biddle Manuscripts in the Library of Congress. The original authorization in 1830 was informal, but this "verbal understanding" was officially confirmed by the board of directors on March 11, 1831 (extract from the Minutes of the Board of Directors of the Bank of the United States, March 11, 1831, in the Cadwalader Manuscripts in the Historical Society of Pennsylvania).

[17] *Ibid.*

have not been abused for political purposes, and that towards him and his administration, the Bank has acted frankly, fairly, and cordially." He assured Lewis that many of those concerned with the administration of the Bank were decided personal and political friends of the President, and added: "To them, as well as to a larger body of citizens, it would be exceedingly gratifying to know the feelings of the president towards the Bank at the present moment, because some of his injudicious friends and many of his opponents seek to make an impression that such is his rooted dislike to the institution that he would refuse his sanction to a continuance of the Bank, were the charter renewed by both houses of Congress."[18]

Lewis replied that the report of Jackson's determination to veto the recharter did not tally with what he had heard him say on the subject. Only a few days before, the President had expressed the opinion that a national bank ought to be established that would be preferable to the existing Bank of the United States, but he had also said that "if Congress thought differently, and it was deemed necessary to have such a Bank as the present, with certain modifications, that he should not object to it." Further evidence that the President was changing his mind was supplied by Joseph Nichol, president of the Nashville branch. After a long conversation with Jackson at the Hermitage in July, 1830, Nichol assured Biddle that the President would "not interfere with Congress on the subject of renewing the charter of the Bank." Jackson told this old friend that he was generally pleased with the management of the Bank and its branches and that he was "satisfied that politicks have no influence in Bank or in the choice of directors." He spoke of Biddle "in the most exalted terms" and acknowledged that "there is no gentleman that can be found would manage the Bank better or do the Bank and country more justice."[19]

Biddle received other indications of this change in Jackson's opinions and, at the end of the summer, decided to make formal application for a recharter at the approaching session of Congress, thus preventing this question from becoming "involved in the controversy for the presidency." He gave as his reasons that there was "a decided majority of both houses of Congress favorable to the renewal of the charter," that those closely associated with the President "studiously disclaim all participation in the opinions announced by him," but, more importantly for the reason that "the worthy person who first made the attack, looks at the matter now with different feelings."[20] Biddle's assumptions were correct in all particulars except one. The opinions of "the worthy person who first made the

18 N. Biddle to W. D. Lewis, May 8, 1830, in the Biddle Manuscripts in the Library of Congress.

19 W. D. Lewis to N. Biddle, May 25, 1830; J. Nichol to N. Biddle, July 20, 1830, in the Biddle Manuscripts in the Library of Congress.

20 N. Biddle to A. Gallatin, September 9, 1830, in the Biddle Manuscripts in the Library of Congress.

attack" had not changed. Jackson still hoped that the Congress would accept his proposal of a government-controlled bank, and he had heard nothing to lead him to alter his suspicion and fear of the existing Bank. Biddle's error was understandable. The President, confronted by opposition from most of his political and personal associates, had ceased talking about his substitute bank or the Bank of the United States, and those close to him thought he was changing his mind. In occasional private letters, however, he still was denouncing the Bank as a "hydra of corruption" which was destroying the morals and inhibiting the freedom of the American people, but Biddle had no access to this information.

~ 15 ~

Propaganda

and

Counterpropaganda

*B*iddle abandoned his decision to apply for a recharter at the approaching session of Congress almost as soon as it was made. His friends in the Jackson party counseled delay, as did Henry Clay, nominal leader of the opposition. Clay, convinced that Van Buren was determined to make abolition of the Bank the issue in the next presidential election, warned Biddle that he would play into Van Buren's hands if he applied for a recharter without being certain of support from the executive as well as the legislative branch of the government. In replying to Clay, Biddle carefully avoided all reference to party matters. His letter dealt entirely with the technical question of the recharter and with his reason for postponing the application, which was the ease with which the question could be delayed in the short session. "My impression is," he wrote, "that nothing but certainty of success should induce an application now. To this I am the more inclined because time is operating in favor of the Bank by removing prejudices, and diffusing a general conviction of its utility."[1]

Time did seem to be working in favor of the Bank. Thoughtful men in politics and business, recalling what had happened to currency and credit when the first Bank was not rechartered, feared that the calamity would be repeated if the second Bank met a like fate. Albert Gallatin was more frightened than most. As Secretary of the Treasury in 1811, he had been the official responsible for the financial health of the nation at the time that the first Bank of the United States had been allowed to die. He be-

[1] H. Clay to N. Biddle, June 14, September 11, 1830; N. Biddle to H. Clay, November 3, 1830, in the Biddle Manuscripts in the Library of Congress.

lieved that this serious mistake was about to be repeated, and he accepted an invitation from Robert Walsh, editor of the *American Quarterly Review*, to prepare an article on the American currency with a view to warning the country of its danger. Gallatin was not an uncritical champion of the national bank or its currency. In economic theory he was a classical liberal and a bullionist, but, like McDuffie, he knew that so fundamental a change in the American monetary system was impossible.[2]

Could he have had his way in the existing situation, he would have stopped the issuance of notes, bills of credit, or any other paper currency by state banks through the imposition of a federal tax. And he would also have limited the notes of the Bank of the United States to denominations of one hundred dollars and up and would have used copper and silver coins, containing less metal than their nominal value, for change, and gold coins, at their true value, for other transactions. This reform program, he realized, was impossible. The Congress would not attempt to proscribe the issuance of notes by state banks, and there was no security against over-issue except state laws and the Bank of the United States. And though he said he was aware of the objections to "a powerful moneyed institution," the Bank of the United States or some other based upon the same principles was, in his opinion, the nation's only "security for preserving a proper standard of value."[3]

Biddle was in fundamental disagreement with Gallatin's monetary views. He believed that a metallic currency, even if politically possible, would prove unsatisfactory and that the existing mixed currency was the best that could be devised for the United States. Pragmatically, however, they agreed that the national bank was necessary under existing conditions because it alone could control the other banks and the currency. Throughout the summer of 1830 they exchanged letters covering all phases of banking and monetary history and theory, but the article and the conclusions presented in it were Gallatin's alone. The worst plan of all, he thought, was that proposed by Jackson to turn the national treasury into a banking and trading company, and, rather than have it or the direct issue of paper money by the government, he would prefer to let "the state banks run wild and suspend their payments." His single interest was the provision of a sound currency, which he considered a constitutional and a moral duty. "With a debased coinage or a fluctuating depreciated paper," he wrote, "you subvert every private and public engagement, impair the perform-

[2] A. Gallatin to R. Walsh, April 27, 1830; A. Gallatin to N. Biddle, August 14, 1830, in the Gallatin Manuscripts in the New York Historical Society.

[3] A. Gallatin to G. V. Verplanck, May 22, 1830, in Henry Adams (ed.), *Writings of Albert Gallatin* (Philadelphia, 1879), II, 427–29; *American Quarterly Review*, VIII (1830), 441–528. The Gallatin-Biddle correspondence on banking, money, and the history of the Bank of the United States is to be found in the Biddle Manuscripts in the Library of Congress and in the Gallatin Manuscripts in the New York Historical Society.

ance of every contract, make invariably the ignorant and weak, dupes of the shrewd and wary, and demoralize the whole community. What are the means to prevent this under existing circumstances? . . . I will congratulate you and the country if you can discover any safe means of attaining the object otherwise than through a Bank of the United States."[4]

Gallatin's article was distributed as widely as had been Smith's and McDuffie's reports, and many old Republicans had a second thought about the Bank. But not the old Republican in the White House. Jackson still thought that there should be a government bank. He requested James A. Hamilton to prepare a new plan shortly after the first message was sent to the Congress, and Hamilton did what he could to comply. The existing Bank, he said to the President, was unconstitutional and dangerous to liberty, but, surprisingly, he then admitted: "It cheapens and facilitates all the fiscal operations of the government. It tends to equalize domestic exchange and to produce a sound and uniform currency." This was a direct refutation of the charge that Hamilton himself had written that the Bank of the United States had failed to establish "a uniform and sound currency," but neither he nor the President thought this worthy of comment.[5]

In January, Hamilton prepared a plan about which Jackson said that it was "the only safe outline for a bank or government deposit," but both apparently had forgotten this proposal in the following May, when the President reopened the correspondence. Jackson was bitter about McDuffie's report, which he considered a disloyal defense of the Bank of the United States, and he denied that he had ever contemplated the creation of such a bank as that which the committee described. "I have often spoken," he wrote, "of a national bank chartered upon the principles of the checks and balances of our federal government, with a branch in each state, the capital apportioned agreeably to representation, and to be attached to and be made subject to the supervision of the secretary of the treasury, and an expose of its condition to be made annually in his report to Congress, as part of the revenue; which might be a bank of deposit only, which I have always thought more consistent with our government than that it should become a brokers or banking establishment for discount and deposit."[6]

This proposal was sufficiently confused, but he made it even more so by stating that, though a national bank of deposit was all that the country should have, "a national bank of discount and deposit may be established upon our revenue and national faith pledged, and carried on by salaried

[4] A. Gallatin to R. Potter, December 3, 1830, in Adams (ed.), *Writings of Gallatin*, II, 440–43.

[5] J. A. Hamilton to A. Jackson, January 4, 1830, in Bassett (ed.), *Correspondence of Jackson*, IV, 111–14.

[6] A. Jackson to J. A. Hamilton, May 3, June 3, 1830, in Hamilton, *Reminiscences*, pp. 164, 167–68.

officers, as our revenue is now collected, with less injury to the morals of our citizens and to the destruction of our liberty, than the present hydra of corruption, and all the emoluments accrue to the nation as part of the revenue." Hamilton did not approve of any of the President's new suggestions. He did not believe that any bank should be "exclusively in the hands of the government and its paid officers," for it would be exposed to the danger of having its funds loaned to irresponsible persons. The officers and directors appointed by the President would be tempted to use their financial power for political ends, and control of the bank would become one of the great reasons for seeking office. The only safeguard against such abuses was that used by the creators of the Bank of the United States, and that, according to Hamilton, was "the untiring watchfulness of individual interest, always better managers of pecuniary concerns, simply, than governments are."[7]

Jackson did not reply to Hamilton's letter, and, if he was disappointed by the essential defection of his financial adviser, he gave no external sign. He became silent about the whole matter of banking reform throughout the rest of the summer and fall, and the single statement reported to Biddle was that to Nichol in praise of the existing Bank. The Jackson party press, it was true, had followed the President's line in denouncing the institution as unconstitutional and dangerous, but almost none of these editors gave substantial support to the proposal of a government-controlled bank. But their columns were opened to all who had real or fancied grievances against the Bank of the United States, and its enemies among the politicians, the brokers, the state bankers, and the speculators took full advantage of this opportunity. Biddle was not particularly worried by this development. He knew that these same newspapers, dependent as they were upon political advertising, would change their editorial attitude if Jackson changed his, and he was also aware that the overwhelming majority of the members of the financial and business community, including the most influential leaders of the farmers, were enthusiastic admirers and supporters of the national bank.

His decision not to apply for a recharter at the approaching session of Congress was made for technical reasons, primarily the difficulty in getting affirmative action in the short session, and he did not expect the President to reopen the issue. Again he was mistaken. Jackson asked Hamilton to return to Washington in November to aid in the preparation of the second message, and he insisted that it should include a more extended recommendation of the substitute bank. His "suggestions as to the bank," Hamilton wrote to a friend, "I do not approve; his plan is impracticable. I made efforts to amend and omit, neither would do." The Cabinet was not consulted, nor were congressional or other party leaders. The Presi-

[7] J. A. Hamilton to A. Jackson, June 7, 1830, in Hamilton, *Reminiscences,* pp. 168–69.

dent alone made the decision, and the message recommended to the Congress that it create a bank as a branch of the Treasury which would be prohibited from making loans or purchasing property. It was not to be a corporate body, so it would not violate the Constitution, and, since it could not "operate on the hopes, fears, or interests of large masses of the community, it would be shorn of the influences which make the Bank formidable."[8]

The sole banking functions that this strange institution would perform were the purchase and sale of bills of exchange and the acceptance of deposits—a role more like that of private bankers or brokers—and those who dealt with it would be deprived of any recourse to the courts because, as a branch of the Treasury, it could not be sued. Not a single member of the Congress and only a few persons in the country gave this proposal the slightest consideration or support, and apparently the sole effect of Jackson's reintroduction of the subject was to make Biddle reconsider his decision not to apply for a recharter. He wrote Joseph Hemphill, a member of Congress from Philadelphia, to suggest that the message gave him and other members of the Committee on Ways and Means the opportunity to say "that this is a question which must not be left in its present position, that all the great interests of the country are hazarded by the suspense, and although they did not intend to stir it, yet now that it had been agitated it ought to be put at rest." The committee could then properly ask the directors on what terms they would accept the renewal, and the question would be presented not as an application by the Bank but "as a financial measure introduced by the financial organ of the House."[9]

Hemphill and the rest of the committee paid no attention to this request. A majority in both houses of Congress were in favor of the recharter, but they were in no mood to take up this or any other controversial issues. A fundamental realignment of political factions was being worked out within the Jackson party, which would have a decisive effect on the choice of its candidates in 1832, and most of the attention of congressmen during this short session was concentrated on these political maneuvers.[10] The administration party seemed united on the surface, but everyone knew that the rivalry of Calhoun and Van Buren for the succession was being decided. Biddle had no interest in this dispute, since the Bank of the United States was not an issue between the rival factions, and his only

[8] Hamilton, *Reminiscences*, p. 191; James D. Richardson (ed.), *Messages and Papers of the Presidents* (Washington, 1896–99), III, 1091–92.

[9] N. Biddle to J. Hemphill, December 14, 19, 1830, in the Biddle Manuscripts in the Library of Congress.

[10] J. Norvell to N. Biddle, December 16, 19, 1830, in the Biddle Manuscripts in the Library of Congress.

connection with it was his irritation at the fact that it kept Congress from considering the recharter of the Bank.

Both Calhoun and Van Buren had remained quiet in regard to the institution throughout the preceding year, and their opinions in regard to Jackson's attack upon it, if they had any, were carefully concealed. The Vice-President, on the basis of his past record, was considered to be a friend of the Bank, whereas Van Buren, respecting whose views there was no evidence of any sort, was frequently described as an enemy. Biddle did not know what to believe. "Of Mr. Van Buren's opinions," he wrote, "I know nothing except that he disapproved of that part of the message, but how he is inclined to the Bank generally I cannot say." But in all his calculations about the Secretary of State, he kept constantly in mind an early warning he had received from Alexander Hamilton: "Have no confidence in Van Beuren; as an aspirant for the Chief Magistracy, he is without principle, and totally destitute of sincerity. In the West, especially in Kentucky, the friends of the administration are against you, and on a majority in this state . . . these are sufficient causes to govern this gentleman; he may smile and seem gracious, it will only be to deceive." And Van Buren, as if to confirm this hostile judgment, replied to a question about the Bank by Senator Smith, "I have never yet given an opinion on the subject."[11]

Calhoun, had he been questioned, could have answered in almost identical language, and his and Van Buren's followers in the Congress, some of whom favored the recharter and some opposed it, did not want to raise this extraneous issue. The only member of Congress to share the desire for legislative action that Jackson and Biddle, for contrary reasons, had recommended was Thomas Hart Benton, and he had to resort to an ingenious parliamentary maneuver to gain the floor of the Senate. At the beginning of February, 1831, he asked leave to introduce a resolution that in the opinion of Congress the Bank of the United States should not be rechartered, and then, while still on his feet, delivered a set speech under the guise of giving his reasons for making the request. Calhoun ruled him out of order, but the Senate reversed the Vice-President, and Benton was permitted to proceed.[12]

The speech was not intended to influence Congress. It was, as Benton boasted, "a speech to be read by the people, the masses, the millions; and was conceived and delivered for that purpose." He spoke not a word concerning the purposes or functions of the Bank or of the reasons why Congress had granted it the great powers that it possessed, and he denied that it served the government or the public in any useful or effective way.

11 A. Hamilton to N. Biddle, December 10, 1829; N. Biddle to S. Smith, January 2, 1830; S. Smith to N. Biddle, December 19, 1830, in the Biddle Manuscripts in the Library of Congress.

12 *Register of Debates* (21st Cong., 2d sess.), pp. 50–75.

In ranting tones he made such statements as these: "This mass of power, thus concentrated, thus ramified, and thus directed, must necessarily become, under a prolonged existence, the absolute monopolist of American money, the sole manufacturer of paper currency, and the sole authority (for authority it will be) to which the federal government, the state governments, the great cities, corporate bodies, merchants, traders, and every private citizen, must, of necessity, apply for every loan which their exigencies may demand."[13]

Benton made many such demagogic charges in his speech, but nowhere did he supply evidence of any actual abuses of authority by the national bank or its branches, nor did he mention the numerous effective restraints that existed to prevent it from engaging in improper activities. Instead, he charged that "a great moneyed power" was necessarily favorable to "great capitalists," it being "the principle of money to eschew the needy and unfortunate," but he did not explain how the elimination of the Bank of the United States would establish an affinity between the poor and money. Biddle tried to persuade Webster to answer Benton but was refused. The opposition did not want to raise an issue that would distract attention from the quarrel between Calhoun and Van Buren that they hoped would weaken the administration party. They contented themselves with denying Benton leave to introduce his resolution by a vote of twenty-three to twenty, with five senators not voting, and the majority included three Jacksonians: Edward Livingston of Louisiana, William Marks of Pennsylvania, and Samuel Smith of Maryland.[14]

When Biddle learned that neither Webster nor any other senator was willing to reply to Benton, he attempted the task himself and published his exposure of Benton's misstatements and misinterpretations some three weeks after the delivery of the original speech. He stated flatly that in it, "from the beginning to the end," there was "scarcely a single statement" which was "not founded upon a want of knowledge of fact, or a total misapprehension of fact," and he proceeded to sustain his contention through a paragraph-by-paragraph analysis.[15] But Benton had accom-

[13] *Ibid.*; Thomas Hart Benton, *Thirty Years' View of a History of the Working of the American Government for Thirty Years, from 1820 to 1850* (New York, 1856), I, 204–5.

[14] N. Biddle to D. Webster, January 30, 1831, in the Biddle Manuscripts in the Library of Congress.

[15] N. Biddle, "Reply to Benton," *United States Gazette* (Philadelphia), February 26, 1831. Biddle's statement, flat and positive though it is, is the literal and exact truth. But Benton's demagogic statement was effective on public opinion. It was reprinted in most of the party newspapers and was distributed widely as a pamphlet in the same manner as Biddle had distributed Gallatin's article and the Smith and McDuffie reports. The money for this distribution of Benton's speech was provided by members of the Jackson party, and Biddle thought that the Bank was justifiably entitled to reply to such misrepresentations and to spend the stockholders' money for this purpose (see Schlesinger, *Age of Jackson*, p. 82).

plished what he wanted to do, and only those people who knew and understood the principles upon which the Bank operated were aware of the extent of his errors. His purpose was not merely to eliminate the Bank of the United States, he wanted to destroy all banks of issue. In his view the only safe currency was one made exclusively from gold, neither paper nor silver would serve, and, to begin the accomplishment of this purpose, he persuaded Senator Nathan Sanford of New York to introduce a resolution increasing the price of gold at the Mint.[16]

The existing regulations valued one ounce of gold as the equivalent of fifteen ounces of silver, but the actual market price of the two metals was in the approximate ratio of one to fifteen and a half. Each, as was to be expected, found its way to the place where it was most valuable, so gold went to the market and silver to the mint, and American coins, though legally either gold or silver, were almost exclusively silver. Biddle was as much opposed to this part of Benton's reform program as to his desire to eliminate banks of issue. He believed that the American currency, consisting of metal and bank notes redeemable in metal, though not perfect, was the best and most adequate in the world. He further believed that a commercial nation should have but one prime standard and that in the United States this standard should be silver, since the one weakness in its monetary system was the prevalence of small notes, less than five dollars in value, issued by banking and commercial firms to meet the ever present need for change. These notes were sometimes issued in denominations as low as five, ten, twenty-five, and fifty cents, and most states had forbidden their use, but so great was the need for change in most areas that relatively severe penalties had not stopped their circulation. The one effective remedy for these small notes, Biddle pointed out, was an increase in the coinage of silver in small denominations; but this would be more difficult to accomplish if the proposed increase in the price of gold was passed by the Congress. This would have a tendency to drive silver out of circulation, and gold coins of less than five dollars were impractical.[17]

The proponents of the change did not press for a vote on the question, and the Congress adjourned without taking action. But this tying-in of the increased price of gold with the attack upon the national bank had one important effect: it induced some of the producers of gold in the newly opened mines of Virginia, North Carolina, and Georgia to begin to support the monetary theories and policies of Benton and Jackson. The political power of this group was not great at the moment, but gold was a

16 *Senate Document* (21st Cong., 2d sess.), No. 96. Jackson and his administration had recommended a year earlier that silver become the exclusive metal in the United States in a report submitted to the Congress by Secretary Ingham (*House Executive Document* [21st Cong., 1st sess.], No. 117).

17 G. McDuffie to N. Biddle, January 29, 1831; N. Biddle to P. P. F. DeGrand, March 8, 1831, in the Biddle Manuscripts in the Library of Congress.

metal that exercised an almost magical influence on the minds of men, and a desire for such an apparently stable measure of value and means of exchange had even affected the thinking of such informed and critical observers as Gallatin and McDuffie. It also was partly responsible for the first theoretical justification and defense of Jackson's attack upon the Bank of the United States, which was written by George Bancroft of Massachusetts and appeared in the *North American Review* at the beginning of 1831. This graduate of Harvard and Göttingen universities had studied the new science of political economy and from his reading had derived the axiomatic conclusion that the sole function of government in regard to the currency was its constitutionally required duty "to coin money and to regulate the value thereof." All else, he insisted, should be left to the natural laws of commerce and trade.[18]

The Bank of the United States was not needed to regulate the issue of notes by the state banks; such regulation was naturally supplied by the "process of free competition, the suspicious shrewdness of those who held their paper, the runs made from malice, or fear, or prudence, or right; the self-restraining principle, which renders it more costly than productive to attempt an excessive issue and which, by making these issues always attended with loss, leaves to banking companies no ultimate option but moderation or bankruptcy." Bancroft illustrated his point by an elaborate metaphor based upon the flow regulator, which was attached to a water-wheel in the mills of New England and which controlled the amount of water that passed through the millrace. "Now would you substitute for such a contrivance," he asked, "the occasional visits of the overseer, absolute dictator though he may be? . . . Will you tell our manufacturers that Congress does not choose that they should employ this simple, and natural, and self-conservative principle, but appoints for them a general agent, to inspect the daily, hourly, momentary flow of the ever-running streams? And yet you propose something of this very sort with reference to the flow of the currency, to the ever-changing transfers of coin and of credit."[19]

This analogy, which equated an ingenious mechanical contrivance with "the method appointed by nature," was an illustration of what Biddle and other proponents of the American System found wrong with the dogmas of classical economics. Biddle knew that unrestrained natural forces were seldom useful. The water mill, of which Bancroft wrote, was a product of the mind and labor of men. It required the construction of a dam, a millrace, a flow regulator, and a water-wheel, but to Bancroft and his school such intervention with the ordinary conduct of a stream was natural, not

[18] George Bancroft, "Bank of the United States," *North American Review*, XXXII (1831), 21–64.

[19] *Ibid.*

artificial. Biddle also perceived a difference between the flow of water through a millrace and the flow of currency and credit through the economy, and he was certain that the device which regulated the one was not properly comparable to that which regulated the other. Irresponsible banking and depreciated paper money could not be prevented automatically. Some form of conscious control had to be created, and, as long as there were state banks of issue, it must be an institution with powers such as those possessed by the national bank.

Bancroft, Benton, and Jackson regarded banks as "favorable to the great capitalists" and injurious to the laboring and productive classes, but to Biddle they were popular and republican institutions which aided the poor to resist the rich. A wealthy man, as Biddle pointed out in the Pennsylvania legislature in 1811, could and would use his money to coerce others into obeying his will, whereas most banks were unambitious and passionless corporations except where profits were concerned. If one of them sought to demand more than prompt payment and legal interest, the borrower could go to another; and if a bank was unwise enough to make loans to persons incapable of repaying them, in order to control them politically, it would soon be stopped by the prompt return of its notes for redemption. But banks, like all other institutions, could be corrupted, so these semiautomatic controls were insufficient. Selfish and dishonest men had many opportunities to create artificial shortages or surpluses of goods and money, and there was need for a publicly responsible agency with power to thwart their plans.

The Bank of the United States had been created to perform this function for the economy and to be responsible for keeping all banks, including itself, in sound condition. In fulfilling this imposed duty it was not hostile to the state institutions. All it ever did or ever could do, as Biddle frequently said, was to correct excesses gently but firmly at all times and in the face of all hazards. The national bank had thus been given great powers and equally great responsibilities, and its creators had also known that wherever there was power, there must be restraint. To guard against the use of monetary influence for partisan ends, the private interests of ownership and the desire for profit had been invoked; but to insure that the Bank would not concern itself with these private interests alone, the Congress and the Secretary of the Treasury had been empowered to check upon the activities of the officers and directors and, if necessary, to remove the deposits or demand the forfeiture of the charter. Other restraints, even more important than these formal powers of government, existed. The Bank was responsible for the condition of the currency and the health of the economy, and hence public opinion was a continuing safeguard against any abuse of its authority. Merchants, state bankers, brokers, manufacturers, farmers, and mechanics were dependent for their prosperity upon the proper operation of the institution, and when some mistaken or inadequate policy was adopted, their protests and complaints made the fact known.

Biddle, as president of this Bank, could not be concerned with theoretically ideal credit and currency systems. His task was to deal with the economy as it was, but Bancroft and Benton were under no such restraint. Under the guise of attacking the Bank of the United States, they were seeking to reorganize the economy so that it would be in accord with the teachings of Malthus, Ricardo, Say, and Mill; and Biddle, if he could have had his wish, would have preferred to conduct the debate on this level. He believed that the people of the United States were satisfied with the Bank and its currency and that they would not accept the deflationary measures required by the doctines of the classical liberals if they could be informed of their cost. He also believed that the defenders of the Bank were abler, better informed, and more influential than their opponents, and he was even more confident that "the great security of all our institutions is in the power, the irresistible power of truth."[20]

He was to learn that he was in error duing the course of the decade that followed, but in 1831 he thought that what was needed was truthful and profound discourses upon the policies and principles of the Bank. Three of the nation's ablest economists volunteered to answer Bancroft's article, and each of them was given aid (not pay) by Biddle. P. P. F. DeGrand of Boston published a direct rebuttal of Bancoft in his commercial newspaper, and George Tucker of Virginia and William Beach Lawrence of New York prepared more general articles, which appeared in the *American Quarterly Review* and the *North American Review*, respectively.[21] They did not have the effect that Biddle expected. The people and politicians were bored by the serious tone of the discussion, and a member of the Pennsylvania legislature humorously advised Biddle that "ballads" were more effective than articles for his purpose. "There is no hostility to deal with," he wrote, "nothing beyond vague fears of what they call a mammoth bank, but the partisans know that Jackson has come out as they call it against it, and you must deal with them according to their worth. . . . Fools here accomplish more than the ablest dissertations in the world, turn your artillery accordingly."[22]

Biddle himself had come to the same conclusion. In returning a pamphlet written in defense of the first Bank of the United States to its author,

[20] N. Biddle to J. Gales, March 2, 1831, in the Biddle Manuscripts in the Library of Congress.

[21] P. P. F. DeGrand to N. Biddle, January 23, 28, 1831; N. Biddle to P. P. F. Degrand, February 1, 1831; G. Tucker to N. Biddle, January 26, April 8, 1831, in the Biddle Manuscripts in the Library of Congress; William Beach Lawrence, "Bank of the United States," *North American Review*, XXXII (1831), 524–63.

[22] C. J. Ingersoll to N. Biddle, March 3, 1831, in the Biddle Manuscripts in the Library of Congress.

Mathew Carey, he said: "The only diminution of one's pleasure [in reading it] is that so much good sense and reason should have been ineffectual, and it is of evil augury for us who are about to resume a similar struggle. My only hope is that although the cause may not be so well sustained as it was on that occasion, the country has had a melancholy experience which will supply the place of argument."[23] More than good sense and true reason was needed. For Biddle was confronted with a powerful enemy who was leader of a great political party and who was determined to destroy the Bank of the United States regardless of whether or not it was useful to the country. A change in sentiment had already begun to occur, and, although Jackson and Benton had not been successful in influencing the opinions of Congress at the beginning of 1831, their party associates in some of the states had joined the battle. The most important scene of conflict in the second year of the Bank war was not Washington at all; it was Harrisburg and Albany, the capitals of the rival states of Pennsylvania and New York.

[23] N. Biddle to M. Carey, May 4, 1831, in the Biddle Manuscripts in the Library of Congress.

~ 16 ~

New York

and

Pennsylvania

$\mathcal{P}$rior to 1831, Biddle had but little concern with state politics or politicians. The Bank of the United States was "a necessary and proper means of exercising some of the delegated powers of the general government," and he could rely on the national courts to protect it from state interference. But when he read Jackson's second message, he realized that one of its purposes was to sound "the tocsin of alarm to the state legislatures," particularly that of New York, and he began preparations to meet this attack. He had long known that the location of the principal office of the Bank in Philadelphia had led many New Yorkers to view it with jealousy, and Richard Rush, at the close of 1828, had warned him that "the frog of Wall Street puffs himself into the ox of Lombard Street, and will not have you abuse him." The following spring, just after Jackson's inauguration, Churchill Cambreleng had been quoted as saying that the Bank would not be rechartered unless its principal office was transferred to New York, but it had not been the New Yorkers in the administration who were responsible for Jackson's decision to denounce it as unconstitutional.[1]

No member of the New York financial community or any of the leaders of the Van Buren party, with the exception of James Hamilton, had supported Jackson in his attack on the Bank, nor had they urged him to undertake it; and Biddle believed that if they had ever been hostile to the institution, they had now changed their minds. Part of this change of opinion had been brought about by Biddle himself. He had tried to conciliate Cambreleng in May, 1829, by employing him as a special agent of

[1] N. Biddle to A. Gallatin, January 1, 1831; R. Rush to N. Biddle, December 10, 1828; R. Colt to N. Biddle, n.d., in the Biddle Manuscripts in the Library of Congress.

the Bank to select the location for an additional branch in western New York and had utilized every opportunity to prove to the Van Buren party that the Bank was politically neutral. The first such occasion was in the spring of 1829, when, for political reasons, the banks in New York City created an artificial scarcity of money and credit. Their purpose was to oppose the newly established Safety Fund System, which required them to contribute annually to a fund for the protection of bank creditors and which also provided for state-appointed commissioners to regulate and inspect banks. This reform measure had been proposed by Van Buren before he resigned as governor to become Secretary of State, and the city banks considered it to be an attempt by his party to create "a mighty engine of political power" through the subjection of the banks to the commissioners.[2]

The city banks threatened to give up their charters and withdraw from business and, to prove their sincerity, curtailed their usual accommodations to the upstate banks and to their local customers. The resulting financial pressure had its inevitable effect on trade in the city and state and, since New York was the commercial center of the nation, upon that in the rest of the country. Interest rates rose, debtors were unable to pay their creditors, and all trade declined. Biddle was not in favor of the Safety Fund principle, but the wisdom of the state's action was not his concern. He was responsible for general economic conditions, however, and he considered it the duty of the national bank to counteract the artificial pressure created by the city banks.[3]

When the pressure first developed, he could do nothing. The New York and Philadelphia offices had expanded their loans to the limit in preparation for the large payment on the government debt at the beginning of the summer, and it was not until he had made certain that the payment would be accomplished smoothly that he could turn his attention to the monetary crisis in New York. He carefully explained to the local officers and directors that the quarrel between the city banks and the state authorities was no concern of the Bank of the United States but that it was the duty of the institution to supply credit to any solvent individual or bank that had been denied it for reasons unconnected with business. The branch immediately increased its loans, publicly announcing that any individual or upstate bank deserving credit could have it; and the city banks, realizing that their plan had been thwarted, abandoned the attempt to coerce the legislature by the restriction of credit.[4]

[2] N. Biddle to M. Robinson, May 28, 1829; N. Biddle to R. Lenox, May 28, 1829, in the Biddle Manuscripts in the Library of Congress; Redlick, *Molding of American Banking*, I, 88–95.

[3] N. Biddle to A. H. Tracy, February 3, March 3, 1830, in the Biddle Manuscripts in the Library of Congress.

[4] N. Biddle to M. Robinson, May 28, 1829; J. G. Bennett to N. Biddle, April 9, 1830, in the Biddle Manuscripts in the Library of Congress.

But they continued their opposition to the Safety Fund System and for the next two years conducted an active campaign for the repeal of the law. Many of the leaders of the Van Buren party became aware of their dependence on the Bank of the United States, and some of them made indirect overtures to Biddle which seemed to indicate that if he continued to protect the upstate banks and the Safety Fund from the pressure of the city banks, the party would support the recharter. One of the sources of his information was James Gordon Bennett, the political editor of the anti-national-bank *Courier and Enquirer*, who in April, 1830, quoted one of the influential Van Buren leaders as saying that the state of monied concerns in New York and their influence on public opinion were very favorable to the United States Bank. If the Wall Street banks again created a pressure upon the country banks either by a call for specie or a curtailment of discounts and the national bank stepped in as it had before, it "would produce in the country banks and their friends a feeling favorable to the national institution, and the feeling would even find its way into Congress."[5]

Biddle used every means he properly could to encourage the Van Buren leaders in this change of opinion about the Bank of the United States. In June, 1830, he strengthened the New York office, so that it could handle the government payment on July 1 and also be ready to thwart any attempt by the city banks to renew the pressure. He also decisively denied all reports which connected Van Buren and his party with Jackson's attacks upon the Bank. "I am satisfied," he wrote, "that Mr. Van Buren was neither the instigator nor the advisor of the President's remarks on the Bank, and I believe that any agency which he may have used on that occasion was rather to discourage than to promote them." He told Walter Bowne, the Democratic mayor of New York and a former director of the Bank, that no one regretted more than he "the indiscretion of ascribing hostility to the Bank to prominent statesmen and particularly to Mr. Van Buren"; and he assured Charles A. Davis, a New York newspaperman, that Van Buren's friends had not the slightest reason to suppose that the Bank was anything but well disposed toward him.[6]

Biddle's purpose in making these conciliatory remarks was to free the question of the recharter "from all party character"; so effective were his tactics that in February, 1831, when resolutions against the recharter were prepared for introduction into the New York legislature, almost all the Van Buren leaders were opposed. Biddle had actually been more successful than he realized, and there was little need for the elaborate intervention into New York politics that he undertook. The reason for his action may well have been his unease and uncertainty concerning the operations

5 *Ibid.*

6 N. Biddle to W. Bowne, May 1, 1830; N. Biddle to C. A. Davis, May 19, 1830, in the Biddle Manuscripts in the Library of Congress.

of politics in this most complicated state, for on an earlier occasion he had written: "Every now and then I make an effort to overtake the current . . . of politics in New York and for a month think myself accomplished in that occult science, but the next tide washes away my marks in the sand and sets me afloat again."[7]

Whatever the reason for the action, he at once started a countercampaign of education and pressure. "I remember very well," he wrote the New York cashier, "that twenty years ago when I was in our legislature and resolutions against the Bank were presented and passed there, the general ignorance which prevailed in regard to the institution. . . . The errors of such a body are always the result of want of information, not of evil design, and I am sure that the legislature of New York could decide rightly if they understood the subject fully." Each of the branches was requested to select one or two persons of the Van Buren party who understood the subject of banking to go to Albany to explain "what might require explanation in regard to the Bank," and John Dun, a brother-in-law of the cashier in New York and "a personal friend of many of the leading Jackson men," as well as two prominent party leaders from Utica, accepted the assignment.[8] Biddle would have been spared many subsequent embarrassments if he had been content with these arrangements, but he wanted to leave nothing to chance, so he opened a correspondence with Silas E. Burrows, a strange and erratic merchant whom he had met a few weeks before.

Burrows had come to Philadelphia with letters of introduction from Samuel Swartwout, collector of customs in New York, and Samuel Gouverneur, the postmaster, and he had talked convincingly to Biddle of his connections and influence with the Democratic party in Washington and New York. He had been on his way to the capital to persuade Jackson and the Congress to make a special appropriation to pay the debts of President Monroe and had stopped by the Bank on his return to report the success of his mission. He had also promised to persuade the former President to write a letter defending the constitutionality and usefulness of the national bank, and these conversations had given Biddle an exaggerated opinion of Burrow's ability and influence. He wrote Burrows on February 7 to ask what could be done to prevent the passage of the resolution by the New York legislature and received an immediate reply. Burrows described all his personal problems, including a casual and offhand reference to the fact that his wife had died shortly before, and closed with the statement: "My father is in Albany and he has taken great interest in doing all his influence

[7] N. Biddle to A. H. Tracy, February 7, 1830, in the Biddle Manuscripts in the Library of Congress.

[8] N. Biddle to M. Robinson, February 7, 1831; M. Robinson to N. Biddle, February 8, 9, 1831; M. Deveraux to N. Biddle, February 12, 1831, in the Biddle Manuscripts in the Library of Congress.

could effect to benefit your institution. He says give yourself no fear. I think nothing will be done to injure the United States Bank or to give an expression as to the renewal of the charter."[9]

The tone of the letter, as well as its contents, should have aroused Biddle's suspicions concerning the responsibility of the writer, but it apparently did not. The connection was continued, and Burrows went to Albany, where he told almost everyone he met that he was there as confidential agent of the president of the Bank of the United States. He wrote long, complicated reports about his activities and assured Biddle that the leaders of the Van Buren party, frightened by the opposition that had been raised against the proposed resolution, had decided that it should not be introduced. The Bank had won a great victory, Burrows insisted, and he urged Biddle to assume the offensive. "Cannot your legislature," he wrote, "be induced to express an opinion favorable to the Bank? If so it would doubtless have great effect. The Jackson party look to Pennsylvania as the great Jackson state, and if that state expresses a warm opinion in favor of the Bank neither the President nor any State Legislature will make war upon her."[10]

Biddle sent this letter to Charles J. Ingersoll, the Democratic leader of the Philadelphia delegation at Harrisburg, and wrote: "My fear for the Bank is not from the West, the South nor the East. My greatest anxiety is from the New York politicians . . . who knowing there must be a Bank hope by a change to have it with them." He warned Ingersoll that "this is a subject on which I very seldom speak and speaking now must not be quoted" and then proceeded to point out the advantages that Pennsylvania received from having the country's monetary operations centered in Philadelphia. Biddle intended that this letter, in spite of its confidential tone, be shown to the leaders of the Pennsylvania legislature, and it also was a prearranged signal for Ingersoll to begin a long prepared political maneuver.[11]

The Pennsylvania Democrats, particularly those in Philadelphia, had been gravely disappointed by the Jackson administration and its attack on the national bank and the rest of the American System. Ingersoll and other party leaders were alarmed by the growing antitariff sentiment in both the Van Buren and the Calhoun faction of the party and by the South Carolina threats to nullify the protective tariff with which the Vice-President, though he had never publicly admitted a connection, was popularly associated. The President's veto of the subscription to the stock of the Maysville Road Company, accompanied as it was by the denunciation of all

[9] S. Burrows to N. Biddle, December 29, 1830, February 8, 13, 17, 1831; N. Biddle to S. Burrows, February 7, 1831, in the Biddle Manuscripts in the Library of Congress.

[10] S. Burrows to N. Biddle, February 17, 1831, in the Biddle Manuscripts in the Library of Congress.

[11] N. Biddle to C. J. Ingersoll, February 21, 1821, in the Biddle Manuscripts in the Library of Congress.

government support for internal improvements, had been another blow to Pennsylvania interests, and some action was needed, Ingersoll and his associates thought, to bring the party back to its true line.[12]

All who participated in these plans, including Biddle, were friends of the administration, and most were to support Jackson for re-election in 1832. But they did not approve of his policies, and it was Ingersoll's purpose to make this disapproval known. He prepared a series of resolutions to prove that the Jackson party in Pennsylvania was still loyal to the American System; the first of these committed the legislature to a repudiation of the doctrine of nullification and to an assertion that the Supreme Court was the final authority on state and national legislation. The others maintained the constitutionality and usefulness of the Bank of the United States, the constitutionality and need for internal improvements at federal expense, and the desirability of a protective tariff. At Biddle's suggestion, Ingersoll also wrote to James Madison to solicit his opinion in regard to the national bank and received a reply which not only defended the existing institution but also explicitly repudiated Jackson's proposed substitute.[13]

The resolutions were introduced into the legislature by Ingersoll on February 24, 1831, and those against nullification and for the tariff were immediately passed. The others were indefinitely postponed, even though Madison's letter was read and Ingersoll warned that the recharter of the national bank was of vital importance to Pennsylvania because "measures were in agitation in a neighboring state to cry down the present Bank in order to establish another of the same kind in the commercial emporium of the United States." He attributed the postponement of the resolution to the ignorance of the legislators and to their fear that it would injure Jackson, but he assured Biddle, "This state is perfectly safe on the Bank question." He also warned, "You must not attack Jackson nor even Van Buren, though I think nothing hits so hard here as the New York interference to supplant us."[14]

Biddle had no desire to attack Jackson or Van Buren, since he still believed that the only chance to obtain a recharter was through the support of their party. The Pennsylvania Democrats had disappointed him by their postponement of the resolution in favor of the recharter, but he had been heartened by the news that resolutions against the Bank in the Jackson party convention of Kentucky had been withdrawn by their sponsors after three delegates, all branch directors, had "vindicated" the institution.

[12] N. Biddle to C. J. Ingersoll, January 15, 19, 1831, in the Biddle Manuscripts in the Library of Congress.

[13] J. Madison to C. J. Ingersoll, February 2, 1831, in the Biddle Manuscripts in the Library of Congress.

[14] C. J. Ingersoll to N. Biddle, February 27, March 2, 1831, in the Biddle Manuscripts in the Library of Congress.

He also had hopes that the Pennsylvania legislature might be persuaded to reverse its earlier action, and he sent John Norvell, a Philadelphia newspaperman, to Harrisburg to estimate the chances. Norvell's reports were optimistic, and he predicted that the resolution would be passed by a large majority before the end of the session. No one, he wrote, had the least idea why he was there: "They think I came merely to look about me. They have been encouraged in this idea. I have been very hospitable to a number of them, inviting them to dine with me, and in two or three instances, lending five, ten, and twenty dollars to them, which I shall probably never get back. Your hundred dollars are pretty well exhausted."[15]

Ingersoll continued to work on his fellow party members, and at his suggestion Biddle paid particular attention to two Philadelphians: Henry Gilpin, a young lawyer who had recently removed to Philadelphia from Delaware, and Joel Sutherland, a member of Congress and the leader of the Calhoun faction in the city. He invited Gilpin to dinner with a number of senators and representatives who were passing through Philadelphia. The flattery was effective, and a few days later Gilpin reported to his father: "I enclose you the Sentinel, in which there is an article of mine on the Bank of the United States. I have been indirectly applied to from that institution to say what I can in favor of it in the Democratic papers." Biddle used other methods on Sutherland, who had returned from Washington after the adjournment of Congress "full of disaffection to Jackson" because of the public break between the President and Calhoun. He pointed out to Sutherland that Van Buren and Jackson were both opposed to the entire American System, which was overwhelmingly popular in Pennsylvania, and that the Calhoun faction could retain its power and influence in the state and nation only by continuing its support of the protective tariff, internal improvements, and the national bank.[16]

Sutherland had been using these same arguments in his efforts to persuade Calhoun to break with his South Carolina supporters. So he welcomed this opportunity to contribute to the embarrassment of Jackson by committing the Democratic party in Pennsylvania to support of the Bank and to bring pressure upon Calhoun to keep him loyal to the nationalistic principles he had previously avowed. Upon his advice, sponsorship of the resolution indorsing the Bank was turned over to Dr. Burden, leader of the Philadelphia delegation, and this arrangement proved decisive. Burden earlier had opposed the original resolution, but Ingersoll had predicted that his hostility could "be muzzled" through the influence of Sutherland,

15 N. Biddle to M. Robinson, March, 3, 1831; J. Norvell to N. Biddle, March 11, 1831, in the Biddle Manuscripts in the Library of Congress.

16 N. Biddle to C. J. Ingersoll, March 1, 2, 3, 5, 6, 1831; C. J. Ingersoll to N. Biddle, March 2, 1831, in the Biddle Manuscripts in the Library of Congress; H. Gilpin to J. Gilpin March 10, 15, 1831, in the Gilpin Manuscripts in the Historical Society of Pennsylvania.

and on March 14 he introduced a new resolution which recommended the recharter of the Bank of the United States "under such regulations and restrictions as to the power of the respective states as Congress may deem right and proper."[17]

The next day it passed the Senate unanimously and, Ingersoll reported, would have passed as quickly through the lower house if what he called an animal, "who is the greatest miscreant here except the tool [Burden?] we have at work," had not added a number of complicating amendments. This action forced the Bank's supporters to recommit the resolution to the Judiciary Committee, which rejected the amendments, and on March 16 the resolution was passed by a vote of seventy-five to eleven.[18] This expression of "a warm opinion in favor of the Bank" by the Democratic-controlled legislature of Pennsylvania did not have the effect expected by Burrows and Biddle. They thought it would frighten the politicians loyal to Jackson and that no state legislature, particularly that of New York, would continue to make war on the national bank, once "the great Jackson state" had spoken. This might have been the result if the attack on the Bank in New York had been instigated by Van Buren or the leaders of his party. Their desire was his advancement to the presidency and their aim the conciliation of as many factions and interests as possible. But their wishes were not controlling, and, though they joined with Biddle in the effort to prevent the introduction of a resolution opposing the recharter, the enemies of the Bank overpowered them.

Three of the most powerful persons in New York politics were responsible for the attack upon the Bank of the United States: Edwin Croswell, editor of the *Albany Argus* and state printer; Thomas W. Olcott, cashier of the Farmers' and Mechanics' Bank of Albany; and Benjamin Knower, principal stockholder in this bank and father-in-law of William Marcy, United States senator from New York. These men had once been accused by William Leggett, editor of the anti-Bank *Evening Post* of New York, of profiting from "the unclean drippings of venal legislation" and had been denounced as "stockjobbers" by James Gordon Bennett, who was also opposed to the recharter of the national bank. Olcott was described by one of Biddle's correspondents as not having "a spotless character if we regard the moral code as a standard of purity" and was considered to be

---

[17] C. J. Ingersoll to N. Biddle, March 17, 1831, in the Biddle Manuscripts in the Library of Congress; *Niles' Register*, XL (1831), 69–70, 73. Burden's reversal and the votes of other members of the Jackson party in favor of the Bank led to charges of "wholesale bribery" in the *New Hampshire Patriot*. Ingersoll and fourteen other Jacksonians pronounced this statement, "no matter by whom made, by whom repeated, or by whom countenanced, to be an unfounded and atrocious libel" (*Niles' Register*, XL [1831], 224).

[18] C. J. Ingersoll to N. Biddle, March 17, 1831, in the Biddle Manuscripts in the Library of Congress.

"the head and front of the opposition to the United States Bank" in New York.

His bank, which was the chief depository of state funds, had paid a dividend of 50 per cent to its stockholders in 1829, and his great influence in state politics had been achieved, it was charged, "by allowing certain persons peculiar advantages in the institution." It had become the central institution in a chain of upstate banks that controlled most of the business in the area, and Olcott, Croswell, and Knower apparently exercised a dominant influence in the selection of the bank commissioners and in the formulation of policies in regard to the administration of the Safety Fund. They also had acquired a substantial interest in banks and other financial institutions in New York City, and it was thought by many persons that their ultimate aim was the domination of all banks in the state and the nation.[19]

Biddle shared this belief. He told Ingersoll that these men were seeking to destroy the Bank "because they know that if the charter is not renewed, after the confusion of a year a new bank will be formed and then it must go, where trade and population are most concentered, to New York."[20] But the public lead in the attack upon the Bank was taken not by these principals but by an agent, Lott Clark, an experienced lobbyist, who was in Albany from the beginning of the session, "bringing the whole force of his clever management to bear upon this question." None of the official Van Buren leaders co-operated with him, and on March 7, eleven days before the Pennsylvania legislature gave its indorsement to the national bank, he turned to an obscure member from Oswego named Morehouse and persuaded him to introduce a resolution against the recharter.[21]

Biddle immediately requested the men who had gone to Albany for the Bank in February to return, and he sought to reinforce them with Saul Alley, a New York director, whose "general reputation," "known political sentiments," and "frank and fearless temper" would enable him "to explain how entirely unconnected with politics the Bank is." Once again he would have been wiser to take no other steps, but he was still under the illusion that Burrows exercised a mysterious power within the Jackson party, so he solicited his aid. Burrows replied at once, "I leave tomorrow for your city. Everything is arranged as you wish it to be." He had earlier written

[19] C. L. Livingston to S. E. Burrows, March 12, 1831; N. Biddle to M. Robinson, March 18, 1831; J. D. Bloodgood to N. Biddle, April 18, 1831, in the Biddle Manuscripts in the Library of Congress; James Mackaye, Manuscript Autobiography, p. 19, in the Mackaye Manuscripts in the Library of Congress; J. G. Bennett to J. Hoyt, August 16, 1832, in William L. Mackenzie, *Life and Times of Martin Van Buren* (Boston, 1846), p. 235; *Courier and Enquirer* (New York), January 7, 25, 1832.

[20] N. Biddle to C. J. Ingersoll, February 21, 1831, in the Biddle Manuscripts in the Library of Congress.

[21] N. Biddle to M. Robinson, March 3, 18, 1831; J. D. Bloodgood to N. Biddle, April 18, 1831, in the Biddle Manuscripts in the Library of Congress.

that "some of the leading party papers in this state *must* be the friends of the Bank. It can easily be affected but must only be talked of. I will take care of this." He explained upon this arrival in Philadelphia that the paper he referred to was the *Courier and Enquirer*, the official New York City organ of the Van Buren party. Daniel E. Tylee, cashier of the Savings Bank of New York and half-owner of the newspaper, had decided to sell his interest, and Burrows assured Biddle that if he would lend Mordecai M. Noah, one of the editors, fifteen thousand dollars to be repaid over the course of six years, Noah would buy Tylee's interest, and the newspaper would change its editorial policy toward the Bank and the recharter.[22]

Such a loan could be made by the Bank at this particular moment. The directors had authorized the exchange committee to take the proceeds of the Bank's holdings of government loans as they were repaid and to invest them in long-term loans to individuals and corporations for capital expansion. No need existed for additional commercial credit, and the directors, under Biddle's guidance, were seeking ways to prevent the government's retirement of its permanent debt from becoming a stimulant to speculation in stocks, commodities, and land. The loan to Noah was exactly the sort of investment the Bank was seeking; but Biddle knew that if he took it to the exchange committee and it was granted and then the paper came out in defense of the Bank, the two facts would be considered to be related and the members of the committee would talk. Biddle also knew, or rather thought he knew, that Noah was the kind of person who demanded this sort of inducement. He had accepted an appointment by Jackson as surveyor of the Port of New York while employed as an editor of a paper supporting the administration, and neither he nor the President had thought such dual employment improper. And then in December, 1829, when the paper had begun its editorial attacks upon the Bank, Alexander Hamilton had written Biddle that Noah was "decidedly hostile and might with a little attention be made as friendly." Five months later Hamilton had returned to the same subject: "I send you the Courier and Enquirer . . . containing a hostile editorial with a marginal note of authorship to which I may add Noah will not write again in opposition."[23]

Biddle also had a strange relationship with James Gordon Bennett, the political editor of the *Courier and Enquirer*, who had written most of the editorial attacks upon the Bank. Bennett, according to his own statement, was an avowed enemy of all banks, but throughout the early years of the Jackson administration he had sent Biddle confidential information concerning the policies and plans of the Van Buren leaders in New York. The

---

22 S. Burrows to N. Biddle, March 7, 8, 1831, in the Biddle Manuscripts in the Library of Congress.

23 A. Hamilton to N. Biddle, December 1, 1829, April 9, 1830, in the Biddle Manuscripts in the Library of Congress.

connection had been sought by Bennett, and it seems certain that he was paid for each letter.[24] Biddle did not know J. Watson Webb, managing editor and co-owner with Tylee of the newspaper, but he had been told by Burrows and others that Webb, though personally in favor of the recharter, had permitted the paper to assume the opposite position in order to keep the political advertising and patronage provided by the Van Buren party. For all these reasons, Biddle was willing to believe almost anything told him about the *Courier and Enquirer* and its editors and owners. He gave Burrows fifteen thousand dollars from his personal funds, and it was not until January 2, 1832, that he turned Noah's notes over to the head of the exchange committee for entry on the books of the Bank. No other loan was ever handled in such an irregular manner, and that its purpose was to procure a change in the editorial position of the paper was made evident by a letter of Burrows in late March: "I send the Enquirer of this morning in which you will see its swinging pivot falling under the lee of old Pennsylvania."[25]

Neither Biddle nor Burrows made a record of their conversation in regard to this loan or referred to it in their subsequent correspondence, but it is virtually certain that Burrows, for personal reasons, gave Biddle false information and that the actual situation was quite different from the one he described. The decision to change the editorial position of the *Courier and Enquirer* in regard to the Bank was made by Webb and Noah without knowledge of the arrangement between Biddle and Burrows, and it was to be almost a year before either of the editors learned that Noah's notes, indorsed by Webb, were in the possession of the Bank. They had approached Burrows, whom they knew as a prosperous merchant and a loyal member of the Jackson party, and had asked him to lend Noah the fifteen thousand dollars. Burrows had told them that he did not have the money but that he would obtain it from his father, Enoch Burrows of Connecticut, if Noah would agree to pay a commission of $2\frac{1}{2}$ per cent in addition to interest and Webb would indorse the notes. They had accepted these terms. Noah had given Burrows ten notes of fifteen hundred dollars, indorsed by Webb and payable at six-month intervals beginning on April 1, 1832, and had received in return the note of Enoch Burrows, which was discounted at a local bank.[26]

[24] This correspondence began in the spring of 1829 and continued until 1833. It is to be found in the Biddle Manuscripts in the Library of Congress. Evidence of Bennett's desire to find out what New York politicians were thinking about the Bank of the United States is to be found in his manuscript diary in the Bennett Manuscripts in the New York Public Library.

[25] S. Brrows to N. Biddle, March 22, 1831, in the Biddle Manuscripts in the Library of Congress; N. Biddle, Testimony before the Clayton Committee, in *House Report* (22d Cong., 1st sess.), No. 460, pp. 84–93.

[26] J. W. Webb to C. C. Cambreleng, March 19, 1832; Testimony of J. W. Webb before the Clayton Committee, in *House Report* (22d Cong., 1st sess.), No. 460, pp. 75–77, 77–83.

This was all that Noah and Webb knew, and from their point of view the loan was a legitimate business transaction. Silas Burrows had been paid three hundred and seventy-five dollars to raise the money, and his father had made a profitable investment secured by the signatures of the owners of a prosperous newspaper. No commitment had been asked or given in regard to the Bank or any other political question, and Biddle's name or that of the Bank of the United States was never mentioned in regard to the transaction. Webb knew, however, that Burrows was an enthusiastic advocate of the recharter, and he talked freely to him, as he did to others, of his belief that Jackson was injuring himself and Van Buren by his attacks upon the national bank. Webb was not alone in this view. Many of the Van Buren leaders in the city and state had come to the same opinion during the previous year, and it was with their consent and approval that Webb had decided to take the course that he subsequently did. This consent and approval were necessary because the *Courier and Enquirer* was not a free agent. In June, 1829, when Webb and Tylee had purchased the Van Buren party's semiofficial *State Enquirer* and merged it with the *Courier,* they had been required to "give up its columns to a political editor appointed by the General Committee" as the price for retaining the political advertising and patronage.[27]

Bennett had been named to his post by the committee, and it was he, not Webb, who had decided in December, 1829, to take the lead in opposing the recharter of the Bank as part of his assigned task of taking "care of the interests of the party and its friends."[28] This arrangement remained unchanged after Noah purchased Tylee's interest, though Bennett, with his own consent, was given a new and better-paid post, and the *Courier and Enquirer* continued to be given its share of the patronage and advertising for more than a year after Webb, on April 1, 1831, came out with an editorial advocating a recharter of the national bank with sufficient modifications to meet President Jackson's objections.[29] Biddle, however, believed that this change had been accomplished by his arrangement with Burrows, and all the subsequent difficulties of the Bank in relation to this newspaper were the result of this erroneous belief, which had been created and fostered by Burrows.

The actual decision to change the editorial position of this official Van Buren paper arose out of a conflict between the political leaders of the party and Olcott, Knower, and Croswell over the Morehouse resolution against the recharter of the Bank. Charles Livingston, Speaker of the Assembly; John C. Spencer, who in 1819 had been chairman of the investi-

27 J. G. Bennett to J. Hoyt, June 7, 11, July 20, 1829, in McKenzie, *Van Buren,* pp. 221–22.

28 J. G. Bennett, signed editorial statement, *Courier and Enquirer* (New York), February 2, 1832.

29 *Ibid.,* April 1, 1831.

gating committee of the Bank of the United States; Senator Marcy; and other influential party leaders agreed with Webb that it would be harmful to Jackson's cause and to that of Van Buren to permit the New York and Pennsylvania legislatures to adopt opposing resolutions in regard to the recharter; and they began a quiet effort to prevent the Morehouse resolution from reaching the floor. Webb was particularly bitter against the Albany triumvirate, who, though they "saw the objections politically to doing so," were bringing the two great Jackson states into opposition from "interested motives" of their own. Their purpose, he believed, was to complete their control of all the state banks by the elimination of the one institution which had the power and will to thwart their plans, and if they succeeded, he predicted, nothing could prevent them "from controlling the politics of the state."[30]

The officers and directors of the New York branches, regardless of their party affiliations, shared Webb's fears in regard to Olcott, Knower, and Croswell, and a number of them joined with him and the other Van Buren leaders to persuade the Assembly to permit the Morehouse resolution to remain in the hands of the committee to which it had been assigned. Their efforts were unavailing, and Speaker Livingston, realizing that a vote was inevitable, told Burrows that he would seek to amend the resolution to read that the existing Bank "with all its present powers" should not be re-chartered. But he also warned that if this move failed, Burrows was "not to be surprised" by the adoption of the original resolution "nor at the vote I may give," and never was there a truer statement. For when the resolution was brought before the lower house on April 6 and the Speaker took the floor to propose his amendment, he voted against a motion to postpone the whole subject indefinitely. Much to his surprise and to that of other observers, the house divided equally, fifty-five to fifty-five, on the motion to postpone, and then Livingston, from the chair, cast the deciding vote to keep the question alive.[31]

Those opposed to the national bank were astonished by this vote on the motion to postpone, and they brought pressure "to drive and compel all Jackson men to join against the Bank" by appealing to the known sentiments of the President. They ignored all the Bank's supporters who were members of the Jackson party and cited the known affiliation of William Rochester and Nicholas Devereaux, presidents of the branches in Buffalo and Utica, with the leaders of the Clay and Anti-Masonic parties, as evidence that the Bank was supporting Jackson's opponents. Webb's editorial advocating the recharter was attributed to a bribe by the Bank, which was also accused of attempting to seduce other editors by reportedly offering

[30] J. W. Webb, Testimony before the Clayton Committee in *House Report* (22d Cong., 1st sess.), No. 460, pp. 77–83.

[31] S. Burrows to N. Biddle, April 6, 7, 1831; N. Biddle to G. C. Verplanck, April 12, 1831, in the Biddle Manuscripts in the Library of Congress.

one a loan of one thousand dollars and promising to provide another with fifty daily subscribers at forty dollars a year. The pressure had its effect, and, though Livingston, Spencer, and many other Jacksonians joined the Anti-Masonic and Clay members in fighting against it, the resolution in its original form passed the Assembly and the Senate on April 11 by a vote of seventy-three to thirty-five in the first and of seventeen to thirteen in the second.[32]

The same day John Mumford, editor of the *New York Standard*, accused Burrows of offering a loan of five hundred dollars from the Bank if Mumford would come out in favor of the recharter. No one who knew Mumford believed the charge. William Beach Lawrence told Biddle that the declaration that "he had refused an offer of money is calculated to throw an air of ridicule over the accusation"; and Alexander Hamilton wrote: "All those friendly to the existence of a general bank feel confident that the whole statement will turn out to be a complete misrepresentation." But Burrows in his letters to Biddle virtually admitted the truth. He accused Mumford of being "a drunken editor" who had been convicted of indecent exposure and at first said that the request for money had come from him but had been refused. The second letter changed the story: "I have done nothing more," he wrote, "than in order to protect my personal property which is to a large amount invested in this Bank offered to make a loan for one year to the extent of $500 if a good endorser could be given to me and remarked that I should not suppose the editor would continue his hostility to the United States Bank."[33]

Biddle, when he received these letters, suddenly realized what a great mistake he had made in enlisting Burrows in his cause. Gulian C. Verplanck, one of the ablest Democratic members of Congress from New York, informed him that Burrows was a wholly unsafe adviser or agent, and Biddle's own experience gave ample confirmation. Verplanck also asked Biddle for authority to contradict these charges of newspaper bribery and said: "I cannot believe that the Bank as a public institution has done anything to give countenance or probability to these reports, whatever may have been done or said by those interested in its stock or who now speculate in it." Biddle immediately gave the requested assurances, telling Verplanck: "If any such propositions . . . were ever made, they were certainly made without the authority, approbation, or wish of any

[32] *Niles' Register*, XL (1831), 114.

[33] *New York Standard*, April 11, 1831; A. Hamilton to N. Biddle, April 13, 1831; W. B. Lawrence to N. Biddle, April 16, 1831; S. Burrows to N. Biddle, April 11, 12, 1831, in the Biddle Manuscripts in the Library of Congress. For Mumford's relations with the Van Buren party see J. G. Bennett to J. Hoyt, June 11 (1833), in William L. Mackenzie, *The Lives and Opinions of Benjamin F. Butler and Jesse Hoyt* (Boston, 1845), p. 93. Bennett here says that the party had aided Mumford "to the extent of $40,000" and that he was sorry to believe that they were more willing to support "a drunken fellow than me."

one connected with the institution."[34] This statement was factually accurate. Neither the Bank nor anyone connected with it had authorized Burrows to aproach editors with such proposals, but Biddle, by soliciting his aid and by participating in the loan to Noah and Webb, had a personal responsibility for all his actions. He could not make this admission, however, for to do so would have injured the institution. The welfare of the stockholders, whose interests he was employed to protect, and of the national economy, which he believed to be dependent upon the continuance of the Bank, were more important to him than the literal and complete truth.

He tried to get a statement from Burrows denying any connection between his actions and the Bank of the United States, and the letter was carefully phrased to avoid wounding the sensibilities of this temperamental person. It began with the statement that the results at Albany were not what they had desired but that Biddle was certain that this unfortunate outcome had proceeded "from no deficiency of kind and disinterested exertions" by Burrows. It then said that Biddle had read certain statements in the *Standard* connecting the Bank with an effort by Burrows to buy support from newspapers and that, though "this story" was so improbable that it must defeat itself, it might be well for Burrows to write and say that "although you yourself are indifferent to the allegations of this writer, yet, lest your silence might be construed into an acquiescence in his statement, you think it right to say that you have never received any authority or request from anyone connected with the Bank to influence by pecuniary or other means the course of any newspaper in New York or elsewhere, and that your efforts to prevent the passage of the resolutions at Albany were altogether your own voluntary exertions growing out of your views of the utility of the Bank to the country."[35]

But the damage had already been done, and no statement from Burrows could repair it. Confused by the complexities of New York politics, Biddle had used the wrong agent, and the Bank's opponents, who before had no evidence to back their charges of political interference, could now point to the accusations of bribery of newspapers and of their apparent confirmation by the change in editorial opinion of one of the leading Jackson newspapers. None of these matters had anything to do with the issue of whether the Bank of the United States should be rechartered or whether it was a useful and necessary institution, but they strengthened the position of those opposed to the recharter by seeming to confirm the fears and suspicions of the ordinary citizen, who understood neither the purposes nor the functions of the national bank.

[34] G. C. Verplanck to N. Biddle, April 18, 1831; N. Biddle to G. C. Verplanck, April 21, 1831, in the Biddle Manuscripts in the Library of Congress.

[35] N. Biddle to S. Burrows, April 14, 1831, in the Biddle Manuscripts in the Library of Congress.

17

The Reorganization

of

Jackson's Cabinet

*T*he reorganization of the President's Cabinet, which began shortly after the passage of the resolution against the recharter by the New York legislature, distracted attention from the subject of bribery of newspapers, but Biddle's difficulties with Burrows had scarcely begun. The requested disavowal was not forthcoming, and the reason became apparent in early May, when Biddle received an incoherent letter of six pages from Burrows which closed with an application for two hundred thousand dollars in India bills, drawn by the Bank of the United States on Baring Brothers and Company of London, for a commercial operation in the Far East. Biddle worded his answer most carefully and told Burrows that the application was the largest the Bank had ever received, that the security offered—the hypothecation of the goods to be purchased—was insufficient, and that the Bank's rules required the application to be submitted in the city in which the applicant lived.[1]

He sent a copy of this letter to the cashier in New York, warning him that the amount was very large and that "the manner in which Mr. B's name has been connected with the Bank would render it specially proper not to depart from our ordinary practice."[2] The New York directors refused to issue the bills, whereupon Burrows wrote to Biddle: "The ne plus ultra has arrived I cannot neither shall I go further. I owe something yet to my own character and my little children, which shall be protected. I am

[1] S. Burrows to N. Biddle, April 16, 1831; N. Biddle to S. Burrows, May 4, 1831, in the Biddle Manuscripts in the Library of Congress.

[2] N. Biddle to M. Robinson, May 5, 1831, in the Biddle Manuscripts in the Library of Congress.

not the author of any result which may take place. . . . For being your friend and agent, confidential agent, I have been grossly insulted." The next day his mood had changed, and he wrote an extravagant letter of apology, stating that he had given up his plans for the voyage to the Far East and was retiring from business. He did not write again until July 2, when he told Biddle of the approaching death of Monroe and inclosed a bill of lading for a box "containing a choice specimen of Canova's chisel," which Biddle was instructed to present to his "good lady and say to her it is from a sincere friend whose heart is allways right, if his head sometimes errs."[3]

Monroe's death on July 4, five years after that of Jefferson and Adams, was another occasion for nation-wide mourning. Burrows and General Winfield Scott were requested by the family to take charge of the arrangements for the public funeral, and Burrows' pleasure over this recognition of his connection with the former President diverted his attention from his personal troubles. His letters to Biddle were few and well balanced, and early in August he came to Philadelphia for a visit. The Bank had just received an application from Webb and Noah for a twenty thousand dollar loan to the *Courier and Enquirer*, and Biddle thought that Burrows had called in order to second this application. He asked him questions about the financial responsibility of the editors, but Burrows' replies indicated that he knew nothing about the application for a loan. Biddle then requested him to keep the matter confidential, and nothing more was heard about it until November, when Webb wrote to protest against Burrows having been told of the loan. He also warned Biddle that Burrows was telling everyone whom he talked to that he was "an authorized political agent of the Bank of the United States and a confidential consultant of its president."[4]

Biddle replied that "this agency and these confidential consultations about the affairs of the Bank, if they exist, are wholly unknown to me." He apologized for his indiscretion and explained that on this occasion he had broken his rule against speaking of one person's financial affairs to another only because he had believed Burrows to be a confidential friend of Webb, interested in the granting of the loan and able to give information which would aid in the securing of it. "The thing has however passed," he added, "and it would be better not to mention it to him, as it would only mortify the feelings of a very good, tho very incautious person."[5] The real reason why Biddle did not want Webb to speak to Bur-

[3] S. Burrows to N. Biddle, May 26, 27, July 2, 1831, in the Biddle Manuscripts in the Library of Congress.

[4] S. Burrows to N. Biddle, July 5, 14, 1831; N. Biddle to J. W. Webb, November 13, 1831; J. W. Webb to N. Biddle, November 17, 1831, in the Biddle Manuscripts in the Library of Congress.

[5] N. Biddle to J. W. Webb, November 13, 1831, in the Biddle Manuscripts in the Library of Congress.

rows about these matters was not concern for Burrows' feelings but rather his own fear of what such an erratic person might do if he became angry at what he could rightly consider an untruthful repudiation.

This caution proved wise, for within a few days Burrows became exceedingly angry at Biddle about other matters. He came to the conclusion that some recommendations he had made of persons to be placed on the board of directors were to be disregarded and that his own nomination to the New York board would be refused. In addition, at about the same time, another application of his for a loan was rejected. He immediately wrote a long and abusive letter which accused Biddle of turning on his friends and fawning on his enemies. He said that he had become poor as the result of his exertions for the Bank and inclosed a statement of account with the Bank of the United States, listing seventeen thousand one hundred dollars that he had expended "by direction of the president at sundry times." Included on this list was the fifteen thousand dollars that had been loaned to Noah to purchase the *Courier and Enquirer,* one thousand dollars that Biddle had advanced him for his political expenses, and eleven hundred dollars which Burrows said he had expended from his personal funds.[6]

Biddle was unwilling to reimburse Burrows for these unauthorized expenses, but he had to be patient and conciliatory. "Indeed my good sir," he wrote, "you put the patience of your friends to a severe trial. . . . So far from sacrificing any interest of yours, the gentlemen who were about to be nominated as directors were with only a single exception all the very persons whom you yourself especially named and recommended, and you would have been satisfied it was better not to go into the local board for the present year, but rather be appointed a government director a place that would do you far more good as a merchant." He even used Burrows' affection for Mrs. Biddle in his appeal and closed with an invitation to dine at four on Tuesday, when he would have an opportunity to "visit that fair and accomplished lady."[7] But Burrows was not to be appeased. He angrily declined the invitation and with great indignation elaborated upon another grievance, namely, that Biddle had been in New York the week before and had not called on him.

"When I found you in the city by report (I could not from our intimacy as a gentleman know you were here)," he said, "and finding by hearsay that you knew everything in relation to my insults, and knowing refused to act, I at once placed myself beyond your power and this damn noble monied monster here, sacrificed five thousand dollars of my property and now enjoy myself far more . . . than to accept any favors from that

6 S. Burrows to N. Biddle, November 19, 25, 1831, in the Biddle Manuscripts in the Library of Congress.

7 N. Biddle to S. Burrows, November 27, 1831, in the Biddle Manuscripts in the Library of Congress.

cold ungrateful heart that never yet complied with a solitary request of mine." In another letter he warned Biddle that he could make a fortune by telling all that he knew about the Bank but assured him that he would not. He claimed great credit for this decision, writing: "If I stood dependent on you in the same way . . . I tremble for the result. The task you assigned me, the nature of the errand, the risque naturally attendant on its execution, and the triumphant result should (instead of a proposition to damn my honor forever) have received from you at least a tribute of approbation. But no, you appear to feel nothing, but what is governed by the sordid influence of monied considerations, and your heart I fear is callous to the motives that now govern my conduct."[8]

The insults did not matter. Biddle, by accepting humiliation, had gotten from Burrows the pledge of secrecy he needed; for, had this story been given to the Jackson newspapers, the results would have been disastrous for the Bank and the recharter. This possibility had been ever present throughout the whole of the correspondence, and Biddle thought that his sacrifice of personal dignity and pride was worthwhile, since during the same period it had come to appear as if the Bank would be rechartered with the support of the Jackson administration itself. The greatest enhancement of the Bank's prospects stemmed from the reorganization of the Cabinet, which had been occasioned by the personal and political break between Jackson and Calhoun. The reason given for the reorganization was the refusal of the wives and daughters of the other Cabinet members to call on Mrs. John Eaton, the wife of the Secretary of War, and it had been precipitated by Van Buren's decision to resign as Secretary of State. Jackson had then requested the resignations of the other members with the exception of Barry, the Postmaster-General, and Biddle was pleased with the change. "In regard to politics and politicians," he wrote on May 4, 1831, "the explosion . . . has given a new aspect to the state of things. I consider it a fortunate change for the Bank by the substitution of an avowed friend Mr. Livingston, for a decided enemy in Mr. Van Buren. The new Secretary of the Treasury is also a known friend and generally speaking the occurrence I consider fortunate."[9]

Jackson's intention, however, had been to strengthen the opposition to the Bank within the administration, and he had told one prospective Cabinet member: "The corrupting influence of the Bank upon the morals of the people and upon Congress are to be met and fearlessly met. . . . Many who you would not have supposed has secretly enlisted in its ranks, and between bank men, nulifyers, and internal improvement men it is hard to get a cabinet who will unite with me heart and soul in the great task of

[8] S. Burrows to N. Biddle, November 28, December 2, 1831, in the Biddle Manuscripts in the Library of Congress.

[9] N. Biddle to J. Hunter, May 4, 1831, in the Biddle Manuscripts in the Library of Congress.

democratic reform." He attributed the difficulties with the previous Cabinet to "the intrigues of Duff Green, Calhoun and Company, aided by all the corrupting influences of the United States Bank," but he did not question any of the new members concerning their views in regard to the Bank.[10] Jackson could hardly have meant to appoint men to office who had been corrupted by the Bank of the United States, but if he meant what he said about the corrupting influence it exercised, this is exactly what he did. The new Cabinet was almost unanimously in favor of the recharter of the Bank. Edward Livingston of Louisiana and Louis McLane of Delaware, who were selected to head the State and Treasury departments, had long been recognized as enthusiastic supporters of the national bank; and Lewis Cass of Michigan, the Secretary of War, Levi Woodbury of New Hampshire, the Secretary of the Navy, and Barry, the only member to be held over, were well disposed toward the institution and generally favorable to its recharter. Roger B. Taney of Maryland, the Attorney-General, was publicly uncommitted, but he was a close friend and political associate of Samuel Smith, Robert Oliver, and other supporters of the Bank in Baltimore, and Biddle believed that Taney would listen to them.[11]

Most of the public was unaware of this support for the recharter within the administration, since the Cabinet members and the party leaders in Congress were loath to oppose the President publicly on an issue about which he had spoken so openly. It was only those Democrats who shared Jackson's views that expressed themselves with respect to the recharter, and the constant attacks on the Bank by them and a large segment of the administration press created the impression that the party was almost unanimously opposed to the recharter. Some of the Bank's officers became convinced that they should join the opposition, among whom were Enoch Parsons, the president of the office at Hartford, Connecticut, who told Biddle that, since the Bank was now so seriously menaced, he questioned the expediency of continuing the policy of neutrality and forbearance in political affairs. Biddle's reply was quick and firm: "I should lament deeply that those connected with the Bank should be active or zealous or conspicuous in political contests. This would be wrong in itself, it is a violation of the perfect neutrality which is the first duty of the Bank. It would be injudicious too, even on calculation, since no advantage to be derived from their efforts would overbalance the general evil from their actual or supposed interference."[12]

[10] A. Jackson to H. L. White, April 29, 1831; A. Jackson to J. Coffee, May 26, 1831, in Bassett (ed.), *Correspondence of Jackson*, IV, 272, 285.

[11] R. Colt to N. Biddle, October 3, 1831, in the Biddle Manuscripts in the Library of Congress. "Mr. O," Colt wrote, "had a conversation with Mr. T on the subject of the Bank. Mr. T says he is in favor of the Bank and the charter must be renewed but with some modifications."

[12] E. Parsons to N. Biddle, February 25, 1831; N. Biddle to E. Parsons, February 28, 1831, in the Biddle Manuscripts in the Library of Congress.

He reprimanded Dr. Joseph Johnson, the president in Charleston, for his active support of Jackson in opposition to Calhoun and the nullifiers and also cautioned William Rochester, president of the Buffalo, New York, branch, who had been named to an opposition party office without his consent. To Johnson he wrote: "The officers of the Bank are still citizens, retaining all their privileges of free thought and free action, nor would the directors presume to control the political opinions of the humblest individual in their service. Yet it is not an unreasonable expectation that they who voluntarily engage in the employment of the institution should conform to its essential policy. . . . The board of directors are therefore extremely unwilling that the officers of the Bank should be zealous or conspicuous at elections." His letter to Rochester, who was planning a trip to the East, was less sharp but equally explicit and said: "The purpose of this note is to suggest that while you will not of course suppress or qualify any opinions which you entertain about men or measures, you will avoid being prominent or conspicuous in politics, or giving any fair ground for supposing that your journey has any other motive than the real one, the benefit of your health."[13]

James Harper, the cashier at Lexington, knew Biddle's rule and its purpose, but even he could not convince Henry Clay that the Bank was not actively opposed to Jackson and his party. He transmitted a request for a contribution to the opposition party in Kentucky which Clay himself seconded. "I know your abstinence from politics," Clay wrote, "still it cannot be unacceptable to you to be informed that *unless we are overpowered by a free use of public money by the Jackson party in the canvass*, we shall I think certainly beat them in this state." Biddle made no reply to Clay, but to Harper he said that he was not ignorant of those who were friends of the Bank or indifferent to their prosperity, but his duty was to the institution, and he believed that its success and usefulness depended on its total abstention from all political controversies and campaigns. "I am the more anxious in regard to this matter," he added, "because on the subject of the branches in Kentucky there exists a most jealous and morbid sensibility. This we believe to be unjust and unfounded, but the knowledge of the fact should make us avoid everything which might afford the slightest countenance to these suspicions."[14]

Biddle had good reason for his caution. In December, 1830, a new administration paper, the *Globe*, had been established in Washington under the editorship of Francis Preston Blair, a former member of the anti-Bank

[13] N. Biddle to J. Johnson, September 27, 1830, in *Niles' Register*, XLI (1832), 478; N. Biddle to W. B. Rochester, June 15, 1831, in the Biddle Manuscripts in the Library of Congress.

[14] L. Combs to N. Biddle, March 9, 1831; J. Harper to N. Biddle, April 22, 1831; H. Clay to N. Biddle, May 10, 1831; N. Biddle to J. Harper, May 10, 1831, in the Biddle Manuscripts in the Library of Congress.

Relief party in Kentucky. Blair's appointment to this position, which had been recommended by Kendall, strengthened the hand of the group around Jackson who were against the recharter, for he was as suspicious of the Bank and its power as the President himself was. "I have always been opposed to the Bank of the United States," Blair wrote shortly after his arrival in Washington. "It is now doing what for many years I predicted it would do, set up to make presidents for the people. It will lend all its influence and spend a million by way of loans to induce the people to crush Old Hickory. It is corrupting the press all over the Union. But sir it cannot corrupt a whole people, if we appeal to the democracy of the nation and not to the aristocracy we shall triumph over this privileged order."[15]

It was not his strong views on this question, however, that had dictated his selection for the post. Duff Green, whose *United States Telegraph* had been the party organ before the *Globe*, had never been derelict in his attacks upon the Bank, once Jackson had come out against it. Green's fault was his loyalty to Calhoun, and the break between the President and the Vice-President was the sole reason for the establishment of the *Globe*. But, as a Kentuckian, Blair had many sources of information within the state, and he soon picked up rumors concerning the negotiations between the Clay party and Biddle. In a bitter editorial he charged the Bank with current political corruption and sustained his contention by the statement that in an 1825 campaign between the Old Court and New Court parties the two Kentucky branches had resorted to widespread bribery of voters. He also revived the earlier refuted charge that the Lexington directors had discriminated between applicants for loans in an effort to influence voters.[16]

Biddle usually ignored such editorial assaults upon the Bank, but Blair's was sufficiently detailed to permit an effective answer. The officers and directors who had served in 1825 published a formal denial of his allegations about the election in that year, and Walter Dun and Ben Taylor, directors in Lexington and members of the Jackson party, once again stated that "men of both political parties, who from solvency and punctuality, were worthy of credit, have been liberally accommodated by loans from the Bank without the smallest regard being paid to their political opinions."[17] But the most decisive refutation of Blair's charges concerning the election of 1825 was made by Warden Pope, a leader of the Jackson party

15 F. P. Blair to ——, May 10, 1831, in the Woodbury Manuscripts in the Library of Congress; Parton, *Jackson*, III, 333–39; William E. Smith, *The Francis Preston Blair Family in Politics* (New York, 1933), I, 103–10.

16 N. Biddle to J. Tilford, June 6, 1831; E. Biddle to E. Shippen, June 6, 1831, in the Biddle Manuscripts in the Library of Congress.

17 W. Dun and B. Taylor to J. Tilford, June 29, 1831, in the Biddle Manuscripts in the Library of Congress; *Niles' Register*, XL (1831), 313–14.

in Louisville, in a personal letter to the President. He said that he did not know "upon whose *veracity*" Blair had relied, but he could assure Jackson that there was absolutely no basis for it, since the money expended was his own and no one else "contributed a cent to it."[18]

Pope, like Lewis, Overton, Carroll, and many others of Jackson's supporters in the West, regretted his opposition to the national bank. On the subject of the recharter, he told the President: "You already know my fixed and deliberate opinion. I fear the recurrence of the events to which birth was given, nearly all over the Union, by the refusal to recharter the old Bank in 1811. . . . If this Bank shall expire, every state will charter banks, the frauds and depreciated paper of which will drive the people, as in 1816, to a like Bank." It would be vain, he insisted, "for anyone to attempt to induce the people to run against the Bank of the United States." Unless a substitute was offered, 90 per cent of the West would support the existing Bank with all its defects. "Those who think differently, do not know the sentiments of the people. If we go against the present Bank, nothing will save us, but a substitute. Without it, we will be beaten and put down."[19]

Biddle had no knowledge of Pope's letter, but all through the year 1831 he was receiving evidence of the refusal of Jackson's supporters in the South and West to follow his lead in regard to the Bank. William R. King and John McKinley, senators from Alabama, told Samuel Smith that they favored the recharter, and Wiley P. Mangum of North Carolina announced that he was a "decided advocate for the renewal." His colleague, Bedford Brown, assured a constituent that he was "strongly in favor of renewing the charter in a modified form." The situation in Georgia was confused, but James M. Hunter, the cashier of the Savannah branch, reported: "I have had the pleasure to find the cause of the Bank of the United States gaining ground and warmly supported by a large proportion of the people of this state." Justice William Johnson, of the United States Supreme Court, gave Biddle similar assurances about South Carolina, and Governor William Carroll of Tennessee was pleased when the legislature tabled a resolution instructing the senators and requesting the representatives "to use all possible means to prevent the rechartering of the Bank of th United States," without a single moment's debate.[20]

Virginia was the only state in the region in which the Bank's opponents had a clear and unequivocal majority, and here the politics was dominated by Thomas Ritchie, the editor of the Richmond *Enquirer*, who, according to one of Biddle's informants, knew little about banks or banking but who

---

18 W. Pope to A. Jackson, June 19, August 6, 1831, in Bassett (ed.), *Correspondence of Jackson*, IV, 297–98, 326–27.

19 *Ibid.*

20 S. Smith to N. Biddle, February 8, 9, 1831; N. Biddle to G. Poe, Jr., February 16, 1831; J. M. Huske to N. Biddle, March 2, 1831, in the Biddle Manuscripts in the Library of Congress.

publicly justified his opposition to the charter by appeals to the Constitution and to the early opinions of Jefferson and Madison. This unauthorized use of his name in a current political debate prompted Madison to publish another public letter on July 13, 1831, in which he said that his opinions had changed between 1791, when he had opposed the charter of the first Bank, and 1816, when he had signed the charter of the second. The constitutional question had been settled by the actions of all three branches of the national government and those of the states and the people. Its expediency had been proved during the War of 1812, and he had signed the charter, he explained, because a veto "would have been a defiance of all the obligations derived from a course of precedents amounting to the requisite evidence of the national judgment and intention."[21]

Madison's letter had great influence. Hezekiah Niles, the Baltimore editor, said that it had convinced him that his constitutional objections to the Bank were not valid, and many others who had accepted the old Republican position without question likewise changed their minds. Biddle became certain that it was an auspicious time to apply for the recharter, and he and Cadwalader, who were preparing a report for the triennial meeting of the stockholders on September 1, decided to include a request for authority to make application whenever the board thought it proper. Cadwalader, who was usually more cautious and pessimistic than Biddle, this time agreed, and on August 26 he wrote to Thomas Wilson and Company of London: "That there will be a majority of both houses in favor of rechartering is a matter of certainty, and the Bank is gaining in popularity every day. All the cabinet are considered as well inclined to use their influence in favor of the institution, and their political friends are decidedly of opinion that the president will not venture to indulge his hostility to the Bank so far as to oppose an expression of the opinions and wishes of the people conveyed through their representatives."[22]

The triennial meeting found the Bank in a flourishing condition, and the stockholders' committee reported that the institution was operating effectively and efficiently in the manner prescribed by its charter. It was faithfully performing "its public trusts toward the government and people of the United States, and its immediate private trusts toward the stockholders." It had established a national currency, as "universally sound" as could be expected, and it had prevented, through its extensive operations in domestic and foreign exchange, all "sudden and violent fluctuations" in commerce. The national Treasury had been aided in the collection and distribution of its revenue, and the large payments on the public debt had

[21] J. Robertson to N. Biddle March 17, July 4, 16, 1831; J. Hunter to N. Biddle, April 23, 1831; R. Smith to N. Biddle, August 9, 1831; W. Carroll to N. Biddle, June 29, 1831, in the Biddle Manuscripts in the Library of Congress; J. Madison to C. J. Ingersoll, June 25, 1831, in Niles' Register, XL (1831), 332.

[22] T. Cadwalader to T. Wilson and Company, August 26, 1831, in the Cadwalader Manuscripts in the Historical Society of Pennsylvania; Niles' Register, XL (1831), 337.

been handled so as not to disturb the ordinary operations of trade or the value of investments. These public services, the committee said, were "the peculiar result of an institution organized and administered as this has been," and they warned their fellow countrymen that "any bank or body whatever, essentially different, would fail in the attainment of most or all of the great objects adverted to."[23]

The stockholders unanimously approved the report and adopted a resolution authorizing the president and directors to apply for a recharter "in the name and behalf of the stockholders, and to accept such terms of renewal as they may consider just and proper." The report and resolution were widely circulated as part of the effort to convince the people that the Bank was not a private monopoly operated for the benefit of the stockholders alone but was a public institution performing important services for the nation. A letter which James Monroe had written to Burrows the preceding January testified to the same essential fact, and it too was released to the public in September. Like Madison's letter, it stated that the doubts its writer had once had concerning the constitutionality of a national bank and the fears of the influence it might exercise on government had both proved groundless and that, after he had witnessed the results of the elimination of the first Bank, he had concurred in the propriety of instituting the new one at the conclusion of the war. William H. Crawford, the former Secretary of the Treasury, also published a letter in which he asserted that he was persuaded that "no man, whatever his preconceived opinions may be, can preside over the treasury one year, without being deeply impressed with the expediency of the Bank of the United States in conducting the finances of the Union."[24]

These letters from old Republicans had their influence on public opinion and were difficult for Kendall, Blair, and other opponents of the recharter to answer. The motives of these men could not be attacked, since all of them were retired from politics and had no reason to speak except their desire to contribute to the nation's welfare. The Bank had not bought them, nor could it, if it had wanted to do so. Theirs was the voice of experience, of knowledge, of reason, not of ignorance, prejudice, and slander, but Jackson was unwilling to listen, and if he read what Madison, Monroe, and Crawford had written, he paid no attention.

[23] Report of the Stockholders' Meeting, September 1, 1831, in *Niles' Register*, XLI (1831), 30, 118. Biddle's joy after this unanimous commendation by the stockholders was shattered a few days later by the news of the tragic death of his brother, Major Thomas Biddle, who had been killed in a duel at St. Louis. The quarrel had been caused by a dispute over the Bank of the United States, and Bray Hammond believes that this incident embittered Biddle's attitude toward the Jackson party. I can find no confirmation of this change in Biddle (Bray Hammond, "Jackson, Biddle and the Bank of the United States," *Journal of Economic History*, VII [1947], 1-23).

[24] J. Monroe to S. Burrows, January 20, 1831; W. H. Crawford to C. J. Ingersoll, December 5, 1831, in *Niles' Register*, XLI (1831), 82-83, 301.

⤳ *18* ⤳

The Application for
Recharter

*P*resident Jackson throughout the fall of 1831 hardly mentioned the Bank of the United States in his personal correspondence. His attention was absorbed by the violent controversy between John Eaton and other members of the former Cabinet over the circumstances of their resignations, and most of his animosity was directed toward Calhoun and Duff Green, who, he said, were responsible for all his difficulties. He listened attentively when McLane, supported by Livingston, advised him to reverse his stand in regard to the recharter and readily gave his permission to the Secretary of the Treasury to make this positive recommendation in his report to the Congress. He also agreed to say nothing at all about the Bank in his own message; but Biddle, when he was informed of these decisions by McLane and Livingston, thought that the President's silence on this question would be misinterpreted. He suggested, instead, that Jackson should include a statement to the effect that "having on former occasions brought the question before the Congress it was now left with the representatives of the people." The way would then be open for McLane, an independent administrative officer in his relations to the Bank as well as one of the President's official family, to recommend the renewal of the charter as a formal spokesman for the administration.[1]

Biddle's advice was accepted. Jackson included the recommended sentence in his message, and McLane, who had always supported the American System, came out for a protective tariff, subsidies for shipping, internal improvements, and other nationalistic measures, in addition to the renewal of the charter of the Bank of the United States.[2] Biddle was pleased

[1] N. Biddle, memoranda of conversations with Secretary McLane, October 19, 1831, and later, in the Biddle Manuscripts in the Library of Congress.

[2] Richardson, *Messages and Papers*, II, 558; *Niles' Register*, XLI (1831), 286–94.

with the report and the message, but he could not make up his mind whether or not to apply for the recharter at this session of Congress. McLane advised him not to. Jackson, he said, was entirely confident of his re-election, all he wanted was a larger vote than he had got in 1828, and if the recharter were presented to him as a question affecting the election when he was so confident, he would be disposed to veto. The members of the opposition to Jackson, on the other hand, were almost unanimous in urging an immediate application, for the reason, as stated by Clay, that if Jackson were "*now* called upon he would not negative the bill, but that if he should be re-elected the event might and probably would be different."[3]

Samuel Smith and other Jackson supporters of the Bank joined McLane in counseling delay. "The message is as much as you can expect," Smith wrote. "It shows that the chief is wavering. If pressed into a *corner* immediately, neither McLane nor myself will answer for the consequences. But we both feel confident of ultimate success if time be given for the president to convince himself of the error into which opinion long formed (prejudice if you please) has committed him." Smith may have thought Jackson was wavering, but Jackson himself did not. "Mr. McLane differs with me on the Bank," he told Van Buren. "Still it is an honest difference of opinion, and in his report he acts fairly, by leaving me free and uncommitted." And in writing to John Randolph, he went further: "You have done me no more than justice when you repelled with indignation the declaration that I had changed my views of the Bank of the United States."[4]

Biddle, of course, did not see these private statements by Jackson, but he was warned by Congressman Charles F. Mercer of Virginia that the President hated the Bank and Biddle with good reason, for "his silly notions respecting it have been exposed with your approbation, and he is mortified or vexed as well as angry." What Biddle feared most, however, was not the President's resentment. This, he thought, could be handled but not the influence of Kendall and Blair. "What I have always dreaded about this new cabinet," he wrote, "was that the kitchen would predominate over the parlor." The editorials in the *Globe* and the two men who set its policy were apparently more powerful than the President's official advisers. McLane's advocacy of the recharter was denounced editorially by Blair. The paragraph as it appeared was severe, but, according to one of Biddle's Baltimore cousins, as it had been written originally it had been

[3] N. Biddle to N. Silsbee, November 21, 1831; N. Biddle to J. Potter, December 3, 1831; H. Clay to N. Biddle, December 15, 1831, in the Biddle Manuscripts in the Library of Congress.

[4] S. Smith to N. Biddle, December 7, 17, 1831, in the Biddle Manuscripts in the Library of Congress; A. Jackson to M. Van Buren, December 6, 1831; A. Jackson to J. Randolph, December 22, 1831, in Bassett (ed.), *Correspondence of Jackson*, IV, 379–80, 387.

so much stronger that McLane had said he would tender his resignation if it were published.[5]

The same person told Biddle that he must not take the message and McLane's report as evidence that the administration had changed its views; but, about the same time, Biddle was informed by the cashier of the Louisville office that Jackson's nephew and private secretary, Andrew J. Donelson, had assured a personal friend that the President did not "consider himself pledged against a renewal" and that if Congress passed "a bill with *proper modifications* of the charter," he would not veto it. In the face of these differing versions of Jackson's opinions and feelings and the contradictory advice received from equally well-informed persons, Biddle found it hard to decide what was the wisest course to take.[6]

He had almost convinced himself that no application should be made when he received positive information from New York that the Van Buren party was ready to indorse the recharter. Silas Wright, its leader during Van Buren's absence as United States minister to Great Britain, had told the president of the Utica branch that, in his opinion, the charter should be renewed, and many lesser figures had said the same thing. They were still worried by their fears for the Safety Fund System if the power of the national bank to check and restrain the city banks was removed, and one upstate banker, who was also an influential Democrat, wrote that it was not to his direct interest to support the Bank, but he nevertheless wished to see it rechartered because it was essential for the national welfare.[7]

General Joshua Whitney of New York, who was introduced to Biddle as "a very honest man," albeit "a great intriguer," was sent to Washington by the Bank and almost at once reported that "now was the time to press the measure," since a majority of the New York delegation favored the renewal. All the Clay, Anti-Masonic, and Calhoun representatives would support the Bank, and if these were joined by the Pennsylvania delegation and a majority from New York, the bill would easily pass. Jackson's friends had made the same calculation and were afraid that if he vetoed the recharter he would endanger his chances of carrying Pennsylvania and New York. They were anxious to avoid such a veto and also the charge that Jackson was inconsistent and for this reason had urged the Bank to remain quiet, but, Whitney insisted, there was only one opinion among

[5] C. F. Mercer to N. Biddle, December 12, 1831; R. M. Gibbes to N. Biddle, December 11, 1831; N. Biddle to R. M. Gibbes, December 13, 1831, in the Biddle Manuscripts in the Library of Congress; H. D. Gilpin to J. Gilpin, November 25, December 19, 1831, in the Gilpin Manuscripts in the Historical Society of Pennsylvania.

[6] E. Shippen to N. Biddle, December 6, 1831, in the Biddle Manuscripts in the Library of Congress.

[7] N. Devereaux to N. Biddle, December 16, 1831; J. Rathbone to J. Rathbone, Jr., January 3, 1832, in the Biddle Manuscripts in the Library of Congress.

the friends of the Bank, and that was "that the time for their success had arrived."[8]

Cadwalader immediately went to Washington to check upon the accuracy of Whitney's report. He arrived on December 20 and remained for eleven days, consulting with the leaders of all parties and factions, and at the close of his investigation he recommended that the Bank should apply. He began with the statement that the President would be as likely to sign at this time as at any future time but that, on the basis of the information he had received, he was convinced that Jackson would never sign. He was also certain that Jackson would be re-elected, regardless of whether he signed or vetoed the bill renewing the charter. "If he is to put on his veto," Cadwalader concluded, "the sooner the country knows it the better. The astounding effect will have time to operate, gaining strength with every moment. A vote of two-thirds being then our only chance, the general alarm ringing through the nation will probably secure it."[9]

This statement cites all the reasons for the decision to apply for a recharter in 1832. Neither Biddle nor Cadwalader thought the application would have the slightest effect upon the President's re-election. Both believed, as did Henry Clay and almost every informed political observer in the United States, that Jackson was certain to win in the fall of 1832, and their decision to apply was based exclusively on what they thought was the wisest policy for the Bank. They had a faint hope that Jackson might sign the new charter if it were presented to him before the election, but they were absolutely convinced that he would never do so if he won re-election without having accepted or rejected the renewal. Their one chance, they thought, was to apply immediately, since the people of the United States gave every indication that they not only wanted Andrew Jackson as president but also wanted the national bank. If this issue was not raised before the election, the candidates for Congress would not have to express themselves in regard to the recharter, but if the question was raised and Jackson vetoed, there was a possibility that two-thirds of the senators and representatives elected in November, 1832, would be forced to commit themselves to vote for the recharter.[10]

The course that Biddle and Cadwalader took was that recommended by

[8] M. Robinson to N. Biddle, December 9, 1831; N. Biddle to R. Smith, December 11, 1831; R. Smith to N. Biddle, December 14, 15, 19, 1831, in the Biddle Manuscripts in the Library of Congress.

[9] T. Cadwalader to N. Biddle, December 22, 23, 25, 26 (two letters), 29, 31, 1831, Wednesday (January 4, 1832), in the Biddle Manuscripts in the Library of Congress.

[10] N. Biddle to T. Cadwalader, December 24, 29, 1831, in the Biddle Manuscripts in the Library of Congress; Edward Everett to Alexander Everett, December 8, 1831, in the Everett Manuscripts in the Massachusetts Historical Society, quoted in Joseph Tregle, "The Jackson Party in Louisiana," an unpublished thesis in the University of Pennsylvania Library. This letter was called to my attention by Mr. Tregle and tells of a gloomy conclave at Washington on December 7 at which Clay "confessed that he thought his chances hopeless." He wanted to withdraw.

Clay, Webster, Adams, and other opponents of Jackson, but the effect it would have on Clay's political fortunes was not a factor in the decision. The first letter Biddle wrote after the directors accepted the recommendation to apply for the recharter was one to Samuel Smith, in which he said: "You will hear, I am afraid with regret, though not with surprise that we have determined on applying to the present Congress for a renewal of the charter. . . . To this course I have made up my mind after great reflection and with the clearest conviction of its propriety." He expressed his regret that he had been forced to go counter to the advice of Smith and McLane but urged them to "disarm their antagonists of their most powerful weapon" by making the cause of the Bank that of the Jackson party. He criticized the contention by some of the Jacksonians that the President would veto the recharter if presented before the election but would sign it if it were postponed, saying that such a course was "much fitter for a humble demagogue than the chief magistrate of a great country," and he insisted that if the bill was in the national interest, it should be signed, regardless of when it was presented.[11]

At the moment Smith received this letter he was angry with Biddle and Cadwalader, not because they had disregarded his advice, but because he thought that they had given a newspaper writer a garbled account of a final conference between Cadwalader, Smith, McLane, and other members of the Jackson party. In the published story Smith was reported to have been opposed to the recharter, and one of the Baltimore stockholders, who knew how generously Smith had been treated by the Bank in its settlement of his indebtedness to it in 1819, had written him "a most insulting letter," accusing him of ingratitude. Biddle immediately apologized. "Whatever the Bank may have done for you," he wrote, "I considered an act of justice. I wished it to be an act of kindness also, but I hope you know me well enough to believe that I never for a moment imagined that it placed you under any obligation, or that it could in any degree interfere with your duties as a public man." He assured Smith that the leak concerning the conference had not come from him or Cadwalader, but Smith had already learned that the source of the newspaper's information was an innocent remark made by McLane to a friend. He wrote Biddle that he was quite satisfied with his apology for the unfortunate letter and promised him to support the recharter unless unexpected circumstances induced him to vote for a postponement.[12]

The day after Smith wrote this letter, January 10, 1832, Senator George M. Dallas, son of the Secretary of the Treasury who had recommended

[11] N. Biddle to S. Smith, January 4, 1832, Biddle Manuscripts in the Library of Congress.

[12] J. McKim to S. Smith, December 31, 1831; S. Smith to N. Biddle, January 4, 8, 1832; T. Cadwalader to N. Biddle, n.d.; N. Biddle to S. Smith, January 6, 1832, in the Biddle Manuscripts in the Library of Congress.

the original charter of the Bank of the United States and a new Jackson senator from Pennsylvania, presented the memorial of the "President, Directors, and Company of the Bank of the United States," requesting the Congress to renew its charter for an additional twenty years. Dallas admitted that his advice had been against making application before the election but said that he was acting as a willing agent in the promotion of a cause that was entitled to every consideration and favor. George McDuffie, who had been the person upon whose advice Cadwalader most relied, introduced the memorial into the House of Representatives, but his motion to refer it to the Ways and Means Committee, of which he was chairman, was opposed by James M. Wayne of Georgia. He insisted that the question should be referred to a select committee, since those on McDuffie's committee were already committed to the recharter by their report two years before. But he also expressed the conviction that the presentation of the memorial, though it had been done by members of the Jackson party, was a measure planned to aid the cause of Henry Clay.[13]

The National Republican Convention had been held shortly before, and its platform pledged its candidates, Clay and John Sergeant, to support the recharter. The party statement had predicted that if Jackson were re-elected, the Bank would be abolished, and "the institution which he has recommended, or something like it," would be substituted in its place. These actions, Wayne said, proved that the presentation of the memorial "was in fact a party measure, intended to have an important operation on persons occupying the highest offices of government"; and he recommended that the question be postponed until after the election. McDuffie, for himself and for the Bank's directors, denied all connection with the National Republican Convention and the political fortunes of Clay. In both houses the lead was being taken by supporters of President Jackson, and the memorial had not been presented until after Cadwalader had consulted with them and prominent executive officers. The majority of the House of Representatives was in McDuffie's favor, and after a prolonged debate his motion of referral to the Ways and Means Committee prevailed by the narrow margin of one hundred to ninety.[14]

The opponents of the recharter made much of the alleged precipitancy with which Biddle and the directors acted, but the question would have been forced on the Congress regardless of what they did. John Quincy Adams, acting as always in what he considered to be the national interest but with a shrewd and humorous eye to the discomfiture of his opponents, had prepared a resolution asking the Ways and Means Committee to report a bill in favor of the recharter. The presentation of the memorial relieved him of the necessity of offering this resolution, an outcome that

13 *Register of Debates in Congress* (22d Cong., 1st sess.), LIV, 1427–31.

14 *Ibid.*

Edward Everett, his colleague and intimate friend from Massachusetts, regarded as most fortunate for the Bank. "This certainly is not the form in which you would wish it to be brought forward," he observed to Biddle, but Adams had been determined. Like many others in the country, he had come to the conclusion that the recharter of the Bank of the United States was too important a question and had been too long agitated to be left unsettled in 1832. If the institution was as dangerous to the fundamental liberties of the country as Jackson said, it should be deprived of its charter and its power to do harm. If, on the other hand, it was as advantageous to the government and the national economy as Biddle and its proponents argued, it should be given the formal indorsement of the Congress and the Executive, in order that the needless newspaper and political agitation for and against it could be ended.[15]

Many of the men who were supporting the attack upon the Bank were convinced that the national Treasury "could not go on for a single year without the Bank" but wanted to replace the existing institution with another. These capitalists were essentially speculators seeking "what they called a new deal," and the most dangerous of these groups was that headed by Olcott, Croswell, and Knower in New York. The leading members of the Democratic party in the state were opposed to them, but they had enlisted the aid of Cambreleng, Hamilton, Jesse Hoyt, and other political and personal friends of Van Buren. They were also supported by the two largest brokerage firms in New York—Brown Brothers and Company and Prime, Ward and King—and they had a strong ally in William B. Lewis, who, despairing that Jackson could ever be convinced that his opposition to the Bank of the United States was a mistake, had agreed in December, 1831, to support this New York project in the event that Biddle applied for a renewal of the charter before the election.[16]

Their petition, though fully prepared, was not presented to the Congress for tactical reasons; but two other groups, one in Portland, Maine, and the other headed by David Henshaw, collector of the Port of Boston, made formal requests that a charter should be given to them rather than to the stockholders of the existing Bank. Theodore Lyman, Henry Lee, and other wealthy capitalists were associated with Henshaw, himself a rich man, and the motivating factor in each of these three groups was the desire to enhance its own interests and power. Most of the leading merchants in New York and Boston, however, supported the established Bank. Thomas H. Perkins, the wealthiest person in Boston, was a leader of the committee of

---

[15] Adams, *Memoirs*, VIII, 457; E. Everett to N. Biddle, January 9, 1832 (erroneously dated and filed, 1831), in the Biddle Manuscripts in the Library of Congress.

[16] W. G. Bucknor to N. Biddle, December 16, 1831; C. J. Ingersoll to N. Biddle, February 3, 1832, in the Biddle Manuscripts in the Library of Congress; W. B. Lewis to J. A. Hamilton, in Hamilton, *Reminiscences*, pp. 235–36; C. C. Cambreleng to J. Hoyt, February 12, 16, 1832, in Mackenzie, *Van Buren*, pp. 232–33; Schlesinger, *Age of Jackson*, pp. 147–48.

merchants who circulated a petition opposing Henshaw's application and asking Congress to recharter the Bank; and John Jacob Astor assured Biddle that he was impressed with the great advantages that had accrued to the country from the Bank, that he was therefore interested in the success of the memorial to Congress, and that he would be happy to promote its passage in any way he could.[17]

Astor's views were those of a majority of the New York merchants, regardless of their political allegiance, but the local bankers were still angry over Biddle's intervention against them in the Safety Fund fight. They refused to sign the Bank's petition, but in most cities the lead in the defense of the Bank was being taken by the state bankers and the brokers and merchants, and this virtual unanimity was itself a refutation of the charge that the Bank had been oppressive and harsh in its dealings with the state banks and the financial community. The Bank of Mobile, by formal resolution, expressed a wish to see the charter renewed, and the directors of the state-owned Bank of Alabama voluntarily testified to the "beneficial influence" of the national bank. Similar resolutions were passed by the Louisiana State Bank and the privately owned banks of New Orleans, and other expressions of approval of the application for renewal were given by state bankers in other parts of the South and West.[18]

Many large farmers and planters also asked that the charter be renewed, but the Bank had less support among the regions dominated by small farmers, few of whom had occasion to use its facilities or to become familiar with its operations. The most interesting deviations from this pattern existed in Georgia and South Carolina, where support for the Bank was as weak in the cities and rich farming areas as, if not weaker than, elsewhere. The officers of the branch in Savannah told Biddle that it would be inexpedient to circulate a petition because it would engender a counterpetition. "In that event," they predicted, "the signatures would greatly out-number ours, and amongst them, all our public men, stockholders and officers in the local banks, would be most prominent." Part of this opposition in Georgia was attributable to the old feud between the local banks and the branch, which had started under Cheves, but most of it was inspired by loyalty to Jackson, whose Indian policy was universally popular, and by the fact that for any politician to oppose him on any issue almost inevitably meant political defeat.[19]

In South Carolina, on the other hand, the opposition to the Bank was led

[17] W. B. Astor to N. Biddle, January 17, 1832, in the Biddle Manuscripts in the Library of Congress; Hammond, *Banking and Politics,* pp. 386–87.

[18] I. Lawrence to N. Biddle, January 30, 1832; G. Poe, Jr., to J. L. Tindall, February 11, 1832; J. L. Tindall to G. Poe, Jr., February 23, 1832; S. Jaudon to N. Biddle, February 11, 1832, in the Biddle Manuscripts in the Library of Congress.

[19] J. Cumming to N. Biddle, January 27, 1832, in the Biddle Manuscripts in the Library of Congress.

by those who had no political allegiance to Jackson, and the papers and societies there which advocated free trade looked on the Bank and the general government as their two most powerful enemies. Biddle received many reports in early 1832 about this opposition to the recharter in South Carolina, including one from Charles J. Ingersoll, who was in Washington on legal business, saying that he would not be surprised if "among the mutations of Mr. Calhoun's mind, that of aversion to the Bank should have taken place."[20] One reason for this change of opinion in South Carolina was the almost unanimous support given to Jackson and the Union party in that state by the officers and directors of the Charleston branch, but there were other and more important reasons less directly connected with party politics. The merchants and planters of South Carolina had begun their opposition to the protective tariff because they were convinced that it was harmful to their economic interest. They, like the merchants of New England, New York, Philadelphia, and Baltimore, were against any measure which tended to restrict the import and export trade, but such opposition was not attended by loyalty to any particular economic theory.

The absence of theoretical justification handicapped them in their appeals to the country, since their opponents were armed with the persuasive neo-mercantilist arguments of the American System. The proponents of the protective tariff spoke not of individual profits but of national strength, high wages for workingmen, a secure home market for farmers, and roads, canals, and schools paid for by invisible taxes on imports. Those opposing the tariff were made to appear as selfish men seeking to advance their individual interests at the expense of the national welfare.

Thomas Cooper, president of the College of South Carolina and earlier Jefferson's friend and economic tutor, provided the needed theoretical support for the nullifiers by his lectures and books on political economy. His theories were not concerned with the tariff alone. They also called for a bullion currency and the elimination of the national bank as the regulator of money and credit; for, like the other classical liberal economists, Cooper believed that the general interest was best fostered by a natural, unregulated economy. His arguments were gradually taken over by most of the political leaders of the state, but Calhoun at first was reluctant to accept this fundamental change of view, which would require him to repudiate the legislative accomplishments of his earlier years and most of what he had previously said.[21]

Once he began the reversal, however, his logical mind carried him rapidly to the extreme laissez faire position, with all its implications, including

20 J. Johnson to N. Biddle, January 24, 1832; C. J. Ingersoll to N. Biddle, January 26, February 6, 1832; J. Potter to N. Biddle, January 18, 1832, in the Biddle Manuscripts in the Library of Congress.

21 David F. Houston, *A Critical Study of Nullification in South Carolina* (New York, 1896), pp. 53–58.

opposition to the national bank. In addition, he was interested in the acquisition of gold-producing lands in the former Cherokee country in Georgia, and this personal economic interest would before long be an added incentive for him to advocate an exclusively gold currency.[22] Characteristically, Calhoun concealed this change of opinion and denied that it had occurred. But he took no part in the fight for or against the recharter, and the other opponents of the Bank, with the exception of Benton, also remained quiet in the first few weeks after the presentation of the memorial. Benton was impatient and angry. He had not been consulted by the administration, and he was worried by the possibility that Jackson might be won over by Smith, McLane, Livingston, and other Democratic supporters of the Bank. For this reason, he began to work independently and became the creator of the tactics that ultimately defeated Biddle and his hopes for the recharter.[23]

"Our course of action became obvious," Benton was later to write, "which was to attack incessantly, assail at all points, display the evil of the institution, rouse the people, and prepare them to sustain the veto. . . . We determined . . . to force the Bank into defences which would engage it in a general combat, and lay it open to sideblow as well as direct attack." He began this campaign on January 20 by an attack on the branch drafts issued as currency by the Bank of the United States. Biddle had devised these substitutes for bank notes in 1827 when the Congress had refused to amend the charter so that persons other than the president and cashier of the principal office could perform the laborious and time-consuming task of signing every note issued by the Bank in every part of the United States. The drafts were drawn upon the Bank in Philadelphia and were signed by the branch officers, but otherwise they were indistinguishable from the bank notes and were used in an identical way. The Treasury accepted them in all payments to the government, and state and federal courts had declared them to be legal, enforcible obligations of the Bank. Millions of them had circulated for more than four years without loss or injury to any person, and the Bank accepted and redeemed them not only at the branch where they were issued and at the Bank in Philadelphia, where they were made payable, but also at the other branches.[24]

Benton's purpose in attacking the branch drafts was not to force the Bank to discontinue their use and revert to bank notes. Had he wanted to do this, he would have had Biddle's co-operation, for all that was needed was a simple amendment to the charter authorizing someone other than the two busiest officers in the Bank to sign the notes. His purpose was

---

[22] Fletcher M. Green, "Georgia's Forgotten Industry: Gold Mining," *Georgia Historical Quarterly*, XIX (1935), 93–111, 210–28; Charles M. Wiltse, *John C. Calhoun, Nullifier, 1829–1839* (Indianapolis, 1949), pp. 320–21.

[23] Benton, *Thirty Years' View*, I, 220–24, 235–36.

[24] Catterall, *Second Bank*, pp. 114–31.

rather to arouse the fears and suspicions of the uninformed concerning the Bank, and he denounced the branch drafts as dangerous, knowing well that any reply to his charges would either be ignored or misunderstood. In his speech, as Biddle had said about the one he delivered the year before, there was "scarcely a single statement . . . not founded upon a want of knowledge of fact, or a total misapprehension of fact"; and it was Benton's deliberate intention for this to be so. He believed that the national welfare required the elimination of the Bank and the establishment of a gold currency and that, to attain these ends, any methods, including deliberate misrepresentation, were justified.

The other senators were aware of Benton's purpose, and none of them thought his arguments worthy of answer. Once again they listened with impatience to his demagogic harangue and, as soon as he had finished, turned to other matters. The Ways and Means Committee, meanwhile, was preparing its report on the Bank's memorial, and McDuffie, early in February, presented its recommendation that the charter should be renewed with minor modifications to meet the administration's objections. The President was authorized to appoint one public director in each branch in addition to the five on the board of the parent bank, and the Congress was empowered to terminate the charter after ten years, if it gave three years' advance notice. The bonus was not to be a specific amount but was to be paid annually as interest on the government deposits, and drafts or checks of twenty dollars or less were prohibited. The Bank was also forbidden to issue branch drafts, the need for them being eliminated by a provision authorizing the employment of special officers to sign notes. The final modification, which required each branch to redeem any note issued by the Bank, was already a feature of the Bank's practice and regulations but was now to be made law.[25]

Two members of the committee—Mark Alexander of Virginia and Nathan Gaither of Kentucky—submitted a minority report opposing the renewal of the charter on the grounds that it was unconstitutional and that the corruption and influence that the Bank might exert upon every department of the government—executive, legislative, and judicial—were "calculated to destroy the purity, virtue, and independence of our political institutions." Gulian Verplanck of New York also voted against presenting the recommendation of the recharter, but he carefully dissociated himself from the reasons given by Alexander and Gaither. He believed that the Bank was constitutional and necessary and voted against McDuffie and the majority of the committee only because he thought that the debate on the application should be postponed until after the election.[26]

The presentation of McDuffie's report and recommendation came at a

[25] *House Report* (22d Cong., 1st sess.), No. 283.

[26] *Ibid.*

decisive moment when Biddle was almost certain that the Bank's charter would be renewed. The Pennsylvania legislature, controlled by Jacksonians, had passed a resolution—unanimously in the Senate and by a vote of seventy-seven to seven in the House—instructing the senators and requesting the representatives to support the recharter; and President Jackson himself had reportedly assured Secretary Livingston that his objections to the Bank were not constitutional and that he would be willing to sign a bill rechartering the institution if proper modifications were made. Biddle's long effort to persuade Jackson to forget his personal objections to the Bank and to recommend its recharter as a necessary adjunct to the national Treasury seemed on the verge of success, and the center of the Bank's interest and efforts was turned from the Congress to the Executive.

～ *19* ～

The Last Attempt at Compromise

*C*harles J. Ingersoll, one of the most influential Jacksonians in Philadelphia, was the source of Biddle's information concerning the President's apparent change of mind. He was so confident that he convinced Biddle, who immediately requested him and Horace Binney, the Bank's official representative in Washington, to persuade Senator Dallas to make a formal offer of compromise. Dallas wanted to be Pennsylvania's candidate for the vice-presidency in opposition to Van Buren, and to promote his candidacy, Biddle wrote, he should identify himself with all the Pennsylvania interests that Van Buren was thought to oppose. He should go to the President and say: "You are not opposed to this Bank essentially; you mean to agree to it with certain modifications. Now let me mediate between you and the Bank. . . . You will take from your adversaries their most formidable weapon, and secure the ascendancy of your friends. If the President will do this, his success is certain; if Mr. Dallas will do this, besides sustaining his father's work and conferring a great blessing on the country, he will assure to himself distinguished consideration through the country."[1]

Dallas was not to be tempted. He had already jeopardized his standing with Jackson by sponsoring the memorial in the Senate, and, anxious though he was to obtain the vice-presidential nomination, he was unwilling to be further identified with the Bank. Biddle, disappointed by Dallas' refusal, turned back to Ingersoll and, in the middle of February, wrote, "My reliance is now on you." He sent Ingersoll a series of letters to be shown "to those who may be well disposed," in which he said: "I have

[1] C. J. Ingersoll to N. Biddle, January 31, February 2, 4, 6, 1832; J. B. Wallace to N. Biddle, February 3, 1832; N. Biddle to H. Binney, February 6, 1832; N. Biddle to C. J. Ingersoll, February 6, 1832, in the Biddle Manuscripts in the Library of Congress.

[181]

reached the conclusion that either I am deranged, or the president's friends are. . . . Here is the Bank which most assuredly has been in its proper sphere, perfectly true and faithful to the administration; and which has never suffered itself even while it believed itself very unkindly treated, to be betrayed into the slightest departure from its duty to the government." The whole matter, he thought, could be settled in five minutes. "The President wishes some modification in the charter. Well let him take the charter and make any changes he likes. Let him write the charter with his own hands, I am sure we would agree to the modifications; and then let him and his friends pass it. It will then be his work. He will then disarm his adversaries, he will gratify his friends, and remove one of the most uncomfortable and vexatious public questions that can be stirred."[2]

In thus negotiating and offering concessions, Biddle was not betraying the opposition to Jackson. He had not asked the National Republican Convention for its indorsement of the recharter, and he and Cadwalader had made it clear that, in applying to Congress in 1832, they were acting in accordance with their view of the interests of the Bank and the nation, not those of any political party. Biddle restated this position in his letter to Ingersoll: "You know I care nothing about the election. I care only for the interests confided to my care, and so far from having the least ill will toward the president, so far from wishing to embarrass the administration, I will do everything consistent with my duty to relieve it from trouble, and will go nine tenths of the way to meet him in conciliation."[3]

Ingersoll knew that Biddle's statement was accurate and truthful on the basis of their long and close personal friendship and his own leadership of the Bank's cause in the Pennsylvania legislature the preceding year. He was a distinguished lawyer, a former United States District Attorney in Philadelphia, and a loyal member of the President's party. He would not have been a party to any corrupt or questionable enterprise, and he was not employed, nor had he been bribed, by the Bank. His sole reason for acting as the Bank's representative was his conviction that the charter should be renewed, and he conducted a shrewd and intelligent campaign. He concentrated his attention on Taney, the only member of the official Cabinet opposed to the Bank, and on Blair, Kendall, and Lewis, and the argument he used was that Calhoun was opposed to the recharter. "I am sure," he told Biddle, "that the president's reactions against whatever the vice-president designs is one of the strongest impulses we can actuate."[4]

Calhoun had indicated that he was at least cool toward the Bank, and Ingersoll made effective use of this fact and of the known opposition to

[2] N. Biddle to C. J. Ingersoll, February 13, 1832, in the Biddle Manuscripts in the Library of Congress.

[3] *Ibid.*

[4] C. J. Ingersoll to N. Biddle, February 9, 18, 1832, in the Biddle Manuscripts in the Library of Congress.

the recharter by a majority of the South Carolina delegation. He told Livingston, Lewis, and Blair that Calhoun's "deep design" included destruction of the national bank, and the first results of this effort seemed promising. Secretary Livingston hoped to convert Taney, Kendall was wavering, and, Ingersoll proudly reported, "My good understanding with the editor of the Globe is well settled." Livingston and Ingersoll, on February 23, had a most significant conversation. After they had talked of general matters for some time, the Secretary finally said, "I suppose that you'll see Biddle at Philadelphia and let him know how matters are as to the Bank." When Ingersoll replied that he would, Livingston added, "I wish you would ascertain from him whether the Bank will agree to the President's terms for a new charter." The whole object of the negotiation seemed accomplished, for what Jackson, according to Ingersoll's report of Livingston's conversation, demanded was, first, to have the government sell its stock in the Bank; second, the President to be empowered to appoint a director in each branch; third, the states to have the power to tax the real and personal property of the Bank at the same rate as they taxed those of the local banks; and, fourth, the Bank to hold no real estate except what it had to take in settlement of debt, which must be sold within a reasonable time.[5]

None of these modifications would interfere with the proper operation of the Bank, and Biddle, convinced that Jackson had finally been persuaded to accept the recharter, enthusiastically wrote Ingersoll: "You are the Coryphaeus of ambassadors. Talk not to me of Tallyrand or Luchhesini or even the great magician of New York." He accepted the four amendments suggested by Jackson and also another that Livingston proposed which called for the capital of the Bank to be increased so that there could be new subscriptions to the stock. When Ingersoll reported Biddle's acceptance to Livingston, he was assured that the President would settle the question during the current term. "If such a bill goes to him as he can sign," Livingston said, "he will sign it without hesitation. If not, he will be equally prompt to reject it." Biddle was not satisfied with these verbal assurances. Ingersoll had said: "Thus we have the mind of the president without doubt, if Mr. Livingston's word is to be taken, of which I have not a particle of misgiving and I feel confident that his is the predominating influence"; but what Biddle wanted was "some overt act, some decisive committal, for the extreme mobility of the principal person in our drama makes me anxious to see him fixed, irretrievably committed." No such act was forthcoming. Livingston, like Lewis in 1829 and 1830, had interpreted Jackson's silence as approval of what he himself believed to be the proper course for the administration, and he too was mistaken. The President,

[5] C. J. Ingersoll to N. Biddle, February 21, 23, 1832, in the Biddle Manuscripts in the Library of Congress.

regardless of what he said or did not say to Livingston, did not intend to sign a bill renewing the charter of the Bank.[6]

An undated memorandum in Jackson's handwriting, which was almost certainly written in January, 1832, began with a recapitulation of classical state rights doctrine and concluded with the statement that the Constitution forbade the incorporation of a national bank. Conceding that in this instance, as in all others, "necessity creates its own law," Jackson nevertheless insisted that if a banking institution was necessary, it "must be exclusively national having no concern with corporations" because "the general government cannot consistent with any power granted, become a member of any corporation Congress may create." The national bank must be an adjunct of the Treasury, as the customs houses were.[7] Livingston could not have seen this memorandum of Jackson's views. Of his proposed amendments, only the first, stipulating that the government was to have no financial interest in the Bank, had any relation to it; but the opponents of the Bank within the administration, appeared to be fully informed and confident that Jackson was on their side. Never once during the negotiations between Ingersoll and Livingston did they manifest the slightest doubt as to the President's position, and they turned out to be right.

These opponents of the Bank were united by their common hostility to the existing institution, but, on what was to replace it, their desires were different and contradictory. Benton wanted a gold currency; Cambreleng, a national bank with exactly the same powers as those of the Bank of the United States, but with its headquarters in New York; and Blair and Kendall, Jackson's Treasury bank; but these differences in aim and purpose did not separate them. Benton's attack upon the branch drafts in the Senate was the first blow in their campaign, and when this failed in its immediate purpose, they transferred their activities to the other house. They decided to ask for an investigation, knowing, as Benton later averred, that "whether resisted or admitted by the Bank majority," it would be certain to have an effect against the institution. "If the investigation was denied, it would be guilt shrinking from detection; if admitted, it was well known that misconduct would be found."[8]

The source of this confidence that an investigation would be rewarding came from information supplied by Reuben Whitney, a former director, who had been excluded from the Bank's board by Biddle after he had failed in business. He believed that he had been unjustly discriminated against, and he kept Kendall and Blair informed of all that went on in the Bank. This information was given to him by John T. Sullivan, a gov-

[6] N. Biddle to C. J. Ingersoll, February 25, 1832; C. J. Ingersoll to N. Biddle, March 1, 1832, in the Biddle Manuscripts in the Library of Congress.

[7] A. Jackson, memorandum, n.d., in Bassett (ed.), *Correspondence of Jackson*, IV, 389–90.

[8] Benton, *Thirty Years' View*, I, 236.

ernment director, who had been appointed to the board at the beginning of 1832 on Whitney's recommendation, and none of these moralistic denunciators of Biddle as the corrupter of free institutions and men thought it improper for Sullivan to violate his oath as a director. They eagerly scraped together the information and misinformation he supplied and handed them over to Augustine M. Clayton, a new member from Georgia, who had been chosen to ask for the investigation. Benton was to claim that it was he who "conceived this movement and had charge of its execution," but others were also involved, including Cambreleng, the spokesman for the New York bank. On February 16 he wrote Jesse Hoyt concerning their prospects of gaining what they desired, saying: "Judge Clayton of Georgia has a resolution prepared and will offer it as soon as he can. It will cover the object in view. I shall see the president tonight, who has a confidential director on the spot. You need not fear but what we shall take care of the mammoth in some way or the other."[9]

Clayton gained the floor a week later and moved that a select committee be appointed to examine into the affairs of the Bank of the United States, justifying his request by reference to the many flagrant abuses which had been discovered in 1819 by the Spencer committee. The two situations were not comparable. The first investigation had been ordered in a period of financial crisis when the Bank was on the verge of suspending specie payments and virtually all economic activity in the country had halted. The stockholders, led by Stephen Girard, were alarmed and disgusted, and the committee, of which Biddle was an official adviser, co-operated with them, President Monroe, and Secretary Crawford in bringing about a change of administration and fundamental reforms. In 1832, however, the country was prosperous, it had a sound and elastic currency, and none of the economic groups which were affected by the operations of the Bank had any complaints of a substantial nature. The stockholders were eminently pleased with the administration of the Bank, and the only demand for an investigation came from its political opponents, some of whom had selfish reasons of their own for wanting it destroyed.[10]

Biddle viewed Clayton's request for an investigation as a delaying and harassing tactic—"postponement in disguise," he said to John Quincy Adams—and he hoped that it would be denied by the Bank majority in the House. Most of the Bank's supporters agreed, but McDuffie, the legislative sponsor of the recharter, was inexplicably conciliatory at this stage of the conflict. He persuaded Lewis Williams of North Carolina to withdraw a motion to lay Clayton's resolution on the table, and he also prevented John G. Watmough, a Philadelphia congressman completely devoted to Biddle

[9] *Ibid.*; C. C. Cambreleng to J. Hoyt, February 16, 1832, in Mackenzie, *Van Buren*, pp. 232–33; T. Cadwalader to N. Biddle, April 10, 1832, in the Biddle Manuscripts in the Library of Congress.

[10] *Register of Debates in Congress* (22d Cong., 1st sess.), pp. 1846, 1874–76.

and the cause of the Bank, from introducing an amendment that would have turned the investigation over to the Ways and Means Committee. This last action angered Ingersoll, who wrote to Biddle: "Immediately after adjournment I went to Binney's apartment to condole and rail with him over McDuffie's infatuation, and there we talked, scolded and drank till I was almost beside myself. In the evening I had a conversation with Mr. Adams whose language may give you some idea of the prevailing sentiments: I have long suspected and watched McDuffie, said he with great warmth, and his ignoble, disgraceful flight today . . . satisfied me that he is politically either a coward or a traitor."[11]

Ingersoll could not subscribe to such an extreme denunciation, but he did express surprise that McDuffie, "with a clear, confident, ascertained majority," had surrendered without a fight. The only explanation that Ingersoll could give was that McDuffie had other game in sight. "There is anti-Jacksonism and there is disunion always fermenting in his mind and unconsciously perhaps he tries to defend the Bank not for itself alone but as an engine to destroy the president." The reason for McDuffie's action was simple, and, when Ingersoll finally talked to him, he admitted it. He did not want the Bank bill voted on until after the tariff bill had been passed, and in this objective he was aligned with Clayton and other opponents of the protective system rather than with Adams or Ingersoll. "Thus you perceive," Ingersoll wrote Biddle, "that McDuffie and Clayton agreeing in opposition to the tariff, and that the tariff is the first consideration, have, no doubt without concert, contrived between the resolution of the one and the concession of the other to postpone the Bank lest it should by its combination of votes interfere with their primary objective."[12]

Ingersoll, who wanted to defeat this attempt to lower the tariff, recommended a complete change of tactics for the Bank. He suggested that the directors themselves request an investigation and, as soon as the committee was selected in the House, press for action in the Senate, where Dallas' committee was almost ready to report its bill renewing the charter. This bill could then be passed by the Senate and sent to the House before the tariff was brought up for debate, thus opening the way for some Pennsylvanian to propose a compromise. The state delegation would yield something on the tariff to Virginia and the Carolinas in return for their support of such a modified Bank as the President would approve.[13]

Secretary Livingston, Ingersoll reported, approved this change in tactics. He still believed that Jackson would sign a renewal of the charter and that he would already have made a public announcement to this effect if the

[11] N. Biddle to J. Q. Adams, March 4, 1832; C. J. Ingersoll to N. Biddle, March 1, 1832, in the Biddle Manuscripts in the Library of Congress.

[12] C. J. Ingersoll to N. Biddle, March 2, 3, 4, 6, 1832, in the Biddle Manuscripts in the Library of Congress.

[13] *Ibid.*

Clayton resolution for an inquiry had not been introduced into the House. "I have not heard him say so," Livingston admitted, "but I have good reason to rely on it"; and Ingersoll predicted that Jackson would be pleased if some Pennsylvanian took the lead in proposing a reduction of the tariff in return for southern support of a modified Bank. But Biddle had lost faith in Livingston's ability to influence the President, and he was as unwilling to tie the recharter of the Bank to the tariff as to the fortunes of any political party or candidate. On March 5 he, Cadwalader, and Binney conferred with Joel Sutherland, the leader of the Philadelphia delegation in the House, and all agreed that for the directors to ask for an investigation would smack of bravado. They decided instead that McDuffie's recharter bill should be sent back to the Ways and Means Committee with instructions to inquire into Clayton's charges against the Bank, and they requested Edward Everett of Massachusetts to initiate this action.[14]

Everett immediately replied that it was too late to do so. He thought the best course left for the Bank's supporters was to vote for an amendment proposed by Erastus Root of New York, which called for election rather than appointment of the special committee. If this amendment passed, Everett said, "we shall have a majority willing to investigate fairly and candidly, and not turn the enquiry into . . . an engine of hostility or delay." Root's amendment, after being debated for two days, came to a vote on March 13. The House was equally divided, and the Speaker, Andrew Stevenson of Virginia, cast his ballot against the amendment, which left the choice of the committee to him. Everett was disappointed and recommended that the demand for the committee, "now avowedly made for the sake of delay," should be voted down. "I have no idea," he told Biddle, "that one vote is to be propitiated by yielding to the enquiry."[15]

At this point Sutherland took control of the Bank's tactics, in the conviction that further resistance to the demand for an investigation would arouse popular suspicion. He persuaded the Bank's supporters to vote for an amendment, proposed by Adams, which left the naming of the committee to the Speaker, but required it to complete its investigation and report back to the House by April 25. This amendment was adopted on March 14, and the resolution authorizing the investigation was finally passed the same day. Biddle had hoped to the last that the resolution would be defeated. "All that I can perceive at this distance," he wrote on March 14, "satisfies me that the resolution should be killed. Then if expedient we may ask an enquiry."[16] What was bothering him was his secret and irregular

14 N. Biddle to C. J. Ingersoll, March 5, 1832; C. J. Ingersoll to N. Biddle, March 10, 1832, in the Biddle Manuscripts in the Library of Congress.

15 E. Everett to N. Biddle, March 7, 13, 1832, in the Biddle Manuscripts in the Library Library of Congress.

16 N. Biddle to C. J. Ingersoll, March 14, 1832; N. Biddle to J. Sutherland, March 14, 1832, in the Biddle Manuscripts in the Library of Congress; *Register of Debates in Congress* (22d Cong., 1st sess.), pp. 2129, 2163–64.

arrangement with Burrows to lend fifteen thousand dollars to Noah for the purchase of Tylee's interest in the *Courier and Enquirer*, and he was afraid that somehow, somewhere, positive knowledge of this loan had been obtained by the Bank's opponents.

The payments he had made to editors and printers of newspapers and periodicals for the publication of articles favorable to the Bank did not trouble Biddle. The Bank had formally admitted and justified these payments in the Philadelphia *Sentinel* in June, 1831, and many of the recipients of such payments had published full details. Gales and Seaton, publishers of the *National Intelligencer*, reported that they had circulated twenty-five thousand extra papers at the expense of the Bank, and Robert Walsh, editor of the *United States Gazette* and the *American Quarterly Review*, stated that his publishers had been paid a thousand dollars for approximately forty thousand reprints of various articles. He insisted that neither he nor his staff had been "subsidized to write for the Bank," and he indignantly denied a report started by the Albany *Argus* that Gallatin had been "employed" to write his article. "The Bank," Walsh wrote, "employed no one to write for the Review; no one has received any remuneration for so doing; Mr. Gallatin refused even the compensation which the publishers allow per page to the literary contributors; he has accepted nothing from any quarter."[17]

The opponents of the recharter, Biddle was certain, would hardly risk raising this issue in view of the large number of party newspapers that were being directly subsidized by political patronage. Niles, under the heading "Bribery," described the organized Jackson press, "more than one hundred and fifty" of whose editors had been "rewarded with offices or fat jobs of printing." Newspapers, he said, had long been sufficiently violent and abusive, but now a falsehood manufactured or a calumny forged ran through the whole line of hired presses. "The whole group," he insisted, "have latterly been arranged to wheel and fire . . . at the word of command. This corps is 200 strong, and whether located in Maine or Georgia, on the borders of the Atlantic or beyond the Mississippi, they are united by a common interest, and act together as if with the soul of one man."[18]

Blair was the commander of this army of newspapers, and he was more vulnerable than most to questions regarding the sources of his capital and profits. He had been heavily in debt as an indorser of other men's notes when he was invited to come to Washington to edit the *Globe*, and the only reason he was not forced to fail was that the Bank of the United States, with intelligent generosity, had extended to him the same privilege it had afforded many of its unfortunate debtors in Kentucky and accepted

[17] J. Gales, Jr., to N. Biddle, June 23, 1831, Biddle Manuscripts in the Library of Congress; A. Gallatin to N. Biddle, December 8, 1830, in the Gallatin Manuscripts in the New York Historical Society; *United States Gazette* (Philadelphia), July 2, 1831.

[18] *Niles' Register*, XLIII (1832), 39.

a small payment in discharge of his very large and old debt. By 1832 he was in possession of a profitable newspaper and a flourishing printshop, the capital of which had been raised by subscription among the principal officers of government and others indebted to the administration for political favors. Officeholders of all ranks were advised that they were expected to subscribe to the *Globe* and to solicit subscriptions from others; and much of the departmental printing was turned over to Blair by the simple expedient, devised by Lewis, of issuing an executive order requiring each member of the Cabinet to report quarterly the amounts expended for such printing and the name of the firm to which it had been paid.[19]

Enough was publicly known about these matters to make it unlikely that the investigating committee would criticize the Bank's practices severely, and Biddle was equally certain that no political capital could be made from its ordinary loans to newspaper and editors. They were entitled to borrow, and throughout the years many such loans had been made to Robert Walsh, Jasper Harding, Gales and Seaton, Thomas Ritchie, and others. More had actually been loaned to papers favorable to the Jackson administration than to those which opposed it, and, though this result was accidental, as Biddle said, "the accident shows the absence of all disposition to favoritism." The only large loans to editors in 1831 were one of twenty thousand dollars to Duff Green and two to Noah and Webb, who, ignorant of the source of the funds they had obtained from Burrows, had applied for and been granted twenty thousand dollars in August and fifteen thousand dollars in December. No political conditions were attached to the loans, and those to the *Courier and Enquirer* had been made on the recommendation of Walter Bowne, Democratic mayor of New York, who, writing as a member of the Jackson party, said that this administration paper had been denied loans by the city banks because it supported the recharter of the national bank. Webb continued to support the party after the loans were made, and, in January, 1832, he indignantly denied a charge made by Jesse Hoyt that he was "falling off" in his loyalty to the administration. He answered that no individual in the United States was "more honestly and disinterestedly attached to Van Buren and General Jackson" than he; and a few weeks later, when Van Buren's nomination as minister to Great Britain was rejected by the Senate, he said that he would like "to get hold of the rascals" who voted to reject.[20]

These loans could be explained and justified, but not that made through

[19] Parton, *Jackson*, III, 338; Smith, *Blair Family*, pp. 66–67. Blair was an indorser of unpaid notes totaling more than twenty thousand dollars and was permitted to settle this debt for the equivalent of ten cents on each dollar. L. Combs to N. Biddle, July 21, 1831; N. Biddle to J. Watmough, April 23, 1832, in the Biddle Manuscripts in the Library of Congress; Catterall, *Second Bank,* p. 171, n 1.

[20] N. Biddle to J. Hemphill, February 10, 1831, in the Biddle Manuscripts in the Library of Congress; J. W. Webb to J. Hoyt, January 19, February 12, 1832, in MacKenzie, *Van Buren*, pp. 230–32; *House Report* (22d Cong., 1st sess.) No. 460, pp. 8–11, 75–107.

the agency of Burrows, and more than anything else this made Biddle anxious to prevent the investigation. Only one thing could be done, and that was to take the notes out of the Bank. Swallowing his pride, Biddle invited Burrows to come to Philadelphia at the beginning of March, and once again no record was made of their conversation. But Burrows was persuaded to pay off the original notes, and Biddle in return arranged for the New York board to lend Burrows thirty thousand dollars on ninety-day terms for his mercantile operations. Webb knew nothing of this transaction, but he was concerned about his other two loans. "I am desirous of knowing," he wrote Biddle, "whether some mode cannot be devised to keep our names and the name of our journal from appearing without in any way compromising the safety of the loan or distorting the honorable character of the transaction." Since the loans had been recorded on the Bank's books, Webb's request could not be granted, but so anxious was he to improve the appearance of the situation that he raised fifteen thousand dollars "with some little inconvenience," and on March 15 paid off the December loan.[21]

The same day he wrote again to Biddle: "A gentlemen just informed me that he had seen a letter from you to S E B urging his immediate visit to Philadelphia. . . . The query was what is the matter and why will Mr. Biddle write such letters to one who exhibits them for the purpose of giving importance to himself. Another friend has informed me that the same person boasts of having got $30,000 out of the Branch for a friend at a moment when our most substantial firms could get nothing. Now you know what I think of B's heart, it is his head that is at fault, and that does much mischief." Biddle was shocked and surprised by this letter. He thought Webb knew why he had to write to Burrows and also that the loan had been granted to pay off the notes signed by Noah. But he discovered how completely mistaken he was three days later, when Webb wrote: "Mr. Burrows has just informed me that Mr. Noah's notes endorsed by me . . . have been by him used in the Bank of the United States, and that they consequently appear upon your books. If the whole transaction could also appear there, I would be well pleased, but as it is, I care much more to have you understand it correctly, than for what the world may make of it."[22]

He recounted the entire story of Noah's negotiations with Burrows and ended with the statement: "I am anxious to have you understand that however much the course of this paper may excite suspicion, yet it is very certain that I have not been induced to change my opinion by the accomodation of the Bank." Biddle thus finally learned that all his secret and irregu-

21 N. Biddle to S. E. Burrows, March 4, 10, 11, 1832; J. W. Webb to N. Biddle, March 6, 12, 15, 1832, in the Biddle Manuscripts in the Library of Congress.

22 J. W. Webb to N. Biddle, March 15, 18, 1832, in the Biddle Manuscripts in the Library of Congress.

lar arrangements with Burrows had been unnecessary and that his one and only departure from his rule to avoid such entanglements had produced no useful results. He could not afford to explain to Webb, however, nor could he complain to Burrows because he was still very much at the mercy of this vain and erratic merchant. Once again he tried to persuade Burrows to accept full responsibility for the loans, and Burrows, somewhat chastened, replied: "All the discounts made at your Bank to me have been for my accommodation and individual benefit. In me you shall find such a friend as was worthy of the introduction I bore from the good Monroe. Never, never through life can wealth allure me to desert a friend in the hour of trial."[23]

Burrows made a secret trip to Washington and, according to his report, "spent the evening with the president." He told Jackson his story of the loan: that the *Courier and Enquirer* was about to be bought by opponents of the Democratic party and that it had been saved by Burrows' appeal to Biddle for the necessary fifteen thousand dollars. Jackson "appeared pleased," Burrows wrote, "I think this stands triumphant." But, lest Biddle begin to feel too secure, he added a disquieting statement: "The moment I knew you had made an entry of those documents, that moment I knew a fortune was at my disposal if I would accept of it, and made without censure by the world as they would justify me for testifying to all. But I view it different, and the monitor in my breast is my only director."[24]

Nothing that Burrows or anyone else said at this moment, however, could add to the humiliation, shame, and regret that Biddle was suffering, for he had already been censured by the man whose opinion he valued most. When the new loan had been made to Burrows, Biddle had informed the directors of the original transaction, and Cadwalader, who had known nothing of it, was shocked and displeased. "The confidential footing on which we have stood and my supposed privity with all the concerns of the Bank," he wrote on March 14, "have placed me in a relation to the institution different from that of any other directors. No censure can fall upon any of its proceedings without affecting me in an especial degree. . . . To resign would be an extreme measure, and perhaps at this critical period not a proper one toward the stockholders. . . . [But] in the meantime you will . . . do me justice to acquit me of all knowledge or participation in the transaction . . . as I from the bottom of my heart do acquit you of any wrong intention, attributing as I do what has taken place to the warmth of your zeal for the interests of the Bank."[25]

23 S. Burrows to N. Biddle, March 19, 1832, in the Biddle Manuscripts in the Library of Congress.

24 S. Burrows to N. Biddle, March 26, 1832, in the Biddle Manuscripts in the Library of Congress.

25 T. Cadwalader to N. Biddle, March 14, 1832, in the Biddle Manuscripts in the Library of Congress.

Biddle replied the same day, and the much corrected draft of his letter is evidence of his personal concern. "I have just read your note of this day with the most acute pain," he said. "Of all that has taken place since my connection of thirteen years with the institution the only circumstance which has caused regret is this matter, not from any consciousness of wrong, but because it is liable to misconstruction and particularly because it has excited unpleasant feelings in your mind." He explained the circumstances under which the loans had been made and then added: "The duty which remains to me I shall endeavor to perform fully and frankly. It is to acquit in the most distinct manner all those gentlemen who were ignorant of these loans and had no participation in making them. Of these the first in every point of view is yourself. You were not present on any occasion when it was mentioned and I believe were not at all aware of its existence. On that subject I shall take any and every occasion to render you ample justice. That I did not mention it to you was certainly not owing to any unwillingness to do it, since with you I have less reserve than with almost any other human being."[26]

"Allow me to say," he concluded, "that no part of the matter has given me such intense pain as the feeling which you have in regard to it. You were the first to remark the anxiety which I could not conceal, and to you I communicated first my own suffering in consequence of it. To that suffering you would add a thousand fold by separating yourself from the institution, a course which I should deeply deplore as equally injurious to the stockholders and to myself. On the contrary my reliance is upon you, that wholly ignorant as you were and as everyone shall know you were of the whole matter, it may be in your power to prevent the ill effects which may arise from it." Cadwalader knew the meaning of this final sentence. He had acted as president of the Bank on frequent occasions when Biddle was absent from Philadelphia, and he would be the natural successor to the office if Biddle was forced to resign. It would be up to him, therefore, "to prevent the ill effects" that would result from disclosure and, for the interests of the stockholders and of the nation, to continue the struggle to win the recharter.

[26] N. Biddle to T. Cadwalader, March 14, 1832, in the Biddle Manuscripts in the Library of Congress.

The Investigation
and the
Veto

*B*iddle gave no outward sign of his fears of the congressional investigation, and no one but Cadwalader was given any hint of a possible forced resignation. He continued to perform his usual duties with his accustomed air of serene self-confidence and prepared for the reception of the committee as if he was absolutely certain that they would find nothing wrong with his administration of the Bank. Much of this confidence was justified. Clayton had listed seven breaches of the charter and fifteen instances of misconduct on the part of the managers of the Bank in the speech which had introduced the resolution of inquiry, but these charges, like those Benton had made the year before, were hardly deserving of an answer. Indeed, it was not Clayton's purpose to expose weaknesses or inadequacies in the organization of the Bank or correctible improprieties in its operations. His purpose was "to take care of the mammoth in some way or another" by arousing the fears and jealousies of the people. The long list of abuses sounded impressive, as it was intended it should, but every count in the indictment was lacking in substance.

One of the violations of the charter listed by Clayton was that the Bank had built houses to rent, with the implication that this stemmed from an intention to hold rental property for income. Actually, the Bank did not want such property and ordinarily sold all lands and houses taken in settlement of debt. But in Cincinnati, the source of Clayton's complaint, it had been confronted with a complex problem. The branch established there during the administration of William Jones had loaned very liberally to purchasers of local real estate at the height of a speculative market, with the result that the Bank found itself in possession of a large amount of the most valuable property in the heart of the city when the market collapsed. It had acepted this real estate only when a monetary settlement had become hopeless, but so extensive were its holdings that a too rapid sale would have injured the whole city.[1]

The Bank would have lost money, but an even greater injury would have been done to other property holders. Consequently, Biddle continued the policy established by Cheves of selling only as buyers appeared on their own initiative. The first agent employed, George W. Jones, had personal holdings and connections in Cincinnati, and he was discharged by Biddle in the belief that he was refusing to sell the Bank's holdings in order to further his own interests. His successor, Herman Cope of Philadelphia, was instructed to sell as rapidly as possible but was given permission to make improvements on certain portions of the property to increase its value and provide income until it could be sold. This policy also increased the value of the property owned by others and contributed to the prosperity of the community as a whole, for, in addition to dwelling houses, the Bank also constructed a canal basin and warehouses on its waterfront holdings.

The loss on the Bank's loans in Cincinnati had originally been estimated at more than eight hundred thousand dollars, but by 1832 it had recovered most of this enormous sum through its real estate operations. And it had accomplished this recovery by aiding, rather than injuring, the city. The results of this system, Biddle was certain, had been "beneficent alike to the Bank and to the community. To the Bank, because it had been enabled to dispose gradually of its property, so as probably to escape any ultimate loss; and to the community, because the sales and improvements of the Bank have kept pace with those of individual citizens, so as not to injure them by competition."[2]

Clayton had also criticized the Bank for making donations to volunteer fire companies, police forces, and such internal improvements as the road from Maysville to Lexington. But in each instance the Bank had property in the area and did only what other property holders did, namely, contribute to those who were protecting it or increasing its value. The amounts involved were small and appropriate to their object, and the directors in authorizing the expenditures were properly applying "the funds of the corporation with a view to the promotion of its interests." Of all Clayton's accusations, however, the one that amused Biddle most was that the Bank was buying 3 per cent government stock at its current market rate as part of "a job" between it and the brokers "to force the government to pay at par for the stock." It was true that the Bank had bought considerable amounts of this stock through secret orders to brokers, but it

[1] T. Cadwalader to G. M. Dallas, December 28, 1831, in the Biddle Manuscripts in the Library of Congress; *House Report* (22d Cong., 1st sess.), No. 460, pp. 6-7, 490-91.

[2] *House Report,* No. 460, pp. 6-7, 490-91.

had done so for the account of the government. In September, 1831, Secretary McLane had asked Biddle to undertake this operation in order to save the Treasury money by purchasing on the open market at ninety-five or below in advance of the time when the government would be forced to redeem at par, and the Bank without compensation had agreed to this proper and legal transaction.[3]

Similar explanations were available for the other practices that Clayton had listed as violations of the charter and could have been obtained by a simple request to the Bank. But this was not his purpose. He wanted to delay the vote on the recharter and to bring out as much damaging evidence against the Bank as he could. His interests were political, not economic, and this was the central weakness of the anti-Bank position. Only a few members of Congress shared Jackson's and Benton's theoretical and constitutional objections to banks and paper money, and Speaker Stevenson, when called on to name a committee of investigation, had some difficulty in finding men willing and able to serve. Clayton as mover of the resolution was named chairman, and associated with him, to make a nominal majority against the Bank, were Cambreleng, Francis Thompson of Maryland, and Richard M. Johnson of Kentucky. The minority on the committee, who represented the views of an actual majority of the House, were Adams, McDuffie, and Watmough.

Adams was the only person appointed who was not a member of the Jackson party. All the rest had voted for Jackson in 1828 and still were numbered among his supporters, though none except Thompson was in full sympathy with his views in regard to the Bank. Clayton had acceded to Benton's suggestion that he present the motion for an inquiry because as a new member it would give him prominence and strengthen him at home; but he was personally favorable to the recharter, and in 1833, when he broke with Jackson over the nullification controversy and the Force Act, he admitted to Biddle that he regretted what he had done. Cambreleng was interested solely in discrediting the existing institution so that it could be replaced by another with headquarters in New York; and Johnson, whose position was the strangest of all, frankly said that he favored the renewal of the charter. He voted with Clayton, Cambreleng, and Thompson to enable them to have a majority, but his sympathies were on the other side.[4]

The committee began its investigations on March 22 in Philadelphia, and its first actions were to subpoena Burrows and Webb and the Bank's records of its transactions with them. Adams and the other members of the minority protested vigorously but unsuccessfully against this invasion of

[3] L. McLane to N. Biddle, September 29, 1831; N. Biddle to L. McLane, October 25, November 29, 1831; N. Biddle to A. Dickins, November 29, 1831, in the Biddle Manuscripts in the Library of Congress.

[4] *Register of Debates* (22d Cong., 1st sess.), pp. 267–71.

the right of privacy, but the results of the investigation were not what the majority wished. Burrows dodged the subpoena and never appeared, and Webb proved conclusively that neither he nor Noah had known where Burrows had obtained the money he advanced. Biddle treated the matter as if it were an ordinary business transaction and disclaimed any intention of bribery. He conceded that the subsequent loans to Webb and Noah were probably too large, but he justified them by the fact that the New York banks, for political reasons, had refused to accommodate the editors of the *Courier and Enquirer*. One of the loans, he reminded the committee, had been paid in full, and the other had been reduced by two thousand dollars at its last renewal.[5]

At this point Clayton was unwise enough to enable Biddle to transfer attention from the *Courier and Enquirer* by asking for a list of all loans and payments made by the Bank to editors, members of Congress, and other federal employees, in the belief that such a list would prove the partisanship of the institution and its administrators. The result was the exact opposite. Newspapers supporting Jackson had received a larger amount of "the favors" of the Bank than those opposing him, and numbered among these were several who were opposed to the recharter. Loans to political officials had also been made without discrimination as to party or attitude toward the Bank, and Biddle, with a feeling of triumph, told Watmough that the list contained "an array of names certainly not expected, and as certainly not agreeable to those who asked for it."[6]

A similar result attended the effort of Clayton and Cambreleng to prove that Biddle had improperly loaned money to a distant relative, Thomas Biddle, without the consent of the directors and without charging interest. This charge, which Adams rightly characterized as an accusation of embezzlement, was made late in the second week of the investigation, and Clayton insisted that it could be proved by the testimony of Thomas Wilson, a former cashier of the Bank. Wilson was immediately subpoenaed, but his testimony did not sustain the charge. He knew of no instance in which Thomas Biddle or any other person had been permitted to use money without payment of interest or of any loan that had been made without the consent of the directors. He admitted, however, that in 1824 he had hinted to Reuben M. Whitney, a director secretly unfriendly to

[5] *Ibid.*, pp. 8–11, 75–77, 84–93, 546–67. The *Courier and Enquirer* was a Democratic newspaper completely loyal to Jackson, and Noah, one of the editors who had been allegedly bribed, was serving as surveyor of the Port of New York by presidential appointment. James A. Hamilton urged Jackson to remove Noah from his place, but the President refused. C. C. Cambreleng to J. Hoyt, March 15, 1832, in Mackenzie, *Van Buren*, p. 234; J. A. Hamilton to A. Jackson, May 7, 1832, in Bassett (ed.), *Correspondence of Jackson*, IV, 437.

[6] N. Biddle to J. G. Watmough, April 30, 1832, in the Biddle Manuscripts in the Library of Congress; *House Report* (22d Cong., 1st sess.), No. 460, pp. 84–93, 424–25, 569–70.

the President, that he thought Biddle had too much influence over the board and had spoken with disapprobation of the fact that Thomas Biddle, a wealthy broker, "had occasionally received discounts upon transferred stocks with checks, which, at the end of an indefinite number of days, were taken up and the cash returned, with regular payment of interest as upon discounted notes."[7]

Clayton and Cambreleng were shaken by this testimony, but they had gone too far to back down. They subpoenaed Whitney, the source of their information, who in sworn testimony stated that Wilson and his assistant, John Andrews, in 1824 had told him of some transactions "which they were not willing should exist without some member of the board being informed of them." They had taken him to the teller's desk, where he had found that Thomas Biddle had received two interest-free advances on stock certificates, one dated May 25 in the amount of forty-five thousand dollars and another the following day in the amount of twenty-five thousand dollars. They had then gone to the discount desk and found a note of Thomas Biddle for thirty thousand dollars, and one of Charles Biddle, Nicholas' brother, for over thirty-eight thousand dollars, both of which, according to Whitney, had been discounted by the president without consultation with the board. He exhibited an old and worn memorandum of these transactions, which corresponded exactly with the Bank's books, and he swore to the committee that the entries had been made only upon his orders to Wilson and Andrews.

He concluded his testimony with the statement that he had then told Biddle what he had discovered and warned him that no repetition of these practices would be permitted so long as Whitney remained on the board. Biddle, who was present while Whitney was testifying, asked him where these conversations occurred and received the reply, "In the area of the banking room, not far from the first teller's desk. . . . I stated to you the particulars I had learned. . . . You did not deny them. You colored up a good deal." In describing his conversation with Biddle, Whitney had gone too far. The memorandum he had made and the entries in the books of the Bank proved that, if what he reported had happened, it must have been on May 27, and Biddle was not in Philadelphia on that day. He had gone to Washington on May 22 and had remained there until June 1. Wilson, Andrews, and the tellers denied the remainder of Whitney's story, and on April 30 the committee by formal resolution declared that "the charges brought against the president of the Bank, of lending money to Thomas Biddle and Company without interest, and of discounting notes of that house and for Charles Biddle, without authority of the directors, are without foundation."[8]

7 *House Report* (22d Cong., 1st sess.), No. 460, pp. 115–19, 126, 131, 132–35, 141–42, 297–314, 384–91, 425–27.
8 *Ibid.*

The minority was more explicit. They stated that "an informer" named Whitney had invented the charges and that his "artfully devised story," which was intended "to blast the reputation of a highminded and honorable man," had been made "to recoil upon the head of its inventor, who must forever stand forth as a blasted monument to the speedy and retributive justice of heaven." The majority of the committee was thus thwarted in its efforts to find evidence that the Bank had violated its charter or been guilty of seriously improper conduct, but they had another object, which was simply delay. Cambreleng took charge of this phase of the inquiry, and he devised a total of one hundred and sixty-two hostilely phrased questions that covered virtually all the past operations and policies of the Bank. He seemed determined to prove that the institution, despite its obvious prosperity, had been managed imprudently and unsafely, but he gave Biddle the opportunity to explain to the country exactly what the Bank did and why.

Cambreleng was surprised at both the speed and the sharpness of Biddle's replies. He protested that he was being treated "unkindly" and "discourteously," a complaint that "only produced a laugh" in the rest of the committee because even those supporting his effort knew that he had been given his just due.[9] The committee was unable to meet its deadline of April 25, and the majority report, even though moderated through the efforts of Johnson, was so offensive that the minority made two replies. The first, signed by all three of the members, was nonpartisan, but the second, signed by Adams alone, was designed to prove that the only way to preserve the Bank of the United States and all other institutions and interests was to defeat Andrew Jackson and elect Henry Clay. None of the reports was of significant importance, nor did any influence a single vote in Congress. But the investigation had the effect that Benton and others had wanted; it raised a great deal of smoke, and where there is smoke, everyone knows, there must be fire.

The reports were presented to the House in the second week of May, and Cadwalader, pessimistic as usual, thought that this delay eliminated any hope for the passage of the recharter. Biddle was more optimistic, and on May 19 he wrote to Webster: "Will you ask your landlord Mr. Gadsby to keep a sitting room and two bedrooms for a traveler who hopes to occupy them tomorrow evening under the name of N. Biddle?" His first conversations in Washington were with Livingston and McLane, and he attempted to convince them that the negative results of the investigation opened the way for the administration to recommend the recharter with the agreed modifications. He had little hope that this final attempt at a negotiated settlement would succeed, but he had to make the attempt. He and Cadwalader were more certain than they had been at the beginning of the

9 J. G. Watmough to N. Biddle, May 11, 1832, in the Biddle Manuscripts in the Library of Congress; *House Report* (22d Cong., 1st sess.), No. 460, pp. 330–67.

year that Jackson would be re-elected. They were almost equally positive that he would never affix his signature to a bill renewing the charter of the Bank. Their one hope was that a sufficient number of Jackson representatives and senators would be convinced of the necessity and utility of the national bank so that they would join with the opposition to override the inevitable veto.[10]

"Our life," Cadwalader wrote, "depends on this session, and getting the veto now, so that the nation may be roused before the autumnal elections." If action were postponed, there would be "no alarm about the Bank," the election would not "turn on the point," as would be the case if the bill were previously rejected. "If vetoed now," he concluded, "I should feel sanguine as to the two-thirds of the new Congress." He urged Biddle to accept any amendments that would help to get a bill through the Congress, for what was needed, he insisted, was to get a charter, any sort of charter, passed. Few of the Jackson supporters of the Bank were willing to join in this attempt, but a sufficient number held firm in both houses to give the pro-Bank forces a majority. Dallas, though reluctant, took the lead in the Senate and was followed by Webster, who made, according to Biddle, "a strong speech ... to which I contributed in a small way after the manner of the man who played the cock in Hamlet." All amendments suggested by the other side were uniformly voted down by the Bank majority, and on June 9 a final attempt to postpone was defeated. The same day a motion to engross the bill was adopted, and Biddle elatedly wrote his wife: "We have a great triumph today on the passage of our bill to a third reading. ... I must stay and see it fairly out and hope to embrace you on Tuesday. So much for the Senate, after all that comes the House of Representatives, after that the President. But before these, thank Providence, will, I hope, come the sight of you and our dear children, whom God bless."[11]

On June 11 the bill passed the Senate by a vote of twenty-eight to twenty, and the next day the House defeated a motion to lay the bill on the table for the remainder of the session. Biddle returned to Philadelphia thinking that all was well, but he soon received from Watmough a communication urgently pressing him to return because of unexpected complications. A severe outbreak of cholera in New York was being used by the opponents of the recharter as an excuse for immediate adjournment, and McDuffie, who was unwilling to permit a vote on the Bank bill until the tariff was settled, was not pressing the issue. Biddle could not leave at

[10] T. Cadwalader to T. Broadwood, May 12, 1832, in the Cadwalader Manuscripts in the Historical Society of Pennsylvania; N. Biddle to D. Webster, May 19, 1832; N. Biddle to T. Cadwalader, May 30, 1832, in the Biddle Manuscripts in the Library of Congress.

[11] T. Cadwalader to N. Biddle, May 31, 1832; N. Biddle to T. Cadwalader, May 30, 1832, in the Biddle Manuscripts in the Library of Congress; N. Biddle to Jane Biddle, June 9, 1832, in the Biddle-Craig Manuscripts in the Historical Society of Pennsylvania.

the moment, but the next week he went down to Washington, and on July 3, the House by a vote of one hundred and seven to eighty-six passed the bill. The Senate concurred in a minor amendment about branches in New York State, and the charter had been renewed as far as the Congress was concerned. "I congratulate our friends most cordially upon this most satisfactory result," Biddle wrote Cadwalader. "Now for the president. My belief is that the president will veto . . . though that is not generally known or believed." And then, in a separate note for Cadwalader's private information, he said, "the president *will certainly veto the bill*."[12]

Cadwalader also foresaw Jackson's veto, but he hoped that it would be "accompanied with qualifying and saving declarations as to the president's disposition to acquiesce in any views that may be manifested by another Congress fully representing the people, and elected mainly by reference to the Bank question." In making this remark he had the interest of the Bank in mind, but he also was concerned about Jackson, whom he had enthusiastically supported in both his previous campaigns. "Such a course," he continued, "would soften the clamour that will otherwise burst forth against him and keep up the confidence of the stockholders and customers, the latter of whom will form the largest portion of the revilers that a naked veto will put in motion against him."[13]

Samuel Smith, apparently without consulting Cadwalader or Biddle, had the same hope. He urged Jackson to sign the recharter and "disappoint those who have pressed the subject, who expect and count on your veto as a means to injure the party." But if Jackson should decide upon a veto, he added, "I pray, beg, and entreat you to do it so as to leave the subject *open* for the decision of the people." He inclosed a letter from his son, John Spear Smith, which advised Jackson not to base his veto on constitutional principles. Instead, it should state that three million people included in the new census were unrepresented in the existing Congress; that the next would be elected after a full debate on the subject; and, finally, that no inconvenience would result from the postponement. These arguments impressed Jackson, and a friend of Biddle's, who had dinner at the White House on June 20, reported that he had "had some conversations with a certain individual on the subject of the Bank. Nothing was said . . . indicative of a *decided* opinion, various difficulties and objections, but none insuperable." And Postmaster Barry, in a letter to his daughter, wrote: "When a charter for a Bank of proper form is presented by a vote of a Congress elected under the new census by the people with a view to this

12 W. Creighton, Jr., to N. Biddle, June 12, 1832; J. G. Watmough to N. Biddle, June 18, 1832; N. Biddle to T. Cadwalader, June 26, July 3, 1832, in the Biddle Manuscripts in the Library of Congress.

13 T. Cadwalader to N. Biddle, July 4, 1832, in the Biddle Manuscripts in the Library of Congress.

question, General Jackson will either sign the bill or retire from his station."[14]

Barry and the other members of the Cabinet, with the exception of Taney, were urging the President to adopt this moderate course, and Jackson prepared a preliminary draft of a veto message which incorporated most of the views and many of the phrases recommended by Smith and his son.[15] The opponents of the recharter around the President were greatly disturbed by this development, and they united in an effort to persuade him to issue an unconditional and positive veto. They were not at all certain that they could accomplish this, and they might have failed if Biddle, who was usually discreet and cautious in his utterances, had not talked too much. He was under great strain and tension and had developed a fixed idea that the sole cause of Jackson's hostility was the Bank's refusal to permit itself to be used as part of the spoils of office. "When these persons first came into office . . . ," he told one of the Bank's supporters in Congress, "they made a combined effort to force us to remove an officer on account of his political sentiments. This was obviously only the commencement of a series, and we took our stand at once. The intractable spirit of the Bank has made it an object of dislike ever since." He repeated this charge once too often, and it was carried to Benton, who immediately transmitted it to the President. All chance of a reasonable veto was eliminated. Jackson denounced the statement as "one of the foulest and basest calumnies ever uttered." The Bank of the United States once again became "a dangerous and corrupt institution" that already controlled "the legislation of Congress," and if it were rechartered, it would "destroy the liberties of the country."[16]

He turned to Kendall and Taney and gave them instructions to make the veto firm, unconditional, and final. They accepted the assignment eagerly, with genuine enthusiasm for their task, and the resulting document defies critical, historical, or constitutional analysis. The major emphasis was on the conflict between rich and poor, and the Congress was accused of passing legislation that made "the rich richer and the potent more powerful." Most of the difficulties of the country were attributed to "the adoption of such principles as are embodied in this act," which "arrayed section against section, interest against interest, and man against man, in a fearful commotion which threatens to shake the foundations of

[14] S. Smith to A. Jackson, June 17, 1832, in Bassett (ed.), *Correspondence of Jackson*, IV, 449; R. Patterson to N. Biddle, June 21, 1832, in the Biddle Manuscripts in the Library of Congress; W. T. Barry to Susan Taylor, July 4, 1832, typescript, in the University of Virginia Library.

[15] A. Jackson, memorandum on the bank veto, n.d., in Bassett (ed.), *Correspondence of Jackson*, IV, 458–59; R. Taney, manuscript history of the bank war, pp. 124–25, in the Taney Manuscripts in the Library of Congress.

[16] A. Jackson to T. H. Benton, n.d., in Bassett (ed.), *Correspondence of Jackson*, IV, 445.

our union." But the message also contained an attack upon the existing stockholders, a fourth of whom were foreigners and the rest, "a few hundred of our citizens, chiefly of the richest class." If the government sold monopolies, the writers asserted, "let them not be bestowed on the subjects of a foreign government, nor upon a designated or favored class of men in our own country. It is but justice and good policy . . . to confine our favors to our fellow-citizens, and let each in his turn enjoy an opportunity to profit by our bounty."[17]

The Supreme Court was denounced as the betrayer of "the humble members of society, the farmers, mechanics, and laborers," and its decisions on constitutional questions were said not to be binding on the other branches of government. The Executive, the Congress, and the Court must each for itself be guided by its own opinion of the Constitution, and the President was thus free to decide whether the act rechartering the Bank was "necessary and proper" and "therefore constitutional," or "unnecessary and improper and therefore unconstitutional." This, the central issue, was stated, but the actual question of whether or not the Bank was a necessary and useful institution was never examined. All that was said was that "suspicions are entertained, and charges are made, of gross abuses and violations of its charter," and this was considered sufficient. The President could not alone "make our government what it ought to be" because of previous "improvident legislation," but he could and did "take a stand against all new grants of monopolies and exclusive privileges, against any prostitution of our government to the advancement of the few at the expense of the many."

He sent the veto message to the House of Representatives on July 10, but he took no action against those in his administration who had favored the "prostitution of our government to the advancement of the few at the expense of the many." Livingston and McLane retained their positions in the Cabinet; Lewis was still one of his most trusted political and personal friends, even though they and many others in his administration and party were among that "corrupt, venial, and self-interested" group that had advocated the recharter of the Bank. If Jackson actually believed what he had written and said concerning the Bank and those who supported it, his retention of these men is exceedingly difficult to explain. But if he did not believe what Kendall and Taney had written for him and made these extravagant and unjustified accusations solely for political effect, then he had indeed, as Biddle charged, adopted "a course much fitter for a humble demagogue than the chief magistrate of a great country."[18]

Biddle was disappointed and angry at the tone and content of the veto message. "It has all the fury of a chained panther biting the bars of his

[17] R. Taney, manuscript history of the bank war, pp. 111–14, 124–25, in the Taney Manuscripts in the Library of Congress; Richardson, *Messages and Papers,* III, 1139–54.

[18] N. Biddle to S. Smith, January 4, 1832, in the Biddle Manuscripts in the Library of Congress.

cage," he wrote. "It is really a manifesto of anarchy, such as Marat or Robespierre might have issued to the mob of the faubourg Saint Antoine." For the first time since he had been elected president of the Bank, he began to take a genuine interest in a political campaign and to care seriously and personally about its results. He knew that any effort was useless. Jackson's re-election was assured, but he nevertheless wrote to Clay: "You are destined to be the instrument of . . . deliverance, and at no period of your life has the country ever had a deeper stake in you. I wish you success most cordially, because I believe the institutions of the union are involved in it." He contributed freely from his personal funds to Clay's campaign and secretly wrote an angry, harsh attack upon Jackson, signed "Simon Snyder," which he had printed and circulated at his own expense. These private and hidden efforts were to relieve his personal feelings, but in his official role as president of the Bank he acted with complete propriety and neutrality. He avoided expressing his views to any but his most intimate friends, and the Bank, though a major issue in the campaign, was not accused of direct participation in politics in 1832 as it had been in 1828.[19]

William G. Bucknor, a New York broker and a large stockholder in the Bank, thought Biddle too fastidious. He insisted that Jackson's defeat could be accomplished if he were opposed by a newspaper of large circulation and influence such as the *Courier and Enquirer*, which he was sure could be persuaded to shift from Jackson to Clay if the Bank would lend Webb the money to buy out Noah. Biddle, of course, had no desire to be entangled again with a newspaper that had already caused him so much pain, humiliation, and worry. He also knew that the directors, a number of whom were Jacksonians, would never approve such a loan. But these were not the operative reasons for his rejection of Bucknor's proposal. He refused to consider the loan because it was improper in principle and would be a direct interference in politics, in violation of the Bank's rules. In his earlier negotiations with Burrows, Noah, and Webb the question of party affiliation had never been raised. All that had been talked about was the paper's editorial position in regard to the charter, theoretically and actually a nonpartisan issue. The loan recommended by Bucknor would have no direct effect on the Bank. It would only contribute to the strength of the Clay party, and Biddle firmly refused, saying that "to interfere in the elections would be a departure from the duty which the Bank owes to the country. This it has hitherto practiced and, whatever may be the consequence, must continue to practice."[20]

His rule against political interference did not prevent his continuing the

19 N. Biddle to H. Clay, August 1, 1832; N. Biddle to R. Conynham, September 24, 1832; "Simon Snyder," "The Day after the Election," in the Biddle Manuscripts in the Library of Congress.

20 W. G. Bucknor to N. Biddle, July 12, 1832; N. Biddle to W. G. Bucknor, July 13, 1832; J. W. Webb to N. Biddle, July 12, 16, 18, August 1, 2, 12, 24, 1832; N. Biddle to J. W. Webb, July 13, 17, August 25, 1832, in the Biddle Manuscripts in the Library of Congress.

circulation of articles and documents explaining the operations of the Bank and answering the attacks made upon it regardless of their source. He thought that the veto message, containing as it did so many erroneous and, to him, ridiculous statements, would be excellent propaganda for the Bank. He distributed it widely, but Clay warned him he was making a mistake, that it was "a common, sometimes fatal error to suppose that the mass of the community is as well informed as the intelligent respecting a given subject." He urged Biddle to employ "the same pen that prepared last year the review of Benton's speech . . . to make a similar review of the veto message," but Biddle was unable to spare the time.[21] He was still president of the nation's bank, and there was not only a political campaign in the summer of 1832 but also economic developments that threatened to cause a financial disaster, and Biddle was forced to turn his attention from political matters to that area in which he was more directly concerned.

[21] H. Clay to N. Biddle, August 27, 1832, in the Biddle Manuscripts in the Library of Congress.

~ 21 ~

"The Bank Is Broke"

$\mathcal{D}$uring all those years when the Bank of the United States was being severely criticized by President Jackson and most of the party press, it was properly performing its duties as the fiscal agent of the national Treasury and as the balance wheel of the national economy. More than fifty million dollars of the government debt was retired between 1829 and 1832, and the payment and reinvestment of that vast sum were accomplished without any disturbance of ordinary business. This was also a period of political and economic disturbance in Europe, and Biddle's management of the Bank in these difficult years of revolution and the threat of a general war was one of his greatest achievements as a public banker. The first serious crisis occurred in the early months of 1831, when the rates of exchange on Europe declined to their lowest point in years, and American importers, seizing the opportunity to buy cheaply, greatly increased their purchases of European-manufactured goods. Biddle encouraged this movement. He thought that war was a certainty and that American balances abroad, including those of the Bank, had become excessive as a result of Europe's increased purchases of American wheat and other foodstuffs and its normal importations of cotton and tobacco. Unless some means of paying these balances was devised, the European debtors must ship specie and reduce their purchases of the new crops. Such a course would have the inevitable effect of lowering prices of southern and western produce and would lead to a disruption of American internal trade.[1]

On February 20, consequently, the Bank of the United States announced that it would sell bills of exchange at the current low and unprofitable rate, and the ships sailing for Europe carried many new orders from American importers. The next news advices from Europe, however, brought the information that all danger of war had passed and that European prices of American agricultural products had declined drastically. The Bank, which

[1] R. Colt to N. Biddle, February 11, 1831; R. Oliver to N. Biddle, February 26, 1831, in the Biddle Manuscripts in the Library of Congress.

in the preceding three weeks had sold more than a million dollars of bills of exchange, was now confronted with a radically different economic situation. The holders of the southern and western crops, hoping for higher prices later, refused to ship them to Europe, and the previously ordered manufactured goods were arriving and being sold at auction in ever increasing amounts. The Bank, instead of having an unprofitable surplus in Europe, was confronted with the possibility of having to borrow at 5 per cent in London and Paris to meet payments.[2]

Biddle ordered an immediate increase in the rate of exchange, but he did not succeed in persuading the American holders of produce to ship to Europe or in preventing the importers from continuing to order European goods. He was forced to wait until the normal currents of trade brought about the natural and inevitable remedy. The rate of exchange rose steadily throughout the summer and in September reached the point where the export of specie began. This, as always, was his signal for action, and he immediately ordered the Philadelphia and New York boards to confine their loans to merchants who had customs bonds to pay on goods already imported and to refuse all applications from those who intended to place new orders in Europe. At the same time he lowered the Bank's rate of exchange below the specie point, so that he could supply all potential shippers of silver with bills on London and Paris.[3]

These gentle measures were just beginning to take effect when, on October 6, the national Treasury announced, without prior notice to the Bank, that all holders of the government stock due for redemption on January 1, 1832, could have immediate payment by presenting their certificates to the Bank of the United States. The Bank was thus faced with a potential cash demand for six million dollars at a moment when it was combating an already severe financial pressure. Biddle had no choice but to order an immediate curtailment of loans at all the eastern offices, which had the effect of increasing the monetary pressure. The rate of exchange went back above the specie point, and the local banks, confronted by this threat to their silver, curtailed their loans. The measures adopted had an immediate effect. The branches at which payment of government certificates could be demanded were completely prepared by October 24, and Biddle once more instituted his previously ordered relief policy. Within a week, all danger of panic had passed, but money and credit remained tight because of the continued arrivals of imports from Europe and the slower countermovement of American crops.[4]

[2] N. Biddle to P. P. F. DeGrand, March 8, April 15, 1831; N. Biddle to M. Robinson, March 22, 1831, in the Biddle Manuscripts in the Library of Congress.

[3] N. Biddle to R. Lenox, September 20, 1831; R. Lenox to N. Biddle, September 21, 1831; I. Carow to N. Biddle, September 21, 1831; N. Biddle to T. W. Ward, October 6, 1831, in the Biddle Manuscripts in the Library of Congress.

[4] N. Biddle to S. Alley, October 24, 1831; N. Biddle to L. McLane, November 29, 1831; N. Biddle to A. Dickins, November 29, 1831, in the Biddle Manuscripts in the Library of Congress.

Critics of the Bank seized upon this temporary period of difficulty in the fall of 1831 as the basis for attacks upon the institution. Roswell Colt wanted to answer these charges with a newspaper article on the Treasury order, but Biddle requested him not to do so. "I would not for any consideration," he wrote, "say anything about Mr. McLane's management of the Treasury for he has behaved in the most handsome manner in regard to the Bank. . . . I consider it a very unfortunate measure, but I know that it was not designed against the Bank and therefore I defend it and bear the blame of its consequences. Do not therefore say a word, and do not write a word, above all, do not publish a word against it." Biddle himself wrote McLane to explain to him the effect of his order. "When large sums are to be paid," he said, "the fixing of a period ahead so as to allow the Bank to accumulate its funds at that time, is much preferable to a general and vague demand which obliges the Bank to keep itself always ready and prevents it from using advantageously to the community, the funds which it thus holds in suspense."[5]

Neither McLane nor Asbury Dickins, his chief clerk who had issued the order, had intended to embarrass the Bank or to bring pressure upon the financial community. Their purpose had been to relieve the pressure, and they had thought that the advance payment would free money and credit instead of having the unfortunate effect that it did. The following March they made certain that a similar result would not occur, and notified Biddle four months in advance that the administration had decided to begin the redemption of the large 3 per cent loan by paying half of each certificate on July 1, 1832. Dickins, who was acting secretary because of McLane's illness, wrote that if any objections occurred to Biddle as to the amount or the mode of payment, he should feel free to mention them. Biddle had many objections to the proposal, but none of them had any connection with the Bank's ability to make the payments. So far as the institution itself was concerned, it was sufficient that the government had the necessary funds; but for the general interest of the commercial and financial community, there were definite reasons for postponing the proposed payment. It would also have a serious effect on the government's ability to collect from its debtors because the Bank would be forced to curtail its loans through April, May, and June, the very moment when importing merchants would need credit to make payment to the government for customs duties. The collector of customs in New York had requested a special extension of loans to this class of customers in February, in order to prevent failures, and Biddle thought that another would be necessary in June and July, a period when large sums were due to the Treasury.[6]

[5] R. Colt to N. Biddle, October 26, November 4, 1832; N. Biddle to R. Colt, November 4, 1831; N. Biddle to L. McLane, November 29, 1831, in the Biddle Manuscripts in the Library of Congress.

[6] A. Dickins to N. Biddle, October 14, 1832; N. Biddle to L. McLane, March 29, 1832, in the Biddle Manuscripts in the Library of Congress; Minutes of the board of

Biddle had another reason for postponement, but he was unwilling to mention it. The cholera, which had caused many deaths in Europe the year before, had appeared in Canadian ports, and there was real danger that it might spread to the United States during the spring and summer. If it did, the population of the disease-stricken cities would flee in panic, and there would be a major disturbance of business and finance. So important did he consider this matter that in late March, with the investigating committee in session, he went down to Washington to talk with McLane and Dickins, carrying with him a letter from Cambreleng that recommended a postponement "as necessary to the business community." Jackson was most reluctant to change the administration's plans, and when he at last acquiesced, he did so with the conviction that he had been magnanimously generous to an enemy in trouble. He considered it "the duty of the Bank to keep itself ready at all times to pay the whole amount of the money it held on deposit for the government upon reasonable notice," and he was sure that Biddle would not have requested postponement of the payment unless he had been forced to do so by the condition of the Bank. "I tell you, sir, she's broke," he told William Lewis, "Mr. Biddle is a proud man, and he never would have come to Washington . . . if the Bank had the money. Never sir. The Bank's broke and Mr. Biddle knows it."[7]

Lewis attempted to acquaint him with the actual situation, but the President could not or would not understand. It was true that the United States had the money to pay off the stock, and it was also true that the Bank of the United States could have made the payment. But, as Hezekiah Niles pointed out, the people would suffer from the derangements of business that would be brought about by its "ill-advised payment" at this particular moment. "We have observed," Niles wrote, "that the Bank can pay this money, but have yet to experience the effects of the contraction of the currency that will follow such payment; for it is inevitable that the Bank must . . . reduce its discounts; and that the local banks, for their own preservation, must pursue the same course." Biddle was seeking to avoid this derangement of business, not to conceal the condition or to protect the solvency of the Bank, and in so acting he was fulfilling his duty as a government director of the nation's bank.[8]

He went to Washington as a responsible public officer to consult with the Secretary of the Treasury and the President about a matter of common interest, not as a commander of an opposing army asking for a truce, but the President interpreted his action differently. And when Jackson decided to veto the recharter and to destroy the Bank, he directed McLane to no-

---

directors of the Bank of the United States, March 13, 1832, in *House Report* (22d Cong., 1st sess.), No. 460, pp. 282–83.

[7] Parton, *Jackson*, III, 498; R. Taney, manuscript history of the bank war, p. 5, in the Taney Manuscripts in the Library of Congress.

[8] *Niles' Register*, XLIII (1832), 17–18.

tify Biddle that the government would pay off two-thirds of the 3 per cent stock on October 1 and the remainder three months later. McLane gave this notice on June 29, and in doing so gave Biddle an opportunity to discredit and dishonor the administration in an election year. Nine million dollars had to be collected by the government during the summer to enable the Treasury to have enough money to make the ordered payment. The Bank, by rigidly restricting credit, could cut off a large part of this anticipated revenue and, on the day of payment, announce that the government lacked sufficient funds. Biddle recognized this opportunity, but he refused to take advantage of it. "They, who administer the Bank," he wrote, "administer it for the country, not for any party, and although denounced by these persons in power, instead of avenging themselves, have striven . . . to avert every inconvenience from these measures with quite as much zeal as if they or their friends were the authors of them."[9]

He made a secret arrangement with McLane whereby the Bank, if the public funds were insufficient on the day of payment, would delay the presentation of any certificates under its control, and then he made a genuine and successful effort to insure that the government had the necessary money on October 1. It was not easy. When the notice of payment was issued, the cholera had already invaded New York and Philadelphia and was threatening the rest of the country. Many of the inhabitants were leaving the cholera-stricken towns, "deranging all business and prostrating all industry," and payments and collections—the lifeblood of the economic system—were almost universally suspended. Cadwalader, who was acting president of the Bank while Biddle was in Washington, immediately directed the New York and Philadelphia offices to suspend specie calls upon the state banks and to expand their discounts and loans on government stock. The New York board had issued a call for specie before Cadwalader's instructions were received, and Biddle was indignant. "I am much annoyed," he wrote Cadwalader from Washington, "by the course taken at New York, which is wrong in itself and particularly ill-timed. The true mode of proceeding was so obvious that I only wonder how our friends should commit such a mistake." The newspapers, even those friendly to the Bank, denounced this specie demand, and an officer of one of the city banks wrote that if the branch continued such calls without extending its loans or purchasing bills, it would "produce a more unfavorable effect than for the government to have paid half the amount of the three per cent stocks on the first of July."[10]

9 N. Biddle to T. Cadwalader, June 29, 30, 1832; A. Dickins to N. Biddle, August 4, 1832; N. Biddle to A. Dickins, August 7, 1832; N. Biddle to J. Q. Adams, November 19, 1832, in the Biddle Manuscripts in the Library of Congress.

10 C. W. Lawrence to N. Biddle, June 28, 1832; T. Cadwalader to N. Biddle, June 29, 1832; T. Cadwalader to I. Lawrence, June 29, 1832; N. Biddle to T. Cadwalader, July 1, 1832; N. Biddle to C. W. Lawrence, July 1, 1832; J. W. Webb to N. Biddle, July 8, 1832; N. Biddle to C. A. Wickliffe, December 6, 1832, in the Biddle Manuscripts in the Library of Congress.

Biddle could make no public explanation or admission of error, but on his return to Philadelphia he confirmed Cadwalader's orders to refrain from further demands upon the state banks and urged the New York and Philadelphia boards to make liberal purchases of exchange and loans upon government stock. The cholera continued to spread, and almost all business needed relief. The local banks had to protect their own solvency and credit and could do nothing to ease the pressure; but the Bank of the United States, which Jackson believed to be insolvent, could and did relieve the threatened communities. When its original measures proved insufficient in New York, it offered the local banks a loan of one million dollars to enable them to carry their debtors through the period of panic, and within a few days of this offer financial confidence was restored.[11]

It was still possible that the cholera would spread farther. If it did, another "interposition of the Bank to give relief" would be required. Hence Biddle could not relax his vigilance. The most pressing problem was the payment to be made on October 1, particularly the portion payable in Europe, which must be provided for, regardless of the state of business in the United States. Very few shipments of produce were leaving the cholera-stricken ports for Europe, and Biddle feared that he might be unable to accumulate the necessary funds in London. Recognizing that some arrangement must be made for this contingency in advance if the credit of the United States was not to be injured, he sent Cadwalader to London with instructions "to obtain control of a considerable portion of the foreign stock" before the day of payment.[12]

Biddle also ordered a general and gradual curtailment of loans throughout the institution and directed the western and southern offices to refrain from all purchases and sales of exchange that did not concentrate funds in the Northeast, where the payments would be made. He continued these restrictive orders throughout August and September in the face of protests that they were injurious not only to the economic prosperity of the interior regions but also to the political prospects of the supporters of the Bank. Leslie Combs, the Bank's attorney in Lexington, Kentucky, told Biddle that the oppressive course adopted by the branch on the orders of the parent board would "break down some of the best men in the country, who are perfectly good and using their utmost efforts for the institution," and urged him to turn every enemy of Clay "out of the directory." Self-preservation, he wrote, was the first law of nature, "the Bank must take care of itself and not grind its friends to powder."[13]

J. Watson Webb, on the other hand, assumed that Biddle's restrictive

11 *United States Gazette* (Philadelphia), July 20, 1832.

12 N. Biddle to A. Dickins, August 7, 1832, in the Biddle Manuscripts in the Library of Congress.

13 *Senate Document* (23d Cong., 2d sess.), No. 17, pp. 8–12; N. Biddle to E. Shippen and other branch cashiers, July 30, 1832; L. Combs to N. Biddle, August 30, 1832, in the Biddle Manuscripts in the Library of Congress.

orders had been issued for political reasons, and he thought they would be useful. "You have taught the people," he said, "the consequence of being without the aid of the Bank, and if at this moment when the practical effects of your course are vivid in their recollections, you should change the course and suffer them to feel all the advantages of the institution the effect would be electrical." When Webb's letter was written, on September 30, orders had already gone out to end the restrictions, their purpose having been accomplished. The eastern offices had paid the holders of stock without the slightest effect on ordinary business, and, though some of the businessmen in the South and West had been inconvenienced, few had been seriously injured. Biddle carefully explained to Webb that the orders had not been issued for political effect, that the course of the Bank had been taken in reference exclusively to its own concerns, and that the restrictions had been ended with the necessity which had imposed them.[14]

Cooler weather also brought the cholera to an end, and the Bank, instead of being hard pressed to meet its engagements at the beginning of October, was actually stronger and more liquid than usual. Biddle was immensely pleased over this successful solution of a most difficult financial emergency. He had brought the government and the Bank safely through a large and unwise payment, in spite of the derangement of business brought about by the cholera, and had accomplished his purpose so easily that few outside the Bank were aware of the danger from which they had been saved. But, having surmounted this crisis, he was immediately involved in another of a different kind. Cadwalader, usually the most precise and careful of representatives, made a serious mistake in the arrangement he made with Baring Brothers and Company, the Bank's London agents, to make certain that all European holders of the 3 per cent debt would either be able to obtain the face value of their stock or accept another mutually satisfactory arrangement when it was due.

Cadwalader knew that the Bank's charter forbade it to purchase any of the public debt without the consent of the Congress, but in his agreement with Barings he acted on the assumption that this restriction did not apply to an indirect purchase by the Bank's agent. One part of his arrangement was entirely proper. Owners of the 3 per cent stock were told that if they postponed presentation of their certificates until October 1, 1833, the Bank of the United States would pay the interest for the additional year, but, they were also told, if they wanted to obtain their money immediately, they could sell their stock to Barings as the agent of the United States Bank. When Biddle and the exchange committee were notified of this arrangement, they ratified the first part, but instructed Cadwalader to inform Barings that the Bank could not consent to the purchase of the stock. They agreed, of course, to protect Barings from any loss resulting from the transaction, but their repudiation of the unauthorized and illegal con-

[14] J. W. Webb to N. Biddle, September 30, 1832, in the Biddle Manuscripts in the Library of Congress; *House Report* (22d Cong., 2d sess.), No. 121, pp. 160–71.

tract was prompt and unconditional. Unfortunately, Barings had made a public announcement in London of their agreement with Cadwalader, and the same ship that brought Biddle the formal notice and contract also brought the same information to the New York newspapers. Those opposed to the Bank immediately began an outcry, which was picked up by the politicians, and none of these opponents of the Bank sought to find out why the arrangement had been made.[15]

The principal—almost the only—motive of Biddle and Cadwalader, in arranging for the postponement of the payment of this foreign-held debt, was "to protect the community from a drain to Europe under the existence of a pestilence," and what they did, they did for the country, not to protect the solvency of the Bank of the United States. The precautionary measures proved to be unnecessary; but when Cadwalader had sailed for Europe, no one knew how severe the cholera epidemic would be or how long it would last. If financial conditions had been critical on October 1 and the Bank had not taken these steps to prevent "a large sum from going abroad at a time when it was pressingly needed at home," the loss to the American economy might have been very great. The postponement did not cost the government a cent. Interest on the stock ceased on the payment day whether the certificates were presented for payment or not, and the cost to the Bank itself was inconsequential. As soon as Biddle was certain that the postponement was unnecessary, he instructed Barings to pay off all holders of the stock and to send the certificates to the United States without delay, so that one of the results of this measure was actually to increase the speed of the redemption and payment.

Jackson and those around him who were opposed to the Bank were nevertheless certain that the arrangement with Barings was further confirmation of the insolvency of the Bank, and the party newspapers, led by the *Globe,* sought to arouse the fears of the people so as to instigate runs on the branches. Their imputations of insolvency, on the whole, were not effective, but in Lexington, Kentucky, a politically inspired raid upon the silver reserve of the branch was actually undertaken, and reports that another would be made at Washington were widely circulated in early December. "I am ashamed to say," Biddle wrote a member of Congress on December 6, "that I have tonight directed a reinforcement . . . to Washington to protect the branch against the officers of the executive"; and the next day he told another that "in any other civilized country, a conspiracy between the chief magistrate and the subalterns of the treasury to destroy the monied institution of the country, would be deemed a crime worthy of impeachment. And even here I think it will not pass without a decided rebuke from Congress. It is mortifying to know that the Bank is at this

---

[15] N. Biddle to C. A. Wickliffe, December 6, 1832, in the Biddle Manuscripts in the Library of Congress; *Senate Document* (23d Cong., 2d sess.), No. 17, pp. 8–12; Parton, *Jackson,* III, 497–98.

moment obliged to fortify itself against the agents and partizans of the executive who have been endeavoring to spread alarm over the country. But it will not avail. The Bank is too strong to have its credit shaken by such a combination."[16]

Jackson himself was associated with this effort to break and destroy the Bank. His triumphant re-election had convinced him that his hostility to the institution was approved of and supported by the people of the country, and so great was his power of self-deception that he may actually have believed that the Bank was dangerously insolvent. Whatever his motives were or whatever he believed, his message to Congress contained a deliberate attempt to arouse the fears of the people concerning the Bank. He denounced the arrangement with Barings as a "failure of the Bank to perform its duties" and said that the Secretary of the Treasury had taken such measures as were within his powers "to judge whether the public deposits in that institution may be regarded as safe." He recommended that the Congress should undertake a further investigation "embracing the branches as well as the principal bank" because of the "many serious charges impeaching its character . . . which if true may justly excite the apprehension that it is no longer a safe depository of the money of the people."[17]

A private individual who made such statements about a bank, even if supported by evidence, would have been subject to a criminal indictment, and the fact that he believed them to be true would not have been acceptable as justification. Jackson, the President of the United States, had an even greater obligation to be sure of his facts before presenting to Congress completely unjustified doubts concerning the solvency of the national bank. If all his suspicions had been true and the Bank had been insolvent, the losers would not have been the stockholders, directors, and officers of the Bank alone. The whole economy of the country would have been dangerously injured and shaken, and the government and all the people would have suffered great loss. As it happened, the President was mistaken, and, even more importantly, his charges were disbelieved. No panic was started, and no needless injury was suffered, but Michel Chevalier, a visiting French economist, accurately commented: "If a European government, from motives of this character, on facts thus destitute of proof, should attempt to destroy an institution essential to the prosperity of the country, the cry of despotism would be raised on all sides . . . [and] many persons would charge such an attempt not only with violence but with folly."[18]

[16] N. Biddle to J. Tilford, November 12, 1832; N. Biddle to J. G. Watmough, December 6, 1832; N. Biddle to J. S. Johnston, December 7, 1832, in the Biddle Manuscripts in the Library of Congress; *House Report* (22d Cong., 2d sess.), No. 121, pp. 127–49.

[17] Richardson, *Messages and Papers*, III, 1162–63.

[18] Michel Chevalier, *Society, Maners, and Politics in the United States* (Boston, 1839), pp. 46–55.

~~ 22 ~~

The Western Debts

*J*ackson told the Congress and the people in December, 1832, that the Bank was insolvent, whereas in actual fact the institution was completing one of its most successful years. It had paid off some eighteen million dollars of the public debt for the government and had provided internal and foreign exchange for the business of the country amounting to two hundred and forty million dollars, at a cost of less than one-eleventh of 1 per cent. Its assets of more than eighty million dollars were almost double its liabilities, a balance in surplus and capital that served as "a guarantee to the holders of the notes of the Bank and to its depositors," and its specie holdings totaled almost nine million dollars. The government deposits, which were said to be unsafe, had been more than ten million dollars on several occasions during the year but had been reduced to twenty-two thousand dollars at the beginning of 1833 by the retirement of the debt and other governmental expenditures. The institution had been operated with intelligent precision, expanding and contracting as necessary to meet the fluctuating needs of government and business.[1]

It was, according to Niles, "a splendid pillar in the broad American System." Two-thirds of its loans had been made for the "direct encouragement and extension of agriculture and the mechanic arts, the promotion of internal improvements, and erection of all sorts of buildings." Similar tributes were received from all who were familiar with banking and monetary problems, and a German merchant in Philadelphia testified that in no country in the world had there ever existed "a more beautiful and convenient currency." Jackson, nevertheless, was certain that the Bank was sustaining itself financially and politically by means of corrupt and illegal measures and that without the government deposits it would fail. In November, 1832, immediately after his re-election, he ordered McLane to examine the Bank to ascertain whether the deposits were safe, confident

[1] N. Biddle to J. G. Watmough, January 8, 1833, in the Biddle Manuscripts in the Library of Congress; *House Report* (22d Cong., 2d sess.), No. 121, pp. 175–77; *Senate Document* (22d Cong., 2d sess.), No. 82, p. 2.

that he would receive a report that would justify the removal of the public funds and a request to the courts for a writ of *scire facias* nullifying the charter. Henry Toland of Philadelphia, the Democratic politician selected by McLane to make this examination of the Bank, had not made his report when Jackson sent his message to Congress, so that the only positive recommendation the President made was that the government's stock in the Bank should be sold.[2]

The announcement of the prospective sale of seventy thousand shares of stock, accompanied as it was by an expression of doubt about the Bank's solvency, caused a break in its price. This was foreseen, and some of the Bank's opponents in the administration hoped to profit by it. Shortly before the delivery of Jackson's message, two associates of Reuben Whitney appeared in New York and gave orders for the sale of a substantial number of Bank shares. They continued to sell short as the market declined, and their confident air caused many people to suspect that they had advance information of what the message was to say. James Gordon Bennett, who had extensive knowledge of the political and speculative underground, was later to write: "I accuse Amos Kendall with being in confidential intercourse and communication with certain confederates known to be connected with speculators in stock";[3] and, though the exact details of this financial conspiracy were never disclosed, the plans of this group of what Niles called "profligate swindlers" were frustrated by the appearance of Toland's report. McLane's investigator, who received full co-operation from Biddle, made a thorough examination of the Bank's financial condition and concluded that there could be no question of the security of the government deposits or of the solvency of the institution. The price of the stock immediately rebounded to the level at which it had been previously selling, and the speculative conspirators, much to Biddle's joy, lost what they thought they had made. Jackson had no knowledge of the machinations of this group, but he was as disappointed as they by Toland's report. He dismissed it as Bank propaganda and turned to James K. Polk, a Tennessee congressman, in an effort to force the appointment of another congressional committee to examine the Bank. "The hydra of corruption," he

[2] *Niles' Register*, XLIII (1832), 49–50; Charles N. Buck, manuscript memoirs, p. 197, in the Buck Manuscripts in the Historical Society of Pennsylvania; Mathew L. Bevan, "Report of the Bank of the United States," *United States Gazette* (Philadelphia), February 14, 1833; N. Biddle to J. G. Watmough, January 9, February 15, 1833, in the Biddle Manuscripts in the Library of Congress; Richardson, *Messages and Papers*, III, 1162–63.

[3] J. Cowperthwaite to N. Biddle, December 7, 1832; R. Colt to N. Biddle, December 8, 1832; J. Sergeant to N. Biddle, March 6, 1833, in the Biddle Manuscripts in the Library of Congress; Henry Gilpin, Diary, April 17, 21, 22, 1833, in the Gilpin Manuscripts in the Historical Society of Pennsylvania; J. G. Bennett to A. Jackson, September 10, 1833, in the Woodbury Manuscripts in the Library of Congress; J. Van Buren to J. Hoyt, October 7, 1834, in Mackenzie, *Van Buren*, p. 256; *Niles' Register*, XLIII (1832), 266; XLIV (1833), 176.

wrote, "is only *scotched, not dead.* . . . An investigation kills it and its supporters *dead.* Let this be had. Call upon the Secretary of the Treasury who must agree with me that an investigation by Congress is absolutely necessary."[4]

Polk, who agreed fully with Jackson, did as he was bid and encountered surprisingly little resistance from the Bank's supporters. Neither they nor Biddle had any hopes of gaining a two-thirds majority in this "lame-duck" session of the Congress, and Biddle assured them that the Bank was in such good order and so very strong that an investigation could not "possibly do any harm." At the same time, he said that he was unwilling for the Bank to be again subjected to "another scene of scandalous gossip and misrepresentation such as last spring" and asked them to seek to have the investigation conducted by the Ways and Means Committee and to have it confined to the subjects mentioned in the President's message—the postponement of the 3 per cent stock and the safety of the deposits.[5]

Polk and other administration leaders made only a token objection to these limitations on the scope of the investigations and to its reference to this committee because they believed that the Bank was vulnerable in these areas and also because the Ways and Means Committee had been so reorganized, with a view to the forthcoming debate on the tariff, as to alter its complexion significantly in regard to the Bank. McDuffie, as a Calhounite and nullifier, had been removed from the committee, and his place as chairman had been taken by Gulian C. Verplanck of New York, an opponent of protection and a strong Jackson and Van Buren supporter. Alexander and Gaither, who had written the minority report against the recharter in the preceding session, had been continued on the committee, and their position had been strengthened by the addition of two opponents of the Bank—Polk and Richard H. Wilde of Georgia. The other two members of the committee, John Gilmore, a Jacksonian from Pennsylvania, and Ralph I. Ingersoll, the sole representative of the formal opposition, had, like the chairman, voted for the recharter, but neither was considered an ardent supporter of the Bank.[6]

The committee began its investigations in Washington during the third week in January and received full and complete co-operation from Biddle. All the information and records that it requested were supplied without subpoena, and Samuel Jaudon, who had been brought from New Orleans the preceding summer to serve as cashier of the parent bank, was sent to Washington to represent the institution. "The western debts are the bugbear," he reported to Biddle, "and extraordinary apprehension is pretended

[4] *House Executive Document* (22d Cong., 2d sess.), No. 8; A. Jackson to J. K. Polk, December 16, 1832, in Bassett (ed.), *Correspondence of Jackson*, IV, 501.

[5] N. Biddle to J. G. Watmough, December 18, 1832, in the Biddle Manuscripts in the Library of Congress.

[6] *Register of Debates in Congress* (22d Cong., 2d sess.), pp. 823–34, 840–63.

in regard to them. It seems that the president has been telling the story of the real estate received from Morrell and Walker of Nashville for sixty thousand dollars, which is not worth, he says, six thousand dollars, and gives this as a specimen of what the whole debt is." Jaudon as former cashier at New Orleans knew more about the actual condition of the western loans than anyone did, but his assurances of their safety were ignored by Jackson and his associates, just as Toland's had been when he reported that the western debt was "in a safe and wholesome state."[7]

The President was sure that something was wrong with the Nashville office, as was Alfred Balch, one of his neighbors, who had written earlier: "As to the effects of the office here, they must in the end prove to the last degree calamitous. Those who borrow are encouraged in their extravagant mode of dressing and living. . . . Many are building little palaces, furnishing them in very expensive style, and the children of many are dressed as though they were the sons and daughters of princes. What may remain of the wrecks produced by these splendid follies, will after a few years be seized on by this mammoth Bank." He was not speaking, of course, of Jackson's rebuilding and redecorating the Hermitage or of the extravagances of the President's adopted son and nephews; he was indicting those who were corrupted by credit from the "Monster," not those who, like himself and Jackson, used credit provided by their merchants in New Orleans, which, for some unaccountable reason, was pure. Balch also complained in the same letter of the costs of borrowing from the local branch. "Instead of loaning money here at six per cent," he wrote, "they will buy a bill on the office at New Orleans, charge you one and a half per cent premium and six per cent all payable in advance and the office will charge you one and a half per cent for accepting it there. So the object of this immense institution is to make money, to secure a large dividend for the great stockholders on the other side of the Atlantic."[8]

Balch, Jackson, and Polk assumed that these practices of the Nashville office were the general rule of the Bank, but they were mistaken. The Bank did limit the amount that each western and southern office could lend on discount, and it did prefer the purchase of bills of exchange rather than the making of straight loans, but the object was not profit. Biddle had learned from the experience of the early Bank that it could operate safely in the interior only if it confined itself almost exclusively to operations in exchange. National bank notes and branch drafts, being receivable everywhere, entered the current of trade and found their way gradually from their place of issue to the northeastern cities. Means for the redemption of these notes and drafts had to be provided the northeastern offices, and the

[7] S. Jaudon to N. Biddle, January 21, 1833, in the Biddle Manuscripts in the Library of Congress.

[8] A. Balch to A. Jackson, January 8, 1830, in Bassett (ed.), *Correspondence of Jackson*, IV, 115.

issuing branches could do so only by purchasing bills of exchange based on the produce shipped to these cities for sale.

In most places this system caused no inconvenience. Local banks were available to those who wanted to borrow at simple interest, and they went to the Bank of the United States generally when they had exchange to buy or sell. In Nashville, however, there was no local Bank, and the Bank of the United States, in order to aid the community, had adopted a liberal policy in regard to exchange. Persons with produce to ship from this area, because of its great distance from New Orleans, were permitted to draw bills on their factors at very long dates, frequently up to six months, and the charges on these transactions were the same as those at other offices. The rate of exchange varied from 1 to 1½ per cent, and the factor who accepted the draft paid only the normal 6 per cent interest at the end of six months. But another system was devised to enable the Bank to lend to those who had no produce to ship. They were permitted to draw upon New Orleans, paying both the interest and the charge of exchange, and the New Orleans branch, charging a fee, would accept the draft. At the end of the period, whether two, three, or six months, the bill would be returned for collection to Nashville, or the drawer would buy a bill in Nashville and send it to New Orleans as payment.[9]

Nichol, president of the Nashville branch, Somerville the cashier, and Biddle were all aware of the dangers of this practice, but they were trying to make the Bank as useful as possible to this commercial and agricultural region. The costs of borrowing money had been greatly reduced from the figure that had been prevalent before the branch had been founded, and the proper remedy for this situation, they knew, was the organization of a local bank. They had urged this course many times in the past, but Jackson had used his influence against it, and it was not until 1833 that such an institution was founded. The Bank in the meantime did what it could to provide the city with credit through this expensive method in the belief that the cost would prevent its abuse. The Bank had almost no losses on this business during its first few years of operation, but the growing season of 1831 in the Nashville area was unexpectedly adverse. The crops of cotton and tobacco were short, and, when they were sent to New Orleans for sale, the proceeds were insufficient to cover the bills of exchange that had been previously drawn and sold. The New Orleans factors, in self-protection, had to draw on their principals in Nashville for the difference between the proceeds of the crop and the advances that had been made during the spring and summer; and the branch was forced to decide whether to carry the local planters and merchants through the next

[9] Thomas P. Abernethy, "The Early Development of Commerce and Banking in Tennessee," *Mississippi Valley Historical Review*, XIV (1927), 321; Charles G. Sellers, Jr., "Banking and Politics in Jackson's Tennessee, 1817–1827," *Mississippi Valley Historical Review*, XLI (1954), 74.

season or to return the bills to New Orleans under protest as uncollectible.[10]

Had the branch adopted the latter course, New Orleans itself would have been seriously injured, for, as Nichol pointed out, such a large number of protests would have prostrated "some of the most respectable merchants" in that city. Their failure would have had adverse effects upon the banks and other merchants, and the resulting difficulties would have extended throughout the whole western area. There was no need for the Bank of the United States to take such ruthless action. Most of the men involved were intelligent, able, industrious, and honest, and they possessed property whose value greatly exceeded their debts. They were also friends and neighbors of the President of the United States, who, like them, had become indebted to his New Orleans merchant through the shortness of his crop. All they lacked was money, which, in any other area of the country, they could have borrowed from a local bank on their personal security, so Biddle did not see why the national bank should force them to fail. He consequently permitted these Tennessee merchants and farmers to obtain the money to pay off the bills drawn upon them by their factors in New Orleans by drawing back on these same factors.

Bills of exchange used in this way were termed "racehorse bills," and in most situations they were condemned and prohibited as an unsound banking practice. In this particular situation, however, they were both useful and safe, even though a sudden frost in October, 1832, caused another short crop in the Nashville area and postponed the complete repayment of these old debts until the following year. The Bank was not injured. It collected all but a small percentage of its loans, and it was compensated for its efforts by the charge for exchange as well as interest. It could have had its money earlier, but only at the cost of needless failures, and Biddle had no desire to protect the Bank through such unreasonable and unnecessary severity. He considered this intervention to protect the Nashville area as an instance of the usefulness and desirability of such an institution as the Bank of the United States. He sent full information concerning the operations of the Nashville office to the committee, but he also made it indisputably clear that the rest of the western country had been unaffected by the crop failures in and around Nashville.[11]

The branches in the other cities were in excellent condition and completely secure. During the last six months of 1832 the western offices as a whole had purchased domestic exchange amounting to more than sixteen million dollars. Few of these bills had been protested for non-payment, and on these the actual loss was estimated at a mere fifteen hundred dollars. The total loans and discounts in the area had been reduced by three

[10] J. Somerville to S. Jaudon, October 21, 1832; J. Nichol to N. Biddle, November 22, 1832, in *House Report* (22d Cong., 2d sess.), No. 121, pp. 149–59.

[11] *Ibid.*, pp. 171–75.

and a half million dollars in the ten months preceding January, 1833, without difficulty or serious complaint. The offices had loaned more than thirteen million dollars, and, of this immense sum, only sixty thousand dollars, or less than one-half of 1 per cent, had been lost. All the rest had been made up by the increase in the value of the property the Bank had taken over in extinguishment of debt, and Biddle could look with pride upon such a useful accomplishment.

The Bank and its branches had been of service to all the groups in the area, and it had guarded and protected the interests of communities other than Nashville. Hundreds of letters in its files testified to these activities, of which, one written by Edwin Shippen, cashier in Louisville, is typical. "We have looked with great solicitude on the situation of this country," he wrote, "and the deep stake the Bank has in its welfare. Encouraged by the excessive importations at the east, our merchants have been induced to purchase more largely than their own means or the necessity of the country require; hence the embarrassment which now exists, and from which nothing but the indulgence of the Bank, and the aid of one full year's produce can relieve them. It seems to me all important that every solvent person should be sustained: their purchases have lately been . . . much more limited. The produce business promises well, and, if encouraged, will afford infinite relief; and a few months of prudent operations will place us beyond danger."[12]

Jackson and Polk considered these departures from the normal pattern of operations, temporary though they were, as additional evidence of the insecurity of the whole western debt. Polk eagerly reported to Jackson each instance of extraordinary accommodation that came to his attention, and the opponents of the Bank awaited the committee report with full expectation that it would confirm the President's charge of insolvency. As late as February 19, Biddle was also expecting a hostile report, and he urged Watmough to be ready with strong counterresolutions reaffirming that the Bank was solvent and the deposits safe. Verplanck, chairman of the investigating committee, gave no hint of his personal conclusions during the course of the investigation. He conducted the hearings with impartiality and listened intently to the evidence. He was finally convinced that the Bank was being effectively, safely, and legally managed, and on February 27, Watmough reported to Biddle: "Verplanck met me a few minutes ago and asked me jocosely what we meant to do with our Bank. Sustain her and carry her through triumphantly of course, Mr. Verplanck, and we hope with your aid. He asked me to sit down, I saw he was in a pleasant mood, having been dining out, and gave me an outline of his report. If he is able to carry it through his committee, it will be satisfactory, sustaining the Bank fully on all material points, particularly as to

[12] E. Shippen to S. Jaudon, November 18, 1832, *ibid.*, pp. 144–46.

her solvency. He says he despises the contest about the three per cents and would have nothing to do with it."[13]

The committee met the next day, and Verplanck read his report. The postponement of the payment of the 3 per cent stock was dismissed with the statement that the transaction had been closed by the surrender of all but a few of the certificates of stock and that the question did not present any important or practical object of inquiry or call for or admit any action by Congress. The rest of his report was devoted to an analysis of the financial condition of the Bank and concluded with the assertion that "there can be no doubt of the entire soundness of the whole Bank capital, after meeting all demands upon it, either by its billholders or of the government." Polk followed with a report which contradicted virtually every statement of Verplanck's, citing the postponement of the payment of the 3 per cent stock and the conduct of the Nashville branch as evidence that the Bank was insolvent, and Alexander and Gaither announced their concurrence with his conclusions. They counted on Wilde to join them to make Polk's report that of a majority of the committee, but he surprised them and the rest of the group by refusing. He had not changed his mind about the Bank of the United States, but Jackson's denunciation of nullification and his proposal of the Force Bill against South Carolina had led this Georgia supporter of state rights to break with the administration. He voted with Verplanck as an enemy of Jackson and Van Buren, and his action made the pro-Bank report that of a majority of the committee.[14]

Verplanck proposed a resolution stating that the government deposits could be "safely continued in the Bank of the United States," and this resolution was passed through the House by a vote of one hundred and sixty-nine to forty-six. This outcome was an acute disappointment to Jackson, who laid it to the wicked coalition between Clay and Calhoun that allegedly controlled the Bank and Biddle with all their corrupting power. He charged that the Bank had expended more than half a million dollars in subsidizing newspapers and loans to congressmen that would never be repaid and laid the blame for his loss of a majority in the Congress to these "bribes."[15] The President had lost control of the Congress but not as a result of any action by the Bank. The members elected as Jacksonians who subsequently joined the opposition did so either because of Jackson's selection of Van Buren as Vice-President or because of his recommendation of the Force Bill during the nullification controversy. Those who

13 J. G. Watmough to N. Biddle, February 15, 1833; H. Clay to N. Biddle, February 16, 1833; N. Biddle to J. G. Watmough, February 19, 1833, in the Biddle Manuscripts in the Library of Congress.

14 J. G. Watmough to N. Biddle, February 27, 1833, in the Biddle Manuscripts in the Library of Congress; *House Report* (22d Cong., 2d sess.), No. 121.

15 *Register of Debates in Congress* (22d Cong., 2d sess.), p. 1936; A. Jackson to H. L. White, March 24, 1833; A. Jackson to H. M. Cryer, April 7, 1833, in Bassett (ed.), *Correspondence of Jackson*, V, 46–47, 52–54.

voted for the recharter in 1832, like those who said that the deposits were safe the next year, did as they did because they were fundamentally honest and patriotic men concerned for the national welfare.

Some of these congressmen took advantage of the fact that the Bank was under attack to apply for loans in 1832 and 1833, and most of the loans so applied for were granted. But others, who were accustomed to borrowing, refrained during these sessions, thinking such requests improper, and the total number of the loans was not greatly different from preceding years. One hundred and two loans totaling eight hundred and fifty thousand dollars were made to congressmen in these two sessions, and the entire sum was repaid. Of the loans made to congressmen between 1826 and 1834, only one of four hundred dollars was passed to the suspended debt, and that not from the want of the ability of the discounter to pay but rather from a desire on his part to force the individual for whom the loan was actually made to pay it. Too much was made of this matter of loans by the opponents of the Bank, and in 1834 a senatorial committee reported that it found no evidence that members of Congress "expected or sought favors of the Bank on account of their public character." The report also stated that it could not be reasonably contended that "the mere loan of a sum of money on unexceptionable security, on which, during its continuance, the interest is regularly paid, with the full knowledge that the principal is also to be exacted in due course of time, can be regarded so to operate as to induce a member to forget the obligations he is under to himself, his country, and his God."[16]

Nevertheless, Jackson firmly believed the Bank to be a corrupting influence, just as he believed it to be insolvent, and no amount of evidence could alter these convictions. He dismissed the report of the Ways and Means Committee and the House resolution that the deposits were safe as he had previously dismissed Toland's report to the Secretary of the Treasury, and he clung to his determination to remove the deposits from the Bank and to cripple or destroy the institution itself.

[16] *Senate Document* (23d Cong., 2d sess.), No. 17, pp. 41–44.

23

Planning the Removal
of the
Deposits

B iddle was relieved and pleased by the Verplanck report and the House resolution, which stated what he knew to be the truth: that the Bank was liquid and solvent and the government deposits absolutely safe. This had always been the situation since the spring of 1819, and the Bank's capacity to meet every demand that could be brought against it had been radically and sharply increased after the politically inspired run on the Lexington branch in the fall of 1832. "There is no saying what these miserable people will not do or try to do," Biddle wrote after this unprecedented episode, and he also said: "This kitchen cabinet must be watched quite as much as their more respectable colleagues, the gangs of counterfeiters." He had called a special meeting of the board of directors in November to discuss the general policy of the Bank in view of the veto, Jackson's re-election, and such unprincipled acts as the Lexington run, and it was decided that the only defensive action required was gradually and gently to convert "the line of notes discounted into domestic bills of exchange, which being payable at maturity will give the institution a greater command of its funds."[1]

As a consequence of these measures, the Bank was in a strong and liquid position by March, 1833, and was ready to meet any demand that could be made upon it, including the complete removal of the government deposits. It had done this without imposing any strain upon its customers or the state banks, and not many persons outside the Bank were aware that it had

[1] N. Biddle to T. H. Perkins, November 11, 1832; N. Biddle to J. Rathbone, Jr., November 21, 1832; N. Biddle to R. Smith, April 8, 1833, in the Biddle Manuscripts in the Library of Congress.

sharply reduced the total amount of its discounts and loans. It had been able to accomplish its purpose easily and quietly because of the general prosperity that had followed and been induced by the easing of political tensions in Europe. The passage of the Reform Act in Great Britain and the termination of the revolutionary disturbances on the Continent had revived confidence all over the world, and the volume and prices of American exports had greatly increased. The resulting strength of the Bank of the United States was evident to anyone who examined its financial statements, but its opponents in the administration in Washington believed that such was the corruption and skill of Biddle as a financier that he could give an appearance of solidity to a fundamentally insolvent enterprise.

Some of them had been so certain that the report of the Ways and Means Committee would be adverse to the Bank that they had sent word to New York of the imminent removal of the deposits. John Van Buren, Jesse Hoyt, and others made large wagers on the basis of this information, and they once again sold Bank shares short, expecting to recoup their December losses. Biddle was disturbed by these developments. "I understand that bets about the public deposits continue in your city," he wrote to Swartwout. "I wish the treasury would make the change at once rather than see this disreputable gambling to continue. Why do not you, who are so devoted a friend to the president, let him know how much he is deceived and perhaps betrayed by these worthless intriguers, people whom he would exclude with scorn from his presence if he was aware of their true character." He then stopped and carefully drew a line through the last clause, for he was no longer sure that Jackson was ignorant of the true character of his associates and was certain that they would not be excluded from his presence.[2]

Reuben Whitney, the discredited witness before the Clayton committee, was now in Washington, closely associated with Kendall, and his influence was apparently paramount in all that was done in regard to the Bank. Sullivan, who as a government director had kept Whitney and Kendall informed of all that went on at the Bank, had been reappointed for another year, and Peter Wager, also a close friend and associate of Whitney's, had been given Biddle's customary place on the President's list. Secretary McLane had opposed these appointments, but his protests had been disregarded. He had insisted, however, that there should be one Philadelphia director appointed by the government whose reports he could trust, and, at his urgent request, Henry Gilpin, the district attorney, had been placed on the board. McLane had been forced to break his connection with

[2] J. G. Watmough to N. Biddle, March 16, 1833; N. Biddle to S. Swartwout, March 27, 1833, in the Biddle Manuscripts in the Library of Congress; Parton, *Jackson*, III, 500, 504; William Stickney (ed.), *The Autobiography of Amos Kendall* (Boston, 1872), p. 376.

Biddle, as had most of the administration supporters of the recharter, and when the new board met for the first time, the government directors were greeted coolly and disdainfully by the other members of the board. No distinction was made between Gilpin and his distrusted associates, and the coolness was increased when each of them cast blank ballots instead of voting to elect Biddle as president for another year.[3]

Gilpin was angered by this disdainful treatment and within two weeks he was complaining to Senator Dallas, "I never saw such a board of directors, it is a misuse of the term directed. Really I feel ashamed to sit like a Venetian senator in Othello, as everyone there does. We know absolutely nothing. There is no consultation, no exchanges of sentiments, no production of correspondence, but merely a rapid superficial general statement or a reference to a committee which will probably never report." The meetings of the board had not always been as meaningless as Gilpin found them to be; before January, 1832, they had been characterized by a free and frank discussion of policy and plans. But when Sullivan took his place on the board, a change had to be made. When it became obvious that whatever was mentioned or discussed in his presence was immediately transmitted to Washington and frequently appeared in the *Globe*, Biddle and the other directors began to refer all important and confidential matters to the board's standing and special committees, from which Sullivan was systematically excluded.[4]

No provision of the charter was violated by this procedure, and Biddle made no secret of it. It had been the practice of the Bank, he wrote in answer to an inquiry, to make no distinction between the government directors and those elected by the stockholders, but Sullivan was in a different category. He had come to the board with a reputation of "the worst possible character," a reputation he had amply sustained, and Biddle, "finding him an object of general contempt," had refused to nominate him to serve with the gentlemen on the board in committees. "Mr. Jackson knew perfectly what sort of a man he was when he appointed him," Biddle said, "and if he will send such people he must take the consequences." Wager, a wine merchant in Philadelphia, was not personally so objectionable as Sullivan, and Gilpin was a person of honor and distinction. They were placed on some of the less important committees, but the complete exclusion of Sullivan continued. Nothing of a confidential nature was discussed in open board meetings, and Gilpin's suspicions were aroused. He was apparently unaware of the conflict in the administration between

[3] N. Biddle to G. Poindexter, December 31, 1832; D. Webster to N. Biddle, January 11, 1833; N. Biddle to J. G. Watmough, January 30, 1833; N. Biddle to S. Smith, January 30, 1833, in the Biddle Manuscripts in the Library of Congress; H. Gilpin to J. Gilpin, December 22, 1832, in the Gilpin Manuscripts in the Historical Society of Pennsylvania.

[4] H. Gilpin to J. Gilpin, January 12, 1833; H. Gilpin to G. M. Dallas, January 12, 26, 1833; H. Gilpin to L. McLane, January 28, 1833, in the Gilpin Manuscripts in the Historical Society of Pennsylvania.

McLane, on the one side, and Whitney and Kendall, on the other, and he was not offended in late January when Whitney wrote him about certain allegedly improper practices of the Bank. They would serve him, he replied, "in the inquiries I shall deem it my duty to make as a director and these I shall pursue should I receive the special instructions of the Secretary of the Treasury to which you refer."[5]

He concluded his letter with this statement: "I should have been glad to hear from Mr. Kendall to whom I beg you to present my respects," and it did not occur to him to question the propriety of carrying on a correspondence about confidential official matters with two men who had no legal or moral right to such information. Whitney had carefully fostered the illusion that he was acting with the knowledge and consent of the Secretary of the Treasury, and he and Kendall used the information supplied by Gilpin and the other government directors to counteract whatever impression might have been made on Jackson's mind by the Toland and Verplanck reports. Watmough, who by the end of the session had become completely disgusted with the administration, picked up rumors about what was going on, and he reported to Biddle that "deep and infamous things" were being planned. There was "much trouble among the members of the cabinet"; Cass, McLane, and Van Buren were harassed, unhappy, and low; "Kendall, the Globe, and Hickory" were in the ascendancy, with "Whitney heading the van (a pun without intending it), the Van being no longer desirous to be led, but on the contrary to manage and no longer able."[6]

James A. Hamilton, now federal district attorney in New York, was associated with this effort to persuade Jackson that, despite the House resolution declaring the deposits to be safe, he should cripple or destroy the Bank to prevent it from doing irreparable harm. He warned the President that the Bank had decided to strengthen itself during the next two years by gradually collecting its loans and that, when it had reached the point of complete safety, it planned "by withholding bills, and by other means in its power, to cause exchange to advance so as to cause the exportation of specie and thus occasion a run upon all monied institutions." The state banks would be forced to suspend specie payments, and this would "induce a strong feeling in favor of a recharter of the Bank as the only means of restoring a sound currency." Blair likewise insisted that "the damned bank ought to be put down" and that "the only effectual way of doing it was to take from it the whole of the public money." William

---

[5] N. Biddle to M. Eyre, February 17, 1833, in the Biddle Manuscripts in the Library of Congress; H. Gilpin to R. Whitney, January 31, 1833, in the Gilpin Manuscripts in the Historical Society of Pennsylvania.

[6] J. G. Watmough to N. Biddle, March 16, 1833, in the Biddle Manuscripts in the Library of Congress; Parton, *Jackson*, III, 500, 504; William Stickney (ed.), *Autobiography of Amos Kendall*, p. 376.

Lewis, who had no sympathy with this scheme of his associates in the kitchen cabinet, asked Blair, "Do you really think the president would order the public money to be drawn from the Bank merely for the sake of crippling, or as you say, *breaking* it?" And Blair answered that he thought Jackson would.[7]

Blair was more correctly informed than Lewis, and in early March, when Gilpin came to Washington, he found Jackson violently incoherent in his denunciations of Biddle and the private directors. They had kept the government directors uninformed of what was going on, and the President threatened to expose "their direct violations of the charter" by appealing to the courts. Gilpin tried to calm him by stating that he had no evidence to justify an application for a judicial forfeiture of the charter, but Jackson was unwilling to listen.[8] Lewis, Van Buren, Senator Silas Wright of New York, and other administration leaders who ordinarily served the President as advisers also tried to persuade him to refrain from precipitate action, but their advice too was ignored. It was Kendall, Blair, Hamilton, Whitney, and others who shared their opinions such as Taney and Benton, to whom Jackson was turning because they alone were radical enough in their enmity to the Bank and to Biddle to satisfy his present mood.

Biddle was partly aware of what was going on in Washington, but he did not believe that the deposits would be removed. The Secretary of the Treasury was the only person who could order it, and Biddle was certain that McLane would never consent to such an action, the sole purpose of which, he said, was "to extricate the gamblers at New York by depressing the stock at once." What he did not know, however, was that McLane had already consented to an arrangement to transfer him from the Treasury to the Department of State. Secretary Livingston, in part because of Jackson's position on the Bank, wanted to retire from the Cabinet to become minister to France, so the President had been given an opportunity to promote McLane and to appoint a new Secretary of the Treasury who would more nearly agree with him on the Bank. The plan had been worked out immediately after the election in November, 1832, but its execution had been postponed until some convenient time after the adjournment of Congress. William Duane of Philadelphia, the son of the Republican editor who had been one of the leading opponents of the first Bank of the United States, was chosen to fill McLane's place. He was notified of his selection on December 4, 1832, but he declined on the ground that he did not think himself qualified for the post. Pressure was brought upon him, and he finally and reluctantly consented, but no one in the adminis-

[7] J. A. Hamilton to A. Jackson, February 28, 1833, in Bassett (ed.), *Correspondence of Jackson*, V, 22–23; Parton, *Jackson*, III, 500, 503–4.

[8] H. Gilpin to J. Gilpin, March 7, 1833; H. Gilpin, Diary, March 5, 6, 8, 1833, in the Gilpin Manuscripts in the Historical Society of Pennsylvania.

tration thought to ask him about the removal of the deposits. They assumed that, as a committed opponent of the recharter, he would agree with the measures they planned, and hence he was not informed or consulted about Bank matters in the period between his acceptance and his taking over the place.[9]

Had Biddle known of this arrangement, he would have been less confident, but no less prepared. He was still acting on the assumption that there was no predicting what "these miserable people" would do, and he directed the Bank with informed vigilance throughout the spring. No positive hostile actions were taken, but it was not for lack of trying. Jackson dismissed the opinion expressed by the House of Representatives as unworthy of consideration, and Whitney and Kendall assured him that "nothing had occurred to lessen the fears as to the safety of the deposits." They insisted that a new scheme "to govern the American people by fraud and corruption" had been formulated by Biddle, Clay, and Calhoun through a combination of "the Bank, the public lands, an overflowing treasury, and internal improvements" and that it could be thwarted only by the immediate removal of the deposits. The perpetrators of this scheme, said Kendall, could do nothing so long as Jackson was in office with the power to veto, but they looked to a future time when they would elect as his successor someone who would "agree to be their creature and instrument." It was the President's duty, as a consequence, "to cripple the Bank of the United States and deprive the conspirators of the aid which they expect from its money and power." By this one act he could "weaken if not destroy a powerful enemy and raise up powerful friends; the Bank managers would have full employment in maintaining their own defences instead of affording the administration any annoyances."[10]

This conspiracy, it is needless to say, had no existence outside Whitney's and Kendall's minds, and they were likewise mistaken when they told Jackson that they doubted whether the "utmost exertions" of Biddle could "save the institution from sudden ruin." But Jackson was convinced by their arguments, and on March 19 he presented a formal paper to the Cabinet recommending that the deposits be removed. He began with a statement that the relations between the government and the Bank of the United States were such that a final decision must be made in regard to the institution and that in his opinion the charter ought not to be renewed. Its successor should be established in the District of Columbia, and the government must be given the power to name the president and as many

[9] N. Biddle to R. Smith, April 15, 1833; R. Smith to N. Biddle, April 15, 1833, in the Biddle Manuscripts in the Library of Congress; William J. Duane, *Narrative and Correspondence concerning the Removal of the Deposits and Occurrences Connected Therewith* (Philadelphia, 1838), pp. 2–5.

[10] H. Gilpin, Diary, April, 9, 17, 21, 22, 23, 1833, in the Gilpin Manuscripts in the Historical Society of Pennsylvania; A. Kendall to A. Jackson, n.d., in Bassett (ed.), *Correspondence of Jackson,* V, 41–44.

directors of the principal bank and its branches as was necessary to "secure fidelity and a thorough knowledge . . . of its transactions." Congress should retain the right to repeal or modify the charter "as a security against the corruptions and evils which are now experienced," and the state legislatures should be authorized to control the location and operation of the branches.[11]

In thus reverting back to his old plan of a government-controlled bank, Jackson was apparently only trying to preserve some semblance of consistency, for he went on to say that such a bank ought not to be recommended to Congress until a full and fair experiment had been made to ascertain whether the fiscal affairs of the government could be carried on without a bank. He recommended that a system of state banks be devised "to go into operation at such a time as shall upon careful consideration of the subject to be thought most advisable," and he clearly indicated that the sooner this was done, the better he thought it would be.

He knew that the overwhelming majority of his Cabinet was opposed to either of these measures and that McLane, supported by the other members, would refuse to order the deposits withdrawn unless it could be proved that they were unsafe; he therefore directed Kendall to get positive proof from the government directors of the corruption and dishonesty that he was still certain could be found. The President also wrote a letter to a personal friend in Philadelphia asking him informally to talk to Gilpin, Wager, and Sullivan, and the directors suddenly found themselves being approached in these various ways—but none in the way provided by the charter, which was to have the Secretary of the Treasury officially ask them for information. Gilpin had learned a great deal by his conversations with Jackson, McLane, and others in Washington, and he and Wager, in a respectful letter to the President, declined to make any inquiry without specific instructions from the Secretary. "Without something of this sort . . .," they wrote, "we feel certain that we should be repelled with prompt distrust, our attempt would be defeated, and we should have to bear all the odium attached to a volunteer inquisition not pursued according to the mode prescribed by the law."[12]

Jackson was unwilling to ask McLane to order another investigation, so he abandoned his plans for an immediate removal of the deposits. Robert Oliver, whose sources of information in Washington included Lewis and others close to Jackson, informed Biddle that he had it on "the highest and most direct authority" that the deposits would not be removed before October, and possibly not until Congress convened. "The wily magician [Van Buren]," he said, "is for throwing the responsibility on Congress,

[11] A. Jackson to the Cabinet, March 19, 1833, in Bassett (ed.), *Correspondence of Jackson*, V, 32–33.

[12] H. Gilpin, Diary, April 6, 8, 9, 1833, in the Gilpin Manuscripts in the Historical Society of Pennsylvania.

believing that they will have a sufficient majority to carry this measure."
The cashier of the Washington office interpreted the same reports to mean
that the administration had abandoned its plans permanently and told
Biddle that "the deposits will not be removed. Mr. McLane has taken a
decided stand in favor of the Bank, even at the risk of losing his standing
with the party, but he has succeeded and he now goes into the state department, triumphing in his course."[13] Kendall and Whitney were much
disappointed by the failure of their schemes, and those who had lost money
gambling and selling Bank stock short in New York were indignant at
what they thought was betrayal. They reluctantly accepted the inevitable
postponement but continued to urge Jackson to seek a judicial annulment
of the charter.

Kendall prepared a letter to the government directors, which the President signed, requesting them to furnish evidence for this purpose. Reports
of certain matters had come to the attention of the President, the letter
said, which indicated that the Bank had violated its charter, and he wanted
the directors to confirm or deny these rumors on the basis of their "personal knowledge or observation." A formal investigation at this stage was
not desirable, but if the rumors should be confirmed by the directors' report, not only would he be able to judge what his duty was, but he might
institute through the Secretary of the Treasury "that more formal and
thorough investigation which you request."[14] The letter was based on
information which could have been obtained by Whitney only through
Sullivan, and Whitney himself called on Gilpin and Wager on the day it
was received. He told them he had come at the request of the President,
and when Gilpin sharply questioned "how the proceedings of the board
had become known at Washington," he replied that "such matters would
always leak out."

This casual dismissal of a serious breach of confidence angered Gilpin
and Wager. They refused to discuss the matter with Whitney and were
still angry the next day when Sullivan appeared. They knew it was he
who was responsible for the rumors referred to by Jackson, and they
believed that in sending this information to Washington he had violated
the obligations of his office. But Sullivan was not in the least embarrassed
by their disapproval. He presented to them for their signatures a reply to
the President in the unmistakable handwriting of Whitney, which included data on loans, overdrafts, and other confidential matters about
private accounts that the charter excluded from executive inquiry. When
they refused to sign this letter, Sullivan suggested that they should at least
report all loans made to congressmen, to which Gilpin objected that they

[13] R. W. Gibbes to N. Biddle, April 15, 1833; R. Smith to N. Biddle, April 15, 1833,
in the Biddle Manuscripts in the Library of Congress.

[14] A. Jackson to J. Sullivan, P. Wager, and H. Gilpin, April 14, 1833, in Bassett (ed.),
Correspondence of Jackson, V, 59.

knew nothing of the circumstances of the loans and that the mere fact that a person was a member of Congress did not justify them in making known to anyone outside the Bank the details of his private account.[15]

Sullivan reluctantly agreed to the elimination of all information about the private accounts of individuals, and the formal reply of the government directors to the President, which was written by Gilpin, contained no reference to these prohibited matters or to the irregular and improper intervention by Whitney. It criticized severely the excessive powers that had been given to the exchange committee by the board of directors and the secrecy of its operations. This committee had existed from the beginning of the Bank and, with the officers, had been given responsibility for purchases and sales of bills of exchange. Its transactions had always been reported to the board only after they had occurred because in this phase of its operations the Bank was a competitor of its mercantile directors in some instances, a purchaser from them in others, and also a seller. Knowledge of the committee's plans and current operations had been deliberately hidden from these members of the board, with their consent and approval, and the members of the exchange committee had usually been chosen from among the non-mercantile directors.[16]

Another important task had been given to the exchange committee after the government had begun to pay off and retire its funded debt, and that was the permanent investment of the funds which were repaid to the Bank for that portion of the debt that it held. These additional funds were not needed for the ordinary purposes of the Bank, and the decision had been made to lend them on the security of stocks and bonds issued by states, cities, and internal improvement companies. Advance knowledge of these transactions would also have been an advantage and temptation to members of the board, and, to avoid the appearance and possibility of corruption or improper use of such knowledge, the exchange committee had been given full power to act and then to report to the rest of the board what it had done.

When Sullivan took his place on the board, the powers of the exchange committee were once more expanded, and they were given authority to make other loans and discounts under the same conditions. The directors were consulted only about the ordinary commercial loans and discounts of the Bank, but at each meeting they were also presented with a list of loans that had been made by the exchange committee under this extraordinary grant of power. All that the directors knew was the name of the person who had obtained the loan, the indorsers or other security, and the amount; and, by tacit agreement, no one but Sullivan ever asked for addi-

[15] H. Gilpin, Diary, April 17, 21, 22, 23, 1833, in the Gilpin Manuscripts in the Historical Society of Pennsylvania.

[16] N. Biddle to J. M. Clayton, April 14, 1841, in *House Executive Document* (29th Cong., 1st sess.), No. 226, pp. 491–99.

tional information. Whenever he did, Biddle refused the request, and his refusal was sustained by a majority vote of the board. This practice was continued after Gilpin and Wager became directors, and it was against this that they protested in their reply to Jackson. But such delegation of power to a committee was clearly and explicitly authorized by the charter and by the by-laws of the Bank, and it did not provide the President with the evidence he needed for a judicial annulment of the charter.[17]

Jackson was thus forced to abandon his plan to bring the Bank into court, as he had previously been forced to postpone the removal of the deposits. Biddle and the institution he managed were proving to be more powerful antagonists than the President had supposed, and he wrote to a Tennessee friend: "I loathe the corruption of human nature and long for retirement and repose at the Hermitage. But until I can strangle this hydra of corruption, the Bank, I will not shrink from my duty."[18] It did not occur to Jackson to think that he himself might be wrong, nor did he examine or question the character or motives of those who had joined him in his war with the Bank. Good and evil to him were very simple matters, and the Bank, since it was evil, must be destroyed. Under the strain of this long-continued struggle Biddle was also beginning to over-simplify the problem and the personalities involved. He could no longer distinguish between Jackson, Benton, and a few others whose objections to the Bank were based on principle, erroneous though it may have been, and those who were seeking to profit in one way or another from the destruction of the institution.

"I feel myself," he wrote, "a much more profound jurist than all the lawyers and statesmen of Virginia put together, for in half an hour I can remove all the constitutional scruples in the District of Columbia. Half a dozen presidencies, a dozen cashierships, fifty clerkships, a hundred directorships, to worthy friends who have no character or money. Why, there is more matter for deep reflection in such a sentence than in any twenty of Tacitus or Montesquieu." He denounced the enemies of the institution as "a coterie of gamblers" who wanted the President to withdraw the deposits to rescue them from unfortunate speculative sales of Bank stock on time, and he insisted that "this combination of political gamblers and gambling politicians is the key to the whole history of the relations between the Bank and the Executive."[19]

Biddle had more evidence to justify his charges against his opponents than Jackson had for his beliefs about the Bank, but the truth or falsity of their respective positions was not the important matter in the next conflict

[17] *Ibid.*

[18] A. Jackson to H. Cryer, April 7, 1833, in Bassett (ed.), *Correspondence of Jackson,* V, 52–54.

[19] N. Biddle to J. Barbour, April 16, 1833; N. Biddle to T. Cooper, May 6, 1833, in the Biddle Manuscripts in the Library of Congress.

between them. What was involved here was primarily Biddle's frustration and anger and his determination to expose the ignorance and incapacity of the Jackson administration in financial affairs. The opportunity occurred on April 26, when a protested bill of exchange for approximately five million francs, drawn by the Treasurer of the United States upon the Treasurer of France, was returned to the Bank of the United States. Secretary McLane had begun this transaction the preceding October by asking Biddle to suggest the best means of transferring a payment by the French government to the United States. The Bank had no need of the funds in Europe and did not want to buy, but Biddle had said it would be willing to make the purchase if the government made the formal request. A better means, he thought, was for the Bank to forward the bill to its Paris agent for collection, which would have the advantage that it would enable the government and the Bank to learn whether or not the French treasury had accepted the bill of exchange before a transfer was made on the Bank's books, but this method would deprive the government of all use of the funds until the notice was received.[20]

Secretary McLane, at the beginning of February, chose the first alternative, and the Bank purchased the bill, transferring its proceeds immediately to the government's account, where they were used to pay its current drafts and bills. The Bank still had no need of such a large sum in Paris, so the draft on the French treasury was sent to Baring Brothers and Company in London for sale or collection as they thought best. Barings accordingly sold it in London, and when its new owner presented it for payment, it was refused because no appropriation had been ordered by the legislative branch of the French government. The bill was protested for non-payment, and Hottinguer and Company of Paris, as the agent of the Bank of the United States, paid its holder the whole amount to protect the credit of their principal and the United States government. The Bank, as Biddle pointed out, thus became doubly indebted for the bill: "once in Philadelphia where they paid the money to the government which has been using it, and again in Paris where it is paying five per cent interest on the advance made by Messrs Hottinguer and Company."[21]

As soon as the bill was returned to the United States, Biddle notified McLane, but, instead of merely chiding the Secretary gently for his lack of understanding of banking procedures, as he had done before in not dissimilar circumstances, he informed him that the government would be held responsible for principal, interest, exchange, costs, and the customary 15 per cent damages provided by law for protested bills. In preceding years Biddle had been a government director and as such had thought of himself and acted as an executive officer sharing responsibility with the

[20] *Senate Document* (23d Cong., 2d sess.), No. 17.

[21] N. Biddle to J. McKim, Jr., April 27, 1833, in the Biddle Manuscripts in the Library of Congress.

Secretary of the Treasury for the administration of the government's financial affairs, but Jackson had refused to reappoint him to this office, and he was now acting as a private citizen who was a private director and president of the national bank. The purchase of the government's drafts on a foreign treasury was not one of the assigned public duties of this institution; hence Biddle, no longer a public officer, acted in this instance in accordance with standard banking practice and law.

He made the most of this opportunity to humiliate the Jackson administration. In spite of its emphasis on economy, it had incurred a needless expense of one hundred and seventy thousand dollars. It had said that the Bank of the United States was insolvent, but the Paris agent of this insolvent institution had voluntarily advanced nine hundred thousand dollars to protect it and its government from commercial dishonor. Jackson and his associates were angry, as Biddle had hoped they would be. The President denounced the Bank as an unfaithful agent, and Taney insisted that the claim for damages "has no foundation in law or equity, and ought not to be paid by the government." Biddle, beaming with pleasure, merely said that the government, like other improvident and careless persons, "has drawn when his friends were not ready and must meet the consequences."[22]

The episode in itself was unimportant and had no effect upon the political conflict, even though McLane, chagrined by the publicity and criticism, told the President that he no longer favored the recharter of the Bank. The twenty-seven-page letter in which he announced his change of opinion could not have given Jackson much satisfaction, for the Secretary also said that the Bank of the United States in every instance except that of the French bill had been a useful and faithful auxiliary of the national treasury. It had safely kept the public money and had provided the nation with a uniform and sound currency. No system of state banks could replace this currency, nor could the country, "without a degree of suffering which the people would not and could not bear," introduce a currency composed wholly of coin. The only practicable solution for the United States was a bank organized on the same principles as that already existing, though McLane admitted his embarrassment in making the suggestion after what the President had said in his veto message.

McLane had gone far in thus challenging Jackson's position in regard to the Bank. The long-planned changes in the Cabinet were about to be made, and the letter in effect was his final report as Secretary of the Treasury. He was not breaking with the administration or leaving the Cabinet, he was being promoted, and he had no reason for writing except his concern for the welfare of the country, the Democratic party, and the President. The final part of his letter, which was devoted to the removal of the deposits, takes on for this reason an additional importance, and in it

22 N. Biddle to R. Lenox, May 10, 1833, in the Biddle Manuscripts in the Library of Congress; *Senate Document* (23d Cong., 2d sess.), No. 17.

he made the positive recommendation that the relations between the Bank and the government should remain unchanged until the expiration of the charter. The deposits had been placed in the Bank, he said, not for its profit but to enable it to accomplish the purposes for which it had been created. They should be removed only "for good cause and in the public interest," for there could be no doubt that their removal would incommode the public service, embarrass the community, and "produce serious disorders in the currency and the business of the country."[23]

The removal would not cripple or destroy the Bank. It was strong and solvent and could transfer any demands made upon it to the other banks and the public by curtailing its loans and purchases of exchange. The resulting pressure would injure the government, for, McLane asked, "What would become of the public deposits and what of those benefits which the government and the people now enjoy in regard to the currency and exchanges of the country, amidst the general destruction of credit, distress, bankruptcies, and suspensions of specie payments?" In one way or another Biddle had been asking these questions for the preceding four years, but Jackson and those who supported him in his attacks upon the Bank did not think that the questions were valid or required answering. It was sufficient that they believed the Bank to be unconstitutional; that it was a monopoly controlled by foreign stockholders which in mysterious fashion enabled a financial oligarchy to dominate the nation; and that, unless deprived of the government deposits, it would by means of bribery and corruption elect Henry Clay or John C. Calhoun president of the United States.

They would have done better to consider seriously the final statement in McLane's letter to the President, which said: "All experience shows that the laws which govern human events are not sufficiently known to trace with certainty the consequences of any means . . . and the undersigned, though he may be mistaken as to extent of the evil, entertains no doubt that the ill consequences to be expected [from the removal of the deposits] outweigh all the good to be hoped for." The Bank of the United States was not a perfect institution, nor was Biddle without fault as its manager, but under his direction the Bank did faithfully attempt to perform and fulfil all its duties and responsibilities to the government and the community. Jackson, nevertheless, thought it dangerous to the freedom and liberty of the country, though he never defined the exact nature of this danger. He removed the deposits, and, as McLane predicted, the evil consequences that followed outweighed whatever good was accomplished.[24]

23 L. McLane to A. Jackson, May 20, 1833, in Bassett (ed.), *Correspondence of Jackson*, V, 75–101.

24 *Ibid.*

24

The Removal
of the
Government Deposits

*I*t was not concern for the welfare or solvency of his institution that dictated Biddle's opposition to the removal of the government deposits. The Bank could meet any challenge or attack on the part of the administration. What disturbed him was the prospect of monetary confusion, the disruption of the country's economic relationships, that would ensue. Many of Jackson's own supporters, too, were unwilling to embark a second time on the course that had proved so disastrous in the years from 1811 to 1817; numbered among these was William Duane, the newly appointed Secretary of the Treasury, who took over his office on June 1, 1833. Duane objected to the Bank of the United States on constitutional and ideological grounds, but he also knew that it had been a safe depository for the government's funds. Every cent of the more than four hundred million dollars that the government had deposited in the Bank had been paid, but the Treasury still carried on its books a figure of almost two million dollars that had been lost in the previous experiment with deposits in state banks. The Secretary could see no advantage to the people or the government in taking the "public money from a bank over which there is control" and distributing it "amongst institutions over which no control exists."[1]

He took over his office with the belief that his views and opinions would be consulted, but on the evening of June 1 he was visited by Reuben Whitney, who came, he said, at the request of President Jackson. He told Duane that Kendall was already preparing an executive order transferring the deposits from the Bank of the United States to a group of state banks

[1] William Duane, *Narrative*, pp. 38–58.

and that, when it was issued, it would be accompanied by a presidential statement relieving the Secretary of any official or personal responsibility. Had Biddle been consulted by Kendall and Whitney, he could have suggested no better means of alienating Duane from the administration and arousing his suspicions concerning the proposed action. "The communication thus made to me," he was later to write, "created surprise and mortification. I was surprised at the position of affairs which it revealed; and mortified at the low estimate which had been formed of the independence of my character."[2]

He protested against this irregular mode of procedure in his first interview with the President, and Jackson, though he denied authorizing Whitney to call, did not deny the essential accuracy of Whitney's statement. He told Duane that the removal of the deposits "was of vast consequence to the country"; that unless the Bank was "broken down," it would break down the administration; and that a system of state-bank depositories should be established to prove to the Congress and the people "that the United States Bank was not necessary." Duane was almost overwhelmed by these statements, but when he told Jackson that he did not view the subject in the same light, the President, with great courtesy and gentleness, replied that "he liked frankness, that my predecessor and himself had sometimes differed in opinion, but it had made no differences in feeling, and should not in my case."[3]

No mention was made of the executive order, but at the end of June, the President, ignoring what Duane had previously said, sent him instructions to appoint an agent to select state banks in the principal cities to "receive the deposits . . . and be responsible to the government for the whole public deposits of the United States." These banks as a group, according to Jackson's plan, were to agree to perform without charge to the government any services that could lawfully be required of the Bank of the United States and to pay any expenses incurred by the removal of the deposits. Kendall was recommended as a suitable agent, and inclosed with the President's letter was a document of "formidable proportions" embodying Kendall's view of the history of the relationships between the government and the Bank. The institution, Kendall said, had been an unfaithful agent, and the people had re-elected Jackson to punish it. It was therefore incumbent on him to remove the deposits to "complete the work of destroying the Bank which the veto had begun."[4]

Duane protested once more, but the President was unwilling to listen. His sole object, he said, was to save the liberties and freedom of the country, which would be lost if the Bank were permitted "to exist." Duane

[2] *Ibid.*, pp. 5–9.

[3] *Ibid.*

[4] A. Jackson to W. Duane, June 26, 1833, in Parton, *Jackson*, III, 515–17.

knew of no danger that would threaten the nation if the Bank was used as a government depository for two and a half years longer, whereas he was well aware that much more trivial financial changes than that suggested by Jackson had produced "great commercial convulsions." He was unwilling to risk a financial crisis in what he knew would be a vain attempt to cripple or break the national bank, and he warned Jackson that such a crisis, if it did occur, would work greater havoc in "the cottage of the farmer" than in "the palace of the banker." He urged the President, as Ingham had done in 1829, to take time "for inquiry and for reflection" and for a thorough investigation of banking and monetary problems with a view to devising an effective and safe substitute for the existing Bank.[5]

Jackson did not want such an investigation, he wanted the deposits removed, and on July 20 he officially instructed Duane to appoint Kendall as agent to consult with the state banks. All he desired, he said, was an inquiry to find out whether the state banks would agree to the plan of a mutual guaranty, which, in his opinion, was an essential requirement for the safekeeping of the government's funds. "Until we get information and consider it," Jackson promised, "we shall remain uncommitted." Duane accepted this assurance and prepared a letter of instructions for Kendall which authorized him to make inquiries, but not to conclude arrangements, inasmuch, the letter explicitly said, as nothing had been brought to the attention of the Secretary of the Treasury that convinced him that the deposits should be removed from the national bank. Jackson was not satisfied. Duane's statement implied that, even if Kendall's inquiries should prove the state banks to be a safe depository for the government funds, they would not necessarily be removed from the national bank, and this was the exact opposite of what the President desired. He called Duane to the White House, and the inexperienced and disheartened Secretary capitulated. He not only agreed to the omission of the offending paragraph but also promised the President that "if, after receiving the information and hearing the discussions, I shall not consider it my duty, as the responsible agent of the law, to carry into effect the decisions that you may make, I will . . . promptly afford you an opportunity to select a successor."[6]

He came to Philadelphia immediately afterward to consult with his political friends as to the proper course he should take in view of his experiences in Washington and also to check on the accuracy of the President's indictment of the conduct of the Bank. Biddle greeted him cordially and did what he could to facilitate his investigation. The Secretary was permitted to see the Bank's records and correspondence in regard to such matters as the postponement of the payment of the 3 per cent stock and the protested bill of exchange on the French government, and he was given an opportunity to learn for himself exactly how liquid and solvent

[5] Duane, *Narrative*, pp. 38–58.
[6] *Ibid.*, pp. 84–92.

the Bank was. Duane was also invited to check the condition of the branch in New York; and when he left Philadelphia, Biddle wrote to Swartwout, a former political ally of the Secretary's father, asking him to give Duane information about Whitney and his New York associates. "You have the means," Biddle said, "of doing much good by frank communication with Mr. Duane. He I believe knows and feels that the toils of these gamblers are spread for him, and he ought to be helped in his honest efforts to disentangle himself. If these practices could once be brought home to the gang so as to satisfy the President and the Secretary of their schemes, the country might be much benefitted."[7]

What Duane learned was not recorded, but it was sufficient to cause him to say to Gilpin on his return to Philadelphia that Kendall "was not his agent, had not been appointed by him, and he would never appoint him to any agency." He added that he was still opposed to the recharter but that he did not intend to "go out of his way to put down" the Bank by an unjustified removal of the deposits. Kendall, when he arrived in Philadelphia, revealed to Gilpin the wide difference that existed between Jackson and Duane on this question. He said that the President had decided on the removal of the deposits and that if Duane continued to oppose it, he would have to withdraw, accompanied by Secretary of State McLane. The tone of this conversation, as recorded in Gilpin's diary, was harsh and authoritative and lends credence to a hostile account of Kendall's conduct in Philadelphia, written by James Gordon Bennett, that said: "The august personage, A. Kendall; who held the whole power of the government in his hands, spoke for the President, and constituted himself his mentor, his prophet, his what-not; gave audience in one of his parlors, and received the attentions of the faithful. . . . Mr. Whitney managed in these conversations the department of the finances and currency, and Mr. Kendall the question of power as regarded the President, Secretary, and the approaching Congress. Mr. Kendall showed the propriety of the removal taking place before the meeting of Congress, for the purpose of interposing the President's veto to prevent their retention. If, said he, the measure should be left to Congress, it might be possible to achieve it; but by removing the money now we have the veto in our possession. Whitney joined in these opinions, and stated that the members of Congress would not dare to oppose the old hero after he had taken the first step. . . . Whitney also showed how easy it would be for the government, when the deposits should be removed, to break a branch either South or West, and thus make a good case for Congress to act upon."[8]

[7] N. Biddle to R. Lenox, July 30, 1833; N. Biddle to S. Swartwout, July 30, 1833; S. Swartwout to N. Biddle, August 1, 1833; N. Biddle to C. Chauncey, August 2, 1833, in the Biddle Manuscripts in the Library of Congress.

[8] H. Gilpin, Diary, August 2, 5, 11, 1833, in the Gilpin Manuscripts in the Historical Society of Pennsylvania; J. G. Bennett, "The Kitchen Cabinet Laid Open to the People," *Pennsylvania Inquirer* (Philadelphia), reprinted in the *United States Gazette* (Philadelphia), January 7, 1834.

Kendall's journey had not been successful. None of the state banks had been willing to accept the provisions for group action and responsibility that Jackson had said were essential, and most of the stronger banks were unwilling to accept the deposits on any terms. They knew that these deposits had not been as profitable to the Bank of the United States as many uninformed persons had thought, because of their extreme variability in amount. They had seen the government's deposit fluctuate from more than ten million dollars to only a few thousand in the course of a very few months, which had not bothered the national bank but which would be unsettling for an ordinary bank. Enough banks had agreed to accept the deposits, however, for Kendall to be able to claim success, and the party newspapers, led by the *Globe*, confidently predicted that the deposits soon would be transferred.[9]

Many of the Bank's directors and friends were alarmed, and Biddle was flooded with inquiries as to what this new move portended for the Bank. He answered them all with calm confidence and pride and assured them that he was "ready at a moment's notice to propose the whole system of measures which must follow any hostile movement by the treasury." Using nautical language, he said that the convoy was under easy sail and could take in reefs whenever it was necessary. The debt of the western branches had been reduced by five million dollars during the course of the year, and everywhere else the Bank was "as snug as may be." He requested the branches to lend out only the amount that they collected from payments on loans, to keep the state banks in their debt, and to be ready to meet any demands that could be brought against them. "For the present," he concluded, "it is better that you should do it, than that I should say it, for when once we begin, we shall have many things to do, which will crush the Kitchen cabinet at once."[10]

On August 13 he felt that the proper time had arrived for the Bank to adopt measures which would make it entirely safe. Each branch was directed not to increase its loans, to limit bills of exchange to ninety-day terms, and to collect the balances due from state banks in specie or in drafts on the Atlantic cities. The five western offices were ordered not to draw on one another but to confine their exchange operations to the purchase of bills payable in the Northeast. He had postponed the adoption of this restrictive course for as long as he could, and he issued the orders with the intention of modifying them as they accomplished their purposes. He had no desire to bring needless pressure upon the community, but he had to prepare the Bank and each of the branches to meet any demands that could be brought against it. He knew as well as did Whitney that the removal of the deposits would give the government or interested indi-

[9] Duane, *Narrative*, pp. 96–103.

[10] N. Biddle to R. Lenox, July 30, 1833; N. Biddle to D. Webster, August 13, 1833, in the Biddle Manuscripts in the Library of Congress.

viduals an opportunity "to break a branch either South or West" unless these protective measures were taken, and he made certain that this did not happen.[11]

The August 13 meeting of the board of directors was also the occasion of an open conflict between Biddle and the government directors over the expense account of the Bank. Wager was a member of the dividend committee, which had to examine the details of all the general accounts, and in the course of this examination he discovered some entries of "a very extraordinary character." During 1831 and 1832 the Bank had spent a total of eighty thousand dollars for the preparation, printing, and circulation of documents, of which twenty thousand dollars had been paid on the orders of Biddle "without any account of the manner in which, or the persons to whom, they were disbursed." Wager immediately told Gilpin and Sullivan what he had discovered, and they made a report to the President. He instructed them to make an investigation, and Gilpin, at the August 13 meeting, formally requested Biddle to lay the expense account before the directors. When this was done, he demanded an explanation of the twenty thousand dollar entry, but Biddle refused. The private directors upheld the right of the president of the Bank to make this refusal and then proceeded to express their "perfect confidence" in Biddle and authorized him "to continue his expenditures."[12]

This act of defiance was deliberately adopted by Biddle and the private directors in the belief that the suspicion aroused by concealment would be less useful to the administration than the detailed facts. Part of the money had been used to pay lobbyists who had been sent to Washington, Harrisburg, and Albany to work for the Bank, and the rest had been expended by Silas Burrows, Alexander Hamilton, William Beach Lawrence, and Biddle himself to encourage newspaper editors in New York and Pennsylvania to defend the institution. None of it had been spent to influence elections, but this distinction, though a real and valid one, would have been forgotten if the names of the persons involved had been disclosed. The total sum, twenty thousand dollars, was obviously too small to have had any effect upon the national political campaign, and when this expenditure was made known, it was ignored by friends and opponents of the Bank.

Jackson, however, thought that the report of the government directors confirmed all his suspicions regarding the Bank. He was more determined than ever to end its power to do harm, and in mid-September he announced his decision to remove the deposits. He presented the directors' report to a Cabinet meeting and asked the assembled department heads, "How shall we answer to God, our country, or ourselves, if we permit the public money to be thus used to corrupt the people?" The Cabinet mem-

[11] H. Gilpin, Diary August 13, 29, 30, September 1, 1833, in the Gilpin Manuscripts in the Historical Society of Pennsylvania.
[12] *Ibid.*, July 2, August 12, 13, 15, 16, 19, 1833.

bers were given a week in which to study the report of the government directors, and the President concluded this initial meeting with the statement: "Observe, I do not want immediate action, but I desire a day to be
fixed. Nor do I want to touch a dollar of the money that is in the Bank;
but I do want that the money coming in may be put where it will be
safe."[13]

Duane was thus placed in an inescapable dilemma. He had promised the
President that he would carry out his wishes or resign, but he had also been
given specific assurances that the deposits would not be placed in the state
banks without adequate guaranties for their safety. Now Jackson had forgotten these assurances. Kendall's agency had been completely abortive.
The President's plan for group responsibility had been unanimously rejected by all the state banks that had been approached. Most of the substantial banks had refused to act as depositories under any circumstances,
and those that had accepted, Duane was certain, were those that had "the
least ability to pay their own responsibilities in coin." He had to decide
whether to remain loyal to his pledge to the President or to attempt to
protect the country from what he thought to be certain disaster.

The administration, in his opinion, was planning to risk chaos in the
"fiscal concerns of the country at a moment when they were conducted
by the legitimate agent with the utmost simplicity, safety, and dispatch,"
and this, he also believed, at the instigation and urging of a self-interested
group of speculators and gamblers. Duane might have kept his promise to
resign if his original distrust of the motives of Whitney and Kendall had
not been succeeded by anger and hatred as a result of the actions of the
Globe and other administration newspapers. During August and September he was attacked in articles published in areas as widely separated as
Washington, Concord, Boston, New York, Albany, Trenton, and Cincinnati, and he was certain that Kendall was entirely responsible. He was in
great distress throughout the week that intervened between the two Cabinet meetings, and he had not come to a final decision when he took his
place with the other department heads in the President's office. He heard
Taney argue for immediate withdrawal and Woodbury urge the postponement of all action until the summer of 1834. Cass refused to comment upon
a matter that must be decided by the Secretary of the Treasury alone, and
McLane was the sole supporter of Duane's contention that the deposits
could not be legally removed from the Bank of the United States unless
they were deemed to be unsafe.[14]

The meeting adjourned for the day without a decision, but the next
morning Jackson began by reading a formal paper that reviewed all the
transgressions of the Bank. He disclaimed any intention of requiring "that
any member of his cabinet should, at his request, order, or dictation, do

[13] Duane, *Narrative*, pp. 86–103.
[14] *Ibid.*

any act which he believes unlawful, or in his conscience condemns," but, he insisted, his own conception of public duty forbade him to "refrain from pressing upon the Secretary of the Treasury his view of the considerations which impel to immediate action." No member of the Cabinet made a comment, and all but Duane departed. He asked the President whether he was being directed to remove the deposits. Jackson replied that such was his desire but that responsibility for the action was to be publicly assigned to the Executive, not to the Secretary.[15]

He made no attempt to force Duane into an immediate decision, and the two parted with mutual expressions of affection and good will; but the next day the Secretary was visited by Andrew J. Donelson, the President's nephew and secretary, who told him that the *Globe* the day after would carry the announcement that on October 1 the government would cease to deposit its funds in the Bank of the United States. The announcement appeared, and the publication of this authorized story fixed Duane's determination. In a painful interview with the President he stated that he would neither resign nor order the change in the depositories. Jackson tried to dissuade him, renewing an offer previously made to appoint him minister to Russia, but Duane refused. Neither of the men was angry with the other, and it was with genuine regret that Jackson, on September 23, reluctantly signed a letter addressed to Duane in which he said: "I feel myself constrained to notify you that your further services as secretary of the treasury are no longer required."[16]

The *Globe* and its editor had no such regrets. "Mr. Duane was dismissed for faithlessness to his solemn written pledges," said the paper editorially, "and for the exhibition of bad feeling, which made him totally unfit for the station to which he had been elevated. He was *not* dismissed merely for refusing to remove the deposits." McLane and Cass planned to resign from the Cabinet in protest against Duane's dismissal, but Lewis, who was also opposed to the removal of the deposits as well as jealous of the growing influence of Kendall, persuaded them to see the President first. Jackson was his most charming and lovable self, and with no difficulty persuaded them to remain. The administration was thus protected from additional discredit, and, so far as the public knew, Duane was the only member of the Cabinet who opposed the President's action.[17]

Taney was appointed Secretary of the Treasury. He designated Kendall as agent for the removal of the deposits, and they, with the assistance of Woodbury, prepared the order of September 25, stipulating that after October 1 all government deposits were to be placed in the selected state banks. This order was accompanied by an explicit pledge that the funds

[15] A. Jackson, paper read to the Cabinet on September 18, 1833, in Richardson, *Messages and Papers*, III, 5–19.

[16] Duane, *Narrative*, pp. 86–103.

[17] Parton, *Jackson*, III, 501–3, 532.

already deposited with the Bank of the United States would be withdrawn gradually as needed for the expenditures of the Treasury and that no funds would be transferred from the Bank of the United States to the state-bank depositories.[18]

This Treasury order fundamentally altered the responsibilities of the Bank of the United States. For almost two decades it had been directly responsible for the condition of the currency by virtue of a contract between its stockholders and the government which gave it the custody and use of the public funds in return for the performance of certain public functions. But now this contract had been abrogated by the Secretary of the Treasury, and those who had taken charge of the government deposits were responsible for what happened to governmental and private finances. "Henceforward," Biddle wrote, "the Bank is the property of the stockholders to be administered for their interests, and whether they shall continue to lend that property or ask for its return . . . are questions for them, and for them alone."[19]

Some of those connected with the Bank urged him to use this changed status as justification for a rigid curtailment of the Bank's activities and, by bringing pressure upon the community and the state banks, to discredit the administration and its financial policy. They recommended that loans be drastically reduced throughout the institution, that it avoid any transactions that would entail a new issue of notes or drafts, and that each branch refuse to redeem any notes or drafts other than those for which it was legally responsible. Such measures would have discredited the administration, but they would also have wrecked the national economy, and Biddle, though he had declared the Bank to be free from all public responsibility, was unwilling to precipitate a needless crisis. "After a great deal of reflection," he answered one who had proposed this ruthless policy, "we are all satisfied that the best thing to be done is to do as little as possible." The Bank continued to collect its loans in the interior by forcing the borrowers to substitute ninety-day bills of exchange on the Atlantic Coast cities, but no change was made in the policy of having each branch accept or redeem all notes and drafts regardless of where they were legally payable.[20]

He justified his inaction by the condition of the Bank and also by reference to the pledges that had been voluntarily given by the President and the Secretary of the Treasury to use the funds on deposit for ordinary expenditures of the Treasury, but many of the Bank's supporters thought he

[18] S. Jaudon to M. Robinson, September 30, October 3, 5, 1833, in *Senate Document* (23d Cong., 2d sess.), No. 17, pp. 120–21.

[19] N. Biddle to A. Hamilton, February 1, 1834, in the Biddle Manuscripts in the Library of Congress; N. Biddle to J. A. Stevens, February 22, 1834, in the Dreer Manuscript Collection in the Historical Society of Pennsylvania.

[20] M. Robinson to S. Jaudon, October 2, 1833, in *Senate Document* (23d Cong., 2d sess.), No. 17, pp. 120–21; N. Biddle to R. Lenox, October 1, 1833, in the Biddle Manuscripts in the Library of Congress.

was being unduly optimistic. "You are dealing with a desperate man," Alexander Hamilton warned from New York, "and therefore ought to be prepared, as you cannot tell when or where you are to be attacked." In this instance he was better informed than Biddle, since Taney, with Jackson's consent, was in process of violating his pledge not to transfer government funds to the depository banks. On October 4 the Secretary of the Treasury issued drafts which totaled two million three hundred thousand dollars to five depository banks in Baltimore, Philadelphia, and New York; and on the next day one of these institutions, the Union Bank of Baltimore, presented two of these drafts for immediate payment.[21]

Thomas Ellicott, president of this bank, was a close personal friend of Taney and his trusted adviser on all financial affairs. The Secretary himself was a stockholder in the Union Bank and had been its attorney before entering the Cabinet. Biddle was forced to believe that this withdrawal of deposits by means of unannounced transfer drafts was an attempt by the administration to break or embarrass the Bank. He could not have known, nor was he told, that Ellicott, in presenting the drafts, had violated Taney's specific instructions to use them only if he was subjected to an unreasonable demand by the Bank of the United States. No such demand had been made, but Ellicott, whose bank was in a dangerous condition as a result of his personal speculations with its funds, had presented the drafts as soon as they reached his hands. Taney did not want to admit this. In view of all that had been said about the danger of trusting government funds to the state banks, he was loath to confess thus early that the bank in which he had a personal interest was in such dire straits.[22]

All Biddle knew was that the Treasury had violated its agreement within a week of its public announcement, and he could not find out how many of these drafts had been drawn, to whom they had been made payable, or why the government had changed its mind. He called a special meeting of the board of directors on October 7 and proposed a general curtailment of loans throughout the Bank amounting to six million dollars to prepare the institution for sudden and unannounced withdrawals of the deposits. Some of the directors protested that more should be done, but Biddle insisted that the curtailment was sufficient, and the board acquiesced.[23]

[21] A. Hamilton to N. Biddle, September 26, 1833, in the Biddle Manuscripts in the Library of Congress; S. Jaudon to J. White, October 8, 1833; S. Jaudon to J. Campbell, November 5, 15, December 9, 1833, in *Senate Document* (23d Cong., 2d sess.), No. 17, pp. 123, 354–61. Jackson told Van Buren on September 29 that the depository banks had been given drafts on the Bank to be used in retaliation against any undue pressure. "A good general," he wrote, "will always keep his enemy in check. We have the bank now checkmated." A. Jackson to M. Van Buren, September 29, 1833, in Bassett (ed.), *Correspondence of Jackson*, V, 213.

[22] Carl B. Swisher, *Roger B. Taney* (New York, 1935), pp. 240–43; Stickney (ed.), *Autobiography of Kendall*, p. 389.

[23] *Senate Document* (23d Cong., 2d sess.), No. 17, pp. 14–22, 94–95, 222–24.

Until this moment the policies adopted by the Bank to meet the removal of the deposits had not seriously injured the national economy. Numerous persons had been inconvenienced, some few had failed, but, in general, the local banks had been able to take care of those persons who were denied accommodation by the national bank. Biddle had meant for this situation to continue. He was determined to protect the solvency and credit of the Bank, but he sought to avoid a general crisis. Jackson and Taney had made this impossible. They had told Duane and others that "if the Bank of the United States did not conduct itself in the manner that would be satisfactory, the state banks would be able to reserve its paper received for revenue, and break in succession every one of its branches"; and now they had begun the attack. But, despite General Jackson's experience in war, he had made a cardinal error, he had underestimated the strength of his opponent, and the nation and all its people were to suffer the consequences of his mistake.

~~ 25 ~~

Attack and Counterattack

$\mathcal{T}$he curtailment of loans reluctantly ordered by Biddle on October 7 came at the worst possible moment for New York and the other importing cities. The tariff act passed by the Congress the preceding spring had changed the time for the payment of duties. Previously the merchant had been able to postpone payment until after he had sold the goods, but under the compromise act of 1833 the full duty was due at the moment of importation. More bank credit was needed than usual, but the Bank of the United States, instead of lending to merchants, reduced its loans by five and a half million dollars in less than two months. It also insisted upon regular settlements in specie of all adverse balances by the state banks in each city, and, to meet these demands, the state banks had to collect from their borrowers rather than make new loans. The depository banks in the northeastern cities, at Taney's request, tried to take up the slack by expanding their loans, but their strength was insufficient. They too had to curtail, and, on November 23, Biddle was told by Jackson's collector of customs in New York that, unless the Bank of the United States came to the rescue by extending its discounts, there would be numerous failures.[1]

Biddle was almost ready to respond to this request. Four days earlier, he had said to a New York congressman that the Bank in a very short time would be "entirely beyond the reach of any mischief from the Treasury," but, just as he came to the decision to begin a moderate expansion, he received a report that the Savannah branch was being subjected to a run on its specie "of great force and bitterness." At the height of the run a government paymaster from Charleston had appeared with a Treasury draft which he presented for payment in specie, and he refused to explain why he was cashing it in Savannah instead of in his own city. The local officers were certain that the run was politically inspired, and Biddle had no reason to question the accuracy of their information. Only two weeks before, on November 14, Blair had warned him in an editorial that if he

[1] *Senate Document* (23d Cong., 2d sess.), No. 17, pp. 94–95, 222–24; S. Swartwout to N. Biddle, November 23, 1833, in the Biddle Manuscripts in the Library of Congress.

continued to press the community, "we will by every means we can lawfully use or suggest make the Bank feel the effect of his reckless course." No secret was made of what Blair thought to be lawful means, and he closed his editorial with the statement: "The trepidation displayed in the Bank hive when the people in a portion of Kentucky by a spontaneous movement began last year to cash its paper, has taught us how to war with effect whenever the conduct of the Bank shall make it necessary or expedient."[2]

Biddle knew who had been behind the "spontaneous movement" in Kentucky, and he thought that the same people were responsible for the run in Savannah. He abandoned his plans for an extension of loans in the northeastern cities, and when the Congress assembled at the beginning of December, a financial crisis was raging with ever increasing severity. The administration throughout the fall had refused to admit that there was any real difficulty. It had dismissed the complaints being voiced all over the country as Bank propaganda, but now it had to abandon this untenable position, and Jackson and Taney, in their reports to the Congress, attacked Biddle and the Bank for the curtailment of loans as if it had been ordered for the sole reason of causing inconvenience to the country. The President in his annual message said nothing about the reputed insolvency of the Bank, which had been the burden of his comments the preceding year. Apparently, he no longer believed that "an exposure of its true condition would discover that it was not competent to meet its engagements."[3] Instead he complained of its great strength and the "almost unprecedented amount" of specie in its vaults and charged that "by a curtailment of its accommodations more rapid than any emergency requires . . . it is attempting to procure great embarrassments in one portion of the community while through the presses known to have been sustained by its money it attempts by unfounded alarm to create panic in all."

He justified the removal of the deposits not on the ground that they were unsafe but as an action necessitated by the August report of the government directors, which had presented "unquestionable proof" that the Bank was being "converted into a permanent electioneering machine," though he admitted that he had been urging the Secretary of the Treasury to take such action for "some months" before receiving this report. The question at issue, he insisted, was "whether the people of the United States are to govern through representatives chosen by their unbiased suffrages

[2] N. Biddle to G. Verplanck, November 19, 1833; N. Biddle to H. Binney, December 3, 1833; N. Biddle to J. G. Watmough, December 12, 1833, in the Biddle Manuscripts in the Library of Congress; *Globe* (Washington), November 14, 1833; *Niles' Register*, XLV (1833), 295, 299–300. The raid, Biddle later learned, was made by Beers and Company, a brokerage firm in New York, for its own purposes, but he did not have this information when he was making his decisions.

[3] A. Jackson to H. L. White, March 24, 1833, in Bassett (ed.), *Correspondence of Jackson*, V, 46–47.

or whether the money and power of a great corporation are to be secretly exerted to influence their judgment and control their decisions."[4]

Taney's report to the Congress increased the confusion. He first said that the deposits had been removed to prevent the Bank from causing a panic when its charter expired in 1836. The Bank, he charged, had increased rather than decreased its loans after the veto, in order that, upon the expiration of the charter, "the country would be compelled to submit to its renewal or bear all the consequences of . . . a severe pressure for the immense claims which would then be due to the corporation." But then Taney remembered that it was the Congress he was addressing and that if the prevention of a panic several years hence was the only reason for the removal, he might well have waited until the session opened. He started on a new tack and blamed the removal of the deposits upon the Bank's restrictive orders in August that had deprived the business of the country of nine million dollars of credit. The deposits had been removed to stop this curtailment, which, if it had been permitted to continue for "two months longer," would have further decreased credit by nineteen million dollars, and "a widespread scene of bankruptcy and ruin must have followed."[5]

These confused and contradictory explanations by the President and the Secretary of the Treasury made it clear that nothing in the Bank's condition, its conduct, or its plans had anything to do with the administration's decision to remove the deposits. The Bank had been operating throughout 1832 and 1833 with what Biddle rightly called "inoffensive usefulness" and had devoted itself to the purposes for which it had been created: "the restoration of the currency, the maintenance of the general credit, and the accommodation of the internal and foreign trade of the country." It had not interfered with the elections in any part of the country, and if "the money and power" of this "great corporation" were "secretly exerted to influence [the people's] judgment and control their decisions," not a single politician in the country or any newspaper knew where or how this power was exerted or this money spent.[6]

The deposits were removed from the Bank of the United States with the expressed intent of crippling or destroying the institution, not for any other reason, and Jackson and Taney were bitterly disappointed when their ruthless and unprincipled scheme failed. They had underestimated the strength of their powerful opponent and its ability to transfer the pressure from itself to the rest of the community and were genuinely surprised when the Bank of the United States at the beginning of December was stronger and more liquid than it had been at the close of September.

4 Richardson, *Messages and Papers,* III, 1249–51.

5 *Senate Document* (23d Cong., 1st sess.), No. 2.

6 N. Biddle to H. Binney, December 9, 1833; H. Binney to N. Biddle, December 10, 1833, in the Biddle Manuscripts in the Library of Congress; *Report of a Committee of Directors of the Bank of the United States* (Philadelphia, n.d.).

Almost ten million dollars in government deposits had been withdrawn without injuring the Bank, and the severe financial crisis that had accompanied this transfer of deposits had been attributable solely to their violation of their pledge not to issue transfer drafts. If Jackson and Taney had abided by this pledge, there would have been no general curtailment of loans, and the removal of the government deposits from the Bank, like earlier payments of the national debt, would have been accomplished without a major disturbance of ordinary business.

Many observers thought that the crisis was over when the deposits had been completely transferred, and businessmen brought powerful pressure on Biddle and the Bank to force them into an expansion of loans. Many of the directors of the parent bank and of the branches were members of the business community. They were customers of the Bank themselves as well as representatives of customers, and it was they and their fellow businessmen who were bearing the burden of the Bank's curtailments. They had not protested against the original decision to initiate the drastic reduction of loans, and they did not object to the continuation of the restrictive policy, so long as it was necessary to thwart the administration's attempts to break the Bank or one of its branches. But they were watching its financial statements with informed intelligence, and, by the middle of December, it had become evident that the Bank had arrived at the point where it could end its restrictions unless the administration made a new attack upon it. These business directors recognized that Biddle was justified in regarding their interests as secondary to his first and greatest duty, the preservation of the solvency of the Bank, but they did not intend to continue to bear the burden of the curtailments, once the Bank was assuredly solvent.

Biddle substantially agreed with these directors, and during the latter part of December he began a quiet and unpublicized increase in loans to holders of stock. This relief to selected individuals was of some general effect, but it was counteracted by a rapid and severe curtailment of loans by the depository banks. They were notified on December 13 that the government's funds in the national bank were almost exhausted and that they must be prepared to meet the Treasury's drafts for the ordinary expenditures of the government and the completion of the payment of the government debt. Some of these institutions, like the Union Bank of Baltimore, had sought the government deposits to rescue them from a dangerously extended position. Others had not needed the deposits for this purpose but had responded to Taney's urgent request to expand their loans to counteract the curtailment by the national bank. The Secretary had given no warning of the rapid exhaustion of the government's balances, and when the depository banks were sent this very late notice, all had to curtail loans sharply and drastically.[7]

[7] P. P. F. DeGrand to N. Biddle, December 18, 1833; C. A. Davis to N. Biddle, December 20, 1833; N. Biddle to R. Oliver, December 28, 1833; N. Biddle to H. Binney,

The resulting pressure was clearly the responsibility of the administration, but it was to Biddle and the Bank of the United States that the pleas for relief were addressed. All that Jackson and Taney would have had to do in this situation to force Biddle to relax his restrictions was to remain quiet, make no threats, and take no hostile actions, but they were too angry to adopt such a reasonable policy. At the beginning of January they ordered the Bank to turn over the pension funds to presidentially appointed agents, and they became indignant when Biddle contemptuously refused to obey an order that was a flagrant and open violation of the law establishing the Bank of the United States as the sole agent for the payment of pensions. The administration press denounced the Bank for this refusal to obey the President's illegal order and published moving and completely true accounts of the suffering inflicted on the pensioners who had been deprived of their expected payments by this conflict between the administration and the Bank. But Biddle had not sought or begun this dispute, and the Bank's duty to retain the pension books and funds was clear and unquestionable.[8]

The amount of money involved was inconsequential. The sole importance of this dispute was the evidence that it provided of the administration's intransigent attitude, and Biddle was reluctant to abandon the restrictions on the Bank's operations so long as the President and Secretary of the Treasury seemed determined to harass and worry the Bank. On January 2 he told a representative of the New York business community that nothing would give him greater delight than to come to its relief, and he promised that, as soon as he thought such a measure proper, he would embrace it with the utmost promptness. But he did not think that the proper time had come. "It has not come for the Bank, it has not come for the country," he insisted, "and I believe that the Bank itself and all the great interests connected with it would be put to hazard by any immediate change in its present course." Two weeks later, however, the situation had changed, and to another inquirer concerning the possibility of relief he wrote: "The difficulty is to know when to change and this must be studied from day to day. As yet I do not think the time has come."[9]

It was well that he waited, for Jackson's indignant anger, always in his view righteous, had been further aroused by the dispute over the pensions,

---

December 31, 1833; N. Biddle to M. Robinson, January 9, 1834, in the Biddle Manuscripts in the Library of Congress; Swisher, *Taney*, p. 265; Smith, *Economic Aspects of the Second Bank*, p. 164.

[8] N. Biddle to H. Clay, January 23, 1834; D. Webster to J. G. Watmough, n.d., in the Biddle Manuscripts in the Library of Congress; *House Report* (23d Cong., 1st sess.), No. 263.

[9] N. Biddle to S. Swartwout, January 2, 1834; N. Biddle to C. A. Davis, January 15, 1834; N. Biddle to B. R. Morgan, January 15, 1834; N. Biddle to J. McKim, Jr., January 15, 1834, in the Biddle Manuscripts in the Library of Congress.

and he made new threats against the institution. This time it was about the branch drafts, ten million dollars of which were in circulation. On January 17, Biddle was told by "an unimpeachable source" that within sixty days the Treasury, on Jackson's order, would instruct the depository banks not to accept the branch drafts in payments to the government. Any doubts that may have existed as to the accuracy of this information were resolved shortly afterward, when Jackson rebuked a committee of merchants from Philadelphia who had dared to ask him to return the deposits and said: "I have no hostility to the Bank ... but if it does persist in its war with the government, I have a measure in contemplation which will destroy it at once, and which I am resolved to apply, be the consequences to individuals what they may. The Bank has in circulation ... checks which I have no doubt are illegal, and which I will direct the state banks to refuse in payment of the public revenue. These checks will then be returned upon the Bank, and will drain her of the specie she is hoarding."[10]

Biddle did not doubt that the administration was serious in this new threat to attack the Bank, and on the day that he received confirmation of the President's statement he told a New York director that he was "beginning a new plan of diminishing our business throughout the establishment." The curtailment order, issued on January 23, called for an additional reduction of loans of three million dollars, and almost immediately there were numerous failures in all parts of the country. In New Orleans alone twenty-one mercantile firms suspended, and in New York three of the leading brokerage firms closed their doors. At first, the financial and business community blamed the Bank for these new difficulties. A cashier of a New York bank reported rumors that the branch was planning a further reduction of between one and two million dollars, and he warned Biddle that such a reduction would produce incalculable distress and alienate many friends. "The alarm," he wrote, "would be given that the city is to be sacrificed, and opposition, I am certain, would be manifested where friendly dispositions exist." Biddle assured him that the reports of the curtailment were exaggerated. All that had been contemplated was a reduction of about five hundred thousand dollars in New York, and this had been made necessary by "the present state of the Bank" and the "new measures of hostility to it in meditation by those who govern the executive." He expressed his regrets but insisted that the entire safety of the banks and other institutions of the country depended "on the failure of the individuals now in power in their efforts to break down the Bank."[11]

[10] N. Biddle to S. Jaudon, January 17, 1834; N. Biddle to R. Lenox, January 17, 1834; N. Biddle to C. A. Davis, January 21, 1834; N. Biddle to J. Tyler, October 18, 1834, in the Biddle Manuscripts in the Library of Congress.

[11] N. Biddle to R. Lenox, January 17, 1834; N. Biddle to P. Allen, January 25, 1834; J. Rathbone to N. Biddle, January 25, 1834; M. Robinson to N. Biddle, January 25, 1834; G. A. Worth to N. Biddle, January 28, 1834; N. Biddle to G. A. Worth, January 29, 1834; N. Biddle to J. McKim, Jr., February 10, 1834; S. Stilwell to N. Biddle, February 11, 1834; N. Biddle to J. Sergeant, February 12, 1834; J. Montgomery to N. Biddle,

Shortly thereafter Jackson gave public confirmation of these "new measures of hostility," thus fixing responsibility for the second curtailment on the administration rather than on the Bank. Public opinion once again turned against the President, and Biddle believed that the country was learning a useful lesson from its economic difficulties, that never again would it permit such experiments with money and banking as those Jackson was making. Biddle was a patriotic nationalist concerned for the welfare of his country, and he was not thinking selfishly of his institution alone when, in the midst of the second series of curtailments, he wrote: "All the other banks and all the merchants may break, but the Bank of the United States shall not break." He believed in 1834 as he had in 1819 "that experience has demonstrated the vital importance [of the national bank] to the fiscal concerns of this country and that the government which is so jealous of the exclusive privilege of stamping eagles on a few dollars, should be more tenacious of its rights over the more universal currency, and never again abandon its finances to the mercy of four or five hundred banks, independent, irresponsible, and precarious."[12]

Many state bankers in all sections of the country shared this opinion, and in New York at least half the directors of the depository banks were reportedly in favor of the return of the government funds to the national bank. One of them was quoted to Biddle as saying that "no relief could be afforded to the mercantile community until the deposits were made as formerly in the United States Bank," and petitions requesting the administration to reverse its policy were signed by politicians of all parties, unemployed mechanics and craftsmen, merchants, bankers, and brokers. James G. King, a leading broker and a proponent of a substitute national bank with headquarters in New York, was named chairman of the committee to take these petitions to Washington, and James A. Hamilton, now district attorney by Jackson's appointment, accompanied the committee as political adviser. Their first interview was with Van Buren and Silas Wright, and they were abruptly informed that "no modification in the system of state banks" would be permitted by the administration. The deposits would never be returned to the Bank of the United States, nor was there any chance that the President would recommend a substitute national bank. Van Buren was reportedly as bitter as "Whitney or Amos" in his comments on Biddle, and he warned King and Hamilton that "the time was not far distant when every man who advocated the Bank or the restoration of the deposits would be held in as great detestation as the members of the Hartford Convention."[13]

February 9, March 20, 1834; N. Biddle to H. Clay, February 2, 1834; N. Biddle to A. Gallatin, March 15, 1834, in the Biddle Manuscripts in the Library of Congress.

[12] N. Biddle to J. G. Watmough, February 8, 1834; N. Biddle to J. C. Spencer, January 27, 1819, in the Biddle Manuscripts in the Library of Congress.

[13] J. W. Webb to N. Biddle, January 11, 1834; J. Rathbone, Jr., to N. Biddle, January 22, 29, 1834; R. Colt to N. Biddle, January 25, February 20, 23, 1834; S. Stilwell

Jackson was even sharper. He dismissed the committee's appeal for relief with the injunction: "Go to Nicholas Biddle. We have no money here, gentlemen. Biddle has all the money. He has millions of specie in his vaults at this moment, lying idle, and yet you come to *me* to save you from breaking."[14] They went back to New York to report the failure of their mission, and Charles A. Davis, a newspaper writer, predicted to Biddle that the state banks would suspend specie payments within thirty days. The expected banking crisis in New York came to a head in the middle of February as an almost direct result of the failure of Benjamin Knower, the leading stockholder in the Farmers' and Mechanics' Bank of Albany and the father-in-law of Governor William Marcy. Knower's failure had created doubts as to the solvency of this bank and of its long list of affiliated institutions throughout upstate New York. If these banks failed, the Safety Fund itself would be endangered, and numerous appeals were sent to Biddle to come to their aid. Nicholas Devereaux, the president of the Utica branch, had gone to Albany at the beginning of the month, and he had been told that if the Bank of the United States would protect the Safety Fund in this moment of crisis, the New York banks and politicians would petition the administration for a return of the deposits to the national bank. Devereaux warned Biddle, however, that nothing but necessity would compel the New York politicians to challenge the administration's policy, and he recommended that their request for aid be rejected.[15]

Biddle followed this recommendation. No aid was forthcoming from the Bank, and runs were started on the upstate banks by their noteholders and depositors. For self-protection, these banks were forced to withdraw their funds on deposit in New York City, and Biddle was told that if the crisis continued and the panic was not stayed, there would be many failures. J. Watson Webb, now in total opposition to Jackson and Van Buren, took great satisfaction in what was happening and, with complete cynicism, advised Biddle: "The time has now arrived when through some of your confidential friends, two or three of the weaker safety fund banks must be made to suspend specie payments. It can easily be effected without fear or suspicion and if you would benefit by the present state of the times it must be resorted to."[16]

---

to N. Biddle, January 27, February 1, 2, 1834; A. Hamilton to N. Biddle, January 29, 31, 1834; N. Biddle to H. Binney, January 27, 29, 1834; C. A. Davis to N. Biddle, February 11, 1834, in the Biddle Manuscripts in the Library of Congress; *House Executive Documents* (23d Cong., 1st sess.), Nos. 3, 4, 5.

[14] Parton, *Jackson*, III, 549–50.

[15] H. Clay to N. Biddle, February 2, 1834; N. Biddle to H. Clay, February 4, 1834; N. Devereaux to N. Biddle, February 12, 15, 1834; N. Biddle to N. Devereaux, February 15, 1834; C. A. Davis to N. Biddle, February 20, 21, 1834; J. Rathbone, Jr., to N. Biddle, February 20, 1834; A. Hamilton to N. Biddle, February 22, 1834, in the Biddle Manuscripts in the Library of Congress.

[16] C. A. Davis to N. Biddle, February 24, 1834; J. W. Webb to N. Biddle, March 7, 1834, in the Biddle Manuscripts in the Library of Congress.

There was nothing that Biddle wanted more at this moment than the suspension of payments by one of these banks. It would lead, he was certain, to a general suspension by the rest of the banks in the state, including those that had the custody of the government deposits, and would be followed almost inevitably by a suspension in the South and West. Jackson's system of state banks would be exposed in all its weakness and inadequacy, but, great as this temptation was, Biddle was unwilling to cause needless failures by making secret and unnecessary demands. If the banks suspended specie payments, they must do so as a result of the general pressure rather than as a result of a deliberate attack by the Bank of the United States, and he rejected Webb's proposal out of hand.

Instead of precipitating the crisis, Biddle came to the aid of the threatened state banks, though he did so reluctantly because he knew that, by abandoning his restrictions, he was risking the loss of the support of the Whig party as well as any chance for an immediate restoration of the government deposits. At this moment Biddle was certain what the correct political course was for the Bank. Most of the people were ascribing the monetary difficulties to the removal of the deposits. They were contrasting their former situation, when the "monster" had possession of the government funds, with that produced by the "experiment with pets," and they were beginning to call for a return to the prosperity they had enjoyed under their "oppressor and briber." He had received word from Washington that "if there is any sentiment here that can be called a general one, it is that it will be entirely impossible to carry on the business of the country and of the government by the state banks." Not only would the deposits be restored, but also a recharter would be passed, and Biddle was determined that the Bank would be "neither frightened or cajoled from its duty by any small drivelling about relief to the country." Only "the evidence of suffering abroad," he was certain, would keep public opinion in its true line and have any influence on the Jackson majority in the House of Representatives. If the Bank permitted itself to be coaxed into any relaxation of its restrictions, this relief would be cited as evidence that the removal of the deposits had not been injurious or oppressive.[17]

But Biddle, despite his determination, knowledge, and desire, was not free to follow the most expedient political line. The second curtailment had placed the Bank in a position to meet any demand that could be brought against it, including the discrediting of the branch drafts. It had eleven million dollars of specie in its vaults, with more on order in Europe, and the weakened condition of the banks and merchants in all areas of the country made it unlikely that even Jackson or Taney would make a new attack upon it. No reason existed for the continuation of the Bank's re-

[17] N. Biddle to W. Appleton, January 27, 1834; J. Hopkinson to N. Biddle, February 11, 19, 1834; N. Biddle to J. Hopkinson, February 21, 1834, in the Biddle Manuscripts in the Library of Congress.

strictions, and the merchants, the state bankers, and brokers were not willing to suffer financially to enable Biddle to force a restoration of the deposits or to gain the recharter. The first break came in Boston, where, on
February 19, Biddle reluctantly consented to a relaxation. He insisted that
every motive of safety and expedience was against any enlargement of the
Bank's business, but he could not deny the directors' contention that the
Boston office was no longer in danger.[18]

For a brief time he hoped that this expansion of loans could be confined
to Boston alone. New England constituted essentially a separate financial
province in the United States, one in which the national bank was less
important than in other areas, and he tried to keep this action from becoming a precedent for the rest of the institution. But he underestimated the
strength and determination of the New York financial community. On
February 11 the King committee had reported to a mass city meeting its
lack of success in Washington, but the endangered community, instead of
admitting defeat, joined together and decided to rely upon itself and the
Bank of the United States. A Union Committee of Bankers and Merchants
was organized, with Gallatin, president of the National Bank of New York,
as its head, and they announced their decision to apply to the Bank of the
United States for aid.[19]

Biddle regretted the establishment of this committee. He requested the
advice of John Rathbone, Jr., and Robert Lenox, the most influential members of the New York board, and told them that any reply to a request
from the Union Committee would "require great delicacy in our movements so as to preserve our present attitude and yet not offend by declining a cooperation with other banks." Rathbone and Lenox agreed with
Biddle that any relaxation of the curtailments would jeopardize the
solvency of the Bank, and they urged him not to make any commitments
to expand loans or to cease demanding the immediate settlement of balances in specie. Gallatin, though head of the committee, shared the views
of the New York directors. He told Rathbone that he thought the branch
had already expanded its loans too much, and he feared that if it stopped
its curtailments, it would "accelerate the suspension of specie payments" in
New York. Paradoxically, he was opposed to all that the Union Committee had been organized to obtain, but King and John A. Stevens, his associates on the committee, did not agree with their chairman. At their in-
sistence a formal communication was addressed to Biddle on February 15
in which he was asked whether the Bank of the United States would increase its loans in co-operation with the local banks of New York and

[18] N. Biddle to W. Appleton, February 19, 1834; N. Biddle to A. Lawrence,
February 19, 1834, in the Biddle Manuscripts in the Library of Congress.

[19] S. Stilwell to N. Biddle, February 10, 1834; N. Biddle to J. Rathbone, Jr.,
February 14, 1833, in the Biddle Manuscripts in the Library of Congress.

whether it intended to continue the universal receipt and redemption of branch notes and drafts.[20]

Biddle delayed answering as long as he reasonably could, but on February 22 he replied that under existing conditions the Bank could not increase its loans and that the "universal receipt of the branch notes is a measure the continuance of which depends on contingencies." He hoped that this positive refusal would end the pressure upon him, but he was disappointed. The announcement of the relaxation in Boston strengthened the determination of the New York committee. King and Stevens came to Philadelphia to renew their requests for relief, and one of their associates wrote: "The intelligent portion of the community (a small number I confess) cannot shut their eyes to the fact that it is in the power of the Bank to relieve the market and restore confidence at any moment. And I do not hesitate to say (and I say it with good feeling and perfect respect) that if at this time no more than half a dozen of the known friends of the Bank and opponents of the government in whom the publick have confidence should declare their entire confidence in the ability of the Bank to give the necessary relief without danger to itself, it would turn the current of popular feeling into an unfavorable channel."[21]

Stevens and King used the same arguments, and Biddle could not counter them. The facts as presented in the Bank's financial statements were too plain to be denied, and on February 26 he tentatively agreed to recommend a plan of co-operative relief to the board of directors. The next day he changed his mind out of pique at an unexpected political development in Pennsylvania. Governor Wolf, who was considered to be friendly to the Bank, had been planning for some time to send to the legislature a message on the crisis which Biddle had reason to believe would attribute the state's financial difficulties to the removal of the deposits. Instead, the Governor, using obscure language and cautious phraseology, seemed to indicate that it was the Bank of the United States, not the government, that was responsible. Biddle was indignant. "It is melancholy," he wrote, "to see a Governor of Pennsylvania thus aiding in the destruction of Pennsylvania interests," and he announced that, instead of coming to the relief of New York, he had told the committee that "the conduct of the Governor of Pennsylvania obliged the Bank to look to its own safety."[22]

[20] J. Rathbone, Jr., to N. Biddle, February 17, 1834; M. Robinson to N. Biddle, February 20, 1834; in the Biddle Manuscripts in the Library of Congress.

[21] N. Biddle to J. A. Stevens, February 22, 1834, in the Dreer Manuscript Collection in the Historical Society of Pennsylvania; J. Rathbone, Jr., to N. Biddle, February 25, 1834; G. A. Worth to N. Biddle, February 28, 1834; in the Biddle Manuscripts in the Library of Congress.

[22] S. Breck to N. Biddle, February 26, 1834; N. Biddle to J. Rathbone, Jr., February 28, 1834; N. Biddle to G. A. Worth, February 28, 1834; N. Biddle to J. G. King, February 28, 1834; N. Biddle to S. Breck, March 1, 1834, in the Biddle Manuscripts in the Library of Congress.

The leaders of the New York committee conceded that the Governor's message was unfortunate, but they denied that it justified abandoning the relief plans for New York, inasmuch as it posed no new threat to the security or solvency of the Bank. Biddle was warned that public opinion would not consider the reasons he gave as sufficient to warrant continued postponement of relief measures, and Cadwalader, who had undertaken no missions for the Bank since his unfortunate agreement with Barings in London, went to New York to confer with the committee. He recommended that the requested relief be given, but Biddle was still unwilling. On March 11, however, he received a warning from a Philadelphia merchant visiting in New York which forced him to act. He was told very frankly that the committee was willing to wait three or four days for his consent to their plan, but if he refused, this fact would be stated publicly. On the other hand, he was told, if he came to the relief of New York, the committee would show its gratitude by a public indorsement and defense of the national bank.[23]

Biddle himself visited New York on March 14 and, while there, agreed to suspend all curtailments in the city until May 1. The public announcement was made on March 16, but the danger of crisis had already passed. The presence of Biddle in New York and the obvious satisfaction displayed by Gallatin, King, and Stevens after their conference were enough to convince the community that an agreement had been reached.[24] The curtailments and calls for settlement in other areas did continue, but all danger of a general suspension of specie payments was past. The relaxation at the center of the nation's trade and commerce spread rapidly, and only one local crisis of importance developed subsequently. This occurred in Washington and Baltimore as a result of the failure, in late March, of the Bank of Maryland. The Bank of Washington, the Bank of Alexandria, and the Farmers' and Mechanics' Bank of Georgetown suspended payments, creating a situation, wrote John Quincy Adams, such as he had "never witnessed in this nor indeed in any other country. The District Banks are all breaking in rapid succession and their breaking is all charged to your Bank." The Washington branch was approached for aid to the local banks at the beginning of this crisis, but Biddle ordered it to refuse. "If we begin," he said, "by venturing prematurely to the support of the institutions which may be embarrassed, we may ourselves become too much weakened to make decisive efforts at a later stage of the disasters which are coming."[25]

23 J. G. King to N. Biddle, March 1, 1834; N. Biddle to J. Rathbone, Jr., March 10, 11, 1834; L. Hodge to N. Biddle, March 10, 1834, in the Biddle Manuscripts in the Library of Congress.

24 J. Rathbone, Jr., to N. Biddle, March 1, 17, 1834; W. Hoskins to J. W. Webb, March 15, 1834; J. G. King to N. Biddle, March 18, 1834, in the Biddle Manuscripts in the Library of Congress.

25 N. Biddle to S. H. Smith, April 2, 1834; S. H. Smith to N. Biddle, April 11, 12, 1834; R. Colt to N. Biddle, April 12, 13, 14, 1834; J. McKim to N. Biddle, April 16,

The reason he did not want to intervene in this crisis in the political capital and its neighboring city was the hope that it would spread. The Bank of the United States had not been responsible in any way for the failure of the Bank of Maryland, and he still wanted to see the complete discrediting of the state-bank depository system. But though he would not come to the aid of the threatened institutions, he did not attack them, and the other Maryland and District banks were saved through vigorous efforts by the national Treasury and its depository bank, the Bank of the Metropolis. The relaxation of the Bank's restrictions in New York was thus the real end of the crisis which had been precipitated by the removal of the deposits, and the only gain that resulted to Biddle and his institution was the frustration of the administration's unprecedented attempt to break or destroy it. Jackson and Taney, having learned their lesson, made no new attacks upon the Bank, and the nation gradually recovered through the spring from its needless economic and financial injuries.

1834; J. G. Watmough to N. Biddle, April 13, 1834; J. Q. Adams to N. Biddle, April 16, 1834, in the Biddle Manuscripts in the Library of Congress; Swisher, *Taney*, pp. 267–68, 279–83.

Biddle and the Whigs

*B*iddle's decision to acquiesce in the demands of the Union Committee of New York was, as he knew it would be, bitterly resented by many of the members and leaders of the Whig party. Alexander Hamilton said immediately after the relaxation that "if the [Democratic] party are not defeated here, it will be your fault," and J. Watson Webb wrote that "the rise in stocks in New York has placed the [Democratic] party in great spirits. They say the 'experiment' has succeeded." Part of Hamilton's and Webb's disappointment was attributable to monetary losses. They, according to Webb, had relied upon Biddle's positive assertions that the Bank would not be diverted from its course until the deposits were returned, and they had made "large sales on time." The ending of the curtailments had made their speculation unprofitable, and Webb bitterly complained: "Hamilton and myself lost about $3000 and Joseph and myself $11,500." The congressional leaders of the party had not lost money, but they were as indignant as Webb. Horace Binney, who had been an attorney for the Bank and a member of the board of directors as well as its defender in Congress, said that Biddle's action was "a complete reversal of the Bank's policy and an abandonment of its only practical weapon of defense against the administration," and he never spoke again in the House of Representatives in regard to the Bank's affairs.[1]

Most of Binney's colleagues shared his feelings, and at the root of this discord between Biddle and the leaders of the Whig party was the conflict between his responsibilities as president of the Bank of the United States and his personal inclination as a political opponent of Jackson. During the first five months after the removal of the deposits, this conflict had been obscured. The Jackson administration, by its actions and threatened actions, had forced the Bank to curtail its loans and purchases of exchange,

[1] J. W. Webb to N. Biddle, March 15, 1834; A. Hamilton to N. Biddle, March 23, 1834; J. W. Webb to R. Colt, March 23, 1834, in the Biddle Manuscripts in the Library of Congress; Charles C. Binney, *The Life of Horace Binney* (Philadelphia, 1903), pp. 117–18.

and the resulting economic distress had been advantageous to the Bank and the Whig party alike. What Biddle was required to do to safeguard the interests of the stockholders and the solvency of the Bank was in accordance with what he wanted to do as a Whig, but the relaxation of curtailments in Boston and New York exposed the essential incompatibility of his two roles. Clay, Webster, Calhoun, and other leaders of the Whig party were in an equally anomalous situation. As politicians they were primarily concerned with the defeat of the opposing political party and their individual advancement, and they were interested in the Bank and the removal of deposits, as they were in other issues, chiefly as they had an effect upon these more immediate purposes.

The Whig party was united only by its opposition to Jackson and Van Buren. It was a paradoxical coalition of neo-Hamiltonian nationalists and extreme advocates of state rights, and its members called themselves "Whigs" as a symbol of their love of freedom and their scorn of the base subservience to "King Andrew" displayed by those whom they designated "Tories." The nationalists in this coalition, led by Webster and Clay, believed in the principle on which the Bank of the United States was based and wanted it rechartered, but the other Whigs used the removal of the deposits as a weapon against Jackson and Van Buren without defending the Bank. Calhoun, motivated in part by his newly established allegiance to liberal, laissez faire economic principles and in part by his personal economic interest as a producer of gold, was the leader of this second group, and he was now an enemy of all banks of issue, state or national. The three principal leaders of the Whig party were also divided by political ambition. Each wanted to be the party's nominee for President in 1836, and their actions with regard to the removal of the deposits were influenced by this fact.

Biddle had been aware of these divisions within the Whig party from the moment that the strange coalition had been brought together, and in devising his political tactics he sought to find some principle of unity which would hold Clay, Webster, and Calhoun together. He had been warned by Duff Green, Calhoun's chief political lieutenant, that "if the defeat of General Jackson and the success of the Bank is to bring up Webster or Clay and with them the doctrines against which we have arrayed ourselves, we will leave the Bank and General Jackson to fight out their own quarrels," and numbered among the doctrines referred to, Biddle had been certain, was the recharter of the national Bank. For this reason he had decided not to push the question of the recharter at all, and he had been pleased at the beginning of the session when Clay recommended the same tactics. It was Clay's opinion that the Whigs should concentrate upon Jackson's illegal usurpation of powers assigned to the Secretary of the Treasury, and he introduced a resolution censuring the President for his violation of the Constitution and the laws "in relation to the public revenue." He advised Biddle to make no movement "towards a renewal of the charter or the establishment of a new bank." Both these proposals should be ignored and the Whig attack concentrated upon the President's actions. "It is the usurpation," Clay wrote, "which has convulsed the country. If we put it by and take up the Bank, we may and probably would divide about the terms of the charter, and finally do nothing. In the other course the recharter will follow. The country will take care of that."[2]

Webster was not pleased with Biddle's acceptance of Clay's leadership and remained stubbornly silent throughout the early part of the session. The previous year he had joined with the Jackson party to oppose the adoption of the compromise tariff sponsored by Calhoun and Clay, and his silence on the deposit issue was interpreted as support of the administration. Rumors began to be spread that he was planning to ally himself with Jackson and Van Buren, and Biddle was much concerned. "We are annoyed perpetually," he wrote Webster, "by the whispers of exultation which pass among these miserable people that Mr. Webster is to come out for them. Only think now of Whitney's writing that it is perfectly settled that you are to leave your friends and go over to that gang. I wish to see some fair occasion on which you can dispel this illusion and demolish the whole gang." He warned Webster of the dangers that threatened the country and insisted that "the fate of the nation is in the hands of Mr. Clay, Mr. Calhoun, and yourself. It is in your power to save us from the misrule of these people . . . but you can only do it while you are united. It is for that reason that every honest man is anxious that you should not be alienated from each other, and that everything you all do is watched and canvassed with intense anxiety."[3]

Biddle could write so frankly to Webster because of their close personal and business relationship. The men were intimate friends, and Webster, as a regularly retained attorney, had represented the Bank in most of its cases before the Supreme Court. Correspondence and consultation on the complicated issues in these cases had given them an opportunity to know and admire each other, and Biddle was freer in what he wrote to Webster than to any other member of Congress. Webster was similarly open in his relations with Biddle, and in December he wrote: "Since I arrived here, I have had an application to be concerned professionally against the Bank, which I have declined, of course, although I believe that my retainer has not been renewed or *refreshed* as usual. If it be wished that my relation to the Bank should be continued, it may be well to send me the usual retainer." Webster was suggesting nothing improper. He was a lawyer as well

[2] D. Green to N. Biddle, September 22, 1833; H. Clay to N. Biddle, February 2, 1834, in the Biddle Manuscripts in the Library of Congress.

[3] N. Biddle to D. Webster, December 15, 1833, January 8, 1834; H. Binney to N. Biddle, February 4, 1834, in the Biddle Manuscripts in the Library of Congress.

as a senator, and it was customary for members of Congress and even the Attorney-General to represent private clients before the court. But the situation of the Bank at this moment was peculiar, and Webster, though he needed the money, assured Biddle in a private note that he would not take the offered case against the institution. He wanted his usual retainer and asked for it, but he also told Biddle that "if such things have to go before the Board, I should prefer the subject to be postponed."[4]

Biddle thought it wiser not to send the requested retainer. If it were done, he wrote, the news would be in the hands of the editor of the *Globe* in forty-eight hours, and the fact would be immediately announced, or "it would be treasured up to be used on the first occasion when any vote of yours gave displeasure to that gang." He also suggested that it would be advantageous if the Whigs in the Senate refused to consent to the re-nomination of Sullivan, Gilpin, and Wager as government directors on the grounds that it was these men who had made it impossible to conduct any confidential business at open meetings of the board. It was they, he insisted to Webster, who would send the information about the retainer to Washington, for they were the ones "who watch your account and the account of every political antagonist . . . who take no share in the affairs of the Bank, except to report and misrepresent every transaction of every individual opposed to them. Depend upon it these people should be expelled now that you have the power."[5]

Webster and the rest of the Whigs complied with Biddle's request to reject the nominations of the government directors, and, as soon as they went off the board, Webster's usual retainer was sent to Washington. It was the refusal to send the retainer, not its payment, that was politically motivated, for what Biddle and the Bank were purchasing was Webster's legal services. His political allegiance and support could not be bought, and he continued to follow a course in regard to the Bank and the removal of deposits that was contrary to the one that Biddle desired. Webster did not believe that Clay was right in his determination to avoid any discussion of the recharter, and, despite the opposition of Biddle and most of the Whigs, he prepared a bill which would extend the charter for either three, four, or six years beyond 1836 so that the Bank would have more time to liquidate its assets and thus enable it to relieve the existing distress. He

[4] D. Webster to N. Biddle, December 21, 1833, in the Biddle Manuscripts in the Library of Congress.

[5] N. Biddle to D. Webster, December 25, 1833, in the Biddle Manuscripts in the Library of Congress. Webster's letter to Biddle, printed in Reginald C. McGrane (ed.), *The Correspondence of Nicholas Biddle Dealing with National Affairs, 1887–1844* (Boston, 1919), p. 218, has been persistently misinterpreted by historians, who have used it to prove that Webster supported the Bank of the United States for the sake of money. Typical of these remarks is that of Arthur M. Schlesinger, Jr. (*Age of Jackson*, p. 84), which says: "Clay fought for Biddle and his Bank because it fitted in with his superb vision of America, but Webster fought for it in great part because it was a dependable source of private revenue."

received support from some of the pro-Bank members of the Jackson party, but the Whigs were almost unanimously opposed. They called on Biddle to do what he could to persuade Webster to abandon the project, but his efforts were unavailing.[6]

Calhoun was also restive under Clay's leadership, and, as soon as he learned of Webster's proposal, he prepared one of his own. What he wanted to do was to lay the foundations of a system by which the United States could be brought to an exclusively gold currency, and the means he suggested was to raise the value of gold so as to make it the metallic base of the currency instead of silver and to fix some amount from ten to twenty dollars below which no bank bill should be received into the Treasury. Both he and Webster were laying a basis for their claim to the Whig nomination in 1836, and both believed what Calhoun was the one to say in February, 1834, that "the overthrow of Jacksonism is certain and with it Van Buren and his party. His partisans are falling off in every direction and the process must continue . . . till he is utterly prostrated."[7] Much evidence existed to confirm this impression. Many of Jackson's most loyal political supporters had been disheartened by his intemperance and lack of principle in the removal crisis. Postmaster-General Barry told his daughter that the President was "growing old and irritable." He was now "acting upon impulse" and "conforming to the counsels of men wholly unworthy of his confidence," and Barry predicted that "unless the evil is corrected (and I see but little hope of it now) General Jackson may retire to the Hermitage under a cloud."

Barry blamed "the derangement of the currency and the suffering of the community" upon "the removal of the deposits; the manner of it; the agents employed in it; [and] the foolish plan of the secretary of the treasury"; but, despite his objections to these financial policies, he remained politically loyal to Jackson. "I support him and will continue to do so," Barry said, and so did large numbers of his fellow Democrats.[8] Whatever was wrong with the administration was blamed upon Van Buren, and it was to men who shared this conviction that Webster and Calhoun sought to appeal. Both wanted a realignment of political factions and the forma-tion of new parties divided according to the principles that had originally separated the Federalist and Republican parties. Webster was seeking the support of those Whigs and Democrats who favored the Hamiltonian pro-gram of a protective tariff, internal improvements, and a national bank;

[6] J. G. Watmough to N. Biddle, January 20, February 27, 1834; H. Binney to N. Biddle, February 4, 1834; J. Sergeant to N. Biddle, February 17, 1834, in the Biddle Manuscripts in the Library of Congress.

[7] J. C. Calhoun to J. E. Calhoun, February 8, 16, 1834, in J. Franklin Jamieson (ed.), *Correspondence of John C. Calhoun* (Washington, 1900), pp. 331–32.

[8] W. T. Barry to Susan Barry, February 22, 1834, typescript, in the University of Virginia Library.

and Calhoun a similar coalition that was basically opposed to these measures. Clay and his supporters, on the other hand, had a different view of the nature and purpose of American political parties. They wanted to avoid such a clear-cut differentiation in regard to issues, and it was with them that Biddle was aligned.

The cashier of the Bank, Samuel Jaudon, was representing the institution in Washington, and he was instructed to seek to prevent the raising of issues that would split the Whig coalition. He and the other representatives of the Bank were able to keep Webster and Calhoun quiet as long as Biddle was enforcing the restrictive orders. Both were aware that no compromise was possible in the midst of a war, and Calhoun, in contrast to Webster, wanted the curtailments continued. The South, he thought, was suffering "much less than the North," and he told his brother-in-law at the beginning of February, almost with pleasure, that "the pressure on the money market is great and growing, and must continue to increase for months to come. It is causing dismay throughout the country."[9]

From the beginning of the session, Webster had taken a different view. He had advised Biddle that "the Bank ought to reduce as slowly and moderately as they can and occasionally to ease off, when it is requisite to prevent extreme suffering," but he had said nothing publicly so long as the Bank was following a contrary course. When Biddle was forced by the Union Committee of New York to suspend the curtailments, however, Webster felt free to bring forward his compromise proposal, and on March 18 he introduced a bill which provided that the public deposits be returned to the Bank of the United States on July 1, 1834, and that its charter be extended beyond March 4, 1837, when Jackson would retire from the presidency. Clay and Calhoun opposed Webster's suggestion. Clay would accept nothing less than a renewal for a full term of twenty years, and Calhoun, by means of a highly original process of reasoning, decided that twelve years was the proper duration.[10]

The country, he said, had been brought to its "present diseased state" through banks, and twelve years was the exact time needed for "a bank to unbank the banks." He proposed to eliminate all paper money and to prepare for this transformation of the currency by gradually raising the denomination of notes which would be received by the Treasury. He now recommended to the Congress that the mint ratio between silver and gold be raised to sixteen to one, and then, turning to the opposite side of the

[9] J. C. Calhoun to J. E. Calhoun, February 8, 1834, in Jamieson (ed.), *Correspondence of Calhoun*, pp. 331–32.

[10] H. Binney to N. Biddle, February 4, 1834, in the Biddle Manuscripts in the Library of Congress; *Register of Debates in Congress* (23d Cong., 1st sess.), pp. 995, 1004–5. When Biddle found that he could not keep Webster from introducing his plan, he gave it reluctant support, in order to keep from offending Webster and his strong group of supporters in Philadelphia. N. Biddle to E. Chauncey, February 10, 1834; N. Biddle to S. Jaudon, March 11, 1834, in the Biddle Manuscripts in the Library of Congress.

Senate, he said: "If I understand their views as expressed by the Senator from Missouri [Mr. Benton]; . . . the Senator from New York [Mr. Wright]; and other distinguished members of the party . . . I see not how they can reject the measure. They profess to be the advocates of a metallic currency. I propose to restore it by the most effectual measures that can be devised, gradually and slowly, and to the extent that experience may show that it can be done consistently with due regard to the public interest."[11]

The Democrats were unmoved by Webster's and Calhoun's essentially contradictory proposals. Those favoring the Bank of the United States and those who wanted a metallic currency alike remained generally silent and permitted the Whigs to carry on their intramural battle without expressing an opinion pro or con. Party loyalty was stronger than economic principles or interest, and both Webster and Calhoun were proved to have misread the signs of the times. Whether a politician called himself a Whig or a Democrat was determined not by his attitude toward the Bank, the currency, or any other issue but by the political faction within his state and locality with which he was aligned. Opposition to Van Buren as the chosen successor to Jackson was shown to be the only practicable platform for a Whig seeking nomination as the party's candidate for the presidency, and Webster and Calhoun, having tried their independent courses, turned back to Clay's motion of censure.

Webster's proposal was tabled at his personal request, and that of Calhoun was not pressed to a vote. The Democrats, led by Benton, had been able to prevent Clay's motion of censure from being brought to the floor so long as the Whigs were divided, but now a vote on the question could no longer be postponed. On March 28 the Senate by a vote of twenty-six to twenty resolved that "the president, in the late executive proceedings in relation to the revenue, has assumed upon himself authority and power not conferred by the constitution and laws, but in derogation of both."[12] The passage of this resolution by a strict party vote aroused the Democrats to counteraction. Jackson formally protested that the censure was improper, and Benton moved unsuccessfully that it be expunged from the record. The main attack, however, was made in the House of Representatives, where the administration still had a substantial majority. James K. Polk, chairman of the Ways and Means Committee, was in charge of the Jackson forces, and under his leadership four resolutions were introduced and passed. Three of these were merely the expression of the opinion of the House that the charter should not be renewed or the deposits returned and that the system of state-bank depositories was secure and sound, but the

11 *Register of Debates in Congress* (23d Cong., 1st sess.), pp. 1057, 1067.

12 *Ibid.*, p. 1187.

fourth called for an investigation of the "abuses, corruptions, or malpractices . . . in the management of said Bank."[13]

The largest number of votes that the "politically powerful" Bank of the United States could muster against any of these resolutions was one hundred and five, and only forty-two representatives dared oppose the request for an investigation. But the strength and unity exhibited by the Democratic party on this particular issue was not a true reflection of its actual situation. It was as divided as the Whigs by the presidential ambitions of Van Buren, Supreme Court Justice John McLean, Hugh Lawson White, and Richard M. Johnson, each of whom was seeking to establish his claims as the rightful successor to the President. Jackson himself had already made up his mind. His choice was Van Buren, and he looked upon the other candidates and their supporters with suspicion as to their fundamental loyalty to him and his administration. The vote on Polk's resolutions, for this reason, was not an accurate reflection of the Democratic party's attitude toward the Bank but rather was an attempt by the supporters of all the candidates to prove that they could be relied on by Jackson.

Thus Biddle was not particularly disturbed by the vote in the House, nor was he worried by the prospects of another investigation. He had kept himself fully informed concerning the conflicts and tensions within the Democratic party, and he was convinced that Polk's object in the proposed investigation was not to ascertain anything about the operations of the Bank or the means used in its defense. His target was the Democratic representatives and senators who were unwise enough to support some candidate other than Van Buren, in particular John Bell, the member from Jackson's home district of Nashville. Bell had consistently supported Jackson on the issue of the national bank, and he voted with the majority on each of Polk's resolutions; but he had been suspiciously quiet in regard to the removal of the deposits and was thought to favor White, McLean, or Johnson over Van Buren for the presidency in 1836. He had also been the cause of the failure of a plan that had been devised to elect Polk as Speaker of the House of Representatives in December, 1833. The object of this maneuver had been to strengthen the Van Buren forces, and Jackson, to make it possible, had offered Andrew Stevenson, the former Speaker, the appointment as minister to Great Britain. But the Democrats in the House refused to accept Polk. Some favored Sutherland of Pennsylvania, but the largest number wanted Bell, and Jackson, rather than permit the election of either, postponed the appointment of Stevenson.[14]

13 *Ibid.,* pp. 3474–77.

14 Powell Moore, "The Revolt against Jackson in Tennessee," *Journal of Southern History,* II (1936), 1–5; Joseph H. Parks, *John Bell of Tennessee* (Baton Rouge, 1950), pp. 68–73; Francis F. Wayland, *Andrew Stevenson, Democrat and Diplomat, 1785–1857* (Philadelphia, 1949), pp. 104–6; Charles K. Sellers, Jr., *James G. Polk, Jacksonian, 1795–1843* (Princeton, 1957), pp. 235–42.

Throughout the session Bell was subjected to pressure in an effort to persuade him to announce that he would not accept election as Speaker, and on April 19, after the investigating committee had been appointed, he was told by one of its members that they had information about some letters he had written to Biddle the preceding year. Nothing improper had been stated or implied in these letters. Bell's brother, a merchant, had needed to borrow money in Philadelphia, and the Congressman, who was personally acquainted with Biddle, had written two letters in support of the application. But so much had been made of the Bank's allegedly corrupt use of loans to bribe senators and representatives that Bell knew it would be politically damaging for his letters to be published. He complained to Biddle about the careless handling of these private letters but was told in reply that the only way in which knowledge of them could have reached Washington was through the associates of Reuben Whitney, who had been placed in the directorate by Jackson. Biddle was not unhappy at this opportunity to point out to a prominent Democrat the exact sort of tactics that had characterized the Jackson administration's war upon the Bank, but when the committee reached Philadelphia and demanded all correspondence with congressmen, including unanswered letters, he wrote Bell: "I incline to think that the purpose is to injure you. To those who know me it is superfluous to give any assurance that I would never permit the execution of such an order. At the same time it may be a satisfaction to you to possess the two letters . . . and I therefore enclose them to you. No one has read them and no one shall read them, unless you permit them to be read, nor is there any copy or vestige of them here."[15]

No warrant for the committee's demand was to be found in the charter, and Biddle firmly rejected it as soon as it was made. He also refused to permit the investigators to examine the books except in the presence of officers of the Bank, and the committee, unable to obtain the sort of information it desired, returned to Washington, threatening to cite Biddle and the directors for contempt. Biddle, who knew that no such resolution would pass the House, wrote ironically that he would "find it exceedingly pleasant to be imprisoned during the warm weather by the votes of members of Congress because I would not give up to their enemies their confidential letters"; and later, when Jackson had appointed Stevenson as minister to Great Britain and Bell had been elected Speaker, he added: "I have amused myself with the . . . prospect of standing at the bar and receiving a reprimand from Bell for my contumacy." He was worried, however, by the effect that the Bank's refusal to submit to an investigation might have on public opinion, and, to prove that it was not inquiry itself that was feared, he encouraged Senator Samuel L. Southard of New Jersey, a friend of the Bank, to introduce a resolution calling for an investigation by the Finance

[15] J. G. Watmough to N. Biddle, April 7, 19, 1834; N. Biddle to J. Bell, May 2, 1834, in the Biddle Manuscripts in the Library of Congress.

Committee of the Senate. This resolution was passed on the last day of the session, and the committee was authorized to sit during the recess "to inquire whether the Bank of the United States had violated its charter; [and] whether it was a safe depository of the public money?"[16]

Biddle's purpose in encouraging this inquiry by the Whig-controlled Senate was not merely to prove that the Bank did not fear investigation and that he had rejected the demands of the House committee only because they were improper and illegal. He also wanted to show how properly the Bank's affairs had been conducted in exact accordance with its charter and how strong and liquid it was. In spite of all that had happened, he still believed that the Bank would be rechartered. "The question of real and permanent stability to the currency," he wrote on May 9, "is in fact the question of the recharter of the Bank," and he was certain that the need for and the utility of such an institution would be demonstrated by the confusion that would inevitably result "when the several hundred state banks are left to themselves."[17] He was also certain that the Democratic party itself would divide on these matters, as that which called itself Whig had already done. Benton and many others were even more opposed to the state-bank depository system than to the national bank, and they had defended the removal of the deposits only because they had thought that it was the first step toward the creation of a system of government depositories and the establishment of an exclusively metallic currency.

In speeech after speech in the Senate, Benton had expressed his hostility to all banks, state as well as national, and his influence with Jackson was feared and resented by Kendall, Whitney, Taney, and other proponents of the use of state banks as depositories. Benton had been greatly pleased when Calhoun publicly announced his conversion to the cause of gold, and soon afterward he reintroduced his bill to change the mint ratio with silver to sixteen to one. This time he had strong backing from Jackson himself and from the representatives and senators of the gold-producing states in the South. The bill became law, and this substitution of gold for silver as the prime monetary metal was considered a major victory by the proponents of a specie currency.[18] Benton, Jackson, Calhoun, and their supporters thought that the overvaluing of gold foreshadowed the time when the nation could dispense with banks, eliminate debt, and establish a regular and unvarying economic system. Biddle, to whom the change in the relative value of gold and silver was not of immediate concern, took no

16 N. Biddle to J. G. Watmough, May 2, 10, June 5, 1834; N. Biddle to J. S. Barbour, June 3, 1834, in the Biddle Manuscripts in the Library of Congress; N. Biddle to J. Biddle, May 6, 1834, in the Biddle Manuscripts at "Andalusia"; *Register of Debates in Congress* (23d Cong., 1st sess.), pp. 2125–26.

17 N. Biddle to J. S. Smith, May 9, 1834, in the Biddle Manuscripts in the Library of Congress.

18 Benton, *Thirty Years' View*, I 406–11, 423–35, 436–58, 469–70.

position on the matter except to point out to those who inquired that this substitution of one metal for another would not have the effect that its proponents believed it would have. He did not think that the American people would support or endure the deflationary destruction of values that would accompany the establishment of an exclusively metallic currency, and he knew that such an economy would be no more stable than that which already existed.

The increase in the price of gold, paradoxically, made more difficult the elimination of small bank notes, one of the major objects of Calhoun's and Benton's reform. Gold coins could be substituted for notes of five dollars and upward, but only silver could be used for lesser denominations. It was for this reason that McDuffie, among others, had said concerning Calhoun's proposal that "the idea of dispensing with bank circulation altogether is utterly visionary in the actual state of our currency," and Biddle had fully agreed.[19] He was also aware that the substitution of gold for silver as the basic monetary metal in the United States increased the importance of the balance of trade between this country and Great Britain, for it essentially identified the British and American currencies "and rendered each forever thereafter liable to be influenced by the other." Great Britain was on the gold standard, and it accepted and paid out silver only because it was the monetary metal in the United States, India, other areas of the Far East, and parts of Europe. So the change in the relative value of gold and silver in the United States meant that whenever metal was taken from the Bank of England to pay American balances, it would be gold, its own monetary reserve.[20]

British financial authorities were particularly aware of this problem at the moment because during the deposit crisis there had been a large drain of silver to the United States. Credit had been easy in Great Britain and on the Continent, and American produce had been selling in large volume and at high prices in these markets. American purchases of European and British manufactures, on the other hand, had declined drastically, and it had been this favorable balance of trade which had enabled Biddle so easily to build up the specie holdings of the Bank of the United States. This loss of silver was in itself sufficient to cause some apprehension in Great Britain, but the passage of Benton's act created real alarm. The financial editor of the *Times* in London said that this change would add materially to the already too numerous calls upon Great Britain for gold bullion and that the working "of this reform of the monetary system in America is a matter which . . . deserves to be carefully watched."[21]

[19] G. McDuffie to N. Biddle, February 22, 1834, in the Biddle Manuscripts in the Library of Congress.

[20] P. P. F. DeGrand to N. Biddle, October 24, 1834, in the Biddle Manuscripts in the Library of Congress.

[21] *Times* (London), quoted in Smith, *Economic Aspects of the Second Bank*, p. 278.

For these reasons Biddle believed that the easy-credit conditions which had prevailed in Great Britain and the rest of Europe during the preceding year might possibly be ended by the fall of 1834 and that the Bank of England, to protect its bullion, would impose restrictions; hence, during the spring and summer, he tried to make certain that the Bank of the United States would be ready to meet this changed situation. Not all financial experts agreed with him. The American representative of Baring Brothers and Company had suggested in March that, since the Bank had not exercised its right to borrow in London for more than a year, it should surrender its line of credit with the firm. But Biddle unhesitatingly rejected this proposal. The difficulty in the way of acquiescing, as he saw it, was that "in the very critical posture of the country, it is possible or even probable that the Bank may be under the necessity of making some effort for the relief of the community," and foreign credit would be essential for that. He saw no immediate prospect that the line of credit would be needed, but he thought it unwise to relinquish it.[22]

He expected that, when the deposit crisis was over, American importers would place large orders to build up their depleted stocks but that American exporters might well be unable to sell the expected volume of produce because of credit restrictions in Great Britain. If in this situation the Bank of the United States was unable to supply the needed exchange, a counter-movement of specie would begin, and the weakened American banks would be forced to curtail. He wanted to keep his line of credit with Barings and also to build up the Bank's European funds, but his efforts to buy exchange during the spring were frustrated by the increased business which had been fostered by the Bank's relaxation in New York. The banks and merchants of the city were acting as though all their troubles had been removed, and their confidence increased on May 1, the day that the agreement with the Union Committee expired, when there was no change in policy by the Bank. Importers increased their European orders and used the money made freely available by the banks to purchase bills of exchange at ever higher rates. The Bank of the United States was unable to buy bills, and Biddle, for the first and only time in his career, was forced to restrict credit deliberately so that the Bank could purchase exchange.[23]

On May 15 he ordered the New York branch to impose a drastic reduction in loans, but the local banks did not heed this signal. They continued to lend as freely as before, and the branch balances, which had been wiped out in March, rose to more than three million dollars by the beginning of June. The merchants continued to buy all available bills of exchange at rates too high for the Bank, and Biddle, to increase the pressure, ordered

22 N. Biddle to T. W. Ward, March 10, 1834, in the Biddle Manuscripts in the Library of Congress.

23 N. Biddle to J. Rathbone, Jr., May 15, 1834, in the Biddle Manuscripts in the Library of Congress.

the branch to demand an immediate settlement of balances. The city banks now had to curtail their loans, and the Bank, having forced its competitors out of the market, replenished its European funds. No one outside the Bank knew why Biddle had resumed the curtailments, and many of the friends and supporters of the institution thought that the new restrictions had been imposed for political reasons. Some were opposed and some favorable, depending upon what they thought the political effect was, and Alexander Hamilton, strangely, held both views. He began by criticizing Biddle severely but soon thereafter reversed his position when he found that the Bank's contraction of operations was having a desirable political effect. The renewal of the monetary difficulties, he reported to Biddle, was greatly embarrassing to the Democrats, and the leading politicians of the party had sent word to Jackson that "unless something is done to relieve the money market, the party and the government deposits will be sacrificed."[24]

Biddle was seeking neither political advantage nor profit for the Bank. His sole purpose was to have sufficient funds in Europe to meet whatever demand for exchange might develop in the approaching business season, and when he had purchased the desired amount by June 10, he agreed once again to suspend the calls for settlement upon the local banks. The passage of the act increasing the price of gold at the close of June made him more apprehensive, and he renewed the pressure in New York by calling upon the banks for three hundred thousand dollars in specie so that the Bank could further increase its European balances by half a million dollars. This second curtailment, following so rapidly after a relaxation, aroused the fears of the mercantile community. "There is existing here an intense anxiety in relation to the future policy of the Bank," a visitor to New York reported on July 8. "A fearful apprehension seems to prevail that the screws may be applied with such force as to separate it from the Whig cause. . . . I have no doubt that you will be waited on in a day or two [and] I pray your wisdom may direct to such replies as may not wean any of the friends of the Bank from it, nor effect injuriously the great cause of our country's salvation."[25]

A committee was formed to protest against this renewal of the pressure, but, before its leaders could arrange a meeting with Biddle, he wrote to inform them that "we have waited for the adjournment of Congress before taking any final course in regard to the Bank, because till then, the movements of the Government were uncertain." He expressed the opinion that

[24] A. Hamilton to N. Biddle, June 2, 6, 1834; N. Biddle to A. Hamilton, June 3, 8, 1834; E. Everett to N. Biddle, June 8, 1834; G. C. Verplanck to N. Biddle, June 9, 1834; N. Biddle to G. Verplanck, June 10, 1834, in the Biddle Manuscripts in the Library of Congress.

[25] C. A. Davis to N. Biddle, June 16, 1834; N. Biddle to R. M. Blatchford, June 18, 1834; M. L. Bevan to N. Biddle, July 8, 1834, in the Biddle Manuscripts in the Library of Congress.

the Bank had now reached the point "of entire safety," and two days later, on July 11, the board of directors by a unanimous vote instructed the committee on offices to end all curtailments and to permit each branch to increase its loans wherever such action would provide relief for the community.[26] The Bank of the United States had come through a full circle since August 13, 1833, when, in anticipation of the removal of deposits, it had inaugurated its restrictive policy. Biddle's preservation of the solvency of the institution and of each of its exposed branches throughout these eleven months was another of his great achievements as a banker, and a committee of the Senate, in commenting upon it, wrote: "Whether any other moneyed corporation in the world could have stood up against trials so severe, is questionable."

That the Bank of the United States during these attacks upon it by the political administration of the country had not been subjected to panic runs upon its specie was cited as proof of a deeply rooted public confidence in its solvency and in the skill with which its affairs had been conducted, particularly since "doubts and suspicions" concerning it had been raised by the President himself and had been "followed up by the most hostile action."[27] The Bank not only had survived these assaults but had come out with its hold upon the respect and support of the financial and mercantile community unshaken. Well-informed men recognized that it was Jackson's order removing the deposits and his public threats to break the institution that had been responsible for the financial difficulties of the preceding year, not Biddle and his measures to protect the Bank.

"The author of this measure," Gallatin, as chairman of the Union Committee, wrote, "is responsible for the effects. . . . It is idle to say that they were greater than was expected, or made at a different time, or in a different manner from what had been anticipated. If it was impossible for the Executive, or for any human being, to foresee what the Bank . . . might be compelled or inclined to do, and the effects which its acts might have on the currency and commerce of the country, that was a sufficient reason for not adopting a measure in itself wholly unnecessary." Gallatin, a state banker, a bullionist, and a New Yorker, was under no obligation to defend the Bank of the United States, but he justified the curtailments ordered by Biddle as necessary for the defense of the Bank against threatened attacks by the administration. He accused the President and his associates of ignorance, incapacity, and irresponsibility, and he insisted that without a national bank the stability and safety of the whole American monetary system would be in danger. "It is principally," he wrote, "because Congress either has not or will not exercise the power of regulating and restraining

---

26 N. Biddle to J. W. Webb, July 9, 1834; N. Biddle to J. Rathbone, Jr., July 10, 11,; 1834; N. Biddle to M. L. Bevan, July 11, 1834, in the Biddle Manuscripts in the Library of Congress.

27 *Senate Document* (23d Cong., 2d sess.), No. 17, pp. 12–14.

the currency issued under the authority of the several states, that resort has been had twice to the national bank. Until a more direct and efficient mode shall have been suggested, we must look to that institution as the only means through which a sound and uniform currency can be issued. ... We know from the experience of nearly forty years, that so long as a Bank of the United States has been in operation we have had a sound currency; and that it has been thrown into utter confusion when left to the control of the several states."[28]

Biddle's point of view throughout this year of conflict was essentially the same as Gallatin's. He defended the Bank of the United States on the ground that such an institution was indispensable to the economic health of the nation. The failure of the Congress to order the return of the deposits was a great disappointment to him not only as president of the Bank from which they had been taken but also as an American who placed the strength of the country ahead of personal political power and influence or the particular interests of any section or group. He did not despair. He was still confident that the country would eventually return to a national bank. Jackson would retire in 1837, and his successor would find it imperative, if he was to prevent a repetition of the national experience between 1812 and 1816, to call for the re-creation or recharter of this particular kind of banking institution.

[28] *Report of the Union Committee, March 29, 1834* (New York, 1834).

~ 27 ~

Closing
the
Bank

*B*iddle was physically and mentally exhausted by the strains and tensions of the political and economic struggles in which he had been engaged, and, yielding to his wife's pressure, he finally agreed to take an extended vacation, his first since 1822. She reminded him of his unfulfilled contract to take her to Europe, but he protested that so long a trip was impossible. They arrived at a compromise of a journey to Newport and Niagara, and on July 11 "the whole movable household," consisting of Mr. and Mrs. Biddle, Edward, the three smaller children, two nurses, and a dozen trunks, sailed from Philadelphia. Biddle found Newport delightful. "I think it is destined to grow in favor," he wrote to a friend, "and to have all its honors as a watering place renewed and enlarged." But the trip to Niagara was marred by the difficulties of the journey, and at its close he reported: "I would not encourage any friend to undertake such an excursion with three small children and two nurses. The journey occupied three weeks, at the end of which the children as well as Mrs. Biddle and myself were so fagged by the heat and dust . . . that we returned to Newport to cool ourselves."[1]

Almost everyone with whom he talked mentioned the approaching congressional elections, since the Bank of the United States and the removal of the deposits were the principal issues. Biddle himself figured largely in the political controversy, and to many the campaign seemed to be a personal conflict between him and Jackson. Numerous cartoons were lithographed and distributed in which Biddle appeared as "Old Nick," if the artist was a

[1] N. Biddle to S. Jaudon, July 16, 1834; N. Biddle to C. S. Hunt, September 8, 1834; N. Biddle to W. Parson, September 17, 1834, in the Biddle Manuscripts in the Library of Congress.

Democrat, and as the defender of honesty, virtue, and sound banking if he was a Whig. Many of the newspapers opposing Jackson carried each week a column written by Charles A. Davis of New York in which Major Jack Downing of the Downingville Militia, Second Brigade, defended the "Gineral," "Mr. Van Buren," and their associates against "Squire Biddle" in a way that made the administration and its policies appear inept, ridiculous, and, most effective of all, funny. Davis had a genuine wit and the capacity to explain complicated financial problems in simple and homely terms, and his efforts were seconded in another series of columns ostensibly written by Congressman David Crockett, a professional frontiersman from Tennessee who was politically an opponent of Jackson. The Whigs were striving for a level of discourse that would counteract Jackson's popularity with the people, but fate, or whatever it is that rules the realm of political loyalty in the United States, was against them. The Downing and Crockett columns made people laugh, but they influenced only a few of the voters, and when Biddle returned from his vacation, he was almost certain that the Democratic party would again be victorious.[2]

He kept the Bank rigidly neutral throughout the campaign, and none of the officers or employees took any part in the election except to vote. When John C. Weems, a Whig candidate for Congress, applied for a loan to finance his campaign, Biddle immediately refused, both on the ground that it would be improper and also because it would "be impracticable to make such a loan without giving it the notoriety . . . which might subject you to reproach in the present excited state of the country." Even more explicit was Biddle's rejection of a request from Silas M. Stilwell of New York, who had left the Jackson party to become the Whig candidate for lieutenant governor. "On the subject of aid from this quarter," he replied to Stilwell, "the fact is . . . that contributions fall on a very narrow circle of not wealthy people, and . . . they have been completely exhausted. . . . As to the Bank itself, I have always made it a point of duty never to permit its interference in any manner with our political concerns. It was a refusal to become a partizan of the present set in power which has made them its enemies, and it will persevere in the same neutrality to the end, although the temptations to depart from this course are obvious and strong."[3]

Many of the Whigs thought that Biddle was much too moralistic in refusing to come to their aid. "It puts me in mind of a person walking with his head erect but stumbling over the smallest obstacles," one of these politicians wrote, and he bitterly protested against the conduct of the New

[2] Charles A. Davis, *Letters of J. Downing, a Major* (New York, 1834); David Crockett, *A Narrative of the Life of David Crockett of the State of Tennessee Written by Himself* (Philadelphia, 1834).

[3] N. Biddle to J. C. Weems, September 17, 1834; N. Biddle to S. Stilwell, September 17, 1834; R. M. Blatchford to N. Biddle, October 30, 1834, in the Biddle Manuscripts in the Library of Congress.

York branches, where, he said, "our political friends have not been known as such. No desire to aid them has been shown, and some of my personal friends in the West have been treated with a suspicion and coldness that was unwarrantable and unjust." The ordinary voters knew nothing of Biddle's refusals to aid the opponents of Jackson, and numbers of them believed that the Bank was financing the Whig campaign. Their attitude was expressed mockingly in an anonymous letter to Biddle: "Notwithstanding all our efforts we have been defeated. . . . We bet largely, all the money indeed you have sent us, hoping . . . by that means we might influence the election, but we have not succeeded. . . . All hope now lies on bribery! I think some of the members of Congress might be sounded successfully."[4]

The Democrats won the election in a majority of the states, and this meant that there was no longer a chance for the Bank to gain a recharter from the Congress before its present one expired. The voters could not be convinced that the Bank was what it actually was—a useful and necessary institution that facilitated their business transactions and increased their profits. To most of them it represented the money power, which was evil, and it was Jackson who had vanquished it. So widespread was this conviction that the Whigs were about ready to abandon the Bank, and the point of view of many of the party leaders was expressed by Thurlow Weed of New York, who wrote: "We have gone with our friends through three campaigns under a strong and settled conviction that in every issue to be tried by the people to which the Bank was a party, we must be beaten. After staggering along from year to year with a doomed Bank upon our shoulders, both the Bank and our party are finally overwhelmed."[5]

The results of the election strengthened Jackson's determination to continue the attempt to destroy and discredit the Bank, and on November 5 he issued the long-threatened order to stop the acceptance of branch drafts in payments to the government. He followed this action with a strong message to Congress denouncing the Bank and praising the gold coinage. The country, he said, would soon have "a sound and portable currency, which will much diminish the inconvenience to travellers of a want of a general paper currency, should the state banks be incapable of furnishing it." All that was needed to make the American currency as "sound and as little liable to fluctuations" as that of any other commercial country, was that the several states "reform their banking system and prohibit the issue of all small notes."[6] The admissions he made in this description were startling. The currency that had been, and was still being, furnished by the Bank of the United States was both sound and not liable to fluctuations. It was entirely convenient to travelers, being accepted at par almost every-

---

[4] Anonymous letter to N. Biddle, October 16, 1834; S. D. Bloodgood to N. Biddle, November 7, 1834, in the Biddle Manuscripts in the Library of Congress.

[5] H. A. Weed (ed.), *Autobiography of Thurlow Weed* (Boston, 1884), p. 431.

[6] *House Executive Document* (23d Cong., 2d sess.), No. 2, p. 42.

where and sometimes commanding a premium, and, as to small notes, the undervaluing of silver had made them almost an essential if anyone was to have any change. The Treasury itself had been forced to issue small notes in the West in denominations of one and two dollars for the use of its land offices, and many merchants and retailers were ignoring the state prohibitions against the issue of notes by non-incorporated businesses, in order to enable their customers to buy.

The people of the country, if they can be judged by their actions, did not share Jackson's fears and hatred of the Bank. His order forbidding the acceptance of branch drafts had no effect upon their use in all other business transactions, and his violent denunciation of the conduct of the Bank did not affect the price of its stock. The answer to the charges he made in his message was contained in the report of the Senate Finance Committee, written by John Tyler and submitted early in the session. Only one aspect of the Bank's activities—Biddle's expenditures under the resolution of March 11, 1831—was adversely criticized, and even here it was stated that the Bank itself had no objection to making "an ample and minutely detailed disclosure of every item of expenditure" but that it had refrained from doing so in order to protect "others, every way innocent," from "vituperation, malignant aspersion, and peradventure to personal vengeance."[7]

Biddle ordered a large printing of this report, to use, he said, as "an epitaph" when the Bank was "dead and gone," and he was amused a short time later when Tyler, who had been particularly vigorous in his criticism of the Bank for spending money to circulate "documents in its defense," asked for a thousand copies of the report, thus "making the Bank incur an expense in publication which it did not desire."[8] There was little else in the situation at the close of 1834, however, to amuse Biddle. His hopes for a recharter to preserve what he knew was the only practicable means for an effective monetary and credit system in the United States had been frustrated, and the job that was left was to supervise the liquidation and closing of the Bank in such a way as to do as little injury to the national economy as possible.

He would have liked to be called on by the Congress to aid in the task of devising some substitute system for what had previously been centered in the Bank of the United States, but even this limited area of service was denied to him. The Congress was too occupied during the short session with other matters, among them the possibility of war with France over the spoliation claims, to concern itself with the currency or the caretaking of the government's funds, and the President's recommendation that the

7 *Senate Document* (23d Cong., 2d sess.), No. 17.

8 N. Biddle to J. Tyler, December 8, 1834; N. Biddle to D. Webster, December 11, 1834; N. Biddle to J. G. Watmough, February 9, 1835, in the Biddle Manuscripts in the Library of Congress.

government's stock in the Bank be sold and his request for legislative sanction of the state-bank depository system were alike ignored. The administration itself did not press these matters. It was more divided now than it had previously been, and a major debate was being carried on within it. Whitney was the leader of the group which wanted to continue the use of state banks, but Benton, assisted by his economic adviser, William M. Gouge, was urging the establishment of subtreasury offices. Jackson himself was saying nothing, and Levi Woodbury, who had succeeded Taney as Secretary of the Treasury, was trying to hold the balance between these violently hostile groups. Gouge and Benton recognized the inherent weakness of the experiment with state banks and the possibility of corruption and mismanagement within it. Whitney knew that the subtreasury plan was not an adequate remedy and that the metallic currency desired by his opponents would impose insufferable burdens upon the business community. But neither would turn back to the Bank of the United States, which, with its predecessor, had successfully acted as the fiscal agent of the government for almost forty years, had provided a sound and elastic currency, and had none of the weaknesses of either of the substitute proposals.[9]

Biddle was aware of this debate within the administration. He was also certain that, regardless of which group triumphed, the excesses and losses of the years from 1812 to 1816 would be repeated. But he could do nothing about it except to deny that the easy-money conditions which prevailed throughout the winter and spring were proof that the administration's experiment was a success. The Bank of the United States was still in operation, he pointed out, buying and selling domestic and foreign exchange. Its notes and branch drafts were circulating as a national currency, and, until these were retired, there was no experiment at all. The administration could not claim success unless after the dissolution of the Bank it was found that the notes of five or six hundred banks were as safe as those of the Bank of the United States, that internal exchanges were as cheap and regular, and that there pervaded the nation a sound, equal, universally redeemable currency.[10]

He was confident that such a time would never come. In his opinion it was manifestly impossible for the Jackson administration, with its laissez faire views, to devise an adequate substitute for the Bank of the United States and its currency. But the experiment had to be tried, and in March, 1835, he began preparations for the final liquidation and closing of the

[9] R. Whitney to L. Woodbury, March 22, 1835; W. M. Gouge to L. Woodbury, April 2, 1835; T. H. Benton to L. Woodbury, December 28, 1835, in the Woodbury Manuscripts in the Library of Congress.

[10] N. Biddle to J. Reynolds, March 24, 1835; N. Biddle to D. Webster, April 6, 1835, in the Biddle Manuscripts in the Library of Congress; Niles' Register, XLVII (1835), 281.

Bank. The western and southern offices were ordered to begin a gradual and gentle reduction of their loans and to transmit the proceeds to Philadelphia by the purchase of bills of exchange. Shortly thereafter the branches themselves were placed on the market, and during the course of the spring and summer most of them were sold. The terms offered were advantageous to the purchaser and the Bank. The banking houses and the other assets were taken over at their book valuation, and the purchaser was permitted to pay for them in four annual instalments with interest at 5 per cent. The Bank was thus provided with semipermanent investments for its capital, and the banks which took over the branch assets were not called on for the total sum at the time they were beginning business.[11]

The funds accumulated in Philadelphia were not permitted to lie idle. They too were invested in semipermanent loans, secured by stock of the Bank itself or that of other incorporated companies, and this immediate reinvestment of the Bank's capital caused the whole operation to move smoothly. Few persons outside the Bank were even aware that a major transfer of capital was being made from one part of the country to another, and only those well informed in finance could appreciate what great skill was being demonstrated and what careful planning had been required. Cadwalader, no longer a director, watched it with admiration. He paid close attention to the published statements of the Bank and to general financial conditions, and regarded both as so favorable that on June 19 he asked Thomas Wilson and Company of London to join him in a large purchase of stock. "I need only say at present," he wrote, "that the promise is good for the *winding up*. There is a large surplus fund and the July dividend of $3\frac{1}{2}$ will leave an addition to it on the business of the half year of $400,000. The suspended debt in the Western District bears an encouraging aspect owing to the advance in the value of the securities, and the real estate owned by the institution . . . has risen very much on the former estimates."[12]

Cadwalader's judgment and decision were that of a man who had some acquaintance with the actual situation of the Bank and some understanding of what the figures in its statement meant, but there were others watching the Bank's operations who were less well informed. Some of the political opponents of the institution in New York and Washington still believed that it had been badly and corruptly managed, particularly in the West, and they counted upon the liquidation of the debt in these regions to prove them correct. They no longer had their secret informants on the board of directors itself and, as a consequence, did not know that the Bank was re-

[11] N. Biddle to J. Johnson, June 10, 1835; N. Biddle to J. Huske, August 3, 1835, in the Biddle Manuscripts in the Library of Congress.

[12] T. Cadwalader to T. Wilson and Company, June 18, 1835, January 15, 1836, in the Cadwalader Manuscripts in the Historical Society of Pennsylvania; N. Biddle to J. M. Clayton, April 19, 1841, in *House Executive Document* (29th Cong., 1st sess.), No. 226, pp. 414–18, 510.

investing its funds in the East as rapidly as they were collected in the West. The total of its loans, instead of decreasing each month, was becoming ever larger, for it was now lending not only the funds that had been previously loaned in the South and West but also those that had been used in the purchase of domestic exchange. To those who wanted the Bank to be in difficulties, this increase in loans seemed a bad sign, and they became even more certain that something was wrong when in July the branch in New York suddenly began to reduce its loans. They looked on this action as an indication that the Bank was in danger, and they were apparently sustained by the August statement. The stock of specie, which had exceeded fifteen million dollars at the beginning of the year, had been reduced to nine million dollars, and the loans, instead of being decreased by its collections in the South and West, were seven million dollars higher.[13]

Someone who had access to the mail of the Treasury as it was brought into the office—probably Whitney—saw this statement upon its arrival and sent word to confederates in New York. The *Globe*, which usually published the monthly statement immediately after its receipt in Washington, postponed the publication of this one until August 13, and four days later Biddle received a letter from a reliable correspondent in New York which said: "I have it from a source, on which I place great reliance, that individuals here connected with certain persons at Washington were engaged in selling stock very largely on time on the 11th, 12th, and 13th inclusive; more stock I am told was sold on those days than in a like time in a year or two. The operations made and the quarters from whence the orders to sell come render it almost certain that the spring of these movements was information from Washington. I know not when your monthly report was forwarded to the Treasury department, but if it was there so as to be in the hands of these conspirators on the 7th or 8th . . . it would serve to confirm me in my belief."[14]

The stockholders, better informed as a general rule than the conspirators, did not panic in spite of the stories about the dangerous condition of the Bank that were spread by word of mouth and in the Jackson papers in Washington and New York. They dismissed the short selling as a "scheme got up for purposes of fraud" and the newspaper stories as tricks of "the kitchen cabinet and their coadjutors out of doors" to frighten "honest people out of their money." The perpetrators of the scheme lost heavily, and among these, according to an Albany newspaperman, were many of the political leaders of New York. "It is firmly believed at Albany," he wrote to Biddle, "that . . . Jesse Hoyt, the back stairs friend of Van Buren,

[13] N. Biddle to R. Lenox, August 4, 1835; S. Jaudon to N. Biddle, August 8, 1835, in the Biddle Manuscripts in the Library of Congress.

[14] R. M. Blatchford to N. Biddle, August 17, 1835, in the Biddle Manuscripts in the Library of Congress.

is reportedly cleaned out. . . . Olcott is said to have suffered several thousand, so young Van Buren. Hubbell is supposed to be in the same condition with Hoyt and scarcely a member of their regency has escaped."[15]

Biddle had already had reason to be proud of his achievement in making the final year of the Bank so smooth and uneventful, but he derived additional pleasure from the knowledge that the speculators and political gamblers in Washington, Albany, and New York, who had been responsible for so many of the political difficulties of the Bank, had lost their money because they underestimated his skill in liquidating its business. He had not expected this misinterpretation of the increase in loans and the loss of specie, which were directly related to each other, and the temporary curtailment in New York had been merely a technical movement of adjustment dictated by the situation of the balances between the branch and the local banks. The rest of the liquidation moved swiftly and easily, and Biddle's accomplishment of this difficult feat was enthusiastically praised by P. P. F. DeGrand, who had been one of the first to recognize and proclaim his skill as a banker. He told Biddle of his great admiration of the "peculiar felicity and novelty and simplicity" of the plan that had been devised for the liquidation of the Bank, of its commanding success, and "at the contrast between the practical good flowing from it and the direful predictions of those, who, by their misrepresentations of your future course, now find themselves placed in a light supremely ridiculous."[16]

Shortly before Biddle received DeGrand's letter, he had been given a dramatic opportunity to prove to the whole nation the great value of such an institution as the Bank of the United States. On December 16 a fire broke out in the heart of New York which devastated its business center and destroyed not only millions of dollars' worth of goods and property but also most of the records of banks, insurance companies, and merchants. The branch of the Bank of the United States was not damaged, and its officers and directors were beseiged with requests for aid. They urged Biddle to come to New York, but, before their letters could arrive in Philadelphia, he had already taken ship. As soon as he learned the extent of the damage, he saw that the consequences would not be confined to the city alone, that it was, in fact, a national calamity, and when he arrived, he was greeted almost as a savior by the committe of merchants, bankers, and insurers that was dealing with the emergency. He assured them that the Bank would come to their aid, and his offer was immediately confirmed by the board of directors, who authorized the branch to advance two million dollars, with or without security, to the New York insurance companies

15 N. Biddle to R. M. Blatchford, August 19, 1835; R. M. Blatchford to N. Biddle, September 1, 1835; N. Biddle to J. W. Webb, September 3, 1835; D. W. Bloodgood to N. Biddle, September 15, 1835, in the Biddle Manuscripts in the Library of Congress.

16 P. P. F. DeGrand to N. Biddle, December 18, 1835, in the Biddle Manuscripts in the Library of Congress.

for the relief of "their fellow citizens who have suffered by the late calamity."[17]

So prompt an extension of credit could not have been offered by the local banks or by the government. And, once the national bank had acted, the danger of a financial crisis was over. The local banks, freed from the threat of a run on their specie by the support of the Bank of the United States, could begin to make loans, and the insurance companies, given time to liquidate their assets, could pay off their claims. The newspapers in New York, even those opposed to the Bank, were fulsome in their praise of Biddle and the institution, but the Jackson administration was not impressed. Financial relief to a stricken community meant no more to the President and his advisers than did the provision of a uniform currency and regular exchanges. The Bank was unconstitutional, it was an aristocratic institution, and it must die.

But was the Bank going to die? All indications in Biddle's correspondence and in his actions throughout 1835 were that he had no other plan than to go out of business when the congressional charter expired on March 4, 1836, but, by coincidence, the last letter he wrote before he stepped on the boat to sail to New York was addressed to the chairman of the committee on ways and means of the lower house of the Pennsylvania legislature on the subject of a Pennsylvania charter for the Bank of the United States. "The question is not," he wrote, "whether Pennsylvania should have more banks, but whether a certain accumulated mass of capital about to be dispersed, should be held together under the authority of the state."[18] This apparent reversal of plans was never any more adequately explained than this. Many of his friends and supporters had been urging this course upon him for months, but the Bank had continued to make preparations for closing, and he had declined to discuss the matter. Now

[17] C. A. Davis to N. Biddle, December 17, 1835; R. M. Blatchford to N. Biddle, December 17, 1835; N. Biddle to I. Lawrence, December 22, 1835, in the Biddle Manuscripts in the Library of Congress.

[18] N. Biddle to W. B. Reed, December 18, 1835, in the Biddle Manuscripts in the Library of Congress. Biddle's decision to apply for a Pennsylvania charter seemed sudden, and nothing in the Bank's actions during 1835 was inconsistent with the avowed purpose of closing on March 4, 1836. Matthew Clarke, the clerk of the House of Representatives, first made the suggestion in October, 1832, and it was seconded in 1833 and 1834 by Samuel Smith, Thomas Cooper, and Robert Y. Hayne. The first intimation that Biddle was considering this action was in a letter from Colt in November, 1834, which said: "The more I have thought about the Bank, the better I like your idea of applying to your state for a charter." And the first action in pursuance of this object was the attempt by Biddle in the late spring of 1835 to acquire stocks in newly chartered state banks. M. St.C. Clarke, to N. Biddle, October 29, 1832; S. Smith to N. Biddle, January 30, 1833; N. Biddle to S. Smith, February 4, 1833; N. Biddle to P. P. F. DeGrand, February 20, 1833; T. Cooper to N. Biddle, March 22, 1834; R. Colt to N. Biddle, November 13, 1834; J. S. Robert to R. Colt, March 14, 1835; N. Biddle to P. Bacot, May 12, 15, 1835; P. Bacot to N. Biddle, May 22, June 3, 24, 1835; J. Potter to N. Biddle June 13, 1835; E. R. Biddle to N. Biddle, November 18, 1835, in the Biddle Manuscripts in the Library of Congress.

he had changed his mind, and Biddle, having made the decision, embarked on an experiment as dangerous as any attempted by Jackson. He set out to provide a national currency, to regulate the domestic and foreign exchanges, and to protect the economy against internal and external pressures through a state bank unconnected with the national government, and one which was viewed with hostility and suspicion by those in control of the executive and legislative branches. It was true that he thought that the experiment would not be long in duration. He confidently looked for a reversal of public and political opinion, once Jackson had retired, and then he expected that Van Buren or one of his Whig rivals would be forced to recommend the recharter of this or some other institution as the national bank. But in the meantime the Bank of the United States would be operating on a large scale in this nation and abroad without the official standing and connections it had previously enjoyed, and whatever success it attained would be certain to be resented not only by its political enemies but also by its economic rivals.

No thought of danger was in Biddle's mind as he began negotiations with the Pennsylvania authorities. He applied for the charter as a Pennsylvanian "devotedly attached to her interests and fame" and opposed to those of New York, and he had the support of most of the leaders of both political parties in the state. The chief opposition came from Democratic leaders in Washington, who told their party associates that if the Bank of the United States were permitted to continue, it would "break the president's heart." But Jackson was leaving office in little more than a year, and party members were less influenced by the prospect of "this melancholy fracture" than they had once been. Secret emissaries were sent to warn Van Buren that he would be risking the loss of Pennsylvania votes if he intervened in opposition to the Bank, and, though Blair in the editorial columns of the *Globe* threatened to punish any Democrat who voted for the charter, a sufficient number joined with the Whigs and Anti-Masons to effect the passage of "An Act To Repeal the State Tax on Real and Personal Property, and To Continue and Extend the Improvement of the State by Railroads and Canals, and To Charter a State Bank To Be Called the United States Bank."[19]

This Pennsylvania charter cost the Bank a large sum of money, but it was worth every cent that it cost, and when it had been passed, Biddle sent a copy of it to Baring Brothers and Company of London with the statement: "To European eyes it will seem a strange composition, but you are aware of the difficulty of making any arrangements with legislative bodies without conciliating a variety of interests. . . . Substantially however it is a very good charter, better in many respects than the present. It has one

[19] N. Biddle to J. McIlvaine, January 7, 1836; N. Biddle to J. Q. Adams, January 10, 1836; J. McIlvaine to N. Biddle, January 16, 1836, in the Biddle Manuscripts in the Library of Congress.

extraordinary merit. It is the triumph of good sense over the idle prejudice against foreign capital . . . and no further action is necessary on the part of the foreign stockholders who will come in of course for as many shares in the new Bank as they hold in the present."[20]

The charter may have been a "triumph of good sense," but it was also attributable to Biddle's political realism and skill. He had been forced to learn the methods through which legislators were influenced in American politics, and, though he did things he knew were wrong, he was not too fastidious to employ the necessary means to achieve his desired ends. He bribed in this instance, as he had done before, but his purpose was to gain something useful for the Bank, not to influence elections or to enhance the strength of either political party. As a young man he had been determined to restrict his course to one "founded on honor," but "honor," he had learned, was not an easily defined term. He was convinced that a national bank was absolutely essential to the economic health and security of the nation, and he thought that the only way in which one could be obtained from the political authorities was to keep the United States Bank in existence. He may have been wrong in his analysis, but all that he did, he did for the country, including the purchase of the charter by improper as well as proper means.

Part of the price was a bonus of two million dollars paid outright to the state of Pennsylvania. The Bank also agreed to lend the state up to six million dollars for the completion of its canal and railroad and to subscribe to the stock of any private railroad or canal company that the legislature "would like to encourage." So many of these specific subscriptions were demanded by Thaddeus Stevens, the anti-Masonic speaker of the lower house, that Biddle playfully complained: "Lord help us, one feels like Isaac the Jew in the Castle of Front de Boeuf. They call Mr. Stevens an inquisitor. I am not very sympathetic about the Masons, but he is certainly very expert at the rack." Other legislators made different demands. One prominent Democrat, the chairman of the Committee on Banks in the Senate, would not vote for the charter until he was promised that a branch would be established in his home county of Beaver, and another wrote in a private letter to Biddle: "I shall expect you will place me in a fair footing with others engaged in this all important question and to you I look for that advocate my merits deserve."[21]

Some support was obtained by the Bank's lobbyist in Harrisburg in ways of which he said in his reports that it would be better not to describe,

[20] N. Biddle to Baring Brothers and Company, February 23, 1836, in the Biddle Manuscripts in the Library of Congress.

[21] J. McIlvaine to N. Biddle, January 5, 1836; N. Biddle to J. McIlvaine, January 23, 1836; J. B. Wallace to E. Chauncey, March 1, 1836; J. B. Wallace to N. Biddle, May 26, 1836; J. McIlvaine to N. Biddle, June 13, 1836, in the Biddle Manuscripts in the Library of Congress; *United States Gazette* (Philadelphia), January 23, February 25, 1836.

and so skilfully did he operate that two investigations during the session of charges of bribery completely exonerated the Bank. The only evidence to prove that the Bank had, in fact, paid certain legislators to vote for the charter was that carefully preserved by Biddle in his private files, and this he did not turn over to the investigating committees. Biddle thought that he had made a good bargain for the stockholders. The total cost of the charter, including the loans to the state and the subscriptions to the stock of the internal improvement companies, was only slightly in excess of his first offer, and for each additional demand upon the Bank he exacted some additional concession from the legislature. He refused to accept any amendments to the charter that would impede the operations of the Bank, and whenever it appeared that some unreasonable demand would be made, he would threaten to move the Bank to New York, Delaware, or Maryland.[22]

Politicians and other interested persons in each of these states had expressed interest in having the Bank there, and each time that an unacceptable proposal was made, he accompanied his rejection with a quiet hint that, if it were pressed, the Bank would go elsewhere. He used this method when Stevens and the governor, Joseph Ritner, aware of the widespread suspicion of the Bank that had been aroused by its payments to printers and newspapers, suggested a charter provision prohibiting this practice. But Biddle would not acquiesce. "I lose no time in stating to you," he wrote, "that if such provisions, or anything in the remotest degree resembling them, shall be put in the charter, it will be instantly rejected by the stockholders. They have not asked for this charter, and certainly would not accept it on terms which might be construed into a reproach on their past administration of its affairs." He also rejected an amendment empowering the legislature to repeal the charter, on the ground that this would "force the Bank to take an interest in the composition of the legislature, to feel anxiety about their elections, and in short to mingle itself with party contests and strive to be always on the strong side. This is a false position. . . . If the Bank depends for its continuance on the laws of the country, there can be no difficulty in its course . . . but I cannot bear

---

[22] N. Biddle to ——, January 7, 1836 (misdated 1835); N. Biddle to J. McIlvaine, January 10, 16, 1836; N. Biddle to W. B. Reed, January 15, 1836; J. McIlvaine to N. Biddle, January 16, February 1, 1836; R. M. Gibbes to N. Biddle, February 1, 1836; J. McKim, Jr., to N. Biddle, February 3, 6, 1836; N. Biddle to J. Todd, February 10, 1836, in the Biddle Manuscripts in the Library of Congress. William B. Reed, a member of the legislature, wrote an unsigned, undated letter to Biddle, marked "confidential." It also contained the statement, "As this is for your own eye, burn it after you read it." But Biddle, instead of complying, marked it as from William B. Reed on February 9, 1836, and placed it in his confidential files. The total spent by the Bank's three lobbyists seems to have been around $400,000, which included compensation for them of $25,000 each. *House Executive Document* (29th Cong., 1st sess.), No. 226, pp. 424, 527.

the idea of making the institution a political machine by depending on the caprice of the legislature."[23]

The contrast between his activities and interests during the first six years of his administration of the Bank and those between 1829 and 1836 was present in his mind when he wrote this letter. Granted that a bank, like all institutions and persons, needed to be checked and controlled for its own interests as well as those of the community, the proper agency was not the legislature, the executive, or any other politically elected person or agency. Some means independent of party and politics was called for if banks were to be properly regulated and controlled, and Biddle, limited by his experience, could think of nothing but a national bank with predominantly private ownership and control. He sought a state charter for his institution to keep it alive, so that when Jackson retired from the White House, it could be restored to its former position as the publicly responsible and chartered means for the provision of a national currency, the safeguarding of the Treasury funds, and the protector and regulator of the other banks and the national economy.

Until the institution could thus be reinstated, he was taking a gamble that it would not be crippled by the dislocations that would inevitably result from an essentially undirected and unprotected currency and credit system. He had no misgivings, he said, as he contemplated the future, while "preparing both the funeral baked meats and the marriage table of the 4th of March." Again, varying the metaphor, he wrote: "For myself, I am in a sort of a chrysalis state, about to lay down my character of a dying worm and come out perhaps a smart butterfly with all the colors of the Pennsylvania rainbow." His actual goal, however, was not either of these new things. What he wanted was a rebirth, like the phoenix, of the Bank of the United States and its reappearance as the national bank with exactly the same status and powers that it had possessed before Jackson began his attacks.[24]

[23] N. Biddle to W. B. Reed, January 15, 1836; N. Biddle to J. McIlvaine, January 10, 15, 16, 1836, in the Biddle Manuscripts in the Library of Congress.

[24] N. Biddle to J. Q. Adams, January 10, 1836, in the Biddle Manuscripts in the Library of Congress.

~~ 28 ~~

The Bank Is Dead
Long Live the Bank

*W*hen the stockholders and their representatives assembled in Philadelphia to accept the charter granted by the state of Pennsylvania, they were more interested in the past than in the future. John Sergeant, the principal speaker, eulogized Biddle for his defense of the Bank against "unlawful aggression." As a director and attorney for the Bank and a member of Congress, Sergeant was familiar with all the details of the war between the Bank and the political administration, and he looked upon its conclusion as "a victory won at last by integrity and truth over unmerited and unmeasured calumny." For this course, he went on, chief credit must go to Biddle. With "unvarying courtesy and kindness," "cheerful good humor," and "undaunted firmness," he had retained the support of officers, employees, stockholders, and many "whose political affinities would have inclined them in the opposite direction." If he had offended, it was because he would not tamely surrender the rights of the Bank or its independence "at the bidding of any man, however powerful." An enemy of the Bank, Sergeant said, "he never made. Enemies indeed he has none that I know of, but such as have become so because he would not betray or surrender the trusts confided in him by the stockholders." He had been equally faithful to the national interest and had, with "extraordinary skill and talent," invariably reconciled "the patriotic care of the common concerns, especially the concerns of the great mercantile portion of the United States . . . with the interests of the stockholders." He had been the creator of "the best currency in the world," and under his leadership "when danger threatened, when credit was trembling, when confidence was shaken, whenever, in a word, a revulsion was threatened with its disastrous train of consequences, this Bank, strong in its power, stronger in its inclination to do good, anticipated and averted the crisis."[1]

[1] *United States Gazette* (Philadelphia), February 25, 1836.

Sergeant's high opinion of Biddle's administration of the Bank was shared by many others. Eliakim Littell, editor and publisher of an international scientific and literary magazine in Philadelphia and a regular borrower from the Bank, took this occasion to write: "It will not, I am sure, be unpleasant to you to receive amid the host of congratulations and thanks now poured upon you, those of the *debtors* of the Bank, who feel grateful for the forbearance and liberality with which they have been treated. In my case the Bank has never added anything to the inevitable pain attending a state of debt. On the contrary it has frequently by new loans enabled me to carry on my business and the effect . . . has been to make my debt to the Bank less than it could have been under other circumstances."[2] Similar and less interested praise came from Michel Chevalier, a French economist, who had come to the United States to study its political, social, and economic institutions. He was a follower of Saint-Simon, a reformer and socialist, and such non-political technicians and institutions as Biddle, the other officers, and the Bank seemed to him to be ideals to be struggled for by those seeking to spread democratic freedom. The Bank of the United States, he said, "directed by men of large fortune and established reputation, charged with a vast responsibility, subject to the supervision of the federal government, . . . and officiously watched by an army of journalists," was "in financial affairs, what the vast rivers . . . are in the system of internal communications." It governed credit, regulated the currency, animated or checked commerce by narrowing or widening the channels of circulation, and through this wise control of credit it had covered "the country with roads, canals, factories, schools, churches, and . . . everything that goes to make up civilizations." It was one of the glories of the republic that the farmers were able to buy land, supply themselves with tools and equipment, improve their farms, and finance their crops through loans and advances and in a few years become independent freeholders with substantial means. Manufactures were similarly fostered, and the increased demand for labor advanced wages. Many mechanics were able to raise themselves "to competence or wealth" by the same means as the farmers, but the national bank, which had made these things possible, had been denounced as an opponent of "the liberties of the people."[3]

President Jackson and his followers, in directing their attack upon the Bank of the United States, had confused the cure with the disease, according to Chevalier, for this institution alone could protect the economy from the aggressive and selfish ambitions of the speculators. The nearly universal dependence on credit had made banks an attractive object of speculation, and the state legislatures had been besieged with an irresistible demand for

[2] E. Littell to N. Biddle, February 29, 1836, in the Biddle Manuscripts in the Library of Congress.

[3] Chevalier, *Society in America*, pp. 46–55.

charters. The legislators had tried in various ways to impose restraints upon the operations of these banks, but no practicable method had ever been devised except that of a national bank. The Bank of the United States had been able to keep the state banks in order "by calling upon them for specie or by refusing to receive their bills" when their issues became excessive; but when its control had been eliminated, as during the War of 1812, these institutions had abused the privilege of issuing notes, individuals had abused the privilege of borrowing, and result had been "mad speculations" and "losses by the lender and borrower."[4]

A national bank had been re-created in 1816 as a remedy for this situation, and "the root of the evil was struck on the day that the Bank of the United States went into operation." But this second national bank was also to be eliminated because some men thought it dangerous to liberty. Chevalier could not understand this reasoning. "They fear more," he concluded, "for this land of industry, from the imperceptible tyranny of the Bank, than from a system in which there would be no check on the cupidity of the local banks, and in which they might renew . . . the commercial anarchy which followed the War of 1812." The stockholders were as puzzled as Chevalier by what had happened during the almost eight years of President Jackson's administration, but they wasted no time on useless explanations or recriminations. They had come to Philadelphia to honor Biddle, and the climax of their meeting was a resolution authorizing the directors to present him "a splendid service of plate" with the inscription, "The Stockholders of the Bank of the United States to Nicholas Biddle President in token of their gratitude for his faithful, zealous and fearless devotion to their interests and of his services to the country in establishing the best currency in the world."[5]

Biddle very naturally was more than pleased by this expression of the stockholders' gratitude and of their enthusiastic praise of his previous accomplishments. But he was more interested in what the future had to hold for the United States Bank of Pennsylvania and for the nation than in what had already taken place. His main object was no longer financial, though he believed that the provision of an adequate national currency and an effective and controlled credit system was an absolute essential for the health and welfare of the United States. The battle he was now beginning to fight was political, to drive out of power those who in his opinion had proved themselves entirely unworthy of office. The Jackson administration, he thought, was corrupt, incompetent, and shameless. "For

[4] *Ibid.* Similar praise of the operations of the Bank of the United States is to be found in Alexander Trotter, *Observations on the Financial Position and Credit of the States of the North American Union* (London, 1839), pp. 18, 32–35.

[5] *United States Gazette* (Philadelphia), February 25, 1836; T. Cadwalader to N. Biddle, March 6, 1836; N. Biddle to T. Cadwalader, September 25, 1838, in the Biddle Manuscripts in the Library of Congress.

the last few years," he wrote in indignant anger, "the executive power of the government has been wielded by a mere gang of banditti. I know these people perfectly, keep the police on them constantly, and in my deliberate judgment there is not on the face of the earth a more profligate crew than those who now govern the president."[6]

John Quincy Adams was also concerned over the moral character of these men. Jackson's presidency, he said, "has been the reign of subaltern knaves, fattening upon land jobs and money jobs." He denounced Kendall and Whitney as "political swindlers," who, by playing upon the President's "vanity and thirst of petty revenge," had got "into their hands the overflowing revenue of the country," which they were using "to replenish their own coffers and make princely fortunes." Neither Adams nor Biddle was completely fair in his appraisal of the men surrounding Jackson, but each was expressing his genuine concern for the country. Their anxiety and fears were shared by many others, including George McDuffie, who, shortly after he had become governor of South Carolina, wrote Biddle: "You were probably disappointed in the tone and bearing of my inaugural address. . . . But I have strong convictions that not only in your state, but in most of the middle and northern states, the agrarianism, which is but another name for the Jackson party, will permanently maintain the ascendancy, and God only knows how soon it will come to pass that the multitude will claim the right to live upon private plunder, as their leaders do upon the public offices. An unmixed democracy, without any organic divisions affording a check to secure property against numbers, will prove, I fear, to be a disastrous experiment, and God grant that the time may not speedily come when those who have a stake in society will have to take refuge in the despotism of one man to get rid of the more fearful despotism of the multitude."[7]

The publication a little later of Beverly Tucker's anonymous novel *The Partisan Leader*, which portrayed Calhoun as the patriot dictator and military commander of the South at war with the rest of the country, showed that McDuffie was not alone in his views, and the growing violence in American life was a further source of alarm. Mobs in the cities burned Roman Catholic schools, convents, and churches and attacked abolitionists and other defenders of unpopular causes. Hired thugs and party gangs dominated the polls, and the open buying of votes had become a common practice in municipal, state, and national elections. The republic appeared to be in danger, not from external enemies, but from internal weakness and an incapacity or unwillingness to maintain order. The situation was as dangerous as that which had been mastered by Washington's

[6] N. Biddle to H. Cope, August 11, 1835, in the Biddle Manuscripts in the Library of Congress.

[7] Adams, *Memoirs*, IX, 311–12; G. McDuffie to N. Biddle, January 26, 1835, in the Biddle Manuscripts in the Library of Congress.

administration, and there was the same need for leadership and governmental authority if freedom—the product of internal security—was to be preserved from destruction.

In 1831 Biddle had believed that it was impossible to differentiate between the political parties in the United States. "The truth is," he told Alexis de Tocqueville, "there aren't two practicable ways of governing this people now, and political passions can only be exercised over small administrative details, not over principles." Adams, a former President, and two members of the federal judiciary were present when he made the statement, and none of them contradicted him. But his opinions had changed by the close of the Jackson administration, and he wrote to Adams: "The most uncomfortable symptom of the strange distemper which now afflicts the country is the conduct of some of our public men, who seem to vibrate perpetually between two fears: the dread of offending the executive; and the terror of the populace. . . . Our people seem to be running wild with all sorts of infatuation, and never required more than now to be rebuked into sobriety. I pray you not to renounce that very necessary though irksome function, which no one can perform so successfully as yourself and so let us enjoy frequent manifestations of that intellect which cannot be repressed and will not be suppressed."[8]

Biddle himself had few opportunities to express his personal views of the political situation. His responsibilities to the Bank virtually forbade his writing or speaking except in his official capacity, and he was forced to decline most of the invitations he received. He made an exception in the summer of 1835 when Princeton offered him an honorary degree and invited him to make the commencement address. Here was an appropriate place for a serious discussion of national problems in the guise of advice to the graduating Seniors, and Biddle accepted. He began with a discussion of education but soon turned to the subject that was closer to his mind. He cited Julius Caesar and Robespierre as examples of men who, acting in the name of the people, had destroyed freedom, and he warned his listeners that "the same arts which succeeded of old, may not be unavailing here. A conspiracy of profligate men, pandering to the passions of the people, may inflame them to their ruin, and the country, betrayed into the hands of its worst citizens, may be enslaved with all the appearance of freedom."[9]

He did not think that the danger lay in the strength and ambition of the political leaders but in their weakness. They did not seek places "to obtain power, but power to obtain places," and the secret of their success

[8] Pierson, *Tocqueville*, pp. 535–36; Adams, *Memoirs*, VIII, 425–26; N. Biddle to J. Q. Adams, June 5, 1836, in the Biddle Manuscripts in the Library of Congress.

[9] N. Biddle, *An Address Delivered before the Alumni Association of Nassau Hall on the Day of the Annual Commencement of the College, September 30, 1835* (Princeton, 1835).

was "adroit management." Their whole purpose was to advance themselves and their political associates by stratagems and combinations, and they ended as "mere demagogues wandering about the political common without a principle or a dollar and anxious to dispose to the highest bidder . . . their only remaining possession, their popularity." A republic, he thought, needed a different sort of leader. The true American statesman must rebuke as well as praise the people, guide and restrain them as well as execute their wishes. Biddle was arguing for an aristocratic approach in what he knew was a democratic age, but the aristocracy he was advocating was based not on wealth or birth. It was produced by "talent and education" and expressed itself in the personal independence and uprightness of public men. Much of his speech was reminiscent of Biddle the student at Princeton writing of the demagogues of the ancient world. The extravagance of his language and imagery was caused in part by the defeat he had suffered at the hands of the administration, but the problem he was concerned with was a real one, and the dangers he described were always present. His fears, viewed from the vantage point of more than a century later, seem exaggerated, but he was speaking from a very brief experience with American politics and its constitutional system, and he was aware of the almost universal failure that had attended previous attempts to establish a free government.

He still believed, as he had when he delivered the eulogy of Jefferson, that among all men "the first place must be conceded to those gifted spirits who after devoting their youth to liberal studies are attracted to the public service," and he urged each of his listeners to prepare himself for "the high and holy duty of serving his country" rather than to seek "mere abundance of fortune." They must see to it that the "vulgar dominion of ignorance and profligacy" should be ended, the laws re-established, and "these banditti" driven back "to their caverns," so that the "only remembrance which history" would preserve of them would be "the energy with which you resisted and defeated them." The Bank of the United States was in Biddle's mind and those of his hearers as he made these remarks, but his concern was much broader, for what he thought was at stake was the whole cause of popular, free government.[10]

When Biddle made his address at Princeton in the early fall of 1835, he believed that the Whig party had a chance to defeat Van Buren the following year but not to elect a candidate of its own. Its objective, he thought, should be to throw the election into the House of Representatives, and for this reason he recommended that different candidates should be selected for each of the sections of the country. "It is manifestly advantageous," he wrote, "to let Mr. Webster lead the New England forces, Mr. White, the Southwest or South, and . . . if General Harrison will run better than anybody else in Pennsylvania, by all means unite upon him." He also believed

[10] *Ibid.*

[293]

that each of the candidates should do as Jackson had done and refuse to commit himself on any issues. "If General Harrison is taken up as a candidate," he advised, "it will be on account of the past, not the future. Let him then rely entirely on the past. Let him say nothing, promise nothing. Let no committee, no convention, no town meeting ever extract from him one single word about what he thinks now or what he will do hereafter. Let the use of pen and ink be wholly forbidden as if he were a mad poet in bedlam. General Harrison can speak well and write well, but on this occasion he should neither speak nor write, but be silent, absolutely and inflexibly silent."[11]

Biddle's dilemma, like that of the other Whigs, was born of the rivalry between Calhoun, Clay, and Webster and the different points of view toward the major political issues of the time held by them and their supporters. No one of the three would agree to the nomination of either of the others. The only thing that the Whigs could do was to support men of local reputation and popularity, to set up "men of straw," as John Quincy Adams observed, rather than nominate any one of their "three talented aspirants" for the presidency. Calhoun and his supporters were the first to realize that none of the three principal leaders of the Whig party could win the nomination, and they early committed their strength to the campaign of Senator Hugh Lawson White, the candidate of the anti–Van Buren Democrats. Clay, who did not want to run again unless he could be sure of election, accepted this virtual veto of his nomination, and some of his supporters tried to persuade the whole Whig party to concentrate on White. Webster, however, was unwilling to withdraw from the race, nor would he subscribe to the policy of concentrating Whig strength on different candidates in order to throw the election into the House of Representatives. In November, 1835, his supporters in Pennsylvania blocked the selection of Harrison as the sole Whig nominee and, by insisting that Webster be kept in the race, made it almost certain that the Democrats would carry the state. Biddle was indignant, but there was nothing he could do. He became convinced that, unless some miraculous change in public sentiment occurred, the election of Van Buren was assured. There was no longer any reason for him to participate in the campaign, and he turned his attention away from politics to the problems of preparing the Bank for its operations under the Pennsylvania charter.[12]

Few people in or outside the Bank had any knowledge of Biddle's plans in regard to the new institution. He spoke and wrote as though it was an ordinary commercial bank, but his real goal was to make it a national bank having the same central functions as its predecessor. He believed that such

[11] N. Biddle to H. Cope, August 11, 1835, in the Biddle Manuscripts in the Library of Congress.

[12] Adams, *Memoirs*, IX, 311–12; J. Hamilton to N. Biddle, August 22, 1834; R. Colt to N. Biddle, December 7, 1834; D. Webster to N. Biddle, May 9, 1835; E. Everett to N. Biddle, November 3, 1835, in the Biddle Manuscripts in the Library of Congress.

an institution was required by the other banks and the general economy and that, if one was not supplied by the government, private individuals must take over. He planned to establish branches in each of the commercial cities of the country and to send agents to London and Paris. The flexibility of such a system, he thought, would enable the Bank to exercise a dominant influence in the exchange markets, to establish a national currency, and to sustain or check the other banks as circumstances required. The Bank in Philadelphia, its branches in other cities, and its agencies in Europe would have established sources of credit as well as their own capital in each locality and would be in a position to buy or sell exchange at all times. Merchants in national or international trade could come to the Bank, its branches, or the agencies and buy or sell bills of exchange, and Biddle, by his central control of the whole institution, could keep the rates of exchange essentially uniform.

In its domestic aspects his plan was essentially the same as the one he had introduced when he succeeded Cheves, but in the international area it was much broader and represented almost a complete departure from past practice. His aim was to place the United States in a position of financial equality with Great Britain and France and to release international trade from its virtually complete dependence upon monetary conditions in Europe. As an American, Biddle had long resented the fact that a European who had money in the United States could not draw a bill of exchange for it and sell this bill in London or Paris. If he wanted his money, he had to let it be paid from the United States by a bill of exchange on someone in Europe who had the custody of American-owned funds or was willing to grant credit to an American drawer. Thus all payments depended upon the ability or willingness of European firms to accept drafts from the United States; and the Bank of England, by easing or restricting credit, could control the course of international trade without regard for American interests or needs.[13]

This situation, Biddle believed, could be altered if the United States Bank established its own agents in London and Paris. They could buy or sell bills of exchange drawn by Europeans on Americans and thus establish full reciprocity and complete equality between the countries. He also believed that such resident agents would be entitled to an account and a line of credit with the Bank of England and the Bank of France and that these connections with the leading institutions of the two most important financial powers would enhance the national and international prestige of the United States Bank. He sent Jaudon, the cashier, to Europe in the spring of 1836 to make arrangements for these agencies and to negotiate loans on the security of the debts owed to the United States Bank by the state banks that had purchased the branches. Jaudon was given complete discretionary authority in both matters, for Biddle was not certain that either of the cen-

[13] N. Biddle to J. Sergeant, April 6, 1838, in the Biddle Manuscripts in the Library of Congress.

tral banks would consent to the innovations he planned. If they refused to permit the proposed agents to have an account, Jaudon was to make arrangements with merchant bankers in both cities, similar to those which the Bank of the United States had previously had. The plan to establish a market for American bills in Europe would be temporarily abandoned, and the Bank would exercise a limited control over the rates of foreign exchange by continuing to buy or sell bills in Philadelphia, New York, and other coastal cities.[14]

The directors of the Bank of England were shocked by the request that Jaudon made in the late spring of 1836, and they refused it on the ground that it would be improper for them to permit another bank of issue to have these privileges. The Bank of France likewise refused to permit a "foreign institution" to have an account, and Jaudon, abandoning the agency plan, made arrangements with Baring Brothers and Company in London and Hottinguer and Company in Paris to act as agents for the United States Bank on essentially the same terms as these merchant bankers had served its predecessor. Through their aid Jaudon was able to borrow one million pounds in London and twelve and a half million francs in Paris on the security of the state-bank debts. These, like the debts with which they were secured, were to be paid in instalments, and the United States Bank was thus provided with the working capital it needed to begin its operations.[15]

While Jaudon was in London raising working capital and making arrangements for the European agencies, Biddle was seeking to establish branches throughout the United States by purchasing stocks of newly organized banks, but he was having great difficulty. Money and credit were abundant all through 1836, the price of bank stocks was high, and the stock was difficult to obtain, so he was forced to decide not to use chartered banks as agencies in most places. He made arrangements with local merchants or brokers to act as agents for the Bank and provided them with guaranteed lines of credit with local banks to enable them to buy and sell bills of exchange and to redeem notes of the Bank whenever called on to do so. The only exceptions were the Merchants' Bank of New Orleans and the Insurance Bank of Columbus, Georgia, which became fully owned subsidiaries of the Pennsylvania bank and acted as its branches in their respective localities.[16]

[14] S. Jaudon to N. Biddle, June 15, 1836, in the Biddle Manuscripts in the Library of Congress.

[15] N. Biddle to D. B. Ogden, April 1, 1837, in the Biddle Manuscripts in the Library of Congress; Smith, *Economic Aspects of the Second Bank*, pp. 188–89; Ralph W. Hidy, *The House of Baring in American Trade and Finance* (Cambridge, 1949), p. 202; Sir John Clapham, *The Bank of England* (New York, 1945), II, 159.

[16] N. Biddle to J. Hunter, April 25, 1836; N. Biddle to J. Irwin, June 25, 1836; N. Biddle to G. Poe, Jr., September 28, 1836, in the Biddle Manuscripts in the Library of Congress; *House Executive Document* (29th Cong., 1st sess.), No. 226, p. 423.

The Bank was thus ready in the fall of 1836 to take its place as the principal purchaser and seller of domestic and foreign exchange, but it was prevented from undertaking any extensive commitments by unforeseen financial difficulties in Great Britain and the United States and by the renewal of the political attack upon the Bank by its enemies within the Jackson party. The upward movement of the British and European economies, which had begun in 1832 with the ending of the revolutionary disturbances and the threat of a general war, had continued almost without interruption. The difficulties that Biddle had expected and prepared for in June, 1834, when the United States made gold its principal monetary metal, had not materialized. The Bank of England, instead of checking the expansion of the market by restricting credit, had fostered it by keeping its rediscount rate low, and, by the spring of 1836, the British were once more in the midst of a speculative boom.[17]

In the United States the national debt had been fully paid, but government revenues from the lowered rates of the compromise tariff and from the increased sales of public lands remained high. The depository banks, having what they thought was permanent possession of these large and increasing government funds, expanded their loans and fostered an internal American boom that was as speculative and insecure as that in Great Britain. These surplus government funds and the unhealthy stimulus they gave to domestic speculation in land, commodities, and stocks were a source of great concern to Biddle throughout the time he was deciding to keep the Bank in existence under a state charter. "The accumulation of the revenue," he wrote Webster, "is now the great nuisance, the real disturber, and since my resignation of the character, the only true monster. Can you not . . . make an early division of the fund?"[18]

What Biddle wanted in 1836 and had wanted for more than a decade was the investment of these great government resources in needed internal improvements, but Jackson, by his veto of the subscription to the stock of the Maysville Road Company, had made such a use impossible. He had decided that the government, for reasons of economy, should not build or aid the building of needed roads, canals, railroads, and other improvements and, instead, had permitted these surplus funds to accumulate in the banks, where they fostered unnecessary and harmful speculative investments which did little but raise prices. Benton, Gouge, and other enemies of the paper and credit system, were alarmed by this result of Jackson's experiment, particularly the rapid rise in the price and sales of public lands. Purchases of government land had risen from four million dollars a year to

[17] Arthur D. Gayer, *The Growth and Fluctuation of the British Economy, 1790–1850* (Oxford, 1953), I, 234–38, 242–76; Smith, *Economic Aspects of the Second Bank*, pp. 175, 183–85.

[18] N. Biddle to D. Webster, March 14, 1836, in the Biddle Manuscripts in the Library of Congress; *Niles' Register*, L (1836), 290–91.

five million dollars a quarter, and those who wanted land for farms, Benton protested, were being "outbid by speculators loaded with . . . borrowed paper." He denounced "the rising streams of paper from seven hundred and fifty banks," and on April 22 he introduced a resolution that "nothing but gold and silver coin ought to be received in payment for the public lands."[19]

The Whigs and the Democratic defenders of state banks joined together to defeat this radical remedy for the problem of the surplus and then went on to pass a bill which provided for the distribution to the states of all federal funds in excess of five million dollars. The transfer of these funds, amounting to approximately thirty-six million dollars, was to begin on January 1, 1837, and was to be accomplished in four equal instalments. Jackson signed this bill reluctantly, largely because he did not know what else to do with the money, but he also liked the sound of Benton's proposal. He thought that it would be desirable to increase the use of gold money, and on July 11, after the adjournment of Congress, the Treasury issued a circular ordering the land offices to accept nothing but gold or silver in payment for government land. The two measures accomplished their purpose. The speculative expansion of land, stock, and commodity purchases was brought to an abrupt halt, but once again the administration's remedy for an economic complaint proved to be worse than the disease. A domestic crisis of major proportions was precipitated. Interest rates rose to 24 per cent, and the costs of domestic exchange were five or six times as high as they had been the year before. By November, Biddle said that "the commercial intercourse between the West and the Atlantic is almost wholly suspended, and the few operations which are made, are burdened with the most extravagant expense."[20]

The administration, as usual, tried to blame him and his allies in Wall Street for all the difficulties, but he took comfort in the fact that he was "in no wise responsible for this foolery." The United States Bank had taken no part in stimulating the speculative expansion, and it was not endangered by the attempt to check it. None of Biddle's plans for his new operations had been put into execution, and, when the rest of the financial and mercantile community were desperately seeking aid, he could comfortably say: "The Bank itself fears nothing and suffers nothing. I am putting her in perfect trim, and if any squall comes, or a heavy gale, I mean to lie to and ride it out under a close reefed main sail."[21]

[19] Benton, *Thirty Years' View*, I, 676–78; *Niles' Register*, L (1836), 10–11.

[20] N. Biddle to J. Q. Adams, November 10, 11, 1836, in the Biddle Manuscripts in the Library of Congress; *Niles' Register*, L (1836), 147, 230–31, 243–45, 290–91, 337.

[21] N. Biddle to C. A. Davis, October 19, 1836, in the Biddle Manuscripts in the Library of Congress; *United States Gazette* (Philadelphia), October 4, 1836.

29

Jackson's Panic
or the
Bank of England's?

*T*he monetary crisis in the fall of 1836 gave Biddle an opportunity to point out to the people and to Van Buren, who was elected in November as Jackson's successor, the danger and insecurity of the new fiscal system that had been imposed on the country. Part of his argument was published in the form of two public letters addressed to John Quincy Adams, and the remainder was included in a petition to Congress for the recharter of the Bank of the United States which he prepared at the request of the Board of Trade of New York. In these he insisted that the economy would never be secure so long as the monetary system of the United States was in the hands of "certain corporations called state banks" which directly or indirectly furnished all the currency and negotiated the greater part of the domestic exchanges. These institutions could not control one another, the state governments could not control them, so that there was, in fact, no effective check "on the exercise of a power upon which every man's property depends for its value, and every man's industry for its reward."[1]

What was needed, he insisted, was "a return to that system under which the commerce of our country so long prospered" by the establishment of a national bank, for such an uncontrolled system as that which had been created by the Jackson administration must end in a "total derangement" of the economy. He said that the beginning of this total derangement had

[1] N. Biddle to J. Q. Adams, November 10, 11, 1836, in *Niles' Register*, LI (1836), 230–31, 243–45; S. Draper to N. Biddle, December 16, 1836; N. Biddle to S. Draper, December 31, 1836, in the Biddle Manuscripts in the Library of Congress; "Memorial of the Board of Trade of the City of New York, January 4, 1837," in *Niles' Register*, LI (1837), 343–44.

already been manifested in the monetary confusion induced by Jackson's attempt to check the speculative purchase of public lands. The specie circular and the distribution of the surplus had confronted the depository banks with demands for which they had not been prepared, and each of these institutions, for self-protection, stopped making new loans, brought pressure on their debtors for payment, and used whatever means they could to draw gold from other banks. Retrenchment and curtailment became the pattern for banks all over the country, and merchants who were accustomed to borrowing from these institutions were without money to buy goods or to pay those whom they owed. Prices of stocks, manufactured goods, and agricultural commodities declined drastically, and virtually all economic activity was brought to a sudden halt.

"These troubles," Biddle said, "may not . . . be wholly useless if we extract from them two great lessons. The first is that we can have no permanent financial prosperity while the public revenue is separated from the business of the country and committed to rash and ignorant politicians with no guides but their own passions and interests. . . . The other to distrust all demagogues of all parties who profess exclusive love for what they call the people. For the last six years the country has been nearly convulsed by efforts to break the mutual dependence of all classes of citizens, to make the laborer regard his employer as an enemy, and to array the poor against the rich. These trashy disclaimers have ended by bringing the country into a condition where its industry is subject far more than it ever was before to the control of large capitalists, and where every step tends inevitably to make the rich richer and the poor poorer."[2]

Jackson, Benton, Gouge, Woodbury, and their associates could never understand that the various economic groups were mutually dependent on one another and the prosperity of one contingent on that of the others. They looked with suspicion upon merchants, manufacturers, bankers, and financiers and assumed that the interests of these groups could be adversely influenced without destroying the market for the produce of the farmers or creating unemployment for the workers. Biddle knew that the Jacksonians were wrong, and, since they spoke of their concern for the poor without doing anything to increase their wealth, he called them "demagogues." He believed that the poor could not have jobs or markets unless there was someone to employ them or to buy what they produced and, conversely, that, unless the poor were earning wages or making profits, the wealth of the rich would decrease. Almost alone among public men of his generation, he argued for high wages as a symbol and cause of national prosperity, and he closed an address to a group of farmers with the prayer, "God grant that for many a long year it may be the lot of our countrymen

2 *Ibid.*

who subsist by the labor of their hands to work well, to be paid well, and to live well."[3]

He urged the farmers in his audience to pay high wages and to rejoice with the workers themselves when their incomes increased. An ill-paid worker was "a half-fed, half-clad, wholly untaught, animal with a useless mouthful of carnivorous teeth," but when his wages increased he became a customer of tailors, shoemakers, hatters, and butchers. He and the ones from whom he bought would buy from the farmer and give back to him "with abundant interest" the increase in his costs. "The bounties of Providence," Biddle concluded, "go round a beneficent circle, and after making the laborer better clad, better fed, better taught (in short a better man), the farmer is richer for the very benefits he dispenses."

This beneficent circle through which everyone prospered could, under other circumstances, become one that was vicious in character, and the decreased income of one group become the source of difficulties for all. This had happened in the United States as a result of the sudden check that had been imposed on the speculative purchasers of land, and the whole country was suffering a needless loss. Unemployed men and machines, unsold goods, foreclosed mortgages, and bankrupt businesses were the price paid by the nation for Jackson's decision to accept nothing but gold in payment for public lands. When the specie circular was issued, most of the gold in the country was held by the banks as a reserve to redeem that small proportion of their circulating currency for which holders were accustomed to demand metal. This happened so seldom that a reserve of one dollar in gold for each ten dollars of bank notes was usually sufficient, so that each time that a bank permanently lost one of its gold dollars, the national currency, the actual means of payment, was reduced by ten.

The specie circular in itself was enough to have inflicted a severe blow to the entire national economy, but its effects had been magnified by the preparations made by Secretary Woodbury in the fall of 1836 for the distribution of the federal surplus to the states in 1837. This transfer, as Biddle pointed out at the time, could have been made "without the slightest derangement of trade and without the movement of a single dollar in specie" by giving each state a draft on a depository bank in New York or Philadelphia for its share of the surplus. "There is no individual and no state in the union," he wrote, "that would not prefer payments in New York or the North Atlantic cities to payments anywhere else, and for this obvious reason: money is worth more there than anywhere else. If the state of Ohio . . . had a draft on New York, it could sell it to its citizens, usefully to them and profitably to its treasury." The depository banks under this arrangement, "knowing what they had to pay, would have been ready to

[3] N. Biddle, Address to the Philadelphia Society for Promoting Agriculture, October 7, 1840, typescript in the Biddle Manuscripts in the private collection of Nicholas B. Wainwright.

pay; and up to the hour of payment would have employed the funds usefully, so that in every stage . . . business would be assisted, commercial activity stimulated, and all parties be gainers."[4]

An additional advantage would have been the fact that the drafts that were issued would have been limited to the nine million dollars to be distributed in each quarter, beginning on January 1, and this relatively small sum could have been handled by the banks without serious inconvenience to themselves or their customers. But Secretary Woodbury, in executing the distribution act, had decided to transfer almost the entire amount to be paid in the four instalments from the banks of the Northeast, where it had been deposited, to selected banks in the interior states, because this operation, he said, "reduced the excess in certain banks in certain states, and placed it in the states where it would be paid next year and where before they had not an equal portion of the public money." This large and sudden transfer of federal funds from the sea coast to the interior would have been disturbing in an ordinary fall when the crops were coming to market and money was needed by the northeastern merchants to buy them. The banks in the interior at this season usually possessed more than they needed of New York and Philadelphia funds, so that the Treasury transfers were ordered, as Biddle said, "without reference to the wants of the business of the different sections of the union, the seasons of the year, or the course of trade," and they made "the whole revenue of the country work against the whole industry of the country." They were even more injurious in 1836 than they would have been in an ordinary year because the banks of the interior wanted all the specie they could obtain. They used the Treasury drafts to draw gold from the northeastern cities, and this combination of measures, produced what Biddle called "a double result," with "the interior banks making no loans and converting their Atlantic funds into specie, the debtors in the interior could make no remittances to the merchants in the Atlantic cities, who are thus thrown for support on the banks of those cities at a moment when they are unable to afford relief on account of the very abstraction of their specie to the west."[5]

Biddle and the United States Bank were virtually unaffected bystanders during this crisis. He had announced on May 31, 1836, that the Bank intended to resume its purchases and sales of domestic and foreign exchange on a national scale at the beginning of the business season in the fall. This announcement aroused the antagonism of those whom Cadwalader called "the miserable . . . time serving flatterers of General Jackson," who were willing "to gratify his senseless animosities by the assertion of dogmas equally senseless," and Democrats in Alabama, Louisiana, and Pennsylvania made plans to inhibit the operations of the Bank through political and legal

[4] N. Biddle to J. Q. Adams, November 10, 11, 1836, in *Niles' Register*, LI (1836), 230–31, 243–45.

[5] *Ibid.*

assaults upon its charter and agents. The plans for the resumption of business could not be put into operation as long as the results of these hostile moves were uncertain, and the Bank throughout the fall and winter of 1836–37 made almost no new loans and purchased or sold very little exchange.[6]

The attacks upon the Bank in Alabama and Louisiana were very easily beaten off. In the first state, the Jacksonians sought an injunction to prohibit the Mobile agent from buying or selling bills of exchange on the ground that the state law on agencies forbade such transactions by the agent of an out-of-state bank. Biddle obtained opinions from Webster, Sergeant, and Chancellor Kent of New York, "to put down such heresies by the highest professional authority," and so decisive was their reasoning that the case was dismissed as unworthy of argument. In Louisiana, Democratic members of the legislature introduced a bill which would forbid the Merchants' Bank of New Orleans to issue notes of the United States Bank, but the measure was overwhelmingly defeated by a combination of Democratic and Whig votes. The same lack of unanimity within Jackson's party was demonstrated in Pennsylvania when some of the leaders, on December 23, introduced a resolution that challenged the "unprecedented haste" with which the charter had been passed. A committee of investigation, "composed of the most violent and fanatical enemies of the Bank," was appointed to undo "the work of their predecessors by ascribing to them misconduct which would justify the repeal of the charter."[7]

The misconduct alluded to was the acceptance of bribes, and many of the most influential Democrats were just as unwilling as the Whigs to have this subject seriously or effectively investigated. Confusion and delay were the tactics adopted by those opposing the investigation, and when the committee at the end of January seemed on the verge of getting out of hand, Simon Cameron, one of the leading Democrats in the state, told Biddle that "the intelligent members of the party are tired of the continued war upon the Bank and are willing to get out of it. I go to Washington tomorrow to see if I cannot get some influence to operate from that quarter upon the more violent ones at Harrisburg. It is probable that we can bring about what will be a compromise, which, while it will soothe the pride of some, will do no harm to anyone."[8]

Biddle encouraged these delaying tactics. "Our merit as the guardians

[6] N. Biddle to S. Knapp, May 31, 1836, in *Circular to Bankers* (London), July 8, 1836; N. Biddle to G. Poe, Jr., September 28, 1836; N. Biddle to J. McIlvaine, January 10, 1837, in the Biddle Manuscripts in the Library of Congress; T. Cadwalader to T. Wilson and Company, March 24, 1837, in the Cadwalader Manuscripts in the Historical Society of Pennsylvania.

[7] *Niles' Register*, LI (1836), 273; N. Biddle to J. McIlvaine, January 10, 1837, in the Biddle Manuscripts in the Library of Congress.

[8] S. Cameron to N. Biddle, January 31, 1837, in the Biddle Manuscripts in the Library of Congress.

of great interests," he wrote his legislative representative, "is in patience and forbearance. Our business is to administer narcotics in small doses." And then, getting harsher, he said that if either the friends or the enemies of the Bank tried to force things too rapidly to a conclusion, "I would send them home penniless." Once again he was authorizing the payment of bribes to those legislators who could be appealed to in no other way, but, if he had refused to do so, the Bank, its stockholders, and its employees would have been the ones who were hurt. The nation itself, Biddle also believed, needed such an institution as the United States Bank, with its established agencies in all parts of the country and in London and Paris. It was for these reasons that he was willing to bribe, not to increase his own personal power or wealth, and the morality of his actions is a question not easy to solve.[9]

This combination of pressures from the Bank and the leaders of the Democratic party proved to be too powerful for those on the investigating committee who wanted to propose an act repealing the charter. They soon abandoned their efforts and at the close of the session joined in a unanimous report that acquitted the Bank and the previous legislature of all charges of bribery or improper conduct.[10] President Jackson and his associates were disappointed in the result of this their last effort to prevent the United States Bank of Pennsylvania from assuming the place of its predecessor in all but its position as the fiscal agent of the government, but there was nothing they could do. The domestic crisis precipitated by the specie circular had discredited the whole financial experiment, and the Congress was almost in complete revolt. The issue before it was the sale of the government's stock in the old Bank of the United States. Agents appointed by Biddle and Secretary Woodbury to negotiate the sale had failed to agree on the price, and Congress, to bring an end to the controversy, directed the Secretary to accept the Bank's offer of one hundred and fifteen dollars and fifty-four cents per share, payable in four annual instalments.[11]

This congressional act, reluctantly signed by President Jackson, was considered a triumph by Biddle, who took it as a sign that the course of the Bank in the future would be "relieved from all political difficulties." He had been privately informed that Van Buren was no longer in sympathy with the financial policies of Jackson, and Biddle's hopes for a change in direction in the new administration were strengthened when John Forsyth of Georgia was appointed Secretary of State and Joel Poinsett of South

[9] N. Biddle to J. McIlvaine, January 10, 17, 1837, in the Biddle Manuscripts in the Library of Congress.

[10] J. Erwin to N. Biddle, March 22, 1837, in the Biddle Manuscripts in the Library of Congress; T. Cadwalader to T. Wilson and Company, March 24, 1837, in the Cadwalader Manuscripts in the Historical Society of Pennsylvania; United States Gazette (Philadelphia), March 28, 1837; Niles' Register, LII (1837), 17.

[11] N. Biddle to J. McIlvaine, March 3, 1837; N. Biddle to Baring Brothers and Company, April 1, 1837, in the Biddle Manuscripts in the Library of Congress.

Carolina, Secretary of War. Each of these men was an informed student of national and international finance, a defender of the principle of the national bank, and a close personal friend of Biddle and of his Baltimore kinsman, Robert Oliver. Their influence, he was certain, would be helpful in repairing the damage inflicted on the economy by the financial incapacity of the previous administration, and shortly after the inauguration of the new President he sent an urgent message to a confidential representative in Washington asking him to ascertain "whether the specie circular will be rescinded, and when it will be rescinded."[12]

When Biddle made this urgent inquiry, he already knew that the stricken American economy was about to receive another severe blow as a result of the deflationary pressures generated by the Bank of England during the preceding summer and fall. The extravagant stock and commodity speculations in Great Britain during the winter and early spring of 1836 had provided American exporters and enterprisers with such large amounts of British funds that the rate of exchange had fallen to the point where it was more profitable to withdraw specie than to sell bills in the United States. Gold began to flow out of Great Britain, and the rate of this drain was increased by the loans negotiated by Jaudon for the Bank and by indemnity payments from France, Naples, and Spain to the government of the United States. The bullion reserves of the Bank of England began to decline in March, and by July they had reached the point where, in the directors' opinion, some corrective action was required. On July 21 the rediscount rate was increased to $4\frac{1}{2}$ per cent and to 5 per cent a few weeks later, but the drain continued. The specie circular had been issued in the United States, and so urgent was the demand for gold that the increased costs of obtaining it in Great Britain did not check the rate at which Americans were converting their British funds into metal. Something further had to be done, and the directors, focusing on the trade with the United States as the prime source of their difficulties, denied the rediscount privilege to those merchants and bankers who continued to accept bills of exchange drawn by Americans.[13]

They also advised Baring Brothers and Company to break their connection with the United States Bank on the ground that the purchase and sale of bills of exchange were not proper operations for a bank of issue. Barings

[12] N. Biddle to ——, March 9, 1837; J. Q. Adams to N. Biddle, March 30, 1837, in the Biddle Manuscripts in the Library of Congress; L. Woodbury to H. Toland, March 27, 1837, in the Woodbury Manuscripts in the Library of Congress.

[13] J. Horsley Palmer, *The Causes and Consequences of the Pressure upon the Money Market* (London, 1837), pp. 29–32; Thomas Tooke, *History of Prices* (London, 1838–57), pp. 73–74, 309–10; Clapham, *Economic History*, I, 513–18; R. G. Hawtrey, *A Century of Bank Rate* (London, 1938), pp. 18–19; Clapham, *Bank of England*, II, 147–54; Hidy, *Baring*, pp. 205–9; Gayer, *Growth of British Economy*, I, 269; W. Marston Acres, *The Bank of England from Within* (London, 1931), II, 463; Macleod, *Theory and Practice*, II, 139–40.

rejected this unsolicited advice, and they and the other merchants in the American trade continued to accept drafts from their correspondents throughout the fall and early winter. Gradually, however, the greater strength of the central institution began to prevail, and, in December, three of the weaker houses dealing with Americans were forced to call on the Bank of England for assistance to save them from failure. A leading private banker in London and one of the large incorporated banks in Manchester were also in difficulties, and it was not long before the whole British boom collapsed. The other banks and merchants were forced to curtail operations, and the resulting decline in the sales and prices of stocks and commodities increased the deflationary pressure.[14]

This was the situation confronting Biddle in March, when, with a new administration in power and the Bank's political difficulties apparently resolved, he began to seek ways to protect and rescue the American economy. Whatever there was to be done, must be done quickly, for the combination of pressures from within the American economy, generated by the specie circular and the distribution act, and those from Great Britain threatened to be irresistible. New Orleans was the weakest point, since upon it were centered the most powerful pressures. The banks in the great western valley, where specie was most needed, had used the transfer drafts provided by the Treasury to drain gold from New Orleans; and the banks in this city had been forced to deny new loans to the merchants and factors just at the moment that the news had arrived from Great Britain of the decline in the sales and prices of cotton. The same mail had brought orders to the buyers for British merchants and manufacturers to stop all purchases, and when they had withdrawn from the market, they could not be replaced by American buyers because of the shortage of credit.[15]

Early in March the factors and merchants in New Orleans notified their correspondents that they would no longer accept drafts from the interior in anticipation of sales, but their protective action came too late. The banks, pressed by the demands being made upon them, insisted on the payment of maturing loans, and Herman, Briggs and Company, one of the largest mercantile firms in New Orleans, suspended payments with liabilities of more than four million dollars. Its failure brought down other firms in New Orleans and threatened the solvency of the entire Mississippi Valley. John Somerville, cashier of the Union Bank of Tennessee, wrote Biddle of the dangers to his institution and others and predicted that the nation was about to experience the disasters "from which the Bank of the United States snatched this country in 1826." He requested Biddle to do something to "again save the people from a . . . state of distress" and to prevent the

14 Hidy, *Baring,* pp. 206–7.

15 *Niles' Register,* LII (1837), 33, 49; *Mississippian* (Jackson), March 17, 1837; Reginald C. McGrane, *The Panic of 1837* (Chicago, 1924).

"serious disappointments which will inevitably grow out of the many failures to remit which must take place."[16]

Jackson, back at his Nashville home, viewed these developments with concern, and in a self-defensive letter to Woodbury wrote: "You will find that in the end . . . the treasury order will work well. . . . It was the only weapon in the hands of the executive which he could wield for the benefit and safety of the country, when he saw the overtrading, gambling in stocks, speculating in lands, the storm of destruction and ruin . . . that was about to break upon us. It will ultimate in good. It must give in the end a wholesome currency of gold and silver coins, and throw out of circulation all notes under fifty dollars, and forever hereafter be a check to this gambling in stocks and overtrading as well as overbanking."[17] To Biddle what was happening in New Orleans and the West seemed to be "destruction and ruin," and he knew that under these critical conditions it was impossible to discriminate between the overtraders, the gamblers, and the speculators who, Jackson thought, "ought to fail," and the merchants, bankers, farmers, and manufacturers who were unable to pay their debts only because they could not sell their produce or collect from their debtors. The just and the unjust alike would perish or be saved, and Biddle threw the whole power of the Bank into the fight to prevent a universal suspension of specie payments which he knew was more likely to result from the crisis than "a wholesome currency of gold and silver coins."

At the moment the situation in New Orleans and the Mississippi Valley was beyond rescue, so he concentrated his efforts in New York, which, as the center of national and international trade and finance, was the country's next most vulnerable point. The failure of Herman, Briggs and Company had brought down their New York correspondents, J. and S. Joseph and Company, early in March, just at the moment when a large amount of bills of exchange were returned unpaid and protested from London. The solvent firms in the American trade, unable to obtain credit, had been forced to refuse acceptance of the drafts from their correspondents, and these simultaneous blows from New Orleans and Great Britain destroyed all confidence in private bills of exchange. A drain of gold from the banks for domestic and international payments was added to that created by the specie circular and the distribution act, and the New York politicians, merchants, and bankers joined with Biddle in urging Van Buren to undo the work of his predecessor.[18]

The President said nothing and did nothing. None of the members of his

[16] J. Somerville to N. Biddle, April 28, 1837, in the Biddle Manuscripts in the Library of Congress.

[17] A. Jackson to L. Woodbury, April 27, 1837, in the Woodbury Manuscripts in the Library of Congress.

[18] *Niles' Register*, LII (1837), 49; Clapham, *Bank of England*, II, 156–57; Macleod, *Theory and Practice*, II, 140–42.

Cabinet was aware of what he was thinking, and Secretary Woodbury, who had remained at the Treasury, replied in late March to an inquiry about the repeal of the Treasury order: "The specie circular you know was issued by direction of the president and can be modified or repealed by his direction alone or by Congress. What the final views of the present executive are on the subject have not yet been communicated to me."[19] Biddle and the New York merchants and bankers could not wait for the President to make up his mind. The first of April was upon them, when another instalment of nine million dollars was to be paid to the states under the distribution act, and few of the depository banks were prepared to meet these drafts. Some substitute for specie—a substitute that would be universally acceptable—must be found, and Biddle thought that post notes, simple promises of a bank to pay specie with interest at some future date, would serve the purpose in domestic commerce, and that one-year bonds in small denominations, payable in Europe, would be equally suitable for international payments.[20]

The proposal was greeted enthusiastically, and Biddle was asked to come to New York. He arrived on March 28 for a consultation with the leading bankers and merchants, and the next day in a public letter to the chairman of a mercantile committee he announced his plan for relief. "Recent events in the South and in Europe," he wrote, "have, in concurrence with reasons of an earlier date, produced a paralysis of private credit which deranges the whole system of our foreign and domestic exchanges. For this the appropriate remedy seems to be, to substitute for the private credit of individuals, the more known and established credit of the Bank until private confidence in private stability has time to revive." He agreed to recommend to the directors that the United States Bank issue four million dollars in one-year bonds, payable with interest in Europe, to be used as a substitute for foreign bills of exchange, and to issue four million dollars of post notes for use in the United States.[21]

The directors were doubtful as to the wisdom of this proposal when they were asked to accept it. The specie holdings of the Bank, despite Biddle's efforts to protect them throughout the previous year, had been reduced to a million, four hundred thousand dollars, and the Bank owed its neighboring Philadelphia banks more than three hundred thousand dollars. The directors believed that any expansion of business at this moment would be dangerous, but Biddle quickly convinced them that the post notes and bonds, instead of increasing the demands upon the Bank, would

[19] L. Woodbury to H. Toland, March 27, 1837, in the Woodbury Manuscripts in the Library of Congress.

[20] R. Colt to N. Biddle, March 27, 1837, in the Biddle Manuscripts in the Library of Congress.

[21] N. Biddle to J. A. Stevens, March 29, 1837, in the Biddle Manuscripts in the Library of Congress; Niles' Register, LII (1837), 81.

strengthen it and at the same time give relief to the country. He was certain that excessive caution in the existing situation was the most dangerous policy, and the directors, convinced by his reasoning, withdrew their objections.[22]

Post notes and bonds were put on sale in Philadelphia and New York on April 1 and were eagerly purchased in preference to the best private bills of exchange by those who had foreign or domestic payments to make. The Morris Canal and Banking Company and other banks in the New York area also offered post notes and European bonds on the same terms, and for a very brief time the panic seemed to be allayed. "The past week," the New York *Journal of Commerce* reported, "will long be remembered . . . as the crisis of the great financial troubles that have been gathering for more than a year from the combined influence of speculation, the surplus revenue, bad government. . . . It was a glorious time for panic makers, croakers, and assassins of credit . . . when by a concerted movement between the United States Bank and our local institutions, measures were adopted for the relief of the community; and from that moment the state of the money market had been evidently improving."[23]

Biddle was proud of his accomplishment and carefully explained to his European agents what he was trying to do. "The movement of the Bank," he wrote, "is one of emergency, wholly conservative in its character, and designed to dissipate an alarm calculated to do infinite mischief. To our friends abroad I deem it particularly important. The country is very able and very willing to pay its debts. The causes which delay the payment are accidental and temporary, and I think it better for them to receive such remittances as the country affords at the moment rather than hazard the injury to their interest inevitable from a commercial panic. . . . I have no doubt that as soon as the mercantile community recovers from its momentary despair . . . everything will resume its accustomed course."[24]

He hoped that the Bank's intervention would provide sufficient ease and time for this recovery to take place, but a week after the sale of the post notes and bonds had begun, news arrived from Europe of a further decline in cotton, accompanied by "a vast mass of drafts returned protested from the South and West." The money market was unsettled, many large firms failed, and, though the Bank and its New York allies continued their efforts, the deflationary pressures were too powerful to be overcome by them alone. Panic hoarding of specie was added to the other drains from the banks, and still further pressure was applied when Secretary Wood-

---

[22] M. Eyre to N. Biddle, March 31, 1837, in the Biddle Manuscripts in the Library of Congress.

[23] Quoted in *Niles' Register*, LII (1837), 82.

[24] N. Biddle to Baring Brothers and Company, to Hope and Company, and to Hottinguer and Company, April 1, 1837, in the Biddle Manuscripts in the Library of Congress.

bury, acting in response to political demands, made transfers to protect favored banks. He sent government funds to an institution in New Hampshire at the request of Isaac Hill and responded to many such appeals as that writen in "favor and friendship" by an officer of the Bank of Virginia who had supported the administration in its attacks upon the Bank of the United States. These transfers of deposits did not go unresisted, and Campbell P. White, a powerful Democratic politician in New York, protested against Woodbury's withdrawal of funds from the Manhattan Bank. This bank, Campbell said, "was in its inception Republican in its character, and it has adhered to the Democracy in all its struggles and vicissitude for a period of thirty-eight years."[25]

The weakness of a depository plan which gave to a political officer the power to choose among competing institutions became evident during this crisis. Powerful individuals in all sections of the country brought pressure on Woodbury to aid banks in which they were interested, and these politically motivated transfers were the only positive steps taken by the Van Buren administration in this period of stress. Many of the President's friends and advisers were urging him to take more vigorous measures, to repeal the specie circular, and to postpone the distribution of the July instalment of the surplus, but Van Buren, according to Robert Patterson of Philadelphia, though "conscious of the impending danger," was "anxious to avoid doing anything which might appear to be a departure from the policy of his predecessor." Some of the Cabinet members were becoming impatient with the lack of decision being exhibited by the President, and, on May 6, Joel Poinsett wrote to Biddle, without indicating whether or not he did so with Van Buren's authorization, and asked: "Can you not in your financial knowledge and experience devise some plan by which a wholesome control may be exercised over bank issues, and exchanges be brought back to what they were before the destruction of the Bank? Some measure apart from a national bank . . . although it might be connected with the operations of a great state institution."[26]

Biddle had been hoping to receive such an inquiry ever since Van Buren had been inaugurated, and he was ready with his answer. What was needed, he said, was a return to the same system as that which had previously existed, and this could be accomplished by an executive order designating the United States Bank as the depository of the public revenue in all places where it had subsidiaries or agencies with the responsibility of transferring these funds without cost to the government. Then, without repeal-

---

[25] *Niles' Register*, LII (1837), 81–82; L. Woodbury to I. Hill, March 27, 1837; C. P. White to L. Woodbury, April 13, 1837; J. Borckenbaugh to L. Woodbury, May 1, 1837; A Gallatin to L. Woodbury, May 4, 1837, in the Woodbury manuscripts in the Library of Congress.

[26] R. Patterson to N. Biddle, May 8, 1837; J. Poinsett to N. Biddle, May 7, 1837, in the Biddle Manuscripts in the Library of Congress.

ing the specie circular, the receivers of public funds could be instructed to accept the Bank's notes as well as gold and silver, and these simple changes, he predicted, would restore confidence and credit in a week's time.[27] It would be interesting to see how this experiment would have worked, for what Biddle was envisioning was a relationship between the United States Bank and the United States government that was closely parallel to that already existing between the Bank of England and its government. But the experiment could not be tried. On May 9 Biddle was told that the New York banks would suspend specie payments the next day, and he knew that his and the other Philadelphia banks had no choice but to do likewise. His almost single-handed effort to prevent the suspension of specie payments had not been successful, and the Van Buren administration, if Poinsett wrote with the President's consent, had been too late in deciding to come to his assistance.

[27] N. Biddle to J. Poinsett, May 7, 8 (two letters), 1837, in the Biddle Manuscripts in the Library of Congress.

~ *30* ~

The Monetary Debate

*T*he United States Bank, at the moment it suspended specie payments, was a strong, solvent, and liquid institution. Its sale of post notes and one-year bonds had brought the other banks in New York and Philadelphia into its debt, and through April and May it had increased its specie stock, even though it had deliberately avoided bringing undue pressure on its debtors. Its suspension of specie payments, nevertheless, was unavoidable, once the other banks had acted, for it could not pay specie to redeem its notes when it was unable to replenish its holdings from other banks. The great creditor in the United States, Biddle explained, was the government, which accepted only specie and the notes of specie-paying banks and which, by a self-adopted rule of the Treasury, paid out only specie. If his or any other bank continued to pay specie, its notes would be collected in payment of tariff duties, and immediately the government would demand specie for its own payments, so, until these rules were repealed, the Bank had no alternative but to concur in the general suspension.[1]

Biddle knew that the suspension of specie payments was a dangerous and drastic remedy, one to be applied only when there was no other choice. It would open the way for an expansion of issues by the banks, such as had occurred between 1814 and 1817, and, unless this expansion was prevented, another 1819 would follow. The only justification for the suspension was that it was the lesser of two evils: a greater injury would have been inflicted upon the national economy if the banks, in a vain attempt to resist the pressures that were draining their specie, had continued to demand payments from their debtors—the merchants, manufacturers, and farmers. During the weeks preceding the suspension, Biddle had been mingling, he said, "with men who, sixty days ago, thought themselves beyond the reach of all the accidents of fortune" but who had found "themselves and their families suddenly reduced to ruin" when called on to pay their debts at a moment when they could not collect from their debtors.

[1] N. Biddle to J. Q. Adams, May 13, 1837, in *Niles' Register,* LII (1837), 182.

A period of relaxation was necessary to enable the banks, the merchants, and the producers to work out their tangled relations, and the suspension of specie payments provided this needed ease and time. The banks, no longer under pressure to raise specie, could cease pressing their debtors for payment and even expand loans.[2]

The suspension was thus of immediate benefit to all the economic groups in the country. The farmers could sell their produce, the manufacturers their products, and the workingmen their labor. "If the banks had gone on paying specie to the government and the New York banks," Biddle wrote, "they would have been obliged to cease lending to the merchants, manufacturers, and mechanics, and the consequence would be that all the laborious classes employed by them would have been turned out of employ." The choice was to suspend specie payments or to suspend factories, trade, housebuilding, and roadmaking. And under such circumstances, he insisted, it was better "to suspend specie payments than to stop all industry."[3] Biddle had a right to speak at this moment. No other person or institution had done as much as he and the United States Bank to prevent the specie circular, the mismanagement of the transfers under the distribution act, and the restrictive orders of the Bank of England from having this result. But the combination of these pressures had proved irresistible. Once the suspension had taken place, however, he continued his efforts to restore monetary conditions to the plane where they had been before Jackson began his attacks upon the Bank of the United States, to bring back the currency to what he called "a safe and wholesome condition."

What was needed, he thought, was a return to a nationally chartered bank or, if this proved unacceptable, the designation of the United States Bank and its agencies as the principal depository for the public funds. The Bank, through its great capital and its nation-wide and international connections, could then provide a national currency of uniform value, regulate the rates of domestic and foreign exchange, keep the state banks in order, and lead the way back to a safe and permanent resumption of specie payments. The weakness of these proposals was that each would require Van Buren to repudiate and condemn the policies of his predecessor, and this, it was soon apparent, he was unwilling to do. But there was a possibility that he might be willing to repeal the specie circular as a necessary step for the resumption of specie payments, and most of Biddle's political efforts during the summer were to convince his friends in the administration of the desirability of at least this step.

Had Van Buren chosen this alternative, he would have had the support of a powerful faction of the Democratic party, which had taken the name "Conservative" and was led by Senators Nathaniel P. Tallmadge of New

[2] *Ibid.*

[3] N. Biddle to G. M. Lee, May 18, 1837, in the Biddle Manuscripts in the Library of Congress.

York and William Cabell Rives of Virginia. Forsyth and Poinsett were the representatives of this group in the Cabinet, and they urged the repeal of the specie circular and the continued use of the state-bank depositories as a necessary means for party victory in 1838 and 1840. Their opponents, called "Radicals" or "Locofocos," were more concerned with monetary reform than with party victory, and they urged Van Buren to come out for a specie currency and a complete separation of the government and its funds from banks of any description. These measures, they thought, were the only effective means of protecting the workingmen and farmers from oppression by the merchants, manufacturers, and bankers, and they were under the illusion that the profit made by paper money, "instead of being in any way advantageous to the community, was made at its expense; that it made the rich richer and the poor poorer; and that the whole system was one of fraud and iniquity."[4]

They also insisted that the divorce of bank and state and the adoption of a hard-money currency would serve to diminish economic crises and prevent the establishment of a moneyed aristocracy, and it was here that Biddle most radically disagreed. The separation of the government from the banks and the collection of the revenue in gold and silver, he said, would make "inconvertible paper" the sole and exclusive currency of the country. If the government, which had no specie, was to procure a supply by importing it from Europe or by paying high premiums to hoarders and if it made its payments by warrants redeemable in gold, those who were paid would either draw the specie and sell it or sell the warrants to those who wanted to ship specie abroad. The whole supply would soon have to be replenished, and ultimately, he predicted, the difficulty and high cost of procuring specie would force the government to halt. It would have no alternative but to issue irredeemable Treasury certificates, and in such a situation the banks would have no reason to return to specie payments. They could make larger discounts and greater dividends without it, and the state governments, subject to political pressure by these institutions, would not intervene to compel them to do so. "The government of the United States," Biddle concluded, "will be left alone to perform the work. And what can they do? Compare the amount of public revenue with the amount of the transactions of the country and judge how little influence the mere payment of the revenue in specie, even if it were practicable, would have on the business of the country. The truth is the whole project would be an abortion, which would either break down the country or break down the administration."[5]

A specie currency would not help the workers and farmers but would injure them, for if there was nothing but gold and silver in the country,

[4] Adams, *Writings of Gallatin*, III, 377; Schlesinger, *Age of Jackson*, pp. 227–41.

[5] N. Biddle, memorandum on the crisis, June 26, 1837; N. Biddle to J. Rathbone, Jr., July 14, 22, 1837, in the Biddle Manuscripts in the Library of Congress.

the owners of gold and silver would be the only persons who could employ workingmen. The farmers, mechanics, and manufacturers would be forced to borrow from the wealthy few when in need of credit, and the power and influence of these rich persons would be greatly increased. Biddle still believed, as he had when he was a member of the Pennsylvania legislature in 1811, that the "greatest misfortune to the laboring classes would be to banish the system of credit" because, as he said, "gold and silver are for the rich, safe bank notes are the democracy of currency."

Van Buren took no part in this debate that was separating the country and his party during the summer of 1837. He issued a call for a special session of Congress on the first Monday in September but refused to take any other action or to make any statements before that time. No one was certain with which of the contending groups he would align himself in his message, and each of the party factions brought pressure on him. Biddle was not directly involved. His duties and obligations at the Bank during this difficult summer absorbed much of his time and attention, and, in addition, he had to meet an attack from an unexpected source: the state bankers themselves and some of the members of the Whig party.

In his view, the suspension of specie payments was a severe and drastic remedy for economic difficulties, one to be adopted only when all others had failed. To many others throughout the country the problem was moral, and John Quincy Adams, in a public letter, asked: "What difference is there between the president and directors of a bank [which suspends specie payments], and the skillful artist who engraves a bank bill, a fac-simile of the bill signed by the president and the directors, and saves them the trouble of signing it, by doing it for them?"[6] Few others went so far as to compare those in charge of suspended banks with counterfeiters, but many agreed with Adams that the proper economic remedy to be adopted in this situation was that used by Solon, the application of "a sponge upon the account of debtor and creditor," to wipe out the old scores and begin again. They did not want to do this through formal legislation but rather by permitting the natural economic forces to have their way. The elimi-nation of debt would be accomplished by default, failure, bankruptcy, or partial payment, and the leading spokesman for this point of view was Albert Gallatin of New York. He insisted that the banks should concen-trate their efforts on a resumption of specie payments regardless of the cost to the community, adhering to what a contemporary British economist called "the restrictive principle," which, "by affecting all minor parties

6 J. Q. Adams to W. Foster, July 1, 1837, in *Niles' Register*, LII (1837), 338; J. Q. Adams to N. Biddle, July 18, August 27, 1837; C. A. Davis to N. Biddle, August 1, 1837; N. Biddle to C. A. Davis, August 3, 1837; N. Biddle to J. Q. Adams, August, 1837, in the Biddle Manuscripts in the Library of Congress; Adams, *Memoirs,* IX, 363–64. Adams apologized to Biddle and said that he intended no personal reference. They remained on friendly terms, but Adams did not change his view of the suspension of specie payments.

acting upon credit and greatly enhancing the value of money," would enable the banks to accumulate a sufficient stock of gold to redeem the diminished amount of notes they maintained in circulation.[7]

To adopt this method, Biddle believed, would be to repeat the error that Cheves had made in the later years of his presidency of the Bank of the United States. It would transfer the pressure from the banks to their customers and save the financial institutions by sacrificing the rest of the community. He was also certain that, so long as the specie circular was in force, the banks, however much they curtailed, would still be under pressure if they resumed specie payments and that Gallatin's policy would make it more difficult to achieve a permanent and effective reform of the currency. Biddle's arguments were unheeded in New York, where the moral strength of Gallatin's personality and position was apparently irresistible. The other state bankers, the merchants, and the politicians, almost unanimously, took up the demand for an immediate resumption of specie payments, and in August, just prior to the meeting of Congress, the New York banks issued an invitation for a national convention of bankers to be held in October.[8]

Their purpose was to provide for a co-operative resumption of payments "between the first of January and the middle of March, 1838," when the foreign debt would be so far lessened as to reduce the risk of a large exportation of gold. No mention was made of any action by the government as a prerequisite for the resumption, and this omission, Biddle believed, was a tactical error. If the banks could resume without the repeal of the specie circular, then this Treasury order could not be regarded as the cause of the suspension. Jackson, Benton, and their Locofoco allies were right; it was the weakness of the credit and paper system which was fundamentally at fault. But the chief objection to the New York proposal was not its tactical weakness but rather its rashness. For, in Biddle's opinion, if the banks named a day when they must resume, regardless of the government's action, the state of the country, or the condition of the foreign exchanges, they were promising to do what they might not be able to perform. The more prudent course, he suggested, would be for the banks "to continue steadily their present preparations for resuming specie payments; to wait quietly the action of Congress without interference of any kind; and be ready to give an immediate and zealous cooperation in any measures which that body may adopt for the common benefit of the country."[9]

Any lasting resumption depended "mainly if not exclusively" on the action of Congress, "without whose cooperation," Biddle said, all attempts at a general resumption of payments would be "partial and temporary."

[7] J. H. Palmer to G. Shaw, March 5, 1838, copy in Biddle Manuscripts in the Library of Congress.

[8] *Niles' Register*, LIII (1837), 6–7.

[9] *Ibid.*, p. 9.

He rejected the invitation of the New York banks, and they temporarily abandoned their plans for a national convention. The wisdom of his advice became evident when the President's message was read to the Congress. Van Buren, instead of listening to Poinsett, Forsyth, and the Conservative Democrats, had followed what a correspondent of Biddle's called "the sullen, vindicative, and stubborn mandates" from the Hermitage and had remained "obedient to the shallow, foolish, yet satanic, conceits of Benton." He refused to recommend the repeal of the specie circular and called for the separation of "the fiscal operations of the government from those of individuals or corporations" by the establishment of subtreasuries in various parts of the country for the safekeeping and transfer of government funds. Now a complete advocate of laissez faire, the President complained about the constant desire of some citizens to enlarge the powers of government and to extend its control over subjects and areas with which it should not interfere, and he said that in regard to economic matters all that the government should do was "to regulate by law the commerce among the states and to provide a general standard of value or medium of exchange in gold and silver."[10]

The government, according to Van Buren, had no responsibility to protect the people from the disastrous effects of what he said was "the excessive issues of bank paper." It should not attempt to manage the domestic and foreign exchanges. And if it should ever recharter a national bank, it would "impair the rightful supremacy of the popular will; injure the character and diminish the influence of our political system; and bring once more into existence a concentrated money power, hostile to the spirit and threatening the permanency of our republican institutions." This appeal to the republican traditions established by Jefferson and Jackson disguised the essential harshness of Van Buren's position. What he was saying was that the government of the United States had no responsibility to come to the aid of the people who were without employment or money through no specific fault of their own. There was real suffering in the country during the summer of 1837, and it was not confined to any one economic class or group. Workingmen, farmers, mechanics, manufacturers, merchants, and bankers, each in their own way, were feeling the effects of the economic crisis, as were most of the state governments, which, in the absence of federal support of internal improvements, had embarked on a major program of construction of canals, roads, and railroads.

Van Buren's advocacy of a policy of laissez faire was an act of political courage on his part and was dictated, so far as can now be ascertained, solely by his belief that it was the true principle of conduct. It was not politically expedient or popular, and Calhoun was the only prominent political leader who changed from an opponent of the administration to a

[10] J. Hamilton to N. Biddle, June 16, 1837, in the Biddle Manuscripts in the Library of Congress; *Niles' Register*, LIII (1837), 11-16.

[317]

supporter as a result of the message.[11] Many of the Conservative Democrats, on the other hand, went into open opposition to Van Buren and joined with the Whigs to defeat the subtreasury plan. The administration's opponents were too badly divided to agree on an affirmative program, and the only positive accomplishments of the special session of Congress were the postponement of the final payment under the distribution act; an extension of time to government debtors; and the authorization of an issue of interest-bearing Treasury certificates (irredeemable paper money) to be used in payments to and from the government.[12]

Biddle was keenly disappointed in the failure of Congress to order the repeal of the specie circular. It meant an inevitable delay in the resumption of specie payments by the banks, and also, by arousing suspicion abroad of the soundness of the American economy, it would make more difficult the carrying-out of plans he had made for the reorganization of Anglo-American commerce. He was still determined to break the financial dependence of the United States upon Great Britain and had already arranged for Samuel Jaudon to go to London as agent of the United States Bank in place of Baring Brothers and Company, so that there would be a representative "devoted exclusively to American concerns," who could "lay the foundations" of a reciprocal exchange between the two countries. Biddle believed that he could now count on the co-operation of the directors of the Bank of England, for they had given evidence of their desire to establish an "intimate and very confidential relationship between the two institutions." In March, 1837, Barings had requested the Bank of England to lend them two million pounds to be advanced to the United States Bank so that American payments could be maintained during this emergency period but had been refused. Instead, the Bank of England offered to lend the same sum directly to the United States Bank for the reason that "the directors desired to give the action the appearance of a national concern in which the leading banking institutions of both countries were joining."[13]

Biddle, having already provided for immediate payments by the issue of one-year bonds, did not accept this offer, but he was gratified that the directors' views had changed since the preceding year, when they had refused Jaudon's request for an open line of credit. He was further encouraged in the late summer when the newly appointed American agent of the Bank of England applied for an account in the United States Bank

[11] J. C. Calhoun to J. E. Calhoun, September 7, 1837, in Jamieson (ed.), *Correspondence of Calhoun*, p. 377.

[12] Benton, *Thirty Years' View*, II, 28–42.

[13] N. Biddle to D. B. Ogden, April 1, 1837; N. Biddle to E. R. Biddle, April 25, 1837; R. Colt to N. Biddle, July 10, 1837; N. Biddle to S. Jaudon, January 6, 1838, in the Biddle Manuscripts in the Library of Congress; Hidy, *Baring*, pp. 213–23; Clapham, *Bank of England*, II, 157–59.

and for assistance in the collection of approximately ten million dollars owed by Americans to Liverpool and London firms. The three houses that had been forced to call on the Bank of England for aid in the preceding winter had suspended payments in June, and the Bank had taken over their assets. Biddle complied with the agent's request on the ground of his "anxious desire to protect the interests of the Bank of England, and to promote the honorable discharge of what was due to a foreign nation." But he did not mention the more important reason—the desire to establish another precedent for co-operation between the two institutions, so that he could ask for reciprocal privileges in London.[14]

The suspension of specie payments in the United States and the numerous failures in New Orleans, other cotton ports, New York, and Great Britain had induced him to broaden the scope of the Bank's national and international operations beyond what he had envisioned in 1836. The basic plan was the same. The United States Bank with its subsidiaries and agencies would buy and sell bills of exchange based on shipments of produce within the country and abroad, thus providing the means for domestic and international payments. Jaudon in London, having access to its money market, and the Bank in Philadelphia, with its large capital and established credit, would draw on each other, and for the first time in history, an American institution would have almost complete control over American financial conditions and an equal voice with the Bank of England in international trade. This, the permanent system, was to be supplemented by two additional features made necessary by the emergency conditions of 1837. Some means had to be devised to provide for the payment of what Americans owed abroad; for when the banks had suspended payments, all commercial arrangements between the United States and Europe had been disrupted by the failure of many large mercantile firms on both sides of the water and by the unwillingness or inability of the surviving firms to buy American commodities for shipment abroad. Prices in the American markets were falling precipitously because there were no buyers, and with each reduction in price the ability of Americans to pay their European debts was further diminished.

Biddle was more worried by this aspect of the crisis than any other. Immediately after the suspension of specie payments he had said in a public letter addressed to John Quincy Adams that the first duty of Americans was to pay their foreign debts. They must make certain that the suspension should not appear to be an effort to avoid the payment of what was owed abroad, and, to prevent this from happening, he was willing to employ the full power and credit of the Bank. His concern was not disinterested. The already large European debt of the Bank had been substantially increased by the sale of the one-year bonds in April, and if funds were not available

[14] *Ibid.*

to make these payments when they were due, the Bank itself would fail. There was only one thing to do. The volume and prices of American exports had to be maintained and increased in some way, and Biddle decided to send agents to each of the Atlantic and Gulf ports to buy produce for shipment to Great Britain or France. He also created a new firm, owned by his own son Edward Biddle and May Humphreys of Philadelphia, to handle the sale of that part of the produce shipped to Liverpool.[15]

These operations had to be started before Humphreys or Jaudon could be sent to England, and Biddle turned to the mercantile directors of the Bank in an attempt to persuade one of them to act as the purchaser of cotton and produce in the United States. The Bank was forbidden to make such purchases on its own account, and none of the mercantile directors was willing to accept the personal risk accompanying such large undertakings. But it had to be done, and Biddle, who had never before borrowed from the Bank, undertook the operation himself. He made a contract with A. J. Jaudon, a brother of Samuel, for the use of his name as the borrower of record, and then sent purchasing agents to the southern and southwestern ports with some two million, three hundred thousand dollars, a large part of it in notes of the old Bank of the United States, with instructions to buy cotton. By autumn these agents had purchased more than sixty thousand bales for shipment to Great Britain and France, and their appearance in the market prevented any further decline in price.[16]

This use of the notes of the old Bank was bitterly criticized by the administration press and by the British and American buyers of produce, who, though they had retired from the market, resented the appearance of a new and powerful competitor. Like the branch drafts of an earlier period, these notes were denounced as illegal and fraudulent, but they were eagerly accepted by farmers, merchants, and bankers who had produce to sell or debts to pay or to collect. No other currency available was equally trustworthy, for the United States Bank was legally responsible for all debts of its predecessor, including its notes. Biddle used them instead of the notes of the existing Bank, as he frankly admitted, because under the Pennsylvania charter the United States Bank could be forced to pay 12 per cent damages on each note it refused to redeem in gold or silver, whereas no such damages could be claimed on the notes of the old Bank.[17]

The Bank's critics also spoke of the heavy losses it "must sustain on its tremendous shipments of cotton," and one of them predicted that "if pub-

[15] W. Scarborough to G. Barnsley, June 14, 29, July 17, 1837, in the Barnsley Manuscripts in the Duke University Library; N. Biddle to J. Roberts, July 31, August 9, September 15, 1837, in the Biddle Manuscripts in the Library of Congress.

[16] N. Biddle, statement of purchases and shipments of cotton, August 15, 1837, in the Biddle Manuscripts in the Library of Congress; N. Biddle to J. M. Clayton, April 8, 1841, in *House Executive Document* (29th Cong., 1st sess.), No. 226, pp. 475-76.

[17] N. Biddle to D. Webster, February 19, 1838, in the Biddle Manuscripts in the Library of Congress.

lic opinion runs in a correct channel, Mr. Biddle will find, like Bonaparte, that he has gone once too often to Moscow." The *Globe* joined the attack, and its charges provoked a southern editor to reply that, though the administration organ was much horrified at the atrocious conduct of Biddle in buying up southern cotton to ship to Europe in the discharge of the debt, the southern planters would not thank the *Globe* for this denunciation "while in the improved price of our staple they are realizing the benefit of the operation."[18] Other southerners joined in this praise, and George McDuffie and Robert Y. Hayne of South Carolina were so pleased with the results of the Bank's intervention that they organized a Cotton Planters' Convention, which, through voluntary co-operation would permanently limit the supply of cotton and turn over its sale to a single organization.

Their purpose was to use their monopoly position to effect a complete rearrangement of the cotton trade and to bring to the ports of the South much of the commerce that was now concentrated in "New York, Boston, and other ports of the northern states." They urged the local banks to follow the example of the United States Bank by making "advances on cotton and other produce" and by establishing agencies in Europe to handle the sale of these commodities.[19] It was for this reason that but few of the southern politicians followed Calhoun into the Van Buren party, and even Thomas Cooper, the economic theorist of the nullificationists, said that he had come to the conclusion that "a national bank is an instrument necessary to . . . the fiscal duties of our government, and therefore, as an implied power, is constitutional." Biddle welcomed the support of this unpredictable group, and in his formal explanation of his cotton operations he said that he had intervened in the market because "the derangement of the currency had placed the staples of the south entirely at the mercy of the foreign purchaser, who could have dictated the terms of the sale to the prostrated planter. It was thought proper to avert the evil by employing a large portion of the capital of the bank in making advances on southern produce. This had two effects: the first was to provide remittances to pay its own bonds in England . . . the second . . . to introduce into the market a new competition, and thus prevent the unconditional subjection of the planter to the foreign purchaser."[20]

In private letters he was more frank as to the reasons why he had decided to undertake this operation, and to a friend who had questioned the wisdom of the Bank's becoming so directly involved he wrote: "The Bank

[18] *Mercury* (Charleston), quoted in the *United States Gazette* (Philadelphia), August 19, 1837.

[19] Thomas P. Govan, "An Ante-Bellum Attempt To Regulate the Price and Supply of Cotton," *North Carolina Historical Review*, XVII (1940), 302–12.

[20] T. Cooper to the editor, July 1, 1837, in *Niles' Register*, LII (1837), 325; N. Biddle to J. Q. Adams, December 10, 1838, *ibid.*, LV (1838), 259.

in order to relieve the mercantile distress contracted a heavy debt on the other side. . . . To pay this debt it must buy bills of exchange. Must it buy from the merchants of New Orleans, who have failed, their bills on the merchants of London and Liverpool, who have failed, so that when its bonds fall due next April, it will have nothing to pay them with except a parcel of protested bills?"[21] This initial and essentially emergency operation was terminated on September 15, to give Biddle an opportunity to establish a more permanent and more secure organization. Jaudon and Humphreys began preparations to move to London and Liverpool, and Baring Brothers and Company were notified that their contract as agents for the United States Bank was terminated. Biddle needed a better-known and more responsible name than that of A. J. Jaudon for the more extensive operations that were planned, and on October 19 he requested Bevan and Humphreys, one of the leading mercantile firms in Philadelphia, to serve in Jaudon's stead. All the details of the operations except the transmission of bills of lading to Humphreys and Biddle in Liverpool were to be handled in the Bank under the supervision of Joseph Cowperthwaite, the new cashier, and his assistant, Thomas Dunlap; the risk would be Biddle's; so Bevan and Humphreys agreed to permit the use of their name for a commission of one-eighth of 1 per cent on the amount of purchases.[22]

Biddle's organizational framework was completed, and he issued instructions to his agents in the South and Southwest to begin purchasing cotton. These initial purchases were entirely in the name of Bevan and Humphreys. To prevent too sudden a rise in the market, no advances were made to other buyers. Such caution was necessary because large amounts of money were involved, and Biddle, though the purpose of his intervention into the market was to protect the national economy, did not want to lose money in the operation. But as the season progressed, he modified his instructions. His agents were told to make an advance of two-thirds or three-quarters of the local price to holders of cotton who shipped to Humphreys and Biddle at their own risk and expense. He also supported the Brandon Bank of Mississippi and other banks in the area which made similar advances and received in return the bills of exchange, the bills of lading, and the right to determine the time and conditions of sale in Liverpool.[23]

This restoration of the cotton market in the South and Southwest laid

[21] N. Biddle to C. A. Davis, September 20, 1837, in the Biddle Manuscripts in the Library of Congress.

[22] T. Cadwalader to N. Biddle, October 2, 1837; N. Biddle to T. Cadwalader, October 2, 1837; N. Biddle to Bevan and Humphreys, October 19, 1837, in the Biddle Manuscripts in the Library of Congress; N. Biddle to J. M. Clayton, April 8, 1841, in *House Executive Document* (29th Cong., 1st sess.), No. 226, pp. 441, 475–76.

[23] S. V. S. Wilder to N. Biddle, October 24, 1837; G. D. Blaikie to N. Biddle, October 25, 1837; W. H. Shelton to N. Biddle, November 8, 1837; N. Biddle to W. H. Shelton, December 2, 1837; N. Biddle to J. Minturn, December 7, 1837; M. Humphreys to N. Biddle, December 23, 1837, in the Biddle Manuscripts in the Library of Congress.

the basis for a general recovery of the national economy. Notes of the old Bank of the United States paid to the holders of cotton not only provided the means for the payment of local debts and obligations but also entered into the stream of exchanges and enabled southern merchants to pay what they owed in the Northeast. The bills of exchange based on the shipments of cotton performed a similar function, and in a very brief time the whole normal pattern of interregional trade was restored. The Bank also laid the basis for a revival of the market in stocks and bonds in the northeastern cities by continuing and extending its loans to the holders or purchasers of such securities. New issues of stocks and bonds appeared on the market, and the Bank provided the means for them to be sold in Great Britain and Europe. The owners of the stock would consign them to Jaudon for sale on the London market, and the Bank would advance the needed funds in the United States, charging only a small commission.[24]

The board of directors was told exactly what Biddle was doing, but all these extraordinary transactions were handled by the exchange committee. Nothing concerning them appeared in the records of the board except the name of the person borrowing and the amount, as these were listed in the periodical reports of the exchange committee, and most of the directors were scarcely aware of exactly what was going on. They trusted Biddle completely, were somewhat in awe of him, and readily agreed to whatever he suggested. He in turn was essentially cautious and conservative in all these transactions in produce and securities. His purpose was the restoration of the market, not monopoly, and he was much pleased when, as a result of the Bank's leadership, others engaged in these trades returned to the market and began to provide the facilities for the sale of American produce and securities abroad.

He was as successful in his plans for the restoration of international payments and trade as he was with those for the restoration of the American economy. Jaudon and Humphreys arrived in Great Britain in early November and almost at once were accepted as full and respected members of the financial and mercantile community, even though their initial greeting was cool because many of the merchants and bankers were suspicious of Biddle's plans. Reports from America of the organization of the Cotton Planters' Convention by McDuffie and Hayne had convinced some that Biddle's purpose was to organize a gigantic cotton monopoly, and others were distrustful because of his resistance to the resumption of specie payments. This seemed to them contrary to all sound principles of banking, and rumors were spread that Jaudon was a proscribed man in London. The basis of this report was the Bank of England's refusal to permit him to use its discount facilities or to allow bills accepted by him as the agent of a foreign bank of issue to be made payable at the Bank, but the directors had

[24] Smith, *Economic Aspects of the Second Bank,* pp. 181–82.

not intended this refusal as a reflection upon him or the institution he represented. They greeted him cordially, accepted him as a depositor, and made no objections when Dennison and Company, a large and influential firm, became his general banker.[25]

Other private bankers agreed to make advances to Jaudon when he needed them, and he was soon established as one of the most influential and powerful figures in the financial district of London. A new issue of bonds of the United States Bank was quickly disposed of, as were the other American securities sent to him through the Bank, and one of the great objects of his agency—the establishment of "a current daily market for American securities"—was accomplished. A second object—"a regularly working system of exchange"—followed soon afterward, and Biddle could proudly report that it was now possible to sell bills of exchange drawn on Americans in the London market. No longer would payments between the United States and Great Britain depend solely on British financial conditions. If British merchants would not accept drafts from the United States, the payments could be made by drafts on American debtors sold to Jaudon in London.[26]

Much of Jaudon's success was attributable to the easy financial conditions prevailing in Great Britain. The Bank of England, having stopped the outflow of gold, was anxious to prevent a repetition of the financial disasters of 1825–26, and through the summer and fall of 1837 had gradually removed its restrictions upon credit. Money became so plentiful that virtually all traces of the previous year's difficulties had disappeared, and whatever American securities were offered for sale by Jaudon or one of his competitors were eagerly purchased. Humphreys had similar success. Within a few months of his arrival in Liverpool he had established lines of credit with brokers and bankers which totaled over four hundred thousand pounds, and, though he had been given authority to call on Jaudon for aid, he was never required to do so. Thirty-five per cent of the cotton shipped from the United States to Liverpool between November 1, 1837, and June 15, 1838, was consigned to Humphreys and Biddle, and it was generally estimated that its control of such a large part of the shipments had made "the cotton crop net two pence per pound more than it would have done."[27]

[25] N. Biddle to S. Jaudon, January 6, 1838; N. Biddle to T. A. Curtis, January 12, 1838; T. A. Curtis to N. Biddle, February 22, 1838; N. Biddle to J. H. Cowell, March 23, 1838, in the Biddle Manuscripts in the Library of Congress; *Times* (London), November 28, 1837; *Circular to Bankers* (London), December 1, 1837. Biddle, too, thought that Jaudon and the Bank had been discriminated against and, before he learned better from Jaudon, wrote a very angry letter to Timothy Curtis, governor of the Bank of England.

[26] N. Biddle to J. Sergeant, April 6, 1838, in the Biddle Manuscripts in the Library of Congress.

[27] M. Humphreys to N. Biddle, March 8, July 4, 1838; cotton received at Liverpool between November 1, 1837 and June 15, 1838, in the Biddle Manuscripts in the Library of Congress; Clapham, *Bank of England*, II, 157–59; Hidy, *Baring*, pp. 218–23.

The United States had thus gained approximately fifteen million additional dollars with which to pay its European debts, and Biddle's reputation as a financier was justifiably high. He not only had provided the means for "the liquidation of the large amount of debt due from the merchants in America to their correspondents in England" but had also laid the basis for a renewal of the mutually profitable trade between the two countries. American buyers were sending orders to British manufacturers, and British merchants in turn were increasing their purchases of American commodities. Prices were almost restored to their former figures, the volume of international trade was rapidly increasing, and Biddle's courage, initiative, and intelligence were almost universally hailed by those who had profited. On June 29, 1838, when the first cotton operations were concluded, a British editor said: "Mr. Biddle stands pre-eminent." He alone had clearly seen "the gradual advance of the evil, and sagaciously and dextrously provided the best retreat from its dangers and difficulties. . . . The United States Bank, by endeavoring to lessen the force and violence of the convulsion, and, immediately after the occurrence of the panic and almost universal stoppage, proceeding to repair the damages which they had produced, did all that could be done to merit the approbation and gratitude of the community."[28]

[28] *Circular to Bankers* (London), June 29, 1838.

31

The Resumption
of
Specie Payments

*A*merican opinion concerning Biddle and his policies was just as enthusiastic as that in Great Britain in June, 1838, and a New York newspaperman wrote: "The position of Mr. Biddle is proud and commanding, and the result has demonstrated the soundness of his views and the wisdom of the ground he took and maintained."[1] Such praise was a decided change from what had been the customary mode of discussion of Biddle during the preceding years when he had been the chief opponent of the national administration and the leaders of the New York financial community in preventing what he considered to be a premature resumption of specie payments. Immediately after the adjournment of the special session of Congress, the New York banks had issued a second call for a national convention of bankers to meet at the close of November. Gallatin, in an effort to enlist Biddle's co-operation, had written: "It is still on you that the country must principally rely," stating that, without his co-operation and that of the United States Bank, it was hardly possible for the other banks to come "to a just and satisfactory result." But Biddle was unwilling to attend the convention. He remained in Philadelphia while Manuel Eyre, a director of the United States Bank, led the fight against naming a day for resumption, and the convention decided that the present circumstances of the country were not such as to make it expedient or prudent "to fix the day for a resumption of specie payments." Seven of the delegations at this November convention were in favor of the New York position, and, as a concession to them, the majority agreed not to adjourn the convention

[1] R. M. Blatchford to T. A. Curtis, June 1, 1838, in the Biddle Manuscripts in the Library of Congress.

[326]

sine die but to meet again on the second Wednesday in April, 1838. The New York bankers were not satisfied with this concession and continued their agitation for an immediate resumption. In January they asked the New York agent of the United States Bank to ascertain whether Biddle and the other Philadelphia bankers would agree to "a simultaneous resumption by the banks of the two cities" or, if this was inexpedient, "whether they would enter into any agreement for the liquidation of balances . . . on the principle of mutual forbearance in drawing specie for a limited period after such a resumption by either party."[2]

Flattering statements were made about the influence, power, and prestige of Biddle and the United States Bank, but along with this praise were voiced less gentle reminders that the continuation of the suspension was generally unpopular. If Biddle continued to block the resumption, his agent was warned, the New York banks would make public the fact of their offer and his refusal to accept it. Biddle was angry at their statements. He rejected the proposal and deliberately accepted the risk of popular disapproval. "The Bank," he wrote, "is strong enough not to be afraid of doing right and it will endeavor to do its duty on this as on all other occasions."[3] His purpose was not to continue the suspension of specie payments indefinitely, but he did not believe that the banks could safely resume so long as the specie circular was in effect without inflicting needless losses and injuries on the rest of the community. The policy that he advocated for all the banks and followed in his own institution was to begin a gradual and gentle diminution of loans both to prepare for resumption and to prevent an undue expansion of issues while the restraint of specie payments was removed but also to provide the means through which others could pay their domestic and foreign debts. The suspension had found the United States with large balances from the southern and western cities to the Atlantic cities and with a very considerable debt in Europe. All parties were willing to pay, most were able to pay if they could collect what was owed them, and all that each needed, Biddle was certain, "was time; time to settle; time to adjust accounts; time to send the debtor's crops to market; time to dispose of his property with the least sacrifice; time to bring out his resources to pay his debts."[4]

The country's first concern should be to pay its debts, but not to depreciate the value of its means of paying them, and these had been the guiding rules for Biddle in his whole operation. The Bank had diminished its loans by 10 per cent, it had increased its specie holdings by three million

---

[2] A. Gallatin to N. Biddle, November 23, 1837; M. Eyre to N. Biddle, November 26, 28, 29, 1837; N. Biddle to M. Robinson, January 20, 1838, in the Biddle Manuscripts in the Library of Congress; *Niles' Register*, LIV (1838), 115.

[3] N. Biddle to M. Robinson, January 20, 1838, in the Biddle Manuscripts in the Library of Congress.

[4] N. Biddle to J. Q. Adams, April 5, 1838, in *Niles' Register*, LIV (1838), 98–100.

dollars, and it was ready to resume payments whenever the national administration abandoned the policies which had forced the banks to suspend. But the Bank had also provided "the necessary facilities for shipping the crops of the south and west," it had placed "its own confidential agent in England to protect the great commercial and pecuniary interests of the country" and thus had led the way to the recovery of national and international trade.[5]

The New York banks, under the leadership of Gallatin, had followed a different course. Their single concern had been the resumption of specie payments without regard to its cost, and they had not considered it any part of their responsibility to aid their merchants to sell goods or to collect their outstanding accounts. Between the day of suspension and April 1, 1838, the New York banks had reduced their loans from forty-six million dollars to thirty million and their circulating notes from nine million to two million. These severe curtailments, as Biddle pointed out, made it almost impossible for anyone outside New York to pay what he owed or to buy in the city. A man who had contracted a debt in New York before the suspension now found his ability to provide means for payment reduced one-third and in some cases one-half, and the dollar he paid represented the same amount of value in terms of goods as one and a half or two dollars when he had borrowed.[6]

If the debtor sent produce, the scarcity of money obliged him to sell it at a great sacrifice; if he tried to pay in out-of-town bank notes, their value was reduced by 25 per cent; and if he sent stocks or bills of exchange, he could not dispose of them. The result was that he sent no produce, no stocks, no bills of exchange. His bills were unpaid, and he made no new purchases. Much of the customary trade of the city was being taken over by Philadelphia and Baltimore, and most of the merchants, instead of protesting against this loss of business, considered it moral and right. Local patriotism, political loyalty to Jackson and Van Buren, and jealousy of the United States Bank were also among the forces that motivated the New York business community in supporting a monetary policy that was injurious to its immediate economic interest.[7] Many of its members believed that Biddle's intervention in the cotton market was planned as a permanent policy and that the United States Bank intended to establish a monopoly in this and other commodities and in domestic and foreign exchange. If such was to happen, the center of the nation's trade and finance would be transferred to Philadelphia, and the Bank, as the Jacksonians had predicted,

[5] *Ibid.*

[6] *Ibid.*; A. Gallatin to W. Hall, February 20, 1838, in Adams (ed.), *Writings of Gallatin*, II, 522.

[7] R. M. Blatchford to N. Biddle, March 26, 1838, in the Biddle Manuscripts in the Library of Congress.

would become so powerful that it would be able to control national elections.

Biddle, of course, had no such ambition. All he was striving for was a return to the monetary system under which the United States had for so long prospered, and he had every intention of retiring from his extraordinary activities as soon as the Bank had provided the means for the payment of its foreign debt, the specie circular had been repealed, and normal trade had been restored. Gallatin, however, had a larger purpose in view. Like Jackson and Benton, he was opposed to all credit and debt. He wanted to restrain and restrict the too rapid expansion and development of the American economy, and Biddle was correct when he wrote concerning their dispute: "The credit system of the United States and the exclusively metallic system are now fairly in the field, face to face with each other. One or the other must fall. There can be no other issue."[8] As chief spokesman for the credit system, he wanted to prevent the reconvening of the bank convention in New York on the ground that if the banks resumed payments while the specie circular was still in effect, their notes would be used, as they had been between the summer of 1836 and the spring of 1837, to draw out their specie for government payments. If the banks, by sacrificing the community, were able to maintain payments, this would be used at the next elections "to show that the schemes of the executive are not as destructive as they will prove hereafter," he wrote. "But if they resume and again are compelled to suspend, the executive will rejoice at the new triumph, and they will fall in the midst of a universal outcry against their weakness."[9]

Gallatin and the other New York bankers did not argue the question with him. They merely replied that the act of the state legislature the previous spring, which retroactively had authorized the suspension of specie payments for one year, expired on May 10, 1838, and insisted that the convention be held. The legislature was again in session, and Biddle and the minority of the New York mercantile and financial community who agreed with his views tried to persuade the legislators to renew the act authorizing the suspension. But they did not succeed. The combined power of the national administration, the Locofocos, and the Conservative Democrats and Whigs who sided with Gallatin was too great, and on April 4 Biddle was informed from Albany that it was "utterly impossible to extend the suspension law." The New York banks must resume specie payments or suffer the loss of their charters.[10]

[8] N. Biddle to J. G. Gamble, January 31, 1839, in the Biddle Manuscripts in the Library of Congress.

[9] N. Biddle to J. Q. Adams, April 5, 1838, in Niles' Register, LIV (1838), 98–100.

[10] N. Biddle to S. Jaudon, February 7, 1838; N. Biddle to D. B. Ogden, April 4, 1838; D. B. Ogden to N. Biddle, April 4, 1838; N. Biddle to J. Sergeant, April 6, 1838, in the Biddle Manuscripts in the Library of Congress.

Until this moment Biddle had hoped that his conflict with Gallatin and the New York banks would not come to a showdown. He knew that the differences between them were irreconcilable, but he thought that if the act authorizing the suspension of payments was extended, Gallatin and his associates would be forced to acquiesce. But now Biddle had no choice, he thought, but to refuse the invitation to meet with the other banks, and he persuaded the rest of the Philadelphians to stay away. He justified this action in another public letter to Adams, in which he contrasted his policy with that of Gallatin and condemned the New York banks and the Van Buren administration for their unwillingness to co-operate with him and the United States Bank in the effort to arrive at a permanent solution of the country's monetary difficulties.[11]

His letter was described by his opponents as "a declaration of war against New York and our banks," and it was said to have increased tenfold "the feeling against a further suspension." Many of the Whigs were embittered because the unpopularity of his position threatened to hurt the party in the fall elections. "No doubt you thought," one of them wrote, "that your wise financial letter to Adams just published would have a good effect . . . on the Whig cause. . . . For goodness sake do not try to make yourself more consequential than you are as you do yourself injury and help the Locofoco party." But in his letter Biddle was not addressing a New York audience or members of either of the political parties, rather he was speaking to the merchants, the manufacturers, the farmers, and particularly the bankers who were to meet in convention in New York on April 11. He wanted them to realize what the consequences would be if a day was set for resumption, and he had his reward when, in the convention, the representatives of the New England banks announced that, although their institutions were fully prepared to resume, they opposed any immediate action for the reason that, while the course of the New York banks during the past year had closed New York against them as a market, the opposite policy of Philadelphia and Baltimore had opened these cities to New England manufactures.[12]

Great Britain, if it had been represented in the convention, could rightly have made the same statement. Biddle's policy had as its purpose the restoration of orderly domestic and international trade and payments, and whatever increase in the American gold stock occurred was accomplished gradually as part of the payment for American stocks and commodities. He used the easy financial situation in Great Britain not primarily to increase the gold supply in the United States but rather to finance an exchange of goods, realizing, as he said, that "when the English have bought all the

[11] N. Biddle to J. Q. Adams, April 5, 1838, in *Niles' Register*, LIV (1838), 98–100.

[12] D. B. Ogden to R. Colt, April 10, 1838; J. Williams to N. Biddle, April 11, 1838, in the Biddle Manuscripts in the Library of Congress; *Niles' Register*, LIV (1838), 113, 114.

produce we have to spare, we must . . . buy from them what manufactures they have to spare." The policy advocated by Gallatin, if it had been followed outside New York, would have replenished American gold holdings by making it impossible to buy from foreigners. The restrictions on credit, by enhancing the value of money, would have checked imports from Europe and would have brought back "a considerable amount of bullion in return for the cotton and other products exported from the United States."[13]

It would have been natural to expect the Bank of England, concerned with increasing the sale of British manufactures and with preserving its bullion reserve, to favor the policy advocated by Biddle rather than that of Gallatin, but, as so often in this confused period, the directors did not follow the course which seemed best designed to foster their own and their country's interest. They, like the majority of the New York merchants, thought that a resumption of specie payments by the American banks, regardless of its cost in terms of trade, was a desirable and moral thing; and they joined with Baring Brothers and Company and Prime, Ward and King of New York in a joint shipment of one million dollars in specie to the New York banks so that they might safely resume payments.[14]

This shipment arrived shortly before the bankers convened, but it had little effect on those from the South and West. They had the same feelings as the New England bankers, and, in addition, they were not prepared to resume. Some provision had to be made to protect their scanty gold holdings from purchasers of government land if they were to issue notes redeemable in specie, and they also had to be assured of a market in the northeastern cities for the produce and bills of exchange from the interior. The balance of payments was against them, and, unless they were certain that their specie would not be drained for the purchase of manufactured goods from New York, Philadelphia, and Baltimore, they could not resume.

So great were the influence and prestige of Gallatin and so determined the support given to the cause of resumption by Van Buren and his supporters that few of the banks were quite willing to say that they had no present intention of renewing their obligations to pay specie. But they were determined not to acquiesce in the New York demand for an immediate resumption, and they masked their refusal by adopting a resolution which recommended that all the banks of the country should "resume specie payments on the first Monday of January next without precluding an earlier resumption on the part of such banks as may find it necessary or deem it proper."[15]

[13] N. Biddle to J. Q. Adams, April 5, 1838, in *Niles' Register*, LIV (1838), 98–100.
[14] Hidy, *Baring*, pp. 243–45; Clapham, *Bank of England*, II, 164–65.
[15] *Niles' Register*, LIV (1838), 113, 114.

This resolution was, in fact, a victory for Biddle and his position. He wanted resumption just as much as did Gallatin if it could be accomplished without harm to the American economy or to the cause of a safe and wholesome currency. But only a few persons in the United States and Great Britain believed him when he made such statements. The majority of people, even well-informed people, thought that he had opposed the resumption of payments not because it was inexpedient and unwise at the particular time but rather for the reason that such an action would have been disadvantageous to his personal interests and disastrous to the Bank. They did not believe him when he said that the United States Bank, with only six million dollars in notes in circulation and with four million dollars in specie and ten million dollars on deposit with its agents in Europe, was more nearly prepared for resumption than any other bank. But Biddle was entirely truthful when he said: "Our principles incline us to an early resumption, our preparations would justify it, and if we were at all influenced by the poor ambition of doing what others cannot do so readily, or the still poorer desire of profiting by the disasters of others, the occasion would certainly be tempting. But the Bank of the United States makes common cause with the other banks and the character and prosperity of the country. . . . They must stand or fall together, and it is of vital importance that the banks . . . should not suffer themselves to be driven by the dread of being thought weak into rash and hazardous enterprises."[16]

Within a few weeks of the adjournment of the bank convention, the doubters and questioners were to learn that they were mistaken in believing that Biddle was unalterably opposed to resumption. The Van Buren administration was in a difficult position all during the spring of 1838. Its one affirmative proposal, the subtreasury system, passed the Senate by the narrow margin of two votes but was defeated in the House, and the Congress, divided into fiercely contending factions, failed to provide sufficient funds for the government's operations.[17] Biddle saw an opportunity in this situation to establish a new pattern of co-operation between the Bank and the administration. The one asset that the government possessed was the six million dollars owed to it by the Bank in payment for the stock of the Bank of the United States which was payable in three instalments in September, 1838, 1839, and 1840.

If these six million dollars were made immediately available to the government, it could pay its current obligations, and Biddle, on April 30, wrote to Secretary of State Forsyth to suggest that the Bank might "anticipate these payments at once and put the government in funds for its pressing wants." The first effect of such an arrangement, he said, "would be to quiet the minds of the people," since it would be "a return to something

[16] N. Biddle to J. Q. Adams, April 5, 1838, *ibid.*, pp. 98–100.
[17] R. M. Blatchford to N. Biddle, April 24, 1838, in the Biddle Manuscripts in the Library of Congress; Benton, *Thirty Years' View*, II, 124–25.

like the ancient habits of intercourse between the Bank and the government." The existing Bank was essentially the same as the old, and the whole machinery could be remounted in twenty-four hours. It could without difficulty "engage to receive and disburse the public funds in every part of the United States without charge" and so relieve the administration of its connection with "a multitude of banks," which was a "fruitful source of trouble and political danger" and also of the constant agitation for the re-charter of a national bank.[18]

The first result of this negotiation was unpromising. Forsyth replied that he did not see that anything useful could be done. Any arrangement made by the Bank and the administration would necessarily be injurious to both, but he assured Biddle that "the administration as a whole desires that your Bank would be to it as other banks are." He also added the warning that he would be uncandid not to state that there were members of the administration who believed something was to be gained "by appealing to public prejudice against the Bank, and that considered as an enemy, it will be more useful than admitted to be a friend."[19] Another politician was also aware of this continuing prejudice against the United States Bank. Henry Clay, who throughout the long and ineffectual session of Congress had sought to find some means of restoring the national currency, decided that the hostility engendered by Biddle's stubborn refusal to resume specie payments might be a means through which the specie circular could be repealed. On April 30, the same day that Biddle wrote to Forsyth, Clay introduced in the Senate a joint resolution providing for the repeal of the circular, and he told everyone that his purpose was to help the New York banks resume specie payments.

He pretended to share the popular hostility to the United States Bank, and on May 21, when presenting a petition for the re-establishment of a national bank, he denied that he wished to see the charter "granted to an existing state institution which has an eminent individual at its head." He had no such purpose in view, he insisted. He and his friends were "not particularly attached to this or that individual, to this or that existing bank, but to principles, to the thing itself, to the institution, to a well organized Bank of the United States under the salutary operation of which the business of the country has so greatly prospered." He spoke well of Biddle but added that there was another person in whom he would have equal confidence, and that was Albert Gallatin.[20]

The speech had exactly the effect that Clay intended. Democrats and Whigs alike were deceived. "The bank project is a project to get New

[18] N. Biddle to J. Forsyth, April 30, 1838, in the Biddle Manuscripts in the Library of Congress.

[19] J. Forsyth to N. Biddle, May 29, 1838, in the Biddle Manuscripts in the Library of Congress.

[20] *Congressional Globe* (25th Cong., 2d sess.), VI, 344, 396–97.

York," Webster wrote indignantly. "Our illustrious friend seeks his great object by connecting himself with some one grand idea. In 1823 that idea was the establishment of an American system. In 1833 the idea was to bargain away that system. In 1838 it is to make a Bank of the United States on certain principles (principals?) which see." James Buchanan, Democratic senator from Pennsylvania, charged that Clay and his friends were "in favor of an establishment of a new bank in the city of New York," but Clay himself wrote to Biddle: "You will have seen and you will comprehend the object and benefit of the movement I made."[21]

Calhoun, Benton, and a few others suspected a trick, but most of the administration senators voted for the repeal of the specie circular. The House concurred on May 30, and the next day Biddle, much to the surprise of the Van Buren leaders, announced: "I rejoice . . . at the termination of this unhappy controversy, and shall cordially cooperate with the government by promoting what the banks are, I am sure, anxious to effect, an early resumption of specie payments throughout the Union." The long and painful struggle was essentially over. The banks, now that the government had abandoned its attempt to impose a metallic currency on the country, could safely resume specie payments, and the supporters of the Bank were enthusiastic. "I have hardly ever seen so much excitement in Wall Street," one of them wrote Biddle, "and those friends who have stood by you and your policy have now their triumph." The same person told the governor of the Bank of England that it was solely due to Biddle that this great triumph had occurred. If he and the banks in the South and West had agreed to the New York demand for the premature resumption, "we should have still been oppressed by that blighting circular and the administration would have persisted in their Quixotic experiments."[22]

Van Buren and his supporters immediately realized that they had been outwitted by Clay and Biddle, and, in an effort to prove to the Locofocos and other radicals that the administration had not deserted the cause of monetary reform, they reintroduced the bill establishing the subtreasury system. Biddle was angry and disturbed. "The rumor of the intended effort to carry the subtreasury bill," he wrote, "has already shaken the confidence which was reviving. It will undo everything . . . and bring us back to where we were a month ago. I, for one, shall be thus influenced. I have said in print that in consequence of the repeal, I would 'cooperate with the government in promoting an early resumption.' That is the extent of my engagement. Now if I find the government relapsing into hostility,

21 D. Webster to N. Biddle, May 24, 1838; H. Clay to N. Biddle, May 30, 1838, in the Biddle Manuscripts in the Library of Congress.

22 *Congressional Globe* (25th Cong., 2d sess.), VI, 416, 417; N. Biddle to J. Q. Adams, May 31, 1838, *Niles' Register*, LIV (1838), 226; R. M. Blatchford to N. Biddle, June 1, 1838; R. M. Blatchford to T. A. Curtis, June 1, 1838, in the Biddle Manuscripts in the Library of Congress.

I shall return to my old position whence I shall not stir until the sub-treasury bill is negatived, or, what is better, till Congress adjourns without any further tampering."[23]

He sent representatives to Washington to lobby against the bill, and on June 25 it was defeated by a vote of one hundred and twenty-five to one hundred and eleven in the House. The Congress then authorized the Secretary of the Treasury to sell the bonds of the United States Bank and adjourned. All that Biddle had demanded as conditions for the resumption of specie payments was fulfilled, and on July 10 the governor of Pennsylvania, after consulting with Biddle and other state bankers, issued a proclamation requiring all banks in the commonwealth to resume the redemption of their "notes, bills, and other obligations in gold and silver" on or before August 13, 1838. The next day the Philadelphia banks announced that a general convention of bankers would be held in the city on July 23, and, when they assembled, all but those in the southwestern states agreed to resume on August 13 or shortly thereafter.[24] These interior banks, very properly in Biddle's view, were unwilling to move forward their date of resumption from the first Monday in January, 1839, and much of his effort during the rest of the year was devoted to the task of making it possible for them to resume specie payments without curtailing their support of the cotton and other commodity markets.

The government co-operated with Biddle during most of the rest of the year. Secretary Woodbury, immediately after the adjournment of Congress, advertised for bids on the bonds of the United States Bank, but only one was submitted. That was from the Bank itself, and the negotiation was conducted in the friendliest and most co-operative spirit. "What befell you may imagine, since we came out good friends," Biddle facetiously reported to Jaudon, "and after a little coquetry and a little flirtation, I think it not improbable that Mr. (not Mrs.) Woodbury and I will be tender and true." The Bank agreed to advance four million dollars immediately for two of the bonds, leaving one in reserve for later needs, and in return the Treasury agreed to withdraw the funds gradually in notes of the United States Bank for expenditures by the Secretary of War in the interior of the country.[25]

In the short space of fifteen months Biddle had thus led the United States out of one of the severest financial crises in its history. There had

23 N. Biddle to J. Barney, June 5, 1838; N. Biddle to J. Sergeant, June 5, 1838; N. Biddle to S. Jaudon, June 9, 1838, in the Biddle Manuscripts in the Library of Congress.

24 *Niles' Register*, LIV (1838), 305, 320, 344; N. Biddle to J. Sergeant, June 15, 1838; O. F. Johnson to O. Barrett, June 28, 1838; N. Biddle to T. Stevens, July 3, August 28, 1838; N. Biddle to J. Ritner, July 23, 1838, in the Biddle Manuscripts in the Library of Congress.

25 *Senate Document* (25th Cong., 3d sess.), No. 31; N. Biddle to S. Jaudon, August 3, 1838, in the Biddle Manuscripts in the Library of Congress.

been numerous suspensions and postponement of payments by mercantile and other firms, but only a few failures, and no major losses had been sustained. The economy was strong and solvent; and the general reputation and credit of the country was high. Its great foreign and domestic debt had been liquidated by payments, not by bankruptcy and failure, and it had gained the distinction, almost unique in Biddle's opinion, "that while the government of the United States is the only government that has ever paid to the last cent its national debt, the people of the United States have discharged their private engagements with an unexampled fidelity."[26]

The Bank, having provided the means for the payment of these debts within the country and abroad by its advances on stocks and commodities, could, Biddle thought, retire from its extraordinary activities, now that the crisis had passed. He instructed Humphreys to sell the cotton being held in Liverpool, and Jaudon was told to bring his business into a more manageable compass as rapidly as he judiciously could. Biddle's purpose was to return to the customary pattern of business, and an authorized statement was published in London that, after the close of 1838, "no merchant will have a reasonable cause for complaint against the United States Bank for departing from strict banking usage in their transactions."[27] He could make no promises for the period from August through December, for during these months the southwestern banks had to be placed in a position that would enable them to resume specie payments with safety. He had already begun negotiations with the Union Bank of Mississippi to advance five million dollars on state-guaranteed bonds and to lend an additional million and a half dollars to other banks in the Southwest, which would be repaid by cotton shipped to Humphreys and Biddle. To insure that the price of cotton would remain stable throughout the fall, he instructed his purchasing agents to be ready to step in whenever the market weakened. They bought very little, some forty-five thousand bales costing some six hundred thousand dollars, but this purchase was sufficient to convince the other buyers for domestic and foreign users that nothing was to be gained by waiting for a break in price.[28]

Through the early fall of 1838 Biddle thought that his political difficulties were over. The collector of customs in New York had begun depositing some of his funds in the newly established and audaciously named

[26] N. Biddle to J. Q. Adams, December 10, 1838, in *House Executive Document* (29th Cong., 1st sess.), No. 226, pp. 404–8.

[27] N. Biddle to M. Humphreys, October 3, 1838; N. Biddle to S. Jaudon, October 19, 1838, in the Biddle Manuscripts in the Library of Congress; *Circular to Bankers* (London), June 26, 1838.

[28] M. Humphreys to N. Biddle, September 7, 1838; N. Biddle to E. C. Biddle, October 1, 1838; N. Biddle to S. Jaudon, October 19, 1838, in the Biddle Manuscripts in the Library of Congress; N. Biddle to J. Q. Adams, December 10, 1838; N. Biddle to J. M. Clayton, April 8, 1841, in *House Executive Document* (29th Cong., 1st sess.), No. 226, pp. 404–08, 475–79.

Bank of the United States in New York (which had been organized under a recently passed statute that permitted individuals to incorporate a bank by application to the executive authority of the state rather than to the legislature), and the rest of Biddle's relations with the administration were universally pleasant and co-operative. In August when Secretary Woodbury, by a careless mistake, ordered the transfer of part of funds on deposit with the Bank to another eastern bank, it was immediately corrected. Secretary Poinsett told him that the agreement with the Bank was "that not more than $500,000 would be required monthly and that at points in the south and southwest," and Woodbury apologized to Biddle.[29]

Biddle actually believed that the administration was now ready to make the United States Bank "the general depository of the government funds," and he went to Washington in September, where he was told that Van Buren had instructed Blair to refrain from attacking the Bank or Biddle in the *Globe* any more. Poinsett wrote an article for the official paper, "explaining the late circular by the government directing the officers to disburse the notes of the Bank," and Blair published it without change; though he added some remarks of his own, Biddle said, "to save his consistency."[30] This change in the political climate, as well as the improved financial prospects, convinced Biddle that he could safely do what he had long contemplated—resign from the Bank when the resumption of specie payments had been completed throughout the country. He had made this decision several times in the past, but now he was determined to carry it through, for his health had begun to break under the strain and responsibilities of his position. He was only fifty-two years old, but the long years of political warfare had taken their toll. Two or three times each year he had been attacked by illness, usually simple exhaustion, and he looked forward to the time whein he could be free from the multitudinous details that engulfed him.

On October 3 he made a record of the pecuniary transactions which fell under his notice on that single day and was almost dismayed to find that he had been required to accept or reject proposals involving twelve and a half million dollars. Whenever he came into his office, he felt a fresh shock of surprise "at the multitude of things which I have to do and the number of

29 J. Poinsett to L. Woodbury, August 19, 1838, in the Woodbury Manuscripts in the Library of Congress; N. Biddle to S. Jaudon, October 19, 1838, in the Biddle Manuscripts in the Library of Congress. This New York statute, which was called the "Free Banking Law," is described in Redlich, *Molding of American Banking*, I, 187–204, and in Bray Hammond, "Free Banks and Corporations: The New York Free Banking Act of 1838," *Journal of Political Economy*, XLIV (1936), 184–209. If such an act had been in existence in Pennsylvania when the United States Bank was chartered, there would have been no necessity for bribery of the legislators, since they would have had nothing to say about the charter and the Bank could not have sought special privileges.

30 N. Biddle to E. C. Biddle, October 1, 1838; N. Biddle to S. Jaudon, October 19, 1838, in the Biddle Manuscripts in the Library of Congress.

people I have to see in the course of a day," and he contrasted this situation with the occasional days he had on his farm, when his only cares were the condition of his grapevines, his horses, and his cattle.[31]

He sought retirement with rest and relaxation from the summer of 1838 on, and he endeavored to bring the Bank into such a position that his successors could operate it either as a large commercial bank or as an institution recognized and used by the government in the same manner as the first and second banks of the United States. He was seeking to free the Bank from entanglement with the stock and commodity markets and to make peace with its political, commercial, and financial enemies. But fortune, which had brought him victory in all that he desired except the literal recharter as a national bank, now deserted him. Few of the things he hoped to accomplish before his retirement actually materialized, for pressures were developing in the national and international economy which made it impossible for the United States Bank to become a simple state bank or the central institution in a restored national system of banks.

[31] N. Biddle to J. Hamilton, October 25, 1837, in the Biddle Manuscripts in the Library of Congress; N. Biddle, memorandum, October 3, 1838, in the Biddle Manuscripts in the Historical Society of Pennsylvania.

⤳ 32 ⤳

Preparing To Leave the Bank

*B*iddle was confronted with two major tasks in the fall and winter of 1838–39; the first was to provide the means so that the resumption of specie payments by the banks of the Southwest, when it occurred in early January, would be permanent and the second was to dispose of the large amount of cotton he owned in the warehouses of Humphreys and Biddle without a crippling loss. Both proved to be more difficult than he had expected. The sale of the cotton was hindered by a renewal of monetary troubles in Great Britain. Throughout this fall and winter the British were once again losing bullion, but this time the American trade was only a minor factor. The first and most important cause of the drain of gold was the failure of the corn crop. Large quantities of foodstuffs were imported from other European countries just at a moment when political and economic disturbances on the Continent and in other areas of the world lessened the purchases of British goods. In South America the French were blockading Buenos Aires, destroying trade in an effort to collect mercantile debts, and in China the dispute over the opium trade eliminated this profitable market. The ambitions of Mehemet Ali were disturbing the Mediterranean area, and in India the Afghan border was seething with intrigue and unrest. Other causes of discord were the Chartist movement in Great Britain itself, the Anglo-American dispute over the Maine boundary, and the rivalry between the French, the British, and the Americans as to which of these countries was to have the most influence in the newly established Republic of Texas.[1]

Western Europe, especially the new kingdom of Belgium, had just experienced the close of a boom in all branches of banking and trade, and the Banque de Belgique had been forced to suspend payments. Runs had been started in Paris on the house of Lafitte and other banks, and throughout the country there were a general collapse of commercial credit and a wave of

[1] Clapham, *Bank of England*, II, 165–67; Leland H. Jenks, *The Migration of British Capital to 1875* (New York, 1927), p. 96.

bankruptcies. French and Belgian prices and exchanges fell and made it profitable for British merchants to buy in these markets rather than to sell.

The market rate of discount in London responded to these changes in the political and economic situation, rising from 2½ per cent early in 1838 to 3¾ per cent in the fall, but the directors of the Bank of England exhibited no concern. Instead of checking the drain of bullion when it began, they seemed determined to encourage it, and on November 29 they offered to make the usual quarterly advances on bills of exchange and other securities at the existing rate of 3½ per cent. This evidence of confidence immediately eased monetary conditions in Great Britain, and Biddle, who had expected to take a loss on his cotton, was able to realize a large profit. In October, expecting lower prices later, he had ordered all the holdover stock sold, but Humphreys, who was in touch with the market, refused to be hurried. He too had been pessimistic earlier in the season. Demand had been slight all through the summer, and Edward Biddle, who had arrived in Liverpool in August, reported to his father that there seemed little hope for any profitable sales.[2]

Biddle did what he could to comfort his son. "You have done all that you were expected to do," he wrote; "and now, whatever happens, you and Mr. Humphreys must make up your minds and close the sales. If this year's business does not end as well as you hoped; next year's may. Above all you must not make yourself unhappy about the result. We want the money and therefore must take our chance of good or ill fortune." Toward the close of October demand began to increase. Humphreys and Biddle, who were the only house in Liverpool that had held on to cotton, were able to sell largely at ever increasing prices, and Humphreys triumphantly wrote, "Never was a position more completely reversed than ours." He had been denounced as foolish and obstinate in refusing to sell when all other firms were getting rid of cotton, and it had been freely predicted that he would be left with an undisposable surplus on his hands. "These sneers," he reported to Biddle, "were freely indulged in from the Bank parlour in London to the pot house in Liverpool," but his profitable sales during recent weeks had proved him to be right.[3]

Biddle was pleased at this happy result. What he wanted, however, was for Humphreys to dispose of the cotton so that at the end of the year an announcement could be made that all the Bank's extraordinary advances for the purchase of commodities had been repaid. He was thus disappointed that his orders for immediate sale had been disregarded, but there was

[2] M. Humphreys to N. Biddle, July 4, 5, 20, 24, September 7, 1838; E. C. Biddle to N. Biddle, August 5, September 6, October 1, 19, 1838; N. Biddle to J. W. Webb, October 13, 1838; N. Biddle to S. Jaudon, October 19, 1838, in the Biddle Manuscripts in the Library of Congress.

[3] N. Biddle to E. C. Biddle, October, 1838; M. Humphreys to N. Biddle, November 30, 1838, in the Biddle Manuscripts in the Library of Congress.

nothing he could do from Philadelphia to hurry his agents. He had to wait for their action, and, in the meantime, he had more than enough to keep him busy in the United States. He had to make certain that the south-western banks would be able to resume specie payments, a difficult operation because it required money and credit to be kept easy in the Southwest so that cotton and other commodities would flow to the market and, at the same time, to make certain that in the Northeast there were not enough money and credit to finance an undue expansion of the imports and sales of manufactured goods. The drain of specie from one section of the United States to another and from the United States to Europe was what he was trying to prevent, for, if either occurred in substantial amounts, the south-western banks would be unable to resume.

He imposed restrictions on credit in the Northeast by requiring all borrowers from the Bank or its agencies to reduce their old loans by 15 per cent every sixty days, and he rejected all new applications for loans except those that would encourage the purchase of commodities or exchange from the interior. But the other eastern banks refused to follow his lead. They acted on the assumption that their financial difficulties were over, and, they freely made loans to all who were in position to borrow, regardless of the purpose for which the money was to be used. The merchants, anxious to increase their depleted stocks of goods, placed large orders in Europe and pressed the imported goods upon their customers in the interior. Had Biddle still had control of the government deosits, he could have checked this movement before it became dangerous by calling on the other banks to settle their balances, but he could do very little in the existing situation. His advances to the banks in the southwestern states had placed his institution in debt to the other eastern banks, and he had to stand by idly as they financed a growing boom in imports.[4]

The volume of exports was low. American prices as the result of the easy-money and easy-credit conditions in the southern and southwestern ports were generally higher than the current quotations in Great Britain and Europe. There had been relatively few purchases, so that there was less British and European exchange available than there were debts to pay. The importing merchants began to compete with one another for this limited supply of exchange, and the rates were driven upward to the point where the export of specie was about to begin. This movement, if carried too far, would make it impossible for the southwestern banks to resume payments, and Biddle, who had hoped to go through the fall without increasing the debt of the Bank or selling any substantial amount of exchange, was forced to intervene.

The critical moment came on November 20. The ship "Great Western" was to sail three days later, and no exchange was for sale on the New York

[4] N. Biddle to T. Dunlap, December 6, 1838, in the Biddle Manuscripts in the Library of Congress; Smith, *Economic Aspects of the Second Bank*, pp. 212-13,

market. Individuals and firms with debts to pay become frantic, and reports spread that a major export of specie would occur. Thomas Dunlap, assistant cashier of the Bank, had been sent to New York in anticipation of this crisis, and on the day that the rates jumped upward, Biddle sent him four hundred and ninety-eight thousand dollars in drafts on Jaudon and Hottinguer, but asked him to "bring them back safe and unused to me unless in your cool and collected mind you see a strong necessity for using them for the public safety." These restrictive instructions were reinforced the next day when Biddle wrote: "I hope you have not been obliged to use the $498,000, not a dollar of it. I hope you will not be obliged to use the $75,000 sent today, not a dollar of it. There will be frights among some of those around you which would induce them to wish for the immediate use of the funds. You will not yield to the use of them except in case of extreme need."[5]

The extreme need, in Dunlap's opinion, did develop, and he sold the bills of exchange. There was no substantial export of specie, and P. P. F. DeGrand, observant and well-informed financial writer that he was, congratulated Biddle on his "great plan of lifting the whole country into specie payments and on your excellent move in aid of this plan, checking the export of specie by selling in New York the needful amount of exchange." Biddle was also pleased with this apparent success. "The events of the day," he wrote Humphreys, "satisfy me that for the security of this country we must stop the exportation of specie, which, if it continues, will convulse the banks a second time. That exportation to a very great extent has been prevented wholly by the Bank of the United States."[6]

He expected this specie crisis to make money scarce in New York, but he turned out to be wrong. The banks continued to discount the notes of importers, and Biddle, to increase the monetary pressure, sold bonds of the United States Bank and other securities in New York. He also told Dunlap to sell bills of exchange in sufficient quantities to keep the rate below the specie point, but none of these measures had the expected effect. "I am puzzled to know," he wrote in early December, "whence comes the money to buy all the exchange we sell"; in another letter he said: "These banks seem to be insane that they do not immediately make money worth two per cent, but what will not crazy people do when their keeper is locked up. I flatter myself that I know one of the keepers who shall be nameless, who, when he is able to leave his room, will make a stir among the maniacs."[7]

[5] N. Biddle to T. Dunlap, November 20, 21, 1838, in the Biddle Manuscripts in the Library of Congress.

[6] P. P. F. DeGrand to N. Biddle, November 29, 1838; N. Biddle to M. Humphreys, November 21, 1828, in the Biddle Manuscripts in the Library of Congress.

[7] N. Biddle to T. Dunlap, December 5, 6, 1838, in the Biddle Manuscripts in the Library of Congress.

The New York banks began to curtail immediately afterward. The Bank's sales of stocks, bonds, and exchange had increased its balances against them, and, when payment was demanded, they had to restrict their loans. The rates of foreign exchange declined below the specie point, the pressure upon the interior was relaxed, and the banks of the southwestern area resumed payments as scheduled. Throughout the fall Biddle had intended to use this decisive event as the occasion for announcing not only his personal resignation but also the Bank's permanent retirement from the stock and commodity markets. He had hoped also to declare that all the Bank's political controversies were over, but, as things had developed, this hope had to be abandoned. He could not resign at this moment because the Pennsylvania Democrats, encouraged by Van Buren, were making a new assault on the Bank's charter. Biddle knew too much about politics to have expected the President to acknowledge that he and Jackson had been wrong in the various experiments with banks and the currency, but it had not semed impossible that Van Buren would refer approvingly in his annual message to the aid given by the Bank in bringing about the resumption of specie payments.

In an effort to persuade the administration to adopt this course, Biddle, on November 27, had written identical letters to Forsyth and Poinsett which said: "The course of the government during the last few years has made it more sincere friends than it can ever gain by continuing these clamors about a metallic currency and the subtreasury; and these friends will fully indemnify it for any political defections from the ultras and vagabonds who make these outcrys." The country needed and wanted repose. It would thank no man, esteem no man, who continued to war on the banks.[8] Van Buren had not wanted to hear such advice. He did not listen to Biddle, to the conservative Democrats, or to Poinsett and Forsyth in preparing the financial paragraphs in his message. Instead he remained loyal to Jackson, Benton, and the Locofocos and recommended anew the subtreasury system for the safekeeping and transfer of government funds. In regard to the recharter of the national bank he wrote: "We have been spared the mortification of seeing the distresses of the community for their third time seized on to fasten upon the country so dangerous an institution. . . . The scenes through which we have passed conclusively prove how little our commerce, agriculture, manufactures, or finances require such [a bank], and what dangers are attendant on its power; a power, I trust, never to be conferred by the American people upon their government, and still less upon individuals not responsible to them for its unavoidable abuse." The rapid recovery from the crisis and the resumption of specie payments were cited as examples of the free working of "private capital, enterprise, and prudence" when left to the guidance of natural economic laws, and no

[8] N. Biddle to J. Forsyth and J. Poinsett, November 27, 1838, in the Biddle Manuscripts in the Library of Congress.

mention was made of the ingenious program worked out by Biddle which had enabled these laws to have this result.[9]

This renewal of the war upon the banks and the credit system was not limited to the harsh words in the message. The Treasury began to withdraw the deposits from the United States Bank, not by expenditures in the South and West, but by transfer drafts to the eastern banks, and a new move to challenge the constitutional validity of the charter was started in the Pennsylvania legislature. Instead of replying in kind to Van Buren and his party, Biddle did all that he could to maintain an appearance of peace. He made no reply to the President's message except by persuading Webster to say in the Senate that Van Buren had been wrong when he attributed the resumption of specie payments to the free operation of economic laws. It had been made possible through the co-operation of the government and the United States Bank in the sale and purchase of the bonds the preceding summer and by the use of the Bank's notes for government payments in the interior of the country.[10]

Biddle himself did publish another long public letter at the close of 1838, but in it he made no allusion, explicit or implied, to Van Buren's message. It had been written as a statement to accompany his resignation, but he published it earlier because of another unexpected development at the beginning of December. The cotton-purchasing agents, who had been sent back to the South and Southwest in the fall of 1838, had been given few orders to buy, and these only at the most important markets. The others, among whom was John Ingersoll of Natchez, had been given authority to make advances of two-thirds of the current price to any holders of cotton who would ship it at their own risk and expense to Humphreys and Biddle for sale, but this offer was insufficient to attract any takers. Ingersoll, a young and inexperienced cotton dealer, was disappointed at the results of his season's work, and, to attract the attention of the holders of cotton, he published a circular in which he claimed to be an agent of Humphreys and Biddle and expressed a willingness to make advances with an agreement that the cotton would not be sold until the following summer, in order, he explicitly said, that the owner could "realize the best market price of the season."[11]

Ingersoll apparently did not understand his own situation. His contract was with Bevan and Humphreys, who were acting for Nicholas Biddle, and he had no connection of any kind with Humphreys and Biddle. He did not mean to do anything improper; all he was trying to do was to get some commissions, and he thought he could do so by styling himself an agent of

[9] *Niles' Register*, LV (1838), 227–28.

[10] N. Biddle to J. Poinsett, December 31, 1838, in the Poinsett Manuscripts in the Library of Congress; N. Biddle to D. Webster, January 21, 1839, in the Biddle Manuscripts in the Library of Congress.

[11] *Journal of Commerce* (New York), December 4, 1838.

Humphreys and Biddle. He was also unable to distinguish between an expression of desire by a Liverpool merchant to hold the cotton for a profitable sale and the unconditional offer contained in the circular to hold for a specified time. But his unauthorized publication did great harm. It seemed to confirm all the fears and suspicions that had been aroused by the Bank's cotton operations, and an editorial in a New York commercial paper interpreted it to mean that "Mr. Biddle is again in the cotton market, sweeping largely at the highest prices." The writer predicted a disastrous end to this new intervention by the Bank to enhance the price of cotton and justified his conclusion by saying, "The laws of trade are the laws of One greater than Nicholas Biddle."[12]

A newspaper in Liverpool, previously friendly to Humphreys and Biddle, said: "Should this kind of operation be allowed to succeed it will drive the independent merchant out of the trade, and place the English manufacturer entirely at the mercy of the banking monopolists in America." And the governor of the Bank of England, usually not an alarmist, expressed his belief that the United States Bank planned to gain complete control of the cotton market "and thus establish any future price that Mr. Biddle chose to put upon it in Europe." Old friends of Biddle were shocked by the circular. Some who had defended the previous purchases of cotton called for an alliance of English and American merchants and banks to defeat the projected monopoly, and Charles A. Davis, the author of the Jack Downing letters, wrote Biddle: "I am free to say that if I thought any bank . . . contemplated a habitual system, such as charged in this instance, I'd grind my axe and go into conflict."[13]

This unfortunate publication seemed likely to do the Bank more harm than Van Buren's renewal of hostilities; indeed, it promised to alienate from the Bank the entire financial and mercantile community of the United States, Great Britain, and Europe.[14] The simple denial of Ingersoll's authority to act in the name of Humphreys and Biddle, issued immediately upon the appearance of the circular, did not seem a sufficient answer to the distrust and suspicion that had been aroused, so Biddle decided to publish his previously prepared statement. He made no direct reference to the circular, confining himself to a positive statement of what he had planned and accomplished: the payment of the American debt in Europe, the repeal of the specie circular, and the general resumption of specie payments. "Of the future," he wrote, "it is difficult to speak, but in that future

12 *Ibid.*

13 C. A. Davis to N. Biddle, December 6, 1838; R. Colt to N. Biddle, December 8, 11, 1838; M. Humphreys to N. Biddle, January 7, 1839, in the Biddle Manuscripts in the Library of Congress; *Times* (Liverpool), December 25, 1838.

14 Bevan and Humphreys to the Public, December 7, 1838; N. Biddle to E. C. Biddle, December 22, 1838, in the Biddle Manuscripts in the Library of Congress; J. Ingersoll to the editor, *Free Trader* (Natchez), August 12, 1839, quoted in *Journal of Commerce* (New York), August 26, 1839.

the Bank of the United States will no longer occupy its past position. . . . It has no longer any responsibility for the Union. It has no longer any controversies with the government of the Union. It now desires only repose, and will take its rank hereafter as a simple state institution, devoted exclusively to its own affairs."[15]

He assured the other bankers and the merchants that the Bank would not continue its advances on cotton, other commodities, and stocks and that it would no longer compete with brokers and merchants. These measures had been undertaken because of the disturbed situation of the country; they were essentially temporary emergency measures, "adopted in the midst of a public calamity, and to be discontinued with the necessity which caused them. As soon, therefore, as the capital and industry of the country had time to subside into their accustomed channels, these operations were relinquished, and now they have totally and finally ceased." The final paragraph was a personal statement in which he spoke of his approaching retirement. He rejoiced, he said, that "this position of the Bank absolves me from many cares and duties. In the general confusion of affairs during the last two years, it has been my lot to be more prominent than my own inclination prompted, and often assume a station which would have better fitted others. But public calamities justify the apparent forwardness they require, as great dangers are best met by defying them. My task is now ended, and I gladly withdraw from these responsibilities, carrying with me the only satisfaction I ever sought in them, the consciousness of having done my duty to the country as a good citizen."[16]

Once this letter had been published, Biddle felt as if his retirement was an accomplished fact. "This abdication of mine is quite refreshing," he wrote. "I feel like Sylla I suppose felt when he renounced his authority, and my worthy fellow citizens may now sleep in peace, satisfied that I shall buy neither cotton nor men." For more than ten years he had been essentially a public man, almost an institution, for he and the Bank of the United States had been so closely identified in the world's eyes that he had little private life of his own. He was now like a boy released from school, and he sought adventure and recreation. Both were supplied by the sudden appearance in Philadelphia of a notorious, exciting, and beautiful European adventuress by the name of Amerigo Vespucci. She had come to America to advance her fortunes, and she hoped that a grateful Congress would make an appropriation of public lands to her as a descendant of the great navigator for whom she and the continent alike had been named.[17]

She was staying at the home of one of Jane Biddle's closest friends,

[15] N. Biddle to J. Q. Adams, December 10, 1838, in *House Executive Document* (29th Cong., 1st sess.), No. 226, pp. 404–8.

[16] *Ibid.*

[17] "Diaries of Sidney George Fisher, 1838–1839," *Pennsylvania Magazine of History and Biography*, LXXVI (1952), 49.

Adele Segoigne, and through the Biddles she was introduced into the city's society. Her behavior was proper and discreet, but the young bachelors of the town reported to one another that, according to the "story" from New York, she was no better than she should be. Biddle must have heard these reports, but he was fascinated by the "black-eyed, well-formed Italian lady," who, according to her own account, was the daughter of a Florentine notary and had been the mistress of a Polish noble who had lost his life in the revolutionary troubles in Ravenna and Bologna. She had fought in these same battles at her lover's side, dressed as a man, and she had a saber scar on her head to prove that her story was true.[18]

Biddle's relationship with Signora Vespucci was essentially innocent, for he had little talent for any sort of romantic intrigue. He took her to inspect the Eastern State Penitentiary and the library of the American Philosophical Society. He brought her to his home for Christmas dinner with the family and danced with her at a "large and gay" party given by Miss Segoigne. It was, nevertheless, a romance, and when she left Philadelphia he wrote in his journal: "Vespucci went this morning to Washington. . . . Let me recall what I have seen of her." He never saw her again, though he became treasurer of a fund raised for her by private subscription among the representatives and senators in Washington. Amerigo, disappointed in her efforts to get an appropriation of public lands, turned to more profitable fields. She became the mistress of Prince John Van Buren, who, having lost all his money to George Parish in a poker game, put her up as a final stake, and she closed her career as "Parish's fancy woman," living in "utter loneliness" at his mansion in Ogdensburg, New York.[19]

This romantic interlude was the one bright spot in Biddle's life during the early months of 1839, for it was proving to be unexpectedly difficult for him to get the Bank in such a position that he could conscientiously resign. There were no major problems but a number of nagging details, chiefly the defeat of the political attack on the charter and the winding-up of the cotton operations. The first of these was easily handled. The Bank's agent in Harrisburg made much of the fact that the government, by selling the bonds to the Bank and using it as a place of deposit, had effectively recognized its legitimacy, and many of the rank and file of the party were converted to "the opinion that the monster has ceased to be offensive." Others were appealed to on a different ground, but here it proved advisable to move cautiously, for, as the agent reported to Biddle, unless he concealed how much he had to spend, such was their avariciousness that he

18 N. Biddle, manuscript journal, in the Biddle Manuscripts in the Historical Society of Pennsylvania.

19 N. Biddle to S. R. Wood, December 24, 1838, in the Gratz Manuscript Collection in the Historical Society of Pennsylvania; N. Biddle to J. Vaughan, January 2, 1839, in the Manuscript Collection of the American Philosophical Society; Vincent Nolte, *Fifty Years in Both Hemispheres,* p. 434; *New York: A Guide to the Empire State* (New York, 1940), p. 534.

"would be literally devoured." The number that demanded bribes in this session, as in others, was relatively small, but the Bank again purchased immunity from the Pennsylvania legislature by a loan to the state treasury to enable it to pay interest on its previously issued bonds. The hostility engendered by Van Buren's message evaporated as the realities of Pennsylvania's financial position became clear, and the legislature adjourned without taking any action in regard to the Bank or its charter.[20]

Biddle also took steps to insure that the resumption of specie payments would be relatively permanent. The large imports from Europe in the fall and their distribution throughout the country made this task more difficult because the merchants and banks of New York, pushed by the monetary shortage brought about by the Bank in December, were attempting to collect what was owed in the interior without buying any of the produce. Once again Biddle had to do two contradictory things at the same time: to keep money easy in the areas where the banks had just gone through the painful process of resumption and tight in New York and the East to prevent an expansion of imports.

The Bank sold post notes, stocks, bonds, and foreign exchange in New York to dry up surplus funds and simultaneously eased the situation of the southwestern banks by postponing collections of debts owed to the United States Bank. These policies proved effective, and for a brief period in February and March it seemed as if the United States had effectively surmounted its financial difficulties.[21] Biddle had little to do except wait for the final reports from Humphreys, and at the close of February he decided to visit Washington. He had no business there, but he was received so cordially by the President and the members of the Cabinet that many persons believed that the administration was about to change its position. Biddle had no such illusions, but he did want peace, and he was pleased to be able to report to Jaudon: "All the traces of our recent hostilities are wholly effaced, and I may perhaps be able to bring about something useful to the country through the agency of the Bank." He had dinner at the White House, but Van Buren gave him no opening to discuss any of his hopes and plans. All the company present were opposed to the administration, and the chief subject of conversation was one of the President's

[20] D. M. Brodhead to N. Biddle, January 13, 1839; C. S. Boker to N. Biddle, January 12, 20, 22, 25, 30, 1839; N. Biddle to C. S. Boker, January 18, 19, 31, 1839; N. Biddle to C. B. Penrose, January 31, 1839, in the Biddle Manuscripts in the Library of Congress.

[21] J. Wilkins to J. Hagerty, January 19, 1839; J. Hagerty to J. Wilkins, January 19, 1839; J. Hagerty to N. Biddle, January 21, 25, 31, February 1, 1839; N. Biddle to J. Cowperthwaite, January 26, 1839; J. Cowperthwaite to N. Biddle, February 24, 1839; N. Biddle to E. R. Biddle, February 24, 1839, in the Biddle Manuscripts in the Library of Congress.

favorite topics, "the maintenance of friendly feelings and intercourse with those opposed to us politically."[22]

Exactly what Biddle had hoped to accomplish by this visit to Washington was never made clear. He may have had no other purpose than that which he avowed—to pay a friendly visit—but immediately after his return, without any previous discussion or warning, he decided to close the agency in London. On March 8 he wrote Jaudon: "The objects which occasioned your visit to Europe have been accomplished. . . . Our wish therefore is that you should . . . open a negotiation with some house in London to do the business of the Bank." His stated reason for this decision was that he did not wish to "prolong an establishment which seems at variance with the views of the Bank of England," and he apparently believed that if Baring Brothers and Company or some other established firm would take over the agency, including its large stock account, much of the increasing British hostility to the Bank and to American enterprise generally would be overcome.[23]

Shortly afterward he received word from Humphreys that all the cotton from the preceding year's crop had been sold, with the last lot going "at the highest rate of the week," which was an appropriate conclusion to this courageous and constructive venture.[24] In the summer of 1837, Biddle had risked all that he possessed to make a market in the South and Southwest for American produce as the only method through which domestic and foreign debts could be paid. He had undertaken this personal venture reluctantly. The Bank, forbidden by its charter to purchase commodities, could not do so, and none of the directors of the Bank had been willing to accept the risk. Opponents and critics of the undertaking had freely predicted that it would end with great losses and that it would destroy the solvency of the Bank; but, when the accounts were closed, the Bank had been repaid all its advances with interest, and there was a surplus of one million, four hundred thousand dollars.

Had there been a loss, Biddle would have had to make up the deficiency; so legally and morally he was entitled to the profits. He had not entered the venture for profit, but there it was, and it was embarrassingly large. Some disposition had to be made of it, and Biddle divided it into four parts. The largest—six hundred thousand dollars—was left with the Bank "to provide against all possible contingency"; two parts of two hundred thou-

[22] R. Smith to N. Biddle, February 21, 1839; N. Biddle to S. Jaudon, February 23, 1839, in the Biddle Manuscripts in the Library of Congress; N. Biddle, manuscript journal, in the Biddle Manuscripts in the Historical Society of Pennsylvania; Hamilton, *Reminiscences*, p. 312.

[23] N. Biddle to S. Jaudon, March 8, 1839, in the Biddle Manuscripts in the Library of Congress.

[24] M. Humpreys to N. Biddle, January 25, February 5, 12, 25, March 20, 1839, in the Biddle Manuscripts in the Library of Congress.

sand dollars each were given to Joseph Cowperthwaite and Thomas Dunlap, cashier and assistant cashier who had attended to all the details of the operation; and the remaining four hundred thousand dollars were deposited in Biddle's personal account.[25]

This final division occurred after Biddle had left the Bank. On March 29, 1839, twenty years and two months after he had first been appointed a director by President Monroe, he tendered his resignation to the directors on the ground that his long years of service had given him "the right to claim the relaxation and repose which approaching age and precarious health require." He assured his son that this was the only reason for his decision, but there were those who did not believe him. Thomas W. Ward, the American agent of Barings, reported that Biddle had taken "advantage of a temporary improvement in the affairs of the Bank to escape from a difficult situation"; and the *Times,* hostile as always, stated that, whatever truth there might be in the plea of ill health, it was more probable that the "uncertain prospects of the Bank" were the real cause of his resignation, for Biddle was "too sagacious not to perceive that a new crisis in American banking is threatened and all but inevitable." These statements seemed prophetic six months later, and subsequent observers have accepted not only them but also the harsher judgment of Charles Ingersoll, who charged that when Biddle resigned "the whole system was rotten and the Bank ruined."[26] To his policies as president of the United States Bank were attributed all the damage that the American economy suffered during the world-wide depression of 1839–44.

But if any single institution or group of men was responsible for this economic catastrophe, it was not Biddle and his associates, but the Bank of England and its directors. As one American merchant put it, they exhibited neither caution, sagacity, nor boldness in exercising their responsibilities as the central bank of the country that was the center of world commerce and finance. They were incautious when prudence was indispensable, alarmed and timid when great boldness and skill were required, and periodically during these disturbed years they produced commercial revulsion which carried distress across the Atlantic. Biddle was indebted to their lack of caution in the fall and winter of 1838–39 for the great profits he had derived from the sale of his cotton; but their

[25] Report of the Stockholders' Committee, April 3, 1831; N. Biddle to J. M. Clayton, April 8, 1831, in *House Executive Document* (29th Cong., 1st sess.), No. 226, pp. 275–82, 419–20; *Judge Barton's Opinion in the Case of Nicholas Biddle and Others vs. Henry Morris,* corrected proof-sheets in the Biddle Manuscripts in the Library of Congress.

[26] N. Biddle to the Board of Directors of the Bank of the United States, March 29, 1839, in the Biddle Manuscripts at "Andalusia"; N. Biddle to E. C. Biddle, April 19, 1839, in the Biddle Manuscripts in the private collection of Nicholas B. Wainwright; T. Ward to Baring Brothers and Company, April 2, 1839, quoted in Smith, *Economic Aspects of the Second Bank,* p. 213; the *Times* (London), May 1, 1839; Ingersoll, *Historical Sketches,* II, 285.

failure to take adequate steps to stop the export of bullion was to force them to curtail too drastically and suddenly in the spring. They set in motion a series of pressures which were to bring on a new crisis in the summer of 1839. Biddle had not foreseen this crisis when he resigned. As he told the directors on the day he left his office, he was confident that he was leaving "the affairs of the institution in a state of great prosperity and in the hands of able directors and officers."[27]

[27] J. C. Levy to N. Biddle, January 17, 1838, in the Biddle Manuscripts in the Library of Congress. For British criticism of the Bank of England from 1836 to 1841 which confirms this harsh judgment by a Charleston, South Carolina, merchant see testimony of Samual J. Lloyd, Horsley Palmer, George W. Norman, and others in *Reports of the Select Committees of the House of Commons on Banks of Issue, 1841, 1842;* the weekly letters of Henry Burgess in *Circular to Bankers* (London); Tooke, *History of Prices;* and Clapham, *Bank of England,* II, 159–85.

Retirement?

*B*iddle's plea of ill health, though not disingenuous, was only one of the reasons for his decision to resign. He had no organic disability. He was suffering from fatigue of body and mind brought about by the strains and tensions of the preceding ten years, the thousands of details of which he had had to be cognizant, and the complicated problems he had been forced to solve. He did need a period of rest and recreation, but he was not yet of an age to think of total retirement. His secret ambition was to be elected President of the United States, and when he left the Bank in the spring of 1839, it did not seem impossible. The Whigs were seeking a candidate who would arouse the enthusiasm of the nation in a manner that neither Harrison nor White had been able to do in the previous campaign. Clay, of course, was the obvious choice, but Webster, his perennial rival, would not give his consent. Webster himself lacked sufficient strength in the South and West to win his long-coveted prize, but Biddle, in spite of his eastern residence, was more popular in these interior regions than anywhere else.[1]

Biddle's candidacy, if it could be called that, was that of a nationalist seeking to advance the freedom and strength of America, and the reason for his opposition to Jackson and Van Buren was his firm belief that their policies weakened the nation. Both wanted personal power, he was certain, not national strength, and he looked upon them and their associates as demagogues who were betraying the people they pretended to love. He was speaking the truth in the spring of 1838 when he told a friend in the Senate: "I cordially unite with you in the hope that the dominion of these miserable people is verging to its close. Certainly no civilized country was ever so long subjected to a misrule . . . so contemptible." He similarly told Jaudon that it was the great consolation of his life that "in the highest and palmiest state of this colossal power, I never in thought, word, or deed capitulated to it or compromised with it," for this, he insisted, "was the

[1] N. Biddle, manuscript journal, in the Biddle Manuscripts in the Historical Society of Pennsylvania.

path of honor and ultimately the road to safety however hazardous it might appear."[2]

His reputation had been made as a public banker, and the recharter of the national bank was one of the objectives that motivated him, but he was also an uncompromising advocate of internal improvements through the united efforts of city, state, and national governments in close co-operation with private individuals. He thought that Jackson's veto of the bill subscribing to the stock of the Maysville Road Company was one of the unwisest acts of that unwise administration; after it had occurred, the Bank, through direct and indirect aid to private companies and states had tried to take the place of the national government. It had contributed "to the internal improvements of the United States at least fifteen million dollars" through purchases of stock, advances, and loans; and each of these local roads, railroads, and canals, in Biddle's opinion, had helped in the solution of "the great problem of free institutions, how to create a central power at once not too strong for freedom, yet strong enough to radiate vigorously to the extremities." It was not merely the exchanges of commerce that were facilitated by these improvements but the more important interchange of knowledge and acquaintance between distant sections. Men were enabled to meet together, overcoming personal prejudice, local rivalries, and party passions, harmoniously blending their various and peculiar interests into the spirit of political union.[3]

Biddle's nationalist views also made him an enthusiastic supporter of territorial expansion. According to Senator Henry S. Foote of Mississippi, Biddle did not at all doubt that in time, perhaps in a few years, all the North American continent, including the islands of the Gulf of Mexico, would be brought under "the Stars and Stripes"; in personal conversations Biddle urged with great force that "until the Mexican Gulf should be made our Mare Clausum, all the commerce of the western states and territories, floating down the Mississippi and its tributaries, would be constantly exposed to foreign molestation." To facilitate this territorial expansion, Biddle supported every projected road, railroad, or canal through the Middle American Isthmus that was proposed by Americans, and he favored the immediate annexation of Texas. He was alarmed by the diplomatic overtures being made to the new republic by Great Britain and France, and he warned Secretary of State Forsyth of the importance of this "immense cotton country" to these nations.[4]

2 N. Biddle to J. M. Clayton, March 4, 1838; N. Biddle to S. Jaudon, August 3, 15, 1838, in the Biddle Manuscripts in the Library of Congress.

3 Niles' Register, LII (1837), 358–59; United States Gazette (Philadelphia), June 4, 1840.

4 N. Biddle to J. Forsyth, November 27, 1838; V. Nolte to N. Biddle, March 28, 1839; N. Biddle to C. A. Davis, July 31, 1839, in the Biddle Manuscripts in the Library of Congress; Niles' Register, LI (1836), 69; Henry S. Foote, Casket of Reminiscences (Washington, 1874), pp. 46–49.

Neither the Van Buren administration nor its opponents were willing to risk offending the antislavery opponents of the annexation of Texas before the election, and Biddle, in an effort to prove to the Texans that the United States was their "best friend," invested his personal funds in its lands and bonds. He became the unpaid financial adviser of the republic and did all that he could to aid it to raise funds in the United States and Europe. This support of territorial expansion strengthened Biddle's popularity in the South and West.[5] And it was Thomas Cooper of South Carolina who was the first to mention his name as a presidential candidate. "Why not look to the presidency?" Cooper asked. "Can your name be brought forward at a time more advantageous than the present? . . . If needful command my services such as they may be. I am, and so may you be, in the odour of political sanctity in this state: and this state is the south."[6]

Biddle made an immediate reply. "In relation to the friendly suggestion which formed the purport of your letter," he wrote, "I have received from various quarters intimation of a disposition to connect my name with the next election of president. These I have never considered seriously, nor indeed noticed at all: but to you I will speak for the first time and without reserve." He preserved this traditional tone of reluctance throughout the rest of the letter but ended with a positive consent: "I believe that the prosperity and character of the country require that those who now govern it should be removed and that all true men should unite to expel them: each taking the position either of chief or subaltern, which the general voice assigns him. I am quite sure that I have not the least affectation in saying that to myself personally, the office has not the slightest attraction. Its dignity has been degraded by the elevation to it of unworthy men, and as to mere power, I have been for years in the daily exercise of more personal authority than any president habitually enjoys. But I stand ready for the country's service. If therefore you think that my name can be productive of good, I am content to place it, as I now do, at your disposal."[7]

Others besides Cooper were thinking of Biddle as a candidate. Clay himself said to a friend that Biddle had been "spoken of as a fit person to run against Van Buren" and that he was prepared to support him heartily, "if, with him, it shall be thought we can drive the Goths from the capital." And J. Watson Webb, reporting conversations with newspapermen and

[5] S. F. Austin to N. Biddle, April 9, 1836; N. Biddle to J. Hamilton, January 23, 1838; D. Webster to N. Biddle, September 9, 10, 1838; H. Clay to N. Biddle, September 14, 1838; J. Forsyth to N. Biddle, November 29, 1838, in the Biddle Manuscripts in the Library of Congress.

[6] T. Cooper to N. Biddle, April 29, 1837, in the Biddle Manuscripts in the Library of Congress.

[7] N. Biddle to T. Cooper, May 8, 1837, in the Biddle Manuscripts in the Library of Congress.

financiers in London, told Biddle: "I am sure it will not either flatter or astonish you to learn that you are in truth considered to be the ablest financier of the age and that they look forward with confidence to you being president of the United States." Men of all ranks and stations from every section of the country paid tribute to Biddle. Francis Lieber, the political economist, wrote that few citizens had ever acquired "such celebrity founded upon private civic valor, circumspect genius and prudent tenacity." There had been "shrewd, wise, bold financiers" before, but none who had acquired importance both as financiers and as citizens; and John S. Skinner, editor of the *American Farmer*, described him as that "truly great (yea among the greatest of the great) little man sitting in the marble palace, cool as a summer morning."[8]

Charles Ingersoll, who had known Biddle since boyhood, wrote: "No American had such European repute; Jackson's was the only one comparable, and that far inferior to it. Flattered, caressed, extolled, idolized in America, Biddle was praised and respected in Europe as the most sagacious and successful banker in the world." This appraisal was confirmed by James Silk Buckingham, who, after traveling all over the United States, wrote that Biddle appeared to him the most perfect specimen of an American gentleman. He had not only "a mind of great force and originality" but also an "excellent education, highly polished manners, great urbanity, and a freedom from all those peculiarities which more or less mark the citizens of every class in this country." His private hospitalities were conducted in the best possible European taste and in a style that the most fastidious could admire, but in "his patriotism, frankness, simplicity, and application to business" he was thoroughly American.[9]

Biddle's situation was such that he could take no steps to further his candidacy until he left the Bank, but at least one of his closest associates believed his election as President was a real possibility. When the cotton operations were closed, Humphreys, speaking of the political as well as the commercial importance of this commodity, wrote: "If hereafter it should be your lot to occupy as conspicuous a position in administering the affairs of government, as you have of late years in guarding the commerce of our country, you may remember, what I now assert, that cotton bags will be much more effectual in bringing John Bull to terms than all the disciplined troops America could bring into the field." The United States, if it wished to inflict a deadly blow on Great Britain, could not resort to a more effective process than by withholding one-third or more of any one year's cotton crop. The immediate effect would be to force

[8] F. Lieber to N. Biddle, January 18, 1838; J. S. Skinner to R. Colt, February 16, 1838; J. W. Webb to N. Biddle, August 27, 1838; A. T. Burnley to N. Biddle, December 5, 1838, in the Biddle Manuscripts in the Library of Congress.

[9] Ingersoll, *Historical Sketch*, II, 285; James Silk Buckingham, *America, Historical, Statistic, and Descriptive* (New York, 1841), pp. 445–46.

prices up to a point that would suspend consumption "and thus throw out of employment an immense multitude of the most turbulent population in the world, when insurrection if not revolution might follow."[10]

Biddle did not share Humphreys' anti-British sentiments, and one of the principal reasons for his desire to get the Bank out of the stock and commodity markets was to eliminate the fears of an American monopoly that had developed in the minds of the British political and financial leaders. He did not approve of monopoly and had intervened in the markets only as a temporary measure for the common benefit of Great Britain and the United States. But his internationalistic action had been applauded by nationalists such as Humphreys, just as in a parallel circumstance his nationalistic intervention in the produce markets had been supported by the most extreme defenders of state rights.

He was too much of a political realist to overestimate his chances of gaining the Whig nomination, and he gave no outward indication that he desired anything but rest and recreation as a retired man. He went out to "Andalusia" immediately after his resignation and deliberately stayed away from Philadelphia so that his successor, Thomas Dunlap, would have complete independence. The only business problems that occupied any part of his attention were those connected with his personal obligations to the men who had helped him to carry the Bank and the nation through the economic crisis—Jaudon, Humphreys, and the cotton-purchasing agents in the South. Biddle had always thought of Jaudon as his choice to succeed him as president of the Bank. He had recommended Dunlap, a relative newcomer as an assistant cashier at the Bank and husband of a distant cousin of Biddle's, only because Jaudon could not be spared from London. But now that Jaudon was making arrangements to turn over his agency to a London firm, Biddle told him that when he returned he could have his choice of his old position as cashier or be elected president of the subsidiary in New York. In either position, Biddle said, Jaudon's authority would be equal to Dunlap's, and he added that he was making this firm offer with the complete concurrence of the board of directors and of Dunlap.

Jaudon was in need of such assurance. The sudden decision to close the London agency followed almost immediately by the announcement of Biddle's resignation had made him uncertain about the future; for a time, he thought that none of the respectable and strong firms in London would take over the agency. "I cannot . . . help thinking," he complained to Biddle, "that your name would have assisted me in this movement, as independently of the mere profit to arise from the business of the Bank, there was not a little attraction in the idea of an association however distant with yourself." His pessimism was unfounded. In May, 1839, Baring Brothers

[10] M. Humphreys to N. Biddle, January 25, 1839, in the Biddle Manuscripts in the Library of Congress.

and Company agreed to resume the agency on condition that the Bank would not again sell bonds and post notes, and, as proof of their desire to return to their former position, they advanced Jaudon two hundred thousand pounds for six months to enable him to make current payments.[11]

Jaudon would thus be free to return to the United States as soon as the contract with Barings was signed in Philadelphia. In similar fashion, though by different means, Biddle tried to repay what he thought was due Humphreys and the cotton-purchasing agents by risking some of the profits that he, Dunlap, and Cowperthwaite had made in the earlier operations. Throughout the winter and spring Humphreys complained about the small amount of cotton being shipped, and the southern agents were likewise dissatisfied with the paucity of purchases. Their commissions, the sole source of their income, were far less than the previous year, and Biddle thought it only fair to engage in a new speculation, now that he was retiring from his office and the Bank could not be held responsible. He ordered new purchases a few weeks before his formal resignation, and the purpose of this operation was to provide commissions for Humphreys and Biddle in Liverpool and the purchasing agents in the United States, not to make profits for Biddle or to meet any need of the Bank.[12]

The competing American and British merchants, however, did not recognize or appreciate this distinction, and, as soon as Biddle's agents began their purchases, it was reported that the Bank of the United States was back in the market. At first, Biddle, who thought of himself as a private citizen free to buy and sell as he pleased, ignored this criticism. But the spinners in Manchester, convinced that the price of cotton was being artificially sustained in the United States, decided to retaliate by going on short time and confining their purchases to their immediate needs. George McDuffie and James Hamilton, two of the organizers of the Cotton Planters' Association in the United States, were in Liverpool when the Manchester spinners made this decision. They were disappointed and angry because their purpose was to lay a foundation for a direct trade between the planters and manufacturers, with no intermediate charges, and they had hoped that the British manufacturers, if assured of direct access to the southern markets, would not object to the other part of the association's program, which, as McDuffie informed Biddle, was based upon "the plan first adopted by you." Their purpose was to take the cotton trade "out of the hands of moneyless and gambling speculators and give steadiness to prices" by concentrating control of the crop in the

---

11 S. Jaudon to N. Biddle, May 17, 1839; N. Biddle to S. Jaudon, July 4, 1839, in the Biddle Manuscripts in the Library of Congress; Hidy, *Baring*, pp. 276-77.

12 M. Humphreys to N. Biddle, March 20, July 4, 1839; N. Biddle to J. Hagerty, March 6, 1839, in the Biddle Manuscripts in the Library of Congress; *House Executive Document* (29th Cong., 1st sess.), No. 226, pp. 419-20.

association, which, sustained by the local banks, would release cotton for export only as it brought a profitable price.[13]

The manufacturers were unwilling to listen to any such proposals. The offer of direct trade to southern ports was no inducement, since they much preferred the situation as it was, with New York as the prime port of entry for their goods into the United States. Volume of sales was a more important consideration to British manufacturers than an increase in price, and the established facilities for marketing in New York made it possible for this port to absorb whatever was shipped to it. There were no delays because imported goods were sold at auction as soon as they arrived; none of the southern ports could provide similar assurances. The other part of the cotton planters' program—control of the price of the raw material— was exactly what the British manufacturers most feared. They had suspected that this was Biddle's purpose in 1837, and it was for this reason that they and the newspapers devoted to their interest had been violent and continuous critics of him and the Bank.

They had thought from the beginning of the cotton planters' association that Biddle was behind it, and this belief became a certainty on June 5, 1839, when, with Biddle's agents still buying in the South, an anonymous circular was issued from the New York office of S. V. S. Wilder, the American representative of Hottinguer and Company, the Bank's correspondent in Paris. The circular stated that an advance of fourteen cents a pound would be offered to any shippers of cotton to Humphreys and Biddle during the next season; assurances were given that this house would be supplied with "unfailing, adequate, and collateral aids, sufficiently powerful . . . to hold over until a greater part of the present stock of cotton in England is worked off at an advanced price." If the new crop was short, the shippers would make a large profit; but if it turned out to be abundant, the circular predicted, the excess holdings of Humphreys and Biddle "would probably induce the great and powerful interest which sustains them to enter the market in the United States early in the autumn."[14]

Biddle was as much surprised by this circular as the British manufacturers and merchants. He had not been consulted before it was issued, and it was not until several weeks had passed that he learned the names of its authors. What had happened was that McDuffie and Hamilton had returned to the United States determined to retaliate against the British manufacturers and had written the circular without the knowledge or consent of Biddle, the officers of the United States Bank, or Humphreys

[13] G. McDuffie to J. Hammond, March 31, 1839, in the Hammond Manuscripts in the Library of Congress; G. McDuffie to N. Biddle, July 26, 1839, in the Biddle Manuscripts in the Library of Congress; Govan, "An Ante-Bellum Attempt To Regulate the Price and Supply of Cotton," *North Carolina Historical Review*, XVII (1940), 302–12.

[14] *Times* (London), April 18, May 1, 1839; *Hazard's Commercial and Statistical Register*, I (1839), 89–90; *Journal of Commerce* (New York), June 6, 1839.

and Biddle. The Bank, as soon as the circular appeared, issued a denial of any connection with the scheme, and Wilder, from whose office it had appeared, published a statement averring that the proposal did not emanate from Humphreys and Biddle and that "the Bank of the United States had nothing whatever to do with it."[15]

These denials would not have been believed if Biddle had continued his purchases of cotton, so he instructed his agents to stop, and Jaudon, whose arrangements to close up the agency had been hindered by the renewed criticism of the Bank, was pleased. "I think it very important," he wrote, "that the Bank should get back as soon as possible to the old strict line of business. . . . Nor is it for the Bank only that I am anxious. . . . I feel great anxiety that you and Dunlap should not hazard the very large fortunes that you have acquired. You succeeded last year by a coincidence of circumstances that seldom happens, and exactly such will never happen again."[16]

Thus in June, somewhat unwillingly, Biddle retired from all business activity, but it was not to be for long. A new period of financial crisis was about to begin, brought about, as had been its predecessor in the spring of 1837, by a coincidence of pressures upon the banks of the eastern United States from Great Britain, on the one hand, and from the interior of America, on the other. The Bank of England had done nothing the preceding winter to protect Britain from the effect of the Belgian and French failures in December, nor had it shown alarm when between January and March it lost one and a quarter million pounds in specie to Europe and other areas of the world. The directors did advance the buying rate of gold by one and a half pence on February 1, but they renewed their offer to make quarterly advances on bills of exchange and other securities at the unchanged rate of $3\frac{1}{2}$ per cent.

Speculation in stocks and commodities, which had begun to slow down, was given a new stimulus, and Humphreys reported to Biddle that the announcement by the Bank had given instant relief to the money market. He utilized this opportunity to get the firm in comfortable shape and made arrangements with his brokers for an additional credit of one hundred thousand pounds. He also sent Jaudon a hundred and fifty thousand pounds to use for the Bank's payments but warned Biddle that he expected a change. He thought that the finances of Great Britain and Europe were in a critical condition and that the continuance of the existing rediscount rate had been "a bold political maneuver" by the Bank of England to enable the Chancellor of the Exchequer to obtain a needed loan.[17]

15 *Journal of Commerce* (New York), June 10, 11, 1839; *Times* (Liverpool), June 25, 1839; *Times* (London), June 29, 1839.

16 S. Jaudon to N. Biddle, July 5, 1839, in the Biddle Manuscripts in the Library of Congress.

17 M. Humphreys to N. Biddle, March 7, April 6, 1839, in the Biddle Manuscripts in the Library of Congress; Clapham, *Bank of England*, II, 167–68; Hidy, *Baring*, pp. 273–75.

Humphreys proved to be a true prophet. In April the Bank of England began to sell exchequer bills and exchange to dry up surplus funds, and on May 16, after all the government's needs had been met, it advanced the rediscount rate to 5 per cent. This increase in the cost of money made it almost impossible for Jaudon to sell American securities or for Humphreys to dispose of cotton. Barings and other merchants could sell at discounts, but Jaudon and Humphreys were reluctant to force the owners of the stocks and commodities to accept a loss. They remained out of the market as prices declined, but their holdings at this time were such a small percentage of the total American trade with Great Britain that the protection thus afforded was inconsequential. The pressure on the money market in London and Liverpool steadily increased. It reached America in June, and here it met the domestically induced pressures brought about by the resumption of specie payments by the interior banks.[18]

Biddle had made plans in the fall of 1838 to take care of this transition period during which the banks in the South and Southwest would be forced to curtail temporarily until they and the community around them could become adjusted to the changed situation. The means of payment of debts in the Northeast was to be provided in part by notes of the United States Bank expended in the interior by the government and in part by the owners of cotton, who, deprived of local credit, would ship to markets in the Northeast or Great Britain and thus produce bills of exchange. Neither of these means had been available. The government, instead of expending its deposits in the Bank of the interior, as it had agreed to do, withdrew them by transfer drafts in the East; and the owners of cotton, instead of shipping in quantity, had been enabled to hold on in the hope of higher prices through the refusal of the banks to curtail.

What happened in the United States in the spring of 1839 illustrated clearly how much the country needed a national bank and demonstrated the truth of a statement made by one of Biddle's correspondents that "the destruction of our regulator has disarmed us of power over our . . . currency. . . . In the loss of the Bank we no longer have sword, shield or helmet to meet the blow when it comes."[19] Had the United States Bank possessed the government deposits, it could have forced the interior banks to curtail and, at the same time, have had the power to handle the other side of the domestic problem—the unnecessary scarcity and tightness of money and credit in New York and the East. The excessive importations in the fall and early winter had been brought to a halt by Biddle's corrective actions, but the New York banks, which had overencouraged this movement by an undue expansion of loans and discounts, responded to the changed monetary conditions by a drastic and oversevere curtailment. The

[18] *Niles' Register*, LVI (1839), 161, 243, 273.

[19] J. C. Levy to N. Biddle, January 17, 1838, in the Biddle Manuscripts in the Library of Congress.

importers and other merchants, pressed for the payment of what they owed, passed the pressure on to their customers in the interior, who could not obtain notes of the United States Bank or bills of exchange with which to pay.

The sole resource was specie, and the only source for this was the newly resumed banks. Agents of the northeastern merchants who had been sent into the interior to make collections were paid with notes of local banks, and, as soon as they obtained possession of these notes, they presented them to their issuers for specie. "You northern bankers and brokers," a south-western banker complained, "have been acting towards our banks ever since the resumption as though a second suspension was inevitable. . . . If anything could have caused a second suspension, it would have been the course thus pursued."[20] He had hardly made this statement when the Commercial and Railroad Bank of Vicksburg was forced to suspend specie payments, and creditors of neighboring banks, instead of lessening the pressure, began panic withdrawals and collections. The banks in turn had to press their debtors, and many of the weaker merchants failed. The most spectacular of these failures was that of Vincent Nolte in New Orleans, whose inability to pay for forty thousand bales of cotton, shipped to Liverpool and Havre, aroused suspicions concerning the solvency of everyone in the cotton trade. Soon completely solvent merchants were unable to raise money and were forced to suspend payments. Their creditors were similarly brought down, and by the beginning of June another panic was on.[21]

The New York banks stopped lending, announcing their determination to carry themselves through any contingency which might possibly occur without a suspension of specie payments, and interest rates fluctuated between 12 and 15 per cent. The week ending June 22 was described as the severest "experienced since the great pressure," but the New York banks resisted the demands of the merchants for an expansion of loans. The United States Bank followed the opposite course through the early stages of the developing crisis. Biddle's successors, in April and May, prevented the export of specie to Europe by selling bills of exchange on Jaudon and Hottinguer and avoided, as far as possible, forced collections from its debtors in Philadelphia, New York, and the interior cities. It continued this protective policy through the early part of June, but then it slowed down its sales of exchange because of Jaudon's exposed position in London and also because Hottinguer protested "at the heavy amount of drafts from the Bank." The Paris agents did more than protest; they warned the Bank

[20] S. Duncan to Jackson, Todd and Company, April 8, 1839, in the Jackson-Riddle Manuscripts in the Southern Historical Collection in the University of North Carolina Library.

[21] Niles' Register, LVI (1839), 161, 243, 273, 326.

that if it again overdrew, as it occasionally had in the past, its bills would be rejected.[22]

As the Bank gradually stopped its sales of exchange, it began to lose specie, more than a million dollars by the first of July, and shortly thereafter Dunlap wrote to Biddle: "I should be happy to see you here if you can accomplish a visit to town without inconvenience. Our matters press somewhat heavily and the benefit of your good counsel would be most acceptable. If you cannot be in town, I must take an opportunity to come to you." Where they met and what they said to each other are not matters of record, but the events that followed are among the most confusing and difficult to explain in all the history of the Bank. The initial situation was clear. If the Bank did not stop the drain of its specie, it would be forced to suspend payments. Jaudon's contract with Barings forbade the Bank to sell post notes or bonds, and the state of its Paris account deprived it of the power to draw bills on Hottinguer. The choice with which Biddle and Dunlap were confronted was between strengthening the Bank by pressing its debtors, thus aggravating the American crisis, and selling bills of exchange on Jaudon with the expectation that if he could not borrow sufficient funds to meet them, he would call on Humphreys to sell Biddle's cotton.[23]

Any policy adopted at this moment involved risk, but the one that seemed least dangerous was to sell bills of exchange on Jaudon, and this the Bank began to do. The purpose of these sales was to prevent a general suspension of specie payments led by the United States Bank, but, as Biddle knew when the Bank began the operation, the balances thus accumulated against the New York banks would place them in danger. If it happened, as it might, that specie drafts by the Bank forced the New York banks to suspend payments, the other banks would follow as they had in 1837, but the responsibility for leading the suspension would fall on those who were known to be uncompromising opponents of such a remedy. If, on the other hand, the New York banks met these demands without faltering, then the United States Bank and those dependent on it might also be able to maintain specie payments.

The critical moment came in the first week of August. "The slope of 'the declivity,' " Dunlap wrote Biddle, "becomes more precipitous every moment and my specie draft of three hundred and fifty thousand dollars in New York on Thursday nearly closed the drama there; perhaps on Monday I can complete it if need be or prove the possibility of averting it altogether. After drawing yesterday the Bank of the United States in New York was creditor two hundred and thirty-six thousand and on Mon-

[22] Hottinguer and Company to J. Cowperthwaite, May 14, 1839, cited in Smith, *Economic Aspects of the Second Bank*, pp. 215, 300.

[23] T. Dunlap to N. Biddle, July 9, 1839, in the Biddle Manuscripts in the Library of Congress.

day it will probably be at least three hundred thousand." Nothing happened on Monday. The New York banks paid the checks drawn upon them without apparent strain, and Biddle thought that the crisis had passed.[24]

What happened next is a mystery that has never been fully explained. Biddle and Dunlap until this moment had been apparently in full agreement about the correct policy for the Bank. The tone of Dunlap's letters was frank and deferential, and Biddle, without interfering, was a willing counselor and guide. But now their paths parted. Dunlap and the exchange committee began what Biddle was later to call a deliberate attempt "to break down the banks of New York" and embarked on a course that was to end in disaster for the United States Bank. They may have thought that what they were doing was only a logical extension of the policy adopted in July, but what they actually did was to make it impossible for Jaudon to give up the London agency or for the Bank to retire from the stock and commodity markets. Without telling Biddle or asking his advice, they began to sell post notes in New York, Philadelphia, Boston, and Baltimore at discounts ranging from 12 to 20 per cent and also sold bills of exchange on Hottinguer, as Biddle subsequently charged, "without having a dollar of funds in their hands, without having any authority to draw for a dollar, without a line of explanation of these unexpected drafts, and without even the usual commercial notice that such bills had been drawn."[25]

The purpose of these sales was to accumulate sufficient demands upon the New York banks to force a suspension of payments, but they failed to produce the contemplated effect. These banks had almost a dollar in specie for every outstanding liability, and in the last two weeks of August they paid over to the United States Bank almost one and a quarter million dollars in gold. Lesser amounts were withdrawn from Boston and Baltimore, and all this specie was immediately shipped to Europe to meet the previously drawn bills. The conduct of the Bank at this moment puzzled the editor of a New York commercial newspaper, who could not understand why any institution would draw and sell bills of exchange at a heavy loss when all it did with the gold thus obtained was to send it to Europe to be used to pay these same bills. Someone more influential apparently was not puzzled. The whole operation was stopped almost as abruptly as it had started. On August 30 the United States Bank, without offering an explanation of its previous conduct, sent a letter to New York "full of assurances of good feeling" and saying that no more specie would be drawn. The sale of post notes and of bills of exchange was halted, and the Bank retired

24 T. Dunlap to N. Biddle, August 3, 1839, in the Biddle Manuscripts in the Library of Congress.

25 J. Cowperthwate to N. Biddle, March 23, 1841; N. Biddle to J. M. Clayton, April 9, 14, 1841, in *House Executive Document* (29th Cong., 1st sess.), No. 226, pp. 488–89, 493.

into semiactivity to await the inevitable moment when it must suspend specie payments.[26]

The most probable explanation of this sudden halt to the attempt to force the New York banks to suspend payments is that implied in the paragraph above—that Biddle, shocked and indignant, intervened. No one connected with the Bank ever told the whole story, but, from the beginning of September, 1839, until the final failure of the Bank, Biddle, though he never resumed his office, was only nominally retired. He came in from "Andalusia" and for the next sixteen months did what he could to save the Bank from insolvency and dishonor. It was too late to warn Jaudon and Hottinguer of the flood of bills they were about to receive. All that could be done in Philadelphia was to hope that, between them, these European agents would work out their immediate problems. But plans had to be made to pay the European debts of the Bank and the country after the suspension of specie payments through the maintenance of the prices of American stocks and commodities, just as in 1837, and these were the matters about which Biddle was thinking, as he waited with almost desperate anxiety through September to hear from Paris and London.

[26] *Journal of Commerce* (New York), August 30, 31, 1839; *Niles' Register*, LX (1841), 121; Bray Hammond, "The Chestnut Street Raid on Wall Street, 1839," *Quarterly Journal of Economics*, LXI (1947), 605–18.

~ 34 ~

The Second Suspension

of

Specie Payments

$\mathcal{T}$he summer of 1839 was a period of difficult and disturbed financial conditions in Great Britain as well as in the United States. The drain of British bullion to Europe, which had begun the preceding year, continued at an average rate of a million pounds a month, and for a time it seemed as if the Bank of England itself would be forced to suspend specie payments. It was saved by bankers in Paris and Amsterdam, who, the last week in July, responded to a desperate appeal by Governor Timothy Curtis for assistance in order to prevent this international financial catastrophe; and these European bankers, for an identical reason, joined with Barings and other British banking firms to help Jaudon carry the London agency of the United States Bank through this same crisis. Many harsh statements about Jaudon, Biddle, the Bank, and American investments were made in newspapers and private conversations; but, regardless of what was said or thought about Americans and their business methods, they had to be supported by the European financial community to protect itself from disaster. The sales of American stocks and bonds in Europe had created a powerful interest which had no choice but to protect the credit of the United States Bank and American credit in general.[1]

The establishment of such an interest had been one of Biddle's purposes in encouraging the sale of American securities in British and European markets, and its existence was the reason why he had been willing for the

[1] Hidy, *Baring*, pp. 275–76; Clapham, *Bank of England*, II, 168–69; Jenks, *Migration of British Capital*, p. 95.

Bank to draw so freely on Jaudon. His confidence was justified by the event. Throughout the summer of 1839 Jaudon met one crisis after another through a brilliant combination of audacity and courage. The overdraft about which Hottinguer had earlier protested he eliminated by borrowing from Rothschild and Son in Paris and from Barings in London; but he had no sooner placed this account in acceptable shape than the Bank began its heavy and unannounced drafts on London. He turned once again to Barings, who gave him a temporary respite by guaranteeing the payment of one hundred and fifty thousand pounds of past-due bonds held by Overend, Gurney and Company. On August 23, however, Barings abandoned all hope of Jaudon's continued solvency. They canceled the contract to resume the Bank's agency, which had never been signed in Philadelphia, and refused to lend Jaudon any more. The only assistance they were willing to give was to engage with Hope and Company of Amsterdam in a joint purchase from Jaudon of two hundred thousand pounds of state bonds at a discount of 50 per cent; Jaudon accepted this loss because he was desperate.[2]

He sent word to Humphreys that he must have another fifty thousand pounds. "If I do not get this," he wrote, "I get none; for all are contingent on my making up my estimates; everything, therefore, turns upon what you can do, for here I am exhausted." What was at stake, he flatly stated, was "life or death to the Bank of the United States," and he told Humphreys: "If 5000 bales of cotton must go, let them go, be the loss what it may; it cannot be so great as a loss from a protest, and must be borne by owner or Bank, as they may settle the matter between them." The "all" of which Jaudon spoke was a loan of more than three hundred thousand pounds from four London bankers, and it was fortunate for the Bank at this juncture that Biddle had resumed his cotton operations in the spring. Humphreys could sell this cotton without question as to the willingness of the owner to accept the loss, and he was able to furnish the needed money.[3]

Jaudon, though under pressure to meet his own engagements, also rescued the Bank from the adverse effects of Dunlap's decision to begin selling bills of exchange on Paris and converted what could easily have been a major disaster into a financial triumph. Hottinguer and Company refused to accept the more than five million, five hundred thousand francs of bills of exchange when they were presented in September, but Rothschild and Son, believing that the United States Bank owed too much to too many people for it to be permitted to fail, came to its rescue. They agreed to accept the bills, and this substitution of the leading banking firm in Paris for the relatively obscure house that had previously handled the Bank's account was the decisive event in changing Jaudon's position from that of

[2] Hidy, *Baring*, pp. 277–80.

[3] S. Jaudon to Humphreys and Biddle, August 22, 23, 1839, in *House Executive Document* (29th Cong., 1st sess.), No. 226, pp. 478–79.

a desperate seeker of funds to one of relative ease. As soon as it became known that he was supported thus powerfully, other bankers came to his aid, and he was able to negotiate large permanent loans in London, Paris, and Amsterdam, to be paid in instalments in 1841, 1842, and 1843.[4]

Back in the United States, Biddle could do nothing during September but wait to learn what was to happen in Europe. The Bank itself remained essentially inactive, waiting for the inevitable moment when it would have to suspend specie payments. Day by day the pressure mounted, and finally, on October 9, the country was notified that the United States Bank and its Philadelphia neighbors would no longer redeem their notes and other obligations in specie. The next day, news arrived of Hottinguer's refusal to accept the bills of exchange, and few observers believed that the Bank would survive two such blows to its credit. It was thought to be totally insolvent, and responsibility for this situation was almost universally attributed to Biddle.[5]

"Have been amused," a Philadelphia diarist recorded, "to hear people talk about Biddle, once the idol, the god of Philadelphia, upon whom for years every specimen of flattery and attention was accorded, and whom not to speak of as the greatest man of these latter times was regarded as flat blasphemy." Now he was reviled and despised. He was called a knave or a fool by many who had previously "joined in the chorus of servile adulation," and these men, remembering his infatuation with Amerigo Vespucci, also said that he was "sensual and much addicted to enjoyments not permitted a husband and father." No charge was too harsh to be brought against him. The dangerous condition of the banks, the embarrassment of business, and the distress of the community were all blamed on him, and it was said that, having "got out of the scrape just in time," he was "retired with an immense fortune, and among his books and gardens at Andalusia, will probably not feel very deeply the sneers and reproaches of merchants and stock brokers and may well despise alike the favor or hate of the fickle multitude."[6]

Biddle was, in truth, unmoved by these sneers and reproaches, but he felt that, despite his resignation from the Bank, he was duty-bound to make an attempt to lead it through the present crisis. His successor had been his own choice for the post and thus had a right to Biddle's support, however unwise and incautious he might have been in his direction of the Bank's policy and actions. Dunlap himself eagerly accepted this offer of aid, and during the fall and winter of 1838–39 Biddle acted almost as if he had resumed his former place at the Bank. Few people outside the institution were aware that he had thus taken charge, and many within the Bank

[4] Hidy, *Baring,* pp. 277–80.

[5] *Hazard's Commercial Register,* I (1839), 267, 269.

[6] "The Diaries of Sidney George Fisher, 1839–40," *Pennsylvania Magazine of History and Biography,* LXXVII (1953), 78.

itself, including the directors, thought that Dunlap was still the operative, as well as the nominal, head. It was Biddle, however, who was making the effective decisions in regard to the basic policy followed by the Bank. He prepared a public letter to be issued as a statement for all the Philadelphia banks in which he justified and explained this second suspension of specie payments by a restatement of the principles that had governed his actions in previous crises. The proper remedy for disturbed economic conditions, he insisted once more, was relaxation and moderate expansion by the banks to enable solvent individuals and companies to pay what they owed and to collect from others. The suspension of specie payments was the only remedy available under existing conditions, for, pressed as the American banks were by the credit restrictions in Great Britain, they could not have expanded without endangering their specie reserves.[7]

They had been confronted with the choice "either to force the community by sacrifices of its property to pay its debts in gold and silver, to be shipped forthwith to England, or else to resort to a temporary suspension, until the community as well as the banks, could have time to recover." The suspension had already facilitated the collection of debts by Philadelphia merchants and increased their sales in the South and West, for it had, to use the words of one of Biddle's correspondents, "greased the wheels to enable the country's produce to move to Philadelphia." If the banks in New York and New England followed the example set by those in Philadelphia, as had most of the banks in the South and West, the suspension of payments would not last very long, and the country would quickly recover from the effects of the crisis without a major catastrophe. The states and private companies which had embarked upon extensive internal improvements would be able to maintain their interest payments and borrow more, instead of being forced to abandon these projects half-completed and unpaid for.[8]

Biddle's arguments were unheard and his advice disregarded in New York and New England, where the banks were determined to maintain specie payments regardless of the cost to the general community and told protesting merchants, manufacturers, and mechanics that no relief would be granted that was not "compatible with the paramount duty of maintaining a sound currency." Philadelphia and New York, Biddle and Gallatin, and their respective theories of political economy were once again in conflict, but this time both principals were acting behind the scenes. Gallatin, as tired as Biddle, had resigned from his position as president of the National Bank of New York, but his New York associates remained loyal to his views and dismissed Biddle's letter as an *ex parte* statement which

---

[7] T. Dunlap to N. Biddle, October 16, 1839; John A. White, chairman, to the People of Pennsylvania, October 23, 1839, in the Biddle Manuscripts in the Library of Congress.

[8] P. P. F. DeGrand to N. Biddle, November 3, 1839, in the Biddle Manuscripts in the Library of Congress.

merely attempted to excuse a suspension brought about by unwise and improvident policies.[9]

This charge, though partly true, did not invalidate Biddle's arguments and conclusions. The productive groups in society (the farmers, the mechanics, the manufacturers, the merchants, the states, and the private companies that were building and operating internal improvements) did profit from the suspension of specie payments. The banks in most areas of the country commenced issuing and lending bank notes, economic activity increased, prices rose, debtors were able to pay their creditors, and purchasers to buy. Whereas the policy adopted by the banks in New York and New England had exactly the reverse effect in their areas. Loans and bank notes in circulation decreased, prices fell, and almost all buying and selling stopped. Mortgages were foreclosed; debtors failed; and yet, so strange and inexplicable is human conduct that, even though every individual's interest, creditor as well as debtor, was adversely affected by this stubborn adherence to specie payments, Biddle could truthfully say that the New York position was supported by the overwhelming majority of the American people and by both political parties.

Biddle's purpose was to convince this hostile majority that their prejudice for silver and gold was injurious to their economic interest, that a prolonged and unrelieved depression was a needless and incorrect remedy for the overexpansion of credit, and that the nation, if it wanted to, could quickly recover from the financial crisis. He did not say, "You shall not crucify mankind upon a cross of gold," nor would he necessarily have agreed with the reasoning of the man who did say it, but this phrase expressed exactly the basis of his opposition to Gallatin and the New York and New England bankers.

What the country needed, according to Biddle's views, was the adoption of measures to restore the market for securities and commodities, to maintain prices, and to provide means for payment of interregional and international debts. Such a policy, he was certain, would be best for the nation, but also he knew that, unless it was followed, the United States Bank would fail. It was overextended in both its domestic and its foreign operations, and it could not survive unless the deflationary pressures in the United States and in Europe were overcome. The first step that the Bank took after the suspension of specie payments had as its prime purpose the re-establishment of its own strength, and it issued an order that all debts to the Bank must be paid in full at the maturity of each note. This apparent harshness was meliorated by an accompanying statement which said that post notes, bank notes, and stock of the United States Bank would be accepted at par in all payments and that other bank notes, stocks, and bonds would be taken on favorable terms.[10]

[9] *Hazard's Commercial Register*, I (1939), 314.

[10] *Ibid.*, pp. 302–3; P. P. F. DeGrand to N. Biddle, November 3, 1839; C. A. Davis to N. Biddle, July 31, 1834, in the Biddle Manuscripts in the Library of Congress.

This order created a demand for securities and the circulating liabilities of the Bank where there had been little before, and also it enabled the Bank to substitute its own stock, that of other solvent companies, and bonds for unsecured promissory notes. The Bank thus set in motion a countervailing pressure against the deflationary forces within the domestic economy at the same time that it increased its own strength. A similar stimulus was needed in the cotton market, but Biddle was understandably reluctant to engage once more in the type of operation that had brought so much criticism against the Bank. For a period of six weeks after the suspension of specie payments he explored all possible alternatives, but in the end he decided that there was no other way to provide funds for the payment of the foreign debts of the United States Bank. American stocks and bonds were unsalable in Great Britain and Europe, and the eight million dollars of securities in Jaudon's possession had no realizable value except as collateral for loans. The dilemma was inescapable. Either Biddle would ship cotton, or American credit would be destroyed through the inability of the states, the merchants, and the United States Bank to pay their European debts.[11]

Biddle began this new operation in November by issuing orders to Humphreys in Liverpool to sell the cotton he then held as rapidly as possible and to prepare to receive additional shipments from the United States. In regard to the holdover cotton, bought at high prices the preceding spring, he told Humphreys that it was no longer a question of how to make a profit on it but how to hold the loss to a minimum. But he was nevertheless hopeful that the new operation would be profitable. The price of cotton had fallen just as much in the United States as it had in Great Britain through the absence of buyers, and every sign indicated that the prices in both countries would be higher in the spring. The Bank of England, having stopped the drain of bullion, would probably begin to relax its restrictions on credit, and the cotton manufacturers, with their stocks depleted, would be forced to buy.[12]

Biddle began buying cotton at the close of November. S. V. S. Wilder, Hottinguer's New York agent, replaced Bevan and Humphreys as the borrower of record from the Bank, but otherwise the purchases were made in exactly the same way as those which had occurred before Biddle resigned. Cowperthwaite and his assistants handled all the details of the transmission of the bills of exchange from the purchasing agents in the South and Southwest to Jaudon in London, and Wilder did nothing but receive and forward the bills of lading. This time, however, Biddle did not use notes

11 M. Humphreys to N. Biddle, October 2, 1839, in the Biddle Manuscripts in the Library of Congress.

12 N. Biddle to M. Humphreys, November 14, 15, 1839, in the Biddle Manuscripts in the Library of Congress; *House Executive Document* (29th Cong., 1st sess.), No. 226, pp. 419–20, 461–62.

of the old Bank of the United States for his purchases. He did not want to increase the circulating liabilities of the Bank when it was unnecessary, and, during the previous months, the Bank had collected large amounts of notes of the southern and western banks in payments to its agents in these regions. What Biddle borrowed was these local notes, which would be accepted at par by the holders of cotton but which the Bank itself could not use. It could not obtain specie with them because their issuers had suspended specie payments, and it could not buy bills of exchange, since these were nonexistent in the absence of cotton buyers.[13]

The Bank was thus able to transform uncollectable and unusable assets in the South and Southwest into effective funds in Great Britain, and, if Biddle's operation had done nothing else for the Bank, this one service alone would have made it worthwhile. But it did do more for the Bank and the country. Once Biddle's agents commenced buying cotton, others joined in, and the bills of exchange thus provided were used to pay interregional and international debts. The needed stimulus was given to economic activity in the interior of the country, on the sea coast, and in foreign trade, and, if the other banks and the government had been willing to co-operate, many of the subsequent economic troubles of the nation would have been avoided.

What Biddle was fighting was not so much economic theory clearly understood but rather a mass emotion. The long years of controversy about money and banking had confused most of the people, and the relative simplicity of the hard-money arguments had a general appeal. Jackson, Benton, Calhoun, Van Buren, and their Locofoco supporters had maintained that bank notes and credit were unsafe and unsound, and the economic crises in 1837 and 1839 had apparently proved them correct. So strong was the emotional impact of their hard-money arguments that the merchants and other users of credit in New York continued to praise the banks for their determination "to maintain specie payments" at a time when these same people were saying that "unless some effectual means of relief shall be immediately adopted, we see nothing that can avert the prostration of the mechanical, manufacturing, and commercial classes of the city." The local banks could do nothing so long as they continued to pay specie when all the rest of the country had suspended specie payments, and, in an effort to find some effective means of aid, the New York merchants brought pressure upon the national administration. But once again they failed. Van Buren was unwilling to abandon his hard-money arguments, and the greater part of his annual message was devoted to the dangers of looking to the government for aid in an economic depression.[14]

He ascribed the hard times to paper money and credit, and his argument

13 *Ibid.*

14 *Hazard's Commercial Register*, I (1839), 314; *Niles' Register*, LVII (1839), 279–84.

was a plausible one under existing conditions. All economic affairs in Europe and America were deranged and disordered as a result of unpayable debt. Those who had bought farms, established businesses and factories, and constructed internal improvements with the expectation of profit were faced with debts they could not pay. Each of them was disappointed and confused; he knew that the fault was not his, that something external—the system or the times—was to blame; and it was to this feeling that Van Buren appealed in his attacks on banks, paper money, and credit. He spoke of "a false system," "gigantic banking institutions," and "splendid but profitless railroads and canals" and repeatedly referred to the inevitable and irresistible laws of trade that governed economic affairs. The solution was simple. The country and its people should "cease to run into debt"; but, since this mistake had already been made, there was nothing to do but to accept its consequences. "Indebtedness," he concluded, "cannot be lessened by borrowing more money, or by changing the form of the debt. The balance of trade is not to be turned in our favor by creating new demands abroad." It was only "by retrenchment and reform, by curtailing public and private ependitures, by paying our debts," that the country could "expect effectual relief, security for the future, and an enduring prosperity."[15]

The Congress, badly divided, rejected all proposals for using the credit and power of the national government to relieve the economic situation, including that proposed by Barings and other English bankers for the assumption of state debts by the United States Treasury. In the final weeks of the session, however, Benton, Jackson, and Van Buren had their way, and the independent Treasury, which was to divorce the government from the banks, was established. Biddle was disappointed at the failure of Congress to do anything about the crisis, for he was gravely concerned by the low state of American morale. The depression was bringing out the worst qualities of the population. Politicians had begun to call for a repudiation of state debts, and an increasing number of employees, the newspapers reported, were stealing from private and public employers. Merchants, unable to sell the goods in their warehouses, were apparently turning to the fire insurance companies for money with which to pay their debts, and in almost all the commercial cities large and disastrous fires occurred. Debtors denounced creditors who demanded payment, and creditors accused the delinquents of bad faith and dishonesty. And back of all this was a deep-seated fear, a sense of insecurity, and a profound uncertainty as to whether the nation was capable of working through its problems.[16]

Biddle was given his first opportunity to speak to the country in January, 1840, at a dinner in Pottsville, Pennsylvania, and his theme was the American nation, its great natural riches, and the character, courage, and

[15] *Ibid.*

[16] Benton, *Thirty Years' View*, II, 164–67; Davis, Brooks and Company, Circular to Europe, March 19, 1840, in the Biddle Manuscripts in the Library of Congress.

inventiveness of its people. Other countries were divided between the poor who labored and the rich who were idle, but America, "with few rich men and no idle men," had the distinction of having "the hardest working people on the face of the earth." They worked not merely to accumulate money but rather "to appease the restless spirit within," and what they earned they spent "with a recklessness quite as characteristic." This youthful exuberance, which had engendered their troubles, could also provide the remedy, and there was no need for despair. Pennsylvania had incurred a debt of thirty-two million dollars to build a great system of internal improvements far beyond its immediate wants, but this debt could easily be paid if the state developed the iron and coal fields within her borders. Her railroads and canals would increase their income tenfold, and the resulting prosperity of her citizens would "carry her triumphantly through all her troubles."[17]

He did not mention Van Buren, but his speech was an answer to the President's assertion that the remedy for the depression was retrenchment, reform, and the curtailment of public and private expenditures. He particularly resented the allusion to splendid but profitless railroads and canals, and he continued his attack upon it in a speech delivered at the opening of the Tidewater Canal on the lower Susquehanna River, in which he characterized these assertions as "maudlin lamentations" by a man "unfit to lead a great nation." Political leaders, he insisted, should take pride in American advances in civilization, moral instruction, social improvement, and enterprises for developing resources, instead of complaining about costs and waste "as if, in a career, totally new, young nations, like young men, must not pay for their experience." He similarly denounced those politicians who had suggested the repudiation of state debts, that Americans should "plunder the strangers who have confided in us." He urged his listeners at the coming elections to reject "the miserable demagogues" who were unwilling to ask the people to pay their honest debts and to elect those who "in tone of honest manliness tell us the public wants and ask us to relieve them."[18]

Willingness to pay these debts, Biddle knew, was not enough; default and eventual repudiation would come inevitably unless the debtor states could collect taxes and borrow. And the deflationary pressures set in motion by the demand for an immediate resumption of specie payments was making it impossible for the states to do either. The situation in Pennsylvania was typical of that in the debtor states. On February 1, 1840, the state treasury needed six hundred thousand dollars to pay interest on its bonds, but it had no funds. The only source it could turn to was the United States Bank and other state banks, but these institutions were unable to lend because the lower house of the legislature had just passed an

[17] *Hazard's Commercial Register*, II (1840), 230–31.
[18] *United States Gazette* (Philadelphia), June 4, 1840.

act requiring them to resume specie payments on February 15, or forfeit their charters. None of the banks was in a position to increase its liabilities at this moment, and the state was forced to default.[19]

Governor David Porter, a Van Buren Democrat, was in a difficult situation. His party was committed by its national leaders to a hard-money policy, which was popular with the voters of the state. But he also knew that "the cumbrous public debt" of the state could not be handled unless the banks were able to lend. For this a postponement of resumption was necessary. He had been unable to resolve this conflict between his interests as a partisan and his duty as governor of the state until the actual default forced him to take a stand, but then he sent a message to the legislature urging the senate to reject the resumption act. The United States Bank, convinced that this message would lead to the defeat of the bill, came forward at once and, with the assistance of the Girard and Pennsylvania banks, loaned the state the sum required to pay the interest that was in default.[20]

The hard-money men in the legislature, instead of being grateful for the loan that saved the state from dishonor, continued their attack on the banks. An attempt was made to force every bank subscribing to the state loan to pay its "notes, deposites, and liabilities in specie"; when this was defeated, the senate passed the lower house bill requiring an immediate resumption. This bill had been amended to such an extent that it had to be referred to a conference committee, and, while it was being considered, another bill, prepared at the request of Governor Porter, which postponed resumption until January 15, 1841, was rushed through both houses by very small majorities. All through this session Biddle had been in close touch with Porter through the Bank's representatives at Harrisburg, and he had been able to convince the governor that the attempt to force the banks to resume specie payments would inevitably lead to a decline in prices and economic activity.[21]

Porter and many others who had been captivated earlier by "the doctrine of an exclusive hard currency" were losing some of their enthusiasm when they observed the "reduction of the price of labor and commodities and an entire disorganization of the exchanges" that had resulted from the hard-money policies forced upon the country by the New York and New England banks and the Democratic politicians. The partial suspension of 1839 did not have the same effect as the total suspension of 1837; instead of producing, as many of Biddle's critics had predicted, "a plethora of depreciated currency," it had left the country with "no currency, good or

[19] J. Norris to N. Biddle, March 14, 1840, in the Biddle Manuscripts in the Library of Congress; *Hazard's Commercial Register*, II (1840), 96.

[20] N. Biddle to J. Tilford, February 4, 1840, in the Biddle Manuscripts in the Library of Congress.

[21] *Hazard's Commercial Register*, II (1840), 169–70, 240.

bad." The New York and New England banks, still paying specie, were unwilling to increase their liabilities, and the other banks, under intense pressure to resume payments at the earliest possible moment, were forced to collect the debts already owed them instead of lending more. Everyone was seeking to sell or to collect, and few were in a position to buy or pay. Hence the whole country was confronted with an imminent possibility of a total collapse of the entire economy.

Biddle had been able to convince Porter of the wisdom of postponing the date for the resumption of specie payments, and even this partial abandonment of the hard-money position caused the governor to be censured by his party. A Democratic convention at Bedford, Pennsylvania, denounced "the odious banking law" as a bill deserving "the eternal and everlasting execration of every genuine Democrat" and consigned the apostates who had sold their principles "to the glittering banking institutions" to "merited infamy."[22] Thus the Democratic party, national and local, was totally committed to the hard-money doctrine regardless of its costs to states with debts to pay or to farmers, merchants, manufacturers, and workers, but the country as a whole was now less willing to accept the view that nothing could be done to remedy its economic problems.

In the spring of 1840 the political signs indicated that the recently named Whig nominees, William Henry Harrison of Ohio and John Tyler of Virginia, would win the presidential election in the fall, and the task confronting Biddle and the United States Bank was to hold things together until the new administration was inaugurated on March 4, 1841. After that, some form of relief—assumption of state debts, federal borrowing and expenditure, or the rechartering of a national bank—would be forthcoming to halt depression and liquidation.

[22] *Ibid.*

35

The Revolt
of the
Bank's Directors

*B*iddle in this crisis in the Bank's history, as in all previous ones, acted on the conviction that fear and despair were dangerous counselors. Courage and confidence, he was certain, could accomplish apparent miracles in financial affairs, and the Bank, he believed, was in no danger if properly and confidently managed. The Bank's directors, however, were not so confident or sure. They were frightened by the large losses incurred by the Bank and by the storm of criticism directed against it, and in the spring of 1840 they suddenly decided to take the control of the Bank into their own hands. This decision amounted to a revolution, for, as a committee of the stockholders said later, "it is very apparent that Mr. Biddle, especially during the latter years of his presidency, considered himself the Bank," and this charge, though not in the hostile sense in which it was written, was essentially true. He had exercised unchallenged power and authority within the institution for so long a time that he was not fully conscious of possessing it, and in January, 1839, he had noted almost with surprise that, though "political writers occupy themselves with the manufacture of checks and balances, it is remarkable how entirely these seem to be disregarded when confidence . . . in any individual is established. In my own case I enjoy that confidence in a degree which imposes upon me an intense and fearful responsibility. . . . In preparing for yesterday's election, there were three vacancies in the country class of directors and four for the city. At the election I voted about 2500 votes by proxy, . . . there were two or three hundred other votes, so that in point of fact the whole matter was arranged by myself. . . . The board so chosen met last evening and I was unanimously reelected."[1]

[1] *House Executive Document* (29th Cong., 1st sess.), No. 226, p. 524; N. Biddle, manuscript journal, in the Biddle Manuscripts in the Historical Society of Pensylvania.

The directors had the same trust and confidence in Biddle that the stock-holders had, and throughout his long administration they had accepted his guidance on all matters of fundamental policy. They had given their advice when it was requested and had passed on applications for ordinary loans; but they had asked few questions about matters not brought directly to their attention, nor had they examined with care the reports of the exchange and other committees which were placed on their table at every meeting. The election of Dunlap as Biddle's successor had made no change in the attitude of the directors in regard to their position and function, and they had continued to follow the recommendations of the new president as they had those of his predecessor. The shock of the second suspension of specie payments, accompanied as it was by the news of the rejection of the Bank's bills of exchange by Hottinguer and Company, was the first indication to many of these directors that all was not well with the Bank, and they became even more doubtful as to how it was being managed when the monthly reports throughout the winter and spring recorded regular and increasing losses instead of profits.

Strong leadership at this moment could have convinced the directors that these losses, large though they were, were no reason for excessive caution or concern. But Dunlap was unwilling or unable to supply this leadership. He joined with a small group of directors who, for reasons of their own, wanted to discredit Biddle and his management of the Bank, and between them they set the Bank on a course which ended in insolvency and failure. Manuel Eyre, a long-time director and the principal stockholder in the Schuylkill Navigation Company, was apparently the leader of this group, and Biddle believed that the source of his resentment was the aid given by the Bank to the competing Reading Railroad. "The Bank of the United States," he later wrote, "has been obliged to take for debts a large number of shares in the Reading Railroad, and with a view to protect its own interests, has given facilities to finish the road, so as to make it more productive. Some of the officers and directors were also holders of shares in the road; and, what was still more criminal, Mr. Jaudon, while in England, negotiated some loan and got some iron for the company. Now the owners of the Navigation Company saw clearly that if these persons should be rendered odious, if the Bank of the United States could be broken down, it would carry down this Reading Railroad, and thus increase the profits of the company. This is really the foundation of the whole attack. . . . It is the vengeance of the Schuylkill Navigation Company."[2]

His analysis of Eyre's motives may have been incorrect, but, whatever the reason, Eyre became the center of a small group who convinced the other directors that the officers of the Bank had been permitted by the exchange committee to borrow large amounts for private speculations and

[2] N. Biddle to J. M. Clayton, April 14, 1841, in *House Executive Document* (29th Cong., 1st sess.), No. 226, p. 492.

that it was these losses which had endangered the Bank. The board ordered an investigation, and Biddle soon became aware that some change had occurred, if only because Dunlap was consulting him less frequently. But it was not until June 20, 1840, when the resignations of Joseph Cowperthwaite, the cashier, and John Andrews, the assistant cashier, were suddenly announced that Biddle had any idea how hostile to him and the former officers the board had become. He still was not informed of the source of the trouble, but the directors, unable to suppress their anger and indignation, talked privately to others of what they were learning at the board. Reports reached New York that Cowperthwaite was heavily indebted to the Bank, and one newspaper stated as an accomplished fact that Biddle, unable to pay his personal debt to the Bank, had suspended payments. Scandalous rumors were spread concerning the speculations of the officers, and soon many people suspected that there had been fraud and embezzlement.[3]

There was an element of truth in these charges. Cowperthwaite, Andrews, and Jaudon had each borrowed large sums from the Bank without the knowledge of Biddle and most of the members of the board of directors, and it had been one of Biddle's rules that "officers of banks ought not to be borrowers at all." He wrote concerning Jaudon's borrowings, "I think he committed a great mistake in suffering himself to borrow so much from the Bank," but in making this statement he was not attempting to escape responsibility. Instead he was trying to explain how it happened that in the later years of the Bank's existence this practice had been permitted to develop. It had begun in 1835 when the Bank of the United States, in preparation for closing, had been investing its funds in semi-permanent loans on stocks, and the exchange committee, which was placed in charge of this operation, had permitted the officers to borrow, on the ground that these loans, unlike ordinary loans of the Bank, were made almost exclusively on the credit of the stock without much regard to the personal responsibility of the borrower. In March, 1836, when the new Bank went into operation, Jaudon, Andrews, and Cowperthwaite each owed approximately one hundred thousand dollars, and during the course of the next year they borrowed additional sums to purchase stocks when the market was low.[4]

By this time, both the officers and the exchange committee had apparently forgotten the circumstances under which the original loans had been made. The officers continued to buy and sell stocks with money borrowed from the Bank, and no one questioned the propriety of their actions so

[3] *United States Gazette* (Philadelphia), June 20, 26, 1840; *Hazard's Commercial Register*, III (1840), 24; R. Colt to N. Biddle, July 27, 1840, in the Biddle Manuscripts in the Library of Congress.

[4] N. Biddle to J. M. Clayton, April 18, 1841, in *House Executive Document* (29th Cong., 1st sess.), No. 226, pp. 417, 423, 447–52, 510–11.

long as the balance was amply secured. The reports of the exchange committee with the names of the borrowers were on the directors' table regularly, and each quarter the examining and auditing committee of the board went over every account. The ignorance of Biddle and the other directors was the result of their own inattention, not of concealment; so, as Biddle himself was to point out later, they were as much responsible for the continuation of this improper practice as were the exchange committee and the officers that borrowed.

The loans in themselves were not unreasonable or immoderate, and those owed by Cowperthwaite and Andrews were completely paid off in early 1839 as a result of Biddle's decision to cut down on the proportion of the Bank's resources that was invested in stock loans. Jaudon, since he was out of the country on Bank business, was not called on by the exchange committee for immediate payment, and in June, 1840, when the board began to take notice of the situation, he owed approximately one hundred and fifty thousand dollars. Cowperthwaite, after Biddle had left the Bank, had incurred a new debt of seventy-five thousand dollars, but each of these officers, through the years, had rendered devoted and useful service to the Bank. Each of them had more than enough personal property, even at the depressed prices then prevailing, to pay off his debt, and, manifestly improper as their conduct had been, it called for no more than a reprimand. Someone on the board of directors, particularly Dunlap or one of the members of the exchange committee, ought to have made a defense of the conduct of these officers. But none of them did, and they also remained quiet when the investigating committee began to look into Biddle's cotton operations. Here again the majority of the board was permitted to retain the erroneous impression that no explanation or justification was possible; that Biddle, Cowperthwaite, and Dunlap, for personal profit, had engaged in a gigantic speculation in the name of S. V. S. Wilder; and that this too was proof of how carelessly and recklessly the Bank had been managed.[5]

This operation had proved to be unexpectedly costly, largely because of financial conditions in Great Britain. The Bank of England, though it had stopped the drain of bullion in the fall of 1839, had kept the price of money high during the following winter and spring, which meant that few securities of any kind had been sold except at large discounts and that the price of cotton and other commodities had remained low. Manufacturers had operated on short time, confining their purchases of cotton to their immediate needs, and the speculators, unable to obtain credit, had remained out of the market. But Jaudon in London had been in urgent need of money to meet the bills of exchange sold by the Bank in New York and Philadelphia to Americans with European debts to pay. Biddle, confronted with the choice of sacrificing his cotton at a loss or permitting the Bank's agent in London to default at a moment when, through loans

[5] *Ibid.,* pp. 526–27, 529.

from the leading European bankers, its credit had been completely restored, had not hesitated, to order Humphreys to sell "whenever you can under the belief that prices though low will go lower."[6]

However much these losses might be, he was certain, they would not be so great as the losses which would have been incurred if there had been no cotton to sell. The solvency of the United States Bank had been staked on the ability of Humphreys and Biddle to keep Jaudon supplied with funds. Humphreys had done what he could to meet this need, but by January he had to complain at "the embarrassed situation I am placed in by advances to Mr. Jaudon that he is unable to refund." Humphreys and Biddle, he insisted, were "used up root and branch" and must retire from business unless reinforced. Something had to be done to restore the firm's credit, but no funds were available in the United States, nor could Jaudon, in his straitened circumstances, raise money in London. To Biddle there seemed to be but one answer, and that was to give Humphreys some means of convincing his bankers and brokers that the debt owing to Humphreys and Biddle would certainly be paid. It had been incurred to save the London agency of the United States Bank, and Biddle thought it only right that the Bank should guarantee its payment.[7]

He prepared a letter for Dunlap's signature as president of the United States Bank, addressed to Bevan and Humphreys in Philadelphia, which said: "the state of the debt due by the Bank to Messrs. Humphreys and Biddle has been for some time the subject of great solicitude. . . . We are extremely anxious to repay them, but in the present state of the Bank it is impracticable to do it by direct remittances. We understand however that they still have on hand a considerable amount of merchandise shipped by you, some of which they have already been obliged to sell to meet their most pressing arrangements on account of Mr. Jaudon. As the only remaining method of acquitting the debt due to them, I have to request that you will direct them to raise funds by the sale of any or all merchandise consigned by you to them, and if this sale should be attended with any sacrifice on its cost, we will make up the difference." To justify this action by the Bank, the letter acknowledged the fact that Humpheys and Biddle had sustained Jaudon "when but for their assistance, he would not have been able to extricate himself," and concluded with the statement that, "having no other method of paying a debt of so sacred a character, we must submit to any merely pecuniary loss it must occasion."[8]

[6] N. Biddle to M. Humphreys, November 14, 1839, January 11, 1840; M. Humphreys to N. Biddle, December 24, 1839, January 18, 1840, in the Biddle Manuscripts in the Library of Congress; Clapham, *Bank of England*, II, 170–72, 176–77; Hidy, *Baring*, p. 272; Hawtrey, *Bank Rate*, pp. 18–19; Clapham, *Economic History*, II, 513–18; Tooke, *Prices*, III, 73–74; Thomas Ellison, *Gleanings and Reminiscences* (Liverpool, 1905), pp. 161–64.

[7] M. Humphreys to N. Biddle, January 14, 1840, in the Biddle Manuscripts in the Library of Congress.

[8] T. Dunlap to Bevan and Humphreys, February 5, 1840; N. Biddle to M. Humphreys, February 6, 1840, in the Biddle Manuscripts in the Library of Congress.

When Biddle had written this letter, on February 5, he had not expected that there would be any losses to assume. The preceding day the Bank had provided the loan that enabled Pennsylvania to pay the interest on which it had defaulted, and Biddle had reason to believe that Governor Porter, besides opposing immediate resumption of specie payments, would recommend to the legislature the suspension of the clause in the Bank's charter that permitted holders of its notes to collect 12 per cent damages for any failure to redeem them in specie. He had suspended purchases in February, expecting this change in the Bank's situation, and by the middle of March the market had been right for a new operation which would have made up most of the previously incurred losses. But the legislature had refused to suspend this provision. The Bank had been unable to lend any of its notes, it had used all its southern funds, and so this opportunity to recoup had been missed. There had been nothing left to do but to reckon up the account, establish the extent of the losses, and settle the matter between the owners of the cotton and the Bank.[9]

The letter to Bevan and Humphreys in which Dunlap had assumed these losses in the name of the Bank had not been intended as a final settlement of this question. Its purpose had been to assure the Liverpool bankers and brokers that the debts owing to Humpheys and Biddle would be paid, and Biddle expected that, in friendly negotiation with the directors, he, Dunlap, and Cowperthwaite would return the overadvances to the Bank out of the profits they had made on the earlier operation. But such an easy solution turned out to be impossible. The directors, already indignant at the disclosure of the other loans to the officers and prejudiced against Biddle, thought the letter to be a trick to foist on the Bank the losses incurred in a private speculation. Eyre and those associated with him carefully fostered this impression, and they were aided by Dunlap, who admitted his "error" and told the directors that the letter had been "draughted by Mr. Biddle himself, urged by him upon Mr. Dunlap, and signed . . . with great reluctance." He urged the directors to disregard the letter and sought to atone for his mistake by insisting upon "the liability of the parties to refund the loss, and making the best arrangements in his power to repay his own share, principal and interest."[10]

Dunlap thus succeeded in convincing the directors that he had been misled by the more experienced Biddle, and the committee appointed by the board on July 21 to settle the cotton account did not even consult the former president. They conducted their deliberations and inquiries in secret, and it was not until the second week in September that Biddle was unofficially told that he was to be asked to pay his share of the full deficiency, some six hundred thousand dollars, without any deduction for the

9 S. V. S. Wilder to N. Biddle, March 14, 1840; N. Biddle to S. V. S. Wilder, March 16, 1840; N. Biddle to M. Humphreys, March 18, 1840, in the Biddle Manuscripts in the Library of Congress.

10 *House Executive Document* (29th Cong., 1st sess.), No. 226, pp. 526–27.

losses incurred on the cotton sold for the the use of the Bank. He immediately sent the relevant documents to Chancellor James Kent of New
York, a leading authority on commercial law, and received the unqualified
answer that his claim for the deduction was "well founded in law and
equity." Armed with this opinion, he assumed the offensive. He had every
intention of paying what had been lost on the sale of the cotton, but he
wanted to contest the Bank's claim, so that his representative in the negotiations with the directors would have an opportunity to explain that the
losses had been incurred to enable the Bank "to meet its necessities" after
Dunlap's unfortunate operation had been undertaken for "the purpose of
breaking down the banks of New York." He wanted to discredit Dunlap
and those directors who were seeking to persuade the others that the Bank
was in an almost irretrievable situation and who were recommending policies, Biddle was certain, that would ultimately destroy it.[11]

The Bank's situation, he knew, was neither desperate nor critical. Its
European credit was completely restored, and Jaudon, having turned over
the London agency to James Morrison and Sons, was returning to the
United States. Its notes and post notes were circulating at a smaller discount than those of the other banks which had suspended payments, and
but few of the holders of these notes had taken advantage of the charter
provision to collect 12 per cent damages for the Bank's failure to pay in
specie. It had suffered large book losses, some seventeen million dollars,
on its holdings of stocks and bonds, but this condition was but a temporary
one. The issuers of these securities (the states, banks, and internal-improve-
ment companies) were essentially sound, and, if given time and a revival
of economic activity, would once more be able to pay interest, dividends,
and principal.[12]

Biddle had also determined to endeavor quietly to place Jaudon at the
head of the Bank in place of Dunlap, so that the institution would have a
strong and capable leader during the difficult period that lay ahead. In
private conversations with directors and stockholders he tried to allay
their alarm and to convince them that the Bank's problems could be solved.
The Whigs, he told them, were almost certain to win the election, and the
true position and the only safe policy of the Bank was to wait for that
moment and see what the new administration intended to do for the
country, what relief it meant to afford. It might not at once propose such
a debatable question as that of the rechartering of a national bank and so
would be forced to use existing institutions, chiefly the United States Bank
itself, for the deposit, payment, and transfer of the public funds. Hence
the Bank must make sure that it was in a position of strength on March 4,

[11] N. Biddle to R. M. Blatchford, September 15, 1840; J. Kent to N. Biddle, September 17, 1840; N. Biddle, draft statement, n.d., in the Biddle Manuscripts in the Library
of Congress.

[12] *Niles' Register*, LIX (1841), 308–10.

1841, which would be possible only if the general economy had begun to recover.[13]

So intertwined were the Bank's interests with those of the country as a whole that anything which fostered or injured the one had the same effect on the other. Much depended on the proper management of the institution throughout the fall and winter of 1840–41, and the most dangerous action that it could take, in Biddle's opinion, was to continue the preparations for the resumption of specie payments on January 15, 1841. "It is undoubtedly true," he wrote, "that the only lawful and proper banking is the payment of specie. But where, by any cause, a suspension once takes place, the time of resumption is a question of expediency, depending on many circumstances." If the banks tried to resume specie payments too quickly, they would be in the position of a man who tried to resume his normal activities before completing his recovery from an illness and would almost inevitably suffer a relapse. The United States had gone through a period of too rapid expansion. Too many public improvements had been undertaken simultaneously; too much land had been purchased and turned into farms; too many factories had been built; and too much indebtedness had been incurred. If times and means were provided, this debt could be paid through the normal instruments of goods and money, but if the process of deflation continued, the debt would be eliminated by universal default.[14]

Biddle thought it more important that the economy be restored to prosperity than that the banks pay specie, and the nation seemed ready for such an assertion of confidence in the future. The summer and fall of 1840, despite the depression, were not periods of repining and despair. The Whig campaign, by spontaneous popular action, had become a gigantic mass celebration. Men shouted, "Van, Van, is a used-up man" and roared their preference for "Tippecanoe and Tyler too." They rolled large balls from one town to another, built log cabins in which they drank cider, and forgot their hardships and sufferings. It was to this youthful optimism and vigor that Biddle was seeking to appeal, but the directors of the United States Bank would not listen.

They continued their preparations for the resumption of specie payments, and this addition to the deflationary pressures further reduced prices and economic activity. Mortgages on houses and farms were foreclosed; solvent merchants, unable to collect debts due them or to sell, closed their doors; and there was no money except gold and silver, most of which was locked up in the vaults of the banks. The directors made no attempt to answer Biddle's arguments; indeed, the validity of these

[13] N. Biddle to E. C. Biddle, September 30, 1840, in the Biddle Manuscripts in the Library of Congress.

[14] N. Biddle to J. M. Clayton, April 9, 1841, in *House Executive Document* (29th Cong., 1st sess.), No. 226, pp. 489–90; N. Biddle to D. Webster, August 7, 1840, *Niles' Register*, LIX (1840), 24–25.

arguments was too obvious to be denied. Instead, they merely cited the act of the Pennsylvania legislature that provided for the forfeiture of the charter of any bank that did not resume specie payments on the specified day. This penalty, Biddle replied, could not be imposed on the United States Bank. If it refused to pay specie, there was nothing the state could do, for its charter lacked the usual provision authorizing the legislature "to alter or repeal it at pleasure." The courts had already decided that the Bank's charter was a permanent and unalterable grant of authority; but, even if it had not been thus protected, Biddle insisted, the state authorities would take no action if their legislative injunction was defied. Pennsylvania had another interest payment of eight hundred thousand dollars due on February 1, 1841, and it had no money with which to pay. The governor must once again turn to the banks, which meant, Biddle said, that "the legislature was much more in the power of the banks, than the banks in the power of the legislature." They could say: "The state breaks on the 1st of February unless you can borrow. . . . You can borrow . . . only from us; and if we lend to you and resume specie payments, we inevitably break ourselves. Let us agree that neither shall break. Authorize a suspension beyond the 15th of January and we will protect you on the 1st of February."[15]

The very plausibility of these arguments was one of their weaknesses; for Biddle, in the fall of 1840, was a discredited man. He was considered to be "able, brilliant, agreeable, plausible, cultivated, but not great" by some who had formerly praised him the most, and he was accused of lacking sincerity and truth. "He can persuade, delight, humbug, and beguile," a Philadelphia diarist noted, "but he cannot convince, elevate, inspire, or command. The proof is, the open mouthed, extravagant, fulsome admiration he received during the days of his success, and the disregard, indifference, almost contempt into which he has fallen. . . . If Mr. Biddle had possessed or displayed really great qualities, men would not have withdrawn from him their respect and confidence and admiration when the game turned against him and his prosperity was gone." The directors thus were on guard against Biddle, determined that he should not "delight, humbug, and beguile" them with the persuasiveness of his arguments. They contrasted the situation of the United States Bank, which had protected its borrowers and been forced to suspend specie payments, with that of the New York banks, which had remained on specie by rapid and relentless collections, and they did not question which had followed the better policy.[16]

The banks in New York were solvent and secure, possessing a dollar in specie for every dollar of liabilities, whereas the United States Bank was in

[15] *Ibid.*

[16] "The Diaries of Sidney George Fisher, 1839–1840," *Pennsylvania Magazine of History and Biography*, LXXVII (1953), 93–94.

a precarious condition. If those who had managed the institution from 1837 to 1840 had listened to Gallatin and had followed the restrictive policy he advocated, the national economy might have been worse off, but the Bank would have been safe. The directors now were convinced that everything the Bank had done at Biddle's instigation to support and sustain the national economy had been injurious and that they would be compounding these earlier errors by postponing the resumption of specie payments again. They rejected his advice and were supported in their determination by Dunlap, who wanted to hold on to his place. He had refused to consider Biddle's proposal that he retire in favor of Jaudon, saying that Jaudon was not a suitable person for the office and citing as evidence the loans he had received from the Bank and the large commissions and fees he had collected in London.

Dunlap and those directors who supported him made no acknowledgment of what a leading London banker had called Jaudon's "great exertions" to uphold "an institution, the credit and prosperity of which is so important to the great and varied commercial interests of both countries." Instead, they insisted that he make immediate repayment of his loans and sought to deny him the commissions he had earned by raising money in Europe for the Bank "at the darkest moment of its trials." Biddle was angered by this attempted mistreatment of Jaudon and intervened decisively. The commissions were paid, and Jaudon used the larger part of his money to repay all but one hundred and seventeen thousand dollars of his loan. He posted stocks valued at more than one hundred and sixty thousand as security for the balance of his debt, and, at the same time, Biddle and Cowperthwaite made similar arrangements to settle with the Bank for its overadvances on cotton.[17]

Biddle, convinced that he had failed to persuade the directors either to replace Dunlap with Jaudon or to postpone the resumption, abandoned the fight. The only hope he now had was to build up confidence in the United States Bank by using the credit it still possessed both in America and abroad to procure additional specie so that, when it resumed payments, the holders of its notes would not present them for redemption. The only person in the Bank family who was known and trusted in Europe was Jaudon, but he was reluctant to go, and the directors did not want to employ him. Once again Biddle intervened. He persuaded Jaudon and the directors that, unless additional specie resources were obtained in Europe, the Bank could not hope to survive, and an arrangement was made whereby Jaudon was sent back to Europe as a special representative to procure a new loan.

Not a single word regarding Biddle's opposition to Dunlap had been

[17] J. Morrison to T. Dunlap, December 12, 1839, in the Manuscript Collection of the Library Company of Philadelphia; S. Jaudon to N. Biddle, October 23, 1840; N. Biddle to T. Dunlap, October 26, 1840, in the Biddle Manuscripts in the Library of Congress.

permitted to leak out during the summer and fall. He had realized that if a public fight for control was added to all the Bank's other troubles, the institution and everyone connected with it would be discredited. So much had happened that could not be explained to anyone not fully familiar with the inner workings of the Bank that an open break with his successor was unthinkable. But his opponents were not satisfied with their victory. They wanted to discredit Biddle and his principal subordinates, and they embarked on a course that destroyed all confidence in the Bank. Dunlap called a special meeting of the board of directors for December 21, 1840, which only ten members attended, and here the damage was done. The committe that had made arrangements with Dunlap and the former officers for the settlement of their several accounts made a report which said that the payment and agreement "are neither of them such as the committee labored to obtain; yet the terms are better than at one period of negotiation they could reasonably have expected; and although unsatisfactory in themselves, are acceptable under the peculiar circumstances of the case." This skilfully contrived wording accomplished its purpose. Those directors who were ignorant of the plans of Dunlap and his associates were convinced by the report that Biddle and the other officers had been reluctant to pay, and Dunlap's part in the operation was deliberately concealed. The name of S. V. S. Wilder was substituted for that of the Bank's president, and only one director protested. He strove to get the report amended to include "the name of the person really interested in the one-fourth" for which settlement had been made with Wilder, but this attempt to bring Dunlap into public notice was defeated.[18]

No one outside the board was to be permitted to know that anyone other than Biddle, Jaudon, Cowperthwaite, and Andrews had borrowed from the Bank of which they were the principal officers, and the unanimous ten members then proceeded to adopt a series of resolutions criticizing their conduct and that of the exchange committee, which said that "the business of loaning money exclusively and of right belongs to the board of directors . . . that the loaning or discounting, on the deposite of collateral security or promissory notes of the officers of the Bank, was unauthorized; and . . . that the large advances made by the officers of the Bank, in the periods of 1837–38 and 1838–39, being totally unauthorized and unknown to the board of directors, merits and receives our just censure and condemnation."[19]

Reports of these resolutions spread through the financial community, and almost at once there was a decline in the price of the Bank's stock. It seemed to Biddle that this had been the purpose of the resolutions, and he could not understand, except on grounds of personal enmity, why those charged with responsibility for the Bank's welfare should seek to make the

[18] *House Executive Document* (29th Cong., 1st sess.), No. 226, pp. 420–22.
[19] *Ibid.*

impending task of resumption more difficult by adopting resolutions that were essentially false. Each of the loans criticized had been entered in full on the Bank's books, and any director who had examined the reports of the exchange committee could have learned of their existence. In addition, a standing committee of the board made a quarterly examination of every account, and at no time had it questioned the propriety of the loans to the officers or the very large operations in exchange that had been carried in the names of Bevan and Humphreys and S. V. S. Wilder.

Joseph Cabot, the managing partner of Bevan and Humphreys, had been a member of the board and of the exchange committee from 1838 to 1840; his fellow directors, had they wished, could have questioned him about these advances on cotton, and they could not properly plead ignorance of a fact that was being mentioned almost daily in the commercial newspapers of the United States and Great Britain. The policies that were criticized, if blameworthy, were the common responsibility of the directors, the exchange committee, the officers, and the stockholders, who had intrusted the management of the Bank to these particular individuals. The purpose of the resolutions, however, was to place all responsibility for the Bank's plight on Biddle and his closest associates and to exonerate Dunlap and the directors by admitting that, because of ignorance, inexperience, and neglect of their duties, they had permitted themselves to become the dupes of a shrewd and self-interested conspiracy among the senior officers of the Bank.

The leaders of the London financial committee and the other banks in Philadelphia were more conscious of the importance of supporting the United States Bank through the resumption crisis than were Dunlap and his supporters on the board of directors. In December, 1840, Jaudon arranged an additional loan of three million dollars in London, and the Philadelphia banks agreed to accept four and a half million dollars in post notes, due in eighteen months, in exchange for the same amount of current liabilities.[20] If those responsible for the Bank's management had been as confident and trusting as these outsiders, much that happened later would have been prevented. But for various reasons these opponents of Biddle were unwilling to forget or ignore the past and look to the future. As a result, the Bank and all that depended on it in the United States and Europe were destroyed.

20 *Niles' Register*, LIX (1841), 310.

36

The Failure
of the
United States Bank

*A*fter this December meeting of the board, Biddle abandoned all hope of influencing Dunlap and the directors effectively in the difficult months that lay ahead, and he looked to the incoming Whig administration as the only remaining chance to save the country, and with it the Bank, from failure and default. Reports reached Biddle that Harrison wanted him to be Secretary of the Treasury and that the President contemplated including in his inaugural address a recommendation for the recharter of the national bank; but Biddle believed both to be unwise. As to the post in the Cabinet, he wrote, "I would not go into the treasury for all the money in it"; and with respect to the proposal of the recharter, he doubted whether it was expedient to mention the national bank thus early. It would be better, he thought, to make "some quiet arrangement with the existing institution" and avoid raising an issue "that might be turned to mischief against the new administration before it had time to strengthen itself."[1]

The only position he wanted was the ministry to Austria, for Jane Biddle had never permitted him to forget that in 1815 he had contracted to take her to Europe, and he wrote to Webster, who had already been designated as the incoming Secretary of State: "It is the great wish of my family to travel in Europe, and I should incline to indulge it. But as you know travelling in Europe as a mere private gentleman is a dull business. . . . I would prefer some position within striking distance of all the places on the continent, and on the whole the place which seems best adapted

[1] N. Biddle to D. Webster, December 13, 30, 1840, February 2, 1841; N. Biddle to W. H. Harrison, December 13, 1840, in the Biddle Manuscripts in the Library of Congress.

for that purpose is Vienna. . . . The great interest to be encouraged there is the introduction upon better terms of our own tobacco, and this I could manage better, perhaps, than any mere planter who would carry about him the odour of his 'business.' "

On this matter he could write frankly to Webster because of their friendship, but he said nothing about another interest he wished to further in Europe, namely, the Republic of Texas. He had for a number of years been seeking to negotiate a loan for this strategically situated new country, and James Hamilton of South Carolina, who, partly through Biddle's influence, had been made financial agent for Texas in Europe, had reported that he was on the verge of success in gaining recognition and permission to sell bonds in Great Britain.[2] Biddle knew that Webster could not show too much interest in Texas, nor could any other politician serving as Secretary of State in 1841, and he carefully concealed his own desire to aid the republic, in preparation for the time when it could be annexed to the United States.

As American minister to Austria and as a financier of unparalleled reputation, Biddle could do much to help Hamilton procure the needed loan. But Webster, thinking of the political realities, denied Biddle the post. "Nobody could be better for the country," he wrote, "and nothing could be more agreeable to me. . . . The difficulty will be with the tobacco men." This rejection of Biddle's request and the unprotesting spirit in which it was accepted were attributable to the personal character of the two men and the relation that existed between them. Webster was at this time heavily indebted to the Bank, and Biddle, working indirectly, was trying to arrange a settlement through a partial payment. He continued this effort despite his disappointment at the failure of his application for a diplomatic appointment, and he ultimately achieved his purpose. The Bank lost nothing by this arrangement. Had it pressed for immediate payment in cash, Webster would have been forced to default. Nothing would have been accomplished except to bring financial disgrace upon one of the ablest leaders of the country at a time when his talents were needed as Secretary of State.[3]

Biddle expected nothing personal in return, and Webster, though fully appreciative of the exertions that had been made in his behalf, made no effort to repay them with political favors. These close relations with the members of the incoming administration, nevertheless, were why Biddle was so certain that if the Bank could survive through the strains and

[2] J. Hamilton to N. Biddle, December, 1840, in the Biddle Manuscripts in the Library of Congress.

[3] D. Webster to N. Biddle, December 24, 1840; N. Biddle to E. Curtis, February 2, 1841; N. Biddle to D. Webster, February 7, 1841; N. Biddle, memorandum, March 25, 1841, in the Biddle Manuscripts in the Library of Congress. Webster turned over all his land in the West to the Bank, with the exception of 1,120 acres in Illinois and one-fourth of his mineral lands in Wisconsin, in settlement of a debt of $114,000.

tensions engendered by the resumption of specie payments, it would be permanently safe and secure. His advice would be sought and followed in regard to financial matters, and there were many and varied ways through which an administration, confident of the future, could give positive and effective aid to the depressed economy. Fortune, which for so long had deserted him, now turned in his favor, and he was given an opportunity to resume control of the Bank. Shortly before the annual election of directors, Dunlap informed him that the proxies made out in Biddle's name, which had been turned over to the new president in April, 1839, could be voted only by Biddle himself, since "an old law of Pennsylvania forbade substitutions on proxies."[4]

The effect of this law was to give Biddle the power he had desired all through the fall. But at first he declined to accept this responsibility, having, he said, "withdrawn finally and totally from all share in administering the Bank and not wishing to resume any connection with it." This refusal seems to have been for the record, for, almost immediately, he reversed himself, "went to Mr. Dunlap and told him that having resolved to act, he would act exactly as he thought the interest of the Bank required . . . and that he was satisfied that . . . Mr. Jaudon should be at the head." As on previous occasions, Dunlap refused to resign in favor of Jaudon, whereupon Biddle told him that, while his name would be retained on the list of directors, that of Jaudon would also be included, so that upon his return from Europe he could be elected president.[5]

Dunlap would be permitted to continue until Jaudon's return, but he would be working with a board the majority of whom would be committed to the election of Jaudon and to the support of a new plan for restoring the credit of the Bank. This plan was exceedingly simple. It called for an open admission of the losses that had been incurred by the Bank through a petition to the Pennsylvania legislature for permission to cut down the stock to its true value and then to permit the institution to do business and to pay dividends on this reduced capital. "In short," as Biddle said, "to make a liberal allowance for bad debts and probable losses, and to commence on a new and better system." This reduction of capital was not so weak and inadequate a remedy as it appeared to be. By frankly admitting the extent of the Bank's losses, it would put an end to the exaggerated rumors that were circulating, and the Bank's creditors could see for themselves that they could collect what was due them.[6]

[4] N. Biddle, memorandum on the election of the directors of the Bank of the United States, January 4, 1841; N. Biddle to D. Webster, January 5, 1841, in the Biddle Manuscripts in the Library of Congress.

[5] *Ibid.*

[6] *Niles' Register*, LIX (1841), 310; S. R. Wood to N. Biddle, March 19, 1841; W. Ayres to N. Biddle, March 23, 25, 1841, in the Biddle Manuscripts in the Library of Congress; N. Biddle to J. M. Clayton, April 8, 1841, in *House Executive Document* (29th Cong., 1st sess.), No. 226, p. 475.

What Biddle was seeking was a restoration of confidence in the soundness and stability of the institution, and he was certain that he could persuade the governor and the legislature to give their consent to the proposed reorganization. The Bank had advanced almost eight million dollars to the state in the previous four years and had saved it from certain default. And on February 1 the Bank would again have to bear the principal share of another loan of eight hundred thousand dollars to pay interest on the state debt. For these reasons he was sure that, in return, the state authorities would grant his request and that this approval of the Bank's petition would add to its creditors' confidence by proving that the government of Pennsylvania, instead of being hostile, was supporting the United States Bank.[7]

Most of Biddle's bitterest opponents were not eligible for re-election to the board, and he had to change only four names on the list of directors previously prepared by Dunlap to gain a majority committed to his views. He made his plans in the utmost secrecy, and most observers were surprised when he appeared at the stockholders' meeting on January 4 and cast a majority of the votes. "We learn that Mr. Biddle, the late President of the Bank," a newspaper reported, "came to the election a few minutes before three o'clock, and by means of proxies . . . voted in four directors in lieu of four on the regular ticket. Our informant believes that this act . . . was without the concurrence or knowledge of the present officers of the Bank." The fact of his opposition to Dunlap, indicated in the above account, was confirmed by a second newspaper, which described Biddle's plan to cut down the capital and said, "a change of officers is also talked of."[8]

Having elected the board, Biddle withdrew from the meeting, and here he made a mistake. Dunlap, knowing that he would soon be replaced by Jaudon, apparently determined to make things as difficult as he could for his successor, and, instead of issuing a summary statement, as was usual, he gave the stockholders a printed list of the Bank's assets "calculated to inspire doubt and suspicion as to its solvency." Anyone who could read could ascertain the full amount of the book losses suffered by the Bank on its stocks and bonds simply by checking its holdings with current quotations. So what Dunlap did was to startle the stockholders into the sudden realization that the losses from operations, bad loans, and the investment account were more than seventeen million dollars. Those in attendance at the meeting had just been given this information when Biddle appeared at the meeting, and, as soon as he cast his votes and retired, Joshua Lippincott, a former director of the Bank and the president of the Schuylkill Navigation Company, proposed that a committee of six be elected to ex-

[7] N. Biddle to J. M. Clayton, April 9, 1841, in *House Executive Document* (29th Cong., 1st sess.), No. 226, p. 490.

[8] *Niles' Register*, LIX (1841), 308–10.

amine the report of the president and to ascertain the reason for the Bank's losses.

The motion was resisted, but a majority of the small group of stockholders left in the meeting voted in favor of it, and the mover of the resolution was named as chairman of the committee. Associated with him was Charles Massey, Jr., a partner of Eyre, the principal owner of the navigation company, and four others, three of whom resigned as soon as they were notified of their election, so that the committee, as Biddle pointed out, was "in fact a committee of the Schuylkill Navigation Company," since Lippincott and Massey made the choice of the three new members.[9]

The next day's newspapers published in full the financial statements that Dunlap had given the stockholders and also reports of the stockholders' concern. Nothing more harmful could possibly have been done; the publication of this statement, Biddle was certain, aroused the distrust of all the Bank's creditors and made it impossible for the Bank to survive. His predictions of disaster promptly came true. Creditors, instead of postponing the collection of their claims in order to help the Bank resume payments, came forward immediately to collect what they could before it was too late. On January 14 the Bank was notified that specie demands of two and a half million dollars would be presented when it opened its doors the next day, and a report from New York stated that a strong effort was being made "to get up a panic and cause a run for specie upon the United States Bank."[10]

The Bank did what it could to meet these demands. It sold bills of exchange on London and other assets in New York and used the means thus obtained to draw specie from that city and New England, and the other Philadelphia banks did what they could to sustain the institution upon which their own strength and welfare so much depended. But they could do little. They too were being subjected to pressure from New York and New England, and, contrary to their expectations, they had to meet the storm alone. The banks to the south and west, which originally had agreed to resume payments of specie on the same day as those of Pennsylvania, had decided it was inexpedient to do so. They held on to their specie, and their creditor banks in Philadelphia, which had planned to transfer part of the pressure for specie to them, were thus deprived of an important resource on which they had counted when making their preparations for the resumption of specie payments.

It was not long before individuals, frightened by reports of the reputed insolvency of the United States Bank and some of its neighbors, began panic withdrawals of specie, and it soon became apparent, as Biddle later reported, that so great "was the feeling of hostility to the institution, or,

[9] N. Biddle to J. M. Clayton, April 9, 1841, in *House Executive Document* (29th Cong., 1st sess.), No. 226, p. 491.

[10] *National Intelligencer* (Washington), January 12, 16, 26, February 4, 8, 16, 1841.

what was equally destructive, a pervading distrust of its credit and means" that it could not maintain specie payments unless it "was prepared to meet every dollar of . . . liabilities with a dollar of coin." The final blow, however, was administered by the state of Pennsylvania, which borrowed eight hundred thousand dollars in notes of the United States Bank from that institution and other banks for its interest payment on February 1 and immediately demanded that these notes be redeemed by the Bank in gold or silver. This senseless procedure may have saved the state a few dollars immediately, but it cost the state and its people much more than it saved, for, after meeting this demand, the Bank could go no further. On February 4 its directors announced the third suspension of specie payments, and, with this announcement, the United States Bank essentially closed its doors.[11]

Biddle was almost in despair. "The poor Bank!" he wrote Humphreys. "It grieves me to see it prostrated by the incompetency of its managers, for these are in truth the only causes of its disasters. I endeavoured to place Mr. Jaudon at the head of it, for that would have saved it, but this could not be and it has met its fate." And to Jaudon he said: "Our poor old ship is on her beams end, and all this from the sheerest folly of her officers and crew. The weakness and vacillation, which you saw and lamented, degenerated after you left . . . into absolute imbecility." Jaudon had not foreseen such a disaster when he left the United States, and the success that had attended his initial negotiations had increased his confidence. And on February 3, when he received the news that Biddle was to control the election of directors, he thought the Bank's problems were solved. "I have taken the advice given in your letter . . . ," he replied, "and have not yet made any arrangement that will bind me down to a residence in London. The door is open to a partnership with Mr. Morrison, but I find many reasons which incline me strongly to prefer returning to the United States."[12]

He could not leave London until he had made an arrangement to handle the payment on the Bank's debt that was due on April 15, which he thought could be done, he told Biddle, by paying 10 per cent and continuing the balance for two years. This would give time "for the measures of the new administration to act favorably on state stocks" and would relieve the market, which was "greatly depressed by the apprehension of a large amount to be suddenly forced upon it." But when he received the news of the stockholders' meeting, he knew that all hope for a quiet and smooth resumption of specie payments was gone and, with it, his hopes for

[11] "Report of the Board of Directors of the Bank of the United States, April 3, 1841," in *House Executive Document* (29th Cong., 1st sess.), No. 226, pp. 471–73.

[12] S. Jaudon to N. Biddle, February 3, 1840; N. Biddle to S. Jaudon, March 9, 1841; N. Biddle to M. Humphreys, March 9, 1841, in the Biddle Manuscripts in the Library of Congress.

additional credit in Europe. He blamed the Bank's failure on the publication of the statement and said that if this had not been done, the Bank would easily have surmounted the crisis and would have become the fiscal agent of the national treasury. But now, he predicted, the United States would "have a new national bank with its headquarters in New York."[13]

"I do hope," he continued, "that the committee appointed at the stockholders' meeting will not make matters still worse by unnecessary and exasperating publications. If they confine themselves to a valuation of the assets and to the recommendation of such measures as may tend to restore confidence, and set the Bank in operation again even on a reduced capital, they may do good. I hope your influence . . . may be exerted to prevent mischief." Biddle unfortunately had no influence with the committee. In the beginning he had persuaded the directors "to keep this committee of investigation to their proper sphere of verifying the assets"; but, as soon as the Bank suspended payments, the board, in "alarm and confusion," abandoned this restriction. A resolution was passed which declared that the directors were ready to afford "every facility in the prosecution of any investigation which the committee may be willing to make of the affairs and transactions of this bank, and the causes of its actual situation; and that it is the wish of the board that the committee should make such an investigation."[14]

The directors soon recovered from their panic, but the mischief had been done. Lippincott and Massey, who dominated the committee, directed its investigations toward those aspects of the Bank's history that could be used to discredit its former officers, and soon Philadelphia was alive with rumors concerning these matters. In the meantime, Biddle was making a last effort to save the Bank from complete failure by an appeal to the Pennsylvania legislature for a remission of the penalties imposed by the act calling for the resumption of specie payments. On February 13, the directors, following his recommendations, presented a memorial stating that the suspension of payments had been caused by "a combination of hostile interests, or what, without personal combination, may have been equally effectual, a pervading distrust, stimulated into activity by the public press in another state." In the short space of eighteen banking days "upwards of six million dollars in specie, and in funds equivalent to specie, were demanded and received at the Bank of the United States; and still the demand continued in such force as to make it perfectly certain that it would be fruitless to persevere."

The legislature was reminded that the Bank had paid over three million dollars to the state for its charter; that it had invested almost a million and

[13] S. Jaudon to N. Biddle, February 9, March 18, 1841, in the Biddle Manuscripts in the Library of Congress.

[14] N. Biddle to J. M. Clayton, April 14, 1841, in *House Executive Document* (29th Cong., 1st sess.), No. 226, pp. 492–93.

a half in state-sponsored internal improvements; and that it had loaned to the state more than eight million dollars in the preceding four years. But it was not on the grounds of these past services that the Bank appealed for exemption from penalties which the legislature had imposed and which it could repeal. The directors were looking to future of the state and the nation, and they warned that the imposition of the penalties would inevitably retard the payment of debts and would produce "a wasteful sacrifice of capital," an increase in the "prevailing embarrassment and discredit," and a loss to Pennsylvania itself. If the Bank's charter were forfeited, its stockholders would not be the only ones who suffered loss. Its notes and other liabilities would "become a thing to wager upon at the exchange, blown up one day by hope, thrown down the next by fear, and at all times the subject of contrivances to bring about the gain of one by the loss of another."[15]

The true interest of the public lay in assisting the stockholders to "make the most of their concern in this bank for themselves as well as for their creditors, and they should not be crippled by penal restrictions, nor hunted down by persecution." No risk was involved in permitting the Bank to continue in business, for the sufficiency of its assets to meet all engagements to creditors was a matter of absolute certainty. Its stocks and bonds, now depressed in price, would rise to par and higher if time were provided. The railroads and canals would begin to make profits when the movement of commodities was stimulated, and the states of Pennsylvania, Mississippi, Maryland, Indiana, Michigan, Illinois, and Ohio would be able to pay interest and principal as soon as their citizens could afford to be taxed.

But if "through measures of madness or folly," the Bank was thrown into liquidation, the value of personal securities would be destroyed, real estate would be "dead in the hands of those who own it," and the eight million dollars of Pennsylvania debt held by the Bank would be thrown into the market. "In the face of this contingency," the directors concluded, "what is to be the market price of the public debt . . . held to a great extent by her own citizens? What is to be the ability of the state to complete and bring into profitable operation her public works? What are to be the consequent effects upon all property?" The legislators were impressed by this argument. They did not see how the public could gain by "swelling the mass of stocks, debts, and land for peremptory sale in a market already burdened with more than could be absorbed," and late in March they passed an act exempting the banks from any special penalties for failure to pay specie and authorizing the reduction of the capital of the United States Bank to fourteen million dollars if the stockholders so desired.[16]

[15] "Memorial of the President and Directors of the United States Bank of Pennsylvania, February 13, 1841," *ibid.*, pp. 531–35.

[16] *Ibid.*; *Niles' Register*, LX (1841), 70.

The governor was still considering this act when, on April 5, the stock-holders' committee presented its report. And one Philadelphian, upon reading it, wrote in his diary that it would destroy "the character and repu-tation of Mr. Nicholas Biddle." No doubt existed in his mind as to the complete truth of the charges brought by the committee, and he said that there had been not only "gross mismanagement" but also "culpable breaches of trust" and the "most wanton disregard of the interests of the stockholders." The revelations did not end here. Soon afterward the same diarist noted: "Met Mr. Dobyn, who walked with me for a square or two. He told me there is in the Bank of the United States a promissory note of Mrs. H——t, for twenty thousand dollars, with two hundred shares of Vicksburg Banking and Railroad stock pledged as collateral security. Madame has been for several years on the most intimate footing with Mr. Nicholas Biddle . . . and this discount . . . looks very much like the 'gage d'amitié' as the French say."[17]

The *Spirit of the Times* repeated this charge without mentioning names, and the editor commented: "The whole amount was the price of an in-trigue, a base intrigue of a high officer of the Bank, who . . . glories in his iniquity and defies public opinion." Such stories, magnified and distorted as they passed from person to person, gave to many a satisfactory explana-tion of the economic difficulties of the country. They ascribed their troubles not to general economic conditions but to a single individual and a single institution. And national or state politicians, puzzled and despair-ing in the face of their inability to understand or control the financial crisis, seized upon this easy explanation and joined with the people in the denun-ciation of Biddle and the United States Bank. On April 8 the governor of Pennsylvania vetoed the bill relieving the state banks from penalties for not paying specie, on the ground that it would benefit this discredited insti-tution; and it was after the directors had already made an assignment of assets to preferred creditors that the legislature repassed the bill over the governor's veto.[18]

The directors made no attempt to resume business as a result of this act, which merely assured them that the charter would not be forfeited, and on September 2 they executed a deed of general assignment to a committee of five trustees. The Bank closed its doors, and Charles Dickens, when he visited Philadelphia some months later, looked out from his hotel window

[17] August Pleasanton, Diary, April 8, May 3, 1841, in the Pleasanton Manuscripts, in the Historical Society of Pennsylvania. The truth or falsity of this report made no difference in regard to the verdict of the public on Biddle, but it seems not to be true. When Biddle was infatuated with Amerigo Vespucci, he gave clear evidence of his feeling in his papers and journals. But Mrs. Hunt and her husband were family friends, and there is no evidence of undue intimacy between her and Biddle.

[18] *Niles' Register*, LX (1841), 117–19; "Report to the Stockholders of the United States Bank, January 3, 1842," in *House Executive Document* (29th Cong., 1st sess.), No. 226, pp. 535–43.

and saw "on the opposite side of the way, a handsome building of white marble, which had a mournful ghost-like aspect, dreary to behold." He was puzzled by its appearance. "I attributed this to the sombre influence of the night," he recorded, "and on rising in the morning looked out again, expecting to see its steps and portico thronged with groups of people passing in and out. The door was still tight shut . . . the same cold cheerless air prevailed, and the building looked as if the marble statue of Don Gusman could alone have any business to transact within its gloomy walls. I hastened to inquire its name and purpose, and then my surprise vanished. It was the tomb of many fortunes; the great catacomb of investment; the memorable United States Bank."[19]

[19] Charles Dickens, *American Notes* (New York, 1905), pp. 115–16.

$$\sim_\circ \quad 37 \quad \circ_\sim$$

Depression

$\mathcal{T}$ he failure of the United States Bank destroyed most of what remained of Biddle's reputation and standing among his fellow countrymen. Instead of being welcome in every house, the doors of nearly all were shut against him, and the societies of which he had been a favorite member were annoyed when he intruded among them. Those who as directors, counselors, and borrowers had idolized him, a close friend of Biddle's charged, became his merciless revilers. They turned their demigod into a demon and held him answerable as a culprit for the offenses they had advised, sustained, and applauded. Biddle gave no outward sign that he was aware of his social ostracism and "went abroad as usual" with no change in "aspect, manners, or behavior." His concern was for the institution, its stockholders, and the other officers, particularly Jaudon, who might still have rescued the Bank, had he been elected president immediately after its failure.[1]

Biddle had made no defense of himself or his policies before the committee report was published, and he had been quiet and secretive in his efforts to prevent the resumption of specie payments and to replace Dunlap with Jaudon. The Bank, he had thought, had quarrels enough with outsiders. What it had needed was repose, not recriminations and faultfinding, and he had accepted without protest the responsibility placed upon him for its condition and situation. "I have contradicted nothing and explained nothing," he wrote, "because I could do neither without injury to the Bank." But the publication of the committee's report freed him from this restraint, and shortly thereafter he told Webster that he was preparing an answer to the assault made by the committee on the former officers. "I shall not fail to vindicate Jaudon, the treatment of whom I consider infamous," he wrote. "The real cause of the attack upon him is the desire to put him out of the way for the presidency of the Bank and above all his being the friend of the Reading Railroad which is a mortal sin to those who govern the Schuylkill Navigation Company, a clique which has produced all this

[1] Ingersoll, *Historical Sketch,* II, 286.

mischief and is willing to break down the Bank in order to break down that rival railroad."[2]

The Bank, Biddle believed, could have survived the third suspension of specie payments if all those connected with it had rallied to its defense, for both the state government and the new administration in Washington had reasons to come to its aid. Most of the banks in Philadelphia, Baltimore, and the interior had continued in business after the suspension, and so could the United States Bank, had not the stockholders' committee chosen to vilify all those who had hitherto managed the institution. The committee's report had so completely destroyed the Bank's credit that it had been unable to obtain aid in the United States or in Europe; and state and national politicians of both parties, instead of being free to come to the rescue of this vitally important institution, had been forced by popular feeling to join in the attacks upon it.[3]

The chairman of the investigating committee was later to deny that the report had been "injurious to the stockholders" and insisted that it had been his intention to reassure the stockholders by presenting them with a fair and honest estimate of the probable future worth of the Bank's assets in better times, so that they would be encouraged to hold on to their stock. If such was his purpose, he chose a strange way to accomplish it. The investigation uncovered no evidence of fraud or embezzlement, but the tone and phraseology of the report conveyed this impression. No attempt was made to put any transactions in their proper perspective, and all but the best-informed readers were convinced that the officers had betrayed their responsibilities to the stockholders by using the funds of the Bank almost exclusively to further their personal interests. The large advances on stocks and commodities were described as if they had been routine operations of the Bank rather than expedients to meet a national and international emergency; and the sole reference to disturbed financial conditions all over the world was the admission that the general derangement of financial affairs had had something to do with the high costs of the loans negotiated by Jaudon.[4]

The report made no mention of the specie circular, the distribution act, the pressures generated by the restrictive policies of the Bank of England, of any other of the causes of the crisis and suspension in 1837. It likewise said nothing about the sale of post notes in August, 1839; nothing of the refusal of the Bank's bills of exchange by Hottinguer and Company; and nothing of Dunlap's attempt to make the suspension of specie payments fall first upon the banks of New York. Instead, the committee had concentrated attention on the loans and advances made to the officers during Bid-

---

[2] N. Biddle to D. Webster, April 5, 10, 1841, in the Biddle Manuscripts in the Library of Congress.

[3] *House Executive Document* (29th Cong., 1st sess.), No. 226, pp. 482, 507.

[4] *Ibid.*, pp. 411–24, 446–54, 520.

dle's administration and had aroused the indignation of the stockholders and creditors by obscuring the fact that most of the loans and advances had been obtained to undertake purchases of stocks and commodities for the protection of the Bank and the national economy, not for the profit of the persons concerned.

In Biddle's opinion, the committee, with hostile intent, had deliberately chosen this form of presentation, and he particularly resented its claim to have given "the simple facts without comment." Nine times out of ten, he insisted, "simple facts, without comment, are made to tell the greatest false-hoods. Facts are not truth, they are only the materials of truth; and their value, nay their very meaning, depends on the manner in which they are presented. Forty-nine facts may make a falsehood, until the fiftieth makes truth of the whole; and quite as much deception is produced by misplacing facts, as by total fiction." Biddle's explanation and defense of his policies and administration, which were published in the form of public letters to Senator John M. Clayton of Delaware, were open to this same objection, and the committee, in its reply, said with some sarcasm that the question which separated it and Biddle was "whether the losses of the stockholders are to be ascribed to the policy and measures which caused prostration, as the committee thought, or to the occurrences which made that prostration known to the world, as Mr. Biddle contends."[5]

This statement, strange as it may seem, was the literal truth; for to Bid-dle, more knowledgeable than most of his generation on the subject of credit, it was obvious that few banks, merchants, or farmers, however sol-vent and liquid they might be, could escape prostration if suddenly called on to pay a large proportion of their debts at one time. The difference be-tween solvency and insolvency was frequently the amount of time given a debtor to meet his engagements; and this was particularly true of the United States Bank in 1841, which, through its long-continued effort to protect and support the American economy, had suffered great losses and had been unable to dispose of its assets with sufficient rapidity to meet needless and destructive demands for immediate payment.

When the Bank closed its doors, it was not insolvent, merely illiquid. Its capital of thirty-five million dollars had been impaired, but relatively no more than that of other institutions which survived; and its assets, even at current prices, exceeded its liabilities by a sizable margin. Its European debts were in excellent condition. Jaudon had arranged for their retirement in manageable instalments over a period of years, and a sizable part of its current obligations in the United States had been similarly postponed. What Biddle had wanted Dunlap, the directors, and the stockholders to do at this moment of crisis was to think of the future, not of the past, and, by appearing confident, to inspire faith in the Bank. All efforts, in his opinion, should have been directed toward convincing the Bank's creditors that

[5] *Ibid.*, pp. 519, 520, 522.

they were secure; but his opponents within the institution had followed the opposite course and had completed the work started by Jackson in his first message to Congress. The effect of the publication of the detailed financial statement on the eve of the resumption of specie payments was to destroy all confidence in the United States Bank. Its creditors, instead of delaying their demands, rushed in to get what they could before it was too late, and no bank, particularly one just resuming specie payments, could stand up under such pressure.

The work started by the publication of this statement was completed by the report of the stockholders' committee, and thus Dunlap, Lippincott, Eyre, Massey, and those who supported them succeeded in doing what "the opposition of a whole popular party, led on by a popular chief" had been unable to do—they brought down the United States Bank. In 1811, when the anti-Madison group in the Republican party determined to prevent the recharter of the first Bank, Biddle had compared these politicians to a child "who wishes to wind up a watch to hear the noise and set it going again"; and the same might be said of those, thirty years later, who concentrated upon identifying the causes of their troubles instead of seeking the best means to work out of them. They broke the "main spring" of their own security and prosperity, and within a brief period seven other Philadelphia banks closed their doors. The city, according to one observer, was as quiet as a village. "The streets seem deserted," he wrote, "the largest houses are shut up and to rent, there is no business, there is no money, no confidence and little hope, property is sold everyday by the sheriff at a fourth of the estimated value of a few years ago, nobody can pay debts, everyone you see looks careworn and haggard."[6]

The damage was not confined to Philadelphia alone. States, unable to collect taxes, postponed scheduled payments of interest and principal, and four (Mississippi, Arkansas, Florida, and Michigan) repudiated the whole of their public debt. Prices and wages continued to decline, unemployment increased, and no one profited except the few rich persons who had money to spend or to lend. These few could buy what they wanted at sacrifice prices and make loans at oppressive rates, but the more directly productive groups in society (the workers, the farmers, the mechanics, the manufacturers, the merchants, and the shippers), lacking employers or customers, became poorer as these "monied aristocrats" increased their wealth.[7]

Britain and other European nations were also injured by the collapse of the American economy. The elimination of the United States as a market for manufactured goods led to widespread unemployment among factory

[6] "Diaries of Sidney George Fisher, 1841–1843," *Pennsylvania Magazine of History and Biography*, LXXIX (1955), 217–36; Nicholas B. Wainwright, *The Philadelphia National Bank* (Philadelphia, 1953), pp. 85–89.

[7] Samuel Rezneck, "The Social History of an American Depression, 1837–1843," *American Historical Review*, LX (1935), 682–87.

workers, and the holders of American stocks and bonds suffered from the failure of the states and private issuers to pay interest or dividends. The resulting loss of confidence fostered a feeling of insecurity all over the world, and the Bank of England and other central institutions, instead of relaxing their restrictions on credit, continued them in effect. The decade as a whole became known as "the hungry forties," and, in the long years of depression that followed the failure of the United States Bank, the Chartist movement in Great Britain and the more radical revolutionary movements on the Continent gained increasing strength. The established leaders of these nations seemed incapable of suggesting effective reforms. Instead, they denounced the United States and its republican institutions and blamed many of their political and economic difficulties upon the American failure to pay what was owed.[8]

Pennsylvania was one of the states forced to default on their interest payments, and Biddle, in an effort to show how the state could regain its reputation for financial probity, published a series of letters in a Philadelphia newspaper. He attributed the situation to the influence of Jackson and Van Buren, who for many years had sought to persuade the states to construct internal improvements, and he demonstrated by quotations from messages to Congress, the Maysville road veto, and editorials in the party's official newspaper how Pennsylvania, in constructing railroads, turnpikes, and canals, had simply followed the policy recommended by these national executives. It was they who had encouraged the state to embark with "reckless improvidence" on an overambitious program that ultimately exhausted its funds and destroyed its credit. His primary purpose, however, was not to explain how Pennsylvania's troubles originated but rather to show how they could be surmounted, and, on the day before the letters began to appear, he wrote to James Gordon Bennett: "I am going to make an effort to help the state . . . by satisfying her that she is able to pay her debts and satisfying foreigners that she is willing to pay. At the same time I think it right to rebuke these foreigners for their insolence in denouncing the United States."[9]

In terms reminiscent of Hamilton, he rejected the notion that Pennsylvania or any other state should or would repudiate its just obligations. The present holder of bonds must be paid the face value and accumulated interest, regardless of what the purchase price had been. This he thought the only fair and honorable method because Pennsylvania had already been more than compensated for its expenditures by the increased property values in the areas served by the partially completed transportation net. It

[8] N. Biddle to D. Webster, April 20, 1843; N. Biddle to J. G. Rockhill, April 8, 1843; S. Jaudon to N. Biddle, April 11, 1843; Hartz, *Economic Policy*, pp. 161–64; Reginald C. McGrane, *Foreign Bondholders and American State Debts* (New York, 1935), pp. 65–72.

[9] *Inquirer* (Philadelphia), November 23, 24, 25, December 1, 3, 9, 1842.

was also able now to compete with its neighbors for the trade between the East and the West; the Great Lakes had been opened to the coal and iron of Pittsburgh; and when the whole system was eventually completed, the income from tolls would be more than sufficient to pay the entire debt. It would thus be to the interest of Pennsylvania and its bondholders alike if these internal improvements were completed, and the only persons from whom to seek the needed capital were those who had previously invested in these enterprises. The state's foreign creditors, Biddle said, were reasonable and intelligent men and would "make further advances to complete works, now unfinished and unproductive," if Pennsylvania, through its legislature, proved its willingness and ability to pay its debts by adopting a policy of rigid economy and increased taxes.

The payment of what was justly due to the foreign bondholders would thus have a double advantage. It would save the state and its people from dishonor and give to them an effective system of internal transportation. All that was needed was for the legislators to have the political courage to impose increased taxes, and Biddle, with more than usual eloquence, urged them to do so and the people to accept. "Having spoken thus strongly on the duty of Pennsylvania toward its creditors," he went on, "I shall speak with equal freedom of the conduct of those creditors themselves towards Pennsylvania." He admitted that it seemed a little inappropriate for a debtor in default to reproach his creditor, but in this instance, he insisted, there was justification, for the creditor had played a considerable part "in occasioning the default."[10]

Pennsylvania and other American borrowers, it was true, had acted irresponsibly in accumulating too large a debt in order to undertake too many internal improvements simultaneously and, through careless supervision and construction, had permitted the costs to be at least a third greater than they needed to be. But they had been encouraged in this course by the willingness of the Europeans to lend when economic circumstances had indicated that the proper policy was to contract. In Biddle's opinion, the Bank of England bore the larger part of the responsibility for the undue expansion of the sale of American securities by reducing its rediscount rate in the autumn of 1838 in spite of the large exportation of bullion made necessary by the failure of Britain's crops. It "took in no sail as the squall was coming," he said, but, on the contrary, increased its loans, and "thus to the eye everything in the English monied market seemed rose-colored, money being abundant and stocks high."

It did nothing to stop the drain of specie until May, 1839, and then suddenly, to save itself from destruction, it made "a general ruin about it." The resulting panic "fell with particular violence on American securities," which were then denounced "as one of the principal causes of the trouble." The prices of these declined, and at the same time American commodities,

10 *Ibid.*

which were the sole means of payment, now that access to additional credit was denied, became almost unsalable except at great sacrifice. Biddle by these statements did not mean to cast "the slightest reproach on the administration of the Bank of England, which, though very slow to perceive the danger, overcame it by proper exertions," but he did want to point to the moral: that creditors, if they wanted their debtors to pay, should not, by undue contraction of credit, prevent them from doing so or, by defaming their character, make it impossible for them to borrow elsewhere.

In thus making the Europeans partly responsible for their losses on American loans, Biddle was not seeking to exculpate Pennsylvania itself, which, first, by loading its banks with state securities had forced them to suspend specie payments and then had compounded its error by requiring a premature resumption. The Pennsylvania banks might have complied with this unwise legislative injunction, he reminded his readers, if the state had not at the same time demanded a loan of eight hundred thousand dollars in specie to cover interest payments due fifteen days after the date of resumption. "Had I been in the situation I once occupied," he wrote, "I would not have permitted the resumption, and I think I could have postponed it; for in times of wild excitement, what is most needed is some stern and stubborn will, to resist these heated crowds until they come to their senses; but as a private citizen, I could only reason, and remonstrate, and warn against the design."[11]

When he wrote these words, Biddle was regretting that he had not followed the advice of Lewis S. Coryell, a former director of the Bank, who on December 30, 1840, had suggested that he reassume the office and president. "You alone can bring the Bank up again," Coryell had written, "and prepare it for that universal confidence that it once had over the whole commercial world. There is none that can really be . . . head of this institution but yourself and to restore it to confidence once more would be glory . . . greater than ever fell to any one man in a civil point of view." Biddle had been unwilling to make this sacrifice of his leisure, to use the proxies fortuitously turned over to him as a means to resume the presidency of the Bank, and he knew that he was thus at least partly responsible for all that happened subsequently. With a board of directors committed to saving the Bank, he could have resisted the resumption of specie payments, prevented the stockholders' committee from having access to the personal accounts, and saved himself and the other officers from the discredit which, besides injuring and humiliating them personally, had proved disastrous to the Bank.[12]

His purpose, however, was not to weep over lost opportunities but to convince his readers that the premature resumption of specie payments,

[11] *Ibid.*

[12] Lewis S. Coryell to N. Biddle, December 30, 1840, in the Biddle Manuscripts in the Library of Congress.

which he called "an act of madness," had been totally unnecessary and had cost the state at least one hundred million dollars. It had made Philadelphia "one mass of ruins" without accomplishing a single useful thing, as could be seen, he said, from the example of Virginia, Ohio, Kentucky, and Tennessee, "who were wise enough to wait till they gained strength for resumption," so that they could return to specie payments "without any of the sacrifices" which had prostrated Pennsylvania.

These attempts to transfer the level of discussion from the question of personal responsibility for the crisis to that of banking and monetary policy and theory went unheeded by most of Biddle's fellow citizens. The stockholders were unconvinced by his effort to show that he and the Bank had been victims rather than causes of the depression, and, as a result of their complaints, the Grand Jury indicted him, Cowperthwaite, Dunlap, Jaudon, and Andrews in December, 1841, for fraud and theft in taking and using for their own benefit money belonging to the stockholders. So lacking in substance was the evidence upon which this indictment was based that the court before whom the officers were brought dismissed it without argument; and civil suits brought against the same parties to collect the million dollars and more expended by the Bank between 1836 and 1841 for unspecified purposes were not brought to trial. These expenditures, everyone knew, had been made to obtain the charter and to protect the Bank from legislative attack. All had been "duly examined, reported upon by a committee, and confirmed by the board of directors," and it was therefore improper to blame them on the officers alone. No money had been spent to influence elections in favor of one party or the other; all had been used to further positive and tangible interests of the Bank; and if anything deserved condemnation in this matter, it was not the persons involved but the political system which made such expenditure a necessary and customary act by corporations in all the states.[13]

The stockholders and other sufferers from the depression were in no mood to make such technical distinctions. They resented the fact that Biddle had escaped punishment and uttered many complaints about the apparent luxury in which he lived. At the height of his success, Biddle, perhaps in vanity and pride, had changed "Andalusia" into a mansion in the Greek style by the addition of stone wings and a columned portico copied from the Temple of Theseus.[14] He had also built great forcing houses of stone and glass, heated by specially designed furnaces, in which he raised silkworms, rare grapes, and other plants unsuited to the rigors of the Pennsylvania winter. In his stables and barns he continued to raise thor-

[13] *Inquirer* (Philadelphia), December 15, 1841, May 10, 1842; "Diaries of Sidney George Fisher," *Pennsylvania Magazine of History and Biography*, LXXIX (1955), 230, 358–59.

[14] Thomas U. Walters designed and supervised the changes at "Andalusia" from October, 1834, to September, 1836. The total costs were approximately $15,000, and Walters was paid a fee of $1,050.

oughbred horses, cattle, sheep, and swine; and his carefully cultivated and irrigated gardens and fields gave no outward appearance of any change in his personal circumstances. But the money now being spent to maintain the place was not his own. His personal fortune, which had amounted to almost a million dollars at the time of his retirement, had evaporated in the general collapse of security and land prices and in the payments of debts. He was entirely dependent upon his wife's income from her father's estate, and they retained possession of "Andalusia," her family home, only because he had mortgaged it to the estate as security for money he had borrowed.[15]

His brother and son, as trustees for Mrs. Biddle, foreclosed the mortgage and bought the house in at a public sale in Bucks County for eight thousand dollars. Only six persons outside the family were present when the sale was made—a not untypical circumstance in these depression years—but it led some of Biddle's creditors to charge that the mortgage, foreclosure, and repurchase were part of a scheme deliberately devised to defraud them. He did not deny this accusation, feeling it useless; and he continued to live in his mansion without any outward indication of his inner humiliation. He also remained quiet when he was condemned for the excessive costs of the building for the Girard College for Orphans, which, like "Andalusia" and the Bank of the United States, had been built in the classical style at his instigation. In the spring of 1833, Biddle had been named chairman of the board of trustees of this institution, which had been given an endowment of two million dollars by the will of Stephen Girard, and he had thought it appropriate that such an undertaking should be given a building that was Greek in appearance and spirit.[16]

The plans, originally submitted by Thomas U. Walters, had called for a building which, in Biddle's opinion, wanted "simplicity and purity," and the architect had not been easily persuaded to take the advice of an enthusiastic amateur. Eventually and reluctantly he had consented and took advantage of what Biddle called "this rare opportunity of immortalizing himself by a perfect chaste specimen of Grecian architecture." He prepared new plans for a building in the Corinthian order taken from the Lantern of Demosthenes in Athens, and, if it had not been for delays brought about by the financial difficulties of 1837, the college would have been completed and in operation shortly thereafter. Additional delays occurred, however, and when the Bank failed, the building was only two-thirds completed, one million two hundred thousands dollars had been

[15] J. Biddle to E. C. Biddle, June 7, 1842, in the Biddle Manuscripts at "Andalusia"; J. Fox to J. Cadwalader, October 3, 1842, in the Cadwalader Manuscripts in the Historical Society of Pennsylvania; *Saturday Courier* (Philadelphia), November 26, 1842.

[16] Henry W. Arey, *The Girard College and Its Founder* (Philadelphia, 1866), pp. 30–37; N. Biddle, manuscript journal, in the Biddle Manuscripts in the Historical Society of Pennsylvania; *Hazard's Commercial Register*, III (1841), 113–18, 247–53, 257–63.

spent, and the mayor and aldermen of Philadelphia, as trustees of Girard's estate, indignantly dismissed Biddle as chairman of the board. The citizens of Philadelphia thus had during the long years of depression three monuments to what they described as Biddle's wastefulness, extravagance, and folly, and each was modeled after the Greek. It was no wonder, therefore, that Charles J. Ingersoll, trying to describe the irony and tragedy of Biddle's situation, should have turned to Greek mythology; comparing him to Acteon torn to pieces by the "dogs" who in the days of his prosperity and power had "licked his hands and fawned on his footsteps."[17]

Biddle, who had become inured through the years to such misinterpretation of his motives, purposes, and actions, was less indignant than Ingersoll at these personal attacks. They made his years of retirement less quiet and peaceful than he had thought they would be, but this gossip and slander were not the chief sources of his real grief and concern. What desolated him most was the destruction of the financial system he had created and the national prosperity it had fostered. But, instead of being discouraged by this failure, he continued to work through the few remaining years of his life to restore the United States to the high position it had attained just before its great collapse.

[17] Talbot Hamlin, *Greek Revival Architecture in America* (London, 1944), pp. 83–84; Ingersoll, *Historical Sketch*, II, 286.

~~ *38* ~~

Conclusion

*I*n the early 1840's the American nation seemed to be disintegrating, having lost the will and power to do anything for its own recovery to strength. One cynical observer in Philadelphia said that the whole community was waiting with trembling anxiety for a savior while the "selfish and corrupt politicians at Washington and Harrisburg" did nothing but maneuver and plan to advance the claims "of the rival candidates for the presidency." The Whigs, like the Democrats who preceded them, were hopelessly divided as to the proper measures of relief and recovery. A bill prepared at the direction of President Harrison called for the creation of a national bank that was similar in form and powers to the Bank of the United States, but Clay and the other congressional leaders of the party refused to accept it. They, Biddle said, distrusted "the remedy which has twice restored us to health," resorting instead to "quackery to obtain not the genuine remedy, but something so like it that we may deceive ourselves as well as the world."[1]

When Tyler, who succeeded to the presidency after Harrison's sudden death, vetoed this measure, the Congress prepared another which, in Biddle's opinion, "was on the whole rather worse than the first." It was to be administered "by nine politicians at Washington" in a manner reminiscent of Jackson's treasury bank, and no one, Biddle contended, would subscribe to the stock of such an institution. This bill also was vetoed, and most of the Whigs denounced Tyler as a traitor. All the Cabinet members except Webster resigned their positions in protest, and the congressional leaders introduced constitutional amendments limiting the veto power and restricting each president to a single term. This was too much for Biddle. "If these be the principles of the Whig party," he wrote, "I am glad I am not a Whig for two more mischievous changes could not well be imagined."[2]

[1] N. Biddle, memorandum on politics, n.d., in the Biddle Manuscripts in the Library of Congress.
[2] *Ibid*.

[408]

Once again he deserted a party when it ceased to be nationalist, and he hoped that the split in the Whigs would lead to the formation of "a party of the best men in the country" committed to the advancement of the national interest. He believed that if such a party could be formed, Webster would be its candidate at the next election, and for this reason he urged him to remain in the Cabinet, so that Tyler would not turn to the Locofocos out of enmity to all the Whigs. Biddle also wanted Webster to have the distinction of settling the Maine boundary dispute between the United States and Great Britain, even though he himself, he insisted half-seriously, was no longer an advocate of peace. "I am beginning to think," he wrote to a friend, "that in the present disorders of the country, a little war would be a good thing to put us to rights. Mr. Peters, the British Consul, was at my house last night and I expressed my willingness for a war, offering to be beaten for a year or eighteen months, when it would be our turn to conquer and relieve England of all her American possessions."[3]

The sectional disputes over slavery and the general economic discontent were creating divisions within the country which would probably be overcome if the United States were confronted by a powerful enemy, and war, he was certain, would be less injurious and dangerous to freedom and national strength than internal disunity. He did not seriously want the United States to acquire Canada or even all the Oregon territory, but he did want Texas, and this in the prevailing climate of opinion seemed almost an impossibility. The abolitionists (whom he now denounced as "deplorable" examples of the American tendency to adopt "with equal frivolity the latest English fashion of philanthropy and dress") had organized a powerful lobby against the acquisition of Texas, but he thought that Webster, as a resident of a non-slaveholding state and a personal opponent of slavery, might be able to win the consent of the Senate to the annexation of this strategically important area. "How, when, or where could we have a long talk about Texas?" Biddle asked the Secretary of State in the early winter of 1843. "I have long been of opinion that *there* is the true road of repairing the wrongs of fortune to some of my friends; and the moment I think not far distant. Take it altogether it is the largest question for a statesman now before us."[4]

By this time, he had only small holdings of Texas bonds, for most of those he had purchased earlier had been turned over to the Bank in payment of his share of the cotton losses; but he still had title to substantial tracts of land which might become valuable if Texas came into the United States. This personal interest, however, was not the prime reason for his

---

[3] N. Biddle to R. M. Blatchford, December 5, 1841; N. Biddle to D. Webster, February 24, 26, 1842; January 18, February 27, April 5, 24, 1843, in the Biddle Manuscripts in the Library of Congress.

[4] N. Biddle to C. J. Ingersoll, June 28, 1841; N. Biddle to D. Webster, January 18, 1843, in the Biddle Manuscripts in the Library of Congress.

involvement in this issue. He was an expansionist who wanted the United States to control all the area from ocean to ocean, the islands in the Caribbean, and the approaches to the Gulf of Mexico, including the Isthmus of Panama. "I have long said," he wrote Tyler, "that as the purchase of Louisiana was the glory of Mr. Jefferson's administration; the war of Mr. Madison's; the acquisition of Florida, the pride of Mr. Monroe's; there is yet reserved for another president the brilliant achievement of enlarging the empire by the annexation of Texas. What you think on this subject, I do not know and certainly do not mean to enquire. All that I wish is to apprize you that if you should undertake that measure, you shall find in me a zealous though feeble cooperator."[5]

When Biddle was thus writing to Webster and Tyler about Texas, he had already been stricken with the illness that was to cost him his life. His health had long been a source of concern to his wife and family, and during his last years at the Bank, though he had no specific ailment, he was constantly feeling tired and weak. At least twice a year, usually toward the end of the hot summer and during the severe weather of winter, he was confined to his bed for varying lengths of time, and his physicians had joined his family in urging him to retire. Jane Biddle was particularly insistent. She had never wanted him to be a great man, distracted from his family by the affairs of the world, but had thought that he should follow the example of her brothers, who, having inherited enough money to have pleasant homes, fine horses, and all the pleasures of life, did nothing but manage their estates, entertain themselves and their friends, and travel. She approved of and supported his work with the schools, hospitals, museums, and libraries of Philadelphia, for she too was active in charitable, educational, and religious organizations; and she took almost equal pleasure in all that he did on the farm. But she never permitted him to forget that in 1815 he had contracted to take her to Europe, and when he complained of his fatigue, his weakness, and his great burdens, she gently but firmly reminded him that this contract was as yet unfulfilled.

She was a devoted mother and housewife, efficiently managing the complicated affairs of their city and country households, and was on occasions pleased to note that the reason her household accounts did not balance was that "Mr. B., the great banker," had borrowed in order to have money in his pocket. At another time she employed a maid for seventy-five cents a week whose duty it was to prepare the water for his luxurious marble bath, and with the same teasing humor she wrote that she had promised the maid a twenty-five-cent bonus for "each week that she gives *perfect* satisfaction."[6] If she heard any of the slanderous stories that were circulated about her husband after the failure, she gave no indication of it and loyally

5 N. Biddle to J. Tyler, November 21, 1843; J. Tyler to N. Biddle, November 25, 1843, in the Biddle Manuscripts at "Andalusia."

6 Household account books in the Biddle Manuscripts at "Andalusia."

supported and believed in him during the difficult years that followed. She acted as if all were right with their world, and she made of "Andalusia" a true island of refuge to which he could retire from the frustration and failure that confronted him in Philadelphia.

His unchanged appearance and manner did not conceal from her, the rest of the family, and his intimate friends the deep sadness, the true heart-break, that he lived with, and they were likewise aware of the accompanying physical decline. His periods of illness became more frequent and his recovery more difficult and slow, and in July, 1843, reports were spread throughout the country of an "extreme illness" which had ended with a complete "loss of reason." All that was wrong with him on this occasion was a severe influenza, and he recovered sufficiently to make a ten-day journey to western Pennsylvania and Ohio to inspect his lands. He also visited Roswell Colt in Paterson, New Jersey, during September, and there he became ill once again. He returned to "Andalusia," where he was desperately sick, but on October 9 he reported to Webster that Dr. Chapman said he would recover. The billiard table was brought in from the game house in the yard, friends came out from Philadelphia, and Biddle, though weak and obviously a sick man, renewed his interest in life.[7]

Webster had resigned from Tyler's Cabinet, and Biddle, in alliance with some of his friends, sought to bring the great leader back to the Whig party as the only means through which his talents could be utilized. "For some months past," Biddle wrote, "I have been annoyed at your personal position. I wish to see it changed as I am not content to look at a colossal statue with no pedestal, nor can you expect to do the good you wish without something to stand upon." He supported a movement begun in New York to nominate Webster Vice-President on the ticket with Clay, believing that his influence would help restore the Whig party to its nationalist principles, and, in closing the letter which told Webster of what he had done, he said: "I am, I believe, getting better, but under a very rigorous system of life which forbids talking and dissuades me from much writing, but no medical or other injunction can prevent my adding how truly I am yours."[8]

His disease was bronchitis accompanied by dropsy, but when he died on February 27, 1844, a Philadelphia friend more truly recorded that "there was something extremely touching in this . . . heart-broken death of Mr. Biddle." The Philadelphia papers were kind. "While the Bank was at the height of its popularity and power," one of them said, "no man was more courted or eulogized than its then president. The struggle of the institu-

---

[7] N. Biddle to J. Hamilton, August 6, 1843; R. M. Blatchford to R. Colt, September 16, 1843; R. M. Blatchford to N. Biddle, October 23, November 18, 1843; N. Biddle to D. Webster, October 9, 1843, in the Biddle Manuscripts the Library of Congress.

[8] N. Biddle to J. Gales, January 9, 1844; N. Biddle to D. Webster, January 9, 1844, in the Biddle Manuscripts in the Library of Congress.

tion for a recharter, the unwavering hostility which was waged against it, its career as a state institution, and its inglorious fall: all form portions of the history of the times, to which it is unnecessary to refer in detail. It is now an utter wreck and ruin, and the master-spirit who once controlled it, has passed from the scene of a busy, active, and anxious life. That Mr. Biddle possessed high qualities of intellect, all must concede. Polished in manners, gentlemanly in deportment, gifted with remarkable eloquence, and signally able as a writer, his decease will be regretted by a wide circle of relatives and friends."

The funeral service was read at the house of Joseph Hopkinson on Chestnut Street below Broad, and he was buried in the graveyard of St. Peter's Episcopal Church. Animosities were forgotten as "respectable citizens of every political complexion," old associates at the Bank, and city, state, and national officials followed the plain dark coffin to the grave. And the editor who described the funeral, seeking perhaps to bury some old stories, wrote: "As a son, husband, and father, Mr. Biddle possessed the noblest traits of social and domestic worth; as a friend, he was faithful and kind; and as an American, he was patriotic."[9]

But down from New York came a blast full of animosity and hatred from the Jacksonian editor and poet, William Cullen Bryant, who reported that Biddle had died "at his country seat, where he had passed the last of his days in elegant retirement, which, if justice had taken place, would have been spent in the penitentiary."

Biddle had suffered too long and too much to permit his family to regard his death as anything but a blessed relief, and Jane Biddle, with the brave determination that he so much loved, soon packed her trunks and set sail on her long-postponed trip to Europe. Some unforgiving persons complained because the family had not been reduced to want, ignoring Charles Biddle's true explanation that whatever he paid to cover the outstanding obligations of his father came not from his estate but from that of Mrs. Biddle, which, by an antenuptial agreement between the older Charles Biddle and Robert Oliver, had remained her own. The property, real and personal, left by Nicholas Biddle "was in such unfortunate condition" that no formal executor was appointed, and the large suits brought by the stockholders of the Bank of the United States "slumbered on the docket," thus saving the family and the Bank "the expense and trouble of their trial." There was no good reason why they should have been tried. The Bank, if it won, could collect nothing. If it lost, the belated justification of Biddle would have been of no effect. The nation and its people had already tried him and the institution he headed, and the verdict was against both.

Throughout the rest of the nineteenth century and into the twentieth

[9] *Inquirer* (Philadelphia), February 28, March 4, 1844; *Recollections of John Jay Smith Written by Himself* (Philadelphia, 1892), pp. 205–8.

the laissez faire principles advocated by Jefferson and Jackson were dominant in regard to banks and the currency, and the country suffered the consequences until, finally, some seventy years later, it returned to essentially the same system that had given the United States an adequate, elastic, and sound currency for almost forty of its first forty-seven years. The ten years that intervened between Biddle's accession to the presidency of the Bank of the United States and the removal of the government deposits from that institution were one of the few periods in American history in which the economic community had no valid reason to complain about its banks, its currency, and its domestic and foreign exchange; but Biddle cannot be judged solely on the basis of his successful years as a national banker. He was also the president of a large state bank, the disastrous failure of which had world-wide repercussions. The stockholders lost almost all they had invested, and many of its creditors were only partially repaid. No explanation can erase this fact from the record; but if it is remembered how similar institutions, almost a century later, were sustained through another world-wide depression, it is a temptation to believe that history might have been different.

Between 1929 and 1933 the book losses on stocks, bonds, real estate, mortgages, and commercial loans were staggering in their immensity, proportionately greater perhaps than those of the United States Bank between 1839 and 1841. But most of the banking, insurance, and financial corporations in the later period were protected by the public authorities. Those that survived—and the great majority did—gained back what had seemed lost when, in the recovery that followed, the market price of their holdings was restored to what it had been before. The United States Bank, in the eighteen months between its second suspension of specie payments and its failure, did not need, though it could have used, such help from the national and state governments. It did not even require the cessation of attacks from a hostile political administration. All that would have been necessary to save it from failure was that those directly connected with it as stockholders and directors should have continued to have confidence in its security and solvency and to have refrained from publications that aroused the distrust of its creditors.

Biddle tried to do more than merely keep the Bank solvent. He wanted to restore American prosperity and to make the nation strong and secure. One cannot help speculating what would have happened if those in control of American economic and financial policy in the years after 1839 had dared to follow Biddle's advice to expand currency and credit to counteract the deflationary forces and pressures that destroyed not only the United States Bank but also many other valuable economic enterprises. Unfortunately, this story can never be told. What happened, happened. It cannot be undone. The Bank failed, and so did Nicholas Biddle, and it is by this failure that he has been remembered and judged.

Note on Sources

The chief source for the study of the life and activities of Nicholas Biddle and of the operations of the Bank of the United States is in his personal and official correspondence. The Bank's records and general correspondence, with a few insignificant exceptions, were sold for pulp after its failure and liquidation, and this fact has led to an element of distortion in all historical studies of the period. The loans and other activities of the Bank that were the official concerns of Biddle are almost the only ones of which there is any record at all, and these, particularly the loans to politicians and newspapers that, for obvious reasons, he personally handled, have received undue attention. His own decision to withdraw from the correspondence the letters exchanged between him and his wife have made it difficult to arrive at a clear portrayal of him as a family man living a life outside the Bank. But, despite these facts, the collections of Biddle letters and papers at "Andalusia," the Library of Congress, Princeton University, the Historical Society of Pennsylvania, and in the personal possession of Nicholas B. Wainwright constitute one of the prime sources of knowledge of the early history of the United States. From his youth on, Biddle preserved not only the letters he received but also copies or drafts of the letters he sent, and such was the variety of his interest and concerns that almost nothing that happened in the nation during his lifetime is not touched on somewhere in his correspondence. I have gone outside this correspondence only where it was necessary to check on its accuracy and to gain information about others.

The accompanying Bibliography is restricted to sources actually cited in the footnotes of this book. It does not include all that were consulted in the course of its preparation, and a more complete listing of materials on banking and finance may be found in Fritz Redlich, *The Molding of American Banking* (New York, 1947). For the political story there are bibliographies in the biographies of Jackson by John S. Bassett and Marquis James (New York, 1931; Indianapolis, 1938), and in Arthur M. Schlesinger, Jr., *The Age of Jackson* (Boston, 1945).

Bibliography

Manuscripts

Barnsley Manuscripts in the Duke University Library.

Barry Manuscripts (typescript) in the University of Virginia Library.

James Gordon Bennett Manuscripts in the New York Public Library.

Biddle Family Papers in the Library of Congress.

Biddle Manuscripts at "Andalusia."

Biddle Manuscripts in the Historical Society of Pennsylvania.

Biddle Manuscripts in the Library of Congress.

Biddle Manuscripts in the private collection of Nicholas B. Wainwright, Philadelphia.

Biddle-Craig Manuscripts in the Historical Society of Pennsylvania.

Binney Manuscripts in the Historical Society of Pennsylvania.

Buck Manuscripts in the Historical Society of Pennsylvania.

Cadwalader Manuscripts in the Historical Society of Pennsylvania.

Cheves Manuscripts in the South Carolina Historical Society, Charleston.

Cliosophic Society Manuscripts in the Princeton University Library.

Coles Manuscripts, microfilm in the Historical Society of Pennsylvania of manuscripts in the private collection of Edward C. Robbins.

Dreer Manuscript Collection in the Historical Society of Pennsylvania.

Ford Manuscript Collection in the New York Public Library.

Gallatin Manuscripts in the New York Historical Society.

Gist-Blair Manuscripts in the Library of Congress (cited as "Woodbury Manuscripts").

Gratz Manuscript Collection in the Historical Society of Pennsylvania.

Gilpin Manuscripts in the Historical Society of Pennsylvania.

Jackson-Riddle Manuscripts in the Southern Historical Collection in the University of North Carolina Library.

Mackaye Manuscripts in the Library of Congress.

Manigault Manuscripts loaned to the Historical Society of Pennsylvania by Miss Anna W. Ingersoll.

Manuscript Collection of the Library Company of Philadelphia.

Monroe Manuscripts in the Library of Congress.

[415]

Pleasanton Manuscripts in the Historical Society of Pennsylvania.
Poinsett Manuscripts in the Library of Congress.
Princeton Manuscript Collection in the Princeton University Library.
Taney Manuscripts in the Library of Congress.
Vanderlyn Manuscripts in the New York Historical Society.

Published Correspondence

ADAMS, HENRY (ed.). *Writings of Albert Gallatin.* Philadelphia, 1879.

BASSETT, JOHN S. (ed.). *Correspondence of Andrew Jackson.* Washington, 1926–33.

FORD, PAUL L. (ed.). *The Works of Thomas Jefferson.* New York, 1904.

JAMESON, J. FRANKLIN (ed.). *Correspondence of John C. Calhoun.* Washington, 1900.

McGRANE, REGINALD C. (ed.). *The Correspondence of Nicholas Biddle Dealing with National Affairs, 1807–1844.* Boston, 1919.

WASHINGTON, H. A. (ed.). *The Writings of Thomas Jefferson.* Washington, 1853.

Books and Articles

ABERNETHY, THOMAS P. "The Early Development of Commerce and Banking in Tennessee," *Mississippi Valley Historical Review,* XIV (1927), 311–25.

ACRES, W. MARSTON. *The Bank of England from Within.* London, 1931.

ADAMS, CHARLES FRANCIS (ed.). *The Memoirs of John Quincy Adams, Comprising Portions of His Diary from 1795 to 1848.* 12 vols. Philadelphia, 1874–77.

ADAMS, HENRY. *History of the United States in the Administrations of Thomas Jefferson and James Madison.* 9 vols. New York, 1889–92.

———. *The Life of Albert Gallatin.* Philadelphia, 1880.

ALLEN, PAUL (ed.). *History of the Expedition under the Command of Captains Lewis and Clark.* Philadelphia, 1814.

AREY, HENRY W. *The Girard College and Its Founder.* Philadelphia, 1866.

BANCROFT, GEORGE. "Bank of the United States," *North American Review,* XXXII (1831), 21–64.

BARKER, JACOB. *The Conspiracy Trials of 1826 and 1827.* Philadelphia, 1864.

———. *Incidents in the Life of Jacob Barker.* Washington, 1855.

———. *Letters Developing the Conspiracy Formed in 1826 for His Ruin.* New York, 1827.

———. *The Speeches of Mr. Jacob Barker and His Counsel on the Trials for Conspiracy.* New York, 1827.

———. *Trial of Jacob Barker, Thomas Vermilye and Matthew L. Davis.* New York, 1827.

BATES, WILLIAM N. (ed.). "Nicholas Biddle's Journey to Greece," *Proceedings of the Numismatic and Antiquarian Society of Pennsylvania,* XXVIII (1919), 167–83.

BENTON, THOMAS HART. *Thirty Years' View; or, a History of the Working of the American Government for Thirty Years, from 1820 to 1850.* 2 vols. New York, 1956.

BIBLIOGRAPHY

BIDDLE, EDWARD (ed.). "Joseph Bonaparte in America as Recorded in the Private Journal of Nicholas Biddle," *Pennsylvania Magazine of History and Biography*, LV (1931), 208–24.

BIDDLE, JAMES S. (ed.). *Autobiography of Charles Biddle, Vice-President of the Supreme Executive Council of Pennsylvania, 1745–1821*. Philadelphia, 1883.

BIDDLE, NICHOLAS. *An Address Delivered before the Alumni Association of Nassau Hall on the Day of the Annual Commencement of the College, September 30, 1835*. Princeton, 1835.

——. "An Address Delivered before the Philadelphia Society for the Promotion of Agriculture," *Niles' Register*, XXII (suppl.) (1822), 1–9.

——. *Eulogium on Thomas Jefferson Delivered before the American Philosophical Society on the Eleventh Day of April 1827*. Philadelphia, 1827.

——. *Oration Delivered before the Pennsylvania State Society of the Cincinnati on the Fourth of July MDCCXI*. Philadelphia, 1811.

——. *Verses*. Philadelphia, 1889.

—— (ed.). *Commercial Regulations of Foreign Countries with Which the United States Have Commercial Intercourse*. Washington, 1819.

BINNEY, CHARLES C. *The Life of Horace Binney*. Philadelphia, 1903.

BOLLES, ALBERT S. *The Financial History of the United States from 1789 to 1860*. New York, 1894.

BROWN, KENNETH L. "Stephen Girard, Promoter of the Second Bank of the United States," *Journal of Economic History*, II (1942), 125–48.

BUCKINGHAM, JAMES SILK. *America, Historical, Statistic, and Descriptive*. New York, 1841.

CATTERALL, RALPH C. H. *The Second Bank of the United States*. Chicago, 1903.

CHEVALIER, MICHEL. *Society, Manners, and Politics in the United States*. Boston, 1839.

CLAPHAM, JOHN H. *The Bank of England*. 2 vols. New York, 1945.

——. *An Economic History of Modern Britain*. 3 vols. Cambridge, 1939.

CLARK, WILLIAM BELL. *Captain Dauntless: The Story of Nicholas Biddle of the Continental Navy*. Baton Rouge, La., 1949.

COLLINS, VARNUM L. *Princeton*. New York, 1914.

CROCKETT, DAVID. *An Account of Colonel Crockett's Tour to the North and Down East, 1834*. Philadelphia, 1835.

DAVIS, CHARLES A. *Letters of J. Downing, a Major*. New York, 1834.

DICKENS, CHARLES. *American Notes*. New York, 1905.

DUANE, WILLIAM J. *Narrative and Correspondence concerning the Removal of the Deposits and Occurrences Connected Therewith*. Philadelphia, 1838.

ELLIS, HAROLD M. *Joseph Dennie and His Circle: A Study of American Literature from 1792 to 1812*. Austin, Tex., 1815.

ELLISON, THOMAS. *Gleanings and Reminiscences*. Liverpool, 1905.

FOOTE, HENRY S. *Casket of Reminiscences*. Washington, 1874.

GABRIEL, RALPH H. *The Course of American Democratic Thought*. New York, 1940.

GALLATIN, ALBERT. "Considerations on the Currency and Banking System of the United States," *American Quarterly Review*, VIII (1830), 441–528.

GALLATIN, ALBERT (chairman). *Report of the Union Committee, March 29, 1834.* New York, 1834.

GAYER, ARTHUR D. *The Growth and Fluctuation of the British Economy, 1790–1850.* Oxford, 1953.

GILCHRIST, AGNES A. *William Strickland, Architect and Engineer, 1788–1854.* Philadelphia, 1950.

GOVAN, THOMAS P. "An Ante-Bellum Attempt To Regulate the Price and Supply of Cotton," *North Carolina Historical Review,* XVII (1940), 302–12.

———. "Banking and the Credit System in Georgia," *Journal of Southern History,* IV (1938), 164–84.

———. "John M. Berrien and the Administration of Andrew Jackson," *Journal of Southern History,* V (1939), 447–67.

———. "Nicholas Biddle at Princeton," *Princeton University Library Chronicle,* IX (1947), 49–61.

——— (ed.), "The Death of Joseph Dennie: A Memoir by Nicholas Biddle," *Pennsylvania Magazine of History and Biography,* LXXV (1951), 36–46.

——— (ed.), "An Unfinished Novel by Nicholas Biddle," *Princeton University Library Chronicle,* X (1949), 124–36.

GREEN, FLETCHER M. "Georgia's Forgotten Industry: Gold Mining," *Georgia Historical Quarterly,* XIX (1935), 93–111, 210–28.

HAMILTON, JAMES A. *Reminiscences.* New York, 1869.

HAMLIN, TALBOT. *Greek Revival Architecture in America.* New York, 1944.

HAMMOND, BRAY. *Banks and Politics in America from the Revolution to the Civil War.* Princeton, 1957.

———. "The Chestnut Street Raid on Wall Street, 1839," *Quarterly Journal of Economics,* LXI (1947), 605–18.

———. "Free Banks and Corporations: The New York Free Banking Act of 1838," *Journal of Political Economy,* XLIV (1936), 184–209.

———. "Jackson, Biddle, and the Bank of the United States," *Journal of Economic History,* VII (1947), 1–23.

HAMMOND, JABEZ D. *The History of Political Parties in the State of New York.* 2 vols. Albany, 1842.

HART, LOUIS. *Economic Policy and Democratic Thought: Pennsylvania, 1776–1860.* Cambridge, Mass., 1948.

HAWTREY, R. G. *A Century of Bank Rate.* London, 1938.

HENDERSON, HELEN W. *The Pennsylvania Academy of the Fine Arts.* Boston, 1911.

HERRING, PENDLETON. *The Politics of Democracy.* New York, 1940.

HIDY, RALPH W. *The House of Baring in American Trade and Finance.* Cambridge, 1949.

HIGGINBOTHAM, SANFORD W. *The Keystone in the Democratic Arch: Pennsylvania Politics, 1800–1816.* Harrisburg, 1952.

HILLARD, G. S. *Memoir and Correspondence of Jeremiah Mason.* Cambridge, 1873.

HOUSTON, DAVID F. *A Critical Study of Nullification in South Carolina.* New York, 1896.

INGERSOLL, CHARLES J. *Historical Sketch of the Second War between the United States and Great Britain.* 2 vols. Philadelphia, 1845–49.

BIBLIOGRAPHY

JAMES, MARQUIS. *The Life of Andrew Jackson.* Indianapolis, 1938.

JENKS, LELAND H. *The Migration of British Capital to 1875.* New York, 1927.

JORDAN, WEYMOUTH T. *George Washington Campbell of Tennessee.* Tallahassee, Fla., 1955.

KLEIN, PHILIP S. *Pennsylvania Politics, 1817–1832.* Philadelphia, 1940.

KONKLE, BURTON A. *Thomas Willing and the First American Financial System.* Philadelphia, 1937.

LAWRENCE, WILLIAM BEACH. "Bank of the United States," *North American Review,* XXXII (1831), 524–63.

LIVINGOOD, JAMES W. *The Philadelphia-Baltimore Trade Rivalry, 1780–1860.* Harrisburg, 1947.

LOCHEMES, SISTER M. FREDERICK. *Robert Walsh, His Story.* New York, 1941.

LONGACRE, JAMES B., and HERRING, JAMES (eds.). *The National Portrait Gallery of Distinguished Americans.* 4 vols. Philadelphia, 1856.

McGRANE, REGINALD C. *Foreign Bondholders and American State Debts.* New York, 1935.

———. *The Panic of 1837.* Chicago, 1924.

MACKENZIE, WILLIAM L. *Life and Times of Martin Van Buren.* Boston, 1846.

———. *The Lives and Opinions of Benjamin F. Butler and Jesse Hoyt.* Boston, 1845.

MACLEAN, JOHN. *History of the College of New Jersey.* Philadelphia, 1877.

McLEOD, HENRY D. *Theory and Practice of Banking.* 2 vols. London, 1893.

MOORE, POWELL. "The Revolt against Jackson in Tennessee," *Journal of Southern History,* II (1936), 335–59.

MOTT, FRANK L. *A History of American Magazines.* Cambridge, 1938.

NOLTE, VINCENT. *Fifty Years in Both Hemispheres: The Memoirs of Vincent Nolte.* New York, 1934.

OBERHOLTZER, ELLIS P. *The Literary History of Philadelphia.* Philadelphia, 1906.

PALMER, J. HORSELY. *The Causes and Consequences of the Pressure upon the Money Market.* London, 1837.

PANCAKE, JOHN S. "The 'Invisibles': A Chapter in the Opposition to President Madison," *Journal of Southern History,* XXI (1955), 17–37.

PARKS, JOSEPH H. *John Bell of Tennessee.* Baton Rouge, La., 1950.

PARTON, JAMES. *Life of Andrew Jackson.* 3 vols. New York, 1861.

PIERSON, GEORGE W. *Tocqueville and Beaumont in America.* New York, 1938.

RANDALL, RANDOLPH C. "Authors of the Port Folio Revealed by the Hall Files," *American Literature,* XI (1940), 379–416.

REDLICH, FRITZ. *The Molding of American Banking: Men and Ideas.* 2 vols. New York, 1947, 1951.

REZNECK, SAMUEL. "The Social History of an American Depression, 1837–1843," *American Historical Review,* LX (1935), 662–87.

ROSENBERGER, FRANCIS C. (ed.). *Jefferson Reader: A Treasury of Writings about Thomas Jefferson.* New York, 1953.

SCHLESINGER, ARTHUR M., JR. *The Age of Jackson.* Boston, 1945.

SCOTT, NANCY N. (ed.). *A Memoir of Hugh Lawson White.* Philadelphia, 1856.

SEARS, LOUIS M. *Jefferson and the Embargo.* Durham, N.C., 1927.

SELLERS, CHARLES G., JR. "Banking and Politics in Jackson's Tennessee, 1817–1827," *Mississippi Valley Historical Review,* XLI (1954), 61–84.

SELLERS, CHARLES G., JR. "Jackson Men with Feet of Clay," *American Historical Review*, LXII (1957), 537–51.

——. *James K. Polk, Jacksonian, 1795–1843*. Princeton, 1957.

SHELLING, RICHARD K. "Philadelphia and the Agitation in 1825 for the Pennsylvania Canal," *Pennsylvania Magazine of History and Biography*, LXII (1938), 175–204.

SIOUSSAT, ST. GEORGE L. "Tennessee Politics in the Jackson Period," *American Historical Review*, XV (1908), 51–69.

SMITH, ALBERT H. *The Philadelphia Magazines and Their Contributors*. Philadelphia, 1872.

SMITH, JOHN JAY. *Recollections of John Jay Smith Written by Himself*. Philadelphia, 1892.

SMITH, WALTER B. *Economic Aspects of the Second Bank of the United States*. Cambridge, Mass., 1953.

SMITH, WALTER B., and COLE, ARTHUR C. *Fluctuations in American Business, 1790–1860*. Cambridge, Mass., 1935.

SMITH, WILLIAM E. *The Francis Preston Blair Family in Politics*. 2 vols. New York, 1933.

SPILLER, ROBERT E., *et al.* (eds.). *Literary History of the United States*. 3 vols. New York, 1948.

STICKENY, WILLIAM (ed.). *The Autobiography of Amos Kendall*. Boston, 1872.

SWISHER, CARL B. *Roger B. Taney*. New York, 1935.

THWAITES, REUBEN G. (ed.). *Original Journals of the Lewis and Clark Expedition, 1804–1806*. 8 vols. New York, 1904.

TOOKE, THOMAS, and NEWMARCH, WILLIAM. *History of Prices*. 6 vols. London, 1838–57.

TROTTER, ALEXANDER. *Observations on the Financial Position and Credit of the States of the North American Union*. London, 1839.

TYSON, JOB R. *Sketch of the Wistar Party of Philadelphia*. Philadelphia, 1898.

University of Pennsylvania: Biographical Catalogue of the Matriculates of the College, 1749–1893. Philadelphia, 1894.

WAINWRIGHT, NICHOLAS B. *The Philadelphia National Bank*. Philadelphia, 1953.

WAYLAND, FRANCIS F. *Andrew Stevenson, Democrat and Diplomat, 1785–1857*. Philadelphia, 1949.

WEED, H. A. (ed.). *Autobiography of Thurlow Weed*. Boston, 1884.

WERTENBAKER, THOMAS J. *Princeton, 1746–1896*. Princeton, 1946.

WETERAAU, JAMES O. "Branches of the First Bank of the United States," *Journal of Economic History* (suppl.), II (1942), 66–100.

——. "New Light on the First Bank of the United States," *Pennsylvania Magazine of History and Biography*, LXI (1937), 263–85.

WILLIAMS, CHARLES R. *The Cliosophic Society, Princeton University*. Princeton, 1916.

WILTSE, CHARLES M. *John C. Calhoun, Nationalist, 1782–1828*. Indianapolis, 1944.

——. *John C. Calhoun, Nullifier, 1829–1839*. Indianapolis, 1949.

WRIGHT, DAVID McCORD. "Langdon Cheves and Nicholas Biddle: New Data for a New Interpretation," *Journal of Economic History*, XIII (1953), 305–19.

Index

INDEX